October 17–21, 2010
Reno/Tahoe, Nevada, USA

I0060959

**Association for
Computing Machinery**

Advancing Computing as a Science & Profession

SPLASH'10

ACM International Conference on
Systems, Programming, Languages, and Applications:
Software for Humanity

SPLASH'10 Sponsored by:
ACM SIGPLAN & ACM SIGSOFT

Onward! 2010 Sponsored by:
ACM SIGPLAN

Supported by:
**Cisco, Google, IBM Research, Addison-Wesley, Prentice-Hall,
InformIT.com, and Wiley Publishing**

Association for Computing Machinery

Advancing Computing as a Science & Profession

The Association for Computing Machinery
2 Penn Plaza, Suite 701
New York, New York 10121-0701

Copyright © 2010 by the Association for Computing Machinery, Inc. (ACM). Permission to make digital or hard copies of portions of this work for personal or classroom use is granted without fee provided that copies are not made or distributed for profit or commercial advantage and that copies bear this notice and the full citation on the first page. Copyright for components of this work owned by others than ACM must be honored. Abstracting with credit is permitted. To copy otherwise, to republish, to post on servers or to redistribute to lists, requires prior specific permission and/or a fee. Request permission to republish from: Publications Dept., ACM, Inc. Fax +1 (212) 869-0481 or <permissions@acm.org>.

For other copying of articles that carry a code at the bottom of the first or last page, copying is permitted provided that the per-copy fee indicated in the code is paid through the Copyright Clearance Center, 222 Rosewood Drive, Danvers, MA 01923.

Notice to Past Authors of ACM-Published Articles
ACM intends to create a complete electronic archive of all articles and/or other material previously published by ACM. If you have written a work that has been previously published by ACM in any journal or conference proceedings prior to 1978, or any SIG Newsletter at any time, and you do NOT want this work to appear in the ACM Digital Library, please inform permissions@acm.org, stating the title of the work, the author(s), and where and when published.

OOPSLA ISBN: 978-1-4503-0240-1

Additional copies may be ordered prepaid from:

ACM Order Department
PO Box 11405
New York, NY 10286-1405

Phone: 1-800-342-6626 (USA and Canada)
        +1-212-626-0500 (all other countries)
Fax: +1-212-944-1318
E-mail: acmhelp@acm.org

OOPSLA'10 ACM Order Number 548105

Printed in the USA

Introducing *the* ACM International Conference on Systems, Programming, Languages, and Applications: Software for Humanity (SPLASH)

It is my pleasure to welcome you to SPLASH, the next step in the evolution of the well-known OOPSLA conference. SPLASH is the premier forum for practitioners, researchers, educators, and students who are passionate about improving the state of the art and practice in the development of software systems and applications through improved programming tools and languages.

SPLASH is a new name for the overall OOPSLA conference, which includes workshops, panels, tutorials, co-located conferences, posters, and a doctoral symposium. The OOPSLA name is being retained for the technical research track that is the core of SPLASH. It would have been easier to just rename OOPSLA to be SPLASH, but that would lose continuity with the strong OOPSLA brand. As a result, we have adopted a phased approach where both names will be used for the foreseeable future.

Although SPLASH/OOPSLA has its origin in object technologies, SPLASH is no longer explicitly tied to object-oriented programming. There is an implicit connection, however, since most modern software development incorporates or builds on ideas from object-oriented programming. From its inception, OOPSLA has incubated new technologies and practices. Dynamic compilation and optimization, software patterns, refactoring, aspect-oriented software development, agile methods, service-oriented architectures, and model-driven development (to name just a few) all have roots in OOPSLA.

SPLASH 2010 continues and strengthens this tradition. SPLASH has as its foundation the most successful software development theories and practices, yet is always striving to find new and better techniques which will define the future of software development.

SPLASH is pleased to host a range of co-located conferences. Onward! is more radical, more visionary, and more open to new ideas, allowing it to accept papers that present strong arguments even though the ideas in the paper may not be fully proven. The Dynamic Languages Symposium (DLS) discusses dynamic languages, including scripting languages. The Pattern Languages of Programming (PLoP) conference explores patterns of software and effective ways to present them. The International Lisp Conference (ILC) is focused on Lisp, a language with a great history and future. The Educators' and Trainer's Symposium and Doctoral Symposium focus on the essential task of educating the next generation of software developers and researchers.

In the end, SPLASH is about people, not technology. While SPLASH inherits SPLA from OOPSLA, it adds a new twist on the end: Software for Humanity. While this may seem an afterthought, I have come to realize over the last year that it is the most important idea in the new name. Our community is strong and diverse. Even as we promote diverse technologies, we share deep values that enable us to work together. One is the simple idea that software can improve the daily lives of humans all around the planet. Like any technology, software has the potential for great benefit and also great harm. Let's try to use it for good.

Organizing SPLASH required hard work from many individuals. As budgets have tightened, we were asked to do more with less. The talent and enthusiasm of the people working on SPLASH have made this year's conference a great success. I am very thankful for all the work performed by the Conference and Program Committees. I am grateful also to the SPLASH Steering Committee for their guidance and support, to our corporate supporters, and to SIGPLAN and ACM for sponsoring the conference. Finally, I would like to thank all of the people who took part in SPLASH 2010. Thank you!

William Cook
SPLASH 2010 Conference Chair
University of Texas at Austin

OOPSLA/SPLASH 2010 Program Chair Statement

Martin Rinard

Massachusetts Institute of Technology
rinard@mit.edu

Abstract

This Program Chair's Statement discusses the paper review process and outcome for the 2010 OOPSLA/SPLASH Research Papers. Based on my experience reviewing papers and interacting with researchers in the field, I believe the current conference-based publication system provides inadequate publication bandwidth for the large amount of high-quality research that the field is currently producing. This problem is especially acute for disruptively creative research, to the extent that the current publication system discourages researchers from performing such research. Accordingly I, working with the OOPSLA/SPLASH Steering Committee, made several changes to the standard conference review process in an attempt to make this process more welcoming to papers that present creative research, especially research that identifies new directions or goes against the standard value system in the field. But while such changes may improve the current conference-based publication system, in the end a more productive course of action is to abandon the current system and shift to the combined conference/journal publication system that prevails in most established scientific and engineering fields.

1. Introduction

This proceedings contains the Research Papers presented at OOPSLA/SPLASH 2010 the ACM Conference on Systems, Programming, Languages, and Applications: Software for Humanity (SPLASH) held in Reno/Tahoe, Nevada.

The program committee met for two full days at the Massachusetts Institute of Technology, selecting 45 papers for presentation at the conference out of 164 papers submitted for review, for an acceptance rate of 27%. All of the papers received at least three written reviews.

2. Scope of OOPSLA/SPLASH 2010

OOPSLA was established in 1986 as a forum for researchers working in the field of object-oriented programming. Over the next several decades object-oriented programming became mainstream, with researchers settling many of the important research questions that originally motivated the establishment of a conference in the field. During the same time period developments opened up many new and interest-ing questions in other areas of programming languages and software engineering. One of the goals this year was therefore to increase the scope of the conference to include all of programming languages and software engineering, broadly construed. The final set of OOPSLA/SPLASH 2010 Research Papers reflects this broadened focus, containing papers from a wide variety of subfields of both software engineering and programming languages.

3. Review and Acceptance Process

In recent years the current conference-based publication system in computer science has become increasingly controversial [1–4, 6–9]. The salient features of this system include a one-time program committee assembled for the specific purpose of reviewing the papers submitted to the conference (with each program committee member typically assigned tens of papers to review), a several month review process, a several day program committee meeting in which the committee makes the accept/reject decisions, and a selective review process that routinely rejects qualified papers, ostensibly for space reasons.

When I agreed to serve as program chair for OOPSLA/SPLASH 2010, one of my goals was work with the OOPSLA/SPLASH Steering Committee to change the review process, to the extent feasible, to address some of the weaknesses of the current system.

3.1 Unilateral Paper Acceptance

Because conferences receive more high-quality papers than they are willing to accept, the selection process becomes so competitive that any significant uncertainty or opposition (even on the part of a single program committee member) is usually enough to get a paper rejected. Papers that open up new directions or go against the established value system in the field are routinely rejected, either because they are controversial or because the program committee finds it difficult to evaluate the paper with the same degree of certainty as more mainstream papers.

In my view, this situation has become severe enough to seriously hamper the development of the field. Conferences become filled with papers that are certainly well-executed, often creative and interesting within the dominant flow of the field, but in the end wind up reinforcing the established status quo. Because researchers are well aware of the difficulties that disruptively creative research faces under the current publication system, they tend to skew their research portfolios (consciously or unconsciously) toward more easily publishable incremental research. Perhaps even worse, this situation discourages ambitious young researchers who aspire to do truly innovative research from even entering the field in the first place.

I had no illusions that changing the process for one year in a single conference would remedy this situation. I did want to make sure, however, that if someone did happen to submit a controversially innovative paper, that the committee would be able to accept the paper. Each program committee member was therefore given the unilateral right to accept one paper regardless of the opinion of the rest of the committee.

In the end, the program committee wound up accepting 6 of the 45 accepted papers via this mechanism. My expectation was that the unilateral accept papers would, in the end, turn out to be the most influential papers in the conference — controversy is often the sign of a new and powerful idea that has the potential to change the field's perspective (one of the hallmarks of an important publication). And in fact, several of these 6 papers were truly controversial, with some committee members strongly in favor of accepting the paper and others strongly opposed. Interestingly enough, however, most of the unilateral accepts were apparently efforts on the part of program committee members to correct perceived injustices — the committee member felt that the paper had not been given a fair hearing in the review process (given the reviewing loads and time pressures associated with the current conference review process, such situations occur frequently), thought the paper worthy of publication, and decided to accept the paper.

3.2 Standard Scientific Review Criteria

The standard review criteria for scientific publications focus on the following three questions: Does the publication present new results or techniques? Does the publication contain errors? Are the presented results or techniques significant, interesting, or intriguing?

Most conferences are selective enough that they reject many papers that fully satisfy the standard criteria for scientific publication. The accept/reject decisions tend instead to be driven by the subjective emotions of the program committee members — i.e., how much they like or dislike each paper. Over time, this fact has skewed the review process away from focusing on the standard scientific review criteria to instead focusing on the reasons why the paper does or does not appeal to the individual reviewers.

One of my goals was to move the focus back to the standard scientific review criteria. The discussion of each paper started with a determination of whether or not the paper satisfied the standard scientific review criteria. Only then did the committee move on to consider the accept/reject decision. During the program committee meeting the committee placed each discussed paper into one of the following categories: High Priority Accept (papers that satisfied the scientific review criteria and were a high priority to accept into the conference), Low Priority Accept (papers that satisfied the scientific review criteria but with lower priority to accept into the conference), Low Priority Reject (papers that largely satisfied the scientfic review criteria but were perceived to have some significant weakness), and Tools (papers whose value was primarily in an interesting tool they presented). Given the time constraints on the program committee meeting, there was not enough time to discuss every paper. Before the meeting I therefore established a Not Discussed category for papers whose written review ratings were so low they had little or no chance of acceptance. During the program committee meeting I scheduled a time for individual program committee members to initiate a discussion of any Not Discussed papers they thought merited discussion. None were nominated for discussion.

Based on my records, there were 37 High Priority Accept papers, 13 Low Priority Accept papers, 19 Low Priority Reject papers, 2 Tools Papers, and 93 Not Discussed papers. The program committee accepted all of the High Priority Accept and Tools papers. 4 of the Low Priority Accept and 2 of the Low Priority Reject papers were accepted by individual program committee members via the unilateral accept mechanism. The remaining papers were rejected.

3.3 Reproducibility

The ability to reproduce the presented results is a fundamental property of scientific publication. Given the complexity of the systems that many computer scientists work with, the fact that many of the components in such systems change rapidly (with older versions quickly becoming effectively unavailable), and the strict page limits that conferences impose, reproducibility has always been a problematic issue for the field [5]. Specific issues include whether or not the paper presents sufficient detail for another researchers to reimplement the system (almost all do not, given the complexity of the systems involved), whether the researchers make the reimplementation issue moot by making their data and/or artifacts publicly available via dissemination mechanisms such as the Internet (many but by no means all researchers do this), or whether, given the speed with which the field moves, reproducibility is even a relevant goal or not for most papers. The program committee did not attempt to address this issue in any detail other than to simply apply prevailing reviewing standards.

One issue did, however, come up during the program committee meeting. The computer science research community in general, and the programming languages/software engineering community in particular, currently has strong participation from communities (for example, researchers working in industrial research labs) that often work with proprietary software systems. Because such systems are not available to the broad research community, it is in general not possible for others in the community to reproduce the reported results — the data and/or artifacts required to reproduce the results are not available (and will never become available) to others. While the program committee was not entirely comfortable accepting papers that present such results, it was at least as uncomfortable with requiring industry researchers to present only results that others could reproduce.

Given the central importance of reproducibility to scientific inquiry and the current ambigious status of reproducibility in the field, I think it is important for the field to come to a more explicit understanding of what degree of reproducibility is acceptable. In particular, I believe the field needs to come to a decision on the acceptability of results that others are inherently unable to reproduce because of the proprietary nature of the relevant data and/or artifacts.

3.4 The Huddle Mechanism

One way to get an unfortunate accept/reject decision is to have a program committee member take a strong but misguided position on a paper in front of the full committee during the discussion of the paper. Having taken such a position, it is then difficult for the program committee member to back down in the face of evidence that contradicts his or her position. Especially when combined with the time pressure of the program committee meeting, the resulting conflict and confusion can make it difficult for the committee to fairly evaluate the paper.

Experienced program committee members therefore often attempt to resolve potential disagreements individually before the paper comes up for discussion, either via email before the program committee meeting or in informal discussions during breaks. I decided to formalize this process as follows. I organized the discussion sessions into six-paper blocks. Before each block, I allowed five to ten minutes for the reviewers on each paper to discuss the paper in a small group among themselves to better understand each others' position and hopefully resolve any misunderstandings. I found this mechanism quite effective in eliminating counterproductively polarized paper discussions when the paper was subsequently discussed in front of the full committee. Note the word counterproductively — there were definitely polarized discussions, but these discusssions arose because knowledgeable reviewers genuinely disagreed about the paper in question, not because a reviewer committed to a misguided position in front of the full committee before understanding the positions of other reviewers.

This mechanism did, however, raise some concerns. Some program committee members felt that it resulted in a less thorough paper discussion in the full committee and that they therefore had less of a sense of the overall set of papers in the conference. Others felt that this mechanism facilitated the application of different quality standards for different papers, especially papers in different areas with non-overlapping sets of reviewers. Finally, there was a concern that this mechanism exposed the reviewer identities to people with conflicts on the paper (for convenience reasons I listed the papers and reviewers for the next block on the whiteboard).

3.5 Program Committee Member Submissions

Some conferences allow program committee members to submit papers to the conference, others do not. Those that do typically hold program committee member submissions to a higher standard than other submissions, although it is never completely clear what this higher standard is. In my experience serving on program committees, what this higher standard usually boils down to is that accepted program committee papers must be even less controversial than other accepted papers.

Because I was not interested in encouraging the submission of even more conventional papers, I was not willing to allow program committee submissions but hold these submissions to a higher standard than other submissions. The OOPSLA/SPLASH Steering Committee indicated that they would not support a decision to hold program committee submissions to the same standard as other submissions. I therefore decided to forbid submissions from program committee members.

The standard concern is that this policy makes it difficult to put together a high-quality program committee. I did not encounter any such difficulty — while several researchers declined invitations to serve on the committee, only one or two cited a desire to submit a paper as the reason for declining.

3.6 Page Limits

Almost without exception, conferences impose a page limit on submissions. The goals of this policy include keeping the reviewer load reasonable and ensuring that accepted papers fit into the conference proceedings. There are two main drawbacks to this policy. First, research that does not fit within standard page limits is essentially unpublishable. This problem is especially severe for new or groundbreaking research since it can take space to present a new perspective or approach. Second, researchers waste a significant amount of time manipulating their papers to make them fit within page limits.

OOPSLA has traditionally had the most liberal page limit policy of any top computer science conference (20 two-column pages). Nevertheless, I decided to impose no page limit whatsoever on OOPSLA/SPLAH submissions (while informing authors that the committee would not accept papers whose content would not fit in the proceedings, which would limit papers to 20 pages). To address the reviewer load issue, the call for papers stated that program committee members were under no obligation to read overly long or boring papers — it was the obligation of the author to keep the reviewers interested and motivated to read the paper. In practice virtually all of the papers fit in less than 20 pages and overly long papers were not an issue.

3.7 Recommendations

Based on my experience in the program committee meeting, I have the following recommendations for future program chairs and program committees:

- **Unilateral Accept Policy:** I was overall very happy with how well the unilateral accept process worked out and strongly advise other conferences to adopt a similar unilateral accept policy. Ideally, the universal adoption of such a policy would encourage researchers to engage in more creative and innovative research.

  The unilateral accept papers and the committee member that accepted the paper into the conference are identified as such in the conference proceedings. I initially was happy to support this policy because I thought it might help conference attendees and other researchers identify particularly interesting papers. But given that the mechanism was used primarily to correct perceived injustices in the review process, it is not clear to me how useful this identification is for this purpose. Discussing this policy with others has also made it clear to me that identifying the committee member who unilaterally accepted the paper has the potential to raise a host of problematic issues. While I do not believe any of these issues became operational in the OOPSLA/SPLASH 2010 review process, I advise future program committees to keep the committe members who decided to unilaterally accept papers anonymous.

  I advise one change to the process I used in the OOPSLA/SPLASH 2010 program committee meeting, in which all unilateral accept papers were accepted in a single short session at the end of the program committee meeting. I advise extending the opportunity to unilaterally accept papers for several days after the program committee meeting. This extension would give program committee members time to read papers that they did not review and to consider their decisions at leisure away from the sometimes hectic environment that prevails in most program committee meetings. If we had adopted this process, I am sure we would have accepted at least several more very worthwhile papers through the unilateral accept mechanism.

- **Scientific Review Criteria:** The focus on standard scientific review criteria helped keep the paper discussions focused on relevant topics and helped minimize (to the extent possible) the intrusion of inappropriate review criteria. I therefore advise future program chairs to keep the paper discussions oriented around these criteria (while maintaining reasonable expectations about the extent to which focusing on these criteria can improve the overall process).

- **The Huddle Mechanism:** I found this mechanism to be effective in avoiding counterproductive paper discussions in front of the full committee. I would use this mechanism again, perhaps with adjustments to help make the broader committee more informed about papers they did not review and to help reviewers from being inadvertently exposed to the identities of the reviewers on papers with which they have a conflict.

  But as long as program committee members are aware of the issue and are proactive in engaging in small-group discussions to resolve misunderstandings before the paper comes up for discussion in the open program committee meeting, a less formal approach may be able to provide many of the same benefits. I advise future program chairs to be aware of this issue and be ready to use some mechanism (formal or informal) to head off potential misunderstandings and counterproductively polarized discussions when the paper comes up for discussion in front of the full program committee.

- **Program Committee Submission Policy:** In my experience this policy did not hamper my ability to put together a high-quality committee. I advise future program chairs to adopt this policy.

- **Page Limits:** The elimination of page limits for submissions caused no problems in the review process and may have saved authors significant time and effort that would otherwise have been spent attempting to make papers fit within the page limit. I advise future program chairs to adopt this policy.

- **Uniform Submission Requirements:** There is, however, another consideration. For a variety of reasons, many papers are submitted to multiple conferences. The lack of uniformity in page limits and paper formatting instructions causes a large amount of needless rewriting and reformatting. I therefore advise the community to settle on a single standard for page limits and formatting instructions. In my opinion having a single standard (whatever it is, although I advise at least generous and ideally no page limits) is more valuable than eliminating page limits.

3.8 Shift to a Standard Conference/Journal System

At the end of the day, however, I believe the current conference-based publication system has outlived its usefulness to the field. It is time to move to the standard conference/journal publication system that prevails in most scientific fields. There are several reasons to hope that this system would be more effective in encouraging innovative research:

- **Multiple Author/Reviewer Interactions:** Papers that propose new directions or go against the value system of the field elicit many more questions and concerns than papers that fit within the mainstream. The standard journal review system enables the multiple author/reviewer interaction cycles required to resolve these questions and concerns and enable the reviewers to accept the paper. With the standard conference review system, on the other hand, the paper gets a new set of reviewers every time it is submitted to another conference. The author and reviewers never have the opportunity to engage in the interactions required for the reviewers to understand, appreciate, and accept the paper for publication. Journals may therefore be more effective than conferences at publishing those (relatively few) papers that help the field progress in new and important directions.

- **Space for Qualified Papers:** Practical considerations (primarily the need to allocate time for an oral presentation of each accepted paper) limit the number of papers that conferences as currently organized can accept. Because there is never enough room to take all papers that satisfy the standard scientific evaluation criteria, the key accept/reject decisions are driven by other considerations that work against controversial papers.

  Reputable journals, on the other hand, are typically organized to accept all qualified papers. So a reviewer who wants to reject a paper cannot simply say he or she does not like the paper — he or she must argue that the paper does not meet one of the standard evaluation criteria. The hope is that this policy would make it easier for reviewers to accept papers that present valid results but challenge the standard value system in the field.

- **More Liberal Page Limits:** Many reputable journals have flexible page limit policies — if the reviewers feel that the paper deserves a certain number of pages, the journal can often accommodate that number. And even if the journal has a page limit policy, the limits are typically much larger than standard conference page limits. Authors are therefore much more likely to have the space they need to adequately present their idea (an advantage, by the way, for all kinds of papers, not just papers that present disruptive new ideas).

One argument against journals is the long review cycle that currently prevails in most computer science journals [8]. Journals should, however, be able to offer a much shorter review cycle than conferences — conference reviewers must synchronize their reviews of tens of papers with tens of other conference reviewers. Journal reviewers, in contrast, can send out each review as soon as it is ready, with only several other reviews required to provide a complete set of reviews to the authors. An emphasis on prioritizing journal reviews should enable the field to significantly shorten the current journal review cycle. There is also reason to hope that such a system would produce higher-quality reviews — while the total reviewing load across the field might not decrease, it would be more evenly distributed over time and reviewers, placing reviewers under less pressure and perhaps enabling them to produce higher-quality reviews.

3.9 Increased Conference Acceptance Rates

For the shift from the current conference-based system to a more standard conference/journal system to succeed, the field will need to shift its reviewing effort from conferences to journals. The conference review system should become an abbreviated review designed only to identify and accept all reasonable papers. Conference acceptance rates would go up, which would have a number of positive consequences:

- **Appropriate Publication Bandwidth:** Whenever I review papers or talk with researchers, I invariably come away impressed with the quality of research that our field, across the board, is currently producing. Unfortunately, the current system rejects much research that is worth publishing. Increasing acceptance rates would provide a more appropriate balance between the amount of quality research that is produced and the amount that is rejected.

- **Timely Dissemination:** Papers that do not fit into the mainstream of the field must often be submitted to multiple conferences before the research becomes well enough known for a committee to accept the paper. Going through multiple conference submission cycles delays the dissemination of such research. Increasing acceptance rates would shorten the dissemination time by decreasing (ideally to one) the number of submission cycles required to publish the paper.

- **Venue Consolidation:** Higher conference acceptance rates would make it possible to consolidate the large number of conferences that currently serve the field into fewer (ideally one) large conferences. This change would reduce travel overhead (cost and time) and facilitate productive interactions between researchers in subfields that, under the current fragmented conference system, have little opportunity to exchange ideas and/or techniques. Consolidation would also make it easier to perform literature searches.

- **Reduced Reviewing Load:** Reducing the number of submission cycles per paper would also reduce the total reviewing load required to accept the paper.

- **Priority Clarity:** The current conference review process often confuses the issue of who should receive credit for a given research idea or advance. I am aware of multiple occurrences when the credit for an idea has become confused, either because the program committee decided to accept only one of multiple papers presenting similar ideas or because a paper presenting an idea happened to be accepted at one conference while another paper presenting a similar idea was rejected at other conferences. Increasing the number of accepted papers would reduce the number of times this unfortunate situation occurred.

- **Enhanced Satisfaction with the Field:** Based on interactions with my colleagues, one of the major sources of dissatisfaction with the field is the fact that rejections of clearly publishable papers are often accompanied by low quality, misguided, or even overtly mistaken reviews. Reducing the number of reject decisions would reduce this source of dissatisfaction.

I agree with many of the arguments that others have put forward criticizing various aspects of the current conference-based publication system in computer science [1, 3, 6, 9]. For me, however, a particularly important reason to move away from the current system is the negative impact it has on disruptively creative research.

4. Acknowledgements

I would like to thank the members of the program committee for the hard work they put in reviewing the papers, the judgment they exercised in selecting the accepted papers, and the time and effort they invested in attending the program committee meeting. For many program committee members attending the program committee meeting required a significant amount of travel. I would also like to thank the conference chair, William Cook, and the members of the OOPSLA/SPLASH Steering Committee for their support. I ran the review process using the CyberChair conference management program, which helped to make the submission and review process run smoothly. Stelios Sidiroglou, Vijay Ganesh, Sasa Misailovic, Michael Carbin, and Deokhwan Kim provided invaluable assistance during the program committee meeting. Finally, I would like to thank Mary McDavitt for her help organizing the program committee meeting. Thanks to Mary, the program committee was well fed and able to devote their full attention to the papers under review!

References

[1] K. Birman and F. Schneider. Program committee overload in systems. *Communications of the ACM*, 52(5), 2009.

[2] J. Crowcroft, S. Keshav, and N. McKeown. Deadline-driven research. *Communications of the ACM*, 52(1), 2009.

[3] L. Fortnow. Time for computer science to grow up. *Communications of the ACM*, 52(8), 2009.

[4] J. Mogul, editor. *Proceedings of the Workshop on Organizing Workshops, Conferences, and Symposia for Computer Scientists*, San Francisco, CA, Apr. 2008.

[5] T. Mudge. Report on the panel: How can computer architecture researchers avoid becoming a society for irreproducible results? *Computer Architecture News*, 24(1), 1996.

[6] D. Patterson. The health of research conferences and the dearth of big idea papers. *Communications of the ACM*, 47(12), 2004.

[7] M. Vardi. Conferences vs. journals in computing research. *Communications of the ACM*, 52(5), 2009.

[8] M. Vardi. Revisiting the publication culture in computing research. *Communications of the ACM*, 53(3), 2009.

[9] J. Wing. Deadline-driven research. *Communications of the ACM*, 52(12), 2009.

Onward! Chair's Welcome

Onward! is a place for presenting high-potential, innovative, even radical, ideas for programming languages, software engineering and applications. We are at a fascinating time in the evolution of computing, where the mind-boggling power of mobile devices, embedded devices and wireless communication are providing serious platforms for further explosion of ideas for applications that change the way people live – the way we communicate, socialise, entertain and learn. Business is also changing, with significant innovation in mobile application marketplaces. Computing has permeated people's lives in fundamental ways, and is now at a crossroads where a sea-change is needed in the way we think about, and produce, software. Onward! is therefore open to thought-provoking influences from multiple disciplines, such as art, music, sociology, psychology, biology, anthropology, economics, politics and indeed, pretty much any other discipline.

The pace of technology change is staggering, and is not matched by the time required to bring research ideas to the required standard of empirical validation in other eminent conferences. Onward!'s contributions are well-argued, though early-stage, with the goal to provide a forum where revolutionary ideas can provide fodder for deep thought and discussion of the future of our profession, amongst the thought-leaders, the attendees, of Onward! and Splash.

This year, we have two Keynote Speakers: Benjamin Pierce is both an eminent scientist in the field of programming languages' foundations, and a gifted photographer; Kenneth Stanley studies natural evolution in consideration of astronomically complex structures. Other contributions to the Onward! programme take a number of different forms. Intriguing new ideas are presented in the research papers (long and short) and essays sessions. We welcome back a workshop covering the evaluation and usability of programming languages and tools. Continuing last year's successful Green panel, this year's panel is on Green Software. Features and short films round out the conference with the presentation of software systems and ideas from unusual perspectives.

Siobhán Clarke
Onward! 2010 General Chair
Trinity College Dublin

Table of Contents

Practitioner Reports

Educators' & Trainers' Symposium Paper

Student Research Competition

Doctoral Symposium

Posters

Panels

Workshops

SPLASH 2010 Conference Organization

General Chair	William R. Cook, University of Texas at Austin
OOPSLA Program Chair	Martin Rinard, MIT
Onward! General Chair	Siobhán Clarke, Lero @ Trinity College Dublin, Ireland
Practitioner Reports	Steve Marney, HP Enterprise Services
Educators' and Trainers' Symposium	Ed Gehringer, NC State University
Doctoral Symposium	Gary T. Leavens, University of Central Florida
Student Research Competition	James Hill, Indiana University-Purdue University Indianapolis
Student Volunteer	Ciera Jaspan, Carnegie Mellon University
Tutorials	William R. Cook, University of Texas at Austin
Workshops	Jeff Gray, University of Alabama
Panels	Aki Namioka, Cisco Systems
Posters	James Hill, Indiana University-Purdue University Indianapolis
Website and Content Management	Henry Baragar, Instantiated Software Inc.
Treasurer	Torsten Layda, SIX Swiss Exchange
Corporate Support	Shail Arora, Adayana, Inc. Gail Harris, Instantiated Software Inc.
Steering Committee Chair	Richard P. Gabriel, IBM Research
2011 Conference	Cristina Lopes, University of California at Irvine
Liaison with ACM	Ashley Cozzi, ACM
Operations	Rebecca Mebane, MeetGreen
Registration	Carole Mann, Registration Systems Lab

SPLASH 2010 Conference Organization —Committees

OOPSLA Program Committee

Ali-Reza Adl-Tabatabai, Intel
Elisa Baniassad, Australian National University
Emery Berger, University of Massachusetts, Amherst
Hans-J. Boehm, HP Labs
Michael Bond, University of Texas, Austin
Cristian Cadar, Imperial College
Robert Cartwright, Rice University
Wei-Ngan Chin, National University of Singapore
Jong-Deok Choi, Samsung
Theo D'Hondt, Vrije Universiteit Brussel
Brian Demsky, University of California, Irvine
Kathleen Fisher, AT&T Labs Research
Richard P. Gabriel, IBM Research
Robert Hirschfeld, Hasso-Plattner-Institut Potsdam
Antony Hosking, Purdue University
Maria Jump, King's College
Christoph Kirsch, University of Salzburg
Patrick Lam, Waterloo
Gary T. Leavens, University of Central Florida
Ondrej Lhotak, Waterloo
Benjamin Pierce, University of Pennsylvania
Bill Pugh, University of Maryland
Shaz Qadeer, Microsoft
Jakob Rehof, University of Dortmund
Dirk Riehle, Friedrich-Alexander-University of Erlangen-Nurnberg
Martin Rinard, MIT (chair)
Vijay Saraswat, IBM Research
Koushik Sen, University of California, Berkeley
Dave Thomas, Bedarra Research Labs
Eli Tilevich, Virginia Tech
Frank Tip, IBM Research
Westley Weimer, University of Virginia
Eran Yahav, IBM Research
Kwangkeun Yi, Seoul National University
Lenore Zuck, NSF, University of Illinois at Chicago

Practitioner Reports Committee

Rob van den Berg, TomTom
Gail E. Harris, Instantiated Software Inc. (chair)
Shan Shan Huang, Logicblox
Steve Marney, HP Enterprise Services (chair)
Bob Marcus, Consultant
Tim O'Connor, Consultant

Educators' and Trainers' **Symposium Committee**	Joel Adams, Calvin College Vladimir Bacvanski, InferData David Bunde, Knox College Jim Caristi, Valparaiso University Curt Clifton, Rose-Hulman Institute of Technology Dan Ernst, Univ. of Wisconsin, Eau Claire Ed Gehringer, NC State University (chair) Dennis Mancl, Alcatel-Lucent Mary Lynn Manns, University of North Carolina at Asheville Barry Wittman, Elizabethtown College
Doctoral Symposium Committee	Jonathan Aldrich, Carnegie Mellon University Gary T. Leavens, University of Central Florida (chair) Kathryn McKinley, University of Texas at Austin Eli Tilevich, Virginia Tech
Student Research Competition **Committee**	Ademola Adejokun, Lockheed Martin Aeronautics Yishai Feldman, IBM Research, Israel James Hill, Indiana University-Purdue University Indianapolis (chair) Michael Richmond, IBM Research Nadyne Richmond, Microsoft Jules White, Vanderbilt University
SPLASH Workshops Committee	Elisa Baniassad, Chinese University of Hong Kong Ruzanna Chitchyan, Lancaster University, UK Sergiu Dascalu, University of Nevada Alessandro Garcia, PUC-Rio, Brazil Aniruddha Gokhale, Vanderbilt University Jeff Gray, University of Alabama (chair) Steve Marney, HP Enterprise Services Christa Schwanninger, Siemens, Germany
Panels Committee	Steven Fraser, Cisco Research Center Ruth Lennon, Letterkenny Institute of Technology, Ireland Aki Namioka, Cisco Systems (chair) Dave Thomas, Bedarra Research Labs, Canada
Posters Committee	Ademola Adejokun, Lockheed Martin Aeronautics Yishai Feldman, IBM Research, Israel James Hill, Indiana University-Purdue University Indianapolis (chair) Michael Richmond, IBM Research Nadyne Richmond, Microsoft Jules White, Vanderbilt University
Tutorials Committee	William R. Cook, University of Texas at Austin (chair) Richard P. Gabriel, IBM Research Torsten Layda, SWX Swiss Exchange

Onward! 2010 Conference Organization

General Chair: Siobhán Clarke *(Lero @ Trinity College Dublin, Ireland)*

Program Chair: Kevin Sullivan *(University of Virginia, USA)*

Panels Chair: Aki Namioka *(Cisco Systems, USA)*

Films Chair: Bernd Brügge *(Technische Universität München, Germany)*

Essays Chair: Daniel Steinberg *(Dim Sum Thinking, USA)*

Workshops Chair: Jonathan Edwards *(MIT, USA)*

Website Chair: Eamonn Linehan *(Lero @ Trinity College Dublin, Ireland)*

Publicity Chair: Alessandro Garcia *(PUC-Rio, Brazil)*

Steering Committee Chair: Elisa Baniassad *(Australian National University, Australia)*

Steering Committee: Robert Biddle *(Carleton University, Canada)*
Siobhán Clarke *(Lero @ Trinity College Dublin, Ireland)*
Geoff Cohen *(USA)*
Richard P. Gabriel *(IBM Research, USA)*
Cristina Videira Lopes *(University of California, USA)*
James Noble *(Victoria University of Wellington, New Zealand)*
Dirk Riehle *(University of Erlangen-Nuremberg, Germany)*

Program Committee: Elisa Baniassad *(Australian National University, Australia)*
Segiru Chiba *(Tokyo Institute of Technology, Japan)*
Yael Dubinsky *(Technion University, Israel)*
Richard P. Gabriel *(IBM Research, USA)*
Jeff Gray *(University of Alabama, USA)*
Ingolf Krueger *(University of California San Diego, USA)*
Jeff Magee *(Imperial College London, England)*
Ana Moreira *(Universidade Nova de Lisboa, Portugal)*
Gail Murphy *(University of British Columbia, Canada)*
Linda Northrop *(Carnegie Mellon Software Engineering Institute, USA)*
Hridesh Rajan *(Iowa State University, USA)*
Peri Tarr *(IBM Research, USA)*

Essays Committee: Kent Beck *(Three Rivers Institute)*
Jutta Eckstein *(IT Communication, Germany)*
Eric Freeman *(The Walt Disney Company)*
Erich Gamma *(IBM Rational Zurich Research)*
Mark Mahoney *(Carthage College)*
Linda Northrop *(Carnegie Mellon University)*
Brian Sletten *(Bosatsu Consulting)*
Glenn Vanderburg *(Relevance)*
Markus Voelter *(Independent / itemis)*
Eugene Wallingford *(University of Northern Iowa)*
David West *(New Mexico Highlands University)*

Workshops Committee: Bruce Horn *(Powerset)*

Films Committee: Roberto Bisiani *(University of Milano - Bicocca, Italy)*
Oliver Creighton *(Siemens Corporation, Germany)*
Ralph Guggenheim *(Alligator Planet, USA)*
Martin Purvis *(University of Otago, Dunedin, New Zealand)*
Maryam Purvis *(University of Otago, Dunedin, New Zealand)*
Harald Stangl *(Technische Universität München, Germany)*

Panels Committee: Steven Fraser *(Cisco Research Center)*
Ruth Lennon *(Letterkenny Institute of Technology)*
Dave Thomas *(Bedarra Research Labs)*

Additional OOPSLA Reviewers

Taweesup Apiwattanapong
Malte Appeltauer
Matthew Arnold
Pavel Avgustinov
Godmar Back
Lujo Bauer
Nels Beckman
Steve Blackburn
Eric Bodden
Elisa Gonzalez Boix
John Boyland
Sebastian Burckhardt
Jacob Burnim
Andoni Lombide Carreton
Hang Chu
Thomas Cleenewerck
John Clements
Pascal Costanza
Florin Craciun
Silviu Craciunas
David Cunningham
Charlie Curtsinger
Alokika Dash
Anupam Datta
Nirav Dave
Cristina David
Hannes Dohrn
Derek Dreyer
Sophia Drossopoulou
Stephane Ducasse
Tudor Dumitras
Christopher Dutchyn
Rochelle Elva
Yong-hun Eom
Erik Ernst

Jon Eyolfson
Manuel Fahndrich
Matthias Felleisen
Stephen Fink
Bruno De Fraine
Vijay Ganesh
Felix Geller
Cristian Gherghina
Neal Glew
Guy Golan-Gueta
Michael Greenberg
Arjun Guha
Sam Guyer
Andreas Haas
Christian Hammer
Tim Harris
Peter Hawkins
Martin Hirzel
Pieter Hooimeijer
Faraz Hussain
Ahmed Hussein
Marc Fisher II
Atsushi Igarashi
Bart Jacobs
Nicholas Jalbert
K. R. Jayaram
James Jenista
Jim Jenista
Pallavi Joshi
Yungbum Jung
Leonardo Uribe Kaffure
Andy Kellens
Sarfraz Khurshid
Heejung Kim
Ik-Soon Kim
Sunghoon Kim

Carsten Kolassa
Soonho Kong
Joeri De Koster
Clemens Krainer
Shriram Krishnamurthi
Lawrence P. Kucera
John Launchbury
Byeongcheol Lee
Jae-Jin Lee
Jupyung Lee
Oukseh Lee
Wonchan Lee
Woosuk Lee
Karl Levitt
Ondrej Lhotak
Calvin Lin
Jens Lincke
Tongping Liu
Eduardo R. B. Marques
Stefan Marr
Jay McCarthy
Ken McMillan
Antoine Mine
Alon Mishne
Gopalan Nadathur
Joe Near
Greg Nelson
Carlos Noguera
Xavier Noumbissi Noundou
Gene Novark
Hakjoo Oh
Bruno Oliveira
Chang-Seo Park
Sungwoo Park

Hannes Payer
Adrian Perrig
Michael Perscheid
Peter Pietzuch
Marco Pistoia
Shengchao Qin
Hridesh Rajan
Noam Rinetzky
Yangwoo Roe
Harald Roeck
Andreas Rossberg
Sukyoung Ryu
Yaniv Sa'ar
Michel A. Salim
Christophe Scholliers
Sangmin Seo
Scott Smith
Manu Sridharan
Friedrich Steimann
Bastian Steinert
Christos Stergiou
Alvin Teh
Bill Thies
Stijn Timbermont
Rainer Trummer
Yves Vandriessche
Martin Vechev
Ronald Veldema
Stijn Verhaegen
Razvan Voicu
Peter Welch
Ben Wiedermann
Jean Yang
Greta Yorsh
Jin Zhou
Yoav Zibin

Additional Onward! Reviewers

Ziyad Alshaikh
Hyun Cho
Bashar Gharaibeh

Richard L. Hudson
Clayton Myers
Eduardo Piveta

Eduardo Rivera
Tyler Sondag
Yu Sun

Pablo Sánchez
Robert Tairas
Alvin Teh

Sponsors & Supporters

SPLASH'10 Sponsors:

SPLASH'10 Supporters:

Onward! 2010 Sponsor:

Onward! 2010 Supporters: IBM Research

Onward! Program Chair's Welcome

Beyond stronger scientific foundations, the research fields of software languages and engineering need bold and promising new ideas. The Onward! 2010 Research Program continues the Onward! tradition of meeting this latter need by attracting, reviewing, selecting and publishing the community's most highly creative new ideas in these areas. Onward! values insightful new research problem formulations and breakthrough solution hypotheses supported by enough evidence and argumentation to justify significant additional inquiry, over rigorous testing of narrow hypotheses yielding higher assurance of validity but for more incremental, and often unsurprising and uninspiring, results.

Onward! 2010 received 39 papers in its initial submission period, of which nine (23%) were selected as full papers to be published in the SPLASH Proceedings. Onward! 2010 received an additional 20 short papers in the second submission period. From the combined 59 papers received in the first and second periods, 8 were selected for publication as short papers in the SPLASH Companion volume.

On behalf of the Program Committee and myself, I thank all of those who submitted papers to Onward! this year. The Program Committee had a difficult job with two submission periods, and I would like to thank each of them sincerely for their commitment and consideration throughout the reviewing process:

Elisa Baniassad	Australian National University
Segiru Chiba	Tokyo Institute of Technology
Yael Dubinsky	Technion University
Richard Gabriel	IBM Research
Jeff Gray	University of Alabama
Ingolf Krueger	University of California San Diego
Jeff Magee	Imperial College London
Ana Moreira	Universidade Nova de Lisboa
Gail Murphy	University of British Columbia
Linda Northrop	Carnegie Mellon Software Engineering Institute
Hridesh Rajan	Iowa State University
Peri Tarr	IBM Research

I would also like to extend my thanks to the co-reviewers who helped with our committee.

We hope you enjoy and benefit from the research papers at Onward! 2010 as much as we enjoyed reviewing and accepting them! Many thanks for your interest. I hope to see you at Onward! 2010.

Kevin Sullivan
Onward! 2010 Program Chair
University of Virginia

now **happens-before** *later* *

Static Schedule Analysis of Fine-grained Parallelism with Explicit Happens-before Relationships

Christoph M. Angerer

ETH Zurich, Switzerland
angererc@inf.ethz.ch

Thomas R. Gross

ETH Zurich, Switzerland
trg@inf.ethz.ch

Abstract

Current compilers are still largely ignorant of the scheduling of parallel tasks at runtime. Without this information, however, they have difficulties optimizing and verifying concurrent programs.

In this paper, we present a programming model where the program contains explicit scheduling constraints in the form of happens-before relationships between scheduled tasks. This model allows for flexible and fine-grained ad hoc parallelism while still enabling us to statically extract an abstraction of the runtime schedule. The result of this schedule analysis can answer the question as to whether two tasks execute in sequence, exclusively, or in parallel with each other.

Categories and Subject Descriptors D.1.3 [*Software*]: [Concurrent Programming]

General Terms Algorithms, Languages

1. Introduction

With the arrival of multicore systems, parallel programming is becoming increasingly mainstream. Despite this, compilers still remain largely ignorant of the task scheduling at runtime. Absent this knowledge, however, a compiler is missing important optimization and verification opportunities.

In a traditional thread model, the lifetime of a thread and its dependencies on other threads are not stated explicitly; rather, they come about as a side effect of executing low level primitives such as signals and locks. For this reason, it is hard for compilers to construct an approximation of the runtime schedule.

Consider the following short Java method:

---
* Supported, in part, by the Swiss National Science Foundation grant 200021_120285.

Permission to make digital or hard copies of all or part of this work for personal or classroom use is granted without fee provided that copies are not made or distributed for profit or commercial advantage and that copies bear this notice and the full citation on the first page. To copy otherwise, to republish, to post on servers or to redistribute to lists, requires prior specific permission and/or a fee.
Onward! 2010, October 17–21, 2010, Reno/Tahoe, Nevada, USA.
Copyright © 2010 ACM 978-1-4503-0236-4/10/10. . . $10.00

```
void begin() {
  this.a = new ThreadA(this);
  this.b = new ThreadB(this);
  a.start();
  //other computations
  b.start();
}
```

Without further information about the lifetime and synchronization of threads a and b, a traditional compiler cannot verify the absence of data races nor can it optimize the parallel code.

One alternative to this unstructured parallelism is to adopt specialized syntactic language features. Systems like OpenMP [20] and Cilk [5, 21], for example, offer lexically scoped fork-join style parallelism in place of ad hoc threads. As a result, these systems are able to better approximate the parallel control flow. Structured parallelism, however, comes at the cost of flexibility, making it difficult to model common patterns such as futures or producer-consumer.

In this paper, we propose a model with explicit task scheduling that keeps the flexibility of threads and enables static reasoning. Given two tasks, a *schedule analysis* can answer the question whether the tasks are sequential, parallel, or exclusive. A compiler can use this information to make parallelism-related decisions during verification and optimization phases.

For representing concurrent programs, we introduce two new primitives to a Java-like language. One primitive schedules a new task and the other explicitly adds a happens-before relationship between two scheduled tasks (Section 3). When executing a program with explicit scheduling, the runtime keeps track of the schedule. The schedule is represented as a graph that exhibits specific structural properties (Section 4). These properties allow us to statically extract an approximation of the runtime schedule (Section 5). We have implemented a prototype and are working on integrating it with an existing Java compiler framework (Section 6).

We build upon a large body of related work (Section 7) for parallel program analysis to design a system that preserves both flexible, unstructured control flow and static analysis of the program schedule. To summarize, this paper makes the following three contributions:

- We define a representation and execution model of parallel programs with explicit happens-before relationships.

- We identify structural properties of abstract schedules.

- We describe an analysis to extract an abstract schedule from a program that was written in or transformed into our representation.

2. The Need for Schedule Analysis

Researchers have developed a wide variety of compiler optimizations and verifications for parallel programs. Adapting such optimizations to parallel programs, however, requires information about what parts of the program might be executed in parallel. The goal of a schedule analysis is to statically compute a mapping $Task \times Task \rightarrow Relation$ to answer the question of how two program tasks relate to each other:

Sequential: Two tasks are sequential if their execution is strictly ordered.

Exclusive: Two tasks are exclusive if they can never co-exist in a single run of the program (e.g., they are scheduled in different branches of a conditional statement).

Parallel: If two tasks are neither sequential nor exclusive, they are considered (potentially) parallel.

Generally, the safe and conservative assumption is to over-approximate the parallelism. As an example, take the detection of data races. Two activations are allowed to write to the same data if and only if they are sequentially ordered. If the sequential execution cannot be guaranteed we must assume that both tasks are potentially executed in parallel and report a data race if they access the same data.

There are numerous examples for optimizations that require or benefit from scheduling information:

Synchronization Elimination aims at removing unnecessary synchronization constructs [22]. A synchronization construct can be removed if all tasks that execute the critical section are sequentially ordered or exclusive.

Region-based Allocation optimizes garbage collection by allocating all or some objects created during a (possibly parallel) computation in a contiguous memory region [24]. The whole region is deallocated as a unit when the computation finishes. To avoid dangling references, however, the compiler must ensure that at the point of de-allocation there are no more parallel tasks that might use the memory.

Polyhedral Analysis tries to automatically introduce parallelism that was not originally specified by the programmer [6]. Parallelism can be increased if, for example, a compiler can show that a happens-before relationship between two tasks can be removed without introducing a data race.

3. Explicit Task Scheduling

Our model is based on lightweight tasks with explicit scheduling. Compared to traditional threads, explicit happens-before relationships simplify the analysis of parallel program schedules while avoiding the limitations of lexically scoped parallelism.

The basic building block of our execution model is a *task*. A task is similar to a method in that it contains code that is executed in the context of a `this`-object (or the class, in the case of `static` methods/tasks). Unlike a method, however, one does not *call* a task, which would result in the immediate execution of the body, but instead *schedules* it for later execution.

As an example, consider a task `t()` that starts a long-running computation `compute()` and schedules a task `print()` that will print the result after the computation has finished:

```
task t() {
  Activation aPrint = sched(this.print());
  Activation aCompute = sched(this.compute());
  aCompute→aPrint;
}
```

A schedule is represented as a graph of $\langle object, task() \rangle$ pairs. The statement `sched(this.print())`, for example, creates a new node with the `this` object and the `print()` task and returns an object of type `Activation` representing that node. Like any other object, `Activation` objects can be kept in local variables, passed around as parameters, and stored in fields.

At runtime, a scheduler constantly chooses activations that are eligible for execution and starts them. The order in which the scheduler is allowed to start the activations is specified by the edges in the schedule graph. If the schedule contains a happens-before edge $\langle o1, t1() \rangle \rightarrow \langle o2, t2() \rangle$, the scheduler must guarantee that activation $\langle o1, t1() \rangle$ has finished execution before activation $\langle o2, t2() \rangle$ is started. The statement `aCompute→aPrint` creates an explicit happens-before relationship between the two activation objects `aCompute` and `aPrint`.

In the code, the currently executing activation can be accessed through the keyword `now`. Whenever a new task is scheduled, the scheduler automatically adds an initial happens-before relationship between `now` and the new activation node. Therefore, in the example the scheduler implicitly creates two additional edges `now→aCompute` and `now→aPrint`. These edges prevent the immediate execution of the new activations and enable the current task to add additional constraints to the schedule before it finishes.

The above example works, as long as `compute()` does not schedule new subtasks. If it does, however, the schedule would not contain any happens-before edges between the `aPrint` activation and those new activations. Therefore, the scheduler would be allowed to execute `aPrint` before the subtasks have finished, i.e. too early. However, there is no place where we could create edges to prevent aPrint from executing prematurely: In t() the subtasks have not yet been created and inside compute() we are missing a reference to aPrint.

To solve this we can pass the aPrint object as a parameter to the compute() task and use it to schedule the new subtasks before aPrint:

```
task t() {
  Activation aPrint = sched(this.print());
  //pass a reference to aPrint:
  Activation aCompute = sched(this.compute(aPrint));
  aCompute→aPrint;
}

task compute(Activation later) {
  Activation aSubtask =
              sched(this.someSubtask(later));
  //schedule our subtask before later
  aSubtask→later;
}
```

In compute() we can pass the reference even further along to aSubtask, thus allowing aSubtask (and its subtasks, if there are any) to push the execution of the aPrint activation further and further into the future until the whole computation is finished. Once the subtasks terminate without inserting new tasks, the scheduler will be able to execute aPrint.

3.1 A Recursive Divide-and-Conquer Example

Figure 1 shows an example of a recursive divide-and-conquer algorithm with explicit scheduling. The algorithm sums the elements of an integer array by recursively dividing the array into a left and a right half before computing their sums. The base case of the recursion is reached for sub-arrays of length 1, in which case the sum is trivial.

The class ArraySum is an implementation of this algorithm. It defines two tasks: sum() divides the work between two children and subtotal() adds their results. Figure 2 shows the changes in the schedule when ArraySum is started with an array of length 3.

Initially, the schedule contains an activation $\langle o1, sum()\rangle$ for an ArraySum object o1 plus an activation $\langle x, y()\rangle$. $\langle x, y()\rangle$ is provided by the client of ArraySum to make use of the result after the computation is finished. A reference to $\langle x, y()\rangle$ is passed to sum() through the later parameter on line 8. In this schedule, the scheduler can choose $\langle o1, sum()\rangle$ because there are no other outstanding happens-before relationships for that activation.

In the first iteration the array length is greater than 1, which leads to the recursive case starting at line 12. In this branch, we first schedule this.subtotal() on line 13. We then add the happens-before relationship subtotal→later on line 14, creating an edge between the nodes $\langle o1, subtotal()\rangle$

```
1   class ArraySum {
2     IntArray arr;
3     int result;
4     Activation left, right;
5
6     ArraySum(IntArray arr) { this.arr = arr; }
7
8     task sum(Activation later) {
9       if(arr.length() == 1) {
10        result = arr.getInt();
11        //end of this task
12      } else {
13        Activation subtotal = sched(this.subtotal());
14        subtotal→later;
15
16        left = new ArraySum(arr.leftHalf());
17        right = new ArraySum(arr.rightHalf());
18
19        sched(left.sum(subtotal))→subtotal;
20        sched(right.sum(subtotal))→subtotal;
21      }
22    }
23
24    task subtotal() {
25      result = ((ArraySum)left.obj()).result
26              + ((ArraySum)right.obj()).result;
27      //end of this task
28    }
29  }
```

Figure 1. Example of a recursive divide-and-conquer algorithm with explicit scheduling.

and $\langle x, y()\rangle$. As shown in Figure 2, this edge defers the execution of $\langle x, y()\rangle$ until the subtotal is available.

Lines 16 and 17 split the input array into two halves and pass them to two new instances of ArraySum. We store references to both instances in the left and right fields so that the subtotal() task can later read their result.

The subtasks left.sum() and right.sum() are scheduled on lines 19 and 20. By passing a reference to the subtotal activation, the recursive child activations of sum() can insert their own subtotal activations on line 14, preventing the parent's subtotal from executing before the children have finished.

The two scheduling statements add the nodes $\langle o2, sum()\rangle$ and $\langle o3, sum()\rangle$ to the schedule and bind their later parameter to the node $\langle o1, subtotal()\rangle$. This is shown in Panel 2 of Figure 2. On the same lines 19 and 20, the two new activations are also scheduled before subtotal, thus creating the edges $\langle o2, sum()\rangle \rightarrow \langle o1, subtotal()\rangle$ and $\langle o3, sum()\rangle \rightarrow \langle o1, subtotal()\rangle$.

The scheduler can now choose either $\langle o2, sum()\rangle$ or $\langle o3, sum()\rangle$ for execution. $\langle o2, sum()\rangle$ hits the base case because its array is of length 1. The base case of the recursion on line 9 does not schedule any new tasks and does not create any new happens-before edges, so the schedule

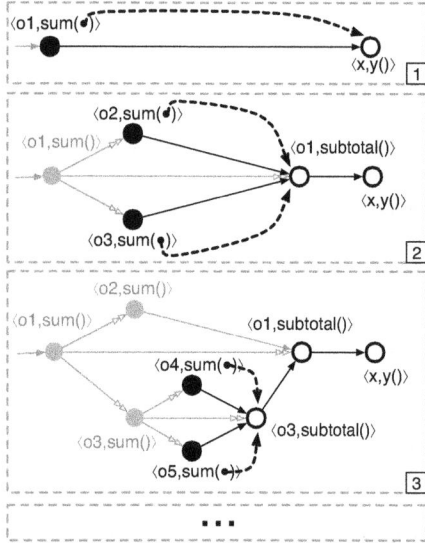

Figure 2. Snapshots of the schedule during execution of the example from Figure 1 for an array of length 3. Satisfied happens-before relationships and already executed nodes are grayed out. Black nodes are eligible for execution. Unfilled nodes have unfulfilled scheduling constraints.

remains unchanged. The execution of $\langle o3, sum() \rangle$, on the other hand, recursively activates three new tasks: two tasks to compute the partial results and one task to add them.

Panel 3 of Figure 2 shows the state of the schedule after $\langle o2, sum() \rangle$ and $\langle o3, sum() \rangle$ have been executed. The scheduler continues to execute $\langle o4, sum() \rangle$ and $\langle o5, sum() \rangle$ in any order and (because of the original array of length 3) both activations hit the base case and leave the schedule unchanged. Therefore, the schedule can execute the remaining linear chain consisting of $\langle o3, subtotal() \rangle$ and $\langle o1, subtotal() \rangle$ before continuing with the caller at $\langle x, y() \rangle$.

4. Structural Properties of Schedules

This section describes structural properties of schedules.

4.1 Well-formed Schedules

A well-formed schedule guarantees that the scheduler can always choose at least one activation for execution (progress) and that every activation is eventually executed (liveness). Both conditions require that the schedule is a directed acyclic graph. A cycle in the schedule would result in a deadlock where two activations block each other and prevent progress. Assuming that the execution of a task always terminates, an acyclic graph ensures that there is always at least one node that has only incoming edges from already executed activations.

Besides being acyclic, a well-formed schedule also restricts the addition of new happens-before relationships. Because activations can be stored in fields, an activation object may reference an activation that has already been executed.

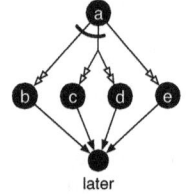

Figure 3. An abstract schedule with a conditional activation. The arc groups the exclusive creation edges.

Imagine that one tries to add a happens-before relationship a1→a2 after a2 has already been executed. The scheduler has no chance of satisfying this edge; since a2 lies in the past, the scheduler cannot retroactively execute anything before that.

To prevent such unresolvable scheduling conflicts, the scheduler allows an edge a1→a2 to be added from within an activation a0 only if there exists an edge a0→a2. This edge ensures that a2 is scheduled after a0 and therefore is still unexecuted at the time of the edge creation. It is not necessary to require an edge a0→a1, however, because it is not a problem if the source of a happens before edge has already been executed.

4.2 Conditional Activation

Conditional control flow can result in a conditional activation of a task. The `if` statement on line 9 of Figure 1, for example, results in three activations in the `else` branch but none on the `true` branch.

At compile-time, the analysis generally cannot determine which branch is executed at runtime. Therefore, all possible executions must be taken into account. Two activations that are created in different branches of a conditional statement are *exclusive* because they cannot co-exist in the same run of the program. Figure 3 shows an example where node b is exclusive to both c and d but parallel to e. Nodes c and d are parallel to each other as well as parallel to e. Graphically, exclusive edges are connected by arcs.

4.3 Creation Tree

The scheduler implicitly adds an edge between the current activation `now` and all the tasks it schedules. Those initial edges are called *creation edges*. We depict creation edges with double arrow heads. Because an activation has exactly one creator, the creation edges form a *spanning tree* that is embedded into the schedule.

The creation tree is a fundamental data structure that enables many of the operations needed during the analysis. Its importance comes from two basic properties:

1. If one activation x is the direct or indirect parent of another activation y in the creation tree, it is guaranteed that x always executes before y because x creates y.

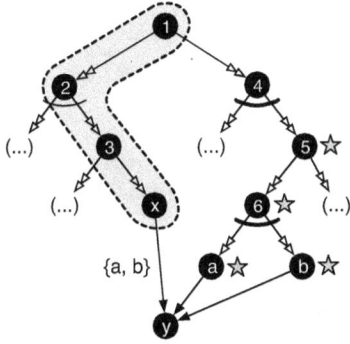

Figure 4. Marking nodes in the creation tree to test if $x \rightarrow y$ is genuine. The fence is circled by the dotted line, marks are shown as stars.

2. If $x \twoheadrightarrow y$ is a creation edge, the existence of the child activation y implies the existence of its parent x, written $y \Rightarrow x$. In fact, this relationship is transitive, thus implying the existence of all parents up to the root of the creation tree (the initial activation that started the program). The inverse, however, is not true. Due to conditional activations, one cannot deduce the existence of a child activation simply from the existence of the parent.

4.4 Genuine Edges

The analysis uses the schedule and its embedded creation tree to decide how two activations relate to each other.

Sequential Activations: If two nodes are connected by a path in the schedule, their execution is ordered and therefore sequential. If there is no such path, the activations are either exclusive or parallel.

Exclusive Activations: If we find that in the creation tree two nodes are connected to their common ancestor by conditional edges, the two activations are exclusive.

Parallel Activations: If two nodes are connected to their common ancestor by parallel edges, the activations are considered parallel.

Because happens-before relationships can be created conditionally, many parts of the analysis only consider genuine edges. A genuine edge $x \rightarrow y$ is an edge where the existence of the source node x implies that the edge exists, denoted $x \Rightarrow x \rightarrow y$. Genuine edges are useful because we know that if the node x executed at all, it executed before y. Edges that are not genuine are ignored by the analysis, thus over-approximating the parallelism.

To determine whether $x \Rightarrow x \rightarrow y$ we record all the activations $creators(x \rightarrow y)$ that unconditionally create the edge $x \rightarrow y$. We can now rephrase the problem to check if the existence of x implies the existence of at least one node c that creates the edge: $\exists c.x \Rightarrow c \land c \in creators(x \rightarrow y)$. This predicate can be approximated using the creation tree.

Figure 4 shows an example of a creation tree. We want to compute whether the edge $x \rightarrow y$ is genuine. The algorithm starts by marking the *fence*. The fence is comprised of all the nodes from the edge source up to the root of the creation tree. As described earlier, the existence of the fence nodes is implied by the existence of x.

The goal is now, to check whether any node in the fence implies the existence of any node that creates the edge $x \rightarrow y$. We do so by iteratively marking nodes, walking up the creation tree, until we either mark a node in the fence, in which case the edge is genuine, or no more nodes can be marked, in which case the edge is not genuine.

The label on edge $x \rightarrow y$ in Figure 4 indicates that the edge was created by activations a and b. Therefore, the algorithm initially marks the nodes a and b and continues with node 6 as the parent of a and b. Because *all* its exclusive children were marked, and thus all possible execution paths are covered, node 6 can be marked as well. The mark on 6 is sufficient to further mark node 5 because node 6 was created unconditionally.

In the example, node 4 cannot be marked because there is a conditional unmarked sibling of node 5. Therefore, there is a program execution that will create node x but not nodes a or b and thus not the edge $x \rightarrow y$. This concludes that $x \rightarrow y$ is not genuine.

If the program was modified to create node 5 unconditionally, the algorithm would eventually mark the fence in node 1, showing that $x \rightarrow y$ were genuine.

4.5 Recursion

Example 1 contains a recursive activation of the task `sum()` on lines 19 and 20. It is important to detect recursion to prevent infinite expansion of the creation tree during analysis.

In our framework, a recursion is detected as soon as an activation of a task `t()` directly or indirectly causes the creation of another activation of the same task `t()`, but possibly with different `this`-objects. Multiple occurrences of the same task `t()` on an execution trace are not automatically considered recursive, however. It is necessary that the recursion is "self-induced"; the second activation of `t()` must be a result from the first activation of `t()`.

For example, a task `s()` could schedule `o1.t()` and `o2.t()` and add a happens-before constraint between the two. In this case, the execution of `o2.t()` is not considered recursive even though it is executed after `o1.t()` because it did not cause the activation of `o1.t()`.

Given a node in the schedule, we can test for recursive activation by walking up the creation tree. If the node represents a recursive activation of a task `t()`, the creation tree will contain a parent with the same task `t()`.

The analysis records recursive activations in the abstract schedule by adding *recursion edges*. Recursion edges are creation edges that are treated specially when testing whether two nodes are exclusive or parallel.

Imagine an activation a that conditionally creates two activations b and c. In the non-recursive case, b and c are considered to be exclusive. If there is a recursion around a, however, a might create b in the first iteration and c in the second iteration. Because the analysis cannot distinguish the individual iterations, it must assume that b and c are parallel.

5. Schedule Analysis

At the core of the schedule-driven analysis is a standard points-to analysis for object-oriented programs such as the analyses presented in [25] or [23]. The points-to information is necessary because we need information about the target object when a task is scheduled. Similarly, because activations are first-class objects, we need the pointer information to compute the sources and targets of new happens-before edges.

A points-to analysis is driven by the control-flow graph. That is, the order in which nodes are visited and the paths of the information flow are determined by the edges of the CFG. In our schedule-driven analysis, the schedule graph augments this (inter-procedural) role of the CFG for guiding the analysis of parallel constructs. During analysis, the schedule determines in what order the nodes are visited and how information flows between them.

The interface between the points-to analysis and the schedule analysis is an *abstract heap*: a data structure containing the points-to information. For the schedule analysis, the abstract heap is a largely opaque data structure that is defined by the points-to analysis at hand. The schedule analysis requires methods for merging heaps and for querying a heap to determine the points-to set for a given variable.

The analysis works by visiting each node in the abstract schedule until a fixed point has been reached. Analyzing a single node is done in three steps:

1. A heap abstraction is computed by combining the heaps flowing into the node through the incoming edges.

2. The combined heap functions as the input to an incremental pointer analysis; the result of this analysis is an updated heap containing the new points-to information.

3. For non-recursive nodes, the points-to information is used to find newly created activations and/or happens-before edges and to incorporate them into the abstract schedule. If the current node is a recursive activation, however, we instead add a recursion edge that feeds back the result heap and re-open the parent for analysis until a fixed point has been reached.

5.1 Combining Incoming Heaps

The abstract heap at the beginning of an activation a must approximate the effects of all the activations that, at runtime, could execute before a. For sequential executions, the execution order is captured by the happens-before relationships in the abstract schedule. The question is, therefore, what in-

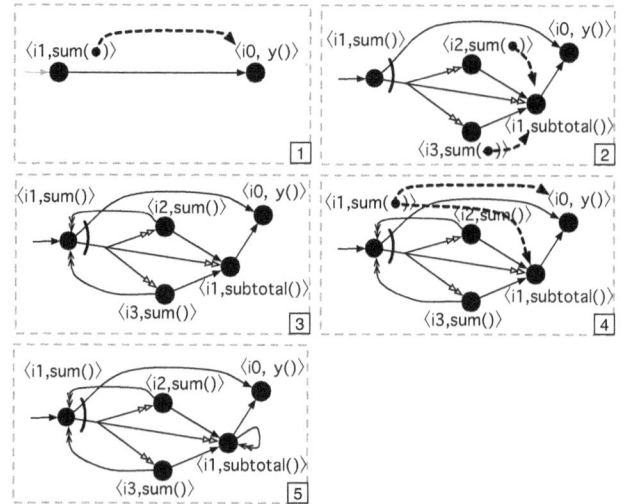

Figure 5. Schedule analysis of Example 1.

fluence can parallel activations have on the initial heap of a?

As it turns out, parallel activations can be ignored if data races are considered to be illegal and if we are willing to 'lazily' detect a data race not in the activations that are directly involved but only in one of their successors. This lazy approach is in contrast to other analyses that iteratively reanalyze threads and update their interference information until a fixed point is reached. For the rare cases where data races should be deliberately allowed we can fall back to such an iterative algorithm, however.

Imagine a special node `exit` that marks the end of the program and happens after all other activations. Then there is always at least one node c for any two unordered activations a and b that happens after a and b: $a \rightarrow^* c \wedge b \rightarrow^* c$. Such a join node c is the point where a data race detection can find concurrent accesses to the same memory locations by comparing the read/write sets of the parallel activations.

Therefore, we can simply assume the absence of data races between a and b because this assumption will be verified later in c. If there is no data race, two activations cannot interfere with each other. For this reason, while analyzing a we can ignore all unordered activations b, c, ... and derive the abstract heap by combining only the heaps of the predecessors connected to a by incoming edges.

5.2 Locks

Synchronizing an arbitrary number of concurrent tasks requires an additional synchronization primitive such as mutexes, atomic compare-and-swap, or locks [11, p.37ff]. Inter-task synchronization requires the analysis to compute the fixed point for the implicit information flow between synchronization points. For space reasons, we do not discuss synchronization primitives but the analysis can be extended to handle them.

5.3 Analysis of the Example

Figure 5 shows how the schedule analysis proceeds for the example of Figure 1. The analysis is at the point where a client has scheduled the sum() task with the abstract object i1. The client further activated $\langle i0, y() \rangle$ to make use of the result later. The relevant part of the abstract schedule is shown in Panel 1 of Figure 5.

The analysis can start to analyze node $\langle i1, sum() \rangle$ because all the preceding nodes have been analyzed. The first step of computing the initial heap is trivial, because there is only one incoming edge. Therefore, we can immediately start the points-to analysis.

Because this was the first time the points-to analysis was started for this node, the resulting abstract heap will contain the three new activations that were created on lines 13, 19, and 20 of Figure 1. Panel 2 of Figure 5 shows the updated abstract schedule after adding the new activation nodes and the corresponding happens-before edges. It is also shown that the later parameters of the two sum() activations are both bound to the same $\langle i1, subtotal() \rangle$ node.

This finishes the analysis of the first node and the analysis consults the schedule to see which node to analyze next. The options are $\langle i2, sum() \rangle$ and $\langle i3, sum() \rangle$ because they are the only nodes that have no unanalyzed predecessors. There is only one incoming edge to either node and the points-to analysis can be started immediately. Because for both nodes we detect a recursion around sum(), we add recursion edges as shown in Panel 3. This re-opens $\langle i1, sum() \rangle$ for analysis.

Back at node $\langle i1, sum() \rangle$, the recursion edges require the analysis to merge the later parameter of the sum() tasks. As shown in Panel 4, due to the recursion, later may point to $\langle i1, subtotal() \rangle$ or $\langle i0, y() \rangle$.

There is more than one incoming edge to $\langle i1, sum() \rangle$; thus we must combine the incoming heaps before we can start the points-to analysis. Looking at the creation tree reveals that $\langle i2, sum() \rangle$ and $\langle i3, sum() \rangle$ are parallel. A data race detection can verify that both tasks can safely run in parallel because both activations access disjoint regions of the array.

Having merged the heaps, the pointer analysis can be restarted for node $\langle i1, sum() \rangle$. In this example, the heap before the pointer analysis is equal to the heap returned by the pointer analysis and we have found a fixed point.

There were no new nodes created, but checking for newly created edges reveals that the statement subtotal→later on line 14 results in an additional recursion edge from $\langle i1, subtotal() \rangle$ to itself because both variables subtotal and later may point to the same $\langle i1, subtotal() \rangle$. This loop represents the chain of subtotal() activations that can occur at runtime.

Panel 5 of Figure 5 shows the state of the abstract schedule after the sum() recursion has been analyzed. The analysis proceeds with computing the fixed point for the recursive node $\langle i1, subtotal() \rangle$ before finishing with node $\langle i0, y() \rangle$.

6. Prototype

We have implemented a prototype of the schedule analysis. The prototype works on a simplified object-oriented language and can be found at http://github.com/chmaruni/XSched. We are now in the process of integrating the analysis with the WALA Java analysis library [28].

7. Related Work

The *happens-before* ordering was first formulated by Lamport [14] and is the basis of the Java memory model [15]. Despite its significance in the memory model, in Java happens-before edges can be created only implicitly, for example by using synchronized blocks or volatile variables.

The goal of a pointer analysis is to statically determine when two pointer expressions refer to the same memory location. Steengaard [26] and Andersen [2] laid the groundwork for the flow-insensitive analysis of single threaded programs. Because points-to analysis is undecidable in the general case, however, researchers developed a large collection of approximation algorithms specialized for different problem domains [12], including parallel programming.

Rugina and Rinard [23] describe a pointer analysis for programs with structured fork-join style concurrency. For each program point, their algorithm computes a points-to graph that maps each pointer to a set of locations. By capturing the effects of pointer assignments for each thread, their algorithm can compute the interference information between parallel threads. Computing the interference information relies on the lexical scoping of the parallel constructs; it cannot handle unstructured parallelism.

By combining pointer and escape analysis, subsequent projects were able to extend their analyses beyond structured parallelism [18, 24]. Both analyses compute points-to information but do not directly answer as to how two tasks are executed with respect to each other. Further, the tight integration of the pointer analysis with the escape analysis and concurrency analysis is contrary to our goal of separating the concerns of schedule analysis from points-to analysis.

A *may-happen-in-parallel* (MHP) analysis can be used to determine what statements in a program may be executed in parallel [19]. Without flow sensitivity, relating two program statements is of limited use for analyzing programs with unstructured parallelism. If two threads execute the same statements but in different contexts, for example, a context insensitive MHP analysis might unnecessarily classify the statements as parallel. When the programming language is restricted to structured parallelism, as has been done for the X10 programming language [1], an intra-procedural MHP analysis can achieve good results, however.

Barik [3] describes a context and flow-sensitive may-happen-before analysis that distinguishes threads by their creation site. Barik introduces a 'thread creation tree', which is closely related to our creation tree. By using threads as their model, however, they must conservatively assume that a parent thread in the tree runs in parallel with each child thread. In our model a parent activation is known to happen before any child activation because the creation tree is a spanning tree embedded in the schedule.

As an alternative to data-flow analysis, many systems apply techniques based on type theory and related formalisms for analyzing parallel programs. Among the many approaches used are typestates [4], ownership types [7], effect systems [9, 16], and access permissions [27].

Actor-based systems [10, 13] avoid many synchronization issues by removing the need for a global schedule altogether. Actors are entities that communicate asynchronously by sending and receiving messages to and from each other. There is no restriction on the order in which messages arrive and an actor has no direct control over the message passing mechanism. This lack of synchronization requires the actor model to avoid mutable shared state whereas our work is based on a shared-memory model. Process calculi, such as the join-calculus [8] and π-calculus [17], permit formal reasoning about systems with autonomous entities.

8. Concluding Remarks

Fully utilizing the increasing number of cores in modern processors requires finer- and finer-grained parallelism. Fine-grained parallelism is characterized by small tasks with only short pieces of sequential code. Many powerful compiler optimizations for single-threaded code, however, become ineffective when the sequential parts are too short. At the same time, new parallelism-aware optimizations require knowledge about the task scheduling at runtime, but this information is not available in current compilers.

Instead of each project inventing its own model of concurrency, we propose an independent discipline of schedule analysis. From this, we expect the same beneficial synergies for future parallel optimizations as with the theory of points-to analysis, which allowed optimizations to focus on their optimization problems instead of computing points-to sets.

We believe that static schedule analysis is a necessary step towards efficient next-generation compilers for multi-core systems.

References

[1] S. Agarwal, R. Barik, V. Sarkar, and R. K. Shyamasundar. May-happen-in-parallel Analysis of X10 Programs. *In PPoPP, 2007.*

[2] L. O. Andersen. Program Analysis and Specialization for the C Programming Language. *Ph.D thesis, DIKU, University of Copenhagen, 1994.*

[3] R. Barik. Efficient Computation of May-Happen-in-Parallel Information for Concurrent Java Programs. *In LNCS, 2006.*

[4] N. E. Beckman, K. Bierhoff, and J. Aldrich. Verifying Correct Usage of Atomic Blocks and Typestate. *In OOPSLA, 2008.*

[5] R. D. Blumofe, C. F. Joerg, B. C. Kuszmaul, C. E. Leiserson, K. H. Randall, and Y. Zhou. Cilk: An Efficient Multithreaded Runtime System. *In PPoPP, 1995.*

[6] U. Bondhugula, A. Hartono, J. Ramanujam, and P. Sadayappan A Practical Automatic Polyhedral Parallelizer and Locality Optimizer. *In PLDI, 2008.*

[7] D. G. Clarke, J. M. Potter, and J. Noble. Ownership Types for Flexible Alias Protection. *In OOPSLA, 1998.*

[8] C. Fournet and G. Gonthier, The Join-Calculus: A Language for Distributed Mobile Programming. *In APPSEM, 2000.*

[9] A. Greenhouse and J. Boyland An Object-Oriented Effects System. *In ECOOP, 1999.*

[10] A. Gul. An Overview of Actor Languages. *In SIGPLAN Not., vol. 21, pp.58–67, 1986.*

[11] M. Herlihy and N. Shavit. The Art of Multiprocessor Programming. *Morgan Kaufmann, MA-USA, 2008.*

[12] M. Hind. Pointer Analysis: Haven't We Solved This Problem Yet? *In PASTE, 2001.*

[13] R. K. Karmani, A. Shali, and A. Gul. Actor Frameworks for the JVM Platform: A Comparative Analysis. *In PPPJ, 2009.*

[14] L. Lamport. Time, Clocks, and the Ordering of Events in a Distributed System. *Commun. ACM 21, 7 (1978).*

[15] J. Manson, W. Pugh, and S. V. Adve. The Java Memory Model. *In POPL, 2005.*

[16] N. Matsakis and T. Gross. Reflective Parallel Programming. *Int HotPar, 2010.*

[17] R. Milner. Communicating and Mobile Systems: The π-Calculus. *Cambridge University Press, NY, USA, 1999.*

[18] M. G. Nanda and S. Ramesh. Pointer Analysis of Multithreaded Java Programs. *In SAC, 2003.*

[19] G. Naumovich, G. Avrunin, and L. Clarke. An Efficient Algorithm for Computing MHP Information for Concurrent Java Programs. *In ESEC/FSE-7, 1999.*

[20] OpenMP Specification: Version 3.0. *http://openmp.org/.*

[21] K. Randall. Cilk: Efficient Multithreaded Computing. *PhD thesis, Dept. of EECS, MIT, 1998.*

[22] E. Ruf. Effective Synchronization Removal for Java. *In PLDI, 2000.*

[23] R. Rugina and M. Rinard. Pointer Analysis for Structured Parallel Programs. *In TOPLAS, 2003.*

[24] A. Salcianu, M. Rinard. Pointer and Escape Analysis for Multithreaded Programs. *In PPoPP, 2001.*

[25] M. Sridharan and R. Bodík. Refinement-based Context-sensitive Points-to Analysis for Java. *In PLDI, 2006.*

[26] B. Steensgaard. Points-to Analysis in Almost Linear Time. *In POPL, 1996.*

[27] S. Stork, P. Marques, and J. Aldrich. Concurrency by Default: Using Permissions to Express Dataflow in Stateful Programs. *In OOPSLA, 2009.*

[28] T.J. Watson Libraries for Analysis (WALA). *http://wala.sourceforge.net*

Emergent Feature Modularization

Márcio Ribeiro   Humberto Pacheco   Leopoldo Teixeira   Paulo Borba

Informatics Center, Federal University of Pernambuco, 50740-540, Recife – PE – Brazil

{mmr3, hsp, lmt, phmb}@cin.ufpe.br

Abstract

Virtual Separation of Concerns reduces the drawbacks of implementing product line variability with preprocessors. Developers can focus on certain features and hide others of no interest. However, these features eventually share elements between them, which might break feature modularization, since modifications in a feature result in problems for another. We present the concept of emergent feature modularization, which aims to establish contracts between features, to prevent developers from breaking other features when performing a maintenance task. These interfaces are product-line-aware, in the sense that it only considers valid feature combinations. We also present a prototype tool that implements the concept.

Categories and Subject Descriptors   D.2.3 [*Software Engineering*]: Coding Tools and Techniques

General Terms   Design

Keywords   Product Lines, Modularity, Preprocessors

1. Introduction

A Software Product Line (SPL) is a family of intensive systems developed from reusable assets. These systems share a common set of features that satisfy the specific needs of a particular market segment [6]. By reusing assets, it is possible to construct products through specific features defined according to customers' requirements [17]. Features are the semantic units by which different programs within a SPL can be differentiated and defined [21]. The set of possible products of a SPL is usually represented through feature models.

Features are often implemented using preprocessors [3, 12]. Conditional compilation directives such as #ifdef and #endif encompass code associated with features. Despite their widespread use, preprocessors have some drawbacks,

including no support for separation of concerns [18]. Virtual Separation of Concerns (VSoC) [12] allow developers to hide feature code not relevant to the current task, being important to reduce some of the preprocessors drawbacks. The idea is to provide developers a way to focus on a feature without the distraction brought by other features [10].

Although this approach is helpful to visualize a feature individually, it does not modularize features to the extent of supporting independent feature maintenance and development [16], since developers know nothing about hidden features. In fact, by visualizing and trying to maintain a feature individually, a developer might introduce errors into the hidden features, since these features eventually share elements — such as variables and methods — with the maintained feature. For instance, the new value of a variable might be correct to the maintained feature, but incorrect to another one that uses this variable. Thus, we have a problem due to the lack of feature modularization: the modification of a feature leads to errors in another one. Moreover, this problem may be worse because this error is only noticed when running the product built with the problematic feature [10].

In this work, we propose the concept of emergent feature modularization, which consists of establishing contracts among feature implementations. We call our approach emergent because the components and interfaces here are neither predefined nor have a rigid structure. Instead, they emerge on demand to give support for specific feature development or maintenance tasks. For example, using the emergent concept, the developer firstly selects feature code to maintain. We associate this selection with a feature, or a combination of features, which we denote as a feature expression. Then, information with respect to the other features and their combinations emerge through an interface.

We also achieve the hiding benefits towards feature comprehensibility. But, while still hiding the feature code, emergent interfaces abstract its details. At the same time, they provide valuable information to maintain the selected code and keep other features and their combinations safe.

This paper makes the following contributions:

- We present the concept of emergent feature modularization to help developers when maintaining SPL implemented with preprocessors-like mechanisms (Section 3);

Permission to make digital or hard copies of all or part of this work for personal or classroom use is granted without fee provided that copies are not made or distributed for profit or commercial advantage and that copies bear this notice and the full citation on the first page. To copy otherwise, to republish, to post on servers or to redistribute to lists, requires prior specific permission and/or a fee.

Onward! 2010,   October 17–21, 2010, Reno/Tahoe, Nevada, USA.
Copyright © 2010 ACM 978-1-4503-0236-4/10/10...$10.00

- A general algorithm to compute emergent components and their emergent interfaces (Sections 3.1, 3.2, and 3.3);

- A prototype tool based on CIDE [12] (a tool that relies on VSoC) to support the concept. It computes and shows emergent interfaces after developers select the code to maintain. Emergent interfaces contain provided/required information to/from other features (Section 4).

2. Motivating Example

Virtual Separation of Concerns (VSoC) reduces some of pre-processors drawbacks, allowing developers to hide feature code not relevant to the current maintenance task [12]. Thus, developers can, to some extent, maintain a feature without the distraction brought by other features [10]. However, we show here that VSoC is not enough to provide feature modularization, which aims at achieving independent feature comprehensibility, changeability, and development [16].

For example, consider **Scenario 1**, where a developer has to maintain the Music feature of the Mobile Media SPL [7]. It implements this functionality using the J2ME standard media API, so that users can play music in formats like *MIDI* and *Mp3*. Basically, the implementation contains a controller (MMController), responsible for handling the play and stop events, and a screen (MMScreen), responsible for painting the buttons and encapsulating the media API. Our scenario consists of adding a new format to play music: the *Ogg* open format. Since the *Ogg* API supports not only play and stop but also pause, rewind and forward events, we need a new controller and screen for it. Figure 1 shows the changes in part of the Music feature code in order to fit this new format.

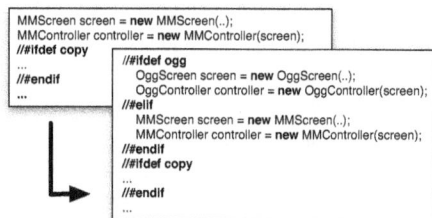

```
MMScreen screen = new MMScreen(..);
MMController controller = new MMController(screen);
//#ifdef copy
...
//#endif
...
          //#ifdef ogg
              OggScreen screen = new OggScreen(..);
              OggController controller = new OggController(screen);
          //#elif
              MMScreen screen = new MMScreen(..);
              MMController controller = new MMController(screen);
          //#endif
          //#ifdef copy
          ...
          //#endif
          ...
```

Figure 1. Adding Ogg format to the Mobile Media SPL.

Notice that there is an #ifdef directive encompassing the code of the Copy optional feature, which allows us to remove that part of the code. Therefore, in the original version of the product line, we have at least two products (possible feature selections): (i) Music without Copy; and (ii) Music with Copy. The compiler raises no errors when compiling the (i) variant in the resulting version of the product line. However, there is a compilation error when we take the (ii) variant into consideration. The Copy feature uses a method (controller.setMediaName(..)) that is only defined in MMController, so that it does not exist in our new OggController class due to a programmer failure. This shows that we have no proper feature modularization: the modification of a feature (Music) breaks another feature

(Copy). In addition, this situation gets worse because this error is only noticed when the developer eventually builds the product line with the problematic feature combination (using Copy).

We do not provide the Copy feature code on purpose in order to simulate a developer that is using VSoC, so that he is not concerned about other features (such as Copy). Consequently, he is neither maintaining nor visualizing the code surrounded by the Copy #ifdef directive. To some extent, this support for hiding features is worthwhile to the independent *feature comprehensibility* benefit, since it may help developers to comprehend a feature individually. Despite this advantage of visualizing features individually, VSoC does not provide enough support for understanding and modifying features in separate. For example, because there is no information about the hidden feature (Copy) when maintaining Music, problems may occur in it. So, the independent *changeability* benefit is not achieved.

In this context, sharing information about two or more features may be a confusing point for two developers, so that achieving the *parallel development* is difficult. For example, consider **Scenario 2**, where a developer is responsible for evolving the Copy feature and another one is responsible for the Music feature. The first developer might decide to use the screen variable for implementing a progress bar for showing the copy progress. Meanwhile, because only one place in the original version of the product line uses the screen variable, the second developer might decide to change MMController(screen) for MMController(new MMScreen(..)) and delete the screen declaration. Since screen is now undeclared, a compilation error will happen in the Copy feature. It happens because there is no "*mutual agreement between the creator and accessor*" [22]. Since this contract does not exist, developers of a feature might actually break another one.

Scenario 1 and **Scenario 2** basically show that conditional compilation, even with VSoC support, does not provide adequate modularization support. Bug reports[1] of systems like Linux Kernel and Mozilla present similar problems (undeclared variables, missing methods, ...) involving different features. Besides these kinds of syntactic errors, as discussed in the remaining of the paper, we also consider semantic errors such as when changing the value of a variable that another feature uses. This way, the new value might be right for the maintained feature but wrong for others. Our approach aims to address these cases as well.

3. Emergent Feature Modularization

To solve the problems discussed previously, we propose the concept of emergent feature modularization, which basically consists of establishing, on demand and according to a given development task, interfaces for feature implementations. It is an uncommon way to think about components and

---

[1] See http://bugzilla.kernel.org/ and https://bugzilla.mozilla.org/

interfaces: they are not predefined by developers, nor have a rigid structure. Instead, we compute them on demand to give support for specific feature development tasks.

For example, in a maintenance task, we consider the feature code to be maintained a component, named *Selection*. The backward/forward paths of the code surrounding it are components too. Paths consider the different feature combinations by the feature model. We name them *dataflows*, since features exchange data among them. Interfaces basically capture data dependencies between these components, and give support to maintaining *Selection* without having to understand the details of code associated to the *dataflows*.

Still using the Mobile Media SPL [7], we now illustrate our approach using a scenario with two optional features, Sorting and Favorites, and a mandatory one, Management, which is the feature to maintain — the *Selection* component. Figure 2 illustrates forward dataflows with arrows. Since Sorting and Favorites are optional features, there are four different feature expressions, each one associated with a *dataflow* component: **d1:** Management ∧ (¬ Favorites) ∧ (¬ Sorting); **d2:** Management ∧ Favorites ∧ Sorting; **d3:** Management ∧ Favorites ∧ (¬ Sorting); and **d4:** Management ∧ (¬ Favorites) ∧ Sorting.

For each component (*Selection* and *Dataflow*), we compute associated interfaces expressing dependencies between them. For example, Figure 2 shows that the dataflow *d3* (associated with Favorites) requires the media variable provided by the *Selection*. These interfaces allow us to change *Selection* abstracting details of the surrounding feature code. At the same time, they provide information to the developer, so that he might avoid implementations that cause problems to other features, like removing media, for instance.

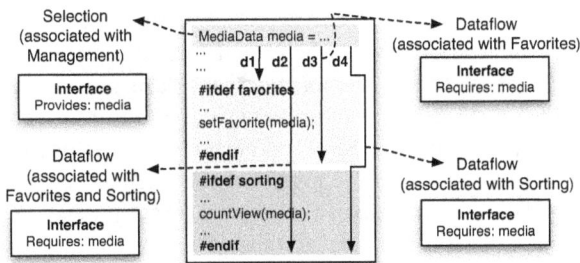

Figure 2. Components and their respective interfaces.

An advantage of using the feature model information is that we can filter which dataflows to take into account. For example, suppose that we associate the *Selection* component with feature *A*, that cannot be present in the same product with feature *B*. This might be due to a constraint in the feature model or by them being alternative features. Thus, we discard dataflows containing both features.

The conceptual model of our approach, depicted in Figure 3, summarizes these ideas. As explained, there are two kinds of components: *Selection*, which corresponds to the

code to maintain (selected by the developer); and *Dataflow*, representing backward (from the beginning of the method to the selection) and forward dataflows derived from the *Selection* component. The dataflows are useful to navigate through the code, being important to retrieve data dependencies among features with respect to the *Selection*. For example, through dataflow *d4*, we learn that the *Sorting* feature uses media, which is a variable declared in the *Selection*. Notice that we discard dataflows in which all code is only associated with the *Selection* feature expression. In this way, *d1* (Figure 2) is not taken into account. So, as mentioned, we associate each component with a feature expression and an interface, which states that components may provide/require elements such as variables to/from other components. These interfaces emerge from the components, establishing contracts between features.

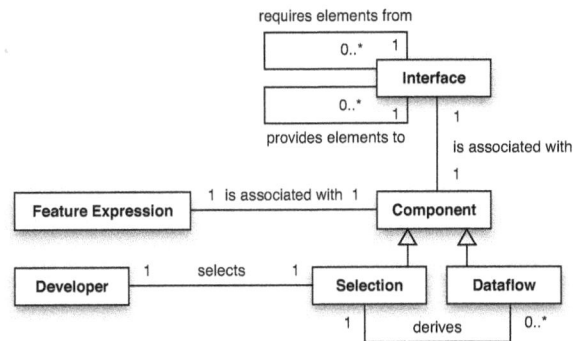

Figure 3. Conceptual Model of our approach.

We now illustrate how our approach might be useful to avoid the problems of the scenarios showed in Section 2.

Scenario 1

In order to add the *Ogg* format, we place both MMScreen and MMController declarations into an else statement. Since the maintenance involves these declarations, developers select them before proceeding with the task, as illustrated in **Step 1** of Figure 4. This is an example of *Selection* component. Additionally, this component is associated with a feature expression, which, in this case, is *Music*. Now, this developer needs information to proceed with the maintenance without damaging other features. For example, which information *Selection* provides (like declared variables and their values) that other features require.

By using the *Selection* component, we derive dataflow components. In Figure 4, arrows from *Selection* towards other parts of the code represent dataflows (*d1* and *d2*). Since Copy is an optional feature, we have the following dataflows with their respective feature expressions: **d1:** Music ∧ Copy and **d2:** Music ∧ (¬ Copy).

After defining the *Selection* and *Dataflow* components, their interfaces emerge in order to establish the contracts. Dataflow *d1* is associated with the Copy feature, which uses the controller variable from the Selection component

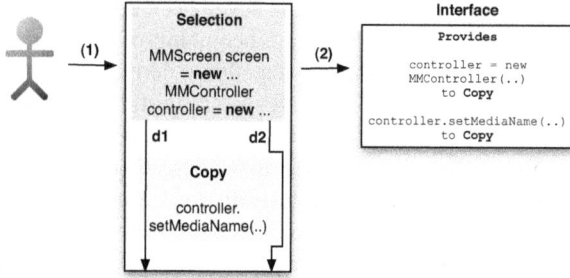

Figure 4. Emergent Interface for Scenario 1.

(see Figure 4). This way, the interface of dataflow *d1* states that Copy requires `controller`. Because the developer is maintaining the *Selection*, he must be aware that there is another feature (and, maybe, another developer) depending on `controller`. In this way, the *Selection* interface emerges (**Step 2** of Figure 4), stating that the Selection component should provide to the Copy feature a variable `controller` assigned to a MMController object and this object must have the `setMediaName(..)` method. This interface might be useful to avoid problems like the one reported in **Scenario 1** of Section 2. Now, looking at the interface makes the developer think twice before assigning the same `controller` variable to an OggController object.

Scenario 2

Figure 5 illustrates two developers working on two different features. Each developer is responsible for a feature, as explained in **Scenario 2** of Section 2: developer *A* maintains the Music feature, whereas developer *B* works on the Copy feature. So, developer *B* selects the Copy code snippet, as illustrated in **Step 1** of Figure 5. Because there is code before and after the selection, forward and backward dataflows are computed. They are, respectively, *d3* and *d4*. Again, these dataflows are helpful to establish the contracts. We can use them to discover other features that share information contained in the *Selection* component of developer *B*.

Now, suppose that the contracts have already emerged (*Selection* interfaces illustrated in **Steps 2** and **Step 3**) and when maintaining Copy, developer *B* decides to use the `screen` variable (from the Music feature) to implement a progress bar for the Copy feature (**Step 4**). Developer *B* now requires a variable provided by another feature (Music). Thus, we update both *Selection* and dataflow interfaces. **Step 5** shows the updated *Selection* interface for developer *B*. This way, when selecting the Music feature before a maintenance, the analogous components/interfaces computations occur for developer *A*, and the *Selection* interface shows information to him (**Step 6**). Now, when looking at this interface, developer *A* would think twice before refactoring new MMController(screen) to new MMController(new MMScreen()).

Therefore, our emerging interfaces should help developers to make some changes in one feature without breaking others, even when they are working on parallel, mitigating the problem illustrated in **Scenario 2**.

Now we present the details on how we implement our emergent approach. Mainly, we defined a general algorithm that consists of three major steps: (i) Compute *Selection* and dataflows components; (ii) Compute their interfaces; and (iii) Match these interfaces.

3.1 Selection/Dataflows Components

The first step consists of computing the *Selection* component and the dataflow components. We associate the *Selection* component with a feature expression and its computation is straightforward: it is the Abstract Syntax Tree (AST) representing the code selected by the developer (see **Step 1** and **Step 2**) of Figure 6. From the *Selection* component, we compute the backward and forward dataflow components. As discussed earlier, we compute dataflows in accordance to the feature expression associated with the *Selection* component and the feature model.

Figure 6 shows a simplified feature model of the Mobile Media product line [7]. It contains the *Management* mandatory feature (filled circle) and the *Copy* and *SMS* optional features (open circles). When maintaining the *Selection* component (associated with *Management*), we compute the following dataflows: **d1**: Management $\wedge$ ($\neg$ Copy) $\wedge$ ($\neg$ SMS); **d2**: Management $\wedge$ Copy $\wedge$ SMS; **d3**: Management $\wedge$ Copy $\wedge$ ($\neg$ SMS); and **d4**: Management $\wedge$ ($\neg$ Copy) $\wedge$ SMS.

Although all these feature expressions are valid according to the feature model, there is a particularity within the code of Figure 6: dataflows *d2* and *d4* are the same because of the two conditional directives: copy || sms and sms. When considering dataflow *d2*, Copy and SMS are present, so that both directives evaluate to *true*, which means that *d2* starts from the *Selection* towards the second #endif directive. The same happens to dataflow *d4*. Because SMS is present, both conditional compilation directives evaluate to *true* as well.

These feature expression combinations are important to alert developers about the impact of their maintenance. By using them, we are able to inform the exact product configurations impacted by a determined maintenance task. For example, if the maintenance assigned a new value to canv (Figure 6), we can inform the developer which SPL products this change may affect. In this case, it affects all possible feature combinations. If the number of possible affected products is high, and if the canv maintenance point is avoidable, developers may opt for another strategy or algorithm to maintain the desired code without causing potential problems in those products.

3.2 Selection/Dataflows Interfaces

Now that the *Selection* and the dataflow components are already defined, we should compute their interfaces. First, we consider the *Selection* interface, calculated by using not

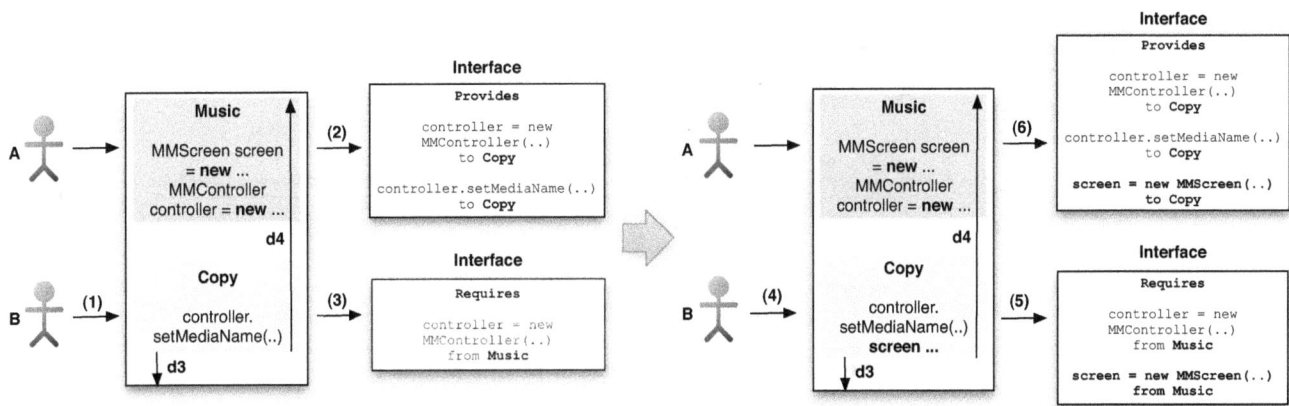

Figure 5. Emergent Interfaces for Scenario 2.

only the *Selection* component, but also the backward and forward dataflow components.

When the developer selects the code associated with the *Management* mandatory feature, we compute the AST of the *Selection* component and navigate throughout it to define the *Selection Elements List (SEL)*. This list plays an important role to define the *Selection* interface. It represents all declarations, assignments and variable uses within the *Selection* component. We illustrate SEL in **Step 3** of Figure 6. For each dataflow component, we navigate through its code searching for elements of SEL. We use some algorithms in this search. Now, we detail two of them:

- **Does any other feature need variable declarations?**

  Taking `canv` variable from SEL as an example, we search in the forward dataflows components for uses of this variable within features other than *Management*. Because this variable appears in three dataflow components (*d2*, *d3*, and *d4*) within other features (*Copy* and *SMS*), we add it to the *Selection* interface. Thus, developers must be careful when dealing with this variable, since there are other features needing it. This way, the *Selection* interface states the following:

  - **Provides** `canv` to:
    Copy ∧ SMS; Copy ∧ (¬ SMS); and (¬ Copy) ∧ SMS

- **Does any other feature need a specific assignment?**

  Now, we consider the assignments present in SEL that reach other features. If there are two assignments to a variable within *Selection*, we only consider the last one. There is only one assignment in SEL: `nextcontroller = this`. This algorithm verifies in the forward dataflows components if this assignment reaches other features. As we can see, it reaches the feature expressions associated with *d2*, *d3*, and *d4*, since each of these dataflows (bold line in Figure 6) uses `nextcontroller` assigned to `this`. Although we reach all feature expressions, the other use of `nextcontroller` (within `#ifdef sms`) is not reached because `nextcontroller` gets reassigned

(italic line in Figure 6). We show the updated *Selection* interface in what follows.

- **Provides** `canv` and `nextcontroller = this` to:
  Copy ∧ SMS; Copy ∧ (¬ SMS); and (¬ Copy) ∧ SMS

Now, the developer of the *Selection* component knows what he should provide in order to keep the other features safe. In addition, this emergent interface abstracts details of these surrounding features, keeping the developer focused on the maintenance task as well as on the elements that may cause problems to these features.

Notice that there is an element of SEL that is not used in any of the dataflows: `storedImage`. This way, removing such a variable or changing its value does not affect other features, but only the maintained feature. Therefore, this variable is not considered in the *Selection* interface.

We consider the dataflow interfaces as follows. We need to compute the interfaces for the dataflow components of Figure 6. Instead of using the SEL as an input, we use the *Selection* interface in order to avoid useless elements, such as `storedImage`. Thus, two elements must be considered: `canv` and `nextcontroller = this`. Now, we search for these elements within each dataflow component.

- *d2*, *d3*, and *d4* **Require**:
  `canv` and `nextcontroller = this` from Management

3.3 Matching Interfaces

Given that we have the *Selection* and *Dataflow* interfaces, we check if they match. That is, if everything that is required by the interfaces is provided. Using the example from Figure 6, suppose that the developer responsible for the *Management* feature now decides to change the value assigned to `nextcontroller`. Thus, `Selection` does not provide `nextcontroller = this` anymore, which interfaces of dataflows *d2*, *d3*, and *d4* require. The contract is now broken, and this should be reported to the developer.

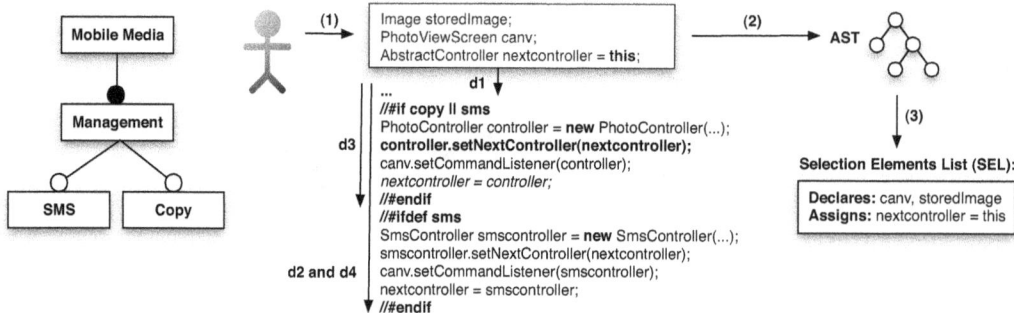

Figure 6. Copy and SMS features of Mobile Media.

4. Supporting Developers

To support developers in charge of maintaining annotative-based SPLs, we present xCIDE (eXtended Colored IDE): a prototype tool that implements the concept of emergent interfaces[2]. We implemented xCIDE as an extension of CIDE [12], a tool that allows developers to use preprocessors in a disciplined manner. Instead of textual comments, it uses background colors to represent features. Thus, given that we already have a SPL implemented with CIDE, our tool can automatically compute the emergent interfaces on demand to support developers that need to maintain a SPL.

As mentioned, the developer must first select code that he wishes to maintain. Based on this selection, the tool computes interfaces for the *Selection* and dataflow components. It presents the *Selection* interface to the developer, in order to prevent him of breaking feature modularity — that is, breaking a feature that he is not concerned while performing the maintenance task. Figure 7 illustrates our tool showing an emergent interface to the developer. As Figure 7 points out, there is hidden feature code, associated with *Sorting* and *Copy* features, respectively. After the developer indicates the code snippet to maintain, the tool shows the emergent interface related to that code — stating that `controller` is provided with a certain value to *Copy*.

4.1 Implementation

Our implementation relies on the three steps showed in Section 3 plus another one to show the emergent interface. The first one uses the Eclipse Java Development Tool (JDT) [1] to retrieve the AST of the selected code and compute the *Selection* component. Based on this selection, we then proceed to retrieve the dataflow components with the aid of Soot [2], a Java optimization framework for analyzing and transforming Java bytecode. This way, we have computed the *Selection* as well as the dataflow components.

The second step consists of computing the interfaces. The AST retrieved is important to compute the Selection Elements List (SEL). We use this list as an input to Soot, which is also used to compute the interfaces, where we analyze the

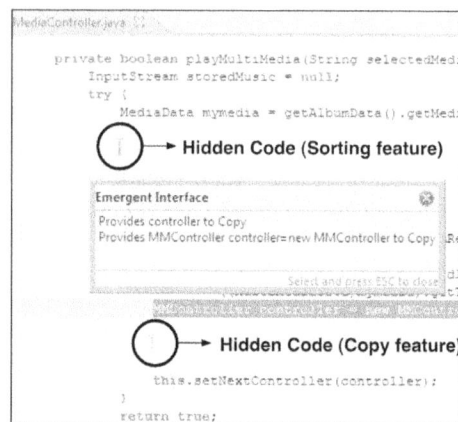

Figure 7. xCIDE screenshot.

dataflow components of our interest. This analysis relies on a variety of algorithms like the ones presented in Section 3.2. Roughly, since CIDE uses background colors to represent feature expressions, these algorithms search for elements of SEL which are in different colors of the feature expression associated with the *Selection* component. If found, we consider them in the *Selection* component interface. Then, we take this interface as an input for Soot to compute each dataflow interface. We match them (third step) and show the *Selection* interface to the user (fourth step).

4.2 Limitations and Ongoing work

Our tool currently implements the general algorithm to emerge interfaces. The main limitation when computing interfaces happens when we have mutually exclusive features. The tool searches SEL elements in all feature expressions (all colors), whether mutually exclusive or not. Improving this computation is an ongoing work.

We are also working on other algorithms, using both intra and interprocedural analysis. An example is the chain of assignments. In this case, changing the value of a variable x in the *Selection* component may produce a chain of other changes that reaches another feature. For instance, we might use the new value of x to define the value of y which, in

---

2 The tool is available at `http://www.cin.ufpe.br/~mmr3/onward10`

its turn, defines the value of z. If another feature uses z, changing the value of x can cause problems to this feature.

5. Related work

Interfaces for non-annotative approaches. This work focuses on interfaces for techniques that annotate code to define feature boundaries, such as conditional compilation. Since this leads to scattering and tangling, researchers evaluated the use of Aspect-Oriented Programming [3, 4, 15] to solve these problems. However, because of problems like fragile pointcuts [19], researchers proposed interfaces between classes and aspects to achieve modularity.

Griswold et al. [8] proposed Crosscutting Programming Interfaces (XPIs) aiming at decoupling the aspects from details of classes, providing better modularity during parallel evolution. Also, there is a notion of provides and requires that XPIs may check. For example, we might define a contract in which aspects cannot change the state of some object. We can write XPIs using AspectJ language constructs. Thus, components and interfaces have a rigid structure: classes, aspects, and XPIs. Unlike XPIs, our approach does not predefine components and interfaces. They emerge on demand, according to a maintenance task. In addition, since emergent interfaces are not written, they do not need language constructs but tools responsible for generating them. Like XPIs, we abstract details of features, being important to make developers focus on the maintenance task.

The AspectScope tool [9] realizes the idea of aspect-aware interfaces in AspectJ [14]. It performs whole-program analysis of AspectJ programs and displays module interfaces according to current deployment of aspects. It aims to help developers understand program behavior with local reasoning. Their concept of presenting interfaces to the developer is similar to what we propose in this work, aiming to facilitate modular reasoning through tool support. However, AspectScope module interfaces are not product-line-aware. As we do, AspectScope provides a visualization of interfaces.

Separation of Concerns. Some approaches aim to provide separation of concerns by hiding information. Mylyn [13] is a task-focused approach to reduce information overload, so that only artifacts (like packages, classes, and methods) relevant to a current task are visible. A task context, created during a programming activity, filters this information. This way, Mylyn monitors tasks aiming at storing information about what developers are doing to complete the task. If the task is not completed, developers can continue them afterwards. When opening the IDE to complete that task, instead of showing thousands of artifacts, developers may select the task and Mylyn provides only the artifacts related to it, improving productivity (developers do not spend time searching for the artifacts of that task) and reducing the information overload. Like Mylyn, our approach also needs a selection. Developers select the snippet in order to maintain it, whereas when using Mylyn they select tasks.

Our interfaces and the task context of Mylyn emerge during maintenance. Finally, we also provide information reduction, since we only show elements shared with other features to the developer through the *Selection* interface.

Colored IDE (CIDE) is a tool for decomposing legacy applications into features [12]. Although CIDE uses the preprocessors semantics (based on the same annotative approach), it avoids pollution of code, which means that *#ifdef* directives are no longer needed. Instead, it relies on the Eclipse editor to define the features boundaries through background colors. CIDE relies on VSoC, so that it is possible to hide code of features not interesting to the current maintenance task. We presented an extension of this tool to improve feature modularization. Our intent is to make developers aware about other features *before* initiating their maintenance tasks. Also, emergent interfaces show the exact product configurations that a maintenance may affect.

Conceptual Module [5] is an approach to support developers on maintenance tasks. They set lines of code to be part of a conceptual module and use queries to capture other lines that should be part of it and to compute dependencies among other conceptual modules. We also catch dependencies, but we go beyond since we consider features relationships. Both approaches abstract details from developers so that they concentrate on relationships among features or conceptual modules rather than on code of no interest, being important for comprehensibility. However, our interest lies not only on providing dependencies, but also information that may be useful during maintenance. For example, interfaces may indicate that hidden features have statements like continue, break, throws, and return. Now, developers are aware about possible control flow changes during maintenance.

Safe composition. Safe composition relates to safe generation and verification of properties for SPL assets: i.e., providing guarantees that the product derivation process generates products with properties that are obeyed [11, 20]. Generating all SPL products to check safe composition turns out to be impractical as the SPL becomes larger.

Thaker et al. present techniques for verifying type safety properties of product lines using FMs and SAT solvers [20]. They extract properties from feature modules and verify that they hold for all SPL members. Safe composition is also proposed for the Color Featherweight Java (CFJ) calculus [11]. This calculus establishes type rules to ensure that CFJ code only generates well-typed programs. CIDE — the tool we extended — implements this formalization.

These works check for type errors on SPL products, being similar to the matching interfaces step of our algorithm, where we catch some of these errors. However, our intent is to use emergent interfaces to prevent errors when maintaining features. Moreover, some elements in our emergent interfaces deal with the system behaviour (value assignment), rather than only with static type information.

6. Concluding Remarks

This paper introduced the emergent feature modularization concept, which might be applied to maintain features in product lines. We call our approach emergent since we do not rely on components and interfaces with a rigid structure, meaning that they are not predefined. Instead, they emerge on demand to support developers when maintaining features.

Our interfaces abstract details from features that are not relevant to the current task (the hidden ones), but at the same time provide valuable information to maintain a feature and keep these hidden ones safe. Because of this abstraction, developers still have the benefits provided by VSoC, in the sense that the feature code of no interest continues hidden.

We also presented a three-step algorithm to compute emergent components and interfaces, implemented in xCIDE. The tool uses the emergent feature modularization concept, so that after a selection, it shows an emergent interface to the developer, keeping him informed about the contracts between the selected feature and the other ones.

As future work, we intend to improve our tool with more robust emergent interfaces. Also, we should conduct an experiment to evaluate our proposal to verify its advantages/disadvantages in terms of developer's productivity.

Acknowledgments

This work was partially supported by the National Institute of Science and Technology for Software Engineering (INES[3]), funded by CNPq and FACEPE, grants 573964/2008-4 and APQ-1037-1.03/08

References

[1] Eclipse Java Development Tools, January 2008. http://www.eclipse.org/jdt/.

[2] Soot: a Java Optimization Framework, April 2010. http://www.sable.mcgill.ca/soot/.

[3] V. Alves, P. M. Jr., L. Cole, P. Borba, and G. Ramalho. Extracting and Evolving Mobile Games Product Lines. In *Proceedings of the 9th International Software Product Line Conference (SPLC'05)*, volume 3714 of *LNCS*, pages 70–81. Springer-Verlag, September 2005.

[4] M. Anastasopoulos and C. Gacek. Implementing Product Line Variabilities. In *Proceedings of the 2001 Symposium on Software Reusability (SSR'01)*, pages 109–117, New York, NY, USA, 2001. ACM Press.

[5] E. L. A. Baniassad and G. C. Murphy. Conceptual module querying for software reengineering. In *Proceedings of the 20th International Conference on Software Engineering (ICSE'98)*, pages 64–73, Washington, DC, USA, 1998. IEEE Computer Society.

[6] P. Clements and L. Northrop. *Software Product Lines: Practices and Patterns*. Addison-Wesley, 2002.

[7] E. F. et. Al. Evolving software product lines with aspects: an empirical study on design stability. In *Proceedings of the 30th International Conference on Software Engineering (ICSE'08)*, pages 261–270, New York, NY, USA, 2008. ACM.

[8] W. G. Griswold, K. Sullivan, Y. Song, M. Shonle, N. Tewari, Y. Cai, and H. Rajan. Modular Software Design with Crosscutting Interfaces. *IEEE Software*, 23(1):51–60, 2006.

[9] M. Horie and S. Chiba. Aspectscope: An outline viewer for AspectJ programs. *Journal of Object Technology*, 6(9):341–361, 2007.

[10] C. Kästner and S. Apel. Virtual separation of concerns - a second chance for preprocessors. *Journal of Object Technology*, 8(6):59–78, 2009.

[11] C. Kästner and S. Apel. Type-checking software product lines - a formal approach. In *Proceedings of the 23rd International Conference on Automated Software Engineering (ASE)*, pages 258–267. IEEE Computer Society, September 2008.

[12] C. Kästner, S. Apel, and M. Kuhlemann. Granularity in Software Product Lines. In *Proceedings of the 30th International Conference on Software Engineering (ICSE'08)*, pages 311–320, New York, NY, USA, 2008. ACM.

[13] M. Kersten and G. C. Murphy. Using task context to improve programmer productivity. In *Proceedings of the 14th International Symposium on Foundations of Software Engineering (FSE'06)*, pages 1–11, New York, NY, USA, 2006. ACM.

[14] G. Kiczales and M. Mezini. Aspect-Oriented Programming and Modular Reasoning. In *Proceedings of the 27th International Conference on Software Engineering (ICSE 2005)*, pages 49–58. ACM Press, 2005.

[15] G. C. Murphy, A. Lai, R. J. Walker, and M. P. Robillard. Separating features in source code: an exploratory study. In *Proceedings of the 23rd International Conference on Software Engineering (ICSE'01)*, pages 275–284, Washington, DC, USA, 2001. IEEE Computer Society.

[16] D. L. Parnas. On the criteria to be used in decomposing systems into modules. *CACM*, 15(12):1053–1058, 1972.

[17] K. Pohl, G. Bockle, and F. J. van der Linden. *Software Product Line Engineering*. Springer, 2005.

[18] H. Spencer and G. Collyer. #ifdef considered harmful, or portability experience with C news. In *Proceedings of the Usenix Summer 1992 Technical Conference*, pages 185–198, Berkeley, CA, USA, June 1992. Usenix Association.

[19] M. Störzer and C. Koppen. Pcdiff: Attacking the fragile pointcut problem, abstract. In *European Interactive Workshop on Aspects in Software*, Berlin, Germany, September 2004.

[20] S. Thaker, D. S. Batory, D. Kitchin, and W. R. Cook. Safe composition of product lines. In *Proceedings of the 6th International Conference Generative Programming and Component Engineering, (GPCE'07)*, pages 95–104. ACM, 2007.

[21] S. Trujillo, D. Batory, and O. Diaz. Feature refactoring a multi-representation program into a product line. In *Proceedings of the 5th International Conference on Generative Programming and Component Engineering (GPCE'06)*, pages 191–200, New York, NY, USA, 2006. ACM.

[22] W. Wulf and M. Shaw. Global variable considered harmful. *SIGPLAN Notices*, 8(2):28–34, 1973.

---

[3] http://www.ines.org.br

Harnessing Emergence for Manycore Programming: Early Experience Integrating Ensembles, Adverbs, and Object-based Inheritance

David Ungar

IBM Research

davidungar@us.ibm.com

Sam S. Adams

IBM Research

ssadams@us.ibm.com

Abstract

We believe that embracing nondeterminism and harnessing emergence have great potential to simplify the task of programming manycore processors. To that end, we have designed and implemented Ly, pronounced "Lee", a new parallel programming language built around two new concepts: (i) ensembles which provide for parallel execution and replace all collections and (ii) iterators, and adverbs, which modify the parallel behavior of messages sent to ensembles. The broad issues around programming in this fashion still need investigation, but, after our initial Ly programming experience, we have identified some specific issues that must be addressed in integrating these concepts into an object-based language, including empty ensembles, partial message understanding, non-local returns from ensemble members, and unintended ensembles.

Categories and Subject Descriptors D.3.2 [**Programming Languages**]: Language Classifications - Object-oriented languages, Nondeterministic languages: D.3.3 [**Programming Languages**]: Language Constructs and Features - Concurrent programming structures, Inheritance : D.1.3 [**Programming Techniques**]: Concurrent Programming - Parallel programming : D.1.5 [**Object-oriented Programming**]

General Terms Design, Human Factors, Languages.

Keywords *object-based inheritance; ensembles; adverb; multicore; manycore*

1. Introduction

Within the next decade, nearly every CPU will have dozens to hundreds of general-purpose cores. How can the vast majority of programmers, perhaps expert in applications, but not so well-versed in the arcane art of parallel programming, easily exploit such extreme parallelism?

Many in our field are exploring ways in which the programmer could continue to write deterministic parallel programs without over-specifying the order of events, or ways in which the runtime enforces determinism [1, 2]. We believe that even such a limited attempt to specify essential determinism will likely run into scaling problems. Others in our field follow a functional approach that frees the result from dependencies upon the order of execution. But if mutable state is needed, a monad is introduced, which makes the temporal dependency quite explicit [3]. We believe this approach to be fruitful, but limited in its ability to directly model systems that are naturally viewed as possessing manifold state.

For example, consider a simulation of a flock of birds, each independently choosing its own path, moment by moment.

At any given time, it seems natural to us that each bird has a state, for instance a definite location. Where is that bird, now? We search for a programming paradigm that can easily model such an interpretation of a massively parallel bird flock. Still others in our field turn to actors to order the chaos of rampant parallelism [4, 5]. However, actors seem to us to merely defer the problem by a constant factor: since an actor can contain mutable state, and since an actor may receive messages from other actors in various orders, we believe that actors do not solve the fundamental problem of taming nondeterminacy. Consider an actor A that holds a bank balance, an actor B that sends A a message to double the balance, and an actor C that sends A a message to add $5 to the balance. The final result is as indeterminate as the order of message passing. Since our field began we have struggled to impose determinism on complex computations, and our languages and programming models have co-evolved with that goal. Significantly easing the challenge of programming with massive parallelism requires a complete shift: instead of resisting, it is time to embrace nondeterminism.

Nature provides us with many examples of massively parallel systems. Without the benefit of any global synchronization at all, these systems manage to solve complex problems and achieve robust behavior. Consider a flock of birds (figure 1), a school of fish, an ant colony, a termite mound, a developing embryo, or even, as some

Permission to make digital or hard copies of all or part of this work for personal or classroom use is granted without fee provided that copies are not made or distributed for profit or commercial advantage and that copies bear this notice and the full citation on the first page. To copy otherwise, or republish, to post on servers or to redistribute to lists, requires prior specific permission and/or a fee.
Onward! 2010 October 17–21, 2010, Reno/Tahoe, Nevada, USA.
Copyright © 2010 ACM 978-1-4503-0236-4/10/10...$10.00.

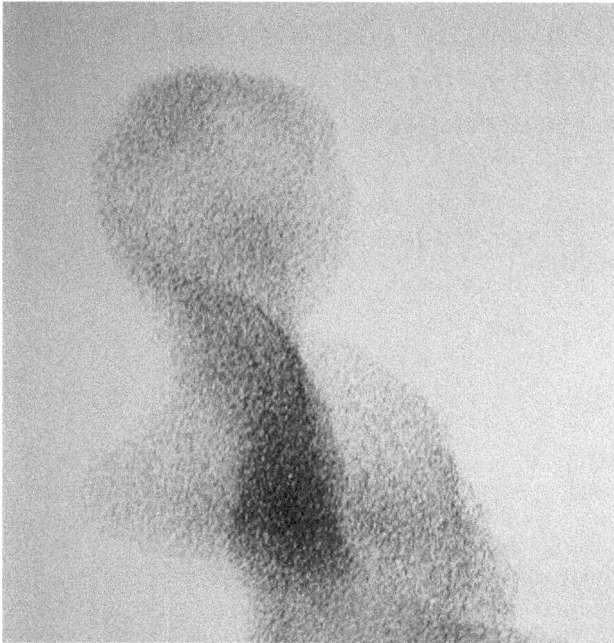

Figure 1. A starling flock

suspect, the phenomenon of consciousness in the human brain [6]. In each case, a large number of individuals, each following local rules, interact asynchronously to exhibit coordinated, robust, distributed behavior of a higher degree of complexity than that of the individuals. This phenomenon is known as *emergence*.

Could a new programming paradigm based on nondeterminism and emergence make it easy for ordinary application programmers to exploit the massive parallelism of future manycore processor chips? To answer that question, we have built a testbed comprised of:

- a Smalltalk virtual machine rewritten to support multithreading and object migration [7], hosting the Squeak IDE;
- a new programming language (Ly) featuring ensembles and adverbs, with object-based inheritance and a JavaScript-like syntax; and
- an integrated development environment including a source-management system and a source-level debugger.

Although still somewhat immature, our testbed, which runs on dual-core Mac laptops; 8-core, 16-hyperthread Mac Pros; and a 64-core Tilera manycore processor, has given us enough experience with these ideas to demonstrate an algorithm running 50 parallel threads with no application-level synchronization. More importantly, this effort has uncovered a number of interesting language issues. We intend to open-source our system so that others may experiment with manycore Smalltalk and our language. This short paper briefly describes our language, its implementation, and those thorny issues.

2. Ensembles and Adverbs

How do you go from a flock of birds to a programming language? Gazing at a flock, you see a constantly changing whole; blink, and you see a collection of individuals, each operating in parallel with its neighbors. Our language includes a concept that models this experience, called an *ensemble*. Our ensemble is a bit like an APL array; it can be referenced as one thing, yet performing an operation on it (i.e. sending it a message) causes each *member* to perform the operation in parallel. Unlike an APL array, which can only contain immutable values (numbers or characters), the members of an ensemble can be mutable objects, or even other ensembles.

Once *ensemble* is admitted to the pantheon of first-class computing concepts, questions arise: For example, in performing a computation over an ensemble, there are many options as to which members are involved: every member, the closest member geographically on the cores, some subset of members? Once the computation has occurred, how shall the results be returned? Shall they be bundled into a resultant ensemble? Discarded? Or reduced by some operation (e.g. averaging)? In order to separate out the specification of these and other questions of execution strategy, we add another concept to our model of computation: an *adverb*. In most object-oriented languages, the tuple required to perform a computation would be receiver-selector-argument(s). In our model, an adverb is added to that mix. Our current syntax denotes an adverb by appending a double-minus ('--') to the list of argument expressions, and following the double minus with an expression supplying the adverb. Perhaps even each argument could have its own adverb. We expect the most common case to be the parallel computation on every member, returning an ensemble of results. Therefore no adverb is needed in that case.

Finally, it is necessary to be able to perform a computation on an ensemble-as-a-whole. For example, sending *size* to a flock would normally return an ensemble of the sizes of each bird; asking the flock for its size (as a whole) would be a different kind of request. We add a second message-passing syntax to indicate this sort of computation: in aFlock..size() the double-dot indicates that the message is to be sent to the ensemble-as-a-whole, instead of to its members. This new variety of *reflection* completes the concepts we explore as a means to embrace nondeterminism.

3. Ly: An experimental programming language

What sort of language would naturally encourage a programmer of massively parallel hardware to embrace nondeterminism via the concepts of ensembles and adverbs? Such a language would have a familiar syntax, such as JavaScript's, and a simple yet powerful object-based inheritance model, such as Self's [8] (more below). Ensembles would be as easy to use as regular objects. Therefore, the concise and familiar message-passing syntax would also be used for ensemble message sends, for example aFlock.turnLeft(), would tell every bird in the flock (ensemble) to turn left simultaneously.

3.1 Object = Ensemble?

Coming from an object-oriented culture, we wanted to bring along all the benefits of that paradigm, so the next decision in the language-design process was how to integrate ensembles and objects. For the sake of uniformity, we wanted a singleton ensemble, for example a flock of one bird, to be indistinguishable from an object, the bird in our example. Following this train of thought, every object would be (in effect) an ensemble containing only itself as a member. Every message would burrow into its destination's member list and go one deep. For example, when sending *name* to a Parrot object named Polly, the message would be received by the parrot, and since she would also be an ensemble, the message would get redispatched to Polly's members, consisting solely of the bird herself. At that point, further redispatching would somehow be avoided, and Polly would answer "Polly", which would itself be an ensemble containing itself (i.e. the string "Polly"). Since Polly the parrot would be an ensemble, the result(s) of the *name* message would have to be returned as an ensemble, and so the one result (the string "Polly", itself an ensemble) would have to get wrapped into a singleton ensemble resulting in a doubly-nested ensemble containing the string "Polly". But this result would have an undesired level of nesting. The gymnastics required to deal with these potentially infinite member-regresses became challenging enough that we backed off: a singleton ensemble in Ly is not the same as the member object.

Still striving for unification, we next considered allowing every Ly object to be an ensemble. In this model, every object would contain slots, a single link to its parent (we hope to avoid multiple inheritance), and a one-to-many link to its members. In this scenario, we faced a choice between two equally plausible alternatives: searching an ensemble's slots before its members, or searching its slots after its members. For example, suppose our flock of birds includes a centerOfGravity method, which would compute the center of gravity of the flock, and furthermore that each bird also includes a centerOfGravity method, returning its own center of gravity. On one hand, the flock's slots could be searched first, so that centerOfGravity() would invoke the flock's center of gravity. On the other hand, the flock's members could be searched first, in order to obtain an ensemble of the individual birds' centers of gravity for a calculation of the polar moment of the flock. Because the choice of lookup order between slots and members seemed arbitrary and hard to remember, and because there might be useful cases for either choice, we decided to design the language so that ensembles could not have slots. Rather, using the power of object-based inheritance, ensembles could be parents of objects and search the slots first, or ensembles could be children of objects and search the members first.

In summary, a *reference* points to either an *object* or an *ensemble*. An *object* contains a *parent reference* and zero-or-more *slots*. A *slot* contains a *name* (i.e. a character string) and (a reference to) its *contents*. An *ensemble* contains a *parent reference* and zero-or-more (references to

its) *members*. By arranging inheritance hierarchies, a programmer can achieve whatever look up behavior is desired.

3.2 Inheritance

Given the cache size and memory bandwidth issues in a manycore system, it seems practical to reify shared behavior by framing inheritance as a way to share parts of objects (just as in Self [8]). So, when a message is sent to an object, if the object has no matching slots, the lookup continues in its ancestors, but even if the match is found in an ancestor, the object that was the original destination of the message is the one bound to *self* or *this*. In contrast, when a message is sent to an *ensemble,* the result will be N parallel invocations, one per member, with each member bound to *self* or *this*. An ensemble may have a parent; if its members do not understand a message, the lookup then proceeds up the ensemble's parent chain, resulting in just one invocation, with the ensemble itself as the receiver. This scheme attempts to integrate object-based inheritance with ensembles while avoiding unintended consequences.

But the intended consequences of this model turned out to be non-trivial: when the lookup dives into an ensemble, it becomes a parallel lookup from each receiver. But if no matches are found, it must back out, reset the receiver to the original object, and continue up the ensemble's parent chain (figure 2).

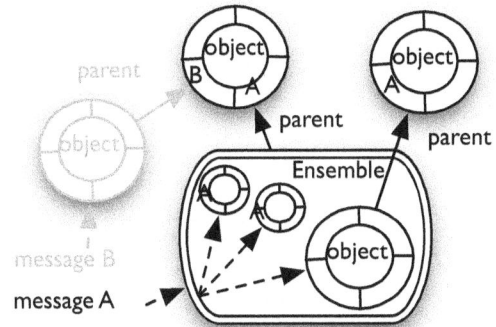

Figure 2. If members don't understand a message, try their parents first, then backtrack to the ensemble parent if necessary.

Figure 3 illustrates this complexity with an example: a message sent to the bottom-left object will first search its slots. If a match is found, there will be one invocation with the bottom-left object as receiver. Next, the members of the left-hand flock are searched, including their ancestors. If matches are found, there will be many parallel invocations, one per bird. If no matches are found, the flock defaults object will be searched. If a match is found, there will be one invocation, with the bottom-left object as receiver. Thus, the bottom-left object allows the turnLeft and turnRight messages to be caught before each bird turns left or right. The flock defaults object allows a default species method to be defined for the ensemble. If the birds understand species, then sending species to a flock will return an ensemble of species. But if they do not, the default species method will invoke the error code.

Pseudocode Description of Ly Lookup in Ly

In order to examine the interesting language issues that arise from Ly's lookup semantics, it is necessary to illustrate those semantics, and this section does so with pseudocode. Ly syntax is used to help the reader gain a feel for the syntax as well as the semantics. The pseudocode ignores many of the features of our actual implementation, including:

- message sends to implicit self,
- message sends to super,
- message sends with an adverb,
- message sends with the double-dot (to the ensemble as-a-whole),
- compile-time lookups (an optimization),
- inheritance cycles (e.g. an object that is its own grandfather),
- membership cycles (i.e. an ensemble that transitively contains itself),
- the extra complexity of maps (an optimization),
- ensembles of ensembles,
- empty ensembles, as discussed below,
- message arguments (the argument count is also used to lookup a method), and
- a pluggable architecture that lets us experiment with different representations of Ly objects.

In the following code, the lookup operation returns an *ensemble* of results, which can then be used for method invocations. Each result will need fields to hold the method to be invoked and the receiver upon which to invoke it:

```
object LookupResult {
    var receiver, var method;
    // In Ly, the empty parentheses can be elided from a
    // method call with no arguments as in "super.new" below
    function new(r, m) {
        var x = super.new; x.receiver = r; x.method = m;
        return x; }
}
```

In order to represent a slot in a Ly object, our pseudocode defines an implementation object to hold a slot's name, its contents, and a function that returns a lookup result if the name matches the selector:

```
object Slot {
    var name, contents;
    function result_if_I_match(receiver, selector) {
        return name == selector
            ? LookupResult.new(receiver, contents)  : nil;
    }
}
```

Finally, here are the objects that implement a Ly object and a Ly ensemble. Common attributes are factored out into LyBase:

```
object LyBase {
    // state & code common to objects & ensembles
    var parent; // nil if no parent
    // Entry point for a lookup;
    // This object or ensemble is both the receiver and
    // the place to start looking.
    // Result is an ensemble of results
    function lookup(selector) {
        return lookup( this, selector);
    }
    // Flexible lookup method; look here,
    // but receiver may be somewhere else
    function lookup(receiver, selector) {
        // local_results is an ensemble
        var local_results = lookup_here(receiver, selector);
        // The dot-dot syntax below redirects the isNotEmpty
        // message to the ensemble-as-a-whole, rather than
        // to each of its members.
        if (local_results..isNotEmpty) return local_results;
        if (parent != nil)
            return parent.lookup(receiver, selector);
        return  Ensemble.new // empty ensemble
    }
}
// a Ly object with slots
object LyObject extends LyBase {
    var slots; // holds an ensemble of distinctly-named Slots
    function lookup_here(receiver, selector)  {
        // The double dash, '--', after the last argument
        // signifies the beginning of an adverb.
        // The 'ignoringNils' adverb filters out the nils
        // from the result ensemble.
        return slots.result_if_I_match(receiver,  selector
                                    -- ignoringNils);
    }
}
// a Ly ensemble with members
object LyEnsemble extends LyBase {
    // holds an ensemble implementing the one-to-many links
    var members;
    function lookup_here(selector, receiver)  {
        // In this case, the receivers will be the member objects.
        return members.lookup(selector);
    }
}
```

Lookup starts by sending the lookup message with one argument, the selector, to the receiver of the message. That method (inherited via LyBase), sends the two-argument lookup message to itself, in order to start searching locally. It also passes in the receiver of the eventual invocation, which will ultimately be bound to "this". If the receiver of the two-argument lookup message is an *object,* its *slots* are searched, and if a match is found, a singleton ensemble holding one result is returned. If no match is found, the search continues with the parent. But if the receiver of the two-argument lookup message is an *ensemble,* its *members* are searched, and the receiver(s) of the eventual invocation (s) is reset to correspond to each member. Only if no matches are found in the members does the lookup continue up the ensemble's parent link with the original receiver.

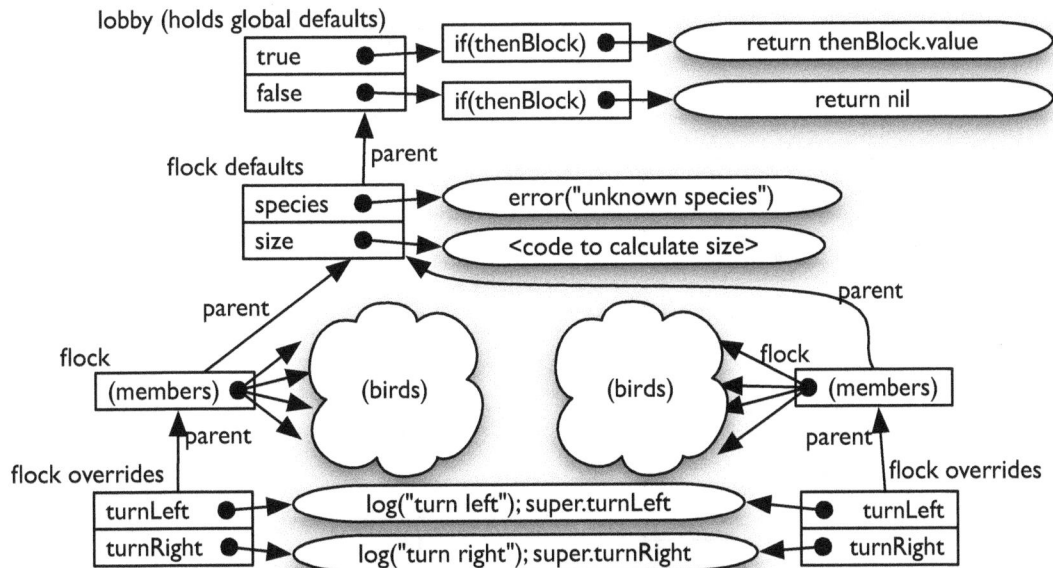

Figure 3. A detailed example of inheritance.

Smalltalk IDE	Ly IDE	Ly Source-to-Smalltalk Compiler	Ly Runtime	Visualization tools
Squeak Smalltalk Virtual Image including class libraries				
Our Renaissance Smalltalk Virtual Machine: multithreading & object migration				
Operating system: Linux, or OS X				
Processor: 64-core Tilera, 16-hyperthread Intel, or 2-core Intel				

Figure 4. The layers of our system

4. Implementation

Using our Smalltalk testbed, we implemented Ly with a hand-written parser designed to give good error messages, a compiler to transform parse nodes into Smalltalk objects, and an interpreter that executes the Ly program represented by the Smalltalk objects. The Ly interpreter, written in Smalltalk, runs atop the Smalltalk VM interpreter, written in C++, which in turn runs atop various platforms: the Tilera hardware, Intel Linux boxes, Mac Book Pros, and Mac Pros. The Mac Book Pro affords two-way parallelism, the other Intel platforms afford 16-way (with hyperthreading), and the Tilera system runs with 56 independent threads of execution. Figure 4 illustrates the layers.

The double-interpretation (i.e. many Smalltalk operations per Ly operation) resulted in intolerable performance, so we implemented several optimizations:

- the capability to use Smalltalk Point and Number objects instead of Ly-level points and numbers,
- compile-time lookups for slots in the current activation record, and
- maps and runtime-lookup caches to transform each run-time lookup from a sequence of hash table probes to an access into a linear array at a fixed offset.

These optimizations improved performance sufficiently to let us implement a simple version of the Boids flocking algorithm [9, 10] with 50 simulated birds ("boids") flying on 56 Tilera cores (figure 5). Boids is an interesting test application for manycore parallel programming in that there is an ever-changing mix of data parallelism and task parallelism that will stress our programming model and virtual machine implementation.

5. Environment

We have also implemented most of an IDE for Ly using Squeak's MVC framework (figure 6). It includes:

- a workspace, in which one can edit, parse, and execute Ly code;
- an object explorer, which allows one to examine and change the contents of Ly object slots and methods;
- a snippet browser, which allows one to store Ly code as text, leveraging the Smalltalk change-management facilities; and
- a source-level debugger, which shows the Ly invocation stack at the Ly source level, and has facilities for single-stepping, etc. The debugger relies on the underlying Smalltalk facilities and a runtime map from the Smalltalk-level execution state to the Ly-level execution state.

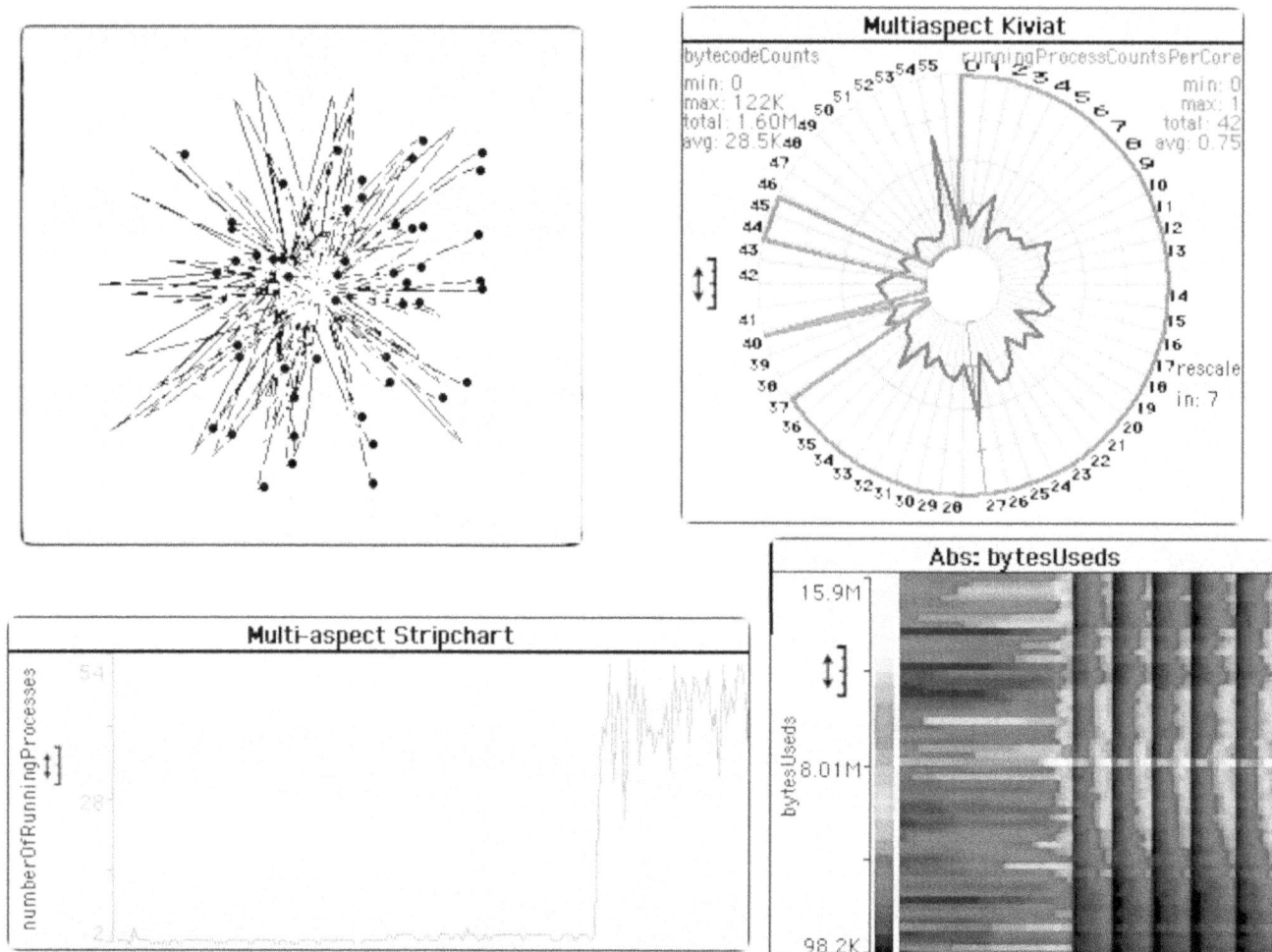

Figure 5. 50 Boids running on 56 cores. Clockwise from the top left: the graphical output of the Boids simulation, the instantaneous execution activity per core, the degree of parallelism vs time, and the occupancy of each core's heap vs time. (Time approximated by samples, so that GC appears to be instantaneous.)

6. Programming Experience in Ly

As of May, 2010, we have written approximately 1,500 lines of Ly code, including many regression tests, a few versions of Boids, and four adverbs: "totally," "pairwise," "serially," and a version of "serially" for ensembles of Smalltalk objects. Figure 5 shows 50 Boids running in 50 threads on 50 cores with several of our visualization tools. This program has no application-level synchronization, yet enjoys 50-way concurrency.

Despite the optimizations described above, Ly's performance on a manycore CPU with a relatively slow memory system led us to investigate other implementation techniques in the past few months, instead of writing many other programs in Ly. However our experience already has uncovered some interesting issues with this model of computation. We do not have all the answers as of yet, but uncovering the following questions may be the most interesting result of our efforts to date.

6.1 Empty Ensembles

For the sake of consistency, a programmer would expect the behavior of an ensemble to remain the same as its membership declined. For example, given a flock of birds, he would expect the turnLeft message to cause each bird to turn left, and, given a flock of no birds, he would expect the turnLeft message to just do nothing (assuming the ensemble's parent has no turnLeft slot). However, given the dynamically-typed nature of Ly, this expectation means that *any* message could be sent to an empty ensemble and the system would just silently do nothing. Later, if a member lacking the method in question were to join the empty ensemble, it would cause a previously running program to incur a "message not understood" error!

What if the ensemble's parent does have a turnLeft slot? In that case, the transition between an empty ensemble and a singleton ensemble would involve a switch from the method in the parent's turnLeft slot to the method in the member's. Such a change could be an unpleasant surprise. These scenarios suggest that Ly's current design is not satisfactory.

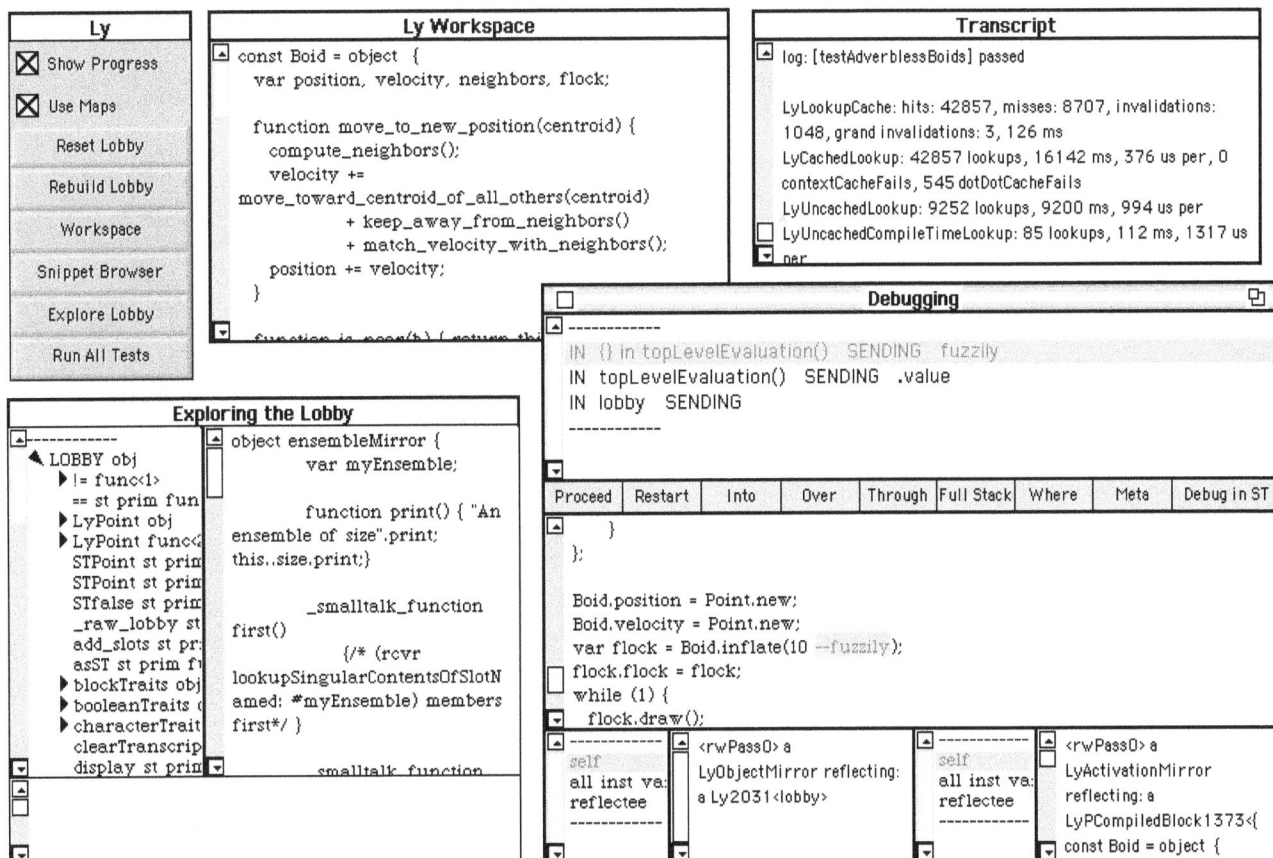

Figure 6. The Ly Environment

6.2 Partial Message Understanding

What if a message is sent to an ensemble and but understood by only some of its members? For example if the program sends "lay eggs" to a flock of birds, should the males silently ignore the request? Or should it result in a global error? Or should special return values come back in the result ensemble? We can see arguments for any of the three possibilities.

6.3 Partial Non-local Returns

Ly includes Smalltalk-like blocks, and as a consequence, a method may be passed a block that, when evaluated, causes the call stack to be cut back to a point above the invocation of said method. This scenario occurs when the block contains a *return* statement, as such statements cause the block to return from its enclosing lexical scope.

Suppose such a block were passed as an argument to an ensemble, so that each member ran a method which received the block as an argument. If some of the members were to invoke the block and it returned, there would be an attempt to cut back the call stack across a fork/join point! Should such non-local returns be an error? If not, what should they do?

6.4 Unintended Ensembles

Unlike the previous three situations, the following one took us by surprise; we were unaware of it until it actually happened to one of the authors. Ly is intended to make massively parallel programming easy, but it became too easy: parallel ensemble computation occurred where none was expected! Our system was executing a method that, like turnLeft in the diagram above, had an ensemble as receiver. Said method contained if (true) doSomething, but instead of invoking doSomething once, it invoked doSomething in parallel for every member of the ensemble! Single-stepping with the source-level debugger exposed the cause of the problem: Ly's compiler treats if(condition) statement as syntactic sugar for condition.if({statement}); that is, it turns the special form into a message sent to the condition, with a block argument. Rather than being built-in, true is merely a slot high up in the inheritance hierarchy. So, when the true message was sent to the current receiver, a match was found in *every* member (because every member inherited the true slot), and an ensemble containing a true for each member was returned. Then, when if was sent to that ensemble, there was a parallel invocation for each true in our ensemble of truth! The result was not what we expected at all: many "somethings" were done.

What can be done about this issue? Recasting true as a literal instead of a slot would merely defer the problem to other cases. Reducing an ensemble containing identical members into a singleton by default would destroy important frequency information.

6.5 Synchronization

On a broader level, Ly's attempt to eschew synchronization and embrace nondeterminism will not be compatible with many classic algorithms. For example, an exchange-based sort would require synchronization to serialize adjacent exchanges. We have started an exploration of alternative algorithms, but do not yet understand their effectiveness or efficiency. We will need to gain significant experience in implementing applications with this programming model before we can assess its efficacy.

7. Related Work

We are not the first to dream of harnessing emergence. Anthony has looked carefully at natural distributed systems and their application to distributed computer systems, and has devised an election algorithm that exploits emergence [11]. Agent-oriented computing also seeks to harness emergence. Varghese and McKee investigate swarms of agents as a means to achieve fault-tolerance [12]. Parunak and Brueckner have taken an information-theoretic approach to understand the conditions under which emergence can be effective [13]. Devescovi et al have devised a computational framework called SelfLets, and incorporated biologically-inspired self-organizing algorithms into it [14]. Finally, Fleissner and Baniassad investigated a programming paradigm based on information diffusion [15], in which there may be a duality relationship between information diffusing across a space with many points, and a system of active individuals in many points in space.

8. Conclusions

We hope to cut the Gordian knot that is manycore programming by embracing nondeterminism and harnessing emergence. To that end, we propose two new concepts: *ensembles,* which capture the notion of a flock or swarm, and *adverbs*, which specify how to perform an ensemble computation and how to treat the results. To test these concepts, we designed and implemented a new language, Ly, adding ensembles and adverbs to an object model loosely based on Self, in a syntax loosely based on JavaScript. Early experience with Ly has uncovered a number of issues which will point the way for our next iteration.

Acknowledgements

We would like to thank Erik Altman, Doug Kimelman, Kristen McIntyre, Leo Ungar for their help with this paper.

References

1. E.D. Berger, et al., "Grace: Safe Multithreaded Programming for C/C++," OOPSLA, 2009.
2. R.L.B. Jr., et al., "A Type and Effect System for Deterministic Parallel Java," OOPSLA, 2009.
3. S.P. Jones, et al., "Concurrent Haskell," POPL, 1996.
4. C. Hewitt, et al., "A universal modular actor formalism for artificial intelligence," IJCAI, 1973.
5. B. Bloom, et al., "Thorn—Robust, Concurrent, Extensible Scripting on the JVM," OOPSLA, 2009.
6. D.R. Hofstadter, *Gödel, Escher, Bach: an Eternal Golden Braid*, Basic Books, Inc., 1979.
7. D. Ungar and S.S. Adams, "Hosting an Object Heap on Manycore Hardware: An Exploration," Dynamic Language Symposium, 2009.
8. D. Ungar and R.B. Smith, "Self: The power of simplicity," *SIGPLAN Not.*, vol. 22, no. 12, 1987, pp. 227-242; DOI http://doi.acm.org/10.1145/38807.38828.
9. C.W. Reynolds, "Flocks, Herds, and Schools: A Distributed Behavioral Model," SIGGRAPH, 1987.
10. C. Reynolds, "Boids," 1995; http://www.red3d.com/cwr/boids/.
11. R.J. Anthony, "Emergence: a Paradigm for Robust and Scalable Distributed Applications," International Conference on Autonomic Computing, 2004.
12. C.A. Moritz, et al., "Exploring Optimal Cost-Performance Designs for Raw Microprocessors," Field-Programmable Custom Computing Machines, 1998.
13. H.V.D. Parunak and S. Brueckner, "Entropy and Self-Organization in Multi-Agent Systems," AGENTS'01, 2001.
14. D. Devescovi, et al., "Self-organization algorithms for autonomic systems in the SelfLet approach," Autonomic Computing and Communication Systems, 2007.
15. S. Fleissner and E. Baniassad, "Harmony-oriented programming and software evolution," OOPSLA, 2009.

Collaborative Model Merging

Maximilian Koegel, Helmut Naughton, Jonas Helming, Markus Herrmannsdoerfer

Technische Universität München, Institut für Informatik

{koegel, naughton, helming, herrmama}@in.tum.de

Abstract

Models are important artifacts in the software development life-cycle and are often the result of a collaborative activity of multiple developers. When multiple developers modify the same model, conflicts can occur and need to be resolved by merging. Existing approaches for model merging require developers to solve all conflicts before committing. The later a developer commits the higher the probability for even more conflicts. This forces the developers to solve every conflict as soon as possible and without consulting the other developer. However, we claim that developers often need to discuss their choice of conflict resolution with another developer in case of a complex conflict, since a conflict also expresses differences in opinion about the model. In this paper we propose to allow developers to postpone a decision of a modeling conflict. We present an approach to make conflicts part of the model and represent them as first-level entities based on issue modeling from the field of Rationale Management. This facilitates the possibility for collaborative conflict resolution and merging. Furthermore, it allows for a complete batch merge instead of interactive merging, where all conflicts are added to the model and then resolved later. To substantiate our claim that developers favor to discuss complex conflicts we conducted a case study.

Categories and Subject Descriptors D. Software [*D.2 SOFTWARE ENGINEERING*]: Version control

General Terms D 2.7 Version Control, D 2.9 Software Configuration Management

Keywords Merging, Collaboration, Model, Operation-based, Issue, Rationale Management

1. Introduction and Motivation

Overview. In a software development project models are important artifacts and they have become more important in recent years, especially with the adoption of Model-Driven Development [21]. Building models is a collaborative activity, where multiple developers participate. Therefore, it is important to control changes to models and to manage conflicting changes by different developers. The activity of integrating conflicting changes into a consolidated model is called merging.

Merging is not only a technical necessity to resolve conflicts. From a broader point of view it is about exploring the design space of a model and about accepting or discarding alternative designs. In this sense conflicting changes are the result of different design choices. Rationale Management is a field in Software Engineering that strives to foster discussion on design choices while trying to capture the underlying design issue, its proposals, and its resolution. Rationale Management Models such as Questions Options and Criteria (QOC) [2] or Issue-Based Information Systems (IBIS) [15] define issues that describe a question or problem that needs to be solved. Issues can have a number of alternative proposals on how to solve them. Proposals can be assessed in different dimensions, which are defined as criteria. Wolf et al. [20] have proposed to integrate rationale management models into existing models for system specification such as UML [13] or SysML [14]. Figure 1 shows the result of such an integrated model using the example of the UNICASE tool [8].

The UNICASE rationale model allows to assign issues to organizational units, for example developers. Issues consist of proposals for resolving the issue and criteria to assess the arguments for a proposal. Furthermore, issues can be annotated to model elements, which they are related to. For example, an issue could be annotated to the use case that is being discussed in the issue.

Related Work. In general, capturing design rationale has long been recognized as beneficial. For instance, Mostow [12] argues for making design decisions as well as design rationale explicit, in order to improve the design process in AI research.

Lee and Lai [10] suggest a design representation language for capturing design rationale. They aim at providing an expressive language, especially tailored to represent design rationale.

Permission to make digital or hard copies of all or part of this work for personal or classroom use is granted without fee provided that copies are not made or distributed for profit or commercial advantage and that copies bear this notice and the full citation on the first page. To copy otherwise, to republish, to post on servers or to redistribute to lists, requires prior specific permission and/or a fee.

Onward! 2010, October 17–21, 2010, Reno/Tahoe, Nevada, USA.

Copyright © 2010 ACM 978-1-4503-0236-4/10/10. . . $10.00

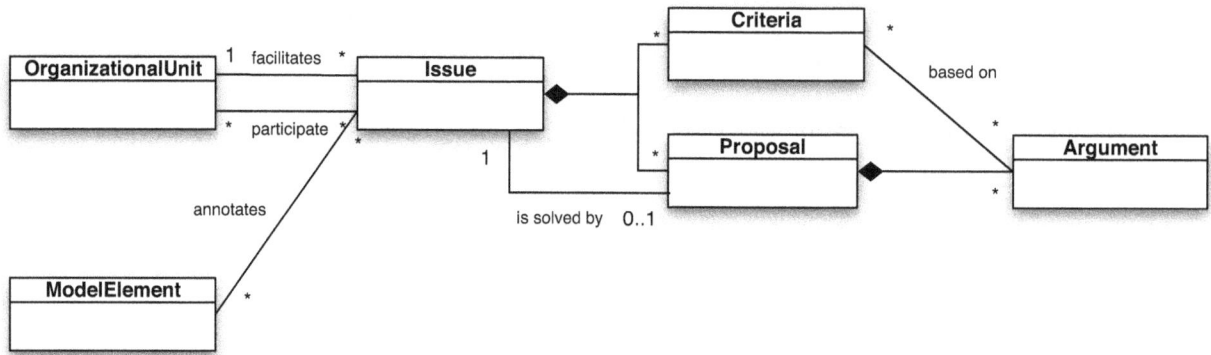

Figure 1. Issue Model of UNICASE (UML class diagram)

In contrast, Lubars [11] argues for representing design decisions as issues (based on the IBIS system of issue modeling), saying their informal manner provides the "necessary flexibility during the early parts of design deliberation, which largely involves analyzing design issues".

DRCS (the Design Rationale Capture System) by Klein [7] uses a "Shared Product Data Blackboard" to capture design rationale, but Klein notes that such rationale capture systems "impose significant overhead on the design process".

Easterbrook [4] extends the idea of modeling design rationale as issues by employing computer supported negotiation models. In his conclusion he emphasizes that "a carefully managed conflict can improve the quality of the requirements specification".

The Timewarp collaborative toolkit was used by Edwards [5] to detect and manage semantic conflicts in artifacts. Description of conflicts is done statically based on the semantics of the application, while conflict handling is independent of them. The strategy pattern is then used to flexibly handle occurring conflicts.

CoObRA by Schneider, Zündorf and Niere [17] uses change tracking of object data to allow for merging at the object level. While the conflict for models detection is similar to our approach, CoObRA does not allow to capture the rationale of design decisions.

Similarly, Ignat and Norrie [6] describe approaches for an operation-based merging approach for asynchronous communication in object-based collaborative graphical editing. They focus heavily on the topic of graphical editing and also do not capture design rationale.

For the domain of viewpoint merging, Sabetzadeh and Easterbrook [16] developed the tool iVuBlender to "explore interactions between different parts of a problem". They conclude by claiming the need for two types of traceability, "one for tracing the elements of the merges back to their sources, and another for tracking down the viewpoint interrelation assumptions behind each unification".

In the field of software architecture, van der Ven et al. [18] argue the necessity of design capture for architectural decisions. They emphasize the similarities between the processes for software design and rationale management. The authors present Archium, a compiler and run-time platform for Java, which is able to capture such rationale, though this is done manually.

Jim Whitehead describes in his paper about collaboration in software engineering [19] the need for better tool support to help with capturing design rationale in the form of an argumentation structure. Such systems "need to be collaborative, allowing many people to modify the evolving argument".

Bagheri and Ghorbani [1] present a Belief-theoretic model for collaborative modeling, focusing on the degree of uncertainty of human analysis and opinions. They also detail how different viewpoints may be merged, but their approach requires annotation of the conceptual model elements to function, which they see as an extra burden.

Cicchetti, Di Ruscio, and Pierantonio [3] in their paper about managing model conflicts in distributed development present a metamodel for conflict management, which allows for the specification of conflicts between different model elements. They focus on the technical side of conflict management and do not provide rationale management for design decisions.

Contribution. In this paper we propose to employ rationale management techniques and methods for model merging. The novelty of our approach is the application and integration of Rationale Management into Model Merging. We call this approach *Issue-based Model Merging*. In this approach conflicts are aggregated into one problem that needs to be decided upon — an *issue*. The alternative choices for resolving the conflicts represent proposals. Issue-based merging addresses the following problems of traditional merging:

Invisible Design Decisions.
Developers make design decisions while resolving conflicts. These decisions are invisible to the other devel-

opers. They are not represented in the model, nor are they captured for rationale management. It is difficult to know the fact that and the reason why a decision has been made.

Isolated Design Decisions.
During merging developers are usually isolated. There is no support for collaborating on merge decisions to make a better decision by involving others such as the developer that made the conflicting change.

Forced Design Decisions.
Without making all merge decisions the developer cannot reintegrate his or her changes into the repository. Either all changes are delayed, resulting in the risk of more merges or the decision has to be made at the time of the merge. This forces the developer to make decisions, that he or she would otherwise have postponed.

Interactive Merge.
From code merging developers are used to a batch merge, where they first produce a merge result and then resolve conflicts in the configuration item the merge occurred in later. To facilitate batch merging for models it is necessary to be able to represent conflicts in the model.

In issue-based merging conflicts are aggregated to issues. The conflicting sets of changes are aggregated to proposals. The issue can even be annotated to the model elements involved and assigned to relevant developers automatically. Developers decide conflicts based on issues. Issues can be persisted directly in the model and thereby make design decisions visible and document the rationale of design decisions. Furthermore, multiple developers can be involved in the decision as merging issues can be resolved in a collaborative effort since they are part of the shared model. Finally, merge decisions may be postponed by generating an issue for the decision and persisting it as an open issue in the model.

Outline. In the following sections we first introduce an algebra for model transformation, which we will use in the remainder of this paper. Then we describe the model for issue-based merging. Furthermore, we present an approach to aggregate conflicts to issues. Finally we provide an empirical study on the need for merging issues when merging complex changes.

2. Operation-based Graph Transformation Algebra

The following algebra for model transformation is used throughout the rest of the paper: *Models* are directed graphs that consist of nodes and edges. Edges can be unidirectional or bidirectional. The graph has exactly one spanning tree based on the containment property of its edges. An edge can be defined to be a containment edge, and the containment spanning tree constraint must be preserved at any time. The

set of all models is denoted with M, while the set of all model element (nodes) is denoted with E. We define the following operators on models for our algebra:

Element Operator $\in: E, M \rightarrow Bool$
The element operator determines whether an element is in a model. It returns a result from the set of boolean values $Bool = \{true, false\}$.

Operations are transformations that transform a graph. An operation may change, create, or delete nodes or edges. We denote the set of all operations with O. We define the following operators on operations for our algebra:

Application Operator $+ : M, O \rightarrow M$
This binary operator applies an operation to a model. The model is transformed as described by the operation.

Conflict Operator $! : O, O \rightarrow Bool$
The conflict operator returns true if two operations are conflicting. A conflict of two operations means that the changes that the two operations inflict on the model overlap. We have defined this operator in detail and more formally in [9].

Requires Operator $\succ: O, O \rightarrow Bool$
The requires operator returns true if one operation requires another operation to be applicable to a model. For example, an attribute change is only applicable after the respective model element has been created. For a more detailed and formal definition please see [9].

3. Merging Issue Model

To facilitate not only solving the technical problem of a conflict but the real conflict of opinions in a development team we propose to use well-known concepts from Rationale Management. A conflict represents different opinions in a development team about a certain part of the model and should therefore not always be solved by only one of the members involved in the conflict on his or her own but by all involved parties in a collaborative effort. Therefore, a conflict is considered to be a merge issue in a project. Its alternative proposals are the conflicting sets of changes. This is very similar to a design issue, where several alternative approaches to resolve the design problem might exist.

Existing Rationale Management Models such as QOC [2] or IBIS [15] provide issues as model elements that describe a question or problem that needs to be solved. We have already introduced an example of these rationale models in the first section. Our issue model is based on these existing models and adds model elements to facilitate modeling of merge issues.

The resulting model is depicted in Figure 2. The added classes are highlighted in grey. An *Issue* is a question that needs to be solved and consists of *Proposals* for solving the issue and criteria that can be used to assess or discuss the different proposals with *Arguments*. A *Merging Issue* is a

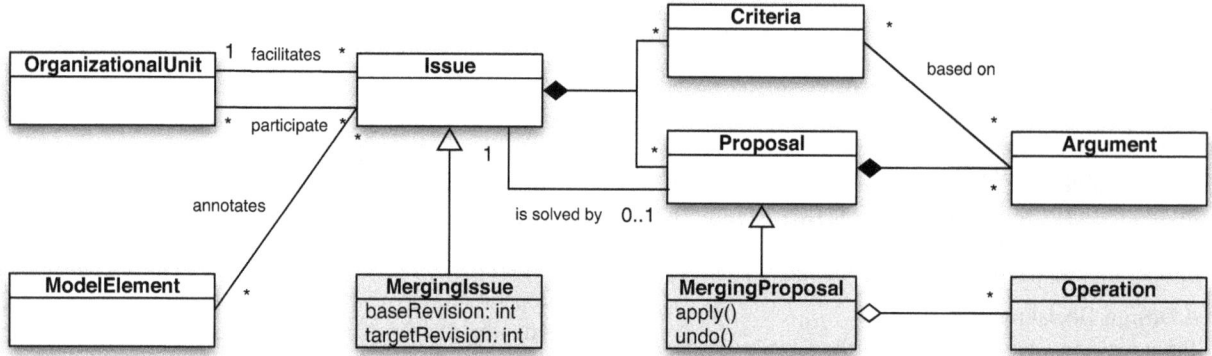

Figure 2. Merging Issue Model (UML class diagram)

subclass of issue that captures additional data such as the base and the target version of the merge it originates from. For discussing a proposal there are arguments that can be based on criteria to support or argue against a proposal. A *MergingProposal* is a subclass of proposal that aggregates the operations which are represented by the proposal. A proposal can be designated to be the current solution of the issue by the *isSolved* association. An issue is *facilitated* by an *OrganizationalUnit* such as a user and many units can participate in solving the issue. For merging issues the assignee and participants are the developers involved in the merge by authoring any of the conflicting operations. Also an issue can be annotated to model elements to which the problem is related. For a merging issue these are the model elements that are conflicting in the merge.

In contrast to regular proposals merging proposals are executable, i.e., they can be applied and undone on a model. On apply or undo, all operations of the proposal are applied to or undone from the model, respectively. When a merging issue is resolved a proposal is designated as the solution and this proposal is applied to the model. When an issue is reopened, the solving proposal is unset and reverted from the model. Conflict detection is applied to ensure that the merge issue solution is not in conflict with any change since its base revision. By applying conflict detection there is an implicit requires and conflicts relation between the proposals. The conflicts and requires relation on the set of all proposals (defined as P) can be deduced from the conflict and requires relation on operations. We define the contains operator $\in$ on operations and proposals such that it returns *true* if an operation is contained by the proposal.

Conflicts Relation on Proposals $! : P, P \rightarrow Bool$
Let $r, s \in O$, p and $q \in P$:

$$p \, ! \, q \Leftrightarrow \exists r \in p, s \in q : r \, ! \, s$$

Requires Relation on Proposals $\succ : P, P \rightarrow Bool$
Let $r, s \in O$ and $p, q \in P$:

$$p \succ q \Leftrightarrow \neg(p \, ! \, q) \wedge (\exists r \in p, s \in q : r \succ s)$$

If two proposals contain any conflicting operations they are defined as conflicting. If two proposals are not conflicting, but contain operations with a requires relation they also share the requires relation in the same direction. If one proposal requires another proposal, it implies that the underlying design choice is depending on the other design choice and can only be realized if the other choice is also implemented. Similarly, conflicting proposals express the fact that their underlying design choices are not compatible. Effectively, we reuse the conflict detection to detect dependencies among design choices.

4. Constructing Merging Issues

Merge issues are constructed to aggregate conflicting operations into problems that can be decided upon independently. A merging issue can also be postponed during merging and is therefore not decided upon. It is then persisted into the model along with the conflict set of operations as described in the previous section. If a merging issue is resolved during merging the developer can still decide to keep the issue and persist it to the model for documenting the decision. In contrast to postponed merging issues it is already resolved with the selected choice of the developer. Regardless whether an issue is persistent or not, it represents a decision that a developer needs to make to complete a merge. The issue consists of several operations and therefore reduces the number of decisions a developer must make during merging. The issues are constructed from the underlying operations with the help of conflict detection. In this section we describe how the sets of conflicting operations are aggregated to issues.

We first set forth the requirements for this aggregation. Our goal is to partition the operations from both lists — the list of incoming operations and the local pending operations — into sets. Each set will represent one issue. The partition must follow two simple rules. First, operations of the same list that are in a requires relation must be in the same set. Second, operations of different lists that are in a conflicts relation must be in the same set. Such a partition obviously exists, since we can just put all operations into one set. However, our goal is to find the partition with the maximum number of sets. The bigger a set is the more complicated the issue is since it involves many operations. Many small sets mean more but simpler issues. In other words, we strive for high cohesion among related operations and low coupling among unrelated operations.

More formally, we have to assert the following properties for the operations partition into issues. We denote I for the set of all issues, I^p for the set of all issues in the partition, O^m for the set of all operations in the list of local operations (*my* operations) and O^t for the list of incoming operations (*their* operations). Furthermore, we write $o \in i$ for an operation o and an issue i if o is contained in the set of operations representing i.

High Cohesion for Conflicts

Let $o, p \in O$, $i, j \in I^p$:

$$\exists o \in O^m, p \in O^t : (o\,!\,p \wedge o \in i \wedge p \in j) \Rightarrow i = j$$

High Cohesion for Requires

Let $o, p \in O$, $i, j \in I^p$:

$$\exists o, p \in O^{m|t} : (o \succ p \wedge o \in i \wedge p \in j) \Rightarrow i = j$$

Low Coupling

Let $o, p \in O$, $i, j \in I^p$:

$$\forall o \in i, p \in j : (\neg(o\,!\,p) \wedge \neg(o \succ p) \wedge \neg(p \succ o)) \Rightarrow i \neq j$$

Basically, the problem of constructing issues from operations resembles the problem of finding connected graphs. The requires and conflict relation on operations define the edges for the graph while the operations are the nodes. Figure 3 shows an example graph of two lists of operations ordered by time. The single arrows denote a requires relation while the double arrows denote conflict relations. Conflicts only occur among operations in different lists, while only operations in the same list may require one another. For example, operation 1 conflicts with operation A while operation 3 requires operation 2. The rectangles labeled with $I1$, $I2$ and $I3$ visualize the three sets of the partition. All sets that only consist of nodes within O^t or O^m do not need to be resolved by a user, i.e., they represent no conflicting design choices and therefore no issues. $I3$ in the example is not an issue, while $I1$ and $I2$ are issues. For each issue, the two proposals are the operations of the set that are in O^t and that are in O^m. The assignees and participants are the involved developers in the merge, while the involved model elements are the model elements the included operations are changing.

5. Empirical Study

To evaluate our approach we wanted to investigate the need for supporting discussion of merge decisions when developers face complex conflicts. Therefore, we conducted an empirical study where we have sampled 778 complex merge decisions from 46 developers. We found that developers favor

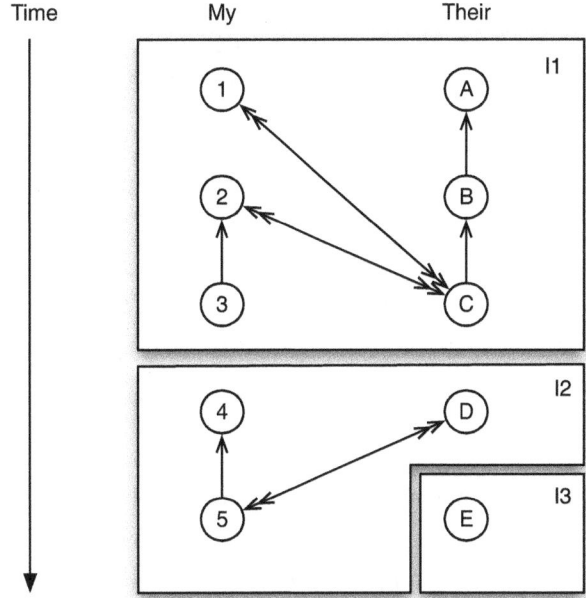

Figure 3. Example for Operations Partition into Issues

to discuss complex merge decisions in 45.47% of the cases and that the need for discussion depends on their selection of how to resolve the conflict. In this section, we present the empirical study. We describe the design of the study, the results, their statistical evaluation and interpretation.

5.1 Study Design

We conducted the empirical study to answer the following research questions:

Would developers favor to discuss complex merges instead of being forced to solve them immediately?
When developers merge models they are normally forced to complete the merge before they can commit their changes to the repository. Would developers favor to postpone a merge decision and discuss the conflict with the involved developer first?

Does the need for discussion depend on the developer's choice on how to resolve a conflict?
When developers reject changes of another developer do they want to discuss this decision more often than if they reject their own change? If they take more time to comprehend the changes do they also want to discuss the conflict more often?

To answer these questions we designed eight different merging scenarios. In every scenario the developer gets a description of the current model state and of the changes that he or she has performed including a rationale for the changes. The developer is then confronted with a merge situation due to conflicts with new changes from the repository.

In the following we will shortly explain one of the scenarios with which the developers were confronted. The example

31

is from the domain of UML class diagrams. In the example, two developers make conflicting changes to a model. The initial model or common ancestor is depicted in Figure 4.

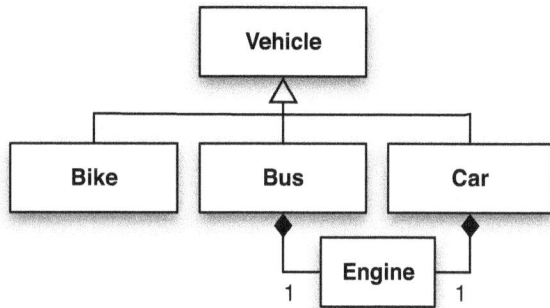

Figure 4. Common Ancestor Model (UML Class Diagram)

We assume that a developer A now performs an extract superclass refactoring on the classes Bus and Car (see Figure 5). This effectively pulls up the composition to $Engine$ from Car and Bus to the new superclass $PoweredVehicle$.

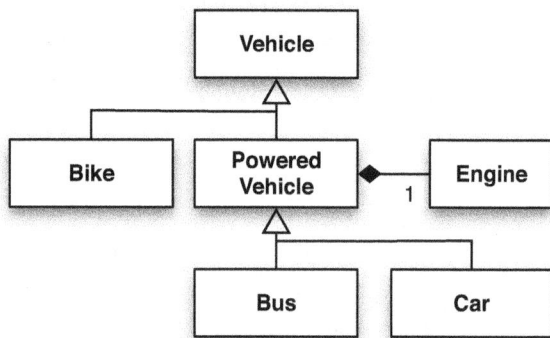

Figure 5. Model after Extract-Superclass Refactoring (UML Class Diagram)

Another developer B also starts with the same ancestor model from Figure 4 but decides to make a different change. The developer changes the multiplicity of the composition from Bus to $Engine$ on the $Engine$ side to unbounded to reflect the fact that buses might have more than one $Engine$ (see Figure 6).

The changes of developer A and B are in conflict since the change of developer A only makes sense if the multiplicity on the aggregations from Bus and Car to Engine are of the same multiplicity. In fact the developers have a different opinion about the model, in this case about how many engines a bus should be able to have.

For each merge scenario such as the previous example the developers had a number of typical choices for merging:

Accept Mine. Accept my change and reject the change from the repository.

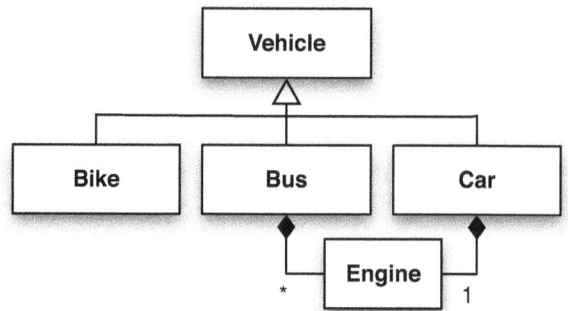

Figure 6. Model after Change of Multiplicity (UML Class Diagram)

Accept Theirs. Accept the change from the repository and reject my change.

Take More Time. Take more time to look at all incoming changes.

Most importantly however the developers could make a selection to indicate whether they would like to discuss a decision with the developer that committed the conflicting change.

Issue. Discuss merge decision with the other involved developer

No Issue. Do *not* discuss merge decision with the other involved developer

This decision is independent of the previous decision.

5.2 Study Result

For the study we interviewed 46 developers by means of an electronic questionnaire. 48% of the developers are professionals and 52% students. 67% of the professionals are software engineers, 29% researchers and 4% other developers. 58% of the students are Bachelor students and 42% Master students, and they all have a Computer Science related major. Figure 7 depicts the experience of developers in years grouped by three areas: Object-Oriented Programming, Source Code Repositories, and Unified Modeling Language.

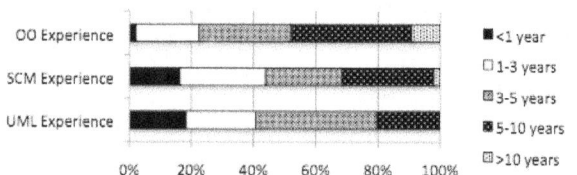

Figure 7. Developer Experience

The 46 developers answered 778 merge questions in total. Figure 8 shows the distribution of the choices for the merge questions. 267 of the choices are to *accept my*, 256 of the choices are to *accept their* and finally 252 are to *take more time*. In effect the choices are almost evenly distributed.

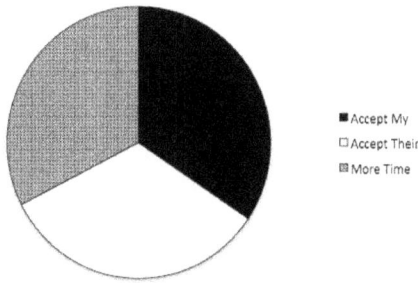

Figure 8. Merging Choices

For all merge decisions, developers had the choice to discuss their decision with the other developer. In 45.47% of merging decisions developers indicated a need for discussion. Figure 9 shows the distribution of the choice of whether or not to create an issue for the three different choices for merge — *accept mine*, *accept their* and *take more time*. While for merge decisions where developers selected *accept mine* or *take more time*, the percentage of created issues was 79.28% and 86.54%, respectively, the same percentage for *accept their* is only 40.34%.

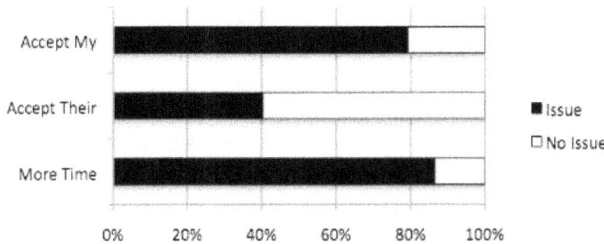

Figure 9. Creation of Issues for the different Merge Choices

5.3   Statistical Evaluation and Interpretation

In this section, we interpret the results in terms of the research question posed previously by applying statistical tests where applicable. In 45.47% of the 778 complex merging decisions developers would have liked to discuss their choice. This shows that the need for discussion support is significant if developers are confronted with complex merge decisions.

The request for discussion is dependent on the choice the developers made in the merge. We expected that developers would discuss decisions more often if they reject a change from the repository or if they request more time than if they just let the incoming changes override their own. This leads to two hypotheses on this correlation. Our first hypothesis is that merge decisions with the choice *take more time* required a discussion more often than decisions with the choice *accept their changes*. Our second hypothesis is that merge de-

cisions with the choice *accept my changes* required a discussion more often than decisions with the choice *accept their changes*.

We have three sample groups, decisions with the merge choice *accept my changes*, *accept their changes* and *take more time* (see Figure 9). The binary random variable is true if there is a discussion request for the decision. Figure 10 shows the 99% confidence intervals for the respective groups. The intervals for the merge *accept their changes* and *take more time* do overlap. This means we cannot assume that the probability for a discussion is different for these groups. However, as expected, the interval of *accept my changes* is disjoint with both other intervals. Therefore, we can accept both of our hypothesis at a 99% significance level.

| Merge Choice | Radius | Interval | |
		Lower Bound	Upper Bound
Accept Mine	0.0595	0.7333	0.8523
Accept Their	0.0748	0.3287	0.4782
More Time	0.0532	0.8123	0.9186

Figure 10. 99% confidence intervals for probability for issue for different merge choice

This means that if developers choose to accept their own changes or take more time for a decision they tend to discuss their choice more often. A selection to accept the incoming change is less often selected for discussion. Both claims are shown on a 99% significance level by the statistical tests. This seems reasonable and we expected this, since a developer will only accept an incoming change over his or her change if he/she understands and approves the incoming change. These decisions require a discussion less often. If a developer selects his or her own change and therefore discards another change it seems more often reasonable to discuss this choice with the other developer. Finally, if a developer chooses to take more time, the decision seems to be difficult, might need to be postponed, and is therefore probably more often suited for a discussion.

6.   Conclusion

In this paper we have proposed an approach to collaborative merging. Our approach allows to represent conflicts explicitly as parts of the model and thereby to postpone them. This facilitates discussion on conflicts and collaborative conflict resolution. We showed how concepts from Rationale Management can be reused to represent conflicts and how these issues can be constructed from a set of conflicts. Finally, we also substantiated our claim that developers favor to discuss complex merge conflicts in a case study. The study shows that developers like to discuss conflicts in a considerable percentage of conflicts. Furthermore, we derived with statistical significance the fact that developers discuss conflicts more often if they would like to reject a change of another developer or to postpone the decision.

References

[1] E. Bagheri and A. A. Ghorbani. Towards a Belief-Theoretic model for collaborative conceptual model development. In *Hawaii International Conference on System Sciences*, volume 0, page 490, Los Alamitos, CA, USA, 2008. IEEE Computer Society.

[2] V. Bellotti, A. MacLean, and T. Moran. What makes a good design question? *SIGCHI Bull.*, 23(4):80–81, 1991. ISSN 0736-6906.

[3] A. Cicchetti, D. Ruscio, and A. Pierantonio. Managing model conflicts in distributed development. In *MoDELS '08: Proceedings of the 11th international conference on Model Driven Engineering Languages and Systems*, pages 311–325. Springer-Verlag, Berlin, Heidelberg, 2008. ISBN 978-3-540-87874-2.

[4] S. Easterbrook. Resolving requirements conflicts with computer-supported negotiation. In *Requirements engineering: social and technical issues*, pages 41–65. Academic Press Professional, Inc., 1994. ISBN 0-12-385335-4.

[5] W. K. Edwards. Flexible conflict detection and management in collaborative applications. In *Proceedings of the 10th annual ACM symposium on User interface software and technology*, pages 139–148, Banff, Alberta, Canada, 1997. ACM. ISBN 0-89791-881-9.

[6] C. L. Ignat and M. C. Norrie. Operation-based versus state-based merging in asynchronous graphical collaborative editing. In *Proc. 6th International Workshop on Collaborative Editing Systems, Chicago*, 2004.

[7] M. Klein. Capturing design rationale in concurrent engineering teams. *Computer*, 26(1):39–47, 1993. ISSN 0018-9162.

[8] M. Koegel and J. Helming. UNICASE. http://unicase.org, 2009.

[9] M. Koegel, J. Helming, and S. Seyboth. Operation-based conflict detection and resolution. In *CVSM '09: Proceedings of the 2009 ICSE Workshop on Comparison and Versioning of Software Models*, pages 43–48, Washington, DC, USA, 2009. IEEE Computer Society. ISBN 978-1-4244-3714-6.

[10] J. Lee and K. Lai. What's in design rationale? *Hum.-Comput. Interact.*, 6(3):251–280, 1991.

[11] M. Lubars. Representing design dependencies in an issue-based style. *Software, IEEE*, 8(4):81–89, 1991. ISSN 0740-7459.

[12] J. Mostow. Toward better models of the design process. *AI Magazine*, 6(1):44, 1985.

[13] Object Management Group. Unified modeling language. http://www.uml.org/, Oct. 2006.

[14] Object Management Group. Systems modeling language. http://www.omgsysml.org/, Oct. 2009.

[15] H. Rittel and W. Kunz. Issues as elements of information systems. Technical report, Institut fur Grundlagen der Planung, University of Stuttgart, 1970.

[16] M. Sabetzadeh and S. Easterbrook. Traceability in viewpoint merging: a model management perspective. In *Proceedings of the 3rd international workshop on Traceability in emerging forms of software engineering*, pages 44–49, Long Beach, California, 2005. ACM. ISBN 1-59593-243-7.

[17] C. Schneider, A. Zündorf, and J. Niere. CoObRA - a small step for development tools to collaborative environments. *IEE Seminar Digests*, 2004(902):21–28, Jan. 2004.

[18] J. Ven, A. Jansen, J. Nijhuis, and J. Bosch. Design decisions: The bridge between rationale and architecture. In *Rationale Management in Software Engineering*, pages 329–348. 2006.

[19] J. Whitehead. Collaboration in software engineering: A roadmap. In *2007 Future of Software Engineering*, pages 214–225. IEEE Computer Society, 2007. ISBN 0-7695-2829-5.

[20] T. Wolf. *Rationale-based Unified Software Engineering Model*. Dissertation, Technische Universität München, July 2007.

[21] Y. Zhang and S. Patel. Agile model-driven development in practice. *Software, IEEE*, PP(99):1–9, 2010. ISSN 0740-7459.

Sonifying Performance Data to Facilitate Tuning of Complex Systems

Performance Tuning: Music to My Ears

Cody Henthorne[1,2]

Raytheon BBN Technologies[1]

chenthor@bbn.com

Eli Tilevich[2]

Virginia Tech[2]

tilevich@cs.vt.edu

Abstract

In the modern computing landscape, the challenge of tuning software systems is exacerbated by the necessity to accommodate multiple divergent execution environments and stakeholders. Achieving optimal performance requires a different configuration for every combination of hardware setups and business requirements. In addition, the state of the art in system tuning can involve complex statistical models, which require deep expertise not commonly possessed by the average software developer. This paper presents a novel approach to tuning complex software systems by leveraging sound to convey performance information during execution. We conducted a scientific survey to determine which sound characteristics (e.g., loudness, panning, pitch, tempo, etc.) are most accurate to express information to the average programmer. As determined by the survey, the characteristics that scored the highest across all the participants were used to create a proof-of-concept demonstration. The demonstration showed that a programmer who is not an expert in either software tuning or enterprise computing can configure the parameters of a real world enterprise application server, so that its resulting performance surpasses that exhibited under the standard configuration. Our results indicate that sound-based tuning approaches can provide valuable solutions to the challenges of configuring complex computer systems.

Categories and Subject Descriptors D.2.8 [*Software Engineering*]: Metrics—Performance measures; D.2.9 [*Software Engineering*]: Management—Software configuration management; C.4 [*Computer Systems Organization*]: Performance attributes

General Terms Experimentation, Performance, Human Factors

Keywords Performance Tuning, Sonification, Empirical Studies, J2EE, Enterprise Application Servers

1. Introduction

A system's performance depends as much on the efficiency of its design as it does on the precision of its configuration. Performance tuning, a key facet of configuration, is the process of choosing those input parameters that achieve the desired level of some performance characteristic. For example, properly choosing the size for a server's thread pool can increase throughput or decrease latency.

Performance tuning is notoriously hard due to the need to accommodate multiple deployment environments and business requirements. Furthermore, pinpointing the exact source of inefficiency in a complex system can be non-trivial. Finally, it is often unclear how the value of a configuration parameter affects system performance.

Existing approaches to performance tuning take advantage of performance profiling [16, 30], visualization [29], and automation using complex statistical models [4]. Because performance tuning remains a standing challenge in the face of the increasing complexity of modern systems, there is great potential benefit in exploring novel tuning approaches that utilize untapped resources. One such resource is using sound to convey performance information.

Programmers have long recognized the utility and value of sound as a cognitive tool for understanding their programs. When dealing with data intensive applications, programmers often listen to the sounds made by hard drives to determine if thrashing is present. When dealing with processor intensive applications, programmers listen to the sounds made by CPU cooling fans to determine if a number crunching phase is in progress. It is worth noting, however, that the overall trend in hardware design aims at silent execution. For example, solid state hard drives are silent, as they do not contain any moving parts.

Permission to make digital or hard copies of all or part of this work for personal or classroom use is granted without fee provided that copies are not made or distributed for profit or commercial advantage and that copies bear this notice and the full citation on the first page. To copy otherwise, to republish, to post on servers or to redistribute to lists, requires prior specific permission and/or a fee.

Onward! 2010, October 17–21, 2010, Reno/Tahoe, Nevada, USA.
Copyright © 2010 ACM 978-1-4503-0236-4/10/10. . . $10.00

But what if executing programs could provide meaningful performance information to the programmer through sound? Furthermore, what if the sounds used were specially designed, so that multiple performance indicators could be effectively discerned by the programmer? This way, the sound would indicate the level of different performance characteristics. Further, in response to the programmer tuning a configuration parameter, the provided sound would immediately reflect if performance was affected by the change.

In this paper, we report on the results of an investigation that we conducted to explore these questions. For the purposes of our investigation, we have tapped into the ability of sound to convey information, otherwise known as *sonification* [19]. Additionally, in order to sonify multiple concurrent streams of performance data, we relied upon the concept of aural focus [23], or the human ability to segregate different aural stimuli in noisy environments (e.g., having a conversation in a loud public space).

Nevertheless, how performance information can be represented effectively within the auditory modality has not been sufficiently investigated. Although prior research has explored using sound and music to represent program execution [26], such results have to be confirmed experimentally to determine their effectiveness specifically as tuning aids.

To obtain reproducible results that can be used by us and other researchers, we conducted a scientific study that evaluated the accuracy with which programmers can perceive sound properties as the means to convey performance information. The survey involved more than 30 programmers with different levels of programming and music expertise. A statistical analysis of the study's results revealed that there are indeed sound properties that are more effective in general sonification.

With these results in hand, we architected, implemented, and evaluated a proof-of-concept performance tuning system that uses sonification to guide the programmer in tuning their systems for improved performance. For our evaluation, we focused on tuning a real world enterprise system—the GlassFish Application Server [22], which is widely used in real world installations. Equipped with our tuning system, all the evaluation's subjects were able to successfully tune GlassFish to achieve a level of performance higher than that provided by the standard configuration.

Based on our results, this paper presents the following novel contributions:

- A systematic user study that assessed the accuracy of sonification to convey information; the results of the study can inform software system designers who want to integrate sonification into their systems.

- A software architecture for tuning software systems with sound; our architecture harmoniously integrates a system under test, a workload generator, a tuning user interface, and a sound rendering engine.

- A proof of concept prototype that demonstrates the utility of our approach and its applicability to real world systems.

The rest of this paper is structured as follows. In Section 2, we describe our user study, and in Section 3 we analyze the results. Then in Section 4, we describe our proof-of-concept tuning system that follows our architecture and present the system's initial results. In Section 5, we compare this work to the related state of the art, and finally in Section 6, we discuss future work directions and present concluding remarks.

2. Investigating Underlying Sonification Parameters

First, we lay out the questions our user study was designed to answer. Then we describe the study's methodology and implementation.

2.1 Study Objectives and Questions

An individual's response to particular sounds is subjective; it depends on factors including one's cultural background, level of music sophistication or training, and frequency of exposure to non-speech audio [11]. Since professional software developers come from all walks of life and have varying cultural and ethnic backgrounds, a sonification approach must be as broadly applicable as possible to be beneficial. This entails choosing those sound characteristic which are interpreted uniformly by a substantial percentage of software developers.

Therefore, one must ask which sound characteristics are most suitable for the task at hand, performance tuning. To that end, we conducted a systematic study that gathered empirical evidence assessing the fundamental affordances of sound characteristics and their effectiveness when applied to performance tuning. Although several prior studies assessed the fitness of sonification techniques for various software engineering tasks [2, 9, 26], our study focuses specifically on how sonification can help performance tuning. In particular, our intent was to design a study that can answer the following questions: (1) Which sound characteristics are most suitable to facilitate perception and comprehension in a performance-tuning context? (2) Which sound characteristics are most effective in expressing whether a value is increasing or decreasing, so maximum accuracy is achieved across different users? (3) How effectively can a user understand a mapping of sound characteristics to the performance metrics of a running application?

2.2 Study Methodology and Design

Our online survey consisted of five sections: Demographic, General, Panning, Mapping, and General Feedback. Each section was specifically designed to help answer the questions above.

The Demographic Section gathered demographic information including years of programming experience, programming environments experience, music background, genre preferences, music listening habits, and hearing impairments.

The General Section determined which sound attributes participants naturally mapped to increasing or decreasing values. Participants listened to eight 10-second audio clips and indicated if they felt the clip represented "something" increasing a lot, increasing a little, staying constant, decreasing a little, or decreasing a lot. The eight clips modified the following sound characteristics: pitch, loudness, panning, and timbre. The questions did not inform the participant which sound characteristic was being exercised or what should be interpreted as increasing or decreasing.

The Panning Section enforced a mapping of sound coming from the left channel as low values and sound coming from right channel as high values. The participant was asked to listen to five short sound clips and indicate on a scale of 1 (lowest) to 100 (highest) what value they felt the clip represented.

The Mapping Section asked participants to interpret a 30-second sonification of program performance data including disk usage, memory usage, and network usage. Each mapping question highlighted different sonification attributes and provided sample sonifications for the participant. The participant listened to sample sonifications and then the full performance data sonification. As the sonification played the participant was asked to indicate on a scale of 1 to 10 where they felt the usage level for each resource (disk, memory, and network) was during the beginning, middle, and end of the clip.

The General Feedback Section collected comments and suggestions about the survey. This feedback was used to gather subjective data from software engineers about using sonification in general and specifically for performance tuning.

2.3 Study Implementation and Deployment

To gather inputs from a large and diverse population of participants, we created a Web-based survey. Participants were recruited by posting to graduate student mailing lists at five universities (Virginia Tech, Georgia Tech, University of Maryland, University of California in Irvine, and University of Rochester) and professional software developer mailing lists at four companies (Google, Amazon, Microsoft, and Raytheon BBN).

The survey was implemented as a Rich Internet Application constructed using the Adobe Flex Framework [1]. The sonification files used for the survey's questions were custom designed using Max/MSP [6] and saved as MP3s. To achieve meaningful results, a comprehensive configuration section guided participants in selecting appropriate volume levels and headphone orientation to be used throughout the survey.

3. Case Study Analysis and Results

In this section, we first analyze the data produced by the study that we described in Section 2. We then explain how the results of this analysis can inform the design of novel software engineering techniques and tools that use sonification.

3.1 Analysis

Overall we had 42 participants in our study. Of these, 33 participants successfully completed the survey. The survey tracked the number of times a participant listened to a sound clip. If a participant did not listen to all the sound clips, all of their answers were excluded from analysis. Except for this restriction, no other data was removed from analysis.

The data collected in the survey was multi-faceted and large. We decided to focus our analysis on primarily finding the three strongest sound characteristics for sonifying performance information. Focusing our analysis allowed us to find the information needed to build a proof-of-concept tuning system quickly. After performing a cursory analysis of all the data, we focused on the general and mapping sections, as they showed the most promise.

Analysis of the general section provided us with a distribution of participants who were able to map increasing and decreasing trends to particular changes in sound characteristics. As described in Section 2.2, the general section of our survey was a collection of multiple choice questions which asked participants to indicate how they felt changes in basic sound characteristics mapped to "something" increasing and decreasing. Analysis of this section was fairly straightforward, as we calculated the distribution of participants that selected each choice for a given question. See Figure 1 for a summary of the analysis of the general section.

The mapping section consisted of 6 major questions each with nine subquestions. These questions asked the participant to rate their observed usage levels of three resources (disk, memory, and network) on a scale from 1 to 10 during the beginning, middle, and end of a 30 second program sonification clip. For simplicity, the nine subquestions when referenced individually, will be referred to as B-DISK, B-MEM, B-NET, M-DISK, M-MEM, M-NET, E-DISK, E-MEM, and E-NET for remainder of this paper. Each question enforced a mapping of particular sound characteristics to resource usage. Since the data collected from this section was large, we have only included the analysis of one question answered with the highest accuracy. The question utilized panning from left to right and from right to left to show increasing and decreasing resource usage, respectively.

To analyze the panning question within the mapping section we calculated the average error for each resource at each location in the clip. The average error was calculated by taking the absolute value of the difference between the average of all the participants' responses and the expected answer

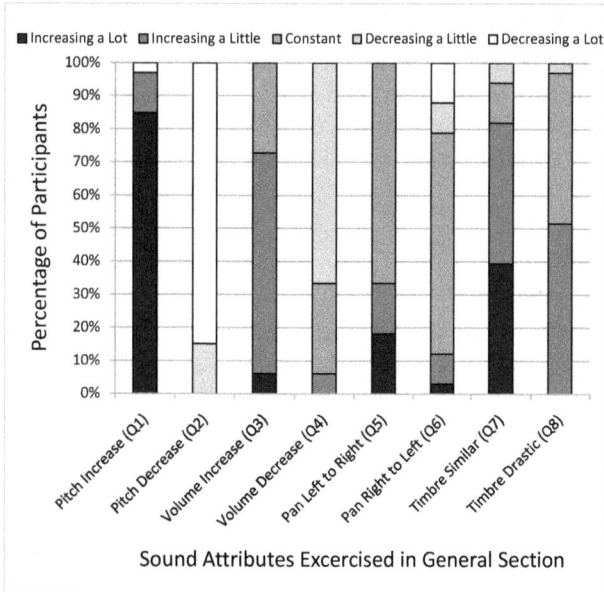

Figure 1. Distribution of participants' responses to all questions in the general section.

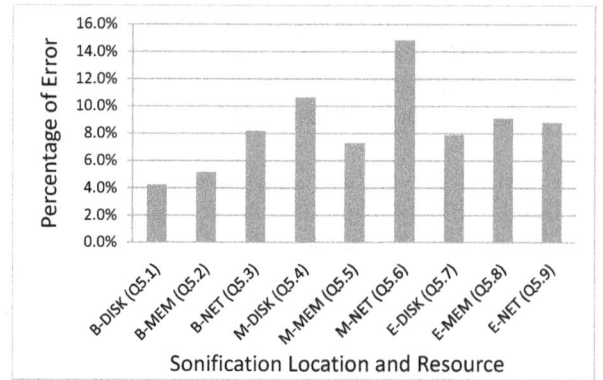

Figure 2. Error in mean participant vs. expected response for each panning subquestion. The persistently low error indicates that panning could provide a high level of accuracy for sonifying information.

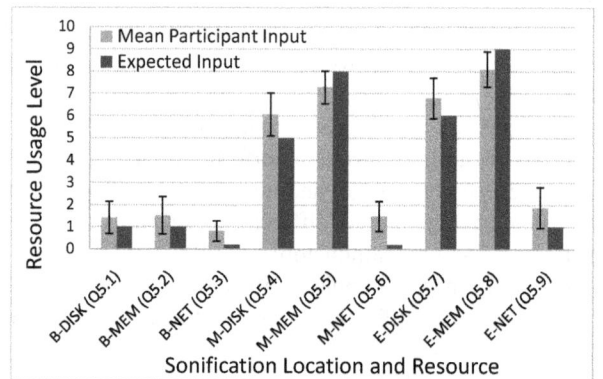

Figure 3. Expected vs. mean participant response with 95% confidence intervals as error bars for each panning subquestion. Since most expected responses fall within the confidence intervals, it shows that users will likely answer consistently and accurately.

for each subquestion. The error analysis is summarized as a column graph in Figure 2.

While the error analysis provides an estimate of the accuracy of using panning to sonify resource usage, it does not indicate any trends across the participant population. We calculated 95% confidence intervals for the average response of each subquestion. Figure 3 shows the confidence interval as error bars for the average participants' response for each subquestion along with the expected response.

3.2 Results

As is evident from the analysis of the general section, 85% of the participants mapped increasing pitch to "something" increasing a lot and 12% mapped increasing pitch to increasing a little. Additionally, 85% of participants mapped decreasing pitch to "something" decreasing a lot and 15% mapping decreasing pitch to decreasing a little. This is a strong indication that most participants already map increasing and decreasing pitch to increasing and decreasing values.

The low error for using panning is an indicator that panning can provide a high level of accuracy for representing changes in sonified data, as long as the participant is aware of the mapping. Analysis of the general section, provided evidence that there is no apparent natural mapping from panning to resource usage; however, if a mapping of panning location to usage level is enforced, panning performs well. Panning is further supported by the confidence interval analysis, as it shows a trend that users will answer consistently within an acceptable level of accuracy.

The general feedback section of the survey provided a form for participants to provide subjective comments about the survey. While this data is subjective, multiple partici-

pants indicated a strong preference for panning based sonifications. We believe this strong preference for panning stems from the user's having been bounded within the left and right limit.

4. Proof-of-Concept

Our proof-of-concept sonification tuning system leverages the insights from our study described in Section 2. The four components of our proof-of-concept are instantiated as follows:

System Under Test (SUT)

The SUT is the system to be tuned. For a SUT to be tunable, it must expose modifiable configuration parameters that can potentially affect some system performance characteristic. As our SUT, we chose a real-world commercial application server, an essential and representative part of modern enterprise infrastructure. An application server provides

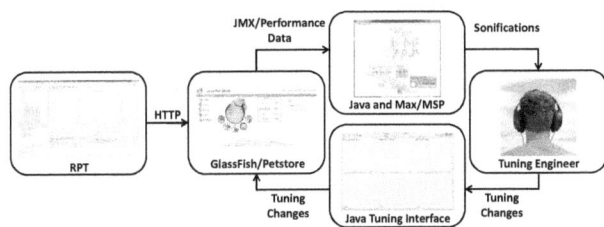

Figure 4. Instantiation of our software architecture for our proof-of-concept demonstration.

a runtime environment for enterprise applications. The performance and reliability requirements imposed on an application server are comparable to that of an operating system. Specifically, we chose Oracle GlassFish v3.0 [22], which has been successfully deployed in commercial installations.

As our enterprise application, we chose a Blueprints J2EE 5 reference application, PetStore 2.0 [13]. The PetStore application is representative of modern J2EE technologies and additionally has been used as an evaluation subject in several other performance tuning-related research and demonstrations [4, 17]. PetStore encompasses the functionality of a typical e-commerce application, in which users can browse, select, sell, and purchase pets.

GlassFish exposes an extensive set of monitoring and performance data via Java Management Extension (JMX). This mechanism provides a standardized avenue through which external clients can obtain information about a running system [20]. External applications can access GlashFish performance data, including processor usage, request rate, and connection queue status through a Java API.

Workload Generator

The SUT is exercised by the workload generator, which emulates realistic usage scenarios. Because our SUT is a Web server-based system, our workload generator emulates clients accessing the SUT remotely across the network using the HTTP network protocol. To reproduce a realistic workload for a typical e-commerce application, we used IBM Rational Performance Tester (RPT)[1]. This flagship testing tool from IBM is used by enterprises to verify whether their applications can handle potential workloads. We used the RPT test generation tools to create 75 virtual users who were exercising the functionality of the SUT under various frequencies commonly observed in practice.

Sonification Engine

The sonification engine continuously takes, as input, the performance data from the SUT and, as output, renders the appropriate sonifications. Our sonification engine comprises two components written in Java and Max/MSP [6], communicating with each other through TCP sockets. The

[1] http://www-01.ibm.com/software/awdtools/tester/performance/

Java component collected performance data from a running GlashFish instance via JMX. Specifically, the performance data our system collected was the average requests per second, CPU usage, and connection queue length. As the Java component collected performance data it dispatched the data as sequences of integers that were received, interpreted, and sonified by the Max/MSP component.

We pursued two key goals while designing the sonifications for our proof-of-concept tool: (1) they must not be "tiring" for the listener during a prolonged tuning session, and (2) their spectral differences must make them sufficiently distinct from each other. Therefore, for our MAX/MSP component, we chose naturally-occurring sounds that were designed as follows: (1) a sustained chord as if it were played by a string instrument, (2) a low hum of a cooling fan, and (3) a filtered sound of a mechanical hard drive.

As our study indicated, pitch and panning were the two sound characteristics that proved most effective for the definitive majority of the study's participants. To take advantage of this observation, we sonified the range of a performance parameter such that it was mapped to a corresponding pitch range. Thus, there was a direct correspondence between the value of a performance parameter and the pitch of the sound used to represent it. For pitch, we chose to use a range of two octaves that provided significantly noticeable difference in sounds while limiting their distortion.

To improve accuracy, we also sonified the range of a performance parameter by assigning the left channel to reflect the smallest value while the right channel the highest one. The panning location of a given sound between channels thus reflected the sonified value.

Tuning Interface

Based on the cognitive feedback received from the sonification engine, the user interacts with the tuning interface. The purpose of the tuning interface is to expose to the end user intuitive controls for manipulating configuration parameters and to relay the user's input into the actual SUT's configuration settings. JMX is a bidirectional interface. In addition to allowing external clients to obtain information about a running system, one can also use JMX to set values in the system. We designed a Java GUI that exposed three GlassFish configuration parameters, number of acceptor threads, maximum request thread pool size, and idle thread timeout to the user. When the user adjusts a parameter via the GUI, the application sends the configuration change to GlassFish.

4.1 Pilot Study: Tuning GlassFish with Sound

The purpose of this pilot study was to investigate whether *sound-based tuning can enable non-experts in either the tuned application's domain or tuning itself to function as effective systems engineers.* In the following, we describe the design, execution, and analysis of our pilot study.

Our study subjects were four professional software developers, employed by a large technology R&D firm. Although quite experienced in their core domain, they only had a cursory knowledge with enterprise infrastructure and vague familiarity with configuring and tunning of application servers. Because all the subjects happened to have participated in our online survey, they were familiar with the general concept of conveying computing information with sound.

The pilot was executed by first exposing each subject to our tuning interface and the available tuning parameters. We were careful though not to recommend or give specific guidelines regarding how the parameters' values should be set. Then each subject learned which sonifications represented which performance metric and how the changing performance data affected the sonifications. In particular, the sonified performance metrics were: requests per second, CPU usage, and connection queue length (i.e., number of requests waiting to be serviced). Finally, each subject was presented with the tuning goal of maximizing requests per second, and the auxiliary goals of maximizing the CPU usage, and minimizing the connection queue length.

The main procedure of the pilot included two runs, during which each subject attempted to achieve the aforementioned tuning objective while being guided by our sonifications. The reason for including two runs was to present an opportunity for the subjects to become more comfortable with our tuning system. Each run lasted for six and half minutes, and only the second run's results were recorded for future analysis. To ensure greater accuracy, the GlassFish server was restarted between runs.

Figure 5 shows the requests per second measurements for all four subjects during the final two and half minutes of the second run. The vertical dashed line designates the time point at which the RPT was winding down its simulation, which reduced the number of virtual users accessing the web application.

The analysis of the results shows that all the subjects were able to specify a tuning configuration that led to a performance level higher than that of the standard configuration (SC). However, the degree to which they were able to outperform the SC differed between the subjects. One subject (P2) consistently outperformed the SC, and toward the end of the second run achieved a configuration that was processing over 400 more request per second than the SC. Another subject (P1) also managed to outperform the SC by the end of the second run, but with more quality fluctuations in the intermediate configurations. Being able to specify a high quality configuration at some point, P1 then somewhat worsened the results but was able to recover toward the end of the run.

The other two subjects (P3 and P4) yielded similar results, which were exemplified with a longer learning curve. Although consistently improving their configuration, they took significantly longer to become comfortable with our tuning system. One way to explain this disparity is that programmers' auditory perception and multitasking abilities

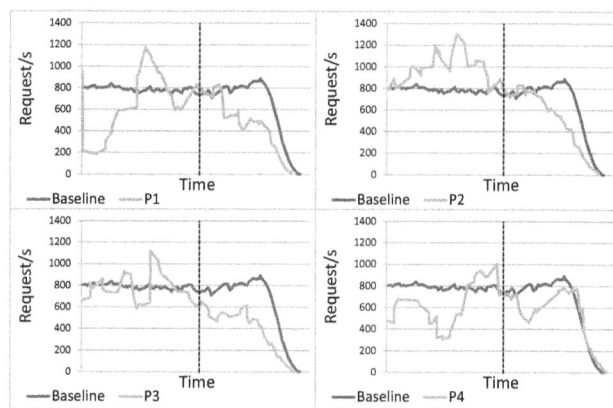

Figure 5. Graphs depicting the four participants' requests/second compared to GlassFish's standard configuration. The data starts at two and half minutes prior to the end of their second run. The vertical dashed line indicates when virtual users began logging off.

tend to differ. P3 explicitly stated that he "was not a good multitasker" and was not even able to listen to music while programming.

We conjecture that the performance of P3 and P4 could have been improved to a greater degree had the run been longer. Based on the trajectory of their results, it is possible that they would be able to eventually achieve the level of performance comparable to that of P1 and P2.

Thus, the results of our pilot study indicate that sound can be effective as a means of conveying performance information to aid tuning. It is certainly worth investigating further the exact human and technical factors that affect the effectiveness of sonification as a cognitive tool.

5. Related Work

Performance tuning, long recognized as a formidable software engineering challenge, has been the target of multiple research efforts. In the following discussion, we first present performance tuning approaches that are similar to ours. Then we give an overview of key sonification concepts and other systems that use information sonification.

5.1 Performance Tuning Approaches and Tools

Jovic and Hauswirth [16] presents an approach to tuning Java GUI applications that profiles event listener latency. Another profiling approach to analyzing performance and tuning applications is presented by Zagha et al. [30]. They provide a framework of counters and profiling tools for tuning systems based on the MIPS R10000 processor.

Other approaches have leveraged visualizations to aid tuning. Walker et al. [29] visualize the large amounts of data collected during the execution of an object-oriented system at the architectural level. Chassin et al. [8] visualize a variety of thread interactions to facilitate tuning multithreaded parallel applications. Jones et al. [15] used profiling and visualizations to aid tuning of parallel applications.

Other approaches have leveraged statistical and stochastic tools to automate tuning instead of simply aiding a manual process. Chen et al. [4] utilize the Markov decision process and a reinforcement learning strategy to discover a system's optimal configuration. Additionally, similar to our work, they also validate their approach by tuning an older version of the J2EE PetStore application. Tiwari et al. [25] present a parallel algorithm for automatically tuning parallel applications. Their work utilizes the automated tuning framework, Active Harmony [5], presented by Ţăpuş et al. as a framework for automated runtime tuning.

5.2 Information Sonification

A good reference that outlines key concepts of sonification research and design is an article by Walker and Nees [28] that defines an *auditory display* as using sound to convey information and *sonification* as an auditory display consisting of non-speech audio. Another definition of sonification is provided by Kramer at al. [19], who define it as "the transformation of data relations into perceived relations in an acoustic signal for the purposes of facilitating communication or interpretation."

Most of sonification research is concerned with identifying those scenarios for which auditory displays provide effective solutions [14, 18, 24]. For example, auditory displays have been particularly effective in rendering complex data patterns and events requiring the user's immediate attention [10, 21]. This is because human hearing excels at identifying temporal information.

A Sonification Design Map presented by deCampo [7] shows quantitative relationships between non-speech auditory displays. A traditional classification of sonification approaches includes audification [18], parameter mapping, and model-based [12]. Categorizing sonification approaches on the basis of their respective data representations results in continuous, discrete, and model-based data. According to this categorization, the sonification approach that we used in this work is model-based. This representation uses a model based on the properties of the data to mediate between the sonified data and the sound. Because the model captures the domain knowledge of the sonified data, it can be applied to different types of datasets.

Several prior approaches have used auditory displays to convey information about computer applications. Vickers and Alty [26] use music to communicate information about which programming language structures are used, to express how programs behave at runtime, and to find potential program defects [27]. They have created the CAITLIN system to aurolize Turbo Pascal programs. One of the most salient insights of their investigation is that music can successfully communicate useful information about computer programs for all users, even for those who have not been formally musically trained.

When representing program constructs using both speech and non-speech audio, Finlayson and Mellish [9] concluded that the two modalities should be used together for maximum benefit. To improve program understanding, Berman and Gallagher [3] sonify program slices.

Compared to the aforementioned auditory displays approaches to convey program information, this work focuses on understanding the performance of a computer application that we treat as a black-box. That is, we sonify the external behavior of an application without any regard for its source code or any other software artifacts. Furthermore, our sonifications are significantly less-structured than music tunes. Finally, we change our sonifications interactively in response to tuning actions of the user.

6. Future Work and Conclusions

This work has explored sonification as a cognitive aid to assist performance tuning. It also opens up several possible future work directions. In particular, we plan to:

- analyze the results of our case study further; correlating the participants' demographics to their answers looks particularly promising. If noticeable differences exist for identifiable demographics, sonification tools can be customizable to accommodate specific users.

- leverage the results of our studies to create approaches that facilitate software engineering tasks other than tuning. As certain sound characteristics can effectively convey software information, we can revisit important software engineering challenges such as program comprehension, analysis, and bug detection.

- evaluate actual performance tuning tools in greater detail. Now that our proof-of-concept tool shown that our general approach is feasible, we would like to further investigate its effectiveness in relation to other tuning approaches.

- combine sonification with other cognitive aids such as visualization. Sonification and visualization have their respective strengths and weaknesses, and when combined together can convey more information better than either cognitive aid in isolation.

The ever increasing complexity of modern computer systems calls for new and more powerful approaches to accommodate these systems for the needs of real users. In that light, tuning systems for optimal performance has come to the forefront of industrial software engineering. This paper has presented a novel approach that leverages sonification to facilitate performance tuning of complex computer systems. We believe that our approach can lay the foundation for a new generation of approaches and tools that use sonification. This powerful cognitive aid can help tame the complexity of engineering computer systems of today and tomorrow.

Acknowledgements The authors would like to acknowledge the contributions of Ivica Bukvic, who built the sonifications for both the case study and the proof-of-concept; Pardha Pyla, who helped with the design of the case study and reviewed portions of this manuscript; and VT LISA for their statistical help.

References

[1] Adobe. Adobe Flex. http://www-sjc0.adobe.com/products/flex/, 2010.

[2] L. Berman, S. Danicic, K. Gallagher, and N. Gold. The sound of software: Using sonification to aid comprehension. In *14th IEEE International Conference on Program Comprehension (ICPC'06)*, pages 225–229, 2006.

[3] L. I. Berman and K. B. Gallagher. Listening to program slices. In *Proceedings of the 12th International Conference on Auditory Display (ICAD)*, 2006.

[4] H. Chen, G. Jiang, H. Zhang, and K. Yoshihira. Boosting the performance of computing systems through adaptive configuration tuning. In *SAC '09: Proceedings of the 2009 ACM Symposium on Applied Computing*, pages 1045–1049, New York, NY, USA, 2009. ACM.

[5] C. Ţăpuş, I.-H. Chung, and J. K. Hollingsworth. Active harmony: towards automated performance tuning. In *Supercomputing '02: Proceedings of the 2002 ACM/IEEE conference on Supercomputing*, pages 1–11, Los Alamitos, CA, USA, 2002. IEEE Computer Society Press.

[6] Cycling '74 Inc. Max/MSP. http://www.cycling74.com, 2010.

[7] A. de Campo. Toward a data sonification design space map. *Proceedings of the International Conference on Auditory Display (ICAD)*, pages 342–347, 2007.

[8] J. C. de Kergommeaux, B. Stein, and P. E. Bernard. Paj, an interactive visualization tool for tuning multi-threaded parallel applications. *Parallel Computing*, 26(10):1253 – 1274, 2000.

[9] J. L. Finlayson and C. Mellish. The 'audioview' - providing a glance at Java source code. In *Proceedings of the 11th International Conference on Auditory Display (ICAD)*, 2005.

[10] J. Flowers, D. Buhman, and K. Turnage. Cross-modal equivalence of visual and auditory scatterplots for exploring bivariate data samples. *Human Factors: The Journal of the Human Factors and Ergonomics Society*, 39(3):341–351, 1997.

[11] D. Hargreaves. *The developmental psychology of music*. Cambridge University Press, 1986.

[12] T. Hermann. *Sonification for exploratory data analysis–demonstrations and sound examples*. PhD thesis, Bielefeld University, Bielefeld, Germany, 2002.

[13] Java BluePrints. Java Pet Store Demo. https://blueprints.dev.java.net/petstore/, 2010.

[14] G. Johannsen. Auditory displays in human–machine interfaces. *Proceedings of the IEEE*, 92(4):742–758, 2004.

[15] D. Jones, Jr., S. Marlow, and S. Singh. Parallel performance tuning for haskell. In *Haskell '09: Proceedings of the 2nd ACM SIGPLAN symposium on Haskell*, pages 81–92, New York, NY, USA, 2009. ACM.

[16] M. Jovic and M. Hauswirth. Measuring the performance of interactive applications with listener latency profiling. In *PPPJ '08: Proceedings of the International Symposium on Principles and Practice of Programming in Java*, pages 137–146, New York, NY, USA, 2008. ACM.

[17] K. Juse, S. Kounev, and A. Buchmann. Petstore-ws: Measuring the performance implications of web services. In *Proceedings of the 29th International Conference of the Computer Measurement Group on Resource Management and Performance Evaluation of Enterprise Computing Systems*, pages 113–123, 2003.

[18] G. Kramer. An introduction to auditory display. *Auditory Display: Sonification, Audification, and Auditory Interfaces*, pages 1–78, 1994.

[19] G. Kramer, B. Walker, T. Bonebright, P. Cook, J. Flowers, N. Miner, J. Neuhoff, et al. Sonification Report: Status of the Field and Research Agenda. 1999. *Prepared for the National Science Foundation by members of the International Community for Auditory Display*, 1999.

[20] McManus, Eamonn. Java Management Extensions Specification (JSR 3). http://www.jcp.org/en/jsr/summary?id=3, 2010.

[21] B. Moore. *An introduction to the psychology of hearing*. Academic Press San Diego, Calif, 2003.

[22] Oracle. Glassfish - Open Source Application Server, 2010. https://glassfish.dev.java.net/.

[23] N. Roman, D. Wang, and G. Brown. Speech segregation based on sound localization. *The Journal of the Acoustical Society of America*, 114:2236–2252, 2003.

[24] M. Sanders and E. McCormick. *Human Factors in Engineering and Design*. McGraw-Hill Science/Engineering/Math, 1993.

[25] A. Tiwari, V. Tabatabaee, and J. K. Hollingsworth. Tuning parallel applications in parallel. *Parallel Comput.*, 35(8-9):475–492, 2009.

[26] P. Vickers and J. Alty. Using music to communicate computing information. *Interacting with Computers*, 14(5):435–456, 2002.

[27] P. Vickers and J. L. Alty. When bugs sing. *Interacting With Computers*, 14:793 – 819, 2002.

[28] B. Walker and M. Nees. *Handbook of Sonification, In T. Hermann, A. Hunt, & J. Neuhoff (Eds.)*. New York: Academic Press, 2009.

[29] R. J. Walker, G. C. Murphy, B. Freeman-Benson, D. Wright, D. Swanson, and J. Isaak. Visualizing dynamic software system information through high-level models. In *OOPSLA '98: Proceedings of the 13th ACM SIGPLAN conference on Object-oriented programming, systems, languages, and applications*, pages 271–283, New York, NY, USA, 1998. ACM.

[30] M. Zagha, B. Larson, S. Turner, and M. Itzkowitz. Performance analysis using the mips r10000 performance counters. In *Supercomputing '96: Proceedings of the 1996 ACM/IEEE conference on Supercomputing*, page 16, Washington, DC, USA, 1996. IEEE Computer Society.

A Recommender for Conflict Resolution Support in Optimistic Model Versioning [*]

Petra Brosch   Martina Seidl   Gerti Kappel

Business Informatics Group
Vienna University of Technology, Austria
{lastname}@big.tuwien.ac.at

Abstract

The usage of optimistic version control systems comes along with cumbersome and time-consuming conflict resolution in the case that the modifications of two developers are contradicting. For code as well as for any other artifact the resolution support moves hardly beyond the choices "keep mine", "keep theirs", "take all changes", or "abandon all changes".

To ease the conflict resolution in the context of model versioning, we propose a recommender system which suggests automatically executable resolution patterns to the developer responsible for the conflict resolution. The lookup algorithm is based on a similarity-aware graph matching approach incorporating information from the metamodel of the used modeling language. This allows not only the retrieval of recommendations exactly matching the given conflict situation, but also the identification of similar conflict situations whose resolution patterns are adaptable to the current conflict.

Categories and Subject Descriptors   D.2.9 [*Software Engineering*]: Management—Programming teams

General Terms   Design, Languages

1. Introduction

Contemporary software engineering is confronted with two major challenges: first, with the complexity of modern software systems and second, with the complexity of the software development process itself. To deal with the first challenge techniques of model-driven engineering (MDE) are employed which benefit from the abstraction power of models [1]. Instead of being artifacts applied for mere design and documentation purposes only, models are successfully leveraged as basis for compiling executable code. The second challenge is faced with adequate tool support enabling the effective management of the software development process to deal with the evolution of developed artifacts.

Very prominent representatives of such management tools are *version control systems* (VCS) supporting collaboration among the team members of a project [7]. *Optimistic version control systems* allow multiple, possibly globally distributed developers to modify the same artifact at the same time and independently of each other. If two modifications do not contradict each other then they may be easily merged into one new version of the artifact [11]. If two modifications are contradicting, a manual resolution has to be performed which is a repetitive, time-consuming, and error-prone task in general. The developer responsible for conflict resolution has to decide for either one of the alternatives or (s)he has to provide a completely new variant. Currently, promising approaches are developed for the conflict resolution in the context of code versioning [8, 9] but for model versioning, no tool support is provided.

Taking advantage of the models' graph-based structure and their rich semantics, we propose a recommender system facilitating the conflict resolution in optimistic model versioning. In [3], we presented a categorization of typical conflicts in model versioning which allowed us to identify an initial set of reoccurring conflict situations and typical resolution patterns. Furthermore, we proposed an approach to automatically mine existing model repositories for the automatic identification of formerly applied conflict resolution patterns [2]. On this basis we obtain a collection of conflicts and executable resolution patterns yielding the knowledge base for the recommender system. Conflicts are represented as models, i.e., in a graph-based data structure. The lookup algorithm realizes not only exact graph matching, but also

[*] This work has been partly funded by the Austrian Federal Ministry of Transport, Innovation, and Technology and the Austrian Research Promotion Agency under grant FIT-IT-819584 and by the fFORTE WIT Program of the Vienna University of Technology and the Austrian Federal Ministry of Science and Research.

Permission to make digital or hard copies of all or part of this work for personal or classroom use is granted without fee provided that copies are not made or distributed for profit or commercial advantage and that copies bear this notice and the full citation on the first page. To copy otherwise, to republish, to post on servers or to redistribute to lists, requires prior specific permission and/or a fee.

Onward! 2010,   October 17–21, 2010, Reno/Tahoe, Nevada, USA.
Copyright © 2010 ACM 978-1-4503-0236-4/10/10. . . $10.00

similarity-aware graph matching as it is done in the context of pattern mining in code repositories [17]. The goal of our approach is supporting modelers during the conflict resolution process in optimistic versioning even if they do not exactly know the necessary resolution pattern at the beginning.

This paper is outlined as follows. In Section 2 we shortly explain our motivation to enrich versioning systems with a recommender component. In Section 3 we introduce a model for conflicts. On this basis we are able to develop a measure for the similarity of conflicts in Section 4, which is applied and evaluated in the similarity-aware graph matching algorithm we use to identify suitable resolution patterns. In Section 5 we discuss the realization of the recommender system supporting conflict resolution in model versioning and conclude with a discussion of related research areas and future work in Section 6.

2. Motivation

When an optimistic versioning approach is followed, each developer works independently on his/her local copy and synchronizes his/her work from time to time with a central repository. As long as the modifications of the different developers do not interfere, i.e., as long as their modifications commute, there is almost no overhead by using the versioning system. The workflow, the two developers—let us call them Sally and Harry—have to pass through, is as follows. Sally and Harry check out the same artifact from a central repository and perform different changes. When Sally is finished, she loads the new version back to the repository. Later Harry also intends to submit his new version to the repository, but unfortunately his changes are conflicting with the changes of Sally. So he has to resolve these conflicts before he is allowed to store his new version into the repository. Instead of doing productive work, he is now occupied by integrating his modifications and the changes of Sally. The resolution of conflicts requires manual intervention because an automatic merge usually yields unsatisfactory results as in the example shown in Fig. 1. The model originally stored in the repository contains a UML Class Diagram consisting of the classes `PublicTransport`, `Subway`, and `Train`, whereas the latter two classes are subclasses of the first and each of them contains the attribute `railtrackWidth`. When Sally introduces a new class `Bus` into the hierarchy (V0') and Harry performs the refactoring `pullUpField` which shifts the attribute `railtrackWidth` common to all subclasses into the superclass (V0''), a naive merge including all modifications would result in a model where a bus inherits the attribute `railtrackWidth` which probably does not reflect reality (V0' + V0'' in Fig. 1).

In order to preserve the intentions of both developers, the conflict resolution of Harry should be as shown in V1 of Fig. 1. A new class `RailVehicle` should be introduced which is a subclass of `PublicTransport` and which inherits the `railtrackWidth` attribute to `Subway`

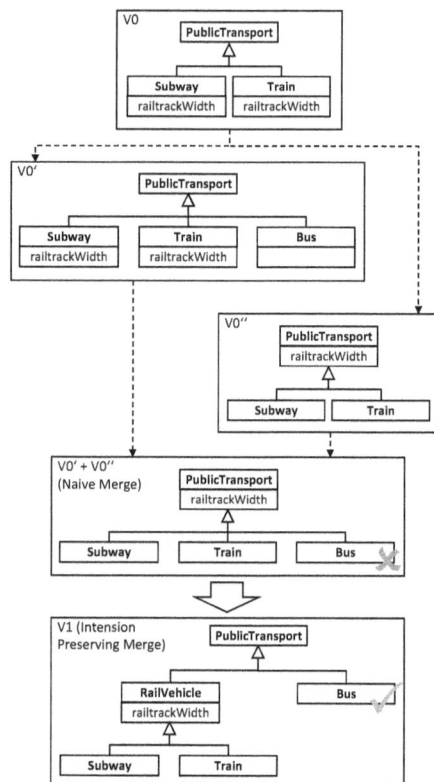

Figure 1. Conflict Scenario

and `Train`, but not to `Bus` which is nevertheless a subclass of `PublicTransport`. This resolution strategy is applicable whenever a conflict of a similar structure reoccurs no matter if the involved classes represent vehicles, creatures, or something else. Therefore, it would be extremely supportive if this pattern is suggested to the developer in charge of the resolution and if the pattern is automatically executed when it is selected by the developer.

Refactoring-aware versioning systems can detect and replay refactorings during the merge process to incorporate newly introduced and modified elements [8, 9]. When modifications violate the refactoring's precondition, a conflict is reported. Current versioning systems usually indicate only, where the modifications have taken place. Advanced conflict resolution support is not provided.

In the remainder of this paper, we present a recommender system as integral component of the adaptable model versioning system AMOR[1]. AMOR's sophisticated change and conflict detection component (the Conflict Detector) delivers precise information on merge problems [2]. Equipped with a repository filled with (conflict, resolution) pairs (the Conflict Repository), where the recommender system looks up suitable resolutions for a reported conflict, (semi-) automatic support for the conflict resolution in the context of model versioning is realized.

---

[1] http://www.modelversioning.org

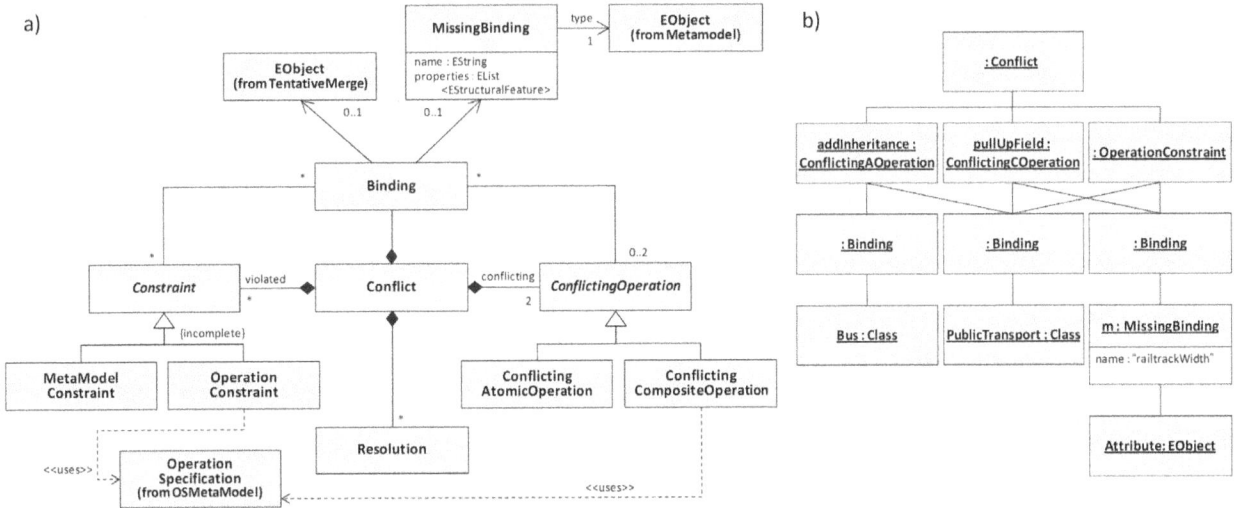

Figure 2. (a) Conflict Model, (b) Instance of the Conflict Model

3. Conflicts in Model Versioning

In the following, we represent conflicts by the means of a model, i.e., we define a UML Class Diagram for describing conflicts. This approach is similar to Cichetti et al. [6], where the authors present a conflict model as an extension to their difference model. Since the conflict detection component of AMOR [4] is able to reconstruct composite changes like refactorings, we obtain a more compact difference report and consequently a compact conflict description. Furthermore, we include status information of the merge process, i.e., we have information about the already integrated modifications given in the *tentative merge* model. The tentative merge consists of the origin version V0 merged with all non conflicting operations performed in the parallel edited versions V0' and V0", hence the tentative merge model is a valid model incorporating the changes identified as unproblematic. Our conflict model is shown in Fig. 2(a). A Conflict always contains two conflicting operations. A ConflictingOperation is either a ConflictingAtomicOperation (e.g., *add*, *delete*, and *update*) or a ConflictingCompositeOperation (e.g., refactorings) which is based on AMOR's OperationSpecification as defined in [4]. The application of these two operations would induce the violation of some kind of Constraint. At the moment, we distinguish between two kinds of constraints: a MetaModelConstraint expresses a well-formedness rule of the applied modeling language. An OperationConstraint refers to an invariant, a precondition, or a postcondition of an operation. Note that a conflict does not contain all possible conditions and constraints but only the ones which are violated and hence important for the definition of the conflict. In fact, our conflict model provides a view on the elements of operation specifications where the elements necessary for the conflict description are included. The constraints and the operations of a conflict

are related to specific bindings which represent their input arguments. These input arguments are expressed by either referring to an element of the tentative merge, or by specifying a MissingBinding if an element is not available in the tentative merge. A MissingBinding points to the type of the missing element in the underlying model and contains additional information about the missing element like its name and other properties. For a complete definition of our conflict model further well-formedness rules would be necessary. For example, it is necessary to ensure that the types of the bound elements of a ConflictingOperation are type compatible with the input parameters of the according OperationSpecification. If a binding is not assigned to an operation, it has to be assigned to at least one constraint. In this paper, we assume that AMOR's Conflict Detector provides syntactical correct conflict descriptions only, hence we omit these well-formedness rules. Finally, an arbitrary number of resolutions may be attached to each conflict.

An example of a conflict instance is shown in Fig. 2(b). The operations pullUpField and addInheritance are conflicting. The bindings point to the involved elements: the class Bus should become subclass of PublicTransport, whereas an attribute Attribute is moved to PublicTransport. Note that we have to deal with a missing binding, as the conflict exists due to the absence of an Attribute with the name railtrackWidth. For the application of the pullUpField operation, the following constraint (expressed in OCL) has to hold:

PublicTransport.subclasses → *forall* (s |
    s.attributes → *exists* (a | a.name == m.name))

The constraint is violated because there exists one subclass of PublicTransport (namely Bus) which does not have an attribute with the according name.

Conflicts as described in this example are returned from the Conflict Detector of AMOR. With such a conflict as input, the recommender system is able to look up suitable resolution strategies in the Conflict Repository using exact as well as similarity-aware matching techniques. When similarity-aware matching techniques are applied, three sources of variability may be considered: (1) the operations, (2) the conditions, and (3) the bindings. As a first step towards a similarity-aware conflict recognition, we consider the bindings in the following.

4. Finding Resolution Patterns

In the following example, we aim at illustrating the need for inexact matching techniques. Assume that the Conflict Repository contains only the conflict and its resolution presented in Section 2. The conflict scenario depicted in Fig. 3 emerges from the parallel modifications where one modeler introduces the new class Penguin into the inheritance hierarchy and the second modeler pulls up the operation getFlightSpeed() of the classes Hawk and Duck into the superclass Bird. A naive merge would produce a model where penguins are able to fly what contradicts reality. The Conflict Detector reports a conflict not due to this common domain knowledge, but due to a violated precondition of the refactoring pullUpMethod. When querying the Conflict Repository, no exact matching conflict is found. In order to find at least the conflict of the previous example (cf. Fig. 1), the ability to handle inexact matches is indispensable.

Unfortunately, existing matching tools (cf. [15] for a survey) or dedicated model diffing tools like EMF Compare are not appropriate for our purposes, since they operate on the model level only and do not consider similarities of the metamodel elements. SiDiff [14] implements a similarity-based algorithm which may be configured by the user. A configuration contains the impact of metamodel features. For example, the name of a class is an higher ranked similarity criterion than the value of the isAbstract feature. So the similarity of two model elements with the same type may be calculated using ranking information for the concrete instantiations. In contrast, we are also interested in the similarity of model elements with different types. Recall that information like the name of a model element is of little help for our purposes because we match the concrete conflict against a generic instance of the conflict model stored in the conflict repository.

Similarity of metamodel elements. One possibility to find a broader range of conflicts is to suspend type information and match on graph structure only. This approach may work well in many situations. The drawback is that structural equality of conflict model instances does not ensure the suitability of their resolution pattern.

A more reliable approach is to apply similarity-aware graph matching techniques [5]. Here the typed graph is analyzed, but inexactness is allowed as long as a minimum

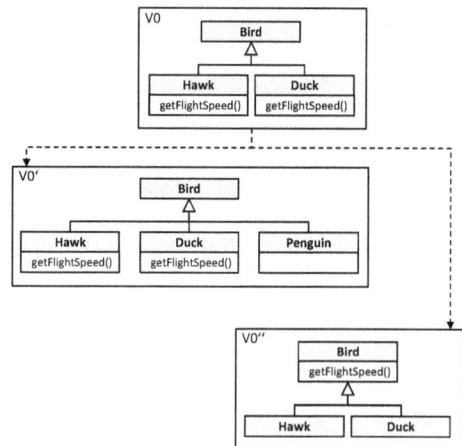

Figure 3. Conflict Scenario Revised

similarity of the compared nodes (i.e., model elements) is given. To faithfully support the generic, modeling language independent approach of AMOR, the necessary similarity measures should not be predefined, but be automatically derived by analyzing the metamodel of the modeling language in use. The taxonomic structure of the metamodel is an indication of the similarity between elements. Unfortunately, considering the inheritance alone is not enough. Some features like the name feature in a Class Diagram (cf. Fig. 4) are inherited to almost every element, hence it is a less valuable indicator for similarity. We propose to calculate similarity by exploiting the internal structure as well as the relational structure of metamodel elements. In fact, properties, relations, and inheritance relations are considered.

DEFINITION 4.1 (Similarity). *The similarity of two metamodel elements is given by the number of their common features weighted by their overall occurrence in the metamodel.*

For decreasing the weight of common features and contemporaneously increasing the weight of rare features, the frequency of the feature's appearance within the whole metamodel is considered like it is done by *term frequency-inverse document frequency* (TFIDF) algorithms [16]. TFIDF is usually used in information retrieval as a measure for the relevance of a term to a document. We use the metamodel as corpus and apply TFIDF as a measure for the relevance of a feature within a metamodel element.

Similarity algorithm. We implemented the algorithm within the Eclipse Modeling Framework (EMF) allowing the calculation of similarity values for every Ecore-based metamodel. A simplified variant of our approach is shown in Alg. 1. First, we analyze the metamodel and instantiate two lists. The list mmElements holds all elements defined in the metamodel, in line 1. The list features holds all distinct features occurring in any metamodel element (line 2). Second, in lines 3-5, we declare convenience functions for accessing

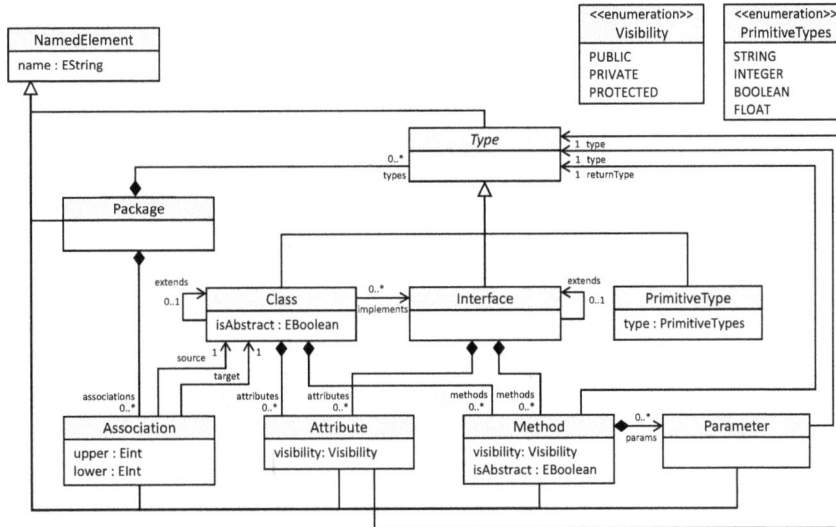

Figure 4. Class Diagram Metamodel

Input: Rootnode *root* of metamodel
Output: Matrix of similarity values for each
        metamodel element pair

```
// variable declarations
```
1   mmElements ← getAllMetamodelElements(*root*);

2   features ← getAllFeatures(*root*);

```
// function declarations
```
3   relevanceMatrix : (EObject, Feature) ↦ float;

4   relevanceVector : (EObject) ↦ float$^{|features|}$;

5   similarityMatrix : (EObject, EObject) ↦ float;

```
// definition of relevanceMatrix
```
6   **foreach** *MmElement* $\mathcal{M}$ ∈ mmElements **do**

7   **foreach** *Feature* $\mathcal{F}$ ∈ features **do**

8   relevanceMatrix($\mathcal{M}$, $\mathcal{F}$) ←
$$\log\left(\frac{\text{countElements}(root)}{\text{getGlobalFreq}(\mathcal{F}, root)}\right) \cdot$$
getLocalFreq($\mathcal{F}$, $\mathcal{M}$);

9   **end**

10 **end**

```
// definition of similarityMatrix
```
11 **foreach** *MmElement* $\mathcal{N}$, $\mathcal{M}$ ∈ mmElements **do**

12   similarityMatrix($\mathcal{N}$, $\mathcal{M}$) ←
     ‖relevanceVector($\mathcal{N}$)‖ × ‖relevanceVector($\mathcal{M}$)‖;

13 **end**

14 **return** similarityMatrix
       Algorithm 1: Similarity Calculation

arrays. Third, we calculate the relevanceMatrix in lines 6-10. The relevanceMatrix is a $n \times m$ array with values describing the relevance of each metamodel feature within each metamodel element. The number of metamodel elements is given by n, whereas m denotes the number of features occurring in the metamodel. The relevance of one feature within a metamodel element is based on the total number of metamodel elements, its occurrence frequency in the complete metamodel, and finally its occurrence frequency within the considered metamodel element. In the last step (lines 11-14), we calculate the similarity for each pair of metamodel elements by the cross product of the normalized relevance vectors. A relevance vector for one metamodel element $\mathcal{M}$ contains the relevance values of all features within $\mathcal{M}$, i.e., it respects to the line of the relevanceMatrix containing the relevance values of $\mathcal{M}$.

An example. In the following we apply the algorithm on a Class Diagram (cf. Fig. 4 for the metamodel). For the sake of readability, the metamodel follows a general design pattern but leaves out specific details. All elements extend directly or indirectly the common superclass NamedElement, enumeration types excluded. Package forms the root element and contains Types and Associations. Class, Interface, and PrimitiveType specialize Type. Both Classes and Interfaces may extend again a Class and an Interface and contain Attributes and Methods. In addition, a Class may be abstract and may implement Interfaces. Attributes and Parameters have a Type, a Method contains an arbitrary number of Parameter and returns a Type. In addition, well-formedness rules are necessary, e.g., neither a Class nor an Interface must extend itself.

The calculated similarity values for the metamodel elements of the Class Diagram shown in Fig. 4 are summarized in Table 1. Values greater than 0.1 are highlighted. As expected, a significant similarity between Class and Interface is found due to their number of common features. Furthermore, Attribute, Method, and Parameter are recognized as similar, because they all have the relation

47

	NamedElement	Package	Interface	Class	Association	Attribute	Method	Parameter	PrimitiveType	Type	Visibility	PrimitiveTypes
NamedElement	1,00	0,05	0,03	0,03	0,04	0,05	0,04	0,06	0,06	0,09	0,00	0,00
Package	0,05	1,00	0,00	0,00	0,00	0,00	0,00	0,00	0,00	0,00	0,00	0,00
Interface	0,03	0,00	1,00	0,54	0,03	0,00	0,00	0,00	0,24	0,37	0,00	0,00
Class	0,03	0,00	0,54	1,00	0,02	0,00	0,09	0,00	0,20	0,31	0,00	0,00
Association	0,04	0,00	0,03	0,02	1,00	0,00	0,00	0,00	0,05	0,08	0,00	0,00
Attribute	0,05	0,00	0,00	0,00	0,00	1,00	0,54	0,29	0,00	0,00	0,00	0,00
Method	0,04	0,00	0,00	0,09	0,00	0,54	1,00	0,00	0,00	0,00	0,00	0,00
Parameter	0,06	0,00	0,00	0,00	0,00	0,29	0,00	1,00	0,00	0,01	0,00	0,00
PrimitiveType	0,06	0,00	0,24	0,20	0,05	0,00	0,00	0,00	1,00	0,65	0,00	0,00
Type	0,09	0,00	0,37	0,31	0,08	0,00	0,00	0,01	0,65	1,00	0,00	0,00
Visibility	0,00	0,00	0,00	0,00	0,00	0,00	0,00	0,00	0,00	0,00	1,00	0,00
PrimitiveTypes	0,00	0,00	0,00	0,00	0,00	0,00	0,00	0,00	0,00	0,00	0,00	1,00

Table 1. Calculated Similarity Values for the Class Diagram Metamodel

to Type, and Attributes and Methods are both contained by the same elements. The inheritance relation of Class, Interface, and PrimitiveType with Type also leads to observable similarity. Since the relevance of features are first weighted by their overall occurrence in the metamodel and normalized within each metamodel element, each specific feature may have a different impact in different metamodel elements. The less features one element has, the higher the relevance of each feature is. Consequently, the similarity of subclasses of NamedElement to their superclass varies, but is nevertheless negligible because so many elements share this relationship.

Finally, we want to emphasize the general applicability of the presented approach. Although we developed the algorithm dedicated for matching conflict descriptions, it may be used for solving any kind of model matching problem if the metamodel of the modeling language is available.

With the components introduced in the previous section, we are able to realize a three-staged comparison algorithm which performs the following steps.

Exact match. The two typed graphs of the conflict models are exactly matched. Therefore, each node (resp. each edge) has to be matched against one node (resp. edge) with exactly the same type.

Match based on type compatibility. If the exact match fails, then the type restrictions are relaxed. Then elements of compatible types (i.e., sub- and superclass) are considered as equal.

Match based on type similarity. Finally, the elements having a similarity exceeding the required threshold are matched. The similarity is calculated once for the metamodel of each modeling language according to the algorithm presented above.

Implementation. The implementation of the presented conflict reasoning approach is mainly based on EMF and on the Java graph library JGraphT. The conflict model and the Class Diagram metamodel are implemented in Ecore and integrated as Eclipse Plug-ins into AMOR. AMOR's

Conflict Detector turns over the conflict model, the tentative merge model, and the actual metamodel to the recommender system. The conflict model links to elements of the tentative merge for describing ConcreteBindings and to elements of the tentative merge's metamodel—in our case the Class Diagram metamodel—for defining the types of MissingBindings.

Before looking up for appropriate conflicts already included in the Conflict Repository, the similarity measures of metamodel elements have to be calculated. As long as the metamodel does not change, these values must be provided only once. The calculation is performed according to Alg. 1.

For comparing the conflict instances with each other in a similarity-aware manner, a graph isomorphism algorithm of the Java graph library JGraphT is used. Therefore, the conflict models are first converted to directed graphs. Model elements are represented by vertices and associations are represented by directed edges. To improve performance, the graph representations are hold in memory. The graph comparison algorithm may be either used to find exact matches, or to find equivalent matches. For finding equivalent matches, an implementation of the Interface EquivalenceComparator has to be provided. In our case, the implemented ModelElementEquivalenceComparator checks for equal types first, and in the case of a concrete binding or a missing binding's type, the pre-calculated similarity value of the type information is used to decide equality.

We are aware of the fact, that isomorph graph matching is assumed as NP-hard problem. As the number of conflicts stored in the Conflict Repository increases over time, the recommendation lookup gets slower. To avoid performance problems, we will use dedicated clustering techniques for graphs [10] to narrow the search space of conflict models in future work.

Experiments. We conducted first experiments to evaluate the applicability of our implementation in various conflict situations. Therefore, we selected a representative set of different conflict situations and matched them with our similarity-aware graph comparison algorithm. The operations involved in the conflicts are all applied on Class Diagrams as

		Conflicts in Repository				
		Cx	C3	C4	C5	C6	C7
Detected Conf.	C1	0					
	C2	0					
	C3		0	0.46	0.92		
	C4		0.46	0	0.46		
	C5		0.92	0.46	0		
	C6					0	0.46
	C7					0.46	0

C1	rename(c1:Class, "name1")
	rename(c1:Class, "name2")
C2	rename(a1:Attribute, "name1")
	rename(a1:Attribute, "name2")
C3	pullUpField(superCl:Class, a1:Attribute)
	addInheritance(subCl:Class, superCl:Class)
C4	pullUpMethod(superCl:Class, m1:Method)
	addInheritance(subCl:Class, superCl:Class)
C5	mvMethodToInt(m1:Method, i1:Interface)
	addInterfaceImpl(c1:Class, i1:Interface)
C6	addInheritance(c1:Class, c2:Class)
	addInheritance(c2:Class, c1:Class)
C7	addInheritance(i1:Interface, i2:Interface)
	addInheritance(i2:Interface, i1:Interface)

Table 2. Edit Distances of Conflict Scenarios.

defined by the previously introduced metamodel. The match is performed using the similarity matrix shown in Table 1.

Table 2 contains a short description of the detected conflicts. For more details we kindly refer to our project website. The conflicts for which resolutions are specified are arranged horizontally. In fact, we match each conflict against each conflict. The numbers in the table cells indicate the total edit distance between the conflict pairs. The edit distance is an indicator of the effort of rewriting the conflict resolution pattern, and is derived by summing up the edit distances of each vertex (1 - similarity). The conflicts C1 and C2 result from an update/update problem, as the name of the same element (a class in C1 and an attribute in C2) are concurrently modified in a different manner. Both of these conflicts are not included in the repository, but as no features of the specific classes are affected, the most general variant, in this case NamedElement, is stored which is denoted by Cx in Table 2. Note that for deducing a general conflict, also the features have to be considered which are involved in the conflict resolution. For matching the conflicts, considering the type compatibility is necessary, which results in an edit distance of 0 in Table 2. The conflicts C3 – C5 are variants of the previously presented motivating example, whereas C6 and C7 cause violations of the Class Diagram's metamodel by introducing inheritance cycles.

The empty fields in Table 2 indicate that no match has been found. All conflicts besides C1 and C2 may not be transformed to a more general form, hence we obtain exact matches in the diagonal (expressed by a 0). Summing up, in these first experiments, the algorithm shows the intended behavior. In future work, we will extend the scope of these experiments in the context of a broader case study.

5. Realization

The recommender system is based on the Eclipse Modeling Framework the and Eclipse Team Support plugin. It implements the basic interplay with the versioning server (cf. (1) in Fig. 5) and offers the possibility to remodel artifacts to resolve conflicts (2). The actual recommender component (3) supports the conflict resolution by providing a list of automatically applicable resolution patterns for each conflict looked up from the Conflict Repository. The resolution patterns in the Conflict Repository are either defined manually or are automatically mined as described in [2]. The proposed resolution patterns may be previewed, rolled back, and manually refined. For easier identification of conflicting operations in the preview mode, the conflicting operations are marked with the dedicated user symbol combined with annotations indicating the application of *add*, *delete*, and *update* on the respective model elements. Recommended resolution strategies are marked accordingly with a system symbol (the cog). Previewing many operations at once may on the one hand overflow the model, but on the other hand may be necessary to understand changes. Therefore, the user may decide which operation should be displayed.

The recommended resolutions are ranked by their relevance. The relevance is calculated by a combination of the edit distance between the current conflict situation and the stored one, the number of applications so far, and the impact of the user who created the conflict resolution, by aggregating the application count of all resolutions created by this user. Resolution specific information is displayed in a dedicated property view (4). The property view contains metadata about the resolution's origin, application and edit distance. Furthermore, since automatically derived resolutions do not have a human understandable name, users may enhance the resolution pattern with additional information.

6. Conclusion

In the context of software engineering, recommender systems support developers in their decision making and particularly in their information finding goals [13]. Recommender systems for software engineering (RSSE) provide guidance for example in programming, i.e., by suggesting code for reuse, in debugging, i.e., by suggesting code for bugfixing, in testing, i.e., by indicating the parts of the program with the probably most defects, and in software maintenance. To support conflict resolution in versioning and especially in model versioning, to the best of our knowledge no recommender systems have been implemented yet. Current research focuses on the detection of differences and conflicts (like, e.g., SiDiff [14]) in order to support the resolution process without offering concrete resolution patterns. Only the ontology merging tool Prompt provides user guidance for a set of hard-coded conflicts [12].

In this paper, we introduced a recommender system enhancing the standard conflict resolution workflow of model

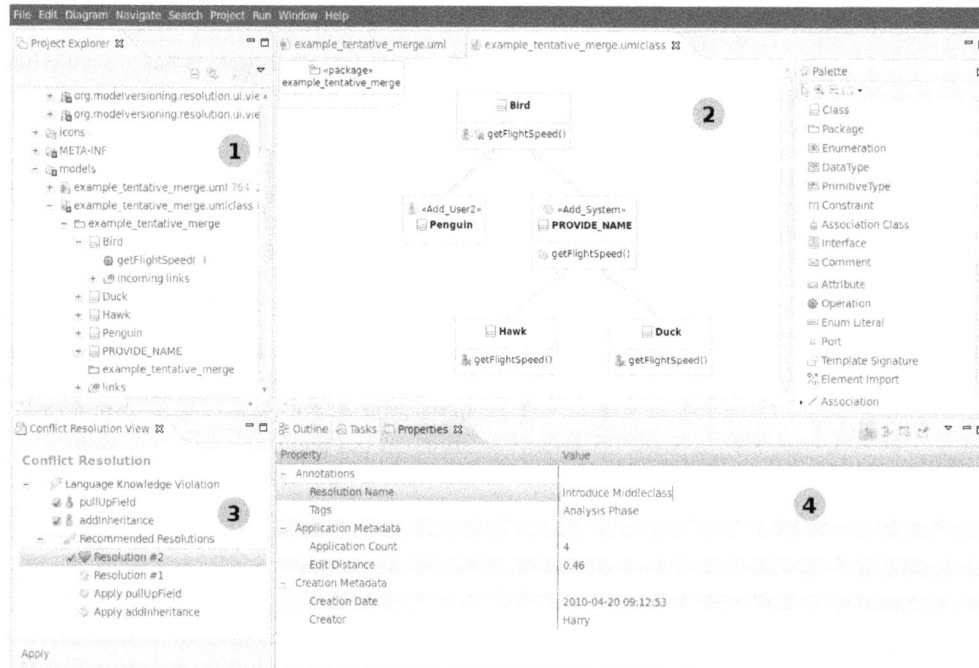

Figure 5. AMOR Conflict Resolver

versioning by suggesting automatically executable resolution patterns. Conflicts are represented as Ecore models and are stored in a conflict repository. For the lookup of suitable resolution patterns we apply a novel kind of similarity-aware graph comparison algorithm allowing for exact matches, type compatibility matches, and type similarity matches.

In future work, we plan to conduct an extensive case study in cooperation with our industrial partner SparxSystems, the vendor of the modeling tool Enterprise Architect. In this context, we will also consider different modeling languages instead of the UML Class Diagram only. The gathered experiences will allow us to fine-tune our similarity calculation and to expand our conflict repository. Furthermore, much emphasis has to be spent on the user interface especially when the models get large. Then specific zooming and advanced filtering mechanism have to be implemented to avoid information overflow of the conflict resolving modeler.

References

[1] J. Bézivin. On the Unification Power of Models. *Journal on Software and Systems Modeling*, 4(2):171–188, 2005.

[2] P. Brosch, G. Kappel, P. Langer, M. Seidl, K. Wieland, M. Wimmer, and H. Kargl. Adaptable Model Versioning in Action. In *Modellierung*, LNI. GI, 2010.

[3] P. Brosch, P. Langer, M. Seidl, K. Wieland, and M. Wimmer. Colex: A Web-based Collaborative Conflict Lexicon. In *Int. Workshop on Model Comparison in Practice*. ACM, 2010.

[4] P. Brosch, P. Langer, M. Seidl, K. Wieland, M. Wimmer, G. Kappel, W. Retschitzegger, and W. Schwinger. Composite Operation Modeling By-Example. In *MODELS*, 2009.

[5] H. Bunke. Error-Tolerant Graph Matching: A Formal Framework and Algorithms. In *Advances in Pattern Rec.*, 1998.

[6] A. Cicchetti, D. Ruscio, and A. Pierantonio. Managing Model Conflicts in Distributed Development. In *MODELS*, 2008.

[7] R. Conradi and B. Westfechtel. Version Models for Software Configuration Management. *ACM Comp. Surv.*, 30(2), 1998.

[8] D. Dig, K. Manzoor, R. E. Johnson, and T. N. Nguyen. Effective Software Merging in the Presence of Object-Oriented Refactorings. *IEEE Trans. on Software Eng.*, 34(3), 2008.

[9] T. Ekman and U. Asklund. Refactoring-Aware Versioning in Eclipse. *El. Notes in Theoret. Comp. Science*, 107, 2004.

[10] S. Günter and H. Bunke. Self-Organizing Map for Clustering in the Graph Domain. *Pattern Rec. Letters*, 23(4), 2002.

[11] T. Mens. A State-of-the-Art Survey on Software Merging. *IEEE Trans. on Software Eng.*}, 28(5):449–462, 2002.

[12] N. Noy and M. Musen. Algorithm and Tool for Automated Ontology Merging and Alignment. In AAAI, 2000.

[13] M. Robillard, R. Walker, and T. Zimmermann. Recommendation Systems for Software Eng. IEEE Software, 2009.

[14] M. Schmidt and T. Gloetzner. Constructing Difference Tools for Models using the SiDiff Framework. In ICSE Companion. ACM, 2008.

[15] P. Shvaiko and J. Euzenat. A Survey of Schema-Based Matching Approaches. Jnl. on Data Sem., 3730, 2005.

[16] K. Spärck Jones. A Statistical Interpretation of Term Specificity and its Application in Retrieval. Jnl. of Doc., 28, 1972.

[17] N. Tsantalis, A. Chatzigeorgiou, G. Stephanides, and S. T. Halkidis. Design Pattern Detection Using Similarity Scoring. IEEE Trans. on Software Eng., 32(11), 2006.

Inferring Arbitrary Distributions for Data and Computation

Soham Sundar Chakraborty *

Tata Research Development and Design Centre,
54-B, Hadapsar Industrial Estate,
Pune, MH, India, 411013
sohamsundar.chakraborty@tcs.com

V. Krishna Nandivada

IBM Research India
Embassy Golf Links Business Park,
Bangalore, KA, India, 560071
nvkrishna@in.ibm.com

Abstract

In the era of mult-core systems, one of the key requirements of achieving better utilization of multiple available cores is that of parallelization of code across multiple distributed nodes; this involves (re)distribution of both data and computation. Such a transformation can be a fairly tedious activity considering the possible dependencies (data, control) and interference between different segments of the code. Further, to keep the data accesses local, computation distribution requires appropriate data distribution and vice versa. And this inter-dependence between distribution of data and computation makes the problem challenging. Another important challenge in this context is that the desired distribution may not be one of the well-known distributions (such as blocked, cyclic etc), and thus reasoning about it can be non-trivial. We present a refactoring framework that can help an application developer to incrementally distribute programs in the context of distributed memory multi-core systems. Given a loop and an array accessed therein, the goal of our framework is to distribute the array based on a specified distribution for the loop (or vice versa) such that the number of remote accessed are reduced. Our framework goes beyond the well-known distributions, and can handle any arbitrary distributions. In our initial investigation, we have used our transformations on varied parallel benchmark programs and have been able to show its applicability along the expected lines.

Categories and Subject Descriptors:
D.3.2 [**Language Classification**] Concurrent, distributed, and parallel languages D.1.3 [**Concurrent Programming**] Distributed programming

---

* Work done at IBM IRL.

Permission to make digital or hard copies of all or part of this work for personal or classroom use is granted without fee provided that copies are not made or distributed for profit or commercial advantage and that copies bear this notice and the full citation on the first page. To copy otherwise, to republish, to post on servers or to redistribute to lists, requires prior specific permission and/or a fee.
Onward! 2010, October 17–21, 2010, Reno/Tahoe, Nevada, USA.
Copyright © 2010 ACM 978-1-4503-0236-4/10/10. . . $10.00

General Terms:
Languages, Performance

Keywords:
User specified Distributions, Automatic redistribution

1. Introduction

Improving the utilization of the available multiple cores is assuming an important role in the era of multi-core systems. The impact can be observed in the context of both legacy and new applications. While the development of new applications needs to take into consideration the multiple available cores, the legacy applications have to be either retargeted or have their runtime (for instance, operating system or hypervisor) modified to be able to take advantage of the multiple cores. The improvements to the runtime are especially exciting to those legacy applications where the source code is not available, or where the runtime parameters greatly influence the performance gains, which are otherwise not known at the source code level. One drawback of this approach is that the operating system or hypervisor may not be able to utilize the structure of the program and the expertise of the programmer who might be able to assist with the task. Thus, rewriting (or porting) existing application to suit the needs of the new multi-core systems is gaining interest. The challenge is compounded in the context of distributed memory multi-core systems; because of the issues arising out of locality of data, parallelization of computation across distributed cores impacts the distribution of data, and vice versa. Thus, such a transformation can be a fairly tedious job, considering the possible dependencies (data, control), and interference between different segments of the code. A tool to selectively refactor parts of the code (legacy or new) to distribute computation and/or data, would be a great help in this direction.

A refactoring tool can be seen as an aid to incremental programming [9], and can be part of an incremental programming environment [13]. Popular programming environments like Eclipse provide a popular platform to incrementally improve programs by applying different refactorings. In this paper, we propose a new refactoring to incrementally distribute existing applications and thereby port applications to multi-core systems; we accomplish these with some minor guidance from the application developer. Another important use of such an approach is to incrementally develop/tune existing applications, wherein the programmer starts from the existing application (legacy or otherwise) and uses the refactoring tool to improve the performance in a trial-and-error method.

In this paper, we present techniques to incrementally distribute programs written in language frameworks, such as UPC [11] and X10 [12], that allow *distribution* of data and code. A distribution is defined as a map from loop or array indices to computing units (cores / *places* in the context of X10). Given an application, the programmer may decide to distribute any particular parallel loop. To ensure that the array accesses in the distributed loop are held in sync with the distribution, it is expected that the arrays would also be distributed (otherwise, the application may have to pay the penalty of remote accesses of the arrays). Which in turn may require further appropriate transformations to other loops accessing the array, and so on.

To illustrate the challenge, we show a snippet of code from the FluidAnimate benchmark from the Parsec 2.1 suite [5] in Figure 1; we have ported the example to X10 for the sake of presentation, and inlined a method. The `foreach` loop creates a parallel loop for each value of `i` (varying from `1` to `threadnum`), and each iteration uses the smoothed particle hydrodynamics (SPH) method to simulate an incompressible fluid for interactive animation purposes. Now, say the `foreach` loop is to be distributed using a blocked distribution (with blocking factor K) then the arrays `grids`, `cells` and `cnumPars` should also be distributed (incidentally using the same blocking distribution, with a blocking factor of K) to avoid remote accesses. Additionally, the array declaration, initialization, and any other accesses should also be suitably modified. The problem of inferring suitable distributions for loops/arrays becomes further challenging in the context of languages like X10, where the programmer is allowed to specify arbitrary distributions. In this paper, we address this challenge by generating a new distribution for a loop(array) based on the programmer specified distribution for the array (loop) and the program syntax such that the number of remote accesses are minimized.

Contributions

- We present an unified algorithm that can distribute a loop based on any arbitrary distribution of an array accessed there in or vice versa. Our approach distributes data and computation in an interleaved fashion - distribution of data may result in distributing computation where the data is accessed, which in turn may require distribution of other data accessed in the computation and so on.

- We present the loop distribution techniques in the context of a refactoring tool that can help in incremental distribution of applications.

```
int main(...){
final Cell [] cells = ...
final int [] cnumPars = ...
final int framenum = ...;
foreach([i] [1:threadnum]) {
 for(int k = 0; k < framenum; ++k) {
 ...
  for(int z=grids[i].sz;z<grids[i].ez;++z)
   for(int y=grids[i].sy;y<grids[i].ey;++y)
    for(int x=grids[i].sx;x<grids[i].ex;++x)
    { int index = (z*ny + y)*nx + x;
      Cell cell = cells[index];
      int np = cnumPars[index];
      for(int j = 0; j < np; ++j) {
       cell.density[j] = ...;
       cell.a[j] = ...; } } ... } } }
```

Figure 1. Snippet of FluidAnimate – a benchmark from Parsec 2.1 [5].

- We have applied our techniques on a varied set of benchmarks and have found our techniques to be useful.

In this paper, we use X10v1.4 as the basis language for discussing the techniques on distributions. However, they can be applied to other language frameworks as well.

1.1 Related Work

Traditional automatic parallelization techniques have been well studied in research [7, 15, 18]. There is also work in the area of refactoring for parallelism [2, 10, 19, 24],which rely on the programmer to specify what loops to transform. Dig et al [10] introduce concurrent libraries via a refactoring mechanism to ensure thread-safety of data types. Markstrum et al [26] present a refactoring tool based approach for incremental parallelization of code in the context of task parallel languages like X10. In this paper, we present a framework to incrementally parallelize programs (by distributing loops and arrays) in the context of distributed memory multi-core systems. Automatic data and code distribution has been a well researched area and the hardness of the problem is well documented [3, 8]. Mace [25] has studied the optimal data storage problem as shapes problem and has proved it to be NP-complete. Most of the prior work deals with finding an ideal distribution for an array or a loop for efficient execution, and thus ensuring a better utilization of resources. Koelbel et al [20] present a functional language called BLAZE that lets the programmer specify data partitions and the compiler automatically does the process partitioning. Rogers and Pingali [27] partition the given set of tasks in a sequential program based on the programmer specified data-partition, to enhance locality of reference. Prior work in distribution of data in the context of HPF [4, 14] dealt with inferring pre-defined data distribution (such as blocked, blocked cyclic, cyclic and so on) for a given a program text. There has been prior work on inferring efficient data distribution from a given distribution of the computation [21, 22], and inferring efficient distribution for a computation from a given distribution for an array [23].

In contrast to these prior works we chiefly differ in the following three ways: (a) We identify that distribution of data and computation are interrelated and present an unified approach to re-distribute both computation and data. (b) Unlike prior work where programmer has no control on the distribution process, we provide the control to the programmer to decide the target computation or array to be distributed. (c) Our approach handles arbitrary distributions of data and computation, even in contexts like X10 that allow specification of arbitrary distributions.

Organization: We first present a brief introduction to X10 language in Section 2. Section 3 presents our techniques to redistribute loops and arrays. We discuss some case studies in Section 4. Finally we discuss some future directions in Section 5 and conclude in 6.

2. X10 Background

In this section we present a brief background to some of the relevant features of X10 for this paper. In this paper, we confine ourselves to simplified X10 programs that have only simple expressions (similar to the expressions in three-address-codes) and every statement has an associated label with it. Details about standard X10 v0.41 can be found in the X10 reference manual [12].

`async (p) S` creates a new child task/activity to execute S, at place p and this new activity runs in parallel with the parent activity. Notions of activities and places become clear through the association of activities to threads of execution and places to processors in the program. Any dereference of an object, created at a place p, is considered local if it is dereferenced in an activity running at place p. The indexical constant `here` evaluates to the place at which the current activity is running. Each object has a final field named `location` that points to the place where the object was created. X10 restricts accesses to remote memory and a run-time exception is thrown if an activity accesses remote data; note that X10 disallows migration of objects and activities.

`future (p) expr` creates an activity to evaluate the expression expr at the place p in an asynchronous way and returns a handler to the activity. The return value of expr is received by invoking the `force()` method on the handler. A `future` is different from an `async` in terms of returning a value; `force` waits for the value to become available before returning. Unlike an `async` the `future` construct is used to evaluate an expression.

`finish S` is a structured barrier statement, wherein S is executed with a surrounding barrier such that all activities created inside S have to terminate (including transitively spawned activities) for the barrier to terminate.

The statement `foreach (point p : R) S` creates a parallel loop iterating over all the points in region R, by launching each iteration as a separate activity executing S. A *point* is an element of an n-dimensional Cartesian space ($n \geq 1$) with integer-valued coordinates and a region is a set of points. A region can be used to specify an array element index space or loop iteration space.

`ateach (point p: D) S` is a parallel loop distributed over the distribution D. A *distribution* is a map from a region (defined by a set of points) to a set of places; both arrays and loops may be distributed. A loop L distributed over a distribution D_L iterates over all points in the domain of the D_L; each iteration of the loop (say, corresponding to a point i) is run at a place determined by $D_L(i)$. Similarly, for an array A distributed over a distribution D_A the location of the array element j is determined by $D_A(j)$. If $A[j]$ is accessed in L (say in the iteration corresponding to point i), then it will result in a remote access unless $D_A(j) = D_L(i)$. For efficient layout of data, X10 defines several standard distributions (such as blocked, cyclic, blocked-cyclic and so on) and also allows a new distribution to be defined as a piece of X10 code in the programmer's code. The signature of an X10 function representing a distribution is given by the function `place dist (point p)`.

3. Code and Data Distribution

Ideally, in the context of distributed memory multi-core systems, the data and the computation should be distributed in sync, such that the data is maximally accessed locally, thereby avoiding the *cost* of data communication across different cores (or *places* in the X10). Depending on the language framework, accessing remote data may be disallowed (X10 explicit syntax) or involve remote communication (X10 implicit syntax, UPC).

In this paper we present techniques, wherein given a loop L and an array A accessed therein, the following two *key challenges* can be answered:
(i) Given a distribution D_A for the array A, derive an *efficient* distribution D_L for L.
(ii) Given a distribution D_L for the loop L, derive an *efficient* distribution D_A for A.
The efficiency of a distribution is measured by the number of resulting remote accesses (fewer the better). Note that the two key challenges are interlinked: redistributing a given loop may require redistribution of the arrays accessed therein, and redistributing a given array may require redistribution of the loops where it is accessed.

Given a distributed loop L, each iteration of it may be running at a different place. An array A accessed in L, may be accessed at multiple program points within it, and at different program points different array elements may be accessed (Say $j_1, j_2, \cdots, j_n$). If the loop has to be distributed over a distribution D_L then for each of the accesses of A in every iteration (with index i) to be local, the array A must be distributed in using a distribution D_A, such that $D_A(j_1) = D_A(j_2) = \cdots = D_A(j_n) = D_L(i)$. In general, it

Arrays	:	Set of arrays
L	:	Set of labels
S-Exprs	:	Set of statement-expressions
Loops⊆L	:	Set of labels of the loops
vExprs	=	S-Exprs ∪ {void}
F	:	Loops × Arrays → P(vExprs)

Figure 2. Helper sets and maps.

```
Vector ⟨Expr⟩ Function F(L, A, success)
Input: Loop L, Array A
Output: boolean success
begin
    Vector⟨Expr⟩ Fk = new Vector⟨Expr⟩();
    success = true;
    foreach index variable e used to access the array
    A and its may aliases do
        L' = label of the statement where A is accessed
        using e;
        Block=Slice(L', L, e);
        if Block contains L' or has side-effects then
            success = false;
            break ;
        Fk.add(Block);
    return Fk;
end
```

Figure 3. Algorithm to evaluate the map F

is not possible to always guarantee that we can generate such a distribution for the array, from the given distribution of a loop (or vice versa). Considering the similarities between the two key challenges, we present a simple unified approach based on data flow analysis, backward slicing, and reverse execution [6] to generate a target distribution so as to reduce the number of remote accesses.

3.1 Definitions

We first present a few definitions in Figure 2. Arrays is the set of array variables from the program, and L is the set of labels in the program[1]. S-Exprs is the set of all possible X10 *statement-expressions*. A statement-expression is defined as a sequence of zero or more statements, followed by an expression, called *last-expression*; the last-expression may be optionally guarded by a predicate. For any loop L and an array A accessed in the loop the map $F(L, A)$ returns the set of all the statement-expressions using which the different elements of A may be accessed in L. Say, V_f is the set of zero or more free variables that L may access (use or define); these are defined in the outside environment of the loop. One or more of the variables from the set V_f may also be accessed in $F(L, A)$. Note the set V_f does not include the loop index variable(s). For any iteration of the loop L and an element $s_e \in F(L, A)$, s_e/V_f (evaluation of s_e in the presence of the environment V_f) returns the indices of the array slots accessed in that iteration, or not return any value (if no array slot is accessed in that iteration).

Figure 3 presents the pseudo-code for the map F. The algorithm takes as input a loop L and an array A, and returns a set of statement-expressions using which the array may be accessed in the loop. For each access of the array A and its aliases (computed using [1]) in the loop L, we first identify the variable e using which the array element is accessed[2] For each of the expression, we compute the corresponding statement-expression, by computing a backward slice [28]; we add this statement-expression to the F map return value. The function Slice(L', L, e) returns a statement-expression corresponding to a backward slice bounded within the region of the loop body of L, starting from node L upto the

statement L', and following the data and control dependence edges induced by e; e depends on this statement-expression.

Figure 4(a) shows an illustrative program, that evaluates the randomness of the builin random number generator. It first generates a large number (10000) of random numbers and stores them in the array A. It creates a two element array sum (initialized to zero). In the first loop, it sums up all the even indexed elements of A into sum[0], and the odd ones into sum[1], and uses these sum values to compute the difference. For a large enough sample space, this difference should approach zero. In the second loop, we copy the generated random numbers into an array of half the size, by summing up two numbers at a time, and do some computation (not shown) on the summed up elements. Figure 4(b) shows the F map.

We use a new program representation, namely a LAG (loop array graph), that helps in efficient code and data distribution. A LAG is a weighted undirectional bipartite graph $G = ($Arrays, Loops, $E)$. An edge $(A_i, L_k) \in E$, *iff* $A_i \in$ Arrays, $L_k \in$ Loops, and A_i is accessed in L_k. Figure 4(c) shows the LAG for the code in Figure 4(a). The weights on the edges are indicative of the frequencies of accesses of the array in each loop it is accessed. We use some conservative static estimates to derive at these frequencies.

3.2 Distribution Algorithm

Considering the interdependencies and similarities between loop and array distributions, we develop an unified approach to answer the key challenges presented at the beginning of the section 3. To distribute a given node n (loop or array) in a LAG G, using a distribution D, we invoke the function redistribute(n, D, G) shown in Figure 5; Initially, all the edges in G are unmarked. For each unmarked edge (n, n'), we first mark the edge. We then invoke GenTD-LA,

---

[1] As discussed in Section 2 we use a simplified syntax wherein every statement has an unique label associated with it

[2] Internally our input program is represented in three-address format. Thus every array element is accessed using a variable only.

```
Region R = [1:10000], R1 = [1:10000];
double []A=new double[R1]
          (point [i]){return random()};
double []sum = new double[[1:2]];
L1: finish foreach (point [i]: R){
  if(i%2==0){sum[0] += A[i];}
  else {sum[1] += A[i];} }
double diff = sum[0] - sum[1];
Region R2 = [1..5000]
double []B == new double[R2];
L2: finish foreach (point [j]: R2){
  B[j] = A[j] + A[j+5000]; ... }
```

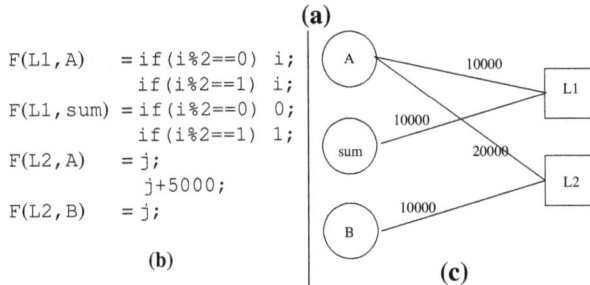

(a)

```
F(L1,A)    = if(i%2==0) i;
             if(i%2==1) i;
F(L1,sum)  = if(i%2==0) 0;
             if(i%2==1) 1;
F(L2,A)    = j;
             j+5000;
F(L2,B)    = j;
```

(b)

(c)

Figure 4. Example program, the F map, and the LAG.

Function redistribute(Node n, Distribution D, LAG G)

// (i) Distributes n using D
// (ii) Distributes any other nodes that
         might get impacted because of (i)

begin
  foreach *edge* $(n, n') \in G$ **do**
    if *edge* (n, n') *is already marked* **then**
    continue;
    mark the edge (n, n') in G;
    if n *is an Array* **then**
    GenTD-LA($n, n', D, success$);
    else GenTD-AL($n', n, D, success$);
    if *success* **then**
    redistribute($n', n'.dist, G$);
end

Figure 5. Distribute loops and arrays

---

or GenTD-AL depending on if the node n' is an array or a loop. The function GenTD-LA generates the target distribution for a loop based on the distribution of an array. Similarly, the function GenTD-AL generates the target distribution for an array based on the distribution of a loop. For each node n' whose distribution gets modified, we invoke the function redistribute to further distribute all the elements that get affected by n'. The input LAG may have cycles; we use the edge markings to avoid infinite-recursion.

Function GenTD-LA($A, L, D, success$)
Input: Array A, Loop L, Distribution D
Output: *boolean success*
begin
  Set $cFunc$ = getDist (L);
  if $cFunc$ == *null* **then** $cFunc$ = GenEmpty ();
  foreach $e \in F(L, A, success)$ **do**
    if $\neg success$ **then** break;
    addCode($cFunc, e, D, success$);
    if $\neg success$ **then** break;
  if *success* **then** setDist($L, cFunc$);
end

Figure 6. Generate Loop Distribution Function

The functions GenTD-LA (Figure 6), and GenTD-AL (Figure 7) use four helper functions: GenEmpty creates and returns an empty set; getDist(n) returns the current distribution of the node n as a set of statement-expressions. setDist (n, S) associates the set S as the code listing for the node n. And addCode ($cFunc$, e, D, $success$) adds the input statement-expression e to the code-listing $cFunc$, if the set of free variables in e are bound to only constant values. Further, the last-expression le is replaced by $D(le)$. The output variable $success$ is set if addCode updates $cFunc$.

The function GenTD-LA includes all the statement-expressions that are used to access the input array, as part of the distribution of the array. These statement-expressions are generated from the enumeration of the map F. The function GenTD-AL is a bit more involved: for each array element access we generate a statement-expression that corresponds to the index of the loop in which the element is accessed; we do this by generating the reverse execution code [6] for the statement-expression of the array index.

Function GenTD-AL($A, L, D, success$)
Input: Array A, Loop L, Distribution D
Output: *boolean success*
begin
  Set $cFunc$ = getDist (A);
  if $cFunc$ == *null* **then** $cFunc$ = GenEmpty ();
  foreach $e \in F(L, A, success)$ **do**
    if $\neg success$ **then** break;
    e' = rev($e, success$);
    if $\neg success$ **then** break;
    addCode($cFunc, e', D, success$);
    if $\neg success$ **then** break;
  if *success* **then** setDist($A, cFunc$);
end

Figure 7. Generate Array Distribution Function

```
   Function emit-dist-map(N)
   Input: Node N
 1 begin
 2 |   cFunc = getDist (N);
 3 |   List CF' = Sort the elements of cFunc in
   |   decreasing order of priority;
 4 |   boolean all-paths-covered = false;
 5 |   foreach statement-expression e in CF' do
 6 |   |   emit-code-element(e, all-paths-covered);
 7 |   |_  if all-paths-covered then break;
 8 |   if ¬all-paths-covered: then
 9 |   |_  emit-code(" return 0;");
10 end
```

Figure 8. Emit Distribution Map

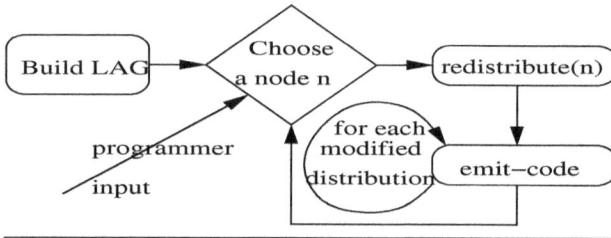

Figure 9. Overall Block Diagram

3.3 Code Generation

The overall block diagram of our framework is shown in Figure 9. After the `redistribute` function returns, we invoke the function `emit-dist-map` (Figure 8) for each node in the LAG whose distribution is modified, to emit the code for the new distribution. We sort the set of statement-expressions in the decreasing order of their frequencies and store in CF'; the frequency of a statement-expression is given by the frequency of the corresponding last-expression. We now construct the body of the distribution map, by emitting the code as given by the elements of CF'. We use an auxiliary functions `emit-code(e)` to emit code; it replaces the last expression $D(le)$ in e, by `return` $D(le)$. If we emit an unconditional `return` statement then the output variable *all-paths-covered* is set and then we stop emitting further code; as all the code following an unconditional `return` statement would become unreachable. A loop L may not access all the elements of an array A. Hence the distribution function of the loop D_L can be used to distribute the only those array elements which are accessed in L, and not others. The algorithm emits an unconditional `return 0` statement to handle any eventuality arising because of this, and guarantees that every element/iteration of the array/loop is distributed using this generated distribution. We emit this unconditional `return` statement, only if we did not encounter an unconditional `return` statement in line 7.

After generating the appropriate distributions for loops and arrays in the programs, relevant portions of the program need to be transformed: (a) For each loop that is redistributed, (i) we modify the loop header to distribute over the new distribution, (ii) for all the scalar variables that are created outside the loop and are accessed inside, we replace the access $v.f$ by $(v.location$ `==` `here`$)?v.f:$ `future` (v) $v.f.$`force()`; (iii) similarly, for all the scalar variables that are created outside the loop and are dereferenced to invoke a function, we replace the invocation

$$v.foo((a_1, \cdots)) \text{ by } \begin{cases} (v.location == here)?v.foo(a_1, \cdots): \\ \{\texttt{final } T_a \ fa_1 = a_1; \cdots; \\ \texttt{future}(v) \ v.foo(fa_1, \cdots).\texttt{force()}\} \end{cases}$$

The arguments to the remote function calls are passed via `final` variables (a syntactic requirement of X10 – only final variables are visible across multiple activities). (b) For each array A that is redistributed using a distribution D_A, we (i) change the declaration of the array, and (b) replace the array accesses $A[j]$ by: $(D_A(j) ==$ `here`$)?A[j]:$ `future` $(D_A(j))A[j].$`force()`;

3.4 Discussion

- It can be seen that, our translation may litter the code with many ternary operator (?:) accesses, to do place-locality checks; which can be fairly expensive. We propose to use the place locality analysis of Agarwal et al [1], to eliminate most of the place checks.

- In Figure 5, it may be noted that we do not specify the order of traversal of the edges of the LAG. The order of traversal has an impact on the resulting distributions. Consider two loops L_1 and L_2 accessing two arrays A_1 and A_2. Say the `redistribute` function is invoked to redistribute L_1. Based on the order of the edges chosen two possible alternatives exist. The algorithm may use the distribution of L_1 to distrbute A_1, then use the resulting distribution of A_1 to distribute L_2, and finally use the distribution of L_2 to distribute A_2. Alternatively, the algorithm may use the distribution of L_1 to distrbute A_2, then use the resulting distribution of A_2 to distribute L_2, and finally use the distribution of L_2 to distribute A_1. Thus the resulting distribution function for A_1, A_2 and L_2 can be different. Identifying the optimal order of edge traversal for a given LAG is a nontrivial problem, and is left as a future work.

- The generation of the F maps forms the backbone of our translation scheme, which in turn depends on alias analysis. Thus, the efficiency of our translation, depends on precision of the underlying alias analysis.

- The complexity of our proposed technique is $O(n^3)$, where n is the number of statements in the program. We pre-compute the F and `rev` maps and reuse these maps in the functions `GenTD-LA` and `GenTD-AL` each of which has a complexity of $O(n)$. Since, there can $O(n^2)$ number of edges in the LAG, the complexity of the

```
dist D = cyclic (R, 2); // dist for L1
// distribution for the array A
Place distA (point i) {
  if (i%2 == 0) return D(i);
  if (i%2 == 1) return D(i);
  return 0; // redundant
}
// distribution for the array sum
Place distSum (point i) { return 0; }
// distribution for the array B
Place distB (point i) { return distA(i); }
// distribution for the Loop L2
Place distL2 (point i){ return distA(i); }
```

Figure 10. Generated dists for the program in Figure 4(a)

---

redistribute function is $O(n^3)$. Finally, the cost of invoking the emit-dist-map function for each modified node is again $O(n^3)$. Thus the overall complexity of our technique is $O(n^3)$.

Illustration

Consider the example code shown in Figure 4(a). Say the programmer identifies the loop L1, and wants it to be distributed using a cyclic distribution over two places. Since L1 is accessing the arrays A and sum, these arrays need to be distributed. It can be seen that the array A is also accessed in loop L2. Once the array A is distributed in the previous step, we have to distribute the loop L2; which in turn would lead to redistribution of the array B. Figure 10 shows the generated distributions. It can be seen that the distribution of L2, B are same as the distribution of A. We can avoid emitting such distributions and reuse emitted distributions. A weakness of our framework can be seen in the distribution of sum. The function GenTD-AL fails (the function rev fails), and thus all the elements of sum are mapped to place 0; a smarter analysis could have done better. In the generated distribution for the array A, the last return statement is redundant – our code generation can be tuned to this effect.

4. Case Studies

In this section, we discuss our experience in applying the techniques presented in this paper onto real world benchmarks. We test the applicability of our techniques on benchmarks spanning three different benchmark suites – Eight benchmarks from Java Grande Forum [17] (JGF), Six benchmarks from HPC Challenge [16] (HPCC), and Ten benchmarks from Parsec [5].

Moldyn is part of the JGF benchmark suite. Figure 11(a) shows the parallel version of a part of the Moldyn benchmark. The goal is to distribute the first loop using a given distribution D. Figure 11(b) shows the transformation by our framework. Our refactoring framework first distributes the loop, then it distributes the array P, and then distributes the second and the third loop (all using the distribution D). It also

transforms the code in the function allreduce; which involves distributing the loop therein, and the modification of the access to the variable t.vir. We have identified similar opportunities in two other benchmarks in the suite (crypt and montecarlo).

RandomAccess is part of the HPCC suite. Figure 12(a) shows the parallel version of the kernel of the RandomAccess program, and Figure 12(b) shows the transformation by our framework; the goal is to distribute the loop using a programmer-specified distribution D over the region R. The loop gets distributed, and so does the array ranStarts (using D). However, the loop also accesses the array table. There is no direct co-relation between the loop iterations and the accesses. And our tool does not change the distribution of table; as the function GenTD-AL returns with the variable *success* set to *false*. Thus, we don't change the distribution of table, and introduce remote accesses. We have identified similar opportunities in FT benchmark of the suite.

BlackScholes is a part of the Parsec benchmark suite; it employs Black-Scholes Partial Differential Equation (PDE) to do option pricing. Figure 13(a) shows the parallel version of the snippet of the benchmark ported to X10. The parallel loop iterates over a region [1:numOption] with a stride of NCO. The goal is to distribute the array prices using a blocked distribution (D) over the region [1:numOption] with a blocking factor of NCO. Our algorithm distributes the array (say using D) and identifies the outermost loop has to be distributed using a distribution:

```
place dist (point i)
{ for (k=0;k<NCO;++k) return D(i+k);}.
```

(This code can be simplified to return D(i+0).) Our algorithm further identifies that the same distribution is applicable to the arrays: sptprice, strike, rate, volatility, otime, and otype. Our algorithm also identifies that the array data has to be distributed, but the function GenTD-AL *fails*. Thus, our algorithm allocates all the elements of data at place 0. Note that, the appropriate distribution for the array data is actually identical to the distribution specified for the array prices. Similar to the BlackScholes benchmark, we have identified similar opportunities in all (ten) of the benchmarks from this suite.

Overall, we have observed that our redistribution algorithm is applicable in many different benchmark programs. We have also observed that there may be cases where our generated distributions sometimes are not concise and needs programmer help for better representation.

Performance gains: We have compared two versions of the benchmarks (i) benchmarks with only the parallel loops distributed, (ii) benchmarks where the parallel loops are distributed, along with other arrays and loops as suggested by our framework. We obtained the execution time numbers and observed significant improvement in performance (upto 100 x, for montecarlo). Due to the lack of space, we avoid presenting the details of these numbers, especially because

```
final region R=[1:NTHREADS];            final dist D=...(R)...;
void run() {                            void run() {
 finish foreach(point [j]:R)             finish ateach (point [j]: D)
        P[j].initialise(...);                    P[j].initialise(...);
 ...                                     ...
 finish foreach(point [j]:R)             finish ateach (point [j]: D)
        P[j].runiters(...);                      P[j].runiters(...);
 ...                                     ...
 finish foreach (point [j]:R){           finish ateach (point [j]: D){
   md myNode = P[j];                       md myNode = P[j];
 ... } }                                 ... } }
void allreduce() {                      void allreduce() {
 finish foreach (point [j]: R) {         finish ateach (point [j]: D){
   for(point [k]: [0:(mdsize-1)]){         for(point [k]: [0:(mdsize-1)]){
     ...                                     ...
     P[j].one[k].zforce = ... }             P[j].one[k].zforce = ... }
   P[j].vir = t.vir; } }                 P[j].vir= future(t){ t.vir} .force(); } }

              (a)                                     (b)
```

Figure 11. (a) Parallel Moldyn, (b) Distributed Moldyn. Changes shown in **bold**.

```
final region R = [0:maxPlaces-1];       final region R=[0:maxPlaces-1];
final int[.] ranStarts=new int[R];      final dist D=... (R) ... ;
for (point p: R) ranStarts[p]=...;      final int[.] ranStarts=new int[ D];
                                        finish ateach (point p: D) ranStarts[p]=...;
...                                     ...
finish foreach (point p : R) {          finish ateach (point p : D) {
 int ran=nextRandom(ranStarts[p]);       int ran=nextRandom(ranStarts[p]);
 for (int count=1; count<=nUpdates;      for (int count=1; count<=nUpdates;
              count++) {                              count++) {
   final int j=f(ran);                     final int j=f(ran);
   final int k=smallTable[g(ran)];         final int k=smallTable[g(ran)];
   final point q = Pt(j);                  final point q=Pt(j);
   atomic { table[q]=table[q] ^ k; }      async(table[q])
   ran=nextRandom(ran);                      { atomic{table[q]= table[q]^ k;}}
 } }                                       ran=nextRandom(ran); } }

              (a)                                     (b)
```

Figure 12. (a) Parallel RandomAccess, (b) Distributed RandomAccess. Changes shown in **bold**.

the importance of data locality in distributed threads is well known. These execution time behaviors were studied only for the benchmarks from JGF and HPCC. The Parsec benchmarks (written in C/C++ which do not support distributions) need to be ported fully to a language like X10 to study the gains; these are large benchmarks and porting them to X10 remains an interesting future work.

5. Future work

Arbitrary distributions: While X10 language description [12] discusses the idea of programmer-specified distributions, an efficient implementation of the language runtime that can support such arbitrary distributions is an open challenge.

Prototype : Implementing the framework in Eclipse type of environment is an involved exercise in itself and is left as future work. Further, making such an implementation applicable to multiple languages is another open challenge.

Optimizations: Our generated code is oblivious to the underlying distribution and thus may loose opportunities for generating efficient distributions. Identifying newer refactoring patterns and possible optimizations in the generated code would be an interesting area to explore.

```
region R=region (1:numOption,NCO);
finish foreach(point [i]: R){
  ...
  BlkSchlsEqEuroNoDiv(i,NCO,sptprice[i],
    strike[i], rate[i], volatility[i],
    otime[i], otype[i], 0);
  for (k=0; k<NCO; k++){
    prices[i+k] = price[k]; }
  ...
  for (k=0; k<NCO; k++) {
    priceDelta = data[i+k].DGrefval
                    - price[k]; }..}
```

Figure 13. Example snippet ported from BlackScholes

6. Conclusion

In this paper, we discuss our preliminary results on distributing arrays and loops using arbitrary programmer specified distributions. We feel that lack of automatic techniques to infer arbitrary distribution of data and computation had been one of the main reasons for programmers to restrict themselves pre-defined distributions. Our paper bridges and important gap in this context and we expect that there will be increased interest in the uses of arbitrary distributions by the application developers.

References

[1] S. Agarwal, R. Barik, V.K. Nandivada, R.K. Shyamasundar, and P. Varma. Static detection of place locality and elimination of runtime checks. In *Proceedings of the APLAS*, pages 53–74. LNCS, 2008.

[2] J. R. Allen and K. Kennedy. PFC: A program to convert fortran to parallel form. In *Proceedings of the Supercomputers: Design and Applications*, pages 186–203, August 1984.

[3] C. Ancourt and F. Irigoin. Automatic code distribution. In *Workshop on Compilers for Parallel Computers*, 1992.

[4] E. Ayguade, J. Garcia, M. Girons, M. L. Grande, and J. Labarta. DDT: A research tool for automatic data distribution in HPF. In *Scientific Programming*, 1995.

[5] C. Bienia, S. Kumar, J. Pal Singh, and K. Li. The PARSEC benchmark suite: Characterization and architectural implications. In *Proceedings of PACT*, Oct 2008.

[6] B. Biswas and R. Mall. Reverse execution of programs. *SIGPLAN Not.*, 34(4):61–69, 1999.

[7] M. Burke, R. Cytron, J. Ferrante, and W. Hsieh. Automatic generation of nested, fork-join parallelism. *Journal of Supercomputing*, pages 71–88, 1989.

[8] S. Chatterjee, J. R. Gilbert, R. Schreiber, and T. J. Sheffler. Array distribution in data-parallel programs. In *Proceedings of LCPC*, pages 76–91. Springer-Verlag, 1994.

[9] W.R. Cook and J. Palsberg. A denotational semantics of inheritance and its correctness. In *Proceedings of OOPSLA*, pages 433–444, 1989.

[10] D. Dig, J. Marrero, and M. D. Ernst. Refactoring sequential java code for concurrency via concurrent libraries. In *Proceedings of the ICSE*, pages 397–407, 2009.

[11] Tarek El-Ghazawi, William W. Carlson, and Jesse M. Draper. UPC Language Specification v1.1.1, October 2003.

[12] V. Saraswat et al. Report on the experimental language X10, x10.sourceforge.net/docs/x10-101.pdf, 2006.

[13] P. H. Feiler and R. Medina-Mora. An incremental programming environment. *IEEE Trans. Software Engineering*, 7(5):472–482, September 1981.

[14] M. Gupta and P. Banerjee. PARADIGM: A compiler for automatic data distribution on multicomputers. In *In International Conference on Supercomputing*, pages 87–96, 1993.

[15] R. Gupta, S. Pande, K. Psarris, and V. Sarkar. Compilation techniques for parallel systems. *Parallel Computing*, 25:13–14, 1999.

[16] HPC challenge benchmark. http://icl.cs.utk.edu/hpcc/.

[17] The Java Grande Forum benchmark suite. http://www.epcc.ed.ac.uk/javagrande/javag.html.

[18] K. Kennedy and J. R. Allen. *Optimizing compilers for modern architectures: a dependence-based approach.* Morgan Kaufmann Publishers Inc., San Francisco, CA, USA, 2002.

[19] K. Kennedy, Kathryn S. McKinley, and C-W. Tseng. Analysis and transformation in the ParaScope editor. In *Proceedings of the ICS*, pages 433–447. ACM, 1991.

[20] C. Koelbel, P. Mehrotra, and J. van Rosendale. Semi-automatic process partitioning for parallel computation. *Int. J. Parallel Program.*, 16(5):365–382, 1987.

[21] P Lee. Efficient algorithms for data distribution on distributed memory parallel computers. *IEEE Transactions on Parallel and Distributed Systems*, 8:825–839, 1997.

[22] P. Lee and W-Y Chen. Generating global name-space communication sets for array assignment statements. Technical report, Institute of Information Science, Academia Sinica.

[23] P. Lee and Z. M. Kedem. Automatic data and computation decomposition on distributed memory parallel computers. *ACM Trans. Programming Languages and Systems*, 24, 2002.

[24] S-W. Liao, A. Diwan, R. P. Bosch, Jr., A. Ghuloum, and M. S. Lam. SUIF explorer: an interactive and interprocedural parallelizer. In *PPoPP*, pages 37–48. ACM, 1999.

[25] M. E. Mace. *Memory storage patterns in parallel processing.* Kluwer Academic Publishers, Norwell, MA, USA, 1987.

[26] S. Markstrum, R. M. Fuhrer, and T. D. Millstein. Towards concurrency refactoring for x10. In *PPOPP, poster*, pages 303–304, 2009.

[27] A. Rogers and K. Pingali. Process decomposition through locality of reference. In *Proceedings of the PLDI*, pages 69–80. ACM, Jun 1987.

[28] Mark Weiser. Program slicing. *IEEE Trans. Soft. Engg.*, 10(4):352–357, 1984.

Ficticious: MicroLanguages for Interactive Fiction

James Dean Palmer

Northern Arizona University

James.Palmer@nau.edu

Abstract

In this paper we provide an experience report where language oriented programming approaches are applied to complex game design. Ficticious is a G-expression based pidgin of several microlanguages designed for describing complex narrative worlds that exist within interactive fiction. G-expression language transformations convert code written in Ficticious to the general programming language Ginger, which is then translated into calls against the underlying machine. In this paper we explore Ficticious's unique object model and demonstrate how dynamic language transformations can be a powerful tool for implementing separation of concerns, rich text markup, complex virtual world design and character interaction.

Categories and Subject Descriptors D.2.10 [*Software Engineering*]: Design—Methodologies; D.3.1 [*Programming Languages*]: Formal Definitions and Theory—Syntax; D.3.2 [*Programming Languages*]: Language Classifications—Specialized application languages

General Terms Design, Languages

Keywords Interactive Fiction, Domain Specific Languages, MicroLanguages, Ginger

1. Introduction

Interactive fiction (IF) is an adventure gaming genre characterized by textual descriptions of characters, objects, game play dynamics, and command based interaction between the player and the virtual world. The genre has its roots in games such as *Adventure* (1975), *Zork* (1977), and a series of commercially successful titles created by InfoCom in the 1980s that included *Planetfall* (1983), Douglas Adams' *Hitchiker's Guide to the Galaxy* (1984) and *The Lurking Horror* (1987). *Zork* begins with the following interaction:

Permission to make digital or hard copies of all or part of this work for personal or classroom use is granted without fee provided that copies are not made or distributed for profit or commercial advantage and that copies bear this notice and the full citation on the first page. To copy otherwise, to republish, to post on servers or to redistribute to lists, requires prior specific permission and/or a fee.

Onward! 2010, October 17–21, 2010, Reno/Tahoe, Nevada, USA.

Copyright © 2010 ACM 978-1-4503-0236-4/10/10. . . $10.00

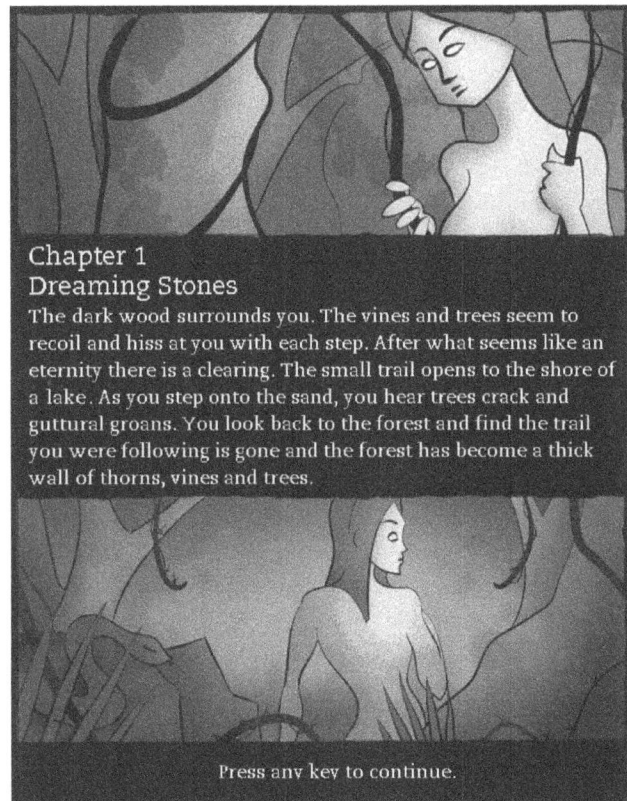

Figure 1. The beginning of a Ficticious based interactive fiction game designed for an eInk display similar to Amazon's Kindle or Sony's eReader.

West of House

You are standing in an open field west of a white house, with a boarded front door. There is a small mailbox here.

> **examine mailbox**

The small mailbox is closed.

> **open mailbox**

Opening the mailbox reveals a leaflet.

> **take leaflet**

Taken.

Here the player interacts in the space using the simple verbs *examine*, *open* and *take* to act on the objects *mailbox* and *leaflet* in the environment. Complex spatial relationships can exist in the virtual world (i.e., the leaflet is in a closed mailbox and is then transferred to the player's inventory) yet this example is extremely basic. Many IF systems support linear, multi-linear, and non-linear story telling, multiple perspectives, temporal events, and physics [11, 14, 22].

IF authors of the 1980s were able to create rich virtual worlds fueled by verbal wit and imagination in an era when home computers were characterized by weak graphical capabilities and extremely resource constrained operating environments. But as home computers became more sophisticated, many IF publishers found it difficult to adapt to a changing marketplace and develop games that took advantage of these capabilities. In 1989 interactive fiction giant, InfoCom, ceased operations and the 1990s saw the general commercial decline of the genre.

After InfoCom's demise, the proprietary "z-code" byte-code and "z-machine" virtual machine that had been developed to run InfoCom games was reverse engineered. This allowed older games to be played on modern hardware and it also enabled the development of new games that could utilize the same virtual machine. Designing languages to target z-code (or similar) interpreters has been an active area of research ever since. Such languages include Michael J. Robert's TADS [21], Graham Nelson's Inform [17] and Inform 7 [16], and Kent Tessman's Hugo [24].

While it's possible to write IF in general purpose programming languages like C, Java, or Python it's extremely uncommon. IF languages tend to be, in some respects, simpler and also support complex systems for representing object hierarchies, conversation, and story state. Consider the following snippet of TADS code taken from Roger Firth's Cloak of Darkness, a story designed as a sort of "hello world" for IF [5]:

```
1  hook: fixeditem, surface, item
2    sdesc = "small brass hook"
3    ldesc =
4    {
5      "It's just a small brass hook, ";
6      if (cloak.isIn(self))
7        "with a cloak hanging on it. ";
8      else
9        "screwed to the wall. ";
10   }
11   noun = 'hook' 'peg'
12   adjective = 'small' 'brass'
13   location = cloakroom
14 ;
```

The same snippet written in C would be littered with `printf`s, hash table assignments and function pointer manipulation. IF languages automatically provide a layer of abstraction that supports custom object systems and high-level string manipulation. IF languages are true domain specific languages and in the case of Inform 7 many conventional constructs of programming languages are eschewed in favor of a much more human language like syntax. The same bit of code rendered by Emily Short and Graham Nelson in Inform 7 reads:

```
1  In the Cloakroom is a supporter called the
2  small brass hook. The hook is scenery.
3  Understand "peg" as the hook.
4
5  The description of the hook is "It's just a
6  small brass hook, [if something is on the
7  hook]with [a list of things on the hook]
8  hanging on it[otherwise]screwed to the
9  wall[end if]."
```

High quality free IF languages and tools have made IF authoring easy and accessible and has helped foster a vibrant community of both indie and amateur IF game developers. While there are a number of important features that have made IF domain specific languages especially suited for their task, one important feature is the ability to programmatically mix text and code. One need only spend a few minutes attempting to write an IF game in Java to see that text management is going to be an issue. Connecting code and narrative is a problem that isn't unique to IF and we have observed that the problem is extremely similar to that of Literate Programming. In Literate Programming one uses narrative to describe and organize code by connecting chunks of code to narrative elements [9, 10]. The goal of an IF language is to do the opposite - connect chunks of narrative to program elements that represent the virtual world.

2. The Ficticious Language

As part of a local game programming challenge we considered the unique problem of designing games for eInk displays and more specifically for devices like the Amazon Kindle, Sony eReader, or Barnes & Noble Nook. Such devices have very high resolution displays but support a limited number of gray-scales and have slow and often distinct refreshes. One game style that we thought should be uniquely suited for the device was interactive fiction. As we began to develop ideas for our game it was the thesis that interactive fiction languages and literate languages should or could be closely related that influenced the development of Ficticious. It should be noted that Graham Nelson (author of Inform) was similarly influenced by Knuth's work on literate programming and that while Inform does not support a CWEB-style language modality it does support chapters, sections and rich output [15].

The design for the game we envisioned involved a somewhat unconventional IF interface with comic-book inspired text and graphic layout and embedded but non-narrative mini-game elements. We decided to approach the problem with what is essentially a language oriented approach to software design. Language oriented programming (LOP) is a phrase that was coined by Martin Ward [25] in 2003 to describe a philosophy of developing purpose-built languages as part of the problem-solving process. In LOP, programmers develop *problem-specific* languages in terms of the concepts of the domain problem they are trying to solve instead of the programming paradigm(s) supported by a general purpose programming language. This is essentially the same strategy that Michael Dunlavey advocated for in 1994 and which he called "problem-oriented languages" [3]. Dunlavey asserts that the number of bugs in a program are, in large measure, directly proportional to the dissimilarity of the language of the program implementation and the domain language that specifies the problem requirements. LOP is a kind of bottom-up design and many of the principles Ward and Dunlavey detailed are similar to the bottom-up programming approach espoused by Lispers like Paul Graham and that has been in practice by Scheme and Lisp programmers for some time [6].

The design methodology we have used in Ficticious involves layering and weaving domain specific languages together to produce an application. We call the resulting language a *pidgin language*. A human pidgin language is a simplified language that allows groups that do not have a language in common to communicate. Pidgin languages incorporate words and rules from other languages in order to support communication. In Ficticious, G-expressions provide the common framework to support sub-languages with different rules thus forming a sort of digital pidgin language. G-expressions have rules similar to S-expressions which are used in Scheme and Lisp but with Python-like spacing and indentation rules for developing groups and hierarchies [19]. In previous work we developed a language that supports literate programming as a core feature of the language [20] and uses G-expression transformations to implement that feature.

G-expressions have a number of nice properties that make them well suited as a basis for domain specific languages. One of these properties is that the syntax closely follows conventions already used in several existing human readable file formats and microlanguages. With minimal to no preprocessing Geomview's OFF files, Voxblast's Poly files, AC3D files, 3D Studio ASC files, Alchemy molecule files, NFF files, Lightwave OBJ files, Stanford PLY files, Vertex-Edge-Face format files, and NetPBM PGM, PBM and PPM files (to name just a few) represent valid G-expressions and can be parsed with Ginger's G-expression reader directly into hierarchical data structures that Ginger can manipulate. In the remainder of this section we describe four microlanguages we designed as part of Ficticious to address problems specific to our game.

2.1 A MicroLanguage for People, Places and Things

While we could use a general-purpose object-oriented (OO) language to develop the objects that populate our game, there aren't many OO languages that directly match the semantics and needs that objects in our world have. We would need to develop support code and boiler plate segments that could lead to more bugs and obscure the semantically imbued elements of our code. Our solution is to develop an object system that matches how objects work in our environment. Many good models for doing exactly this are represented in existing IF languages and we have tried to learn many of the lessons of these languages.

The Cloak of Darkness example discussed earlier could be rendered in Ficticious as:

```
1  object Hook extends: FixedItem
2     set name "hook"
3     set aliases ("hook" "peg")
4     set adjective ("small" "brass")
5     set location 'CloakRoom
6
7     action examine
8        :story It's just a small brass hook,
9        if (isIn cloak self)
10          :story with a cloak hanging on it.
11       else
12          :story screwed to the wall.
```

While Ficticious supports an object system, Ficticious objects always correspond to virtual world objects. One can not, for example, use objects to implement new data structures. Ficticious expects that objects should appear in the game as characters, items or locations and there is no extra code needed to make that happen.

Ficticious uses the words *class* and *object* differently than most languages. In Ficticious, a class is a special kind of object that does not appear in the world. In other words, the object is not and cannot be instantiated. Thus a *class* roughly corresponds to an *abstract class* in Java. Classes allow us to push commonalities in objects higher up a class hierarchy so we can maximize code reuse just as we might in any other object-oriented language. An *object* is a class definition that is also instantiated. In some respects the Ficticious object system is more similar to prototype-based OO systems except that each Ficticious object is based on a definition and objects can not be cloned, duplicated or copied at runtime.

2.1.1 Classes

Ficticious classes and object definitions define and set properties and methods. Properties can be numbers, strings, lists or references to other objects. Ficticious methods are much simpler than their counterparts in general-purpose object-oriented languages. Methods do not take parameters nor do they return values. Methods should not be thought of as functions but rather as *actions* or *observations* that mutate the game state as a whole.

An action method specifies what happens when a verb is applied to an object. Consider an example that defines a Bridge location that responds when it is examined:

```
1 object Bridge extends: Location
2   action examine
3     :story The *bridge* looks forgotten.
```

An observation method specifies an action that is taken when a verb is applied to an external object. In other words it is an action that an object perceives but does not receive. Consider an example that defines a Troll who watches the bridge.

```
1 object Troll extends: RoughCharacter
2   observe examine
3     if (eq? target 'Bridge)
4       :story
5         The troll eyes you suspiciously.
```

When the player commands "examine bridge" the troll will eye them suspiciously if he is present. It's through this mechanism that objects can act in the scene without being directly acted upon. A special verb called time can be used for the object to react each time a player turn takes place.

2.1.2 Game Objects

All game objects are created at initialization. Objects can be identified with their global identifier or using references. While property references can take on other values, global identifier references are immutable. This disallows the author from changing the meaning of objects but still allows object state to be changed.

Objects must have a name, a location and sets of aliases and adjectives that describe it. Each object has its own namespace but can access other objects through a global namespace. In the following snippet of code we ask if the current object (identified with a local variable named self) is the same thing as a character named Alice (a global variable):

```
1 if (eq? self 'Alice)
2   :story Her name was Alice.
```

The global variable is accessed as what is called a "quoted" symbol in Ginger or Scheme. Another advantage of using a domain specific language over adapting a general purpose object-oriented language is that we can hardwire requirements of the objects as language features. This makes it more difficult for the programmer to make mistakes that violate assumptions made for the problem.

2.2 A Microlanguage for Rich Text and Grammar

Beyond the actual organization of our virtual world, we will have to spend a great deal of time describing it. The language for providing narrative needs to let us work without having

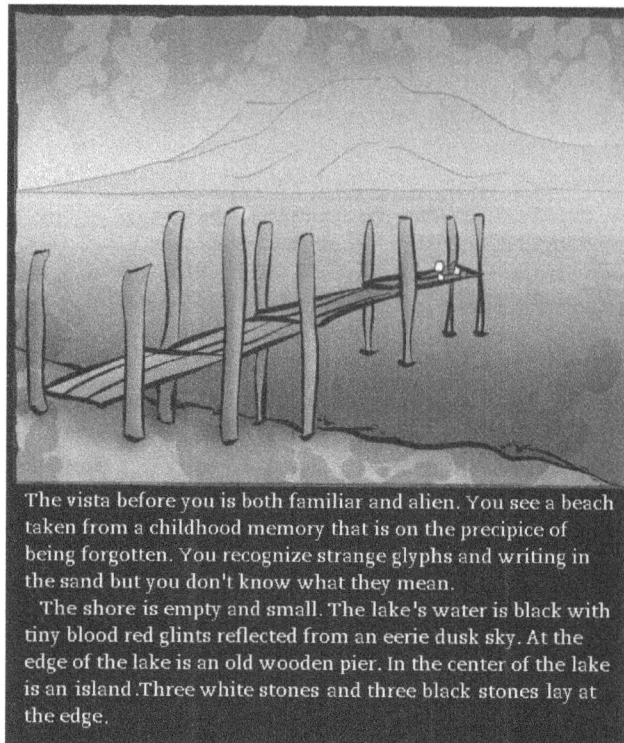

The vista before you is both familiar and alien. You see a beach taken from a childhood memory that is on the precipice of being forgotten. You recognize strange glyphs and writing in the sand but you don't know what they mean.

The shore is empty and small. The lake's water is black with tiny blood red glints reflected from an eerie dusk sky. At the edge of the lake is an old wooden pier. In the center of the lake is an island. Three white stones and three black stones lay at the edge.

Figure 2. A simple layout with only one graphic panel and one text panel.

to worry about a lot of quoting rules but also needs to support text markup and dynamically generated grammar.

We accomplish this by mixing our G-expression colon-quoting feature with a Textile based markup language [1]. Colon-quoting was originally designed to support literate programming in Ginger where the exact same problem exists. Colon-quoting allows quoted blocks of text to enter a quoting mode with a single character (a colon). Blocks become unquoted based on indentation and not based on quotes as they are in C and Java. This makes having to worry about escaped characters less common and conveniently follows ad-hoc conventions that many authors have used in plain ASCII documents. The next fragment demonstrates colon-quotes and the use of Textile markup.

```
1 :story
2   The sign reads "No Loitering" but
3   ironically a cowboy whittles a small
4   piece of wood *right beside* the sign.
```

The quotes used here require no special escaping and asterisks are used to represent emphasis or bolding when the text is actually rendered. Textile has its own rules for escaping characters but we've found it's extremely uncommon to use them in interactive fiction dialog and narrative writing.

Some narrative requires grammatical trickery based on the state of the environment. Consider this line which must change based on the number of rocks present on the shore:

```
1 set $ 'LakeShore.whiteStoneCount
2 :story
3   $It$ almost $$seems$$ to glow with energy.
```

We use a Textile-like convention for marking subjects (surrounded by single dollar signs) and verbs (surrounded by double signs). If the special variable, $, is equal to one the sentence reads "It almost seems to glow with energy," but if $ is greater than one then the sentence reads "They almost seem to glow with energy." We call this the inflection language. This specialized microlanguage helps us avoid some truly deep nested if statements that consider a stream of different inflections for objects, actors and actions in the scene. This inflection language is in turn (and appropriately) written using a mixture of regular expressions and the core implementation language. Thus, it is through a series of language transformations that the final text is rendered.

2.3 A Microlanguage for Page Layout

Unlike many IF games, graphics play an important role in this game. The pages in this game need to be able to have multiple columns of text and graphics. Ficticious has another language specifically for drawing game pages. This language creates panel objects that are created and destroyed on demand (and thus are fundamentally dissimilar from the game objects already described). Commands like setImage and drawImage are unique to this mode and allow us to position the game elements in the frame. At the same time the same language for evaluating expressions is used so we can change the layout or content of the page based on the game state. In the next example, the graphic includes the boatman, Charon, only if he is present:

```
1 panel GamePageLakeShore extends: GamePage
2   property Image panel1
3   property Image panel2
4   init
5     setText 10 445 580 250
6     setImage panel1 "imgs/charonGone.png"
7     setImage panel2 "imgs/charonWaits.png"
8   draw
9     if (eq? 'Boatman.location 'LakeShore)
10       drawImage panel2 7 7
11     else:
12       drawImage panel1 7 7
```

This code generates the panel shown in Figure 2. Program logic and high-level draw operators allow a lot of design flexibility and support complex overlapping multi-panel arrangements. Figure 1, for example, illustrates an instance where three panels are used. The panel language does not care about drawing contexts or low level drawing functions as they are not directly pertinent to describing the scene. The language itself enforces separation of concerns as this functionality is neither visible nor accessible.

2.4 A Microlanguage for Dialog

The final microlanguage we describe is our dialog system. While a number of researchers have considered generative narrative [2, 12, 13, 18], very few have considered generative dialog in an IF context. If we don't care about characters advancing plot points, we could implement non-player characters (NPCs) as chatterbots. But advancing a story places a number of constraints on a dialog system. Players expect that they should be able to explore a conversation systematically. Emily Short has considered this problem and sketched a partial taxonomy of dialog strategies [23, 4]. We expand on her thoughts slightly to develop the following list of commonly used strategies:

1. Unstructured
   - Reactive chatterbots
   - Unreactive or non sequitur chatterbots
2. Static Structure
   - Tree Structured Branching
   - Hub-and-Spokes
3. Dynamic Structure
   - Plan Driven Conversation
   - Atomic Conversation
   - Atomic Conversation with conditions

Each of these techniques describes an organization approach with varying degrees of structure and dynamic engagement. As most of these techniques can be represented as a tree or graph, the actual syntax for implementing any of these techniques could be markedly similar if general enough. Short provides the following pseudocode example to demonstrate quips as atomic entities:

```
1 Quip about Fangclaw's castle:
2   subjects: Fangclaw
3   prerequisite: none
4   followups: only quips that immediately
5     follow this one
```

What Short calls pre-conditions and post-conditions are kinds of dependencies. We argue her example even looks a little bit like one of our favorite dependency languages, Make. While Makefiles were designed for assembling software they have been used for a number of dependency resolution problems unrelated to software construction. This includes actions to manage firewalls, convert files, and manage startup services [7, 8]. Make's dependency resolution format is extremely simple:

```
1 targetToConstruct: list of dependencies
2   actions to perform if dependencies are met
```

and has inspired our own system that names the quip and the action needed to fulfill the quip along with its dependencies:

```
1 conversation on OldMine
2   oldMine "Ask about the old mine."
3     :dialog
4       Sam: I keep seeing an old donkey
5       at the mine.
6
7   donkey "Ask about the donkey." => oldMine
8     :dialog
9       Sam: The donkey comes and goes.
```

Here, the player can't ask about the donkey unless they have already asked about the mine. Dependencies may also include expressions allowing the game state to influence the conversation graph.

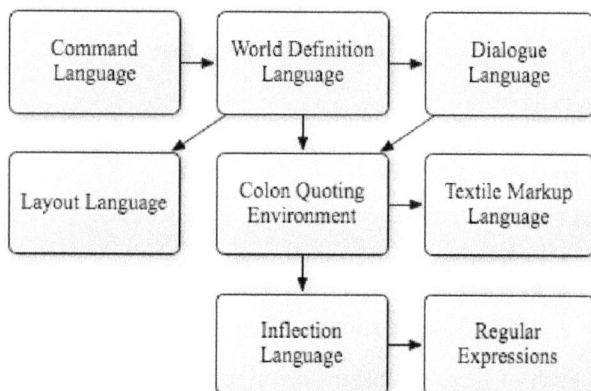

Figure 3. The dependency relationships of languages and environments used in Ficticious.

3.   Implementation

We hope the short snippets of code have been convincing evidence that the game logic is being efficiently and succinctly represented. The one question we must ask is has it been worth it? Has the difficulty in terms of time and lines of code simply been shifted to writing the domain specific languages (DSLs) we have described with no real savings? While we will admit our measure is unscientific, at the beginning of the project we implemented many of the classes we described here using only Java. We then implemented the same functionality using the DSLs we designed and found the number of lines of code was easily improved by two-to-one or better. And subjectively, implementing the world using a series of DSLs was faster and much less torturous. The time to implement the DSLs was honestly nominal. By using Ginger, we got a well tested G-expression parser for free. Developing the semantic transformations and error checking involved only a few hundred lines of code while the number of lines of game logic goes into the thousands.

It's hard for us to even think of Ficticious as a single language. Instead, it represents a collection of context specific microlanguages that are designed to work together to solve a problem. Figure 3 maps relationships between these different languages that we have described in this paper. While the software system is a legion of languages, we beleive the number of bugs have been relatively few because, by design, our DSLs map closely to the problem spaces.

4.   Conclusions

In this paper we have discussed language oriented programming in the context of a complex medium sized game project. This kind of bottom-up programming dramatically reduced the number of lines written to implement our game. We also feel it improved the readability and inspect-ability of the code by laying bare the essential logic associated with each game part and divorcing it from the implementation concerns. While Ficticious was designed to implement a specific IF game, we hope ongoing work on our part to develop new features and documentation will help make it available as a general purpose approach to IF.

References

[1] D. Allen. The Textile markup language.
    `http://textile.thresholdstate.com/`.

[2] L. M. Barros and S. R. Musse. Introducing narrative principles into planning-based interactive storytelling. In *ACE '05: Proceedings of the 2005 ACM SIGCHI International Conference on Advances in Computer Entertainment Technology*, pages 35–42, New York, NY, USA, 2005. ACM.

[3] M. Dunlavey. *Building Better Applications: A Theory of Efficient Software Development/Book and Disk*. Van Nostrand Reinhold, 1994.

[4] B. Ellison. Defining dialogue systems.
    `http://www.gamasutra.com/view/feature/3719/defining_dialogue_systems.php?page=1`,
    July 2008.

[5] R. Firth. Cloak of Darkness.
    `http://www.firthworks.com/roger/cloak/`.

[6] P. Graham. *On LISP: Advanced Techniques for Common LISP*. Prentice Hall, September 1993.

[7] S. Hambridge, C. Smothers, T. Oace, and J. Sedayao. Just type make! - managing internet firewalls using make and other publicly available utilities. In *NETA'99: Proceedings of the 1st Conference on Network Administration*, page 5, Berkeley, CA, USA, 1999. USENIX Association.

[8] J. Hunt. Boot Linux faster. `http://www.ibm.com/developerworks/linux/library/l-boot.html`,
    September 2003.

[9] D. E. Knuth. Literate programming. *The Computer Journal*, 27(2):97–111, 1984.

[10] D. E. Knuth. *Literate programming*. Center for the Study of Language and Information, Stanford, CA, USA, 1992.

[11] N. Montfort. *Twisty Little Passages: An Approach to Interactive Fiction*. MIT Press, Cambridge, MA, USA, 2004.

[12] N. Montfort. *Generating narrative variation in interactive fiction*. PhD thesis, Philadelphia, PA, USA, 2007.

[13] N. Montfort. Curveship: an interactive fiction system for interactive narrating. In *CALC '09: Proceedings of the Workshop on Computational Approaches to Linguistic Creativity*, pages 55–62, Morristown, NJ, USA, 2009. Association for Computational Linguistics.

[14] G. Nelson. Inform 7 extensions. http://inform7.com/write/extensions/.

[15] G. Nelson. Natural language, semantic analysis, and interactive fiction. http://www.inform7.com/learn/documents/WhitePaper.pdf.

[16] G. Nelson. Writing with Inform. http://inform7.com/learn/man/index.html.

[17] G. Nelson. *The Inform Designer's Manual*. Dan Sanderson, 4th edition, 2006.

[18] M. J. Nelson, M. Mateas, D. L. Roberts, and C. L. Isbell Jr. Declarative optimization-based drama management in interactive fiction. *IEEE Comput. Graph. Appl.*, 26(3):32–41, 2006.

[19] J. D. Palmer. Ginger: Implementing a new Lisp family syntax. In *ACM-SE 47: Proceedings of the 47th Annual Southeast Regional Conference*, pages 1–6, New York, NY, USA, 2009. ACM.

[20] J. D. Palmer and E. Hillenbrand. Reimagining literate programming. In *OOPSLA '09: Proceeding of the 24th ACM SIGPLAN conference companion on Object oriented programming systems languages and applications*, pages 1007–1014, New York, NY, USA, 2009. ACM.

[21] M. J. Roberts. TADS: The Text Adventure Development System. http://www.tads.org/.

[22] E. Short. Multilinear IF. http://emshort.wordpress.com/how-to-play/writing-if/my-articles/multilinear-if-older/.

[23] E. Short. Sub-facade. *Homer in Silicon*, 2009.

[24] K. Tessman. The Hugo book. http://www.ifarchive.org/if-archive/programming/hugo/manuals/hugo_book.pdf, 2004.

[25] M. Ward. Language oriented programming. Science Labs Durham, 2003.

Onward! Film Chair's Welcome

Since the inception in 2006, the organizers of the Onward! film track have believed that film can play an increasingly significant role in the development process. Surprisingly, there has so far been little use of film in the software development process, despite the fact that digital video techniques are now well within the time and resource constraints of most software development projects. However, film can be used in software projects in several ways. For example, film can show the interactive nature of a proposed system in a way that goes well beyond the capacity of requirements specifications and use-case diagrams. Film can reveal how a proposed system should or might work, and reveal exceptional circumstances in which the system still must work. There is also an increasing need of describing research projects whose results are difficult to explain to non-experts. The interesting behavior of such systems often stretches into weeks or months and a film might be much more helpful than a real-time demo. Moreover, film can be used as visual scaffolding of how software engineering is conducted in order to help us improve the software development process itself.

I would like to thank the members of this years film program committee, Roberto Bisiani, Oliver Creighton, Ralph Guggenheim, Martin Purvis, Maryam Purvis and Harald Stangl, for their help in the organization of the track and in the review process. I would also like to thank the contributors for their movies which demonstrate yet another set of creative techniques and possibilities of the use of film in software engineering. I hope these films encourage others to get enthusiastic about submitting their own film to Onward! 2011.

Bernd Bruegge
Onward! Film Chair

Physics as Freedom

Seung Chan Lim

Rhode Island School of Design
Providence, RI 02903
slim@alumni.cmu.edu

Abstract

We live in a world full of "things". Much of what we do everyday involves reenacting verbs on things. For example, trimming a piece of paper may be described as reenacting the verb "cut" on the piece of paper. Just as we reenact verbs on things, we o□en times reenact verbs on files. But for the average person, reenacting verbs on files tends to involve many more steps, and takes a much longer time to complete. Yes it's true that you get faster as you get better with the tools, but that's not all. So□ware tools are usually much more expensive than their physical counterparts. To be fair, so□ware tools typically do a lot more than one thing to justify their cost. But the real difference is not in the speed or the cost. It is in having the freedom of choice.

In the physical world, if we don't have a knife to cut with, we can choose to use our own bare hands. If our hands are tied up, we can even use our teeth. Nobody can deny us of this freedom of choice that physics affords us. Why should the digital world be any different?

Categories and Subject Descriptors H.5.1 [**Multimedia Information Systems**]: Artificial, augmented, and virtual realities H.5.2 [**User Interfaces**]: Ergonomics, Graphical User Interfaces, Input Devices, and Strategies, Interaction Styles, Standardization

General Terms Design, Experimentation, Human Factors, Standardization, Languages, Theory.

Keywords *physics, freedom, information, things, human-information-interaction, choice, operating system.*

Copyright is held by the author/owner(s).
Onward! 2010 October 17–21, 2010, Reno/Tahoe, Nevada, USA.
ACM 978-1-4503-0236-4/10/10.

Gource: Visualizing Software Version Control History

Andrew H. Caudwell

Catalyst IT Ltd, Wellington, New Zealand
acaudwell@gmail.com

Abstract

This film demonstrates a tool for visualizing the development history of software projects as an interactive animation, showing developers working on the hierarchical file-directory structure of a project over the course of its development.

Categories and Subject Descriptors H5.2 [*Information interfaces and presentation*]: Graphical user interfaces (GUI)

General Terms Design

Keywords Software visualization, Software development history, Force-directed

1. Film Description

Typically as software is developed, incremental changes to files are grouped together as 'commits' and stored in a Version Control System, maintaining a history of the files changed, by who, and when. In this film we introduce Gource, a tool to visualize this history, playing it back as an interactive animation.

Software development history is displayed by Gource as an animated tree with the root directory of the project at its centre. Directories appear as branches with files as leaves. Developers can be seen working on the tree at the times they contributed to the project.

Scenes produced by Gource are made up of a series of different elements:

- a dynamic tree of the active directories generated by a force-directed [1] tree layout algorithm.

- edges between directories are drawn as splines [2]. The mid point of each spline drags slightly behind the ends, emphasizing the direction of the motion and giving the tree an organic feel.

- files represented by spheres coloured by a hash of the file extension, are laid out in a spiral pattern around the center of the directory they belong to.

- users who are currently contributing to the project float in near proximity to the files they are modifying, sending out beams coloured to indicate the kind of change they are making (green: add, orange: modify, red: delete).

- labels appear above the active files, developers and directories as they appear or are modified, and fade out shortly after, telling the viewer the names of the objects of interest as their eyes are naturally drawn to changes.

- a camera dynamically positions itself to capture the scene. This operates in several different modes, highlighting a specific file or developer, the area of current development activity or an overview of the entire project.

The following projects are highlighted in this film:

- VLC Media Player: http://www.videolan.org/vlc/

- Moodle: http://www.moodle.org/

- Aptitude: http://algebraicthunk.net/~dburrows/projects/aptitude/

- Git: http://git-scm.com/

- The Linux Kernel: http://www.kernel.org/

- Papervision 3D: http://blog.papervision3d.org/

References

[1] P. Eades. *A heuristic for graph drawing*. Congressus Numerantium, 42:149-160, 1984.

[2] I. J. Schoenberg, *Contributions to the problem of approximation of equidistant data by analytic functions*, Quarterly of Applied Mathematics, 4:45-99, 112-141, 1946.

Copyright is held by the author/owner(s).

Onward! 2010, October 17–21, 2010, Reno/Tahoe, Nevada, USA.
ACM 978-1-4503-0236-4/10/10.

Pinocchio: A Virtual Symphony Orchestra Game

Video Presentation

Ruth Demmel

Technische Universitaet Muenchen
Department of Computer Science
Chair for Applied Software Engineering
demmel@in.tum.de

Abstract

The movie shows the evolution of a computer-based game for conducting a virtual orchestra system that enables users of any skill level to conduct a virtual symphony orchestra in real-time. One of the main goals was to enable children to experience classical music in a playful manner by combining an immersive gaming experience with educational aspects. The movie focuses on the exploration of alternative input devices, emphasizing the end users point of view - the conductor's view -, and it illustrates several audio and video processing aspects during the recording sessions with the musicians.

Categories and Subject Descriptors K.3.2 [**Computers and Education**]: Computer and Information Science Education - Computer science education.

General Terms   Human Factors

Keywords Serious Games, Evolutionary development

Description

The first version of the virtual symphony orchestra shown in the movie uses a baton with a colored tip as the input device was developed for an orchestra consisting of four musicians. The baton tracking was done with a standard web camera and the gestures were interpreted by a rule-based system. The orchestra was recorded in four separate audio and video sources. The latency of the system was too high to be acceptable by musicians acting as end users. The second version of the game was developed in 2006 using the eWatch [1] as a baton. The eWatch, developed at Carnegie Mellon University, is a wearable sensing, notification, and computing platform built into a wrist-watch. The eWatch featured two accelerometers and a bluetooth connection that transmitted sensor output to a single desktop computer for further processing. This version reduced the latency significantly and was much less resource consuming than the image processing in the vir-

tual baton tracking method, but the latency was still not acceptable by the musicians. The third part of the movie describes the final version of Pinocchio [2]. The goal of Pinocchio was "0-percent-latency", that is, the game gives the conductor the feeling of an immediate response of the digital orchestra when moving the baton. The input device was an iPod touch serving as the digital baton for conducting the orchestra and as a remote control device for changing properties of the game, such as selecting a specific orchestra configuration or switching between different background images. The audio and video material was created in a professional recording session with the members of the Bavarian Radio Symphony Orchestra. The system was successfully demonstrated to a wide audience ranging from children to music enthusiasts at an open-door event organized by the Bavarian Radio Symphony Orchestra in October 2009. The reaction of the users was very positive. Even children were quickly able to understand how the game works and how to conduct an orchestra.

References

[1] U. Maurer, A. Rowe, A. Smailagic, D.. Siewiorek, eWatch: A Wearable Sensor and Notification Platform, International Workshop on Wearable and Implantable Body Sensor Networks, 3-5 April 2006, Cambridge, Massachusetts, USA 2006

[2] B.Bruegge, C.Teschner, P.Lachenmaier,E.Fenzl, D.Schmidt, S.Bierbaum, Pinocchio: Conducting a virtual symphony orchestra, Proceedings of the international conference on advances in computer entertainment technology, Vol.203 of ACM International Conference Proceeding Series, ACM New York, NY, USA, pp.294 – 295, Salzburg, Austria, 2007.

Copyright is held by the author/owner(s).
Onward! 2010 October 17–21, 2010, Reno/Tahoe, Nevada, USA.
ACM 978-1-4503-0236-4/10/10.

SPLASH Practitioner Reports Chair's Welcome

The original OOPSLA Conference organizers were a practical bunch. They knew theory was important, of course, but they were especially interested in applying theory in the real world. As OOPSLA morphed into SPLASH, the SPLASH Conference organizers continued to share this interest, and so two of the words represented by "SPLASH" are "Systems" and "Applications". The Practitioner Reports are where the SPLASH community looks to hear about what's working (or not!) in leading-edge systems, applications, methodologies, frameworks, patterns, and management techniques. They are a key embodiment of the "reality check" that is an integral part of the SPLASH Conference.

SPLASH Practitioner Reports present actual experience and reflections, together with supporting evidence for any claims made. Of particular interest are reports that discuss both benefits and drawbacks of the approaches used. Reports may focus on a particular aspect of technology usage and practice, or describe broad project experiences. Some reports also focus on people, process, or development challenges.

This year the practitioner reports committee accepted 8 papers that cover a variety of topics related to agile development, large systems and modeling. First of all, I would like to thank the authors for taking this opportunity to share what they're doing, what is and isn't working, and why. I would like to thank my practitioner reports committee for their kind assistance throughout this past year, and for their hard work reviewing papers and providing suggestions for their improvements. I would also like to thank those of you who attended SPLASH and participated in the Practitioner Reports sessions. My hope is that these Proceedings will serve its readers well and that you find the papers interesting and thought-provoking.

Steve Marney
SPLASH 2010 Practitioner Reports Chair
HP Enterprise Services, USA
steve.marney@hp.com

Letters from the Edge of an Agile Transition

Christopher P. O'Connor

University of Michigan
Institute for Social Research
Ann Arbor, MI 48109
cpoconno@umich.edu

Abstract

Starting as a new coach of a team with almost no agile experience and an enormous release pending was quite daunting. Change was slow and at first it seemed like we would not succeed in converting the team and delivering the product. It took patience, support at many different levels of the organization, and hard work from many different people to put this team on the path to becoming a functional and productive agile team. Now the team is growing as a successful and productive agile team. I am proud to have been a part of going from mostly offshore waterfall development to a local agile development team; from one release in about a year and a half to an average of one release per week; from over a hundred open issues to dozens and falling.

Categories and Subject Descriptors D.2.9 [*Management*]: life cycle, cost estimation, time estimation, programming teams, productivity, software quality assurance (SQA)

General Terms Management

Keywords Agile development, agile teams, scrum, XP

1. First Baby Steps

I was brought on by Gale Cengage at the end of May of last year as a developer and coach. The organization was undergoing an agile transformation started by the newly hired CIO. A local consulting firm was brought in to assist with the transformation. I was the second developer and coach brought on directly by the company. I was placed with a team working on a new back end server platform for the company's online products. This platform provides search and retrieval services for educational databases serving the library and university markets, as well as expanding into government and direct consumer markets. The development group was around 40 people, around 30 of whom were developers. They were looking to add an additional 22 people and I was one of the first to be hired.

My first surprise upon starting work with the team was that the team had no idea what was going to happen or what I was there to do. When I arrived it had been just four days since the cube walls had come down. Most of the development team looked shell shocked. Not only were they busy fighting numerous fires in an attempt to get a release out the door, but now the latest new company initiative had descended upon them.

The release itself was over a year in the making and had already been postponed more than once. I arrived with the updated release date only two weeks away. As I began to assess the climate I recall in particular a series of questions I asked that illustrated some of the problems I would face. It started with "Is there a list of what still needs to be done?" "Well we're code complete..." Not quite the answer I was looking for. In an attempt to seek some clarity I rephrased the question. "So what else needs to be done to release to production?" Awkward silence. We were mere weeks from the release and no one person seemed to know what was left to do, yet as I looked around everyone was busy fighting fires.

This lead me to ask about some of the usual suspects: bugs, load testing, and deployment. I learned there was a list of bugs but there was ongoing discussion of which ones were "showstopper" bugs that would hold up the release. Few if any of the bugs had any information on how long they might take to resolve. I was told we wouldn't know until we looked into them. Fair enough, but surely we had an idea of the level of effort involved? "Yes." I moved on to the load tests, which were probably the brightest spot in this line of questioning. Tests were following a plan and ongoing. The catch here was the QA team was waiting for data to be loaded. Loading would take days and may need to be restarted if bugs were found in the loading and indexing process. Not exactly confidence inspiring. Finally I heard the war stories of deployment.

Permission to make digital or hard copies of all or part of this work for personal or classroom use is granted without fee provided that copies are not made or distributed for profit or commercial advantage and that copies bear this notice and the full citation on the first page. To copy otherwise, to republish, to post on servers or to redistribute to lists, requires prior specific permission and/or a fee.

SPLASH'10, October 17–21, 2010, Reno/Tahoe, Nevada, USA.
Copyright © 2010 ACM 978-1-4503-0240-1/10/10...$10.00

I found I didn't know where to begin. Here I had expected a team ready to start an agile transformation and what I found was a team on the verge of both success and failure: success in the sense that they were "done" with all of the requirements for the release and failure in that once again they were not tracking to deploy the new system by the time the business had agreed upon.

I immediately found the only thing I was sure of was the chances of the release happening in two weeks were slim to nil. The individual developers on the team were talented, but they were having trouble closing the existing issues without introducing new problems. They didn't have an automated regression suite so they were forced to do manual regression testing, which was both expensive and time consuming. This also had the effect of exacerbating the problem of bug prioritization. The risk of breaking something and having to restart days of data loading was daunting. If something went wrong during data loading, the risk of not making the release date and having to make additional compromises would skyrocket. Without a list of tasks and estimates it was very hard to figure out how the release was tracking. Many people were trying different ways of planning, but since they were not involving the team with the planning process it was not effective.

For example, another newcomer to the team at this time was originally supposed to lead the performance side of the team. He had a lot of management experience and was also shocked by the state of the team in regards to the release. He spent a week or more generating a reasonably complete list of what needed to be done. It was managed by him and done over email. It was better than before but still was geared more to informing upper management of the state of the release than to aiding the team. While he worked hard to get input from the team, the team was not involved in the process, so data could have been more accurate. It was not directly tied to what the developers were doing so while there was a relationship it was only a reflection of what was going on, a snapshot of what was not accomplished.

I was torn; I knew that many of the agile processes could help but it was also clear that this was not a team that was ready and waiting for a switch to agile. Initially I tried to introduce some basic agile practices I thought might help them get a handle on the release. Given the short time frame, scarce unit test coverage, legacy code base, and general resistance to change, it seemed prudent to focus on practices that were not development-specific. This was especially true since the developers were far more concerned at this point with the release than contemplating changing the way they approached their craft.

I embarked on trying to establish some story cards for the work that was currently being done and to get estimates on that work. The hope was that we would be able to get an idea of how we were tracking for the release even if we couldn't immediately put together a specific plan. Also this was relatively unobtrusive change. Developers could more or less continue working as they had been. The story cards would let the team know when a task was finished. The developers agreed to help out but after a short time it was obvious they weren't keeping up. Cards did not have the time the developer had spent on them marked. Most of the cards remained in the "On Deck" section of our story board. Most of the story cards had estimates greater than a day but were claimed to be "done" at a rate of two or three in a day. The obvious problem was estimation, which shouldn't have been a surprise at all. Asking people who haven't estimated before to estimate, especially when they were already under pressure, turned out to be somewhat of a disaster.

The more subtle problem which would only grow in importance over time was the definition of done. The business and development sides of the team were not on the same page as to what "done" was. It was defined as it is on many teams: done was when time was up and you had to release. I wanted to redefine done as a managed and discussed item that was determined before the task started.

While trying to get my head around this new problem of estimation I realized like many of the team's issues it was not one item that was the problem but a conglomerate. In this case many of the outstanding issues being worked on were bugs. Put this together with the weak test coverage mentioned earlier and it would have been hard even for more experienced agilists to have been very accurate with their estimates. Even estimates on more known quantities such as bugs with a known root cause varied greatly. This is due in part to the nature of work with bugs. The bugs had a tendency to go in fits and starts. Without the unit tests or an end to end regression suite, the risk of introducing new defects was high. This had the effect of pushing up estimates in order to account for time spent manually testing changes. Take these problems and add the more subtle issue of the definition of done and you have a very tough nut to crack.

Over the next weeks the pressure mounted and I found it harder and harder to engage the team in discussions of how to keep making small incremental improvements. Frustration set in. I talked with the team lead and the head of development letting them know I may need some support from them. Basically I needed some help getting the herd moving in the right direction. They were understanding but here I had another unpleasant surprise. They wanted to wait until after the release to start changing to agile. This was not a wise decision for the team. No matter how much pain the team went through I knew it would also reinforce bad habits to continue on the path that was already not working. There was a good chance that instead of thinking "wow do we ever need to change" they would think that they had made it through the worst and were still standing. My thought was if we could introduce some change and actually make their lives better along the way to the release we might be able to use this pain as a springboard for change.

Sadly, I was not able to implement agile changes as early as I thought would be most effective. The team lead tried to give me a hand but with his other responsibilities he was not able to give me enough support. Therefore I was forced to pick and choose my battles very carefully as I waited for the release when the team will be declared "agile." This was probably the lowest point in the transformation. The initial release illustrated many of the challenges ahead. The release did not go out the door for another two months - not weeks.

2. Sparks but No Fire

As we transitioned from dealing with the release to adding new features and enhancements to the product our problem set also changed. Now that people had a moment to reflect they began to question how this new agile process was helping them. What they did not realize was how many more changes the team had to make before they were truly agile. Here we had just started planting the seeds of change and already people on the team were wondering where the crops were. Previous teams I had worked with were more eager for change and therefore were more likely to be excited with the progress they had made instead of wondering why larger rewards had not appeared. The decision to become agile came from management, not from internal team decisions, and the team was not convinced it would benefit them.

As I considered where to begin, I gained my first ally. Another coach was floating from team to team trying to provide support for the transformation. The two of us had many conversations about the problems the team was having and came up with two leading problems to tackle. One: we just did not have enough people with agile experience to lead by example and/or mentor the non-agile developers. The teams consists of around eight rotating contractors, two full time employees in addition to myself, and another couple of newly hired developers. Out of a team of 13, three had agile experience: me with over ten years, one with a couple years, and one with less than two.

The second conclusion we drew was that the team needed a win that would be able to aid the team as it moved forward. This led us to start a project to introduce acceptance and regression testing via FitNesse. This proved to be a challenge as neither of us had the domain knowledge required and we were met with resistance when we attempted to draw in developers. Did I mention the team moved directly from release firefighting to patch purgatory?

Eventually we were able to allocate enough developer time to get the first regression test done. It wasn't much but showed that not only could it be done with agile methods, but that the results were immediately useful.

Given how averse the team was to change, I realized I was fighting an uphill battle to switch the team to agile alone. I had generated some sparks but they were not enough to start the fire. The technical lead of the team was excited about switching to agile; he had experienced enough pain trying to work the old way and saw the potential benefits of a fully agile team. The problem was he wasn't available most of the time. As much as he wanted to change, he also wanted to keep the team moving. Looking back we should have figured out how to support him better and get some items off his plate since he was already an ally in the conversion. The project manager was ready for the change but was also so overloaded that she was constantly fighting to stay afloat. Even though she saw the benefit of switching she had little time to spare to help make it happen. In hindsight she was another ally if she had had more free time. She could have greatly assisted us to help break down/translate requirements into stories.

Both of these examples reinforced a concept that I knew but had not appreciated. People who are already behind or overloaded have great difficulty changing their behavior even if the result would be less work. As a coach you have to find them some time. This meant picking up work from them at times or figuring out a way to head off some of their work upstream. In my case I groomed the board, making sure the PM only had to take the cards I gathered week to week and enter them in a series of spreadsheets and our agile planning tool to generate reports. Unfortunately due to trouble with the company's choice of agile tool even this was too time consuming. Tool problems aside it was difficult to find ways to help these team members without getting drawn too far into their problems. Just taking over some of their work was not going to keep the team moving forward, but it did help.

Basically between budget and the amount of work that was scheduled for the team the team needed to more than double its size. This meant adding six to ten people. Previously these resources had existed in the form of offshore contractors. Now the team was looking to hire local developers with agile experience. This proved challenging. Agile has become quite the buzz word and lots of people claim agile experience. We needed more than just people who had done a little agile; we wanted a good community.

At first the development organization as a whole, not just our team, was able to recruit a number of people through our friends and family network. After that ceased to provide new people the organization starting relying on recruiters. The quality of candidates dropped sharply and the lack of resources started to put projects at risk. Our team was somewhat insulated given that we had just released (even though we still had plenty of work to do), but other teams with dependencies on us were ramping up for releases in the near term that would increase the pressure on us.

3. The Crucible of Growing Pains

One of the problems with integrating new developers was transferring knowledge of the products from the four team members who had been the primary developers on site for the last two to three years. These four developers were essentially giant silos of knowledge, and at first the rest of the team did not know enough to be able to break down tasks. Each of the four knew different areas of the code, so while there was some overlap in their knowledge their specialization was a serious hurdle. Often, we would go to estimate stories and find ourselves bogged down in discussion of the code and trying to figure out why story after story were receiving really high estimates. The overlapping problems of the team were killing us. The four experts knew what needed to be done but were having a lot of trouble translating from their mental task list to estimating the time it would take to complete the story. Our business analysts were running into the same issue one level up. They were not used to providing feature requirements in story form, much less breaking down these "feature" level stories into stories that could be reasonably estimated by the development team. I realized almost immediately the stories were too big, but you can't force immediate understanding. Like any skill, estimating takes practice. We went through many agonizing estimation and story breakdown sessions before we started to get some traction. As we began to build up some historical data this closed the feedback loop. The team was able to see that we were frequently underestimating and that this was directly connected to the trouble we were still having with story breakdown.

The large amount of time we were taking to break down the stories was causing another problem. We had only a few developers who were knowledgeable enough to work with the business analyst to break down the story, and we needed them to do the actual work. To make matters worse this fed the the four domain experts' belief that they just needed to sit down and work through the problem as they coded it the way the had always done it. This attitude that was unfortunately reinforced by the company as they pushed for a follow up release.

It was a very frustrating time. The team was still in the process of learning how to break down stories. The original developers often felt that two of them needed to pair in order to work on particular problems, and this reinforced the trouble we were having integrating the new people. If we had had appropriately sized stories we could have more easily divided up the features and had the experts pairing with the new people. Eventually we did get to this point but along the way we had many instances where the new folks, including myself, ended up trudging along on our own and wasting time with issues that could easily been cleared up by the more experienced developers. When we began to get the stories closer to the right size from the business analysts

it eased the tension between preparing the work to be done and actually doing the work.

In the end we had to convince the business that pairing in the new team members and breaking up the pair of original developers was necessary. By taking some time now to pair in the new team members we would perform better in the long run, even if it would slow us down in the short term. I can't say there was any one thing that convinced the four original developers to start pairing more and helping to transfer the knowledge. I think it was a combination of things. One was simply getting to know the new people better and building team bonding and chemistry. Another was the hard work of the new people, especially one of our team who went on to take a leading role in the implementation of a complex feature. Lastly I'd like to think I had some influence as I reinforced what they already knew but just hadn't accepted; that in order to achieve the benefits of agile we had talked about they needed to change. If the team was to meet the challenges the business was issuing, change was a must.

We continued to have problems with estimation. The combination of the lack of experience, vague task definition, and low team buy in continued to drag us down. Lots of cards were started; few were finished. We started finishing cards, but found that estimates of hours often took weeks. Stories would spawn additional stories in order to reach completion. For example, a story that started with a two day estimate would generate a week's worth of stories (sometimes even more than a week!). Many agile developers would say "Great! That's part of agile." Gaining clarity on a story and understanding that there is more to it is part of the process. Unfortunately this was happening far too often. We needed to translate business requirements into stories and break down these stories into tasks the team could more accurately estimate.

4. Are We Agile Yet?

Despite some agreement from the business that we needed to invest time to change the team, they continued to be concerned about the timeline for the follow on bug fix release. They thought that because we were agile now they would get frequent releases, not understanding that the transition was far from complete. Here was where we got into more tension between keeping development moving and converting the team to be agile. It's one thing to declare agility; it's quite another to be a fully functioning agile team. I would argue many teams never make it and other people would argue that perhaps not every team needs to. That is a topic in and of itself. In our case one thing we were striving for was frequent and meaningful releases. Unfortunately at this point we weren't really ready for either. The legacy code base was making it difficult to turn around features in a weekly time frame. Even if we did, we did not have the infrastructure in place to accomplish a weekly deployment. A week was a difficult to impossible timeline. The developers manually put a new release out on the preproduction environment, and the QA team ran their manual regression testing. Our team was faced with a choice: spend time improving our team or spend time on the release.

Our next battles revolved around planning, estimation, and definition of done. We were just barely managing to put together enough stories with enough clarity actually to plan an iteration. We continued slowly to improve on the estimation front but were really held back by stories that were too big. This was a double edged sword: since our estimation skills still needed development it was harder to discover just how big some of the stories were. Couple that with poor story definition and we spent an inordinate amount of time in estimation for a number of weeks as we fixed these issues. On the story definition side, we carved out some time ahead of planning sessions to vet stories with domain experts. We tried to break down cards as much as possible before estimation. On the estimation side we finally started getting actuals that more or less correlate to amount of work spent on the card. This allowed a synergy to form that got us away from the epic planning and estimation sessions.

We needed to cross train but the business still wanted the best people working on the task. The new team members were not getting enough exposure and the code was complex enough that without a lot of exposure it was difficult for the new people to contribute. At this point one tactic we employed was to start pairing the new hires with the domain experts in the different areas of code. While at first it was slow going and met some resistance, the new people managed slowly to gain knowledge and were more able to help. Some of the pain of only a few developers having all the knowledge started to diminish, but it was not the last we would see of it.

Four months after the start of the transition the entire development team across all projects participated in a multiday training event. It was intended to help build consensus, understanding, and acceptance of agile practices outside the day to day environment.

On the first day we paired the developers up and worked through an exercise on testing comparing two code bases that did exactly the same thing: one written by an individual with no tests in a very procedural, non-object oriented fashion; the second test driven with objects. We asked the developer pairs to add a feature to both, adding tests to prove the new feature worked. All but one of the pairs failed to add the feature to the untested code, all pairs succeed in adding both the test and the feature to the second test driven code. This exercise opened some eyes, but the group as a whole was far from convinced. Could these same results be replicated in their day to day lives with a much larger legacy code base?

On the second day we ran a simulated project complete with product owners and iterations. Each iteration was roughly an

hour and began with an abbreviated planning game, followed by coding. The development group was divided into four teams of six to eight developers and each had a product owner in the form of a agile coach or senior agile developer. This went much better than planned: most teams got through all the cards to build "the game of life" and one even got through the extra wishlist items, fulfilling a suite of unit and functional tests along the way. They saw the value in having a suite of acceptance level tests that let them know when they were done.

After the training there was a definite upturn in the team's opinion of agile. It was a local maximum in terms of the transition but it was not the turning point. The main trouble remaining was getting the team members who were least experienced from an agile perspective the support they needed to reinforce the process. They were willing to test but often saw it as still taking too much time if they could not easily envision a way to test a particular section of code.

They were beginning to get on board with creating acceptance tests to help define what a task's goal was and serve as regression down the road, but only with people helping craft these tests. This fell to the more experienced agile team members. There were almost enough of us, but we were often still short on resources when it came to balancing between mentoring team members and trying to improve tools and processes to foster a more agile development environment.

5. The Turning Point

One critical element to converting a team to agile is gathering enough momentum to change. Two ways to achieve this are having a majority of team members who are motivated to change from the beginning or hiring experienced agilists until they have enough influence and leverage to convert the team. A top down decision without internal team support is unlikely to be successful. In the end, we added three more developers to the team, all with some amount of agile experience. This brought us close to equality based on agile experience. The new folks provided much needed resources and an opportunity to cross train the new members of the team, introducing more consistent pairing to the team.

The best part of the new team members was they were expecting an agile team so they adhered to the practices and actively supported them within the team. This support was key on many levels. They sought to pair because they didn't know the domain and needed the assistance of the domain experts, so they sought them out. When something was not right they were willing to say so. Devoid of preconceptions, they were willing to try things the other developers would not have. They immediately picked up the acceptance and regression testing torch as they went about learning the domain and system. They helped build out the continuous integration server and other agile support mechanisms for the team that had been suffering from lack of resources.

This was a big turning point for the team. New blood and better balance allowed us to provide some social pressure to do more testing, pairing, and evolving as a team. Suddenly I was not the only one advocating for items to improve our development practices. The team started taking the first steps towards policing itself.

The addition of another senior agile developer was the last piece of the puzzle. He tipped the scales so that the experienced agilists comprised more than half the team. After this, I transitioned to one of the other teams feeling confident that while this team still had many challenges ahead they were well on their way to being agile and no team member would go back to the way things used to be.

Acknowledgments

Thanks to Patrick Wilson-Welsh, the Ocean and EI Teams, and all my colleagues at Gale. My time at Gale was a tremendous adventure and learning experience.

Object-oriented Software Considerations in Airborne Systems and Equipment Certification

Michael R. Elliott

The Boeing Company
2401 E. Wardlow Rd. MS 6052-0066
Long Beach, CA 90807, USA
+1 562 645-3355
Michael.R.Elliott2@boeing.com

Peter Heller

Airbus Operations GmbH
Kreetslag 10,
21129 Hamburg, Germany
+49 40 743 73098
Peter.Heller@airbus.com

Abstract

This is a practitioner's discussion of the production of software in airborne systems which operate in civil airspace and the changes impacting it with the introduction of DO-178C/ED-12C, the emerging standard for the development of safety-critical software in airborne systems. A focus is made on the impact of the object-oriented supplement to this document which establishes, for the first time, a standard for the use of object-oriented programming and design in this environment.

Discussion is made of the state of airworthiness certification where software is concerned, the existing standard DO-178B/ED-12B[1], its history, perceived shortcomings, existing practice and how that may change with the new standard. Additionally, an overview is given of how this supplement introduces a formal type theory basis for reducing the amount of verification an applicant for airworthiness must demonstrate in order to provide the necessary safety assurance for an airborne system.

Categories and Subject Descriptors D.1.5 [*Airborne Software*]

General Terms Airborne Software Certification, Safety-critical Software, Object-oriented programming

Keywords DO-178B, DO-178C, Safety-critical, airworthiness, DO-178, ED-12B, ED-12C

1. Introduction

The formal standard *Software Considerations in Airborne Systems and Equipment Certification*[1], known in the industry as DO-178B/ED-12B[1], is used as the means by which government certification authorities such as the FAA[1] and EASA[2] determine that aircraft and engines containing software as part of their operational capability can be granted the necessary airworthiness certification needed for operation in civil airspace. As such it is required reading by thousands of engineers worldwide who produce software for aircraft and the engines which go into those aircraft. It specifies the means by which such software is produced and verified so that airworthiness certification can be granted.

DO-178B/ED-12B[1] was produced by a group of industry practitioners whose goal was to be unknown and invisible; that is, it was fervently hoped that the flying public would go about their business – flying wherever they needed to go, whenever they wished to go there – without the slightest thought as to how safe the software on their airplane was or who had been involved in making it so. Those of us who are creating the new version of the standard strive to maintain that same goal of invisibility.

This most recent effort was completed in 1992 and therefore fails to reflect the great body of advancement in Software Engineering practice which has taken place since the mid 1980's. In late 2004 an effort was begun to produce its successor document, to be known as DO-178C/ED-12C. Special Committee 205 (SC-205) of the RTCA[3] and Working Group 71 (WG-71) of EUROCAE[4] were formed to address the perceived shortcomings of the existing standard from a viewpoint more attuned to modern software practice.

Permission to make digital or hard copies of all or part of this work for personal or classroom use is granted without fee provided that copies are not made or distributed for profit or commercial advantage and that copies bear this notice and the full citation on the first page. To copy otherwise, to republish, to post on servers or to redistribute to lists, requires prior specific permission and/or a fee.

SPLASH'10, October 17–21, 2010, Reno/Tahoe, Nevada, USA.
Copyright © 2010 ACM 978-1-4503-0240-1/10/10...$10.00

---

[1] Federal Aviation Administration (Washington, DC, USA), http://www.faa.gov

[2] European Aviation Safety Agency (Cologne, Germany) http:// www.easa.europa.eu

[3] RTCA, Inc. (Washington, DC, USA) is an organization which creates standards documents for the FAA http://www.rtca.org

[4] The European Organization for Civil Aviation Equipment (Malakoff, France) is an organization which produces documents referred to as a means of compliance for European Technical Standard Orders http://www.eurocae.net

1.1 Object-oriented Technology

The importance of object-oriented technology was recognized as a key element to be addressed and one of the three subgroups formed to address software development practice was Subgroup 5 – Object-oriented and Related Technologies.

> *To date, few airborne computer systems in civil aviation have been implemented using OOT. Although OOT is intended to promote productivity, increase reusability of software, and improve quality, uncertainty about how to comply with certification requirements has been a key obstacle to using OOT in airborne systems.*
>
> *OOTiA[2], 2004*

The mission of this subgroup was to address the needs of the software practitioner in creating object-oriented software for airborne systems, a practice widely seen in the community as being prohibitively difficult under the existing standard. To this end, changes were made to the core document of DO-178B/ED-12B[1] to help facilitate this effort and a supplement to the emerging DO-178C/ED-12C was produced providing additional (and sometimes alternative) objectives, guidance and recommendations to aid the practitioner in the production of airborne software and the certification authorities in approving it as part of a certification effort.

1.2 Object-oriented Technology Supplement

This supplement, as IP[5] 500, was formally approved at the SC-205/WG-71 plenary session in Paris, France on October 29, 2009. It is singularly appropriate that the day the last ever OOPSLA ended – the day that object-oriented programming was considered so mainstream that it was no longer worthy of a special conference – is the day that marked the first formal acceptance of the use of object-oriented programming in the international standards for safety-critical airborne software.

2. Background

Initially, software was viewed as being a way of inexpensively extending the versatility of analog avionics. However, software in the system did not fit easily into the safety and reliability analysis based on mean time between failure and other service history based techniques.

2.1 DO-178

Created to provide a basis for communication between applicants and certification authorities, this initial effort at a standard for software development in airborne systems was a set of best practices. It required applicants to meet "the intent" of DO-178 without giving specific objectives to be achieved or any significant degree of guidance as to how to meet the intent of the document. It did, however, introduce a three tiered system of software criticality – critical, essential and non-essential – and set the level of verification to reflect the criticality level. Additionally, it provided a linkage between software verification and FAA documents such as Federal Aviation Regulations and Technical Standard Orders.

2.2 DO-178A

After the initial experience with certification using DO-178, there was a consensus that a revision was needed. SC-152 of RTCA created DO-178A in 1985, and it turned out to be quite different from DO-178. It introduced rigorous requirements on software process (based on the waterfall method), software production and quite stringent requirements to provide process documentation and history. Certification artifacts were, however, frequently misinterpreted by applicants and certification authorities sometimes causing entire software development efforts to be abandoned. In general, the knowledge of why the certification requirements existed and the purpose of the requirements failed to be understood or appreciated[3].

2.3 DO-178B

The avionics industry became more and more software oriented during the time DO-178A was in use. Many new companies entered the field, producing equipment subject to certification efforts. Lack of experience, documentation and understanding of the basis for satisfying DO-178A brought about a desire for an improved standard. In 1992 this became DO-178B[1], developed in cooperation with EUROCAE as ED-12B[1] by SC-167 and WG-12.

This updated document made many fundmental changes to its predecessor. Salient among these was the introduction of software criticality levels A through E replacing the critcal, essential and non-essential previously used. A strong emphasis was placed on requirements-based testing, which was seen as a more effective way of verification than traditional white-box testing. It also required that these tests and their related artifacts be made available to certification authorities for use as part of their approval process.

2.4 OOTiA

During the eight years after the release of DO-178B/ED-12B[1] and its adoption by industry, concern was expressed that more modern software practices were difficult to employ using that standard. In 2000, the FAA responded to this concern by contacting the representatives of several key companies, Boeing, BF Goodrich and others, to produce an analysis of what it would take to adapt object oriented software procedures to the needs of airworthiness certification.

This process was later opened up to industry in general and workshops were held in order to produce position papers which, it was hoped, would evolve into a best practices

---

[5] Information paper

guide, an FAA Advisory Circular or rolled into the not yet begun DO-178C effort. Meetings were held by the FAA and NASA[6] which eventually resulted in the FAA publishing the four volume *Handbook for Object-Oriented Technology in Aviation (OOTiA)*[2]. This document was never intended to contain objectives or guidance for practitioners and certification authorities, only to contain a set of suggestions as to best practices and warnings about problematic situations.

By 2005, the FAA had decided that it would no longer maintain sponsorship of OOTiA[2] or facilitate any updates or corrections to it. SC-205 of the RTCA was under consideration as a means to upgrade DO-178B[1] and it was considered best to turn OOTiA[2] over to the nascent SC-205 to use as input to the creation of an object oriented supplement to the new standard.

2.5 Rationale

The views of a number of stakeholders, including certification authorities, airframe manufacturers and equipment suppliers, were taken into account in the creation of DO-178B/-ED-12B[1]. A basic tenet of this document was that it be written as much as possible to be requirements oriented; that is, to try to make the document about what has to be achieved rather than how to go about achieving it. A fundamental rationale for this was to try to minimize the impact of technological evolution, as long diatribes such as the best use of blank COMMON blocks in FORTRAN were considered inappropriate in the long term. This brought about the philosophy of creating the document in terms of objectives, guidance and guidelines, to be utilized by the applicant in creating airborne software and the certification authorities in judging its suitability in an airworthiness determination.

A large part of the document is concerned with how software is produced, how source and object code is traced to requirements, how the requirements trace to source and object code, and how the software is tested and shown to have been adequately tested.

2.6 Software certification

There is a perception among those entering this field, or wishing to enter this field, that software is somehow "certifiable" for airworthiness. This may come about through simple observation of the title of DO-178B/ED-12B[1] *Software Considerations in Airborne Systems and Equipment Certification*. However, software is not actually "certifiable". Entities for which airworthiness certification can be granted are aircraft, engines, propellers and, in the UK, auxiliary power units. This means that the effort expended on achieving the "certifiability" of software is in actual practice expended on ensuring the certifiability of the aircraft, engine, etc., that is the subject of the airworthiness certification effort – not that of the actual software involved.

As a result of this, it is not possible to, for example, produce a "certified" version of a real-time executive, or garbage collector, regardless of any statements in the marketing material of a particular vendor. What that vendor may well do, and typically charge a substantial fee for, is to provide the requirements, source traceability, requirements-based tests and test results for a particular software component. This documentation can then be submitted to the certification authority as part of the applicant's request for airworthiness certification of an engine, aircraft, etc.

2.7 Software production process

DO-178B/ED-12B[1] is widely perceived as being process heavy; that is, that it imposes a substantial burden on the applicant to show that a particular process has been followed in the production of and verification of the airborne software which is to be considered as part of the certification effort. Although this has been widely seen as a very expensive activity, almost twenty years of airborne operations have not revealed any major safety flaws. Contrast this with, for example, the maiden flight of the Ariane 5 (Flight 501, June 4, 1996) which was destroyed 37 seconds after launch due to a software coding flaw – the failure to handle an exception raised during the initial boost phase. The Ariane 5 was never subjected to a formal airworthiness certification effort as its flights through civil airspace fall under a different authority – but it serves to illustrate that spectacular disaster certainly can come about through software coding errors.

Nonetheless, it is still widely seen in the airborne software industry that DO-178B/ED-12B[1] makes using less process-heavy techniques such as model based development, formal methods and object-oriented programming difficult to use when certification aspects are considered. The attitude is often one of *"We already know how to create certifiable software the old-fashioned way, why should we change now?"*. There is, therefore, a substantial perceived risk to adopting more modern techniques regardless of the promised reduction in cost, errors and time to market.

3. Rationale for change

The answer to the question given above is that the cost of doing things the old fashioned way is becoming prohibitive. It now costs hundreds of millions of dollars to achieve airworthiness certification for a new large aircraft. That makes even small increases in efficiency lead to a competitive edge for airframe manufacturers and their equipment suppliers who are able to be more efficient in their software production. Object-oriented programming is one means by which substantial increases in efficiency can be achieved – if only it can be used in an approved airworthiness certification effort.

Additionally, the software world has changed. Back in the 1980's, almost all airborne software was written from scratch to run on a single processor. This was a big problem for "commercial off the shelf" (COTS) software as it was

---

[6] National Aeronautics and Space Administration (Washington, DC, USA), http://www.nasa.gov

almost certainly not developed in an airborne software environment and therefore didn't have all the traceability and requirements based test artifacts needed for an eventual certification effort. This, obviously, has an impact on cost.

As far as safety is concerned, there's a real benefit to be realized in investing substantial resources in getting certain things done right in a project independent manner. Consider the wisdom of using a memory management sysem written by a specialist in real-time garbage collectors and used by thousands of developers in place of a pooled memory system written by a specialist in terrain avoidance and used by fifteen developers.

In the 1980's, the desire was to use testing to achieve safety goals. In particular an objective is *"to demonstrate with a high degree of confidence that errors which could lead to unacceptable failure conditions, as determined by the safety assessment process, have been removed"*[1]. The realization that this objective is, by and large, unobtainable in modern software systems has gained substantial consensus. It is widely felt that this view does not scale to the complex systems of current airborne software, let alone future systems, due to both hardware and software complexity; that is, that exhaustive testing of software will not reach the desired conclusion that all necessary errors *"have been removed"*. This, in turn, has brought about a refocusing of the testing effort towards more realistic goals of reaching a reasonable level of confidence that the software is correct, safe and useful rather than that it is completely error free.

3.1 Terms of Reference

This thought process culminated in a desire to:

- Modify DO-178B/ED-12B[1] to become DO-178C/ED-12C with a minimum of changes to the core document.

- Consider the economic impact relative to system certification without compromising system safety.

- Address clear errors and inconsistencies in DO-18B/ED-12B[1].

- Provide recommendations (guidelines) that provide example solutions to expected problems to aid both practitioners and certification authorities in achieving the objectives.

- Provide supplements to amplify and expand objectives, guidance and guidelines for technology specific or methodology specific areas of interest.

Additionally, the desire to change the existing document was reinforced by the observation that the difference between the terms *guidelines* and *guidance* is not only not readily understood in English but apparently they don't translate at all into French[7] as different words. *Guidelines* then became *recommendations*.

4. What's new?

Subgroup 5 – Object-oriented and Related Technologies – took on the challenge of addressing, to a large extent, all coding issues. While issues such as dead and deactivated code, inlining, ad-hoc and parametric polymorphism are not particularly object-oriented, subgroup 5 addressed those issues along with more obviously OO topics such as inheritance, class hierarchy consistency and run-time polymorphism.

The overall aim was to provide clarification of objectives from an OO viewpoint, provide any new objectives which were deemed beneficial to airborne safety and to provide guidance and recommendations as to how to achieve those objectives.

4.1 OOTiA, CAST, FAA and EASA

One of the initial responsibilities of the subgroup was to address all issues raised in OOTiA[2] and either incorporate them into the supplement or decide they were either inapplicable or unfounded. IP 508 was produced by the subgroup to address each individual concern raised by OOTiA[2] and respond to that concern. Additionally, concerns about OO had been raised through CAST[8] papers, EASA CRIs[9] and FAA IPs. All these were also to be addressed by the subgroup.

4.2 Dead and deactivated code

DO-178B/ED-12B[1] disallows dead code, which is basically code which is never executed. Dead code is treated as a software error which should be eliminated. A variant on this is deactivated code which is code which might get executed for a particular configuration but for which that configuration is not the one used in flight. An example of this might be a software controlled radio which includes code to control a military hardware encryption/decryption device but which would not be selected for a purely civilian application. This is already addressed by DO-178B/ED-12B[1]. However, when reusing software components, especially externally developed software components such as class libraries, this comes into play as the abstraction for a component may include more behavior than is actually exercised by the airborne software.

Consider a stack class which is used as a previously developed component and which contains methods for *push*, *peek* and *pop*. All of these methods fit the abstraction for how a stack should work and are not at all out of place in a stack class. The particular airborne software using such a stack, however, might not actually use the *peek* method, for example. The previous standard would have forced the practitioners to actually remove the code for the *peek* method before certification as it would be considered dead code. The new

---

[7] ED-12B, the EUROCAE-produced version of the document, contains both English and French language versions

[8] Certification Authority Software Team, a group of individuals representing several certification authorities, including EASA, FAA, JAA and Transport Canada

[9] Certification Review Item

standard relaxes restrictions on separately developed components and now allows this stack class to be used unmodified.

4.3 Type Theory

Early on, the subgroup decided to provide a type theoretical basis as a rationale for reducing the amount of redundant testing / verification that involved base classes and their derived subclasses. A great deal of this testing and verification can be shown to be redundant and therefore unnecessary through type theoretical arguments which involve class hierarchy design, as long as the type hierarchies in question share particular properties. There is a notable absence of type theory – or, for that matter, any sort of formal computer science – as a basis for decision making in DO-178B/ED-12B[1], so this was perceived by subgroup members as being at some risk of being rejected by the subcommittee as a whole but, in the end, it was accepted.

4.4 The Liskov Substitution Principle

This sort of type theoretical formulation initially manifested itself in the specification of the Liskov Substitution Principle[4] (LSP) as the basis for establishing that verification of the behavior of a superclass could be used as part of the verification compliance of a subclass of that superclass. The point was that only the additional behavior provided by the subclass needed to be verified for the subclass if that subclass conformed to LSP.

Consider the formulation LSP which appears in the supplement:

Let $q(x)$ be a property provable about objects x of type T.

Then $q(y)$ should be true for objects y of type S where S is a subtype of T.

Regardless of the succintness of this, the subgroup felt that a purely theoretical expression of this concept might place too great of a burden on the practitioners.

4.4.1 Explaining LSP

As the supplement neared completion, the feeling was expressed by members of the subgroup that we needed to provide a clearer understanding of LSP than simply providing the definition given above. The inclusion of a Frequently Asked Questions (FAQ) section in the supplement provided a less structured environment into which we could place a question (along with its answer) which we presume will be frequently asked, essentially: *What's the deal with the Liskov Substitution Principle and why should I care?*.

We could have reiterated the concept and continued to claim that it was a good thing – which is true – but probably doesn't get the point across. Based on the idea that seeing a car crash is more conducive to reminding drivers why safety is important than listening to safety lectures, we proposed showing how not following LSP could lead to problematic

behavior. DO-178C/ED-12C is, fundamentally, a document about software safety, after all, so this approach was seen as reasonable.

4.4.2 Creating a counter example

For purposes of the supplement's FAQ, the following situation was proposed: There exists a conceptually abstract hardware speed controller which can be instantiated with the necessary behavior to reflect the actual hardware of multiple different manufacturers. This provides the necessary basis for creating a base class so that concrete subclasses could be created for each manufacturer's particular version – with whatever device-specific low-level hardware interface was necessary. Additionally, it was felt that this example was something that practitioners would see as at least vaguely similar to the sort of software they were developing – software to control a pump for a fuel control system, maybe. A stretch, perhaps, but not an outrageous one.

4.4.3 Preconditions, post conditions and invariants

The argument is made that a number of different manufacturer's speed controllers would be substitutable for the base class as long as they correctly implemented the adjust speed method to communicate the desired increase in speed to the hardware through whatever hardware-specific means necessary.

A class invariant for the speed controller is that an instance's speed attribute is the magnitude of the velocity and therefore can never be less than zero. The base class makes available a means to adjust the speed by giving a speed increment to an adjust speed method (to use the Java terminology). This adjust speed method would have as its post condition that when given a positive, non-zero argument, the speed attribute of the object has increased; that is, it must be non-zero.

4.4.4 Time to divide by zero

Based on this post condition and invariant, a method *time to go*, taking a distance argument, will return the time value (in whatever units are convenient) it takes to traverse that distance. This ultimately reduces to dividing the given distance by the object's current speed attribute then changing to whatever units are convenient.

The situation as outlined above represents a valid use of LSP. Any desired number of subclasses of the speed controller can be created, each of which tailors its behavior to what is required by the underlying hardware. In order to demonstrate the failure of LSP, we introduced an *auto controller*, a subclass of speed controller designed to control a fundamentally different type of hardware, one which is given a desired speed which it will then seek to reach and maintain.

Listing 1. Violation of LSP – Java

```java
1  // ////////////////////////////////////////////////////////////
   // Base class which implements a speed controller
3  class SpeedController {

5      public int getSpeed() {
           return speed;
7      }

9      public void adjustSpeed( int increment ) {
           speed += increment;
11         //code which tells controller hardware the speed increment
           //post condition: speed augmented by 'increment'
13     }

15     // Return the time to traverse the given distance at the current speed
       public int timeToGo( int distance ) {
17         // here we expect that getSpeed() returns non zero value
           return distance / getSpeed();
19     }
       protected int speed = 0;
21 }
   // ////////////////////////////////////////////////////////////
23 // Subclass of Controller which violates LSP.
   // It uses setDesiredSpeed() rather than adjustSpeed() to change the speed.
25 // The now LSP-broken adjustSpeed() does nothing, ignoring its post condition.
   class AutomaticSpeedController extends SpeedController {
27
       public void setDesiredSpeed( int val ) {
29         desiredSpeed = val;
           // Code which tells hardware what the desired speed is
31     }

33     @Override
       public void adjustSpeed( int increment ) {
35         //do nothing
           //post condition: speed doesn't change
37     }
       private int desiredSpeed = 0;
39 }
   // ////////////////////////////////////////////////////////////
41 public class Main {
       public static void main( String[] args ) {
43         final SpeedController controller =
               //   new SpeedController(); // This substitution would have been fine.
45                 new AutomaticSpeedController();  // This substitution violates LSP
           // Taking the traditional view, the speed is incremented by 2 units
47         controller.adjustSpeed( 2 );
           // Expected post condition: speed is non-zero – since we just changed it
49         System.out.println( "Time to go: " + controller.timeToGo( 5 ) );
           // Exception thrown only for instance of AutomaticSpeedController
51     }
   }
```

Listing 2. Violation of LSP – C++[10]

```
   #include <stdio.h>
2  ////////////////////////////////////////////////////////////////
   class Controller {
4  public:
       int Speed() {
6          return speed;
           }
8      virtual void adjustSpeed( int increment ) {
           if (speed + increment > 0)
10             speed += increment;
           }
12     //post condition: speed augmented by 'increment'
       Controller() {
14         speed = 0;
           }
16 private:
       int speed;
18 };
   ////////////////////////////////////////////////////////////////
20 //routine relying on adjustSpeed post condition
   int computeTimeToGo(Controller* controller, int distance) {
22     controller->adjustSpeed( 3 );
       // here we expect that controller.Speed() is non-zero
24     return distance / controller->Speed();
   }
26 ////////////////////////////////////////////////////////////////
   //derived class violating LSP on adjustSpeed
28 class AutoController : public Controller {
   public:
30     int DesiredSpeed();

32     void setDesiredSpeed( int val);

34     virtual void adjustSpeed( int increment ) {} //does nothing
       //post condition: speed doesn't change
36
       AutoController() {
38         desiredSpeed = 1;
       }
40 private:
       int desiredSpeed;
42 };
   ////////////////////////////////////////////////////////////////
44 int main(int argc, char** argv) {
       Controller* controller = new AutoController();
46     int time = computeTimeToGo(controller, 5);
       printf( "Time:_%d\n", time );
48     return 0;
   }
```

---

[10] Contributed by Rob Morris and Thomas Bleichner

Listing 3. Violation of LSP – Ada (1 of 2)[11]

```
1  ─────────────────────────────────────────────────────────
   ── Basic speed controller definition
3  package Speed1 is
       subtype Speed_Type  is Integer range 0 .. 200;
5      subtype Speed_Delta is Integer range −5 .. +5;

7      type Controller is tagged private;
       function Speed (This : Controller) return Speed_Type;
9      procedure Adjust_Speed (This : in out Controller; Increment : Speed_Delta);
       pragma Postcondition (This.Speed = This'Old.Speed + Increment);
11 private
       type Controller is tagged record
13         Actual_Speed : Speed_Type := 0;
       end record;
15 end Speed1;

   ─────────────────────────────────────────────────────────
17 package body Speed1 is
       function Speed (This : Controller) return Speed_Type is
19     begin
           return This.Actual_Speed;
21     end Speed;

23     procedure Adjust_Speed
          (This : in out Controller; Increment : Speed_Delta) is
25     begin
           This.Actual_Speed := This.Actual_Speed + Increment;
27     end Adjust_Speed;
   end Speed1;
29 ─────────────────────────────────────────────────────────
   ── routine relying on adjustSpeed post condition
31 with Speed1; use Speed1;
   procedure Compute_Time_To_Go (C : in out Controller'Class;
33     Distance : Integer; Time_To_Go : out Integer) is
   begin
35     C.Adjust_Speed (3);
       ── Controller's Adjust_Speed guarantees that C.Speed /= 0
37     ── but we have a divide by 0 here if C is an Automatic_Speed_Controller
       Time_To_Go := Distance / C.Speed;
39 end Compute_Time_To_Go;
```

---

[11] Contributed by Cyrille Comar

Listing 4. Violation of LSP – Ada (2 of 2)

```
 1 ──────────────────────────────────────────────────────────
   ── Derived class violating LSP on adjustSpeed
 3 with Speed1; use Speed1;
   package Speed2 is
 5    type Auto_Controller is new Controller with private;

 7    function Desired_Speed (This : Auto_Controller) return Speed_Type;

 9    procedure Set_Desired_Speed
         (This : in out Auto_Controller; Val : Speed_Type);
11    pragma Postcondition (This.Desired_Speed = Val);

13    overriding procedure Adjust_Speed
         (This : in out Auto_Controller; Increment : Speed_Delta);
15    pragma Postcondition (This'Old.Speed = This.Speed);

17 private
      type Auto_Controller is new Controller with record
19       Desired_Speed : Speed_Type := 0;
      end record;
21 end Speed2;
   ──────────────────────────────────────────────────────────
23 package body Speed2 is
      function Desired_Speed (This : Auto_Controller) return Speed_Type is
25    begin
         return This.Desired_Speed;
27    end Desired_Speed;

29    procedure Set_Desired_Speed
         (This : in out Auto_Controller; Val : Speed_Type) is
31    begin
         This.Desired_Speed := Val;
33    end Set_Desired_Speed;

35    procedure Adjust_Speed
         (This : in out Auto_Controller; Increment : Speed_Delta) is
37    begin
         null;
39    end Adjust_Speed;
   end Speed2;
41 ──────────────────────────────────────────────────────────
   ── program raises an exception due to violation of LSP
43 with Speed2; use Speed2;
   with Compute_Time_To_Go;
45 procedure Main is
      Res : Integer;
47    Ctrl : Auto_Controller;
   begin
49    Compute_Time_To_Go (Ctrl, 5, Res);
   end Main;
```

4.4.5 Breaking LSP

Since this new auto controller class no longer needs (and, indeed, has no use for) the adjust speed by a speed increment method, its implementation of the method (which, of course, it must implement) did nothing. Additionally, a *set desired speed* method would need to be introduced to address the new abstraction of this type of speed controller. The point we strove to make was that in having the auto controller's *adjust speed* method do nothing, the post condition would be violated, since invoking the *adjust speed* method on an object with zero speed would fail to make the actual speed attribute non-zero.

While this is a moderately contrived example, we did manage to create a situation where we could have an unexpected exception thrown due to violation of a post condition which came about through failure to ensure the Liskov Substitution Principle was maintained throughout the hierarchy. In order make this more concrete, example code was created in Java, C++ and Ada – see listings 1, 2, 3 and 4.

Originally the code examples we created used floating point values but once we actually ran the code we wrote, we were surprised to find that none of our examples actually threw the expected division by zero exception since all the implementations simply returned infinity when the division by zero occurred. We therefore had to increase the contrivance level a bit more by making all the values integers so we could actually cause the exception we wanted to have thrown, and possibly leave the reader with an image of the smoke and debris cloud ultimately resulting from that unhandled exception on the Ariane 5's maiden flight.

4.5 Local and global class hierarchies

The supplement includes a brief explanation of the concept of hierarchical encapsulation so that it could form the basis for a discussion of class hierarchies which, in turn, brought about discussion of type consistency for local and global type hierarchies.

The supplement uses the term *local type consistency* to provide a means to determine type consistency in a component, independent of the type consistency of code which might utilize that component; that is, that developers could make type consistency determinations with well-defined boundaries facilitating the incorporation of separately (and often externally) developed class hierarchies.

4.6 Taxonomy of polymorphism

Although not really object-oriented in nature – the charter of the subgroup being essentially all coding issues – the notion of polymorphism was approached from a type-theoretical basis as well. With a brief description of the forms of polymorphism as being universal polymorphism and ad-hoc polymorphism, each of these was discussed as being divided into parametric and inclusion polymorphism, coercion and overloading, respectively. Again this was done

by the subgroup with some apprehension but we felt that at least introducing the vocabulary would provide additional means of clarifying situations where polymorphism is used as well as a common vocabulary for practitioners and certification authorities.

A similar philosophy guided our decision to discuss closures as a means of specifying behavior; that is, if we introduce the terms in the supplement an applicant can use the concept with an expectation that the certification authority will at least be on the same page.

4.7 Resource management

One area in which the subgroup expects to have a large impact on software design in airborne systems is the provision of a section on resource management, especially heap management, where automatic garbage collection is permitted for the first time. Garbage collection in real-time systems is a subject where a great deal of religious fervor has been expressed in the software safety community, especially the ongoing theme that garbage collectors are somehow "too complex" and therefore should not be allowed in a real-time or safety-critical situation. A consistent problem we encountered with this view was the inability of any of its proponents (at least the ones with whom we communicated) to express just how complex "too complex" is or even how such complexity should be measured. We found it especially curious that the notion was expressed – and fiercely defended – that garbage collectors were inherently too complex to be used in aviation but that high bypass turbofan jet engines somehow were not.

While rejecting the notion that garbage collection – now and (presumably) forever – was unusable due to some unspecified and undefinable algorithmic complexity in all garbage collectors, we did indeed recognize the potential for heap memory exhaustion in an airborne system and provided guidance to detect it and provide a degraded mode into which the subsystem can transition if such a situation becomes imminent. The idea of throwing an unhandled out of memory exception is still possible (just as is the throwing of an unhandled division by zero exception) but the guidance and recommendations give developers and certification authorities a specific set of criteria to verify.

5. Conclusions

Generally, the subgroup took the view that it should strive to remain language and technology neutral but to use real languages (Ada, C++ and Java, in particular) and technology to provide examples and illustrations of problem areas (for example, static dispatch and violation of the Liskov Substitution Principle). The subgroup also subscribed to the view that this supplement will be the foundation for perhaps two decades of future safety-critical software implementation so the subgroup really needed to be careful and conservative in the resulting document.

This was also done with the knowledge the real-time, avionics and safety-critical communities are quite reluctant to introduce new concepts (garbage collection and run-time polymorphism, for example) so the subgroup needed to provide a basis for acceptability of such ideas to that community by at least furnishing a theoretical base for discussion as well as an analysis of the perceived risks of a given approach as well as recommendations as to how to mitigate those risks.

5.1 DO-178C/ED-12C approval

Although the object-oriented supplement has been approved as part of the overall DO-178C/ED-12C document (along with supplements covering tool qualification and the use of formal methods), the overall core document along with one additional supplement have not yet completed the approval process. In particular, the aviation community has expressed a desire to see a supplement address the means by which model based development can be utilized in airborne software. Subgroup 4 of SC-205/WG-71 has been developing this supplement from the outset and it is hoped that it will be completed in time to become a part of DO-178C/ED-12C.

The approval of the entire DO-178C/ED-12C document (with or without the model based supplement) is expected in the second week of November, 2010, with actual publication by RTCA and EUROCAE shortly thereafter, at which time it will become available as the standard for the determination of airworthiness for airborne systems and and equipment containing software. As more and more practitioners consider this supplement as the means to achieve airworthiness consideration for their products, we – the members of subgroup 5 – will slowly, but eventually, become known as "those idiots" as in the phrase: *What were those idiots thinking of when they wrote . . . .* As long as we remain invisible idiots, we'll be OK with that.

Acknowledgments

The other active members of Subgroup 5 of SC-205/WG-71 who actually wrote and edited the OO supplement, 2005 – 2010:

Thomas Bleichner . . . . Rohde & Schwarz
Jan-Hendrik Boelens . . . . Eurocopter
Jim Chelini . . . . Verocel
John Chilenski . . . . Boeing
Cyrille Comar . . . . AdaCore
Branimir Dulic . . . . Transport Canada
Mark Gulick . . . . Solers
James Hunt . . . . aicas
John Jorgensen . . . . Universal Avionics Systems
Varun Malik . . . . Hamilton Sundstrand
Greg Millican . . . . Honeywell
John Minihan . . . . Resource Group
Rob Morris . . . . CDL Systems
Sven Nordhoff . . . . SQS
Bill St. Clair . . . . LDRA
Robin Sova . . . . FAA
Elroy Wiens . . . . Cessna

References

[1] Special Committee 167 / Working Group 12 of RTCA and EUROCAE. *DO-178B/ED-12B – Software Considerations in Airborne Systems and Equipment Certification*. RTCA and EUROCAE, Washington, D.C., USA and Malakoff, France, Dec. 1992.

[2] Federal Aviation Administration (FAA). *Handbook for Object-Oriented Technology in Aviation (OOTiA)*. Federal Aviation Administration (FAA), Washington, D.C., USA, Oct. 2004.

[3] L. Johnson. DO-178B, "Software Considerations in Airborne Systems and Equipment Certification", *Crosstalk, The Journal of Defense Software Engineering*, 11(10), Oct. 1998.

[4] B. Liskov and J. Wing. A behavioral notion of subtyping. *ACM Transactions on Programming Languages and Systems*, 16(6): 1811–1841, Nov. 1994.

Migrating a Large Modeling Environment from XML/UML to Xtext/GMF

Practitioner Report

Moritz Eysholdt

itemis AG

moritz.eysholdt@itemis.de

Johannes Rupprecht

VSA Group

johannes.rupprecht@vsa.de

Abstract

If you use UML to drive code generation, what do you do when a UML model grows so large that the tool needs 60 minutes to open it? What if it turns out that UML doesn't provide the expressiveness you need? What if your UML editor barely provides feedback about the validity of your models and the turnaround time from modeling to code-generation and compilation is somewhere between setting up a new can of coffee and reading a day's amount of slash-dot.org news? Time to look for a different modeling solution...

This paper reports how *VSA* (Verrechnungsstelle der Süd-deutschen Apotheken GmbH, one of the most well-known billing centers for pharmacies in Germany) migrated their in-house modeling environment and their existing models from UML to an Eclipse Modeling based solution: Models of all five pre-existing modeling languages are now persisted tex-tually and can be edited using Xtext. Models of two chosen modeling languages can additionally be edited graphically using GMF-based editors which store their models textually using Xtext. The modeling environment provides tight inte-gration with the JDT for referencing and navigating to Java elements. Custom validation rules provide the earliest feed-back possible for the modeler. An Eclipse Builder triggers incremental code generation, which keeps the turnaround time to a minimum. This paper describes the old modeling environment, addresses the challenges of the migration and outlines the new modeling environment. Furthermore, it doc-uments how to integrate GMF with Xtext.

The project has been realized in cooperation between *VSA* and *itemis AG*. *VSA* had the knowledge about the ex-

isting modeling environment, *itemis AG*, a consulting com-pany with several full-time Eclipse Modeling Committers, brought in their knowledge about EMF, Xtext, GMF, etc.

Categories and Subject Descriptors   D.2.6 [*Software En-gineering*]: Programming Environments—Eclipse, Xtext, GMF

General Terms   Design, Languages

Keywords   Modeling, Migration, MDSD, DSL, Xtext, Eclipse, EMF, GMF

1. Introduction

The *VSA*, a company of 1.100 employes, based in Germany, which has specialized in billing and IT in the health care business, uses model driven software development for in-house software development. The tool chain which has been established during the last eight years included modeling in UML, exporting the modes to XML and generating Java code from the XML. However, the models grew so large that the UML tool needed up to an hour to load the largest module. It became obvious that due to misuse of UML, modeling in UML was sometimes more complex than in XML.

This paper reports about the project in which new mod-eling tools have been created to replace the existing ones. Furthermore, existing models were migrated to the new in-frastructure.

In cooperation with the company *itemis*, the existing UML- and XML-based languages have completely been re-placed with textual languages (external DSLs, implemented with Xtext [1]). For selected languages, graphical editors (implemented with the Graphical Modeling Framework, GMF [3]) have been developed. The graphical and tex-tual editors operate on the same files. Therefore, the user can freely choose his/her preferred representation and there is neither round-trip engineering nor other synchronization needed to keep textual and graphical representation syn-chronized. Furthermore, mechanisms for a fully-automated migration of the existing models and diagrams have been developed.

Permission to make digital or hard copies of all or part of this work for personal or classroom use is granted without fee provided that copies are not made or distributed for profit or commercial advantage and that copies bear this notice and the full citation on the first page. To copy otherwise, to republish, to post on servers or to redistribute to lists, requires prior specific permission and/or a fee.

SPLASH'10,   October 17–21, 2010, Reno/Tahoe, Nevada, USA.

Copyright © 2010 ACM 978-1-4503-0240-1/10/10... $10.00

2. About VSA Group

The *VSA* (Verrechnungsstelle Süddeutscher Apotheken; The name translates to Clearing House of the South German Pharmacies) was founded in 1983 and is owned by 7000 German pharmacists. The main business units are:

- *VSA*: Clearing for German Pharmacies
- *azh*: Clearing and IT for German health care professionals
- *awinta*: Pharmacy administration systems

150 of the employees are tasked with software development, which is distributed over several projects and several locations. The developed systems include internal systems (e.g. the two clearing systems), online systems for the clearing customers and pharmacy administration systems. Development is mostly done in Java, but also C#, C++, C and Objective-C are used.

3. About itemis AG

Four companies applied for implementing this project, three of them proposed a solution based on Xtext and GMF and *itemis* was chosen due to their competence with Xtext.

Employing 140 people, *itemis* has its headquarter in Lünen (close to Dortmund), Germany and branches in Canada, Switzerland and France. As a Strategic Member of the Eclipse Foundation *itemis* employs several Eclipse committers of which four are working full time on the Xtext project. This put *itemis* in the unique position to extend Xtext with features (such as integration with the Java language and support for incremental building) that were needed for this project.

Model Driven Software Development [4] and Domain-Specific Languages [2] are the main focus of *itemis*. This knowledge is mainly applied in the fields of enterprise applications, embedded systems and mobile devices (e.g. based on the iPhone and Android platform).

4. The Modeling Environment

Around 2000 to 2002, the *VSA* re-implemented their existing systems in Java. This created the need for supporting frameworks and led to the development of custom frameworks for object relational mapping and user interface workflows, since back in these days no viable other frameworks were available. The frameworks grew as well as the projects using them. Multiple database implementations and different UI technologies had to be supported. XML files were introduced from which Java code was generated. This allowed for some degree of platform/technology independence and it allowed to work at a higher level of abstraction. Later, UML was introduced to add another layer of abstraction on top of the existing XML models. The tool of choice was Magic-Draw (by No Magic) and custom plug-ins were developed

to allow the XML export. The name given to this modeling environment is *marvin*.

The following concepts could be described in XML/UML:

- Persistent Objects (entities), including their columns/attributes, inheritance, master-detail-relationships and find-methods.
- Persistent Views, including query statements and find methods.
- Workflows, consisting of activities and steps to describe the paths through user interface masks.
- Masks, to describe forms in Java/Swing and HTML
- ObjectModel, to describe objects for databinding in forms

The following projects are examples for what has been developed with this tool chain: Project *jump* is about administration of pharmacies and project *nProd* is about clearing for pharmacies.

	jump	nProd
Effort (Man Years)	200	?
Lines of code	1.400.000	1.000.000
Classes	20.500	13.300
Persistent Entities	916	560
Persistent Views	369	96
Workflows	278	124
Masks	1.150	612
UML diagrams	2000	1000

5. Problems with the Old Modeling Environment

Modeling in XML was inefficient due to the verbose syntax itself and the lack of good tool support. Tools which could check tags/attributes based on the XML Schema were not sufficient, since the more relevant aspects of assistance are:

- Instant feedback of custom validation rules.
- Instant feedback and content assist for references to other model elements and files.
- Assistance with entering arithmetic/logical expressions, e.g. the conditions used for the find expressions.

Modeling in UML led to additional and similar problems:

- Opening the largest UML module with MagicDraw took up to one hour.
- Opening the largest UML diagram took up to ten minutes.
- Turnaround times were too slow. The process was as follows: Change an UML diagram, export XML files, generate Java files, compile them via ANT. A developer had to go through this process each time he/she wanted to ensure his/her model is correct.

- Modeling was not intuitive since UML was misused to express things UML is not suited for.

- Partly, the UML model was more complex than the corresponding XML file.

- Modeling was occasionally cumbersome, because there was no assistance in editing the models. For example, when other model elements were referenced by their name or when entering arithmetic/logical expressions in a custom, ANTLR-based language.

- Workflow diagrams became too big and thereby hard to handle. The largest workflow had more than 700 nodes.

- Not all functionality of the XML files could be expressed via UML.

- Roundtrip-engineering between XML and UML was not possible. I.e. there was no way to re-create an UML diagram from XML files.

- No custom validation was available in the UML tool.

- No content assist was available in the UML tool.

- Branching was not possible, therefore modeling was restricted to one branch.

- There was no navigation between code and model.

It is out of question that *not* all of the points listed above can or should be blamed on the UML tool. However, re-factoring the existing models to make optimal use of the UML tooling would have required the same or more effort than the project this paper reports about.

6. Objectives for the New Modeling Environment

The objectives for the new modeling environment can be summarized as follows:

- Textual languages for all existing XML-languages based on Xtext.

- Graphical modeling for selected aspects of selected languages based on GMF (no UML!). Furthermore, there should be a mechanism to partition workflow diagrams.

- Integration of the legacy code generator as an Eclipse Builder

- Tooling for a 100% automatic migration of existing projects, including layout information from MagicDraw. Furthermore, the ability to migration one project at a time is needed.

- Support for mixing migrated and not-yet-migrated projects, since projects can depend on each other. It is not possible to migrate all projects at once since they are involved in different release cycles.

7. The Value of Eclipse/XMF/Xtext/GMF

To keep the efforts for this project in an affordable scale, it was imperative to build on existing frameworks as much as possible. Furthermore, since the modeling tools are used in Java projects, it is valuable for them to be integrated with a Java development environment.

This is available with Eclipse: Eclipse's JDT for Java development, Eclipse's extensibility via plug-ins, Eclipse's rich ecosystem of modeling tools and frameworks. For modeling, the Eclipse Modeling Framework (EMF [5]) provides support for XML/XML Schema and is the foundation for integrating textual languages based on Xtext with graphical languages based on GMF.

Furthermore, all these frameworks are available as open source.

8. The Project

To realize this project, two developers from *itemis* and four developers from *VSA* have been working in cooperation. Two of the *VSA*'s developers were working part time. Working in cooperation ensured training on the new technologies for the *VSA* developers. The project's extent was defined in a specification document. Development was distributed over four different locations. A shared infrastructure consisting of a subversion repository and a Trac bug-tracker (which includes a wiki) supported the teamwork. Weekly telephone conferences were held to check the status and discuss problems.

9. The New Modeling Environment

From the five XML/UML based languages, five textual languages with equivalent semantics have been created. For selected aspects, graphical editors have been created using GMF. Since tooling for all textual languages has been created using Xtext, the editors provide a similar user experience as Eclipse's JDT.

The following features are provided. For the very most cases, Xtext's default behavior was just fine. For all other cases, it is mentioned what has been customized:

- Syntax highlighting

- Outline View: Structure, labels and icons have been customized.

- Scoping has been customized. In Xtext, a scope is the list of visible names for one cross reference. Linking and content assist delegate to scoping.

- Content assist, which provides suggestions for keywords and all model elements and Java elements that can be referenced at the current cursor's position in the document.

- Validation of cross references: If a model element or Java element identified by a name can not be resolved, an error marker is created.

- Navigation: If the user holds CTRL and clicks on a cross reference or presses F3, the editor will navigate to the referenced element. If this element is in a different file or is a Java element, a new editor will be opened.

- Find references: When selecting a model element, the *Find References View* provides a list of all model elements that hold references to the selected element. This feature is especially valuable to gather knowledge about existing code before re-factoring it.

- Formatting: Formatting automatically optimizes indentation, line-breaks and white-spaces. Custom formatting rules have been implemented for a well-readable appearance of the source code.

- Validation: In this project many custom validation rules have been implemented using Xtext's declarative API for EValidators. Validation is run as the user types, i.e. the user gets instant feedback about potential errors/warnings. This works well for the moment, but in case longer-running validation rules will be introduced, they should only be run on save or when explicitly triggered.

- *Open Model Elements* dialog: This dialog resembles JDT's *Open Type* dialog. By entering a name or a search pattern the user can quickly identify all matched model elements no matter where they are stored in his/her workspace. Furthermore, navigation to these elements is provided.

- Incremental build: Xtext integrates with Eclipse's Builder infrastructure: Each time a file is modified on the hard disk, the Builder is triggered to update Xtext's index with the modified model elements and run validation. Furthermore, the *VSA*'s existing code generator has been integrated. The user experience is as follows: If he/she modifies and saves a file, the generated Java code is updated in a matter of seconds. Code generation runs only if validation passes without errors.

9.1 Domain.xtext and View.xtext

The language for persistent objects (called *domain*-language from now on) and the language for persistent views build the first group of languages. Both extend a common language named *PersistCommon* which provides constructs that are shared by both languages. Example: Syntax of an expression language for find-methods.

9.2 The Graphical Domain Editor

Furthermore, a GMF-based editor for the *domain* language has been created. Its visual appearance resembles a UML class diagram. Its behavior, however, differs from typical GMF-based editors. Usually one diagram editor operates on one file representing the semantic model. In this case, the diagram is intended to display nodes for all semantic model elements (the ones for which nodes are defined). Deleting

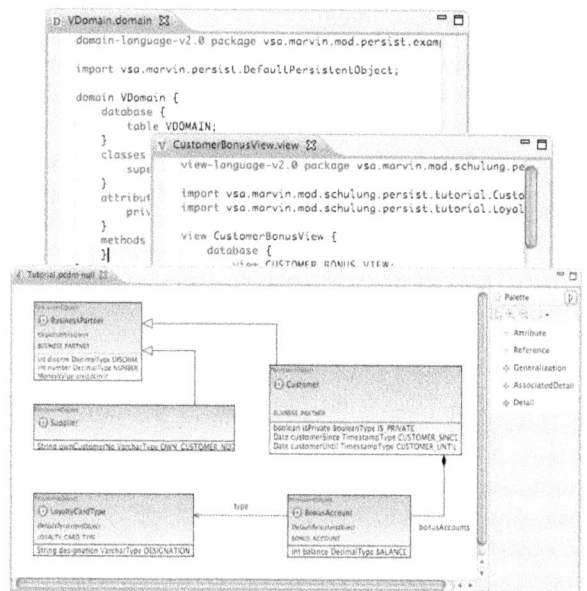

Figure 1. Textual and graphical editors of the persist-languages

a node from the diagram means to delete the element from the semantic model as well. However, the diagram editor developed in this project operates on an arbitrary amount of semantic models. This became necessary since one domain (think of one entity) is persisted in one file and is expected to be one node in the diagram. Therefore, when a new diagram file is created there is initially no semantic model and the diagram is empty. The user may then add nodes to the diagram by drag'n'dropping domain-files from Eclipse's Package Explorer onto the diagram. If nodes are related, edges are automatically added. Furthermore, an action in the context menu can be used to add all related elements of one node.

9.3 Workflow.xtext, ObjectModel.xtext and Mask.xtext

The languages for workflows, object models and masks build the second group of languages. They also extend a common language, named *WorkflowCommon*. *WorkflowCommon* and *PersistCommon* both extend a language named *MarvinCommon* which provides common terminal rules and parser rules, e.g. for import statements.

9.4 The Workflow Diagram Editor

The workflow editor allows to view and edit workflows in an UML activity diagram like style. However, it supports some extended semantics, for example to define a loop, a return back to a previous step or to mark transitions as starting, committing or rolling-back of transactions.

Furthermore, the diagram allows to partition large workflows into multiple nested diagrams, called *WorkflowParts*. It has no impact on the semantics of a model element whether it resides in a *WorkflowPart* or the root-workflow. This mechanism is solely exists to keep the visual appearance of large

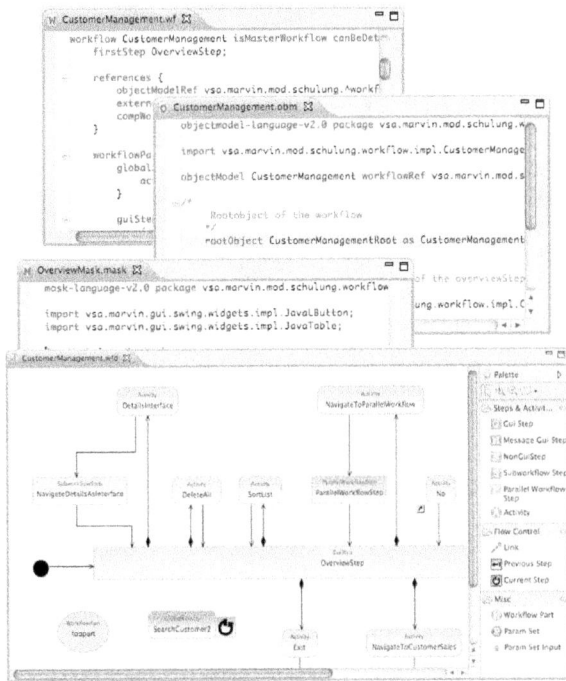

Figure 2. Textual and graphical editors of the workflow-languages

workflows manageable. *WorkflowParts* are represented with their own nodes in the root diagram and on double click the editor for the nested diagram opens. The diagram editor supports cut'n'paste to move model elements from one diagram to another.

This behavior leads to a conceptual challenge of how to display edges when the nodes are in different diagrams. This problem has been solved by dynamically inserting shortcut-nodes so that all edges can be displayed. Shortcut nodes, similar to symlinks in the UNIX file system, allow to have a representation of a semantic element at a position in a diagram that does not correspond with the actual position in the semantic model.

10. From XML to a Textual Language

When an XML Schema and example XML files are available, as in this project, this can be used as a starting point to develop a textual language. The basic idea is to look at an XML file and think of ways how to make the contents more readable. To illustrate this idea, the reader may think of the following steps:

1. Replace all "<sometag>....</sometag>" with sometag {...}. If the object has a name by which it can identified, the name-attribute may be removed and the name inserted behind the tag's name: "sometag elementname {...}".

2. Remove all remaining "<",">" and "/>".

3. Remove directives such as "<?xml.." and metadata such as namespace declarations.

4. Find reasonable default values for attribute values and tags. Remove all attributes and tags from the file that equal the default value.

5. Verify if reasonable default values for attributes or existence of tags can be derived from other values. For example, the Java class name of an entity can usually be derived from the entity's name. Remove all attributes and tags whose value equals a derived default value from the file.

6. Check whether there are values that would have a more concise notation if they would be composed of a common value. For example, in this project the models contained many references to Java files, which were all qualified names. By introducing "import" statements, the simple names of the Java classes could be used.

7. Check whether more restructuring are reasonable. In this project, for example, the *domain* language contained separate listings for table columns and class attributes. This has been re-factored to class attributes containing optional column specifications, because the column specifications can be defaulted in many cases.

By now the file should be much more concise as before. Now it is up to the language designer's good taste to find an well-readable, writable and understandable syntax. In this project we did not follow the process as formal as it is described above. However, it was guiding our mental model.

11. Models are Code!

Models are stored textually in the same folders in the file system as the source code of the project. They only differ from Java source code in the way that Java code is directly transformed to byte-code while models are transformed to Java code which is then transformed to byte code. To consider and to treat models as source code has several advantages:

- Version control works the same for them as it does for source code. They can be stored in the same repository as the source code and do not demand special attention for branching and tagging.

- Comparing and merging of text is well-proven and mature tooling is available.

- Copy'n'paste works across applications.

- Artifacts can easily be exchanged via email, chat or web.

- Textual models integrate seamlessly with existing source code. This is true for the user experience as well as the tooling.

12. Rapid Crafting of a Language with Xtext

In Xtext, every language's concrete syntax is defined by a grammar and every abstract syntax is defined by an Ecore model. Xtext can automatically derive the Ecore model from a grammar or import an existing Ecore model. In this project it proved to be very productive to start with a derived Ecore model since this allows for unrestricted changes of the grammar. With this flexibility and many example documents the language's syntax stabilized quickly. However, even in this phase it was important to keep the Ecore model in mind. The Ecore model is "the core" of a language, since it practically defines the API which provides access to the semantic model. This API is heavily used by the implementations of scoping, validation, outline, transformations, etc. This makes it very valuable to have a concise and understandable Ecore model. Furthermore, in the authors opinion, it is more efficient to specify an Ecore model via an Xtext grammar than it is to use EMF's Reflective Tree Editor.

As soon as the language's concrete and abstract syntax were stable, the Ecore model was moved from the "src-gen" to the "src" folder and Xtext was configured to use the existing one rather than regenerating it every time. This provided the stability of the Ecore model needed to build GMF editors on top of it.

13. Integration of GMF and Xtext

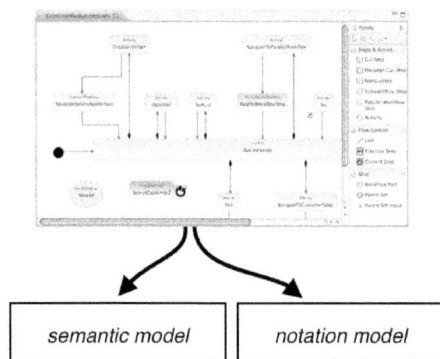

Figure 3. Files persisted by GMF-based editors

To understand how Xtext and GMF integrate one basically has to understand how GMF persists its models: Usually, GMF stores two files: one for the semantic model and one for the notation model. While the semantic model is the "actual" model, the one that is used for code generation and validation, the notation model only contains information about layout and formatting of nodes and edges. To illustrate this, the reader may think of what happens when the notation model is lost for some reason: A new diagram can easily be created from the remaining semantic model and the diagram will contain all nodes and edges the old diagram contained. However, position, sizes, font, color, etc. of nodes and edges will have been reset to default values. GMF usually stores both models as XMI using EMF's *XMIResource*.

To integrate Xtext with GMF, all that needs to be done is to register an *XtextResource* for semantic model's file extension instead of an *XMIResource*. Since the *XtextResource* implements save() the GMF editor will from now on store its semantic model in a textual syntax defined by Xtext. Since the Xtext editor and the GMF editor operate on the same file, synchronization of the editors happens on resource level. Eclipse's default behavior is to notify an editor once the file in the file system has been changed by some other editor. This causes the first editor to reload its contents. To avoid merge conflicts that will inevitably occur when two editors hold modified contents, the user will be warned with a dialog when he/she starts modifying the second editor's contents.

Furthermore, tooltips for diagram nodes were developed in this project. They provide hyperlinks allowing to quickly navigate from the diagram node to the corresponding textual element. This becomes very helpful if some elements are more conveniently editable textually than graphically.

An interesting aspect of this approach is that it eliminates the need to have the GMF editor cover the complete semantic model. The user can always switch to the textual syntax if the GMF editor doesn not (yet) support a certain syntax. This is interesting since the effort of implementation per concept (meta-element) is much lower for Xtext than it is for GMF.

14. A Roundtrip-Architecture

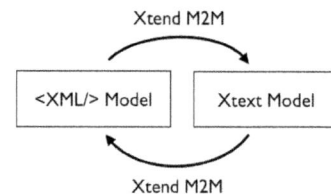

Figure 4. From XML to Xtext and back

For all existing XML-based languages, there was an XML Schema available. Via EMF this could fully-automatically be transformed into an Ecore model. Using this Ecore model, EMF was capable of loading and saving all existing XML files. Using EMF to access XML provided a convenient and proven interface to handle the loaded data. Furthermore, EMF proved to be well-customizable to handle glitches in XML files such as invalid import-schema attributes. The XSD-based Ecore models, however, differed from the ones derived from the Xtext grammars. It was decided to implement two model-to-model transformations in Xtend: One to transform XML-models to Xtext-models and one to transform Xtext-models to XML-models. Xtend is an OCL-like language for model-to-model transformations than integrates well with EMF and Xtext and is part of the Eclipse Xpand project. This allowed to cover three scenarios that were important for this project:

- Migration: To migrate an XML model, the XML file is loaded via an *XMLResource*, the model is transformed to the Xtext-based Ecore model and then saved via an *XtextResource*. Xtext's formatter ensured that the output is a well-readable text file.

- Integrating the legacy code generator: The existing code generator needs XML files as input, since it is not (yet) EMF-based. To keep the scope of the project reasonable, it was decided not to modify the generator. Now the Xtext-to-XML transformation becomes useful to create the XML files needed by the generator: An *XtextResource* loads the textual document, the transformation applied and an *XMLResource* saves the XML to disk.

- Generic Integration Testing: It was imperative for the new tooling to support all existing models. Therefore, it could not be relied on documentation/specification to be accurate or complete. As projects were migrated one-by-one, this test allowed to quickly add error-causing XML files to the test suite. The test, which is a roundtrip test, is implemented as follows:

1. The XML file is loaded.

2. The XML model is transformed to an Xtext model.

3. The Xtext model is saved to disk.

4. The Xtext model is loaded from the disk.

5. The Xtext model is transformed to an XML model.

6. The XML model is saved to disk.

7. The original XML file and the new XML file are compared. If relevant differences occur, the test has failed.

This test is valuable since it involves many aspects of the tooling:

- Both transformations are tested for complete- and correctness.

- The Xtext model is tested whether it is in a state that can be serialized. For example, values for assignments that are mandatory in the grammar must be provided.

- The grammar is tested for completeness.

- It is tested whether scoping can provide names and resolve names for the cross-referenced elements.

- Xtext's lexer and parser are tested if they can read the document.

- Value conversion for terminal and datatype rules is tested.

15. Lessons Learned

15.1 Migration

We have experienced that it was very valuable to have a 100%-automatic migration for existing projects. At the time of writing this, two thirds of the 75 CVS modules have been successfully migrated. In an earlier project phase an automated migration test tool has been developed. This tool is able to check out modules from CVS, migrate them to the new modeling infrastructure and build them. Then, artifacts are compared. All errors and relevant differences are logged. Due to this mechanism, the team was able to detect all (!) migration problems before rollout. However, investigating and resolving the found errors took more time as expected.

15.2 Training

Even for very experienced users it is helpful to be trained on the complete new way to model. For this, an exercise project has been created with tutorials covering the main features. All *VSA* developers (even the Romanian ones) took part in a 4-6 hour training. The result was very few handling problems and low support effort of the *VSA* modeling developers.

16. Conclusion

The issues in productivity the *VSA*'s developers were facing with the old modeling infrastructure have been solved. With the new modeling infrastructure the time span from editing the model to the availability of the generated code has been reduced from minutes to seconds. In the majority of cases, correctness of models can be checked by the validation rules integrated in the editor. Therefore, the user is now notified about potential errors or warnings before code generation has been run. Code generation does not need to be triggered explicitly anymore, since runs now as an incremental builder of Eclipse. Additionally, the editor now provides sophisticated assistance when editing the model, such as content assist, navigation, find-references, and open model element features. Content assist and navigation are integrated with Eclipse's JDT, i.e. they are available for Java elements. The risk that UML model and code get out of sync has been eliminated since models are are now stored textually in the same repository as the source code. The GMF editors allow to edit models where this seems reasonable and existing diagrams have been preserved in the migration. Compared to the UML tool the GMF editors are much less cluttered since they only provide the UI elements that are actually needed by the domain-specific language.

References

[1] S. Efftinge, S. Zarnekow, J. Köhnlein, and M. Eysholdt. Xtext - Language Development Framework, 2010. URL `http://www.xtext.org/`.

[2] M. Fowler. Domain Specific Languages. *Addison-Wesley Professional*, 2010.

[3] R. Gronback. *Eclipse Modeling Project: A Domain-Specific Language (DSL) Toolkit*. Addison-Wesley Professional, 2009.

[4] T. Stahl and M. Völter. *Model-Driven Software Development*. Wiley, 2006.

[5] D. Steinberg, F. Budinsky, M. Paternostro, and E. Merks. *EMF: Eclipse Modeling Framework 2.0*. Addison-Wesley Professional, 2009.

Software Evolution in Agile Development: A Case Study *

Renuka Sindhgatta, Nanjangud C. Narendra, Bikram Sengupta

IBM Research India, Bangalore, India

{renuka.sr,narendra,bsengupt@in.ibm.com}

Abstract

The agile development method (ADM) is characterized by
continuous feedback and change, and a software system developed using ADM evolves continuously through short iterations. Empirical studies on evolution of software following
agile development method have been sparse. Most studies
on software evolution have been performed on systems built
using traditional (waterfall) development methods or using
the open source development approach. This paper summarizes our study on the evolution of an enterprise software
system following ADM. We evaluated key characteristics of
evolution in the light of Lehman's laws of software evolution
dealing with continuous change and growth, self-regulation
and conservation, increasing complexity and declining quality. Our study indicates that most laws of evolution are followed by the system. We also present our observations on
agile practices such as collective code ownership, test driven
development and collaboration when the team is distributed.

Categories and Subject Descriptors D.2 [*Software Engineering*]: Design - *methodologies*; Design Tools and Techniques - *computer-aided software engineering*

General Terms Measurement, Documentation, Experimentation

Keywords Agile Methods, Scrum, Evolution

1. Introduction

Agile development methods (ADM) are characterized by
short "inspect-and-adapt" cycles and frequent feedback
loops [14] through which the software system continually
evolves. These characteristics of ADM clearly distinguish
them from traditional development methods like waterfall

---

* Thanks to Balasubramani Radhakrishnan and Rajesh Thakkar for their
feedback.

Permission to make digital or hard copies of all or part of this work for personal or
classroom use is granted without fee provided that copies are not made or distributed
for profit or commercial advantage and that copies bear this notice and the full citation
on the first page. To copy otherwise, to republish, to post on servers or to redistribute
to lists, requires prior specific permission and/or a fee.

SPLASH'10, October 17–21, 2010, Reno/Tahoe, Nevada, USA.
Copyright © 2010 ACM 978-1-4503-0240-1/10/10. . . $10.00

[2, 7], or more recent approaches like open source development [5, 11, 15]. However, in spite of the increasing
popularity of agile methods in recent years and its many
success stories in practice, studies exploring the evolution of
systems following agile methods are limited. Most of the research work on software evolution till date have focused on
traditional or open source methods, and Lehman's laws of
software evolution [9] have been interpreted and evaluated
in detail in the context of these methods. These laws, dealing with continuous change and growth, self-regulation and
conservation, increasing complexity and declining quality,
of software systems, need to be examined on projects following agile methods, to see if they continue to hold good
across the agile lifecycle.

Towards that end, in this paper we present a case study
on the evolution of a software system in our organization
following the agile Scrum method [13]. The project team
of around 60 members (including some geographically distributed practitioners), was involved in developing a product
on the Jazz[1] platform, over a period of 15 months and 25 iterations or *sprints*, culminating in the first product release
to the customer. We tracked the development of the software product through its lifecycle and studied the applicability of Lehman's laws in understanding its evolution path.
To the best of our knowledge, ours is amongst the first case
studies to investigate Lehman's laws of software evolution
on projects that follow agile development methods. We also
reviewed some distinct practices that often accompany the
agile method, in particular, collective code ownership, test
driven development and team collaboration. We report on
our findings on these practices from the case study.

This paper is organized as follows. In the next Section,
we present the basic definitions that will be used throughout
the paper. Section 3 discusses how Lehman's laws of software evolution apply to ADM. Section 4 presents our observations on agile practices such as collective code ownership,
test driven development and distributed collaboration. Section 6 positions our paper against related work in this area.
Section 5 presents some insights from our case study, which
are potentially useful for project teams following ADM. Finally, the paper concludes in Section 7.

---

[1] https://jazz.net/

2. Overview

2.1 Scrum Agile Development Method

Scrum [13] is characterized by iterative and incremental development. A Scrum project makes progress in a series of iterations or *sprints* which are typically of one to four weeks duration each. At the start of a sprint, team members commit to delivering some number of features that are listed on the project's *product backlog*. This subset of features is called the *sprint backlog*.

At the end of the sprint, the features of sprint backlog are completed - they are coded, tested, and integrated into the evolving system. A sprint review is conducted during which the team demonstrates the new functionality to the product owner and other interested stakeholders who then provide feedback that could influence the next sprint. Scrum also promotes meetings for planning, reviewing and retrospection on a continuous basis.

A project team is supported by a *ScrumMaster* and a *product owner*. The ScrumMaster helps team members use the Scrum framework. The product owner represents the business, customers or users and guides the team toward building the right software system.

2.2 Project Background

We briefly describe the system and the project team. The system was developed using Java and JavaScript programming languages. 90% of development team members were co-located. The remaining 10% of the team including management were located across multiple countries. The system was developed over a period of 15 months, and was broken into 25 sprints of varying duration, as shown in Fig. 1. The first 11 sprints led to an initial prototype of the product that was hardened into a beta release over shorter sprints 12 through 15. This was again followed by a period of concentrated development and enhancement (Sprints 16 through 21), finally leading to release candidates being hardened through very short sprints of about a week each (sprints 22 through 25).

The entire project was divided into smaller teams comprising of 6-7 people based on the functionality. Each functional team had a ScrumMaster for managing the smaller functions/features of the project. The sprint backlog was functionally divided within and further assigned to the respective team members by the ScrumMaster after consulting the team. The project consistently followed the scrum meetings such as daily scrum, sprint review and sprint retrospective.

2.3 Development Platform

The project used IBM Rational Team Concert (RTC)[2] as the development platform. Rational Team Concert provides a mechanism of creating and managing a Scrum-based project. Hence, our study is based on a project using a ma-

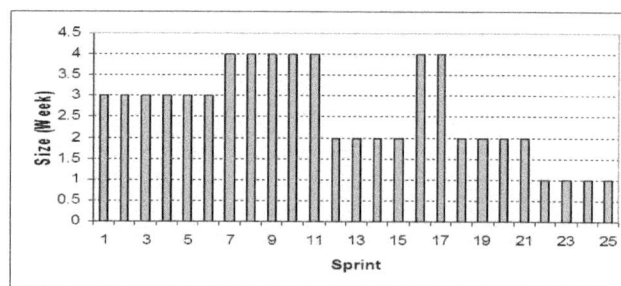

Figure 1. Duration of Sprint Iterations

ture environment for agile development. In Rational Team Concert, a project area refers to a project. Users and their specific roles can be defined. Sprints with their time lines can be defined. A product backlog is associated to project area and further a sprint backlog can also be defined. In Rational Team Concert, the sprint or product backlog is a set of work items. A work item is a unit of work. Work items can be of different types, such as plan, user story, task, defect, enhancement, test case, etc.

Each work item consists of a set of basic attributes that are useful for tracking it; these include, name, unique identifier (ID), description, sprint it has been planned for, creator (name of the team member who created the work item), owner (name of the team member who is responsible for successfully completing the work item), creation date, closure date, priority, estimated effort, actual effort and time spent.

The real benefit of work items, however, accrues from the links that may be established between these items and the corresponding development activity carried out. Each work item can be linked to software development artifacts (code, test cases, designs, plans, etc.). A work item can be linked to files stored in a configuration management system through the definition of one or more change sets. A change set is a collection of files grouped together by the developer in a manner that is meaningful for the project. For example, all GUI-related file changes can be grouped together into a single change set. A changed file can be checked in against one or more work items. This facility is particularly useful for defect work items, since a single set of changes to a file could potentially fix multiple defects simultaneously.

The availability of all the information in the form of work items and linkages with the source code management system allows us to mine and analyze various aspects of software evolution.

2.4 Data Extraction

Figure 2 shows the details of the work item, change set, file and changes that are extracted from Rational Team Concert. The platform's Java client APIs are used to connect to the project repository. The attributes of a work item such as the owner, creator, sprint iteration it has been planned for, duration, etc., are extracted. For each work item, files that were modified and the modification date is extracted. Ratio-

---

[2] http://www-01.ibm.com/software/awdtools/rtc/

nal Team Concert provides a mechanism for identifying if a file was added, deleted, changed or renamed. This information is stored as Change status. Metrics on the file such as the number of non-commented source lines of code (LOC), number of methods in the files, etc., are extracted. Complexity metrics such as the cyclomatic complexity of the file and coupling, i.e., the number of external functions called by the class or script is measured and stored. Similar metrics for the changes made are collected - LOC added or changed, and number of methods added or changed.

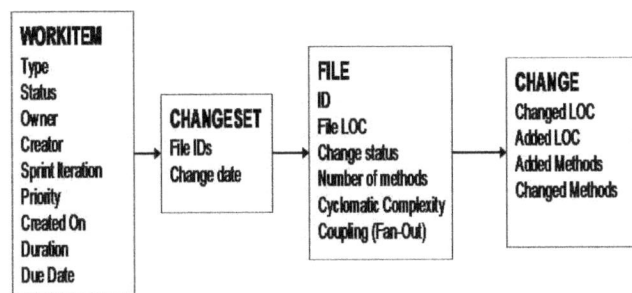

Figure 2. Data Extracted from Work Items

3. Observations on Software Evolution Laws

In this section, we evaluate the laws of software evolution as defined in [9]. For ease of exposition, we have grouped the 8 software evolution laws into four categories. This is motivated by similarities in core concepts across some of the laws, as has also pointed out by Lehman himself [8]. Our categories are:

- The first and sixth laws, viz., Continuous Change and Continuing Growth, have been grouped into a category called "Change and Growth".

- The third, fourth, fifth and eighth laws, viz., Self Regulation, Conservation of Organizational Stability, Conservation of Familiarity and Feedback System, have been grouped into a category called "Self-Regulation and Feedback".

- The second law, viz., Increasing Complexity, has its own category

- The seventh law, viz., Declining Quality, has its own category

During our experiments, we have only analyzed Java and JavaScript files as they are the key contributors to the functionality of the system. Other file types (XML, HTML, CSS, and TXT) have not been considered. In some cases, in a single sprint a file may be added and can further undergo a modification or a file that has been modified may be deleted. In such scenarios, we only consider a file as added or deleted respectively. Also, given that the sprints were of unequal duration, for ease of review, the X-axis in our figures has been scaled to equal sized time intervals (month), while each

data point shown will capture the relevant value for the corresponding sprint. Finally, we have used relative numbers wherever possible to explain the quantitative data, in order to maintain its confidentiality.

3.1 Change and Growth

This category, that subsumes the first and sixth laws, addresses the common issue of change and growth, i.e., to investigate how the software system changes and grows until its release.

The first law specifies that a program must continually adapt to its environment, otherwise it becomes progressively less useful [2]. Change has been characterized by prior work as the number of modules handled in each release [2], system and module size in terms of number of lines of code [5] and function modifications [12]. We track changes across sprints in terms of number of lines of code (LOC) modified and number of files modified. We consider each Java or JavaScript file as a functional module (as an object oriented class can be considered as a module). Although Java Script is not a full blown object oriented programming language, it is object based and the concepts of objects can be applied.

As seen in Figure 3, the cumulative number of changes (for both LOC and files) increases steadily through the lifecycle of the project. As would be expected, the rate of change is higher in the sprints immediately preceding the beta release (sprints 9, 10, 11) and flattens out during the beta release sprints (sprints 12 through 15), but overall, change occurs reasonably uniformly and continuously, with about 40-50% of changes being made around the half-way mark (month 8). Thus Lehman's first law of continuous change was found to hold very well in this project.

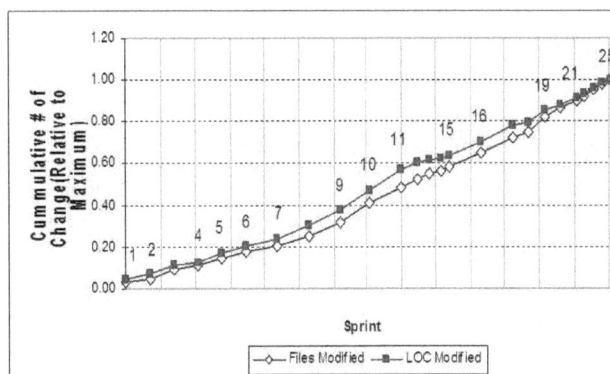

Figure 3. Law #1 - Changes in Files Relative to Maximum

In a similar vein, the sixth law, i.e., continuing growth, states that the functional content of software systems must be continually increased to maintain user satisfaction over their lifetime. We have used number of files and number of methods to measure the functional growth of the software system, since both these measure represent system functionality albeit at different levels of granularity. We found these measures to show very similar growth patterns, and the cumulative number of file additions (and deletions) is shown in Figure 4. Compared to the characteristics of change (Figure 3), we see that growth in functional content occurs more rapidly in the initial stages, with around 70% of all file additions achieved by the half-way mark. This further increases to 80% just prior to the beta release sprints, and then flattens out as the focus shifts to refining existing features rather than adding new ones. Thereafter some new content is added before things are finally frozen for the release sprints. Thus overall, Lehman's law of continuing growth was also found to be followed in this project, with rapid addition in functional content being interspersed with periods where the added content is refined in preparation for a stable release. Figure 4 also shows cumulative deletion of files, which shows very similar behavior to file additions. Interestingly file deletions also occur throughout the project's lifecycle as system functionality is continually re-factored. Finally, we found that the number of files in the system (the difference between file additions and deletions), which captures net functional content at any time, shows a similar cumulative behavior.

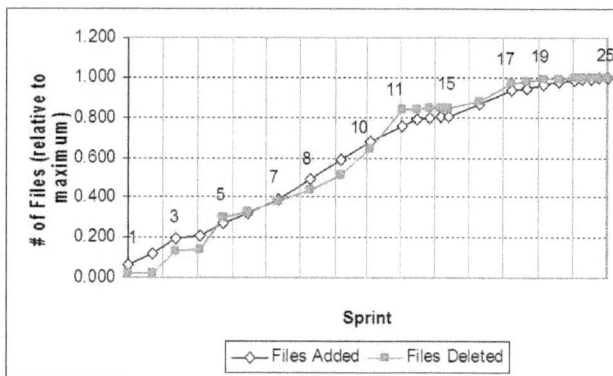

Figure 4. Law #6 - Number of Files Relative to Maximum

3.2 Self-Regulation and Feedback

This category, which subsumes the third, fourth, fifth and eighth laws, viz., Self Regulation, Conservation of Organizational Stability, Conservation of Familiarity and Feedback System, investigates how well the system "stabilizes itself" as it grows. That is, we investigate whether the system is able to maintain a degree of stability even as it grows, so that its development can be managed by the project team.

We start by describing the behavior of the third law. This law states that growth trends in the system are cyclically self regulating over a long time period. As described in [2], the incremental growth in the number of files is measured. The y-axis in Figure 5 shows the increment in the number of files $(N_i - N_{i-1})$, N_i being the number of files in the system for the ith sprint. A similar growth trend is seen when the lines of code or number of methods added are considered. We see that in the ADM lifecycle as followed in the project, there are considerable ripples in the growth. A sprint with a

large increment in number of files is usually followed by one where these is a lesser number of additions, and this pattern repeats, clearly emphasizing the self-regulatory nature of the development process. Interestingly, in some cases, the net number of file additions falls below 0, as more files get removed than added through re-factoring of functionality.

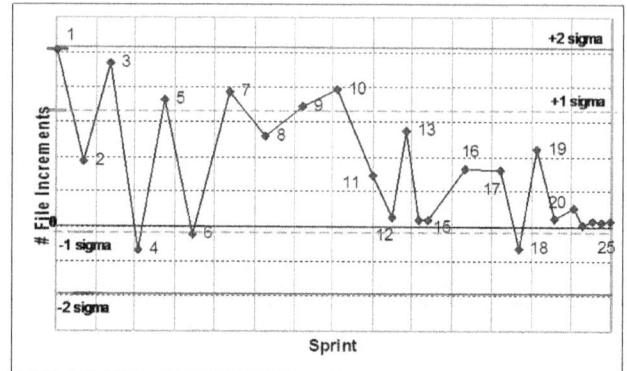

Figure 5. Law #3 - Incremental File Changes over Previous Sprint

Figure 5 depicts the 1-sigma (standard deviation - red-colored line segments) and 2-sigma (twice the standard deviation - black-colored line segments) ranges. It can be observed that most incremental file changes are within the 1-sigma range, with all of them within the 2-sigma range. Thus even when there are ripples in growth, these are regulated within certain bounds. Overall, Lehman's third law of cyclical self-regulation does seem to explain the observed behavior in the project.

The fourth law on *conservation of organizational stability* proposes an "invariant work rate" - that is, the average effective global activity rate on an evolving system is invariant over the product life time. Lehman, et. al. [2] measured the number of modules handled per day (handle rate) for every release and concluded that handle rate is stationary with cyclic ripples. However, studies on the evolution of open source systems have found them failing to comply with "invariant work rate law" because in all of them, the number of developers increases over the system's life time. In our case study, the project team stayed reasonably stable throughout the period of study. We measured the handle rate of a sprint as the average number of files/methods/lines of code changed per day during the sprint. Figure 6 shows the measured handle rate of changed lines of code (loc); i.e., we divide the total number of loc changed during a sprint by the time period of the sprint. While the observed behavior cannot be termed invariant, we do see that the handle rate stays within certain bounds; for example, Figure 6 shows that the work rate largely stays within the 2-sigma bound (black-colored line segments), with most values remaining within the 1-sigma bound (red-colored line segments) itself. Handle rates in terms of files or methods changed were also found to possess similar characteristics.

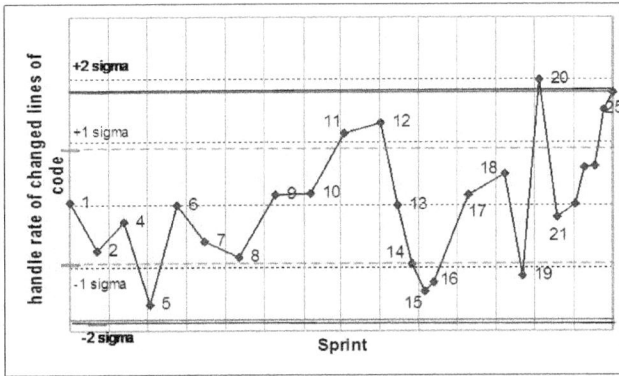

Figure 6. Law #4 - Handle Rate per Iteration

The fifth law on *conservation of familiarity* states that during the active life of an evolving program, the content of successive releases is statistically invariant. As a system evolves, the associated team must maintain mastery of its content and behavior. Excessive growth diminishes that mastery. Hence the average incremental growth remains invariant during evolution. This result follows directly from the law of self regulation, and we have seen a sprint with large increments of files to be generally followed by lesser number of additions. In addition, we also investigated the impact of the agile practice of collective code ownership on the conservation of familiarity in the system. Through collective ownership, multiple developers in the team can update and change the same code. In such a scenario, domain knowledge gets distributed across multiple team members and familiarity is thus shared. We measured the number of users owning (i.e. updating) a file through the evolution of the system. As shown in Figure 7, the percentage of files owned by multiple users gradually increases from 11% to 60%. That is, although the system does keep growing, there are steps taken through the agile development methodology to conserve file familiarity.

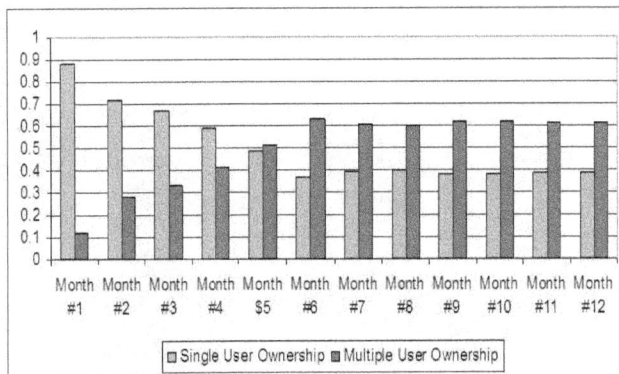

Figure 7. Law #5 - File Ownership throughout System Evolution

Finally, in the eighth law on *feedback system*, Lehman et al attribute the ripple effect of the growth of a software

system as an outcome of the system stabilizing itself due to feedback. In effect, this law, like the fifth law, states that the rate of system growth is self-regulatory, and we have already seen this behavior in our case study. Lehman [8] discussed the effect of positive feedback loops as one of the main reasons for chaotic behavior of a product development process just before product release. In contrast, in our ADM-based project, we noticed increasing stability and decreasing chaos as the product development moved towards release. Based on our interactions with the project team, we believe that this was due to the fact that in agile development, feedback is continuous across sprints, instead of being concentrated around releases. Moreover, although the product backlog changed from one sprint to the next based on the feedback received, it did not change significantly, and was managed well by accommodating whatever was possible within the time-bound release and delivering other high priority items from the backlog in a subsequent release.

3.3 Increasing Complexity

The second law of evolution states that the complexity of the system increases as the program evolves unless steps are taken to reduce complexity. We evaluated different measures of system complexity. The first measure is the percentage of files handled relative to the total number of files, based on the metric used in [2]. In their work, Belady and Lehman used modules instead of files. Here again, we did not consider high-level functional modules or components of the system as they were well defined (based on functionality) and did not increase or decrease through the project's lifecycle. Instead, as mentioned earlier, we considered each Java or Java Script file as a (low-level) functional module. Figure 8 shows that the percentage of files handled reduces through the lifecycle of the system. This is because the size of the system increases rapidly through the initial sprints, but eventually, changes are localized to few files in each sprint based on the product backlog being addressed, hence the relative percentage of files changed reduces. Thus this metric, a direct adaptation (in the context of agile development) of the one proposed by earlier work [2], seems to invalidate Lehman's law of increasing complexity. However, we believe that the measure does not reflect true functional complexity of the system, and hence we experimented with two other metrics, cyclomatic complexity and fan-out of each file, reflecting respectively, the intra- and inter file complexity within the system.

Cyclomatic complexity of a program represents the number of independent paths through it. We measured the percentage of changes where the cyclomatic complexity of the files increased, reduced or remained constant as the system evolved, as shown in Figure 9. The reductions are a result of some refactorings due to the feedback that is given at end of each sprint. As Figure 9 shows, the percentage of changes resulting in an increase in cyclomatic complexity (due to additional functionality) was much higher (and increased sharply

109

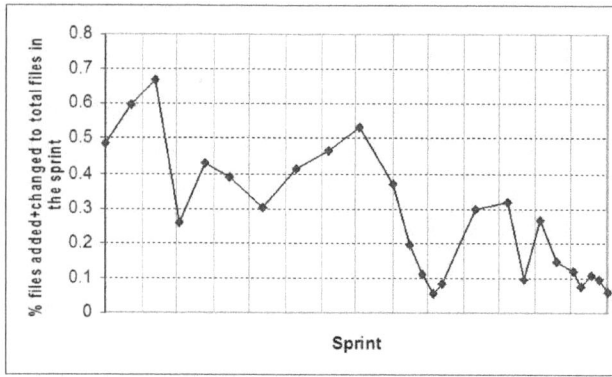

Figure 8. Law #2 - Percentage of Files Added+Changed

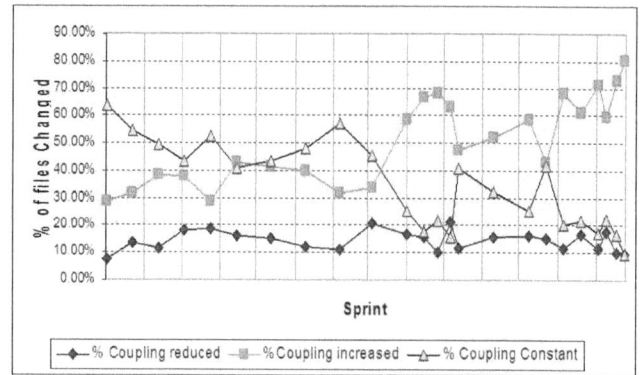

Figure 10. Law #2 - Changes in Coupling across Sprints

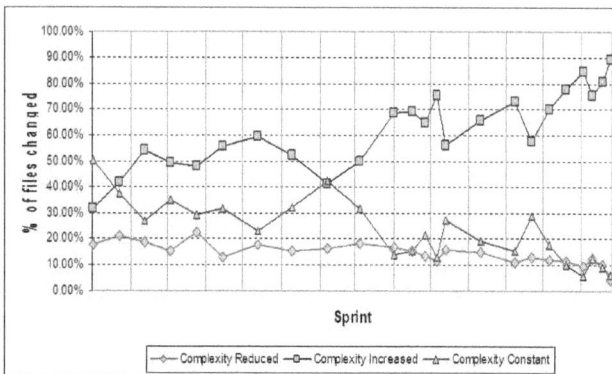

Figure 9. Law #2 - Changes in Complexity across Sprints

through the lifecycle of the project) than those that caused the complexity to reduce or remain constant. As the refactorings were relatively small, their impact on the overall complexity of the system was not significant, and the complexity continued to increase as per Lehman's law.

We also measured the efferent coupling (fan-out) of each file or class which is the number of functions the particular class or file calls. We computed the percentage of file changes where coupling of the files increased, reduced or remained constant as the system evolved, as depicted in Figure 10. We see similar behavior as with cyclomatic complexity. There are a few changes that result in reduction of coupling but these have less impact on the large percentage of changes that result in increased coupling. Hence, the second law of evolution holds good across sprints.

3.4 Declining Quality

This law as defined in [9] states that the quality of a software system will appear to be declining unless it is rigorously maintained. In Rational Team Concert, it is possible to define a unit of work as task, defect or enhancement. A sprint backlog has a set of plans. Each plan would be fulfilled by tasks. If the task does not pass the test case, a defect is raised as a defect work item that needs to be addressed in a specific sprint. If there is additional work that needs to be done for a

given task, an enhancement is created. Hence, it is possible to track the sets of tasks, defects and enhancements defined for each sprint.

As shown in Figure 11, the percentage of defects start increasing as the system is developed. After the a few sprints, the percentage of defects is higher than tasks and enhancements. We classify defects into two types - requirements related and code related. The former defect type signifies a gap in the understanding of a requirement, whereas the latter type signifies a coding error; obviously, the former defect type is considered more a serious defect. In ADM, defects tend to be high because requirements are refined or redefined as the system evolves through short cycles. Hence, features get implemented as tasks and undergo multiple changes (as defects are raised). In the project under study, there are very few work items classified as "enhancements". This is a classification that has not been used frequently. Certain defects may have been enhancements. After the project advances through its life cycle, 80% of the work items are defects (see Figure 11). This is not necessarily an indication of declining quality, but an outcome of rapid prototyping with continuous feedback in ADM, and the fact that the number of task work items corresponding to features, does not increase beyond a point.

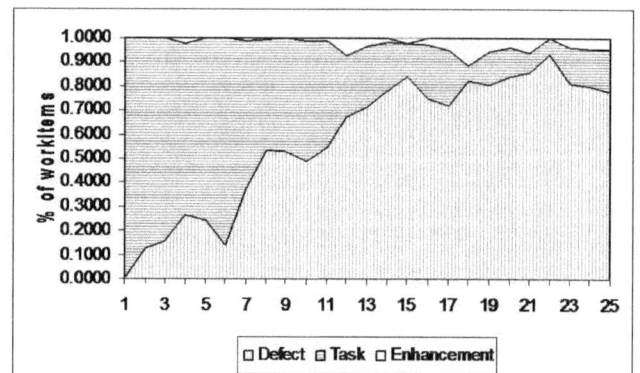

Figure 11. Law #7 - Distribution of Work Item Types across Sprints

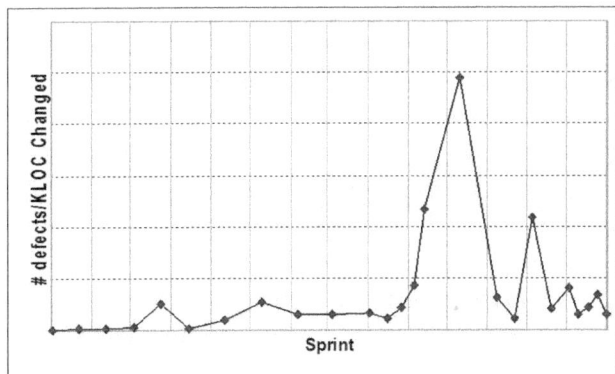

Figure 12. Law #7 - Defect Density across Sprints

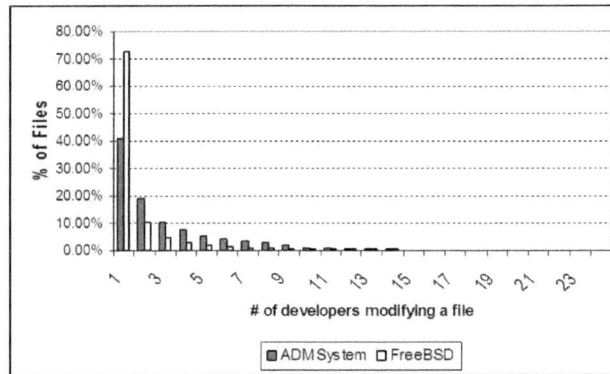

Figure 13. Code Ownership in ADM vis-a-vis Open Source Development (FreeBSD)

Table 1. % Attributed to Test Cases

Type	% Attributed
Files	12%
Methods	12%
Lines of Code	20%

To measure quality, we use the defect density measure defined in [11] as the number of defects per added or changed lines of code. The graph in Figure 12 shows that defect density stays relatively stable through the normal development-and-test sprints, but increases sharply around the beta release sprints. This is due to the fact that during these sprints relatively few lines of code are changed (as shown earlier in Figure 3), but higher number of defects are detected in earlier code through more rigorous testing. As we will discuss in Section 4, a large number of test cases are added or updated prior to the beta release sprints to facilitate this process. Overall, as defects are constantly being identified and addressed in agile development, the quality of the system appears to have been maintained, and the spike in defect density visible around beta release sprints, eventually stabilizes again towards the end of system development.

4. Observations on Agile Practices

In this section, we will summarize our observations on some of the practices followed in the project that are typically characteristic of agile development. These practices are collective code ownership, test driven development and team collaboration.

4.1 Collective Code Ownership

Agile development method promotes collective code ownership which allows any team member to make changes to the code if required. As discussed earlier in the paper, this promotes common knowledge and lends stability to the development process. We measured the percentage of files modified by multiple developers, and compared this with a large open source system - FreeBSD [3]. The modification history of source code files of FreeBSD were extracted from the version repository and analyzed. As shown in Figure 13, although a large percentage - 40% - of files are still owned (modified) by single users in our case study system (depicted as ADM System), the percentage is much higher for FreeBSD (72%). In fact, 30% of the files in the ADM project

had 4 or more people who had worked on them at some point in the project lifecycle and thus had shared knowledge and ownership of these files. Interestingly, on interviewing the developers, we discovered that actual shared knowledge was even more since many developers were experts on files they had never modified by virtue of having performed code reviews - another practice that was diligently followed in the agile project.

4.2 Test Driven Development

Test driven development (TDD) [1] is a practice where each feature is incrementally tested and developed. Hence, test cases become a key aspect where all major public classes of the system have a corresponding unit test class to test the public interface of the class. In the project under study, the user interface code was manually tested in most of the cases. However, the server code which was in Java was tested using the JUnit[4] framework. Table 1 depicts the percentage of files, methods and lines of code respectively attributed to test cases. 49% of the work items that updated Java code updated the test cases. Hence a work item updating the functionality of the component frequently resulted in updating the test cases. Figure 14 shows the number of test case files added or updated in every sprint. As has been pointed out in Section 3.4, the number of such additions/updates increased rapidly prior to the beta release so that the system could be adequately tested and hardened for the release. Post the beta release, further additions/changes were made to the test suite to keep up with the functionality modifications being made and to ready the system for the actual release.

---

[3] http://www.freebsd.org/

[4] http://junit.sourceforge.net/

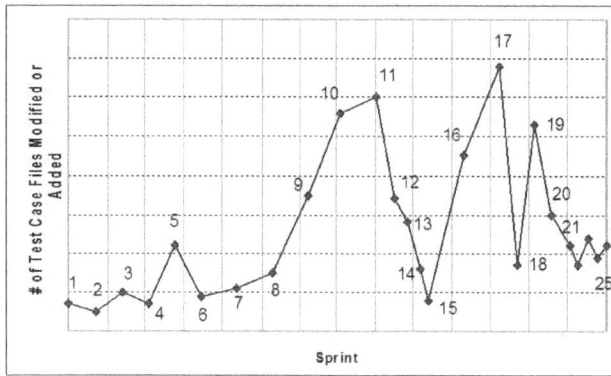

Figure 14. Test Case Files Added/Updated per Sprint

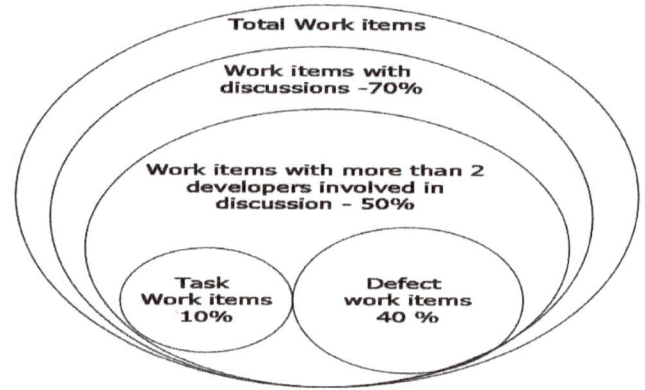

Figure 15. Discussions linked to Work Items

4.3 Collaboration in Distributed ADM

In the project under study, we had 10% of the team distributed. The distributed team consisted of primarily the management, ScrumMaster of a functional component and a few developers. The goal was to identify the use of collaborative development in the distributed agile team. Rational Team Concert provides a mature environment for collaboration. It is possible to associate a set of team members to a work item. The team members can add their discussions and link it to a work item. This enables us track the discussions team members had against each work item. We focused on collaboration around development work items - task, defects and enhancements. In future, we will evaluate other types of work items such as plans, user stories, etc. which depict the requirements planning in ADM.

The following observations are made based on Figure 15. Of the total development work items, 30% did not have any discussions around them within the tool. These work items would have largely involved face-to-face discussions given that 90% of the team was co-located. Of the remaining 70% of work items, there are several where only a single user has added his/her comments. The developers of the team provided the following explanations for this scenario: i) a test team member sometimes adds a discussion to describe a scenario or the context when reporting a defect; or ii) often, a developer who had face-to-face discussions with colleagues, summarizes the inter-personal discussions and links it to the work item for the record, and for the awareness of others who may be interested. As majority of the team is co-located it is common to have such a summary of discussions noted against a work item.

It is also observed that the functional leads (typically ScrumMasters) of each component, the management and the testing team are involved in a large number of discussions. 50% of the total discussions are attributed to them (16 members of the team). The components that are distributed have 45% more discussions against the work items as compared to co-located teams.

The type of work items that have a large number of team members involved in discussion were also analyzed (see Figure 16). There are a few work items that have more than 9 developers (a few have as high as 15 members) which is large considering each functional team has 5-6 members. Large number of developers indicates the work item needed discussions across different teams. 90% of these work items were defects. The lines of code modified for each of these work items was measured. Around 71% of these work items led to more than 100 LOC changed, and 20% had more than 500 LOC changed. This high volume of code change suggests that the work items most probably involved requirements that were refined, and required several members to discuss and arrive at consensus.

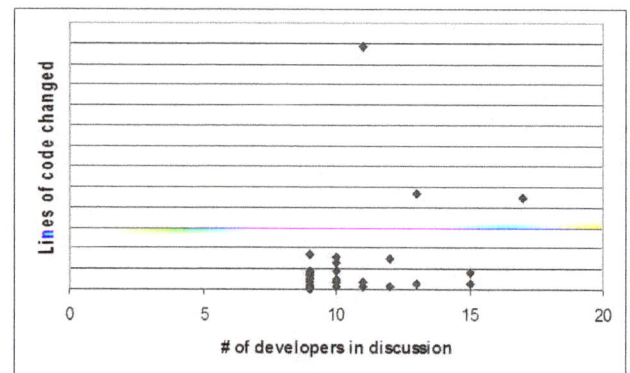

Figure 16. LOC changed for workitems involving large number of developers in discussions

5. Insights from the Case Study

The following are some of the insights we gathered from the case study, which may benefit a team embarking on a new agile development project.

- Projects following ADM are likely to constantly change and refine features already developed. This may occur because understanding of requirements evolve over multiple sprints, and as a result, the number of defects (many of which are requirements related refinements) may be much higher than tasks (new development), as has been observed through Figures 3, 4 and 11. This has important implications for estimation - when a project plans for developing the features defined in the product backlog, a non-trivial effort for change and refinement should to be factored into the effort estimate.

- Evolving requirements causes constant code modifications. As these modifications need to be done in shorter cycles of sprint, the possibility of code decays in ADM is high. Developers need to continuously monitor code complexity of files across iterations and refactor code by detecting duplicate code, large classes, large methods and other "code smells" [4] across iterations.

- Test driven development would require non-trivial effort for developing test cases, and this needs to be factored in while estimating effort for developing the system. For example, in the case study, an additional 10% of code was written in order to accommodate TDD. TDD is essential to ensure that the quality of the system is not compromised due to the frequent requirement changes, hence agile projects should be fully prepared to make this additional investment. In the system under study, majority of the defects were identified during beta release because a large number of test cases were developed prior to the release.

- Distributed agile teams need to use a well defined mechanism for collaboration to ensure that the continuous changes and refinements are properly coordinated. In the case study, the collaborative features of Rational Team Concert platform were widely used whenever teams and work items were distributed. It is therefore a good idea for co-located sub-teams to summarize and record their local discussions.

6. Related Work

6.1 Software Evolution

Laws of software evolution by Lehman and Belady have been defined [2] and revisited over the past 30 years [8, 9]. These laws were focused on so-called "E-type" systems, viz., systems that operate in or address a problem or activity of the real world. The laws were defined in the context of systems developed by proprietary organizations. Software evolution laws were studied in the context of open source system by Godfrey and Tu [5]. Using system lines of code as a metric for size, they concluded that the law of invariant work rate does not hold for open source software. In one of the recent works on the study of open source systems, Xie, et. al. [15] evaluated all the eight laws of software evolution on seven open source systems. They concluded that of the eight laws, Continuing Change, Increasing Complexity, Self Regulation, and Continuing Growth are still applicable to the evolution of open source software. They were inconclusive

of the other four laws on Conservation of Organizational Stability, Conservation of Familiarity, Declining Quality, and Feedback System.

6.2 Agile Development Methods

There have been limited empirical studies on evolution of systems following agile methods. A previous work on such evaluation was by Capiluppi, et.al. [3]. In their work, a study was conducted on a proprietary system (like ours) that used eXtreme Programming (XP). The authors measured the cumulative complexity control work (i.e., amount of work needed to limit complexity of the product) by counting the number of methods that experience a reduction of cyclomatic complexity between two consecutive releases (or weeks). They concluded that the amount of complexity control work accumulates across sprints. We also use this measure to evaluate Lehman's second law of increasing complexity. There have also been studies that have compared the usefulness of different agile methods based on the experiences of the teams using specific agile methods such as Scrum or XP [6, 10] and their benefits to the team and the customer. To the best of our knowledge, our study is the first substantive empirical examination of Lehman's laws in the context of agile software development.

7. Conclusions and Future Work

In this paper, we investigated Lehman's well-known software evolution laws, and tested them on a project team following the scrum agile development method. Unlike earlier work that have focused either on traditional waterfall-type development or open source development, our study looks at how Lehman's laws apply to software development characterized by short iterations and continuous feedback. We found that most of Lehman's laws hold for the ADM-based project in our case study, although some properties expected to stay "invariant" show controlled variation within bounds. We also proposed new metrics to evaluate some of the laws, for example, the laws dealing with increasing complexity and conservation of familiarity. Finally, we reported in our study some of the agile practices being followed in the project, viz., collective code ownership, test driven development and team collaboration. We discovered that a significant share of files have been modified by multiple developers during the lifecycle of the project. A large number of work items had test cases updated continuously indicating a well-defined process that ensured that changes in the functionality (i.e., feature updates) were preceded and succeeded by a test case update and verification. We also found that most of the discussions centered around defect work items, and components that involved distributed team members had significantly more tool-supported discussions as compared to co-located teams who seemed to prefer face-to-face communication. Moreover, discussions on work items that involved a large number of developers very often led to significant code change as well, indicating that the work items were typically concerned with issues such as requirements understanding and refinement. In future, we would like to review Lehman's laws on larger case studies with a view towards validating our initial results. We would also like to generalize findings across multiple agile case studies into laws that may be specific to agile development.

References

[1] K. Beck. *Test-Driven Development: By Example*. Addison-Wesley Professional, 2002.

[2] L. A. Belady and M. M. Lehman. A model of large program development. *IBM Systems Journal*, 15(3):225–252, 1976.

[3] A. Capiluppi, J. Fernández-Ramil, J. Higman, H. C. Sharp, and N. Smith. An empirical study of the evolution of an agile-developed software system. In *ICSE*, pages 511–518, 2007.

[4] M. Fowler and K. Beck. *Refactoring: improving the design of existing code*. Addison-Wesley Longman Publishing Co., Inc., Boston, MA, USA, 1999.

[5] M. W. Godfrey and Q. Tu. Evolution in open source software: A case study. In *ICSM*, pages 131–142, 2000.

[6] H. Hulkko and P. Abrahamsson. A multiple case study on the impact of pair programming on product quality. In *ICSE*, pages 495–504, 2005.

[7] C. F. Kemerer and S. Slaughter. An empirical approach to studying software evolution. *IEEE Trans. Software Eng.*, 25(4):493–509, 1999.

[8] M. M. Lehman. Laws of software evolution revisited. In *EWSPT*, pages 108–124, 1996.

[9] M. M. Lehman, D. E. Perry, and J. F. Ramil. Implications of evolution metrics on software maintenance. In *ICSM*, pages 208–, 1998.

[10] C. Mann and F. Maurer. A case study on the impact of scrum on overtime and customer satisfaction. In *AGILE*, pages 70–79, 2005.

[11] A. Mockus, R. T. Fielding, and J. D. Herbsleb. Two case studies of open source software development: Apache and mozilla. *ACM Trans. Softw. Eng. Methodol.*, 11(3):309–346, 2002.

[12] J. W. Paulson, G. Succi, and A. Eberlein. An empirical study of open-source and closed-source software products. *IEEE Trans. Software Eng.*, 30(4):246–256, 2004.

[13] K. Schwaber and M. Beedle. *Agile Development with Scrum*. Prentice Hall, 2001.

[14] L. A. Williams and A. Cockburn. Guest editors' introduction: Agile software development: It's about feedback and change. *IEEE Computer*, 36(6):39–43, 2003.

[15] G. Xie, J. Chen, and I. Neamtiu. Towards a better understanding of software evolution: An empirical study on open source software. In *ICSM*, pages 51–60, 2009.

Application Frameworks: How They Become Your Enemy

Martin Mailloux

University of Illinois at Urbana-Champaign

martin.mailloux@gmail.com

Abstract

Application frameworks have become a de-facto standard to implement business systems. In most organizations, when choosing either a development platform or a commercial solution, an application framework is part of the overall solution. This paper reviews my personal experience developing a proprietary application framework, its lifecycle, software engineering practices, successes and mistakes through its releases.

Categories and Subject Descriptors D.3.3 [**Programming Languages**]: Language Contructs and Features – frameworks.

General Terms Management, Documentation, Performance, Design, Economics, Experimentation, Human Factors.

Keywords Application Frameworks, Coupling, Evolution

1. Introduction

Application frameworks are central to most system development; they can either greatly facilitate or impair the implementation. Many in-house application frameworks are solution specific to their business domain, they provide the "silver bullet" [1] to the team, making it more productive and improving the quality by resting on the shoulders of previous releases. In most organizations, mastering the proprietary application framework enables greater developer productivity.

In many situations, an application framework will remain in use, as long as a minimal expertise remains within the team. As both the team's personnel change and

Permission to make digital or hard copies of all or part of this work for personal or classroom use is granted without fee provided that copies are not made or distributed for profit or commercial advantage and that copies bear this notice and the full citation on the first page. To copy otherwise, or republish, to post on servers or to redistribute to lists, requires prior specific permission and/or a fee.
SPLASH'10 October 17–21, 2010, Reno/Tahoe, Nevada, USA.
Copyright © 2010 ACM 978-1-4503-0240-1/10/10…$10.00.

the system goes through releases, its usage and longevity may suffer a downturn. Application frameworks can represent challenging design and conceptual work; enticing deep understanding of the technology, complex algorithm, integration with the operating system.

The demise of the American programmer was predicted over a decade ago [10] and with the flattening of the world [6], they are in competition with developers from around the world. Commoditization of IT [3] is an added pressure to increase developer productivity. In this paper I review my personal experience building a proprietary application framework through its releases which spanned many years. The information provided is based on my past experience as a software architect, but it also includes information made available to me by past colleagues. It was a successful development in many aspects for the early releases but the last releases were challenging. I document the successes, failures and challenges that each release brought to the team in terms of software engineering practices, software architecture and organizational structure.

Unlike most research on application frameworks, a study was done independently to evaluate the value of migrating through different releases of the application framework [4]. The study focused on the early releases of the application framework and concluded it was positive in terms of effort versus new functionality.

Application framework just like its counterpart, application system, evolves through time by subsequent chains of minor improvements and a few major (big bang) evolutions. To better understand the architectural changes that occurred through time in the application framework, information regarding the company strategy is provided and the evolution of the software engineering practices.

2. Organization Specificity

The organization was involved in developing website systems for its own usage, and all websites were not only sharing the application framework but some of the business functionality. The websites were Business To Business (B2B) e-marketplace for a specific industry. All websites were online transactional processing (OLTP) systems, requiring high availability, with worldwide clientele (24/7). Specific extension and capability was provided to enable customization of application functionality for each website. The application framework supported the encapsulation of system level functionality but also extensibility features such as business rules specialization found in business oriented application frameworks such as the San Francisco framework [2].

The software development group (SDG) was divided in three distinct teams:

• Software Infrastructure: in charge of the application framework.

• Business Component: in charge of providing generic business components to implement business functionality.

• Website Family: in charge of developing all the websites within a common business domain. Amongst the websites that a website family team was in charge of, many were related to a similar industry in terms of functionality and business requirements. A website family team would implement common functionality into a generic website for its family, which would then be specialized.

3. Releases

3.1 Bare Bones

Description: it represents the initial implementation, with very few websites being developed by the organization; most developers had limited professional experience.

Organization: the overall company had less than 30 employees.

Table 1: Bare Bones Software Engineering Practice

Project planning	None
Project management	• Most specifications could fit on a single page. • Release management was non existent, write code→clean compiled→ship to production→wait for the comeback.
Configuration management	• An excel spreadsheet is used to track who is modifying which file.
	• Development and production environment only.
Software Quality Assurance	No bug tracking tool (except excel).
Change management	None.
Programmer's Life	No enforcing of the few rules, collegiate environment.

Software Architecture: the implementation was divided in 4 layers: template, controller, entity object, entity accessor.

• Template: an html page template was divided in sections, such as header, body and footer. Within the template, placeholders were used to add content at runtime.

• Controller: process a request and implement the business rules, interacts directly with the entity object and entity accessor to execute the request and generate the response using template.

• Entity: an entity represents a Java implementation of a relationnal table. It did not implement any business logic and was a data object (getter/setter) to interact with its entity accessor.

• Entity accessor: an entity accessor was composed of two sections, one generated by the framework and a user defined part. A generator was used to generate both the entity and the entity accessor based on a create table statement.

No factory was used within the system, therefore to begin the implementation of a website, a set of scaffolding classes was available. The scaffolding classes were composed of classes prefixed with "AB" such as "ABUser". Within the code, instantiation of objects were instructed by "new ABUser()". Each Website class was prefixed with a set of specific characters, such as "TEST". The generator processed the class' sources, and generated the specific code for a website (it would generate the class file and rename all AB to the specific prefix for the website).

Lesson Learned:

• Learning curve: the application framework used very basic techniques; therefore it was assimilated very rapidly. If a programmer could do an SQL statement, they could very rapidly code an entity and its accessor, and write a specific method for a controller. The template system, even though proprietary, was very close to other templating systems of that time.

• Protection: there was no protection against programming errors, (ie., not closing a 'PreparedStatement'). An unclosed PreparedStatement by a Controller will not release the resource at the database level and will exhaust in the long run the available resource.

- Maintainability: the website could easily be maintained and the overall classes/code to implement functionality could very rapidly be found and traced by a developer. The code was using specialization to implement specific business rules. There was no indirection in the code and very few abstractions were used in the system.

- Generator: very easy and powerful way to generate the scaffolding code for a website. The drawback was that many classes were generated only to instantiate specific classes. To implement modifications of the application framework could require regenerating the website code.

3.2 1st Abstraction

Description: It was the first release of the application framework, where the 'whitebox' framework was not a set of generated classes specific for each website. A basic Class factory was implemented which required minimal configuration to instantiate the specialized classes by the business components or the website. Specialization of business rules was still based on overloading the method within the class hierarchy.

Organization: the software development group had grown, but was still comprised of less than 30 employees.

Table 2: 1ˢᵗ Abstraction Software Engineering Practice

Project planning	None
Project management	• No development methodology. • Release management: no change.
Configuration management	• Quality Assurance and Pre-Production environment are added to the Development and Production environment. • A proprietary build system is implemented.
Software Quality Assurance	• No bug tracking tool (except excel). • A Quality Assurance Group is in place: QA is on overdrive to pickup the past releases.
Change management	Informal one-on-one coaching
Programmer's Life	• Programming standard emerged. • Code generation for Entity was available. A java program interprets the SQL Data Definition Language (DDL) and based on its specification, generates the properties and the getters/setters.

Software Architecture: A new business object emerged, the Transactional Object (TXO). It will be used to remove some of the business related processing from the controller. Common interface started to be used to specify class signature.

Lesson Learned:

- Learning curve: initial loss of control due to the introduction of the class factory and its added abstraction was an acceptable solution in relation to its cost/benefit.

- Protection: it introduces a purer whitebox framework without code generation. As loopholes were found in the application framework, the correction did not require anymore re-generating the website.

- Maintainability: the drawback of using a factory to instantiate an object is greatly alleviated by the removal of all the repeated code. The business code is not mixed with framework related code.

3.3 Commercial

Description: This iteration of the application framework was in reaction to the business initiative of the company, to facilitate the commercialization of its solution if given the opportunity. The initial application framework was based solely on proprietary technology, from the templating system all the way to the application server itself. Only Java and its components, such as JDBC were used in the application server. As J2EE was becoming the fad of the day, a new direction was set for the application framework. The business entity became J2EE Entity (the Entity and Entity accessor were merged) and the TXO a stateless Session bean. It was decided to modify the proprietary application server to support the J2EE semantic instead of purchasing and migrating the production infrastructure.

Organization: the software development group was growing, and within a year it was over 100 employees.

Table 3: Commercial Software Engineering Practice

Project planning	Websites begin to implement project plan.
Project management	No change.
Configuration management	A configuration manager is implemented.
Software Quality Assurance:	No change.
Change management	Formal documentation: "How-to".
Programmer's Life	A code generator was implemented, to generate the required Interface, Entity and the J2EE proxy object. First release of the Developer Workbench.

Software Architecture: the overall layered architecture remained the same. The modifications implied changes at each level, but their design responsibility remained the same.

Lesson Learned:

- Organization growth: the rapid growth of the software development group requires documenting and formal training on our technology. The original few are spread amongst the teams in an effort to provide in-team support. The average tenure for team members in the company can almost be counted in weeks.

- Learning curve: this release is a major rewrite of the business object implementation, but the overall learning curve is fast as most of the concepts are very similar.

- Inertia: the rapid growth of the software development group and in the number of websites that it must support, adds to the challenge of implementing through the website teams a new release of the application framework.

- Maintainability: having its proprietary J2EE implementation, no commercial IDE is available to help developer productivity. Projects are started to integrate the continuous build platform into a tool (Developer Workbench) to automate and facilitate the tasks of managing the project configuration.

3.4 Advanced Business Function

Description: The software development group initiates the centralization of common business function development to a central business component team. The more complex business functions are redesigned, to implement a configurable workflow system to facilitate the customization across websites.

Organization: the software development group is stable, with a very low turnover.

Table 4: Advanced Business Function

Software Engineering Practice

Project planning	The application framework is following a release management, with planned release and features set (Priority: Required, High, Medium, Low).
Project management	No change.
Configuration management	Documentation for Major/Minor release and overall release policy
Software Quality Assurance	Automated testing is implemented by the websites, but not for the application framework.

Change management	• A preliminary description of each release is communicated to the website teams. • Formal release notes includes: dependency & compatibility, migration activities, fixes & improvement, business layer modifications.
Programmer's Life	TogetherJ is now used as platform for code generation.

Software Architecture: the layered architecture is reviewed to enforce greater de-coupling between the presentation and the business layer. XML serialization of Entity is added and XSLT template is supported alongside with the previous template system. A new business object, New Entity, is implemented to replace the J2EE entity. The New Entity is implemented to fully support inheritance, unlike its DDL predecessor. It is modeled using TogetherJ. TogetherJ code generation is too generic and not specific to the application framework. A custom code generator is integrated with TogetherJ.

Lesson Learned:

- Decoupling: XML provided a very strong decoupling mechanism between the presentation and the business layer. Within the business layer and through the persistence layer, XML processing was more costly to program and also to execute. It could adversely influence performance due to the cost of XPath and/or serializing/de-serializing the objects. In an effort to decouple all aspects of the application system, all dependencies were transferred into configuration elements. Using XML as a decoupling mechanism moved most of the basic validation from the compilation to the runtime realm. Code quality degradation cannot be tracked by using coupling as a criteria [7] with XML as a integration scheme.

- Layers vs Workflow: most designs of a workflow, start with the state machine and the pre/post condition. The workflow system had to be highly customizable to meet the variety of requirements across all the websites. The current layering implementation between the presentation and the business layers is based on using XML as communication protocol. This requires specific processing for the workflow system and creates a dependency in its configuration and its counterpart at the presentation layer. The workflow system may dictate as it changes state the next user interface to be displayed. If a pre-condition is added and adds a user input, the presentation layer configuration must be modified to enable this use case.

- Role Based Access Control (RBAC) [FK92]: to further improve the granularity and customization of the business components, the ACL security control was replaced with a RBAC system. The workflow system was integrated with the RBAC system, to provide greater security in its implementation. The configurable element at both the workflow and at the RBAC level made it almost impossible to predict the dependency between adding a condition in the workflow and the required RBAC modifications. Conflicts arise between achieving a configuration of RBAC at a higher level to simplify its configuration and its impact on the workflow's condition.

- Learning curve: as new technology and abstraction concepts are introduced, the short term productivity is lowered. The strategy is through greater decoupling, the cost of customization should be reduced in the long term.

- Maintainability: decoupling between the components using XML, made the current IDE (Eclipse) ill-adapted. We lost the power of live debugging and checking objects/variables states at run time. Properly writing a configuration file became almost a programming language of its own.

- Configuration: the number of errors caused by the high level of configurable elements in the components configuration, required building a configuration browser/editor. Also, as the configuration became a central location for dependency between components, it was also the main element in configuring the components across the environment (development, quality assurance, pre-production, production). From the original configuration file in XML it grew into a XSLT like file. Where specific keywords could be used within the configuration to specify based on the environment/servers specific parameters to the components (such as database username/password).

3.5 User Experience

Description: To improve the User Experience, we initiated a stronger binding, through configuration and naming convention, between the presentation layer and the business layer. One of the caveats of web development, compared to a 4th generation programming platform, is field validation such as maximum input must be duplicated between the layers. The extent to which a business object will be customized across the website could not be predicted by its designer. The ease of modifying a field's attribute at the configuration level did not have its equivalent all the way to the presentation layer. Basic dynamic binding using 'contract' between the layers was initiated, binding the field's attribute of the persistence layer across all the layers.

Organization: the software development group is stable, with very low turnover.

Table 5: User Experience Software Engineering Practice

Project planning	No change.
Project management	No change.
Configuration management	The business component group is challenged in implementing a release management, with planned releases and feature sets. The customization by some websites makes it too costly to migrate them to the newer version.
Software Quality Assurance	A bug tracking tool is implemented (bugzilla).
Change management	• A preliminary description of each release is communicated to the website teams. • Formal release note includes: dependency & compatibility, migration activities, fixes & improvements, business layer modifications.
Programmer's Life	A developer workbench is developed to integrate the proprietary tools (build system, management console).

Software Architecture: to provide a refined user interface, such as highlighting field in error, a mechanism that enables to customize errors between the layers is implemented. The error management by itself is very complex and costly to use effectively.

Lesson Learned:

- Decoupling: To make the components work together we kept adding more configurations. Architects and designers greatly appreciated the advantage, but developer productivity started to be a challenge.

- Learning curve: more abstraction added more proprietary technology, which required more proprietary tools added to Eclipse to alleviate the development effort. Our development teams were no longer Java specialists, but experts (some will say PhD) in our proprietary technology. Error messages and stack trace were not indicative to the source of the problem, but required interpretation to diagnose the issue.

- Maintainability: in most cases, a runtime error generated a stack trace that included calls only to the framework classes. Most business objects became anonymous and were dynamically configured.

- Configuration: it seems that most developers spent more time trying to decrypt their configuration then doing java coding.

- Contract: the contract system provided a mechanism to manage the difference in specification across the layers. As an example, in a business object 'User' the username may be mandatory. In the search function for users, the username must follow the attribute length, but not inherit that it is mandatory. Contracts were dynamically generated for Create/Read/Update/Delete (CRUD) services on an object, but complex business transactions had to build their contract step by step. At the business function level, the contract represented a Service Oriented Architecture (SOAP), but within the system implementation itself, all operations had become services. Developers on top of configuring the business object had become contract experts.

The standardization of literal values for numbers, strings, dates, was standardized in the earlier release, following the "Whole Value" pattern [5]. The deferred validation pattern was implemented to provide an initial pass of validation for a form. Instead of having each field process all its validation at once, a two phase validation was implemented. The first phase provided basic unit field validation such as: mandatory/optional, length, format. Any error during this phase, produced a feedback to the user about which fields were incorrectly entered. The second phase of validation was related to complex business rules, which included inter-field dependency such as verifying a begin date is before or equal to the end date.

3.6 Going Horizontal

Description: the model of centralizing the development of common business objects, but going through a distributed model for customization became inefficient. The distributed customization incurs a very high cost of training each website team in the specificity of each common business module. Also, the centralized team lacked the opportunity to synchronize the websites' release in accordance to their own schedule. Websites were allowed an 'a la carte' choice, instead of the 'buffet' approach, and therefore would pick and choose to upgrade only a few modules at a time. The cost to manage the diverse version of the common modules, and their inter-dependencies, made it impractical to have an 'agile' response time.

Organization: the software development group was reorganized based on the common business modules that existed. Each team was in charge of a specific set of common business modules and its customization.

Table 6: Going Horizontal Software Engineering Practice

Project planning	Each team plans its activities, with informal inter-dependency scheduling.
Project management	Initial attempt to initiate a Project Management Office (PMO).

Configuration management	No change.
Software Quality Assurance	Quality Assurance was divided across the business modules team.
Change management	An initial training was provided to the development team. The application framework rate of change was so fast, that rapidly the initial training became obsolete. There are no formal meetings/communication channels to funnel the information.
Programmer's Life	The developer workbench/open-source or commercial tools are not providing the proper toolset to enable productive work with this application framework.

Software Architecture: the organization takes this opportunity to expand the Contract system. The primary goals were to leverage emerging open-source technologies and to use a declarative approach. It leveraged the metadata information from the entity as a source to define the contract.

This release of the application framework, unlike the previous release, could not upgrade one website at a time to track the tasks required and fix the problems that arose.

The new organization structure meant it had to upgrade all the business module teams at once, to have one functional website. The major challenges for the infrastructure team were:

- Persistence Layer: major upgrades to the persistence layer are performed to make it more declarative. It is migrated from a proprietary ORM implementation to Hibernate.

- Declaractive programming: very complex processing is added to support the declarative approach across all the layers.

- Website as assembly: websites are not whole anymore. They are an assembly of services. Distributing the workload across servers based on the website must be modified to support the distribution by business module.

- Distribution model: the distribution model is also supported at each layer, distributing the presentation and business/persistence layer across servers.

The overhaul of the application framework is initiated as the functional module teams are created. During the first four months, the functional module teams are involved in requirements gathering across all the websites. Training sessions are organized to bootstrap the team on the technology. As implementation begins, missing functionality or heavy/redundant configurations are modified. No efforts are spared in having an application framework that will require no programming, only declarative configuration. The declarative programming is implemented by specifying all rules in XML. Code walkthroughs are also performed to monitor what is lacking in the declarative programming. The application framework is extended as business modules are developed to support them through declarative programming. The modifications are retrofitted into the current development.

In the first few weeks when the implementation began, developers encountered problems with the application framework that were resolved promptly without many side effects. As the development effort gained momentum, more developers were using the application framework encountering more problems and limitations.

Throughout its lifecycle, the application framework had very limited formal quality assurance performed prior to a website upgrade. Ad-hoc unit tests were performed by each developer on the application framework with each modification. The first website migration was performed by the application framework team, assisted by the website technical lead.

Under the horizontal team structure all the teams had to be affected at once by any changes to the application framework. Any deficiency in quality assurance by the application framework team increased the risk of downturn with all the teams experiencing bugs, stopping them in their tracks. As expected, the downward spiral of having more teams finding more bugs meant tighter deadlines for the application framework team to release fixes, increasing the risk of regression bugs showing up.

The application framework was upgraded every day, with all the teams linking directly to the development version to have access to the latest fixes. One way to minimize the risk was to slow down the rate of releases of the application framework and to stabilize each version prior to release. With increasing pressure to provide the missing functionality, proceeding forward was deemed the best solution.

Lesson Learned:

- Pulling the Carpet: having a whole software development organization developing on an application framework that was modified beneath them was a risky proposition and it was proven to be a costly approach.

- Pilot Project: no pilot project was initiated, or even in this case, a pilot/test website to support future quality assurance activities. The pilot project should have led the way in functionality and been used as a demonstration/teaching platform for the teams.

- Champion: as the application framework team got overwhelmed with the development/bug fixing/support

cycle, having a champion in each business module team would have eased the problems. Champions would have been a key asset in communicating the best practices as well as serving as a single point of communication.

- Toolset/IDE: as new technology is released, having the proper toolset/IDE to support it is essential. As an example, the lack of validation in the configuration makes it very costly to track and fix a problem. Poor support of the developer in repetitive tasks or having complex configuration files, creates a barrier to the adoption of the application framework.

- Weekly gathering: no organized communication structure was established to gather either the technical lead on each team or at the management level.

- Moral: developers did not see it in a positive light, to become a XML specifier instead of a Java developer.

- Quality: an application framework initial quality + support of the developers in their task would be proportional to its acceptance. Each issue encountered slowed the curve of acceptance of the new framework.

- Layering: The new application framework implemented two distribution layers for a website. The traditional distribution between presentation and business layer was implemented between two instances of application servers, but also, across servers for each functional module. Each functional module could be leveraged across multiple websites. The double distribution and dependency across functional modules (i.e., each are dependent on the security module) required complex operational process for upgrades or system restart.

- Remote layering: as a means to provide higher scalability and remove all coupling between servers, each invocation across layers went through a queuing system. The queuing system was implemented using a persistent manager. Each layer was conceptually implementing a service oriented approach, publishing its services and guaranteeing the execution of the request.

SOA: As described in [12], the major goals of a service oriented architecture vs an object oriented analysis-design are:
- Increased Business Requirements Fulfillment
- Increased Robustness
- Increased Extensibility
- Increased Flexibility
- Increased Reusability and Productivity.

With the promised gain of a SOA approach, one can only question why almost the opposite occurred. All aspects of SOA were leveraged: service contracts, coupling, abstraction, reusability, autonomy, statelessness, discoverability and composability. The major misstep came in having a very small granularity level for the service definition. The system was not anymore implemented using an object-oriented approach, but instead services built by aggregating atomic services together. No distinction was done between an internal service required only within one business transaction and one by an external module. An internal service would be implemented in a more straightforward manner through a traditional OO approach. Toolsets to support SOA, especially complex service composition, were not available and had to be scripted manually.

A service orientation architectural direction is justifiable if requirements such as a heterogeneous platform [11] is required. The operational criteria under which the system was deployed did not have such requirements.

3.7 Open-Source

Description: after spending much time, energy and a massive capital investment, the organization judged that the current direction was not achieving its goals and could not be sustained. Conversion to the Going Horizontal application framework was suspended; some functional modules remain implemented with the User Experience release. It did a first prototype based on open-source technology (Spring, Hibernate, JSP), which was then standardized for future development. As the open-source release was deployed, efforts are engaged to break the ties between websites still dependent on the previous release.

Organization: the software development group is regrouped around websites, as it was previously.

Software Architecture: the software architecture is now a mix of three releases, User Experience, Going Horizontal and Open-Source.

4. Conclusion

Application frameworks are part of most systems; some are part of a commercial platform and others a proprietary implementation. In all cases they support a set of implementation patterns relevant to their business domain, with the goal to reduce time to market and cost of development. Our business domain was specific and as such, not very likely to attract the attention of a researcher or of a software provider. Some of the challenges we encountered were common across the industry, such as implementing an Object-Relational-Mapping system. Today, commercial and open-source solutions are readily available for many of the requirements we had.

The area where we encountered the most difficulty, contract management, is the one area where both research and the industry have not advanced to answer our requirements.

Acknowledgments

I would like to thank Professor Ralph E. Johnson at the University of Illinois at Urbana-Champaign, who served as my supervisor for an independent study which was the original bases for this paper.

References

[1] Brooks F. P., The mythical man-month, Addison Wesley, 1995.

[2] Carey J., Carlson B., Graser T., San Francisco Design Patterns: blueprints for business software, Addison Wesley, 2000.

[3] Carr N. G., IT Doesn't Matter, May 2003, Vol 81, Issue 5, p. 41-49, Harvard Business Review, 2003.

[4] Corrales Y., Laporte C. Y., Étude de cas : Évaluation de la Migration d'une Architecture Logicielle d'une Société de Commerce Électronique, Génie Logiciel, N. 82, Septembre 2007.

[5] Cunningham & Cunningham Inc., The CHECKS Pattern Language for Information Integrity, Site reviewed on March 11th, 2009.

[6] Friedman T. L., The World is Flat: A Brief History of the Twenty-first Century, Farrar-Straus and Giroux, 2005.

[7] Subramaniam G. V., Object Model Resurrection - An Object Oriented Maintenance Activity, ICSE 2000, ACM, 2000.

[8] Ferraiolo D. F., Kuhn R. D., Role-Based Access Controls, 15th National Computer Security Conference (1992), Baltimore MD, pp. 554 – 563, 1992.

[9] Weinberg G.M., The Psychology of Computer Programming, Silver Anniversary edition, Dorset House, 1998.

[10] Yourdon E., Decline & Fall of the American Programmer, Yourdon Press, 1993.

[11] Mariani R., Bohling B., Smith C. U. Barber S., Improving .Net Application Performance and Scalability, Microsoft Corporation, 2004.

[12] Erl T., SOA Principles of Service Design, Prentice Hall, 2008.

MDSD for the iPhone

Developing a Domain-Specific Language and IDE Tooling to produce Real World Applications for Mobile Devices

Heiko Behrens

itemis AG

Heiko.Behrens@itemis.de

Abstract

During the last years, code generators and models have become increasingly popular tools to support software development processes in manyfold ways. At the same time, the emerging pervasiveness of domain-specific languages (DSLs) in this field has complemented the idea of raising the level of abstraction by introducing specialized view points of a certain problem space. In combination with a proper set of idioms at the target platform generation-based approaches allow for weaving generated parts of an application with handwritten enhancements and refinements over the whole application lifecycle.

The mobile division of itemis AG has delivered an implementation of such a model-based solution for mobile devices that uses a DSL to completely describe the structure and behavior of data-centric mobile applications. Its tool support reaches from static analysis over code navigation to compiler and simulator integration of the iPhone development platform.

Categories and Subject Descriptors D.2.6 [*Software Engineering*]: Programming Environments

General Terms Design, Languages

Keywords Model-Driven Software Development, Development Environment, Domain-Specific Language, Mobile Devices, Eclipse, iPhone

1. Introduction

The advent of virtual market places for smart phones such as the Apple App Store paved the way for many companies not active in this particular area of business before to participate in the market and to leverage their established infrastructure and customer base. The increasing amount of available applications for mobile devices (*apps*) on the market is versatile and reaches from casual games over comprehensive applications with rich media to unique solutions that take advantage of the uninterrupted availability of the internet in conjunction with a set of advanced sensors not accessible to the consumer market a few years ago. For the most part though, today's mobile applications reuse and deliver existing content in a way suitable for mobile devices. Information retrieval systems for public transportation, mobile clients for social networks and simple shop systems take advantage of existing APIs and make up a successful portion of the mobile market.

Whereas such applications technically could be implemented with modern web standards to allow offline capabilities, caching and advanced animation customers explicitly ask for native applications for platforms such as iOS [3] or Android [1]. We find that the ongoing demand for native apps even for basic scenarios can be derived from to following reasons.

Visibility Till this day the virtual market of mobile applications for the iPhone is solely controlled by Apple. Only apps that fulfill certain conditions will be listed on the App Store and will thereby be accessible to potential customers via this prominent distribution channel. In addition to requirements with regard to its contents Apple only allows native apps to be listed on the App Store.

Extensibility Customers new to the market of mobile applications tend to limit their capital spending and aim for a short time to market with only a minimum set of initial features. The production costs of mobile web applications for this purpose might be lower than those of their native counterpart. But from a technology perspective websites remain less capable. We find that customers are willing to accept higher development costs to protect the investment by allowing for unforeseen additional features currently only possible with native applications.

To streamline the process of prototyping as well as to allow unexperienced developers to start producing mobile

Permission to make digital or hard copies of all or part of this work for personal or classroom use is granted without fee provided that copies are not made or distributed for profit or commercial advantage and that copies bear this notice and the full citation on the first page. To copy otherwise, to republish, to post on servers or to redistribute to lists, requires prior specific permission and/or a fee.

SPLASH '10, October 17–21, 2010, Reno/Tahoe, Nevada, USA.

Copyright © 2010 ACM 978-1-4503-0240-1/10/10...$10.00

applications itemis AG decided to build a textual domain-specific language (*DSL*) in conjunction with a complementary code generator. The amount of chosen concepts of this DSL had been limited intentionally and concentrates on simple, data-centric mobile applications for mobile devices as a wide range of the existing customer base requires. The tools address developers with little or no background of the actual target language Objective-C and the underlying API provided by the iPhone SDK (*iOS SDK*). To support the programmer's learning process the generated code is being geared to the sample code provided by Apple for each implemented aspect. The tool chain integrates with the development tools provided by Apple to support both the learning process of unexperienced developers as well as continuative tasks at a later step of development.

We decided to build a solution based on the Eclipse platform [7] that offers a vast range of available technologies needed for the chosen approach. We chose Xtext [10] to design the DSL and to implement different validation rules. The framework abets the integration of productivity features such content assist and code templates, too. The code generator has been realized with the template framework Xpand [9]. The Eclipse platform itself could be leveraged to implement incremental code generation, compilation of the generated Objective-C code and eventually invocation of the iPhone simulator provided by the Apple SDK without managing external tools manually.

This paper discusses the core concepts of the DSL we have chosen to implement and how well certain details could be implemented with Xtext. It continues on describing the process of development of the code generator with Xpand based on a reference implementation. Finally, the paper presents summary of the achievements and future work.

2. Development of the Domain-Specific Language

2.1 Language Capabilities

The textual domain-specific language we developed at itemis AG is capable of describing simple, data-centric mobile applications. Those applications connect to existing web resources and present the retrieved information in various ways. Asynchronous data fetching as well as established interaction metaphors of the platform has been used in order to take advantage of the mobile platform. The manual implementation of several similar iPhone application led us to the following core concepts we implemented in the DSL.

Application Structure The targeted application aligns itself with the built-in applications of the iPhone and offers a tab bar at the bottom of the screen. The views connected to each tab bar as well as possible navigation actions from each view span trees of reachable views within the described application.

Figure 1. Schematic representation of a data-centric iPhone application as it can be generated from the discussed domain-specific language.

Entities Complex data types enable a static type system within the DSL as well as runtime checks against the retrieved data. The language has support for entities that can be nested.

Content Providers The actual information as it is displayed can be retrieved from existing web resources be it an RSS feed [11] or a REST API [4]. The data retrieval has been decoupled from the views and description of the entities to allow for different data backends. As a result different named services can asynchronously be invoked throughout the DSL using a functional notation.

Views The concept of two different views eventually present the data to the user and offers interaction concepts with the application. The chosen building blocks have been derived from the iOS SDK as these turned out to be very useful in practice. The degree of freedom had been limited according to our demand in the past.

The target platform of the iPhone extensively relies on different callback methods to obtain information about the user interface and to control the user interaction. Those methods are implemented with an imperative paradigm based on Objective-C. We find that this approach is resource efficient but hard to understand and often leads to repetition in code. As you can see in Figure 2 we decided to shape our DSL in a declarative way. Functionality such as memory management, asynchronous fetching of data, or caching is hidden behind the concepts of the language.

```
detailsview SpeakerDetails(Speaker speaker) {
  title= "Presenter"
  header {
    title= speaker.name
    subtitle= speaker.tags
    details= speaker.bio
    image= speaker.photoUrl
  }

  section {
    cell Default foreach speaker.sessions as t {
      text= t.title
      action= SessionDetails(t)
    }
  }

  section {
    cell Value2 {
      text= "blog"
      details= speaker.blog
      action= "http://" + speaker.blog
    }
    cell Value2 {
      text= "mail"
      details= speaker.email
      action=  "mailto:" + speaker.email
    }
  } // 2nd section
}
```

Figure 2. A details view including a list of upcoming talks written in the domain-specific language.

2.2 Implementation and Tool Support

Xtext [10] significantly reduced our effort of developing a textual domain-specific language. It's based on the ANTLR parser [2] and integrates well into the Eclipse platform and EMF [6] where it provides a code editor and several other facilities for custom languages. From our idea of the concrete syntax we created a grammar definition of our language in the Xtext grammar language. As you can see in Figure 3 this grammar definition is similar to the EBNF notation but additionally describes so-called *features* that describe the structure of the parsed abstract syntax tree.

Even though the grammar language of Xtext allows for the definition of cross references to already declared elements the DSL concepts of nested entities, parameters of views and loops for cells required an additional scoping mechanism to control the visibility of symbols. Xtext foresees this demand and enables its adaption via a sophisticated dependency injection mechanism implemented with Google Guice [5].

Once the scoping has been implemented, the framework automatically leverages this information for error messages,

```
DetailsView:
  'detailsview' name=ID
  ('(' content=Parameter ')')?
  '{'
    'title=' title=ScalarExpression
    (header=ViewHeader)?
    (sections+=ViewSection)*
  '}';
```

Figure 3. Excerpt of the Xtext grammar definition that describes the domain-specific language.

content assist and linking of the semantic model. Xtext's built-in support of these features significantly increased the acceptance of the tools throughout the process.

3. Development of the Code Generator

3.1 Reference Implementation

From existing applications of the targeted category we derived a reference implementation as described in [8]. This fully functional mobile application captured any feature we wanted to deliver with our tools and repeatedly opened discussions to further simplify our feature set. Finally, we came up with a set of base classes and third-party libraries that implemented generic functionality such as parsing of various data formats or providing common user interface functionality. The remaining classes and resources have carefully been organized in a way that abets code generation.

3.2 Implementation of the Code Generator

The code generator has been developed with Xpand [9]. It evaluates statically typed templates to produce text from EMF objects as they come from Xtext. A powerful mechanism to extend existing classes with additional polymorphic methods reduces the amount of repetition throughout the templates significantly (see Figure 4).

```
«DEFINE sectionTitleHeader FOR SectionedView»
- (NSString *)tableView:(UITableView *)tableView
      titleForHeaderInSection:(NSInteger)section {
«FOREACH sections AS s ITERATOR i SEPARATOR "else"»
  if(section == «i.counter0»)
    return «s.title.asObjectiveCExpression()»;
«ENDFOREACH»
}«ENDDEFINE»
```

Figure 4. Excerpt of the generator template written in Xpand to produce Objective-C source code.

According to the aforementioned reference implementation we used the domain-specific language to write the corresponding reference model. From there, we gradually implemented the templates to produce the output similar to the targeted implementation. During this process the static typing of Xpand appeared to be invaluable as we constantly had to make smaller changes to the definition of the DSL. Each change in the grammar that resulted in a different model structure has been identified by the Xpand template editor before execution with the exact location and description of the errors.

4. Development Environment

The intention to deliver a development environment that render the knowledge of Apple's development tools unnecessary could partly be realized with the Eclipse platform itself. The editor of the domain-specific language offers comprehensive editing facilities and additional features such as project templates, version control integration are services of the platform itself. To finally make developers independent from a separate development environment we decided to contribute the following additional features:

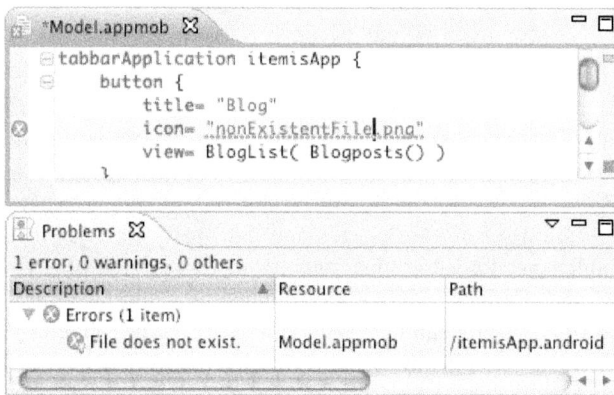

Figure 5. The semantic analysis of the Eclipse-based DSL editor checks for the existence of declared resources.

Symbolic Integration In addition to the reference checks between elements within the DSL that are provided by Xtext some additional validations and strategies have been implemented. External resources in particular are treated as strong as any other reference within that language. Even though the DSL and the target platform treat those references as ordinary strings the specific knowledge of the context allowed us to offer content assist, error markers for unknown files and quick fixes in case of typing errors (see Figure 5).

Incremental Build Code generation can be understood as an unnecessary indirection. To increase the acceptance of our development tool we established a background service that regenerates artifacts as needed. Since it is built upon the builder infrastructure of Eclipse it seamlessly integrates with other other builder steps and can transparently trigger other compilers and builders after its execution.

Invocation of the iPhone Simulator The extension mechanism of Eclipse allowed us to add additional commands at the expected locations of the user interface of the de-

velopment environment. From the developer's perspective the launch of the iPhone simulator from the DSL editor is similar to launching a Java process from a Java file.

In conjunction with minor other features such as code templates the developers were able to implement additional views and test them without leaving the Eclipse-based development environment. The full development cycle of creating, testing and changing applications is covered with this tool chain.

5. Conclusion

Even though the structure of this paper might be suggestive of the order of actions we took to develop the model-driven tool chain throughout the project we implemented the code generator as well as the domain-specific language simultaneously in an iterative manner. This approach allowed us to enhance the language concepts incrementally as we reproduced the reference implementation with the generator output. The static analysis of Xpand supported us by denoting any incompatibilities with the structure of the language concepts.

We find that the use of a domain-specific language is considerably less difficult to learn for technically experienced specialists than acquiring the needed knowledge to build mobile applications with the development tools provided by Apple. The developers only had to learn a limited set of language concepts and were guided by the tools, their extensive validation capabilities but also their constraints. Since the generated project structure including the Objective-C code complies to the official development tools and training materials developers have the chance to broaden their knowledge of the target platform on their existing accomplishments.

The presented results offer a good initial position to master the challenges we face when addressing today's mobile market with its increasing diversity of unequal technical platforms. DSLs and generators could help us to formulate a common feature set across those different types of devices. They allow for detail design and reuse of a shared application model at the same time as they already do with software in the large scale.

After the initial prototype phase of generated apps the implementation usually has to be adapted with common object-oriented techniques to weave in manually written code. In future, we will investigate possibilities to integrate project-specific classes from the DSL directly and leverage the positive effects of the model-driven approach. To do this, we will introduce concepts into the DSL to make existing classes accessible as if their were first class concepts of the language.

References

[1] Android SDK, http://www.android.com/

[2] ANTLR Parser Generator, http://www.antlr.org

[3] Apple iOS SDK, http://developer.apple.com/iphone/library/navigation

[4] Fielding, Taylor, *Principled Design of the Modern Web Architecture*, http://www.ics.uci.edu/~taylor/documents/2002-REST-TOIT.pdf

[5] Google Guice, http://code.google.com/p/google-guice/

[6] Eclipse Modeling Framework, http://www.eclipse.org/emf/

[7] Eclipse platform, http://eclipse.org

[8] Efftinge, Friese, Köhnlein, *Best Practices for Model-Driven Software Development*, http://www.infoq.com/articles/model-driven-dev-best-practices

[9] Xpand language, http://wiki.eclipse.org/Xpand

[10] Xtext framework, http://eclipse.org/Xtext

[11] RSS 2.0 Specification, http://www.rssboard.org/rss-specification

Stop the Software Architecture Erosion:

Building better software systems

Bernhard Merkle

SICK AG
Research & Development
Software Engineering
Erwin-Sick-Str.1
79183 Waldkirch, Germany
bernhard.merkle@gmail.com

Abstract

In lots of software projects unfortunately an architectural erosion happens over time. Modules which were independent, become interconnceted, plugins finally depend on each other, and in general the architecture gets violated more and more. In this paper we will discuss how to avoid such architecture- and design-erosion and how an already eroded system can be fixed again. We will look at three different level of static analysis and examine architectural analysis in detail. Also typical use cases for architectural analysis are examined, followed by a collection of requirements for powerful tool support. The eclipse platform serves as case study and we look if, and how far architectural erosion happened there and if it can be fixed. Finally we discuss pros and cons of architectural analysis and conclude with an out view.

Categories and Subject Descriptors D.2.11 [**Software Architecture**]:

General Terms Architecture, Design, Refactoring.

Keywords *software, architecture, design, erosion, refactoring, simulation, refactoring, static code analysis*

1. Introduction

Static code analysis is often used to improve programs and make them more secure and robust. Complexity and maintainability metrics try to guide a software developer and help him to write better code. However, Software Architects would like to have similar methods and tools. Unfortunately software often decays during its life time and especially in maintenance it is often difficult to find the "right" extension point and get a picture of the underlying architecture. This is where architecture-analysis and -management comes in, internal code quality will be improved and our applications will conform to the intendet architecture.

The remaining chapters are structured as follows: Chapter 2 talks about different levels of static analysis while Chapter 3 defines the term architecture and gives a couple of reasons why architecture erosion happens in projects. Chapter 4 presents several use cases for architecture analysis and Chapter 5 introduces a selection of tools which support theses use cases. A case study, the architecture erosion of eclipse is covered in Chapter 6 and finally Chapter 7 summarizes and concludes.

2. Levels of Static Analysis

Architecture Analysis [1] is usually performed via a static analysis [2] approach. A parser extracts information about the system via code and other artifacts, followed by aggregating the information on different levels. In the further discussion we want to distinguish three levels:

2.1 Micro-Level

The Micro-Level deals with the smallest entities of our program, the code itself. We care about single statements or a single code line or alternatively a combination of only a few statements. Performing analysis on this micro- or code-level tries to spot errors or risky statements embodied in the language, often used unintentionally by the programmer. Fortunately some programming languages document known "issues", e.g. C-Standard [3] Appendix G/ISO summarizes a collection of problems like:

Permission to make digital or hard copies of all or part of this work for personal or classroom use is granted without fee provided that copies are not made or distributed for profit or commercial advantage and that copies bear this notice and the full citation on the first page. To copy otherwise, or republish, to post on servers or to redistribute to lists, requires prior specific permission and/or a fee.
SPLASH'10 October 17–21, 2010, Reno/Tahoe, Nevada, USA.
Copyright © 2010 ACM 978-1-4503-0240-1/10/10…$10.00.

- unspecified behaviour
- undefined behaviour
- implementation-defined behaviour
- locale-specific behaviour

Note however that C is rather the exception: e.g. for C++ there exists no official collection of "problems" by the committee. Errors also result due to incorrect handling of the language. Less Hatton identified several patterns in "Safer C" [4] which can not be found by a compiler e.g.: Misplacement of language constructs, omission and addition, unexpected behaviour and, complexity. To avoid such problems coding-conventions like MISRA-C [5] can be used. Meanwhile also issues for C++ have been collected and published in the MISRA-C++ [6] document. Furthermore most companies have an internal coding guideline.

Checking source code against a coding guideline should definitely be automated because lots of errors can be found by tools. The typical lint-tools like pc-lint[7], splint[8], QA/C/C++ [9] or findbugs[10] perform this task automatically. Additionally files with high or suspicious metric values (e.g. complexity) should be examined in a manual code review.

2.2 Macro-Level

The next level cares about Class- and API-Design. We do not consider a single line of code but rather a complete method, its signature and subsequent implementation. Also sets of APIs or correlation of multiple methods are examined. A typical rule is e.g. that objects should be passed by C++ reference because of efficiency (avoidance of unnecessary calling a copy constructor). Other rules include how to implement a copy assignment operator correctly in C++ or the equals() and hashCode() methods in Java. Books like "Effective C++" [11] or "Effective Java" [12] define a useful set of design- rules on the Macro-Level. A small selection of the rules for C++ follows:

- Prefer const and inline to #define
- Use same form in corresponding uses of new / delete
- Declare copy constructor and assignment operator for classes with dynamic memory
- Strive for class interfaces that are minimal and complete
- Choose carefully between function overloading and parameter default

Comparing these rules with the MISRA-C rules it strikes out that there is often no binary yes/no decision. Instead we find rules which depend on several aspects (e.g. "prefer, choose carefully), or rules which can not be automatically checked at all (rule about completeness of classes / interfaces). Hence in this layer the traditional lint-tools emit more false-positives or "invalid"-warning. This is however not the tools fault, as the rules demand the human designers intelligence and information about the context.

In general the mentioned rules should be known by programmers as they significantly improve code- and design quality and can be checked (semi-) automatically by a lint-tool

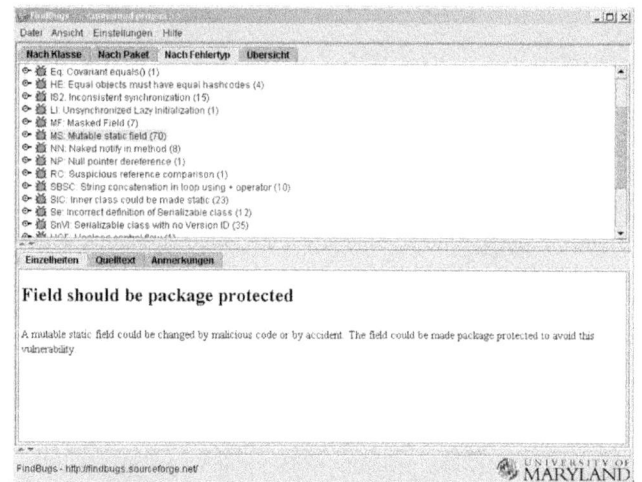

Figure 1. findbugs: static analysis for Micro/Macro-Level

2.3 Architecture -Level

On this layer we finally care about managing the overall architecture and structure of our application. Our unit of examination again gets larger and now we talk about components, subsystems and layers. Components are coarsely grained entities, usually a collection of multiple classes or packages, offering an interface for client usage. Designers and architects talk about components, their interfaces and do not really care about the lower level implementation details (we examined in 2.1 and 2.2).

Furthermore, multiple components can be grouped into subsystem and physically shipped as DLL in C/C++ or Jar-File in Java. OGSI [13] e.g. supports component based development and cares to certain extend about modularity regarding subsystems.

Often the overall architecture is designed as a layered (e.g. 3-tier) architecture. Sometimes also graph-based architectures are used.

There is plenty of literature about good design and architecture, also [14] lists good strategies and metrics for decoupling systems and handling refactorings in the large. Some exemplary rules:

- in layered architecture: no lower layer may use a upper one
- in layered architecture: only access to the n-the lower layer from a upper layer is allowed
- it is forbidden to bypass the public interface
- independent subsystems shall not use each other

Furthermore with architectural analysis we will also examine our system and search for antipatterns[15]. Dependency metrics between components and subsystems can be measured and unwanted dependencies are discovered.

Compared with 2.2 these rules are relatively simple and result in very low false-positive rates. The rules should be defined in a project specific architecture/design-guideline and also verified by a tool automatically. We will discuss the architecture-level in detail in the subsequent chapters along with a concrete case study.

3. Software Architecture and Erosion

3.1 Software Architecture

We define the term "Software Architecture" according to [16]: "The fundamental **organization** of a system, embodied in its **components**, their **relationship** to each other and the **environment**, and the **principles** governing its **design** and **evolution**.".

In this definition I highlighted the important points. Additionally Software Architecture also deals with design principles and guidelines. Kruchten suggests [17] to document them in dedicated artefacts, e.g. the "Software Architecture Document" and the "Software Design Guidelines". Similar to the same way we have coding guidelines on the Micro- and Macro-Level we should have Software Architecture and Design guidelines on that level. Furthermore usage of tools to find areas of erosion is necessary.

3.2 Software Architecture Erosion

The most important word in the definition [16] is "evolution". No architecture is a one time shot. Software always will be changed and adapted to new requirements and new end-user needs. Over time every architecture undergoes an evolution and this is where the erosion happens. During projects the design of a system and its implementation diverge to a certain extend. Robert Martin made the same observations: "Sometimes the developers manage to maintain this purity of design through the initial development and into the first release. More often something goes wrong. The software starts to rot like a piece of bad meat" [14].

One reason is that the initial software architecture often was not built for the new "unforeseen" customer requirement. To satisfy the customer however, some kind of workaround or hack will be implemented and incorporated into the architecture. It is often difficult (economically and/or technically) to change the architecture to satisfy the new emerging demands. Over time more and more violations are built in and the quality of the architecture degrades. At the end, the initial architecture can sometimes even not be recognized anymore.

Another reason for divergence is the lack of documentation and understanding of the "should architecture". Documenting design and architecture and keeping it up to date is a nontrivial task. Developers maintaining a product are often not involved in the initial design. In these cases the lack of

up to date documentation complicates product maintenance and extensibility.

And finally one reason is time pressure in projects. This correlates also with the reasons above but is usually omnipresent in projects. If a release-date comes closer, workarounds are implemented to get the product running or to meet the performance requirements. After release nobody will remove these violations because coding, testing can result in significant effort. Several effects can be shown with eroded software architectures: Programs are more difficult to understand, harder to maintain and also contain anti-patterns.

3.3 Architecture Erosion of findbugs

As a small example we briefly show the architectural evolution (and erosion) of findbugs. We already saw findbugs as a lint-like tool for code- and design-rules. How does findbugs follow the rules of the "next" level? Figure [2] shows an early version of findbugs. Dependencies are still aligned; the package structure and overall design of findbugs can be recognized and is obvious.

Figure 2. findbugs dependencies: version 0.8.6 in 10/2004

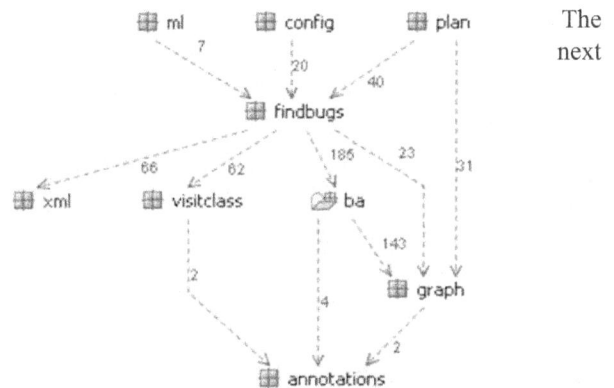

The next

Figure [3] shows findbugs three years later. The project has grown significantly in size, functionality but also complexity. Unfortunately the clean initial architecture can not be recognized anymore. The architecture analysis tool highlights that twelve top-level packages from together a cycle (tangle). That is a bad situation because it degrades the maintainability and extensibility of the software. Also packages like "util" start to have bidirectional dependencies which are a clear indication of a blurred design. Actually findbugs does not have any runtime problems or stability issues but the design and extensibility of findbugs, the internal software quality is not very good anymore. There is a need for architectural cleanup and refactoring in this case.

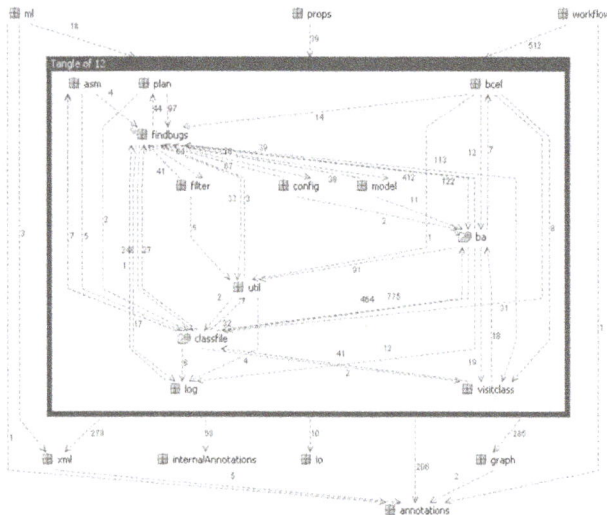

Figure 3. findbugs dependencies: version 1.3.0 in 07/2007

4. Architecture Analysis

4.1 Deviation Analysis / Reflexion Model

The main and most important use case is "deviation analysis". Architects are interested where the "is"-architecture (current code base) deviates from the "should"-architecture (the original design). We need several ingredients as shown in Figure [4]: For the "is"-architecture we need to extract the information mostly from the source code in an efficient way. This information is aggregated and stored for later evaluation.

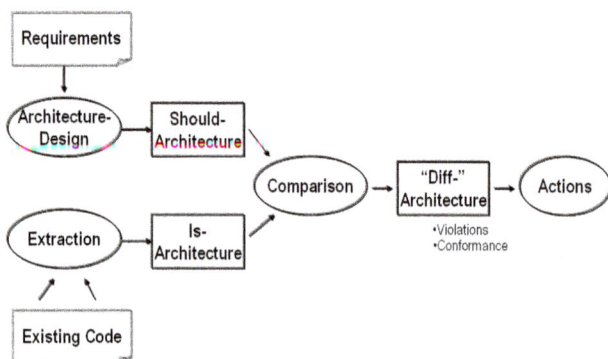

Figure 4. Reflexion model: is- and should-architecture

For the "should"-architecture we need a valid architecture model. Concepts like interface, public/private parts, components, subsystems and layers can be described with an Architecture Description Languages (ADL) [18], additionally with the allowed dependencies. Subsequently both data sets are compared by a tool and we get a report of violations or conformance versus the architecture.

The reflextion model [19] distinguishes between:

- "Convergences": Dependencies which should be present and are present in the is-architecture
- "Divergences": Dependencies which should **not** be present but are present in the is-architecture
- "Absence": Dependencies which should be present and are **not** present in the is-architecture.

Depending on the information you can then take actions and plan refactorings. Note that it is important to visualize the results in a condensed way. We do not want to see e.g. all violations between all classes. First it is important to aggregate them on the right level (e.g. inter component dependencies) and then drill down to lower levels. The amount of violations gives a first rough indication for the developer if it will be easy or difficult to cut a certain dependency. Also the numbers indicate how much the software depends on a certain framework. Additional Filter and navigation facilities are necessary in practice to manage large amounts of packages / classes.

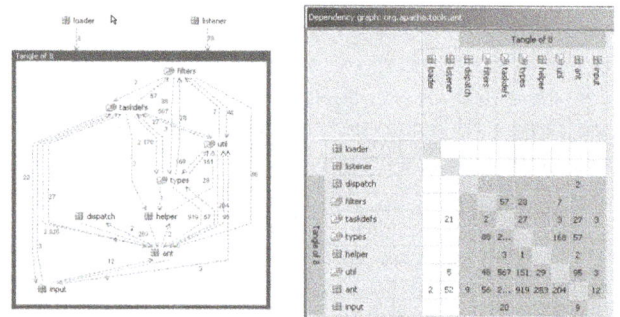

Figure 5. Graphical / numerical dependency visualizations

How to visualize the results (graphically/numerically) depends on the situation. Sometimes a graphical view is beneficial and sometimes a table with numbers is more appropriate. Figure [5] shows both alternative visualization methods: the graphical view uses the number of dependency as physical strength between to nodes. This spring-embedder algorithm can be used to visualize tight coupled packages in a very good way.

4.2 Monitoring changes, trends

An important point is monitoring changes and trends over time.

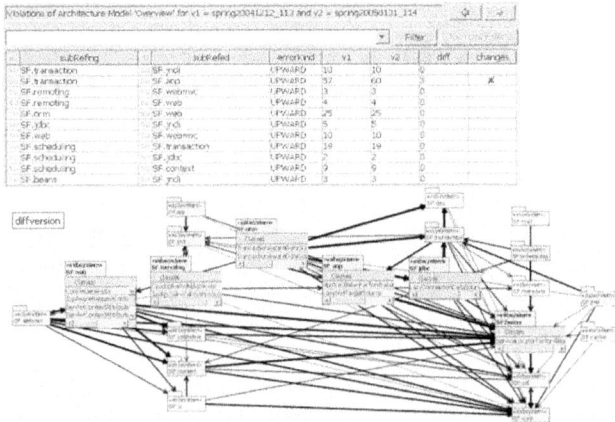

Figure 6. Graphical and numerical trend analysis

To keep track of an evolving architecture we need to have e.g. information like the number of added or removed packages, classes, methods and members. It is important to keep and eye on metrics like coupling and complexity and see if our team introduced new architecture violations. Figure [6] shows a comparison of two spring-framework [20] snapshots, both in numerical and graphical way. The numerical view shows that 3 new architecture violations have been introduces between the SF.transaction and SF.aop subsystem. In the graphical view we have highlighted all packages with new entities, added since the last version. Also the graph shows the overall architecture of spring as layered architecture where the upper layers are on the left and lower layers are on the right side.

5. Tools Overview

In this chapter we will show briefly a selection of architectural analysis tools. The following chapter will apply one of them to conduct an architecture analysis on the Eclipse platform.

5.1 Basic Approaches

One aspect for architecture analysis is dependency management. On a very coarse grained level (e.g. file or library level) this can be done via the "ordinary" makesystem. Some basic architecture analysis tool also uses jdepend as their input data. Also IDEs like Eclipse offer a Java Build Path with opportunities to specify package names for inclusion or exclusion via regular expressions. And component systems like OSGI also support the management of dependencies and specification of public interfaces. This information can also be reused and processed by tools like

Eclipse MoDisco[21] or the PDE Plug-in dependency explorer

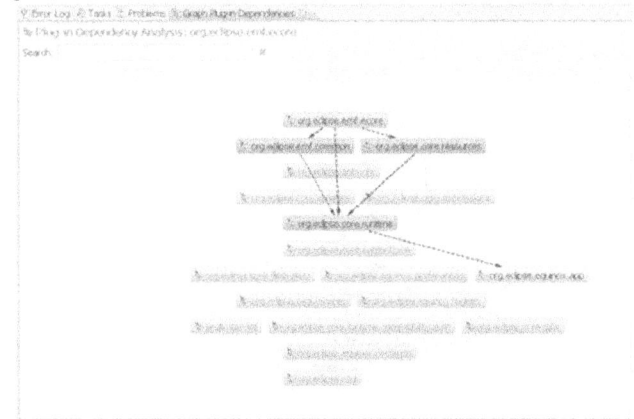

Figure 7. Eclipse PDE dependency visualizer

Note however that these basic approaches are often limited. E.g. the Plug-in dependency explorer currently has no real support for layout algorithms and no drill down functionality (resolve the dependency down to the specific source code line). Also you can not distinguish between different types of dependency (e.g. type usage, call, inheritance, etc). Some tools only parse byte code but the get the full information for traceability we need a real parser. Different languages should be supported (e.g. C, C++, Java, etc) and often additional information sources, e.g. OSGI- or XML-configuration files, database schemas etc. have to be obeyed. Note also because of its static nature, we might not immediately find all dependencies e.g. classes created via Java-Reflection will not be detected and have to be added manually to the dependency model.

5.2 Architecture Analysis Tools

There are various tools for Architecture Analysis. We will briefly describe SotoArc, Bauhaus and Structure101.

5.2.1 SotoArc / hello2morrow

SotoArc[22] is a product from hello2morrow. Various languages like C/C++, C#, Java are supported. A parser extracts source code information and stores it in a mysql database for later analysis. Figure [8] show a screenshot of SotoArc with a possible should-architecture of findbugs. Dependencies between various layers and subsystems are represented as colored arrows counterclockwise, where green means a valid and red an invalid dependency. On the left side the creation of the should-architecture is shown. Most modeling operation are pattern based (e.g. following a java package style structure) and done via menus or wizard. SotoArc has algorithms to offer breaking of cycles; also the most important metrics are displayed. In SotoArc "virtual refactorings" are possible. Restructurings can be simulated before actually performed on the code base which is a major advantage. For trend analysis, extensive metrics and arbitrary model query support there is an more powerful Sotograph which uses the same mysql database information.

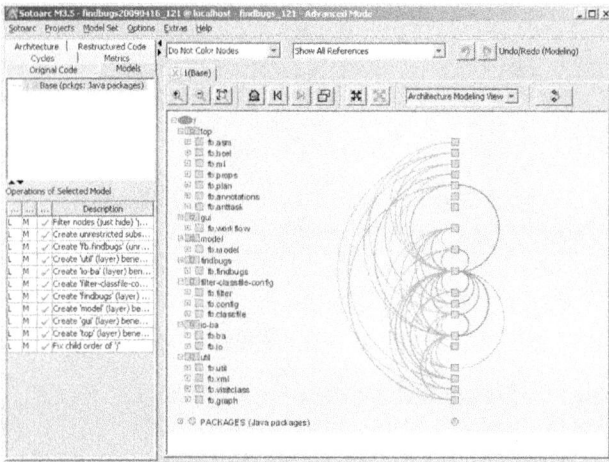

Figure 8. SotoArc ./ hello2morrow

5.2.2 Bauhaus / Axivion

Another interesting tool is Bauhaus[23] from Axivion. It supports the "usual" languages like C/C++, Java but also COBOL, VB and various others. Bauhaus stores its information about the system in iml files (intermediate language) and rfg (resource flow graph). Based in this information various analysis can be performed. Figure [9] shows a deviation analysis with the should-architecture on the left side and the is-architecture on the right side. Modeling the should-architecture is done via the GUI or python scripts. Metrics, trend analysis and user defined queries are also possible. Also you can write your own coding guidelines as the full information about the AST is still available. The MISRA-C guidelines e.g. have been implemented and are available as additional plug-in. The author expects that more and more tools will integrate the three levels of static analysis into one environment over time. Another interesting facility in Bauhaus is support for code clone detection, even modified code clones can be detected to a certain degree (e.g. renamed comments, renamed variables etc). Code duplication and clones often cause problems and new bugs during the maintenance phase of a product.

5.2.3 Structure101 / Headway

Structure101 [24] is a product from Headway software and supports multiple languages (C/C++, Java, .NET). There is also a "generic" support module which allows integrating any programming language, for up to date information check their website. Figure [10] again shows the architecture of findbugs, modeled in Structure101. Upward arrows are architecture violations; the tool allows drilling down to the class where the violation happens.

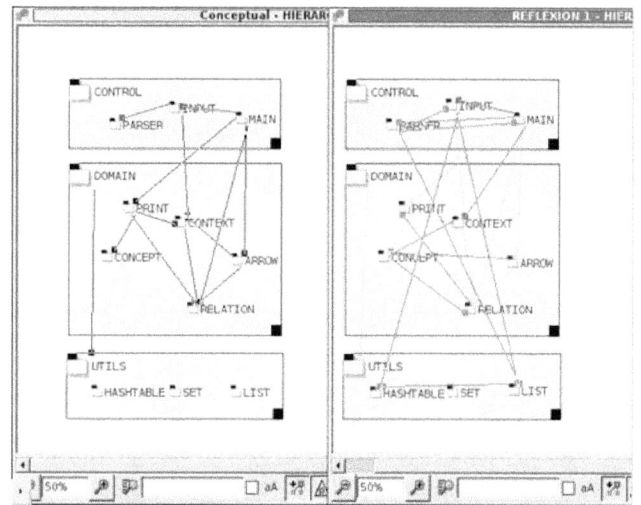

Figure 9. Bauhaus / Axivion

The should-architecture is defined within the architecture perspective. Beside the graphical view there is also support for DSM [25] (dependency structure matrix). Refactorings can be simulated via transformation rules. A trend analysis tracks changes over time and the complexity view lists the most important metrics. To integrate the architecture analysis within your IDE there is also an eclipse and IntelliJ IDEA plug-in.

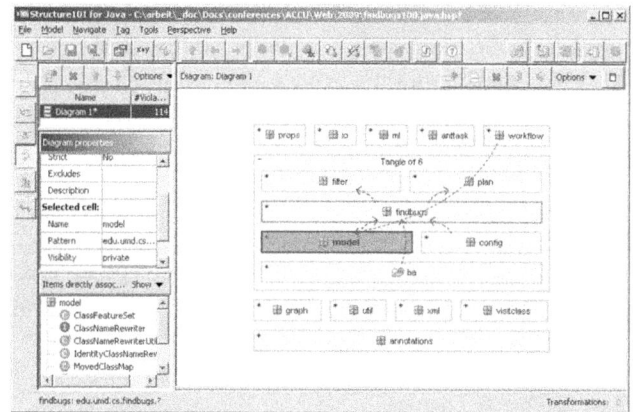

Figure 10. Structure101 / headway

6. Case Study with Eclipse

In this chapter we conduct an architectural analysis of the eclipse 3.4 platform (eclipse + JDT). We examine to which extend the current code base deviates from the initial architecture.

6.1 Eclipse Architecture

Eclipse is a generic platform for application development. It is not only limited to create IDEs for various languages (C/C++, Java, PHP, XML) and modeling technologies but also enables to create complete new RCP Applications (rich client platform). OSIG and the plug-in mechanism are the heart of the eclipse architecture. Figure [11] shows the initial planned layers, a base RCP containing the Platform runtime, JFace and SWT as GUI technologies and the Workbench UI with Editors, Views and Perspectives. Also Help is a part of the base RCP. The optional RCP is layered on top of that and contains the Workbench editor as well as Update and Forms facilities. Finally the next layer is the Workbench IDE with Compare/Search facilities and Team support (among others). Eclipse allows extending the Workbench IDE with your own Tools written again as collection of plug-in. The JDT (Java, Development Tools), CDT (C/C++ Development Tools) and PDE (Plug-in Development Environment) are probably the most well know extensions.

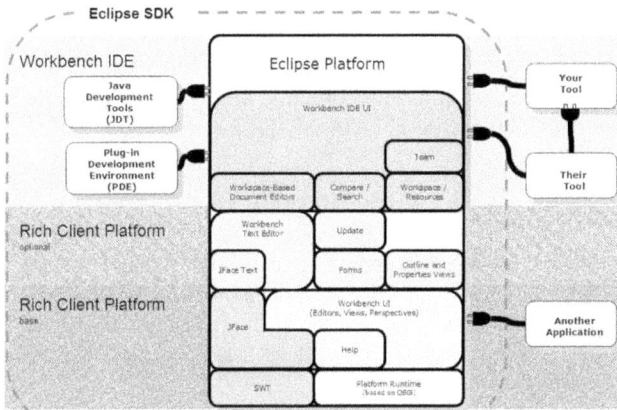

Figure 11. Eclipse architecture with JDT and PDE

We now analyze the architecture of Eclipse with SotoArc. First we parse the source code of the various plug-in (is architecture) and let SotoArc put that information into the mysql database. Based on the plug-in names and the relevant java package names (eclipse follows a consistent naming convention) we assign those to subsystems. A subsystem in SotoArc corresponds to a collection of plug-in belonging together. We distinguish between "unrestricted" subsystems (can use each other) and "independent" subsystem (completely decoupled within a layer). A square represents an "unrestricted" subsystem and a rhomb an "independent". Furthermore the subsystems are assigned to architecture layers, depicted as rectangles. Figure [12] shows the Eclipse architecture modeled in SotoArc; you recognize the layers "Platform", "JDT" and "PDE".

Within those layers we have again layers, e.g. in "PDE" and "JDT" we have an "API", "UI", "Build" and "Core" layer. Within the "Platform" you also recognize again various layers, known from Figure [11]. Each layer contains a collection of several subsystems (unrestricted or independent) and finally each subsystems also has a public API and a private implementation part (which should not be used from outside).

As mentioned before dependencies are drawn as counter

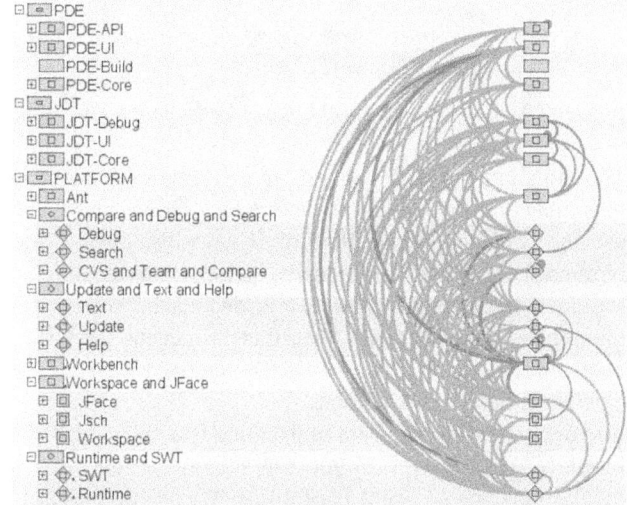

clockwise circles with green for valid and red for invalid dependencies.

Figure 12. Eclipse 3.4 architecture in SotoArc

As we can see we have two kinds of architecture violations:

- arrows on the right side represent layer violations (a lower layer is using an upper layer),
- arrows on the left side represent interface violations (a usage bypasses the interface and uses implementation internals)

We examine a candidate of each kind in the following section.

6.2 Erosion of Eclipse Architecture

We take a layer violation (right side) between Workbench and Help from Figure [12], drill down and focus on the relevant files from these layers. A detailed view (zoom in + focus) in shown in Figure [13] and show that MarkerView, ExtendedMarkerView and the Factory depend on the Interface IContext from Help. IContext represents the context of a help. On further analysis we discover however that IContext belongs to Workbench and not Help, so we move (virtually refactoring) this Interface to the relevant layer. Furthermore IContextProvider contains to the Workbench layer so we move this "down" as well and hence remove the violation.

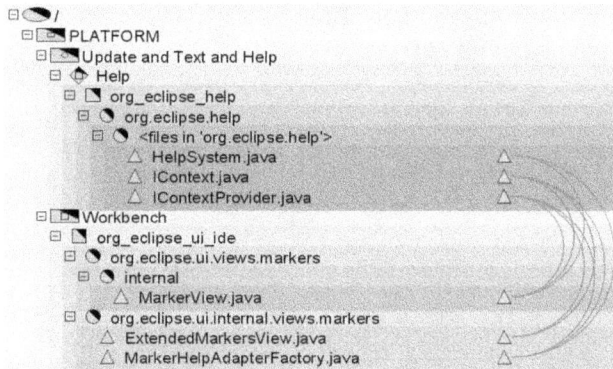

Figure 13. Layer violations between Workbench → Help

The violation to HelpSystem currently remains because in those location the context is determined. However we can use the .getContext() Method of IContextProvider to determine the context. Additionally HelpSystem depends on Interface IHelp which however is deprecated so we can remove it. Note however that this influences backward compatibility. In this case we have removed now all the existing architecture violations.

The next violation we want to examine is a "bypassing the interface". In Figure [12] you can see on the left side an invalid dependency from Platform to Workbench. Calling down the layer is valid; however in this case a private / internal class is called.

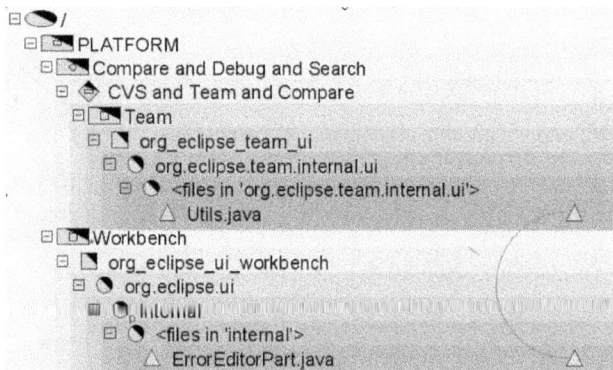

Figure 14. Interface violation Platform and Workbench

We can see this in detail in Figure [14] if we zoom into this dependency. The Java class Utils calls a internal class ErrorEditorPart of the Workbench. Note the small "p" on the internal package. Eclipse follows again a strict naming policy for packages. Internal packages are not allowed to be called from outside; we have modelled this also in SotoArc. If we navigate to the source location where the violation happens, the programmer even has documented that he violates the architecture. The corresponding bug report [26] documents however that this "workaround" causes problems repeatedly.

As can be seen in Figure [12] there are various other violations in eclipse but the number is currently not very dra-

matic and could be reduced via appropriate refactoring. Definitely the number is low because OSGI helps to manage dependencies between plug-ins . However software architecture is more than dependency management. Is is also API-design, well balanced package arrangement, a clear way how to do things (e.g. one meachnism to store config settings or do persistence) and other aspects. A critical point the author sees is the number of code duplication that is in the current eclipse code base. This is not further discussed here because of size constrains but it is possible to show large packages of duplicated code which meanwhile also diverges (bugfixes are not propagated across the copies).

7. Summary

There is definitely a need for software architecture analysis. Every project suffers an architectural erosion or decay at some point and also opensource projects are no exception as we saw. Compared with code- and design-level lint tools, the amount of messages can be better managed on the architecture level. Good tool support is necessary to be able to find violations efficiently and to simulate refactorings. We expect that over the next years, tools will start to combine the different level of static analysis and also integrate much more directly into the IDE.

References

[1] Rick Kazman , Len Bass , Mike Webb , Gregory Abowd, SAAM: a method for analyzing the properties of software architectures, Proceedings of the 16th international conference on Software engineering, p.81-90, May 16-21, 1994, Sorrento, Italy

[2] Foster, J. S., Hicks, M. W., and Pugh, W. 2007. Improving software quality with static analysis. In *Proceedings of the 7th ACM SIGPLAN-SIGSOFT Workshop on Program Analysis For Software Tools and Engineering*

[3] http://www.open-std.org/jtc1/sc22/wg14

[4] Hatton, L. 1995 *Safer C: Developing Software for in High-Integrity and Safety-Critical Systems*. McGraw-Hill, Inc.

[5] MISRA-C 2004: Guidelines for the Use of the C Language in Critical Systems, ISBN 0 9524156 2 3 (paperback), ISBN 0 9524156 4 X (PDF), October 2004.

[6] MISRA-C++ 2008: Guidelines for the Use of the C++ Language in Critical Systems, ISBN 978-906400-03-3 (paperback), ISBN 978-906400-04-0 (PDF), June 2008.

[7] http://www.gimpel.com/

[8] http://www.splint.org/

[9] http://www.programmingresearch.com

[10] http://findbugs.sourceforge.net/

[11] Meyers, S. 2005 *Effective C++: 55 Specific Ways to Improve Your Programs and Designs (3rd Edition)*. Addison-Wesley Professional.

[12] Bloch, J. 2008 *Effective Java: The Java Series(2nd Edition)*. Addison-Wesley Professional.

[13] http://www.osgi.org/Specifications/HomePage

[14] Martin, R. 2006 *Agile Software Development, Patterns and Principles*. Addison-Wesley Professional.

[15] Brown, J. 1998 *AntiPatterns: Refactoring Software, Architectures, and Projects in Crisis*. Wiley.

[16] http://standards.ieee.org/reading/ieee/std_public/description/se/1471-2000_desc.html

[17] Kruchten, P. 2003 *The Rational Unified Process: An Introduction, 3 edition*. Addison-Wesley Professional.

[18] Medvidovic, J. 2000: A Classification and Comparison Framework for Software Architecture Description Languages: IEEE Transactions on Software Engineering Volume 26 , Issue 1 (January 2000)

[19] Murphy, Gail C. and Notkin, David and Sullivan, Kevin, 1997, Extending and Managing Software Reflexion Models University of British Columbia

[20] http://www.springsource.org/

[21] http://www.eclipse.org/MoDisco/

[22] http://www.hello2morrow.com/products/sotoarc

[23] http://www.axivion.com/

[24] http://www.headwaysoftware.com/products/structure101

[25] Sangal, N., Jordan, E., Sinha, V., and Jackson, D. 2005. Using dependency models to manage complex software architecture. In *Proceedings of the 20th Annual ACM SIGPLAN Conference on Object-Oriented Programming, Systems, Languages, and Applications* (San Diego, CA, USA, October 16 - 20, 2005). OOPSLA '05. ACM, New York

[26] https://bugs.eclipse.org/bugs/show_bug.cgi?id=90582

Textual Modeling Tools:

Overview and Comparison of Language Workbenches

Bernhard Merkle

SICK AG
Research & Development
Software Engineering
Erwin-Sick-Str.1
79183 Waldkirch, Germany
bernhard.merkle@gmail.com

Abstract

Domain Specific Languages (DSL) attract more and more users as they are specialized and optimized for a certain problem area. Currently the number of new emerging Programming Languages is significant [1] but GPL (General Purpose Languages) do often not fit the specific need of the end-user. DSL are one way to solve this problem. DSLs can be divided into different independent dimensions: e.g. internal vs. external or textual vs. graphical or tabular. In this paper we focus on textual syntaxes as they have several advantages like easy information exchange via e.g. mail, integration into existing tools like diff, merge and version control and most important the fast editing style supported by the "usual" IDE support like code completion, error markers, intentions and quick fixes. While Fowler described the initial vision of Language Workbenches [2], several mature Textual Language Workbenches have emerged in recent years. In this paper we will compare them with a consistent example and look at pros and cons.

Categories and Subject Descriptors   D.3.3 [**Programming Languages**]: extensible languages, domain-specific languages

General Terms   Design, Languages, Textual modeling, Eclipse.

Keywords   *language workbenches, domain-specific languages, textual modeling, , Xtext, TEF, TCS, EMFText, MPS.*

1. Introduction

Model driven development enables programming/modeling on a higher level, and generate low level stuff via a code generator. Essentially the idea is not really new and similar to the former transition from assembler to high-level programming languages (where code generators were compilers). Meanwhile developers want to express problems for a certain domain more appropriate, hence general programming languages (GPL) are not enough which led to the adoption of domain specific languages (DSL). Textual Languages are beneficial for many reasons. They enable productivity because of their easy and fast editing style, usage of code completion, error markers and other facilities people are used to meanwhile. Textual editors for GPL like eclipse, netbeans, IntelliJ are powerful and set new standards for textual editing. However for a wide adoption of DSL in day to day developments, IDEs for DSL should be easy to create (for language designers) and easy to use (for end-users). Martin Fowler described the idea of Language Workbenches [2], however that term focused on Projectional editing [3]. In this paper we compare the current state of Textual Language Workbenches, mainly based on the eclipse platform.

The subsequent chapters are structured as follows: Chapter 2 talks about various forms and representations of Domain Specific Languages and presents a specific DSL example. Chapter 3 describes a DSL classification model which is applied later and Chapter 4 shortly discusses textual and Projectional editing approaches. Several Textual Language Workbenches are presented and discussed in Chapter 5, following the example and criteria outlined before (in 2+3) and finally Chapter 6 summarizes and concludes.

2. DSL Overview and DSL Example

DSLs can be divided into different independent dimensions e.g. internal vs. external or textual vs. graphical or tabular.

2.1 DSL Overview

Internal DSL are language extensions built with the language itself and directly embedded into the host language. During recent years, several languages like Ruby, Clojure or the

Permission to make digital or hard copies of all or part of this work for personal or classroom use is granted without fee provided that copies are not made or distributed for profit or commercial advantage and that copies bear this notice and the full citation on the first page. To copy otherwise, or republish, to post on servers or to redistribute to lists, requires prior specific permission and/or a fee.
SPLASH'10 October 17–21, 2010, Reno/Tahoe, Nevada, USA.
Copyright © 2010 ACM 978-1-4503-0240-1/10/10...$10.00.

classical Lisp got much attention for supporting internal DSLs. On the other hand it requires a good amount of discipline and unfortunately often convenient features like IDE support (code completion, syntax highlighting, cross-referencing, etc) are typically not supported by internal DSLs. Also fluent interfaces [4] support some kind of internal DSL/API, they even can be generated from a higher level abstraction, like an Ecore model as [5] shows.

Another possibility is embedding a DSL into a general purpose programming language (GPL). A classical example is embedded SQL (or LINQ from C# language) for database access from a host language. A major drawback of this approach is the proprietary GPL extension and usually a vendor lock-in, also editing and debugging support is usually not very good (e.g. often some kind of preprocessor or pre-compiler is required).

External DSLs on the other hand are another approach to support the user with a powerful language, adopted specifically for a certain domain (e.g. state machines). Language designers and end users get support for external DSL with textual [6] and graphical [7] concrete syntax. Most of the tools mentioned in this paper, create or deliver the "usual" infrastructure like parser, model-creation and code-emitters (generator) as well as IDE convenience features for free. The main drawback with external DSL is that they start again from scratch and initially lack constructs like flow-control, type systems and other language features usually expected by end-users or users with a GPL background. Figure [1] shows some textual DSL example.

```
//SQL
SELECT firstname, lastName from
  employee where age = 42;

// Regular Expressions
([+-]?[0-9]*) | ([A-Z][a-z]+)

// fluent interface in java
```

```
public Collection<Student> findByNameAge (String name, int age, {
  return em.createNamedQuery("Student.findByNameAge")
        .setParameter("name", name) .setParameter("age", age)
        .setFirstResult(1) .setMaxResults(30)
        .setHint("hintName", "hintValue") .getResultList();

}
```

Figure 1. examples of textual DSL

While we focus on textual DSL here, often graphical DSL are also used (interestingly most modeling/DSL initially started graphical). As an example for a non-technical or non-IT DSL see Figure [2] where a graphical DSL for music (basso continuo) is used. It saves writing 80% of the notes and several music notes get derived from the sequence of events or numbers below the bass note. Actually this shows that this particular DSL is a combination of graphical (notes) and textual (numbers, symbols) domain syntax.

Figure 2. graphical DSL

2.2 DSL Example

We will present several Textual Language Workbenches [6] in Chapter 5 with a uniform example. It should be a textual language with rules and additional constraints. Chess games often use a textual DSL to exchange and document their moves (e.g. wikis, e-mail, irc etc.). To keep the sample short, we use the shortest tournament game, at the Open Championship of Omaha: Mayfield vs. Trinks. Figure [3] shows the five moves in tabular notation, and subsequently as plain text in two forms (algebraic and spoken move). This is the concrete syntax we want to use for our DSL.

Figure 3. DSL notation of chess game

Analyzing the complete game, written in algebraic and spoken moves statements we can derive the underlying meta-model.

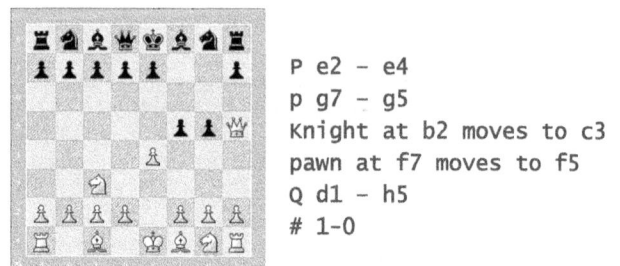

```
P e2 - e4
p g7 - g5
Knight at b2 moves to c3
pawn at f7 moves to f5
Q d1 - h5
# 1-0
```

Figure 4. Concrete Syntax (CS) of chess game

The meta model is represented in an abstract syntax (AS) in Figure[5] and consists of a Game, Moves and Pieces.

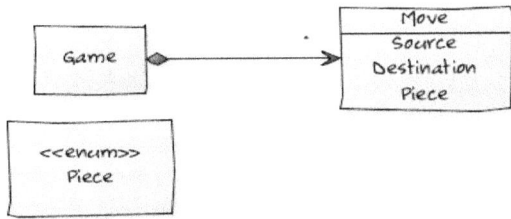

Figure 5. Abstract Syntax (AS) of chess game

3. DSL Language classification

To better compare the textual language workbenches we will first introduce a DSL language classification schema. This schema follows a DSL feature model defined by Langlois [8] and serves for a "as a neutral as possible" comparison. Figure [6] shows that the feature model covers various aspects from a DSL e.g. language, transformation, tooling and process. In this sense we are following the approach of [9] but we compare a different set of textual language workbenches and use a more extensive example.

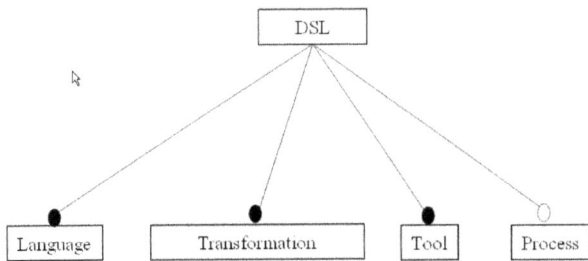

Figure 6. DSL classification model

We focus on the first three criteria as process is optional. An alternative DSL classification model is described in [10]

3.1 Language

The language considers criteria about the abstract syntax (AS) and concrete syntax (CS). Figure [7] show the main parts.

We evaluate which representation is used for the AS (graph or tree), which syntax is used the for definition of the AS (grammar or meta-model), issues about composability and how the AS to CS mapping happens. As we are looking at textual language workbenches only, the representation style of the CS will be text.

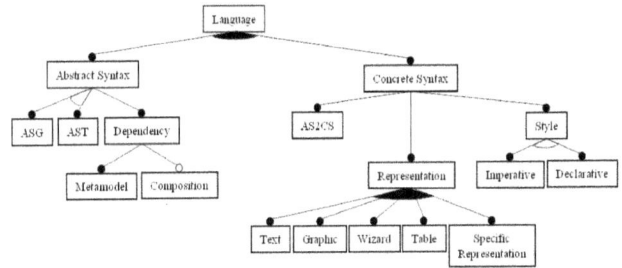

Figure 7. DSL classification model: Language

3.2 Transformation

This section is further divided into aspects about:
- Specification of the Transformation
- Target Asset and
- Operation Transformation

Generally the transformation realizes the correspondence from problem to the solution domain. Because of size restriction we only show Target Asset in Figure [8] as an example.

In Target Asset questions like: which representations of the target asset are possible (text, graphic, binary), and what support of asset update is available (regenerate or incremental) are answered.

In Operation Transformation we look at different transformation techniques, mode for trafo execution (compile vs. interpreted) and also the environment for the trafo (internal or external). Also scheduling, location and automation level are interesting points.

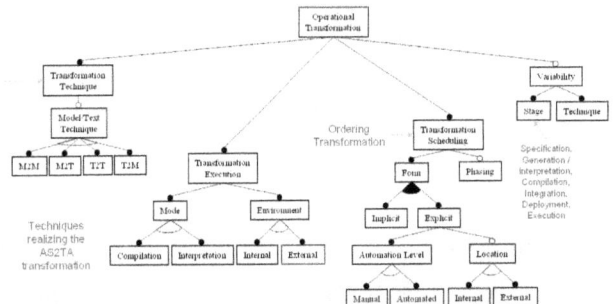

Figure 8. DSL classification model: Transformation

3.3 Tool

This category covers the overall tool support, e.g. what assistance is supported, (static or adaptive), is there process guidance (step or workflow) and what kind of checking is supported (consistency or completeness).

While the mentioned criteria serve as a good comparison catalog other aspects should not be forgotten like documentation, updates, activity of development, support via newsgroups/mail etc. We omitted the Process category as this is often project specific.

4. Textual Language Workbenches

In this chapter we discuss two kinds of Language Workbenches: pure text based (based on the usual scanner/parser approach) and Projectional based with a textual projection.

4.1 Textual Language Workbenches (TLWB)

A number of different TLWB are available, especially on the Eclipse [11] modeling project. Xtext currently is most well-known. It generates an EMF model, a full featured editor and parser from an enhanced EBNF notation. Other examples are TEF (Textual Editing Framework), EMFText and TCS (Textual Concrete Syntax). Most of them use EMF as underlying abstract syntax technology and some kind of scanner/parser technology like ANTLR[12] or RunCC[13]. Especially TCS is interesting as it has a generic editor and interprets the model at runtime, hence avoids as much code generation as possible and enables short turn around cycles during the language development.

4.2 Projectional Language Workbenches (PLWB)

Jetbrains offers an open source solution with MPS (Meta Programming Systems) [14]. Three steps typically define a new language, 1. the "concept" defines the Abstract Syntax (AS), 2. an editor supports the Concrete Syntax (CS) via a cell based editing style and 3. the generator emits new artifacts (e.g. a GPL code like java). The Intentional Language Workbench [15] is a similar solution which is also used for real world projects, especially in the insurance and banking domain, however it is not really widespread and has a higher learning curve for language creators.

Spoofax/IMP [16] is not really a Projectional editor but uses scanner less parsing and also enables arbitrary language composition. In summary the number of PLWB is still relative small but we expect them to increase soon.

5. Workbench Comparison

For creating languages (by a designer) and applying them (by an end user) we need some ingredients. Martin Folwer described this [2] and created the term Language Workbench (LWB).

Essential requirements for LWB are e.g.:
- ability to freely define languages
- which are fully integrated with each other,
- primary source of information should be the abstract syntax,
- DSL is defined by schema, editor and generator
- it can also persist incomplete or contradictory information

Fowler also talks about
- manipulation of the DSL via a Projectional editor

This is a kind of prerequisite for some of the other requirements. While LWB were still in a "visionary stage" in 2005, meanwhile there are plenty of solutions around. Admittedly the variation amongst them is still large but one basic criterion is if it is a text/parser based or a Projectional language workbench. We will discuss pros and cons in the following subchapters.

5.1 Xtext

Xtext [17] is developed actively by a group of developers in itemis' Kiel office and offered as open source. Itemis also offers professional training, consulting and support.

The first version of Xtext was initially developed as part of the openArchitectureWare [18] framework, however after a rewrite of Xtext, it is now a major part of the Eclipse TMF (Textual Modeling Framework) project. Since version 0.7 Xtext is self hosting. The current version 1.0 delivered with Helios is used in lots of projects, also in Eclipse projects itself in B3 [19].

The Xtext supported workflow in shown in Figure[9]. The user starts to describe the AS and CS in the .xtext file. The CS is specified as context-free grammar including the terminal symbols and production rules while the AS is mixed into the same .xtext file and later generated into a corresponding Ecore model. Xtext does not support left-recursive meta-models. Also a corresponding .mwe (Modeling Workflow Engine) file describes necessary build steps like loading the model, run checkers or code generator, transform/layout of generated code. Figure [10] shows the Xtext grammar with our Chess DSL.

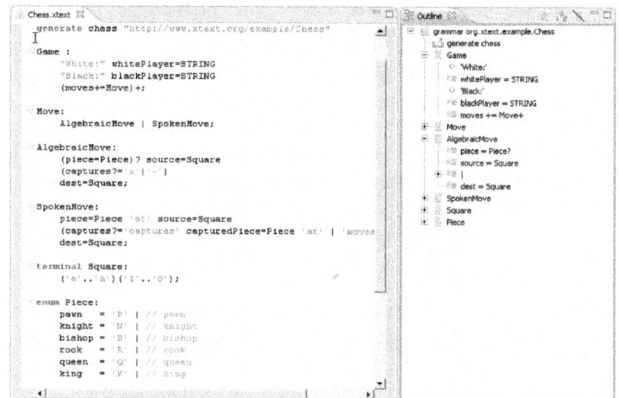

Figure 9. Xtext workflow

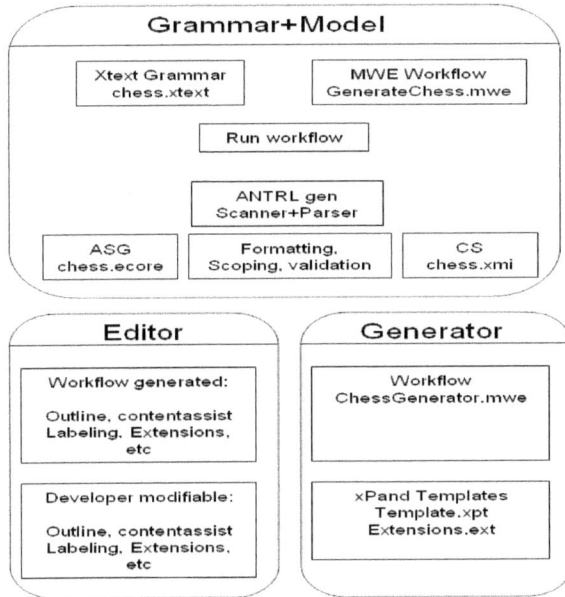

Figure 10. Xtext: Concrete Syntax and Abstract Syntax

From the .xtext file, Xtext generates a ASG (.ecore file), an ANTLR based scanner and parser for DSL-to-model transformation, model-to-text generator with Xpand (.xpt) support and a full fledged editor the DSL based on eclipse. The generated editor supports nearly all features you are used from a textual editor and could compete with the eclipse JDT java editor (without the refactoring support). The editor supports syntax highlighting, code completion, navigation and reference, folding,

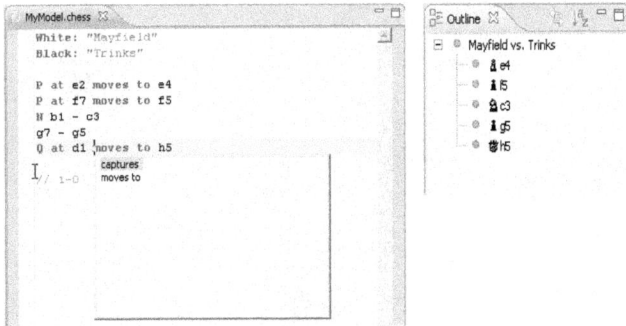

Figure 11. Xtext: Chess DSL Editor

bracket matching, styled label providers, incremental codegen, and much more. Xtext also supports qualified name support and referencing existing java elements from your DSL. Figure [11] shows the resulting Xtext Chess DSL editor.

5.2 TEF (Textual Editing Framework)

TEF (Textual Editing Framework) [20] was initially developed by Markus Scheidgen during is PhD at the University of Berlin. For the concrete syntax (CS), TEF provides a syntax definition language called TSL (textual syntax language). TSL describes the textual notation for an existing Ecore meta-model (AS) is in the .etslt file. Via the usual Eclipse EMF facilities (the gen-model) the necessary EMF support is generated. For DSL-to-model transformation, TEF creates a RunCC parser which is interpreted at runtime (RunCC avoids code generation).

Figure[12] show the TEF workflow and relevant artifacts.

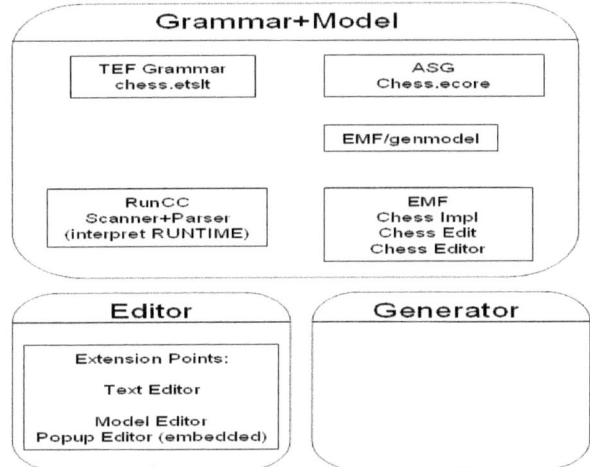

Figure 12. TEF workflow

Figure[13] show the etslt description (CS) for the Chess example. Note that we reference the AS in a Ecore model.

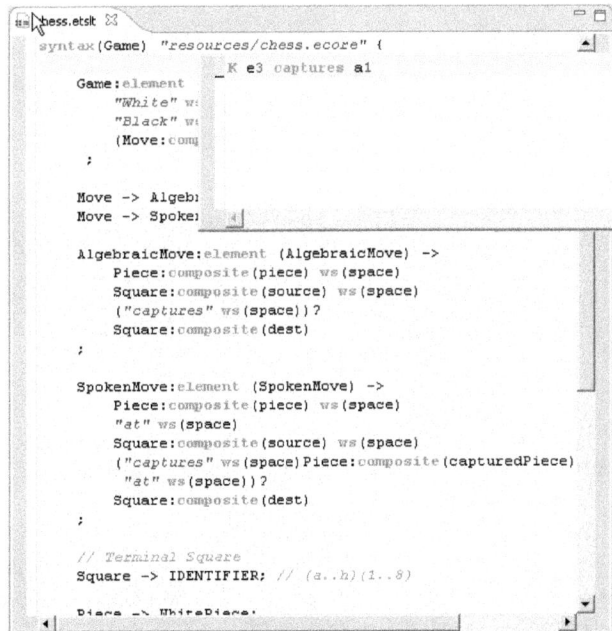

Figure 13. TEF Concrete Syntax

TEF generates three different editors via eclipse extension points:

- a textual editor

143

This editor parses textual models and allows editing them in a comfortable way. Features of the generated editor are outlined below. Figure[14]

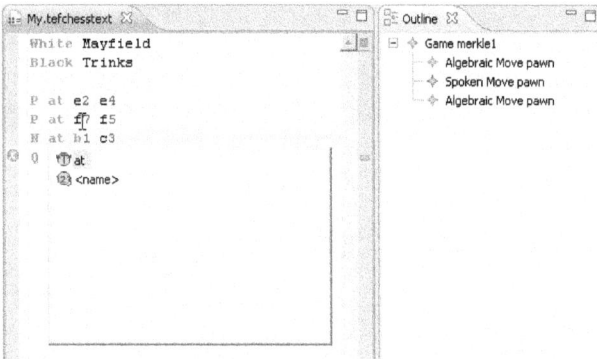

Figure 14. TEF: textual editor with Chess DSL

- a model based editor

The model based editor acts like an enhanced generic Ecore editor. Initially it is a tree based editor but other representations are also possible. Figure[15]. There is no text parsing involved here as the editing "style" does not allow it.

- a embedded editor

This is a textual editor embedded into the model based tree editor. On each model element the user can open a textual editor with a hotkey (Alt-T). Figure[15]. TEF hence combines different editing styles (treebased/textbased). Depending on the situation, the best editor is offered for the user (we call this "convergent" editor).

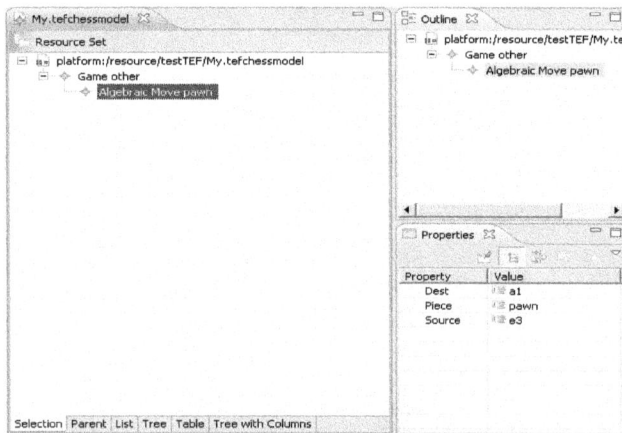

Figure 15. TEF: model editor and embedded text editor

The generated editor supports syntax highlighting, code completion, navigation and reference, folding, error annotation and several other features. Model validation is possible via the Eclipse Modeling projects.

5.3 TCS (Textual Concrete Syntax)

TCS (Textual Concrete Syntax) [21] was developed by Frederic Jouault at EMN (Ecole des Mintes in Nantes) and the ATLAN-Mod team. It is also part of the eclipse TMF

project and used in other eclipse projects, e.g. ATL2 [22]. TCS is also self hosting.

Figure[16] show the TEF workflow and relevant artifacts.

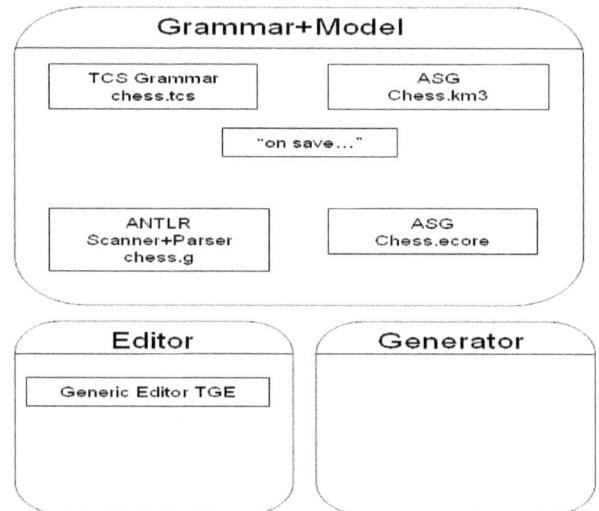

Figure 16. TCS workflow

The abstract syntax is (also) specified in a textual language for meta-modeling, called KM3 [23]. When saved, TCS then generates a corresponding Ecore file on the fly.

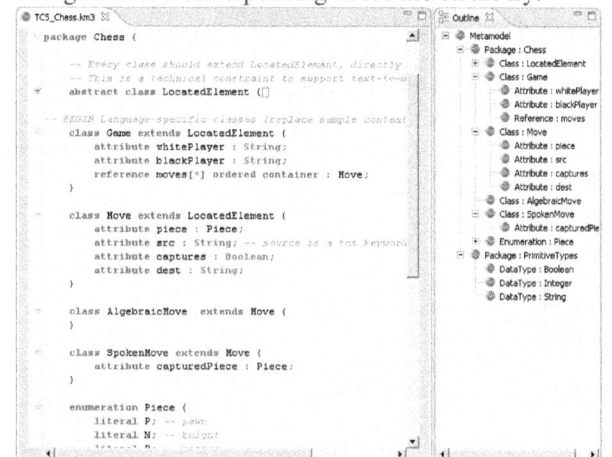

Figure 17. TCS: Abstract syntax

The concrete syntax is specified in a .tcs file. Again, when saved a corresponding ANTLR parser is generated on the fly. TCS hence avoids lots of (unnecessary) code generation often found in other tools.

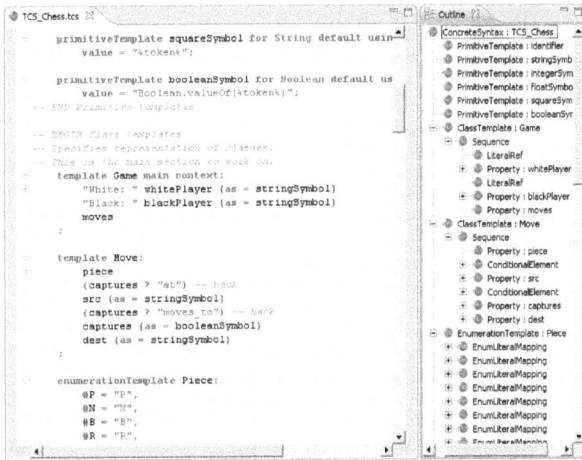

Figure 18. TCS: Concrete syntax

TCS avoids as much code generation as possible and hence allows very fast and short turn around cycles. There is no need to start an additional embedded eclipse instance with the plugin, instead everything is updated "on save" and then reinterpreted.

To edit and create DSL conforming to the one the user specified, TCS offers the Textual Generic Editor (TGE). TGE supports syntax-highlighting, text hovers, hyperlinks, and an outline view for every language that has its textual syntax specified in TCS. If necessary, TGE can be further customized to specific needs/layout. Model validation is possible via the Eclipse Modeling projects or preferably via the ALT language directly.

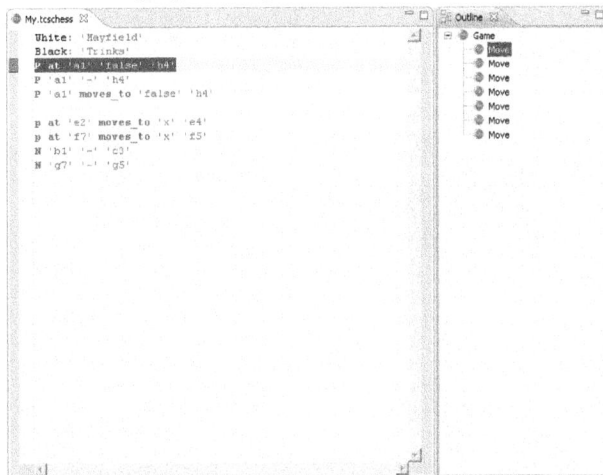

Figure 19. TCS: Generic Editor (TGE) with Chess DSL

TCS supports a language Zoo with over 50 languages on their website. TCS is also reused by Furcas, another TMF tool.

5.4 EMFText

EMFText [24] was initially developed as part of the resuseware composition framework [25] at University Dresden. It was later extracted into an own, independent tool. Similar to TCS also EMFText allows specifying a concrete syntax for an existing EMF model (abstract syntax). Figure[20] shows the main workflow. Note that some of the workflow/ANT properties can be specified in the .cs (concrete syntax) file already (e.g. reload properties).

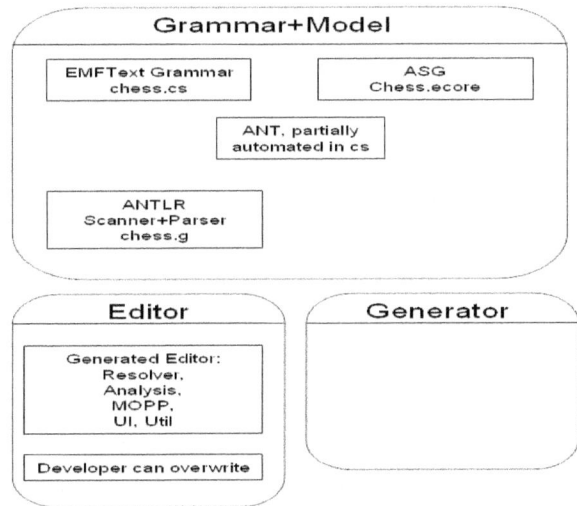

Figure 20. EMFText: workflow

To enable EMFText to use models at runtime, a EMF model plug-in must be generated (following the well-known genmodel).

The concrete syntax specification (.cs file) consists of 3 blocks:

- A configuration block, which contains the name, the base model and the root Meta class (start symbol).
  Optionally other syntaxes and metamodels can be imported and generation options can be specified.
- A (optional) TOKEN section.
  tokens for the lexical analyser can be specified.
- A RULES section, which defines the syntax for each concrete Meta class.

EMFText has some special support for the syntax definition:

- Automatic generation of default syntaxes
- Modular specification
  (Support for abstract syntaxes and syntax imports)
- Default reference resolving mechanisms
- and comprehensive syntax analysis to warn about potential syntax problems

The concrete syntax for the Chess Example is shown in Figure [21].

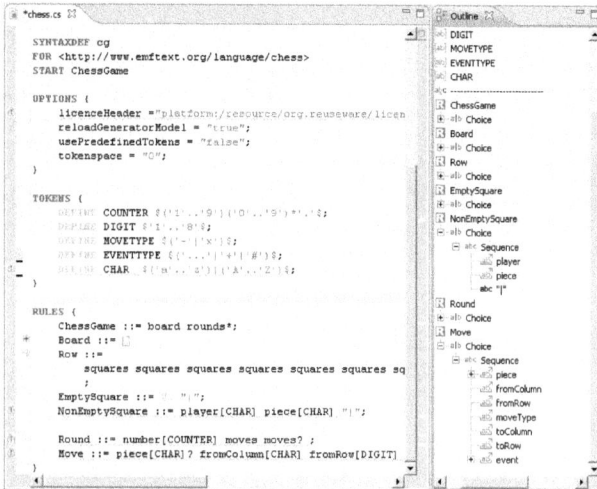

Figure 21. EMFText: Concrete Syntax

Via the build process a default editor is generated by EM-FText. Developers can overwrite or customize special behavior. Out of the box the editor supports several IDE features like outline view, customizable syntax highlighting (also via the .cs file), code completion, bracket handling, text hovers and the usual hyperlink and reference support. Figure [22] shows the EMFText Chess.

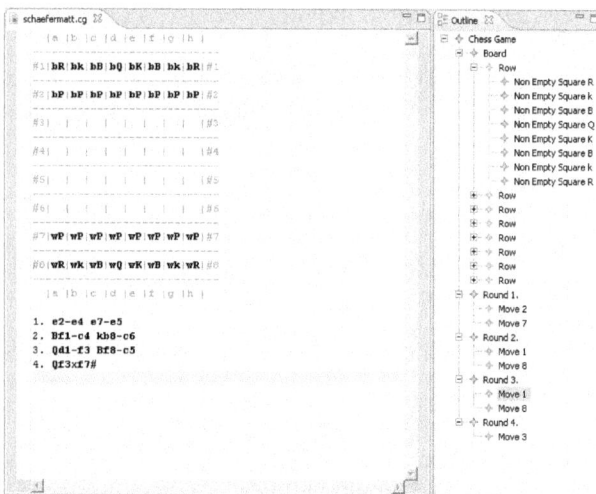

Figure 22. EMFText: Editor with Chess DSL

EMFText supports also a language Zoo with about 50 languages, with real world languages like Java5 or .e.g. a textual Ecore syntax.

5.5 Other text based approaches

On the eclipse platform there are several other interesting text based approaches which should be mentioned like IMP[26], Spoofax/IMP [27] (a project at the university Delft) or ETMOP and CAL [28] (Andrew Eisenbergs PhD.)

5.6 MPS (Meta Programming Systems)

Jetbrains offers an open source solution with MPS (Meta Programming Systems) [14]. Unlike the previous introduced parser based approaches of Xtext, TEF, TCS and EMFText, MPS is a Projectional editor. This approach also follows the "language oriented programming" idiom described in [29].

MPS offers a projection from the Abstract Syntax Tree (AST) to Text, however under the hood the user edits (indirectly the AST). Editing the tree as opposed to "real text" needs some accustomization. Without specific adaptations, every program element has to be selected from a drop-down list and "instantiated". However, MPS provides editor customizations to enable editing that resembles modern IDEs that use automatically expanding code templates. So the user does not really feel that he is editing an AST. Using the Projectional approach avoids a lot of problems like scanning/parsing, refactoring support etc.

Three steps typically define a new language, 1. The "concept" or "structure" defines the Abstract Syntax (AS), 2. An editor supports the Concrete Syntax (CS) via a cell based editing style and 3. The generator emits new artifacts (e.g. a GPL code like java).

Within MPS there is direct support to use the generated Editor or Generator. CTRL-F9 generated/compiles e.g. the DSL Editor and reloads in on the fly. There is no need to start an additional instance (like the eclipse plugins). MPS also supports important features like Constraint checking, support for real type system, etc. The Workflow is depicted in Figure [23]. MPS is self hosting and used for several real world products (e.g. the youtrack MPS bug tracker[30]) and was developed and used for about 7 years internally within Jetbrains. The MPS product is now open sourced.

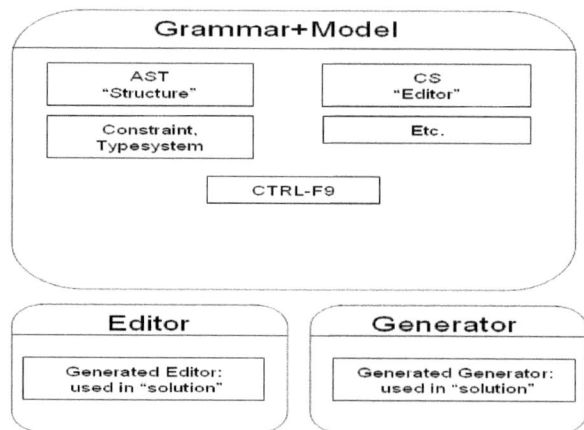

Figure 23. MPS: Workflow

Defining a new language start with the abstract syntax which is called a "concept", located under the "structure" node. As shown in Figure [24], MPS uses also a textual syntax to describe the AS. (n.b. This editor is also described with MPS (self hosting)).

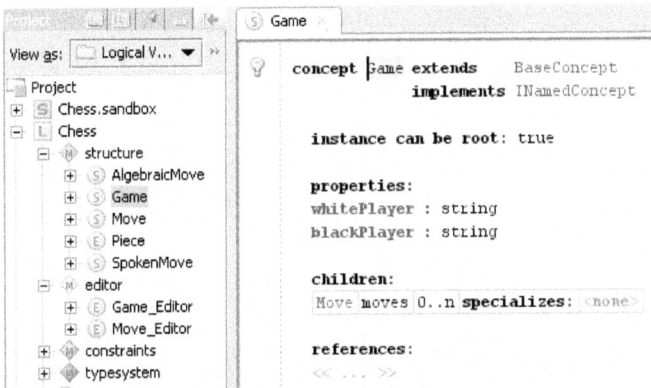

Figure 24. MPS: Abstract Syntax

Next, the concrete syntax has to be defined in an "editor". As MPS uses the Projectional approach there is no parser/scanner. Editing is only based on "cell-editing", hence the programmer describes the cell layout (horizontal/vertical list/collection etc) and the mapping to the abstract syntax. The concrete syntax is shown in Figure [25]. Note that other, alternative projections (e.g. to table, graphs, spreadsheets etc) would be possible.

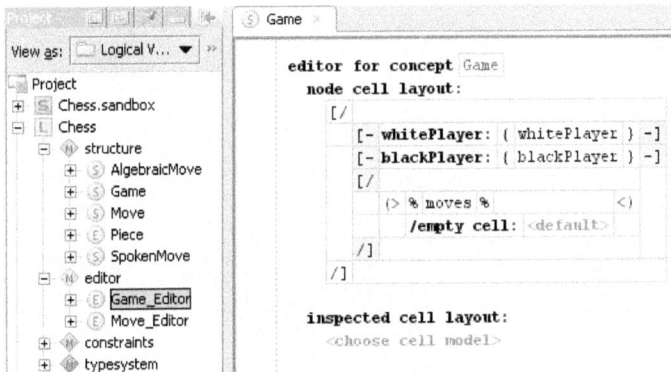

Figure 25. MPS: Concrete Syntax

Finally we can generate a DSL Editor with CTRL-F9 for our Chess language in MPS (Figure [26]) and create the hess game.

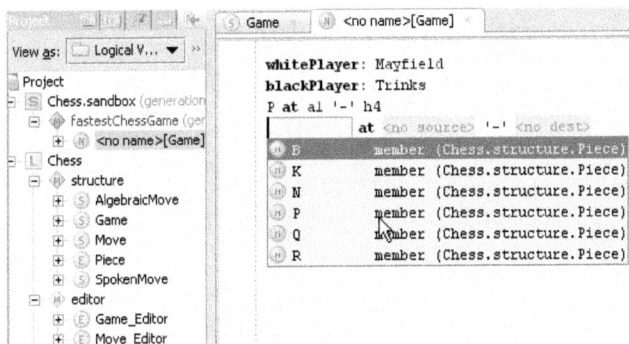

Figure 26. MPS: DSL Chess editor

6.   Conslusion / Summary

In this paper we presented several different language workbenches for textual DSL. Using a feature model for DSL one can compare them on a "neutral" and unbiased platform. However this is not to declare a winner or the "best" textual language workbench.

The number of parser based textual language workbenches is significant in the meantime and eclipse seem to be the common host. However in terms features and approaches we were able to identify several differences (e.g. pure generation based approach of Xtext vs. a generic, interpreted approach of TCS).

While Projectional editors are currently still the exception (MPS and Intentional), we assume that they gain a huge increase of use. The combination of modular languages, different DSLs combined is much easier with Projectional editor and classical parser based approaches will reach their limits. Currently there is not yet a real projectional editor for eclipse but we are sure that this is already on the roadmap.

Acknowledgments

Special thanks go to the developers from Xtext, TEF, TCS, EMFText and MPS. They were very helpful with my questions and bug reports for their tools. Thank you again!

References

[1] Announcing The Emerging Languages Camp at OSCON http://radar.oreilly.com/2010/05/announcing-the-emerging-langua.html

[2] Fowler, M.: Language Workbenches - The Killer-App for Domain Specific Languages?

http://martinfowler.com/articles/languageWorkbench.html

[3] Fowler, M.: Projectional Editing

http://martinfowler.com/bliki/ProjectionalEditing.html

[4] Fowler, M.: Fluent Interfaces

http://www.martinfowler.com/bliki/FluentInterface.html

[5] Garcia, Automating the embedding of Domain Specific Languages in Eclipse JDT

http://www.eclipse.org/articles/Article-AutomatingDSLEmbeddings/index.html

[6] Textual Modeling Tools for ecliplse

Xtext http://ww.eclipse.org/Xtext/

TCS: www.eclipse.org/gmt/tcs/

TEF:http://www2.informatik.hu-berlin.de/sam/meta-tools/tef/tool.html

EMFText: http://emftext.org

[7] Meta Edit http://www.metacase.com

[8] B. Langlois, C.E. Jitia, E Jouenne: DSL Classification. In 7th OOPLA Workshop on Domain-Specific Modeling, 2007

[9] M. Pfeiffer, J. Pichler A Comparison of Tool Support for Textual Domain-Specific Languages, In 8th OOPSLA Workshop on Domain Specific Modeling, 2008

[10] T. Goldschmidt, S.Becker, A. Uhl: Classification of Concrete Textual Syntax Mapping Approaches, In ECMDA-FA 2008

[11] www.eclipse.org/modeling

[12] www.antlr.org/papers

[13] runcc.sourceforge.net

[14] www.jetbrains.com/mps

[15] Intentional Software, Intentional Domain Workbench, http://intentsoft.com/technology/IS_OOPSLA_2006_paper.pdf

[16] L.. Kats, E. Visser. The Spoofax Language Workbench. Rules for Declarative Specification of Languages and IDEs. In OOPSLA 2010

[17] Xtext http://ww.eclipse.org/Xtext/

[18] openArchitectureWare http://www.openarchitectureware.org/

[19] eclipse B3: http://www.eclipse.org/modeling/emft/b3/

[20] TEF: http://www2.informatik.hu-berlin.de/sam/meta-tools/tef/tool.html

[21] TCS: www.eclipse.org/gmt/tcs/

[22] ATL: www.eclipse.org/m2m/atl

[23] KM3: F. Jouault, J. Bezivin: KM3: a DSL for Metamodel Specification, Formal Methods for Open Object-Based distr. Systems 2006

[24] EMFText: http://www.emftext.org

[25] Reuseware: http://www.reuseware.org/

[26] Eclipse/IMP (Safari project) http://eclipse-imp.sourceforge.net

[27] Spoofax/IMP http://strategoxt.org/Spoofax

[28] CAL, http://www.cs.ubc.ca/~ade/research.html

[29] S. Dmitriev: Language Oriented Programming: The Next Programming Paradigm

[30] Jetbrains youtrack bugtracker

http://youtrack.jetbrains.net/dashboard

SPLASH Educators' & Trainers Symposium Welcome

Back in 1986 when OOPSLA started, object-oriented languages had already been around for 19 years, but they were new to most software developers. When the OOPSLA Educators' Symposium began in 1992, objects had become a hot research topic and were increasingly penetrating industry, but most computer-science programs were still teaching C or Pascal. Now, in the Symposium's 19th year, objects are commonplace in pedagogy as well as industry; in fact, it is hard to think of a recent programming language that does not in some way pay homage to the object model. The ubiquity of o-o languages means that o-o does not draw much excitement by itself; rather, it is the use of objects to solve new kinds of problems that's where the action is. And in today's multicore world, no programming paradigm is gaining importance as rapidly as parallelism. For unlike other architectural advances of the past 30 years, parallelism affects the programming model. To teach students to write efficient programs, it is indispensable to teach them to write parallel programs.

Thus, this year's Educators' and Trainers' Symposium focuses on parallelism. Our program consists of a keynote, a panel, an activity, and seven papers, chosen from twelve submissions. We begin with the keynote by Doug Lea, one of the most prominent educators in parallel programming. Next come two papers on teaching various aspects of parallelism.

Software testing is the focus of the next three papers. While software testing is an established research area, relatively little work has been done on testing software written for classwork--and that which has been reported deals almost exclusively with tools for automating testing. But this is not enough. Programmers need instruction in how to write their tests. It is good to see this area finally being addressed.

After a lunchtime poster session, Orit Hazzan and Yael Dubinsky will direct an activity on how to devise grading strategies that reward students for contributing to their team. Their work on teaming is among the best in computer science, if not all of engineering. I am sure that the audience/participants will take away important lessons that they can apply in their own classes.

Another paper session comprises two presentations, one on leveling the playing field in CS1 between students of widely varying backgrounds. If the interest of PC members in reviewing this paper is any indication, it should be one of the most popular presentations at the symposium. The final presentation is on teaching the Strategy pattern in PHP—an application of design patterns to a language that has not often been used to teach this paradigm. The symposium concludes with a manifesto for a new educational programming language by Andrew Black, Kim Bruce, and James Noble, who collectively have many decades of teaching and researching many different object-oriented languages. The symposium session on this is in the form of a panel; the manifesto itself will be presented during Onward!

It is my honor to chair this year's symposium. Whatever innovation it represents is largely creditable to those who have organized the conference and submitted the proposals. Filling the schedule was the easy part! I'm happy to acknowledge the help of William Cook and Dick Gabriel, among others, as well as the inspiration of last year's OOPSLA Curricula for Concurrency workshop, organized by Guy Steele and Vijay Saraswat.

Ed Gehringer
Chairing SPLASH Educators' & Trainers Symposium
North Carolina State University, USA

Active Learning Exercise

Students' Cooperation in Teamwork:
Binding the Individual and the Team Interests

Orit Hazzan

Department of Education in Technology and Science
Technion – Israel Institute of Technology
Haifa, Israel

oritha@tx.technion.ac.il

Yael Dubinsky

IBM Research - Haifa Lab
Mount Carmel
Haifa 31905, Israel

dubinsky@il.ibm.com

Abstract

This Active Learning Exercise aims at increasing the participants' awareness to the importance of cooperation in software teams as well as at guiding instructors of project-based courses in the evaluation process of students' projects. The Active Learning Exercise is based on individual activities, teamwork activities, discussions and reflections.

Categories and Subject Descriptors D.2.9 [Software Engineering]: Management – *Programming teams*

General Terms Management, Measurement, Performance, Design, Economics, Human Factors, Legal Aspects.

Keywords human aspects of software engineering, teamwork, bonus, reward, grading.

1. Introduction

The Active Learning Exercise aims at increasing the participants' awareness to the importance of cooperation in software teams as well as at guiding instructors of project-based courses in the evaluation process of students' projects. The activity consists of three main sections. First, connections between bonus allocation and cooperation are investigated. Second, cooperation in software development processes is examined through the Game Theory framework of the Prisoner Dilemma. Third, based on the understandings gained in the first two sections, a grading policy is constructed, addressing the individual interests, the team interests and the unavoidable need to cooperate in the development of software projects. The Active Learning Exercise is based on individual activities, teamwork activities, discussions and reflections.

2. The Active Learning Exercise

2.1. Bonus Allocation (Hazzan, 2003; Tomayko and Hazzan, 2004)

This part of the Exercise illustrates how students' cooperation can be increased by introducing them to win-win situations. It consists of three stages, each one is followed by a reflective session.

Step 1: Individual work

Task: *Assume that you are a member of a software development team. Your team is told that if the project it is working on is successfully completed on time, the team will receive a bonus. Five options for bonus allocation are outlined below (See Table 1). Please explain how each option might influence team cooperation, and select the option you prefer.*

Table 1. The task

	Personal Bonus (% of the total bonus)	Team Bonus (% of the total bonus)
a	100	0
b	80	20
c	50	50
d	20	80
e	0	100

Step 2: Team work

Each team decides on one option that the team members, as a team, prefer.

Step 3: Individual work – reaction to two situations

A. Your supervisor tells each of the team members, **separately,** that if he or she performs better than the other team members, he or she will be promoted. The team members do not know that each of them is told the same.

- In your opinion, how will this effect team cooperation?
- If you were one of the team members, how would you suggest sharing the bonus now?
- How would you behave in such a situation?

B. Now, your supervisor tells each of the team members, **separately,** that his or her contribution to the teamwork is a major factor contributing toward his or her promotion. The team members do not know that each of them is told the same.

Copyright is held by the author/owner(s).
SPLASH'10 October 17–21, 2010, Reno/Tahoe, Nevada, USA.
ACM 978-1-4503-0240-1/10/10.

- In your opinion, how will this effect team cooperation?
- If you were one of the team members, how would you suggest sharing the bonus now?
- How would you behave in such a situation?

Activity explanation

The task is composed of three steps. Step 1 focuses on the participants' preferences when a neutral situation is described. Step 2 examines how they face possible conflicts between their own preferences and the preferences of the other team members. Before proceeding with Step 2, the participants' written responses to Step 1 are collected in order to ensure that the answers to Step 1 were not changed later on.

Step 3 presented the participants with two cases. The first addresses a situation in which the participants have a personal incentive; the second describes a situation in which there is an incentive to contribute to the teamwork. In both cases, personal promotion is conditional.

Following the completion of all three stages, a discussion takes place. The participants share their feelings, conflicts, and rationales for choosing a particular option of bonus allocation in each scenario. One of the main lessons highlighted during this discussion is that cooperation is vital in software development processes. The discussion is continued with an analysis of the topic of reward allocation by theories taken from Game Theory, mainly the Prisoner Dilemma.

2.2. The Prisoner Dilemma: The Case of Cooperation in Software Teams

See Tomayko and Hazzan (2004) and Hazzan and Dubinsky (2005) for this analysis.

2.3. Grading Policy for Student Evaluation (Hazzan and Dubinsky, 2003, 2008)

The two previous parts of the activity inspired the message that in software development environments the individual interests are bound to the team interests and one cannot achieve his or her targets without taking into the consideration the team interests as well. Further, one theme which enables this binding is cooperation.

At this stage we illustrate how this understanding, which refers to the linked nature of the individual and the team interests in software team, can be reflected in a grading policy constructed for the evaluation of students' software projects.

In general, it is accepted that when a university courses instructor wishes that his or her students follow specific principles that he or she deems important, these principles must somehow be incorporated into the evaluation policy of the course. This is particularly true when a software development method is used in a project-based course. It is reasonable to assume that students naturally devote more effort to what is valued (and graded).

Among different options, we present here a grading policy which has this property, as is described in what follows.

According to this grading scheme the grade is composed of an individual component (35%) and a team component (65%), which was identical for all members of the team (see Table 2). Naturally, such an evaluation scheme conveys the message that both teamwork and individual contribution count. In practice, students are encouraged to contribute to the teamwork on the one hand, and on the other hand, this evaluation scheme affords those wishing to excel, the opportunity to improve their grade through the personal component of the grade.

Table 2. Example of a cooperation-oriented grading policy

Team Component (65%)	Individual Component (35%)
60% - Answer the customer stories and meeting the schedule according to the team time estimations: ✓ **(10%)** for iteration 1 ✓ **(25%)** for iteration 2 ✓ **(25%)** for iteration 3 **25% -** Project documentation **15% -** Team evaluation by the academic coach	**40% -** ✓ Weekly reflection ✓ Student-supervisor pair programming experience ✓ Test-Driven-Development exercise ✓ Weekly presence **40% -** Performance of a personal role: ✓ Actual implementation ✓ Further development and enhancement **20% -** Individual evaluation by the coach

Clearly, instructors can adjust the ratio between the individual and the team components and the specific ingredients of each component according to their teaching goals.

3. Conclusion

This activity suggests utilizing the conflicts and dilemmas rooted in bonus allocation task and the Prisoner Dilemma analysis, as a means for the construction of an evaluation scheme for students' software projects. A similar activity is conducted by us also with software development teams in the software industry.

4. References

Hazzan, O. (2003). Computer Science students' conception of the relationship between reward (grade) and cooperation, Proceedings of the *Eighth Annual Conference on Innovation and Technology in Computer Science Education (ITiCSE 2003)*, Thessaloniki, Greece, pp. 178-182.

Hazzan, O. and Dubinsky, Y. (2003). Teaching a Software Development Methodology: The Case of Extreme Programming, The proceedings of the *16th International Conference on Software Engineering Education and Training*, Madrid, Spain, pp. 176-184.

Hazzan, O. and Dubinsky, Y. (2005). Social Perspective of Software Development Methods: The Case of the Prisoner Dilemma and Extreme Programming, *Proceedings of the Sixth International Conference on Extreme Programming and Agile Processes in Software Engineering*, Sheffield University, UK, pp. 74-81.

Hazzan, O. and Dubinsky, Y. (2008). *Agile Software Engineering*, Springer.

Tomayko, J. and Hazzan, O. (2004). *Human Aspects of Software Engineering*, Charles River Media.

Mutation Analysis vs. Code Coverage in Automated Assessment of Students' Testing Skills

Kalle Aaltonen

kalle.aaltonen@gmail.com

Petri Ihantola   Otto Seppälä

Aalto University, Finland
{petri,oseppala}@cs.hut.fi

Abstract

Learning to program should include learning about proper software testing. Some automatic assessment systems, e.g. Web-CAT, allow assessing student-generated test suites using coverage metrics. While this encourages testing, we have observed that sometimes students can get rewarded from high coverage although their tests are of poor quality. Exploring alternative methods of assessment, we have tested mutation analysis to evaluate students' solutions. Initial results from applying mutation analysis to real course submissions indicate that mutation analysis could be used to fix some problems of code coverage in the assessment. Combining both metrics is likely to give more accurate feedback.

Categories and Subject Descriptors   K.3.2 [*Computer and Information Science Education*]: Computer science education

General Terms   Experimentation, Measurement, Human Factors

Keywords   automated assessment, testing, programming assignments, test coverage, mutation analysis, mutation testing

1.   Introduction

Students taking introductory programming classes are not usually accustomed to perform their own testing. As a result, they tend to focus on the correctness of the output as specified in the assignment and little else. If the program performs unexpectedly, some manual testing is often done to locate a bug instead of using more systematic approaches. We have observed this effect especially when feedback from automated assessment is available. Spacco and Pugh made sim-

ilar observations and suggest giving detailed feedback only after students have tested the code also by themselves [14].

Some automated assessment tools allow grading of student tests making it worthwhile for the students to test. At Aalto University (former Helsinki University of Technology) we have used automated assessment of programming assignments at least since 1994 and assessed students' self-written unit tests with Web-CAT[1] [2] since 2006. In Web-CAT, the assessment of student-provided tests is based on the percentage of the student's self-defined tests passing and the structural code coverage (i.e. statement or branch coverage) of these tests. While coverage provides information for the tester about possible places for improvement it might not tell the whole story - this is because good code coverage does not automatically guarantee proper test adequacy. It is well known from the industry that developers can misuse code-coverage-based test adequacy metrics to create a false sense of well tested software [10]. Not too surprisingly we have observed some students to do just the same to please the automated assessment system.

Although Web-CAT performs static analysis to ensure that tests include assertions, getting a good code coverage can be achieved without strong enough assertions or even by checking the assertions before running the code that was to be tested. For example,

- `assertTrue(1 < 2); fibonacci(6);`
- `assertTrue(fibonacci(6) >= 0);`
- `assertEquals(8,fibonacci(6));`

all achieve the same code coverage in automated coverage analysis, although their ability to tell how well the fibonacci method works is quite different. It is even possible that some students do not even see a problem in the first and second examples, which would be even more worrying. At least there are students following approaches similar to all previous examples. When students are rewarded from the code coverage of their tests, they seem to forget the true reason why tests are written.

Permission to make digital or hard copies of all or part of this work for personal or classroom use is granted without fee provided that copies are not made or distributed for profit or commercial advantage and that copies bear this notice and the full citation on the first page. To copy otherwise, to republish, to post on servers or to redistribute to lists, requires prior specific permission and/or a fee.

SPLASH'10,   October 17–21, 2010, Reno/Tahoe, Nevada, USA.
Copyright © 2010 ACM 978-1-4503-0240-1/10/10...$10.00

---

[1] http://web-cat.cs.vt.edu/

2. Research Problem and Method

To tackle the problem of poor test quality in students' written tests, we decided to seek alternative metrics to evaluate the test adequacy.

Mutation analysis is a well known technique performed on a set of unit tests by seeding simple programming errors into the program code to be tested. Each combination of errors applied to the code creates what is called a *mutant*. These "mutants" are generated systematically in large quantities and the examined test suite is run on each of them. The theory is that the test suite that detects more generated defective programs is better than the one that detects less [1]. This makes mutation testing an interesting candidate for use in automatic assessment of student tests. In this paper we apply mutation analysis to real course data to study how this method would perform in an educational setting.

The exact research questions we address are:

Q1: What are the possible strengths and weaknesses of mutation analysis when compared to code coverage based metrics?

Q2: Can mutation analysis be used to give meaningful grading on student-provided test suites requested in programming assignments?

Suitability of mutation testing for test suite assessment was evaluated with test data from Helsinki University of Technology, Intermediate Courses in Programming L1 and T1, held in Fall 2008. These identical courses both teach object oriented programming in Java and are worth 6 ECTS-credits[2]. They have a 5 ECTS-credits CS1 course as their prerequisite. Automatic assessment is used on all courses but students are not required to do unit testing on the prerequisite course. The exercises count for 30 percent of the course grade. All exercises were originally assessed with Web-CAT. The number of resubmissions was not limited. When the course was given no mutation testing was used.

The research method we applied was to compare the test coverage to the *mutation scores*. Both scores were calculated from existing student solutions to three programming assignments. Mutation scores were calculated using Javalanche [12]. During the course the students were "traditionally" awarded points from test coverage. We further investigated submissions that got full points from the coverage but performed poorly in the mutation analysis. In addition, for test set A, we evaluated the effect of different solutions by calculating the mutation scores of each submitted test against all submitted solutions.

Generating and testing mutants requires processing time. Providing instant feedback using mutation analysis in assessment requires keeping the number of mutants at a reasonable level. Minimum, maximum and average counts of mutants are given for each of the test sets.

---

[2] European Credit Transfer and Accumulation System

3. Related Research

3.1 Automated Assessment of Testing Skills

Both code coverage based metrics and the ability to find faulty implementations are used to automatically evaluate students' tests. Some of the related research conducted before 2006 is summarized in [14].

Assessing the Code Coverage

ASSYST [8] and Web-CAT [2] are perhaps the most widely used tools that combine automated assessment of correctness and tests. Grading in Web-CAT is based on three factors: percentage of teacher's tests passing, percentage of student's own tests passing and code coverage percentage of student's tests. In ASSYST, statement coverage can affect a grade that is originally based on testing the correctness with teachers's tests. Still another system, Marmoset, has been modified to take into account students' tests when grading and giving feedback [14]. By default, Marmoset has the tests grouped into two sets. Feedback from public tests, including test definitions, are given immediately after submission. After the public tests pass, the students can ask for the release tests to be executed. Feedback from the release tests is both limited and delayed. An enhanced version of Marmoset investigates both the code coverage of release tests and student's own tests. As an incentive to test throughly, information about a release test is provided only if student's own tests cover the same as what the release test covers.

Assessing the Ability to Find Bugs

Goldwasser [4] describes an idea where each student on a course provides both a program and a test set - all combinations of which are tried together. Test sets that reveal a lot of bugs and programs that pass a lot of test sets are both rewarded. It is also possible for the staff to seed a faulty implementation to the competition. This also makes it possible to give immediate feedback as students do not need to wait until the exercise deadline when the competition can be performed. Moreover, this allows students to learn from their mistakes. Other papers with similar concept of a competition include e.g. [6, 11]. Elbaum et. al. have created BugHunt [3], a web based tutorial where students write unit tests to reveal problems from given programs.

3.2 Mutation Analysis

Figure 1 explains the process of mutation analysis. Process inputs are the program to be tested and the test suite to be evaluated. In the next phase mutants are generated from the program, and each mutant is tested with the test set. If a mutant fails in the testing it is killed. If it passes all tests, it is called a live mutant. Live mutants are examined in the next phase by hand and split to equivalent and non-equivalent mutants. For example, Listings 2 and 3 are mutants of Listing 1. Note that Listing 2 is functionally identical with the original (i.e. equivalent) whereas Listing 3 is not.

```
int normFib (int N) {
  int curr=1, prev=0;
  for (int i=0; i<N; i++){
    int temp = curr;
    curr     = curr+prev;
    prev     = temp;
  }
  return prev;
}
```

Listing 1. Original

```
int equalFib (int N) {
  int curr=1, prev=0;
  for (int i=1; i<=N; i++){
    int temp = curr;
    curr     = curr+prev;
    prev     = temp;
  }
  return prev;
}
```

Listing 2. Equivalent mutant

```
int mutFib (int N) {
  int curr=1, prev=0;
  for (int i=0; i<=N; i++){
    int temp = curr;
    curr     = curr+prev;
    prev     = temp;
  }
  return prev;
}
```

Listing 3. Non-equivalent mutant

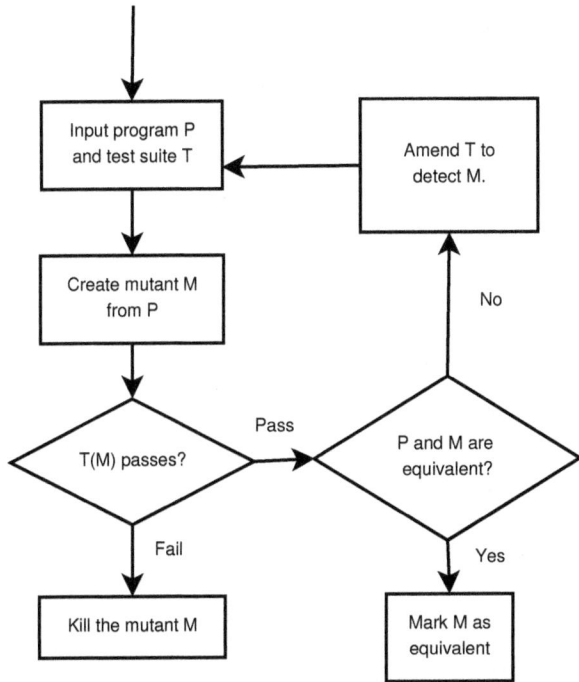

Figure 1. Mutation analysis process

The effectiveness of a test set in mutation analysis is measured by a *mutation score*. This is normally defined as the percentage of non-equivalent mutants killed by the test set. Automated tools often estimate it by dividing the number of *all* live mutants with *all* mutants. The latter is provided by most mutation tools and is also what we have used in this paper.

Mutating Java Programs

Mutants can be generated by modifying a program on different levels – from machine code to interpreted languages with a high abstraction level. Current mutation analysis tools for the Java language generate mutants from the Java source code (e.g. μJava [9]) or from the intermediary bytecode executed by the Java Virtual Machine (e.g. Javalanche [12]), as illustrated in Figure 2. There are pros and cons in both source code level and bytecode level mutants:

- Each examined source code mutant has to be compiled, which is slow.

- Bytecode mutants are difficult to examine afterwards as it's not possible or straightforward to generate the Java source for the mutated bytecode.

- The compiler can eliminate dead code, which in theory can result in fewer equivalent mutants in source code mutants, e.g. if the mutation operation targets a part of the code that's deemed dead by the compiler, the resulting bytecode will be identical with the original.

- Some more advanced operators are significantly easier to implement in Java than in bytecode.

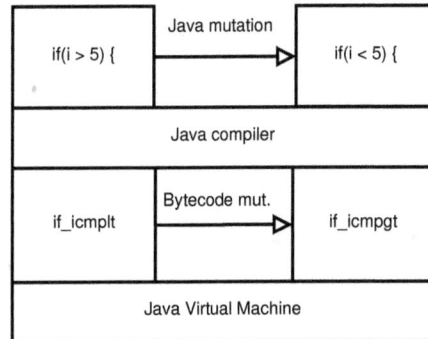

Figure 2. Mutant generation on the Java architecture

μ**Java**[3] is a well known mutation tool for Java, developed since 2003. μJava's mutation operations fall into two distinct classes: method-level mutation operators and class mutation operators. Class level operations are related to encapsulation, inheritance, polymorphism, and some java-specific features (e.g. add or remove keywords like this and static). Method-level operations, presented in Table 1, are very generic and can be applied to other languages.

Javalanche[4] is a simple and effective bytecode level mutation analysis tool. It replaces numerical constants ($x \rightarrow x + 1|x - 1|0|1$), negates jump conditions, omits method calls and replaces arithmetic operators. There are no advanced mutation operators related to visibility, inheritance

---

[3] http://cs.gmu.edu/~offutt/mujava/

[4] http://www.st.cs.uni-saarland.de/~schuler/javalanche/

155

Name	Description	Example
Arithmetic operators	Replace, add, and remove unary and binary arithmetic operators (+, -, /, *, ++, --) for both integer and floating point operators.	x+1 x-1 x*1 x/1
Relational operators	replace different comparison operators (>, >=, <, <=, ==, !=) within the program.	x==1 x!=1 x>=1 ...
Conditional operators	Replace, insert and remove conditional operators (&&, ||, !). Bitwise operators &, |, and ^ are also used as replacements for these operators as they are very common mistakes.	x||!y x|!y x&&!y x||y ...
Shift operators	Replace bit-wise shifting operators (<<, >>, >>>)	x>>1 x<<1 x>>>1
Bitwise operators	Replace, add and move four operators to perform bitwise functions(&, |, ^, ~).	x&~y x|~y x&y x^~y
Assignment operators	Replace the convenience assignment operators provided by Java with another (+=, -=, *=, /=, %=, &=, |=, ^=, <<=, >>=, >>>=).	x+=2 x-=2 x*=2 x/=2 ...

Table 1. Method-level mutation operators in μJava. The last column shows a tree diagram where the child nodes are possible mutants generated by this operation applied on the parent.

and polymorphism as μJava has. Javalanche has been successfully used to run mutation analysis on AspectJ, a large open source Java project (with almost 100 thousand lines of code) in under six hours on a single workstation [13].

4. Test Coverage vs. Mutation Score

We analyzed final submissions from each student to three assignments – called test set A, B, and C later on. We failed to apply mutation analysis successfully on some submissions because:

1. The submission did not compile successfully.

2. The test suite did not pass on the unmutated program.

3. Individual tests were not repeatable and independent of the execution order.

This implies that only submissions where all the student's tests passed are analyzed. Table 2 summarizes how many of the submissions were successfully analyzed and how many mutants, on average, were generated from each assignment.

Name	Mutation analysis			Generated Mutants (per submission)		
	All	Applicable	Mutation score avg.	min	max	avg
Set A	158	131 (83.0%)	80.5%	22	90	44.4
Set B	187	174 (90.0%)	73.7%	79	439	106.9
Set C	193	169 (87.6%)	84.9%	12	93	26.4

Table 2. Summary of the test sets used.

4.1 Test set A - Binary search trees

In this exercise the students were instructed to implement a binary search tree by extending an existing binary tree implementation through inheritance. As with all our exercises, unit-testing the solution was required and code coverage was used as the measure of completeness.

Of the 131 analyzed submissions 125 achieved perfect code coverage. This is an expected result, as the students were awarded for reaching perfect coverage, and in the case of this assignment it was relatively easy to achieve.

The mutation analysis yielded an average of 44 mutations per sample, and it took on average about 12 seconds to run per sample. The best work managed to kill 48 of its 49 mutants, resulting in 97.96% mutation score. The one remaining live mutant was identical on the java source code level and thus unkillable, so this can be considered a perfect score. On average the mutation score was 80.48%, and the worst was 40%. The worst mutation score that had reached perfect code coverage was 54.76%. There were several samples where the tested method could be completely commented out, and the test suite would fail to detect this. This would seem to support our assumption that mutation analysis offers better capabilities in identifying weak test sets.

Figure 3 illustrates relationship between mutation score and test coverage in the set as a scatter plot. Histograms on each axis show the distribution of the respective variables. Code coverage (on the X-axis) was 100% for most submissions. This also explains why the correlation between the variables is small ($\rho \approx 0.1628$).

Effect of Implementation to the Generation of Mutants

The binary tree assignment was more restrictive than any of the others. Not only were the students told which methods to implement but they were not allowed to declare any additional instance variables. This was checked automatically. These restrictions made it possible to combine implementations and tests of different students.

In order to show how much variation does the implementation itself (excluding the tests) cause to the mutation score, we selected 4 example test suites from the ones that had achieved 100% test coverage; the worst, the best, and two random ones. We ran mutation analysis on all the previously analyzed submissions with each of these test sets, and results are shown in Figure 4. Each box plot presents one of the four selected test suites. Labels on the X-axis are the original mutation scores and the box plot visualizes how the mutation score varied when the test was executed against implementation of all the other students.

If we are to use the mutation score as an indication to the adequacy of the test set, this score should not be affected by the implementation, but the implementation does affect the number of equivalent mutants created, which makes the mutation scores of two test suites on two different implementations incomparable. It should be noted that in Figure 4 the distribution of the first two test sets seems to be very similar even though the original score is very different. This is something that needs to taken into account if the students are ever rewarded on basis of their mutation score.

4.2 Test set B - Hashing

This was the first exercise on the course and its main idea was to acquaint the students with unit testing. The code to be tested was a pre-implemented hash table implementation using double hashing. The students only had to add in it a method for finding prime numbers – other than that it was all about testing.

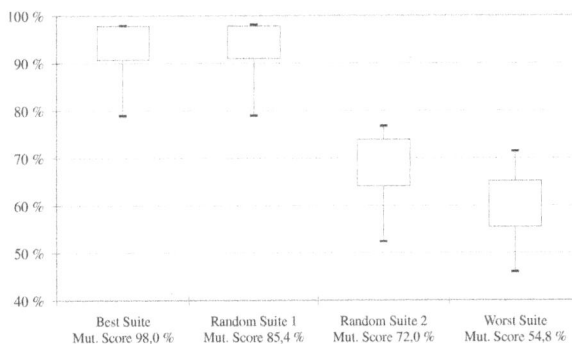

Figure 4. Distribution of mutation scores for the selected test suites as box plot. Displayed are the minimum, maximum 90th and 10th percentiles. X-axis labels are the mutation scores that were achieved when running the mutation analysis on its respective implementation.

Of the 174 analyzed submissions 135 achieved perfect code coverage. This exercise was more complex than test set A, as it yielded on average 106 mutations per sample. Mutation scores of the submissions that achieved perfect coverage score ranged from 42.7% to 89.39% with 73.73% being the average. Mutation scores of the submissions that didn't reach perfect coverage ranged from 24.44% to 85.96% with 63.52% being the average.

The distribution and the relationship between code coverages and mutation scores can be seen in Figure 5.

The best sample reached 100% code coverage and managed to kill 100 out of 112 mutants.

We also examined the sample with the worst mutation score that had reached perfect code coverage: The sample managed to kill 38 of the 89 total mutations, reaching a mutation score of 42.70%. The student generated portion of the test suite had only a single assertion, and half of the unit tests didn't contain any assertions. The test suite is clearly inadequate despite it having perfect branch coverage.

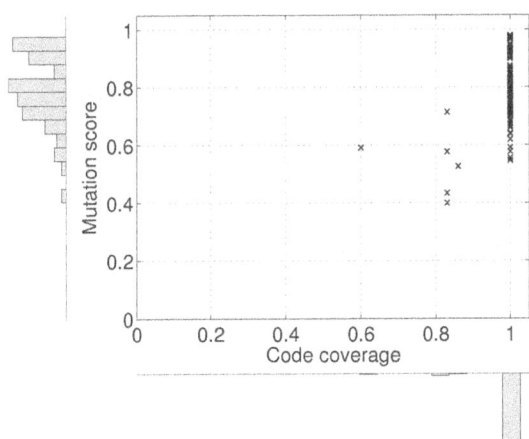

Figure 3. Scatter plot of code coverage and mutation score of the test set A

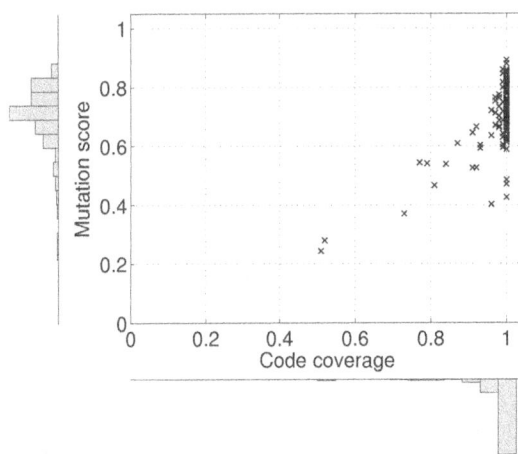

Figure 5. Scatter plot of code coverage and mutation score of the test set B

The distribution seems to be very similar to the distribution seen in test set A (Figure 3), except that the number of samples is higher and there is more variance in the code coverages, $\sigma \approx 0,064$. Pearson product-moment correlation coefficient for the dataset is $\rho \approx 0,669$ indicating a clear positive correlation, unlike in test set A. Major difference with test set A is the maximum mutation score, which was under 90% compared to the practically perfect mutation score achieved in A.

From some submissions we analyzed all mutants that were not killed. Not even the best student generated test suite managed to kill all the non-equivalent mutants.

4.3 Test set C - Disjoint sets

In this exercise the students were instructed to build a simple union-find structure. The exercise allows extracting code shared by different methods into helper methods and has fairly simple recursive and iterative solutions.

Mutation analysis was successfully performed on 169 submissions, of which 144 achieved perfect coverage. Each submission yielded on average 26 mutations. The amount of generated mutants ranged from 12 to 93. Mutation scores of the submissions that achieved perfect coverage score ranged from 38.46% to 95.00% with 84.88% being the average, which is the highest in all the data sets. Mutation scores of the submissions that didn't reach perfect coverage ranged from 21.43% to 90.48% with 67,84% being the average.

The distribution and the relationship between code coverages and mutation scores can be seen in Figure 6.

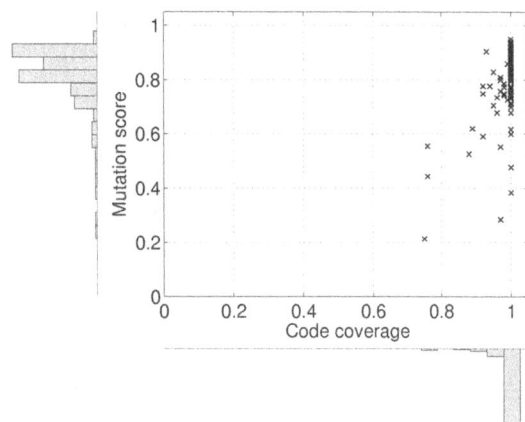

Figure 6. Scatter plot of code coverage and mutation score of the test set C

The best sample had 100% code coverage and killed 19 of its 20 mutations reaching a mutation score of 95.00%, and the remaining mutant was equivalent so this sample should considered mutation adequate.

The submission with perfect code coverage and worst mutation score managed to kill 10 of its 26 total mutations reaching a mutation score of 38.46%.

The distribution seems to be very similar to the distribution seen in the previous test sets (Figure 3 and 5). Pearson product-moment correlation coefficient for the dataset is $\rho \approx 0.6034$ indicating a clear positive correlation.

5. Analysis of Weak Test Sets

We manually examined bottom four samples by mutation score from the samples that had reached perfect coverage. Our initial assumption was that these should be of poor quality by having badly tested or untested functionality. We were not investigating other aspects of test quality, such as style and structural considerations. We also examined the percentage of the teacher's tests passing. It should be noted that all students' tests had to pass their own implementation so that we were able to run the mutation analysis.

5.1 Test set A

All the examined samples had significant problems. For example, none of them tested `printInorder`, at all – although it was fully covered by the tests. Table 3 summarizes our findings from Test set A.

Name	Mutants generated	detected	score	teacher's tests
weak 1	42	23	54.76%	57%
weak 2	54	30	55.56%	86%
weak 3	45	26	57.78%	71%
weak 4	49	29	59.18%	100%

Table 3. Samples with perfect code coverage and bad mutation score of the test set A

5.2 Test set B

All the samples had plenty of untested functionality. Three of the analyzed test sets had only one trivial (although meaningfull) assertion generated by a student. Numerical results from this test set are in Table 4. It should be noted that the most important part of this assignment was to test code that was given. This is why all of the teacher's tests are passing.

Name	Mutants generated	detected	score	teacher's tests
weak 1	89	38	42.70%	100%
weak 2	104	49	47.12%	100%
weak 3	107	52	48.60%	100%
weak 4	90	53	58.89%	100%

Table 4. Samples with perfect code coverage and bad mutation score of the test set B

5.3 Test set C

Unlike in the other test sets, the samples in the test set C were not all of bad quality. Quality of the test of samples 1 and 2 was poor and comparable to test sets A and B. However, tests of samples 3 and 4 were significantly better and it can be argued they only had some corner cases untested but redundant code caused a large number of mutants to be equivalent with the original. Quantitative data from the samples are presented in Table 5.

	Mutants			teacher's
Name	generated	detected	score	tests
weak 1	26	10	38.46%	100%
weak 2	23	11	47.83%	100%
weak 3	25	15	60.00%	86%
weak 4	21	13	61.76%	100%

Table 5. Samples with perfect code coverage and bad mutation score of the test set C

6. Discussion and Conclusions

In the following two subsections we answer to our first research question: *What are the possible strengths (Section 6.1) and weaknesses of mutation analysis (Section 6.2) when compared to code coverage based metrics?* In Section 6.4 we answer our second question: *can mutation analysis be used to give meaningful grading on student-provided test suites requested in programming assignments?*

6.1 Strengths

Automatically assessed exercises are often criticized for not being creative enough. Assessing the functionality of the solution by unit tests written by the teacher implies exercises where students are given the structure of the code. Greening, for example, argues [5, pp. 53–54]:

> Usually, however, the tasks required of the student are highly structured and meticulously synchronized with lectures, and are of the form that asks the student to write a piece of code that satisfies a precise set of specifications created by the instructor. [...] Although some practical skills are certainly gained, the exercise is essentially one of reproduction.

Mutation analysis combines the correctness of the program to be tested (i.e. it can only be applied when tests pass) and the adequacy of the tests. This lessens the need of unit tests written by the teacher and allows more open ended assignments.

In Section 3.1, we described other approaches and assessment tools that also evaluate test set's ability to detect faulty programs. The benefit of mutation analysis over competitions where students' assignments are executed against each other is the ability to give immediate feedback. Immediate feedback would also be possible if faulty programs were generated beforehand by the teacher – as discussed in Section 3.1. However, manual generation of the mutants would prevent automatically assessing more open ended assignments – which mutation analysis could perform. Qualitative analysis in Section 5 implies that mutation analysis is an effective approach for semi-automatic assessment. It could be used with systems like Web-CAT and ASSYST to post-process the submissions and to identify students that may be trying to fool the assessment systems. These submissions could then be manually assessed to ensure this is not the case.

6.2 Weaknesses

One weakness of mutation analysis is that coverage results are easier to interpret and are therefore simpler to use as feedback and assessment criteria with students. While approaches where mutants are used as counterexamples of weak test sets exist, they should be tested in a real course setting to see what is the best way to apply them.

Complex Solutions can be Over-weighted

Complex code creates many mutants and redundant code can cause large numbers of equivalent mutants. This can cause unfairly low mutation scores but can also be used to cheat automatic assessment based on mutation analysis.

When methods contain redundant code or are very complicated the number of mutants blows up. This can lead to a situation where a significant portion of the mutants are from a small untested functionality. This implies that the penalty of not testing that specific funitionality gets too high as demonstrated in Section 5.3.

If students realize that complex code creates many mutants, they may try to fool the mutation analysis system by seeding irrelevant code into their submissions. For example, Listing 4 simply performs the function $f(x) = x + 63$, but the way it is written blows up the number of mutants. This will distort the mutation score. The large number of analyzed mutants can also result in the grading system performing poorly.

```
public static int dummy(int x) {
    x+=3;x+=3;x+=3;x+=3;x+=3;x+=3;x+=3;
    x+=3;x+=3;x+=3;x+=3;x+=3;x+=3;x+=3;
    x+=3;x+=3;x+=3;x+=3;x+=3;x+=3;x+=3;
    return x;
}
```

Listing 4. Sample of an easily testable dummy method, that yields a large number of mutants, and can be thoroughly tested with `assertEquals(63,dummy(0));`.

The number of mutants generated per submission should also be monitored, as it can indicate this kind of cheating, malicious intent in trying to cause the system to perform poorly, or simply an over-complicated solution from where the student should get feedback.

6.3 Testing Unspecified Behavior

Even with assignments where an exact interface to implement is provided, some details of the implementation can be unspecified. For example, how to use return values of methods can be left for students. For students, leaving such unspecified behavior not tested is natural. However, mutation analysis penalizes from this as mutants are also generated from the unspecified behavior. This forces students to specify the otherwise unspecified features through tests.

6.4 Mutation Analysis in Grading

We conclude that mutation analysis can reveal tests that were created to fool the assessment system. Preliminary results indicate that mutation analysis can provide valuable feedback of how well students have tested their software. While the information is most easily interpreted and used by a teacher, the results could be valuable to the students as well. However, to verify this result, a follow up study where students get feedback based on the mutation analysis is needed. An interesting question is if students fool the mutation analysis just like they do for the coverage.

We should also keep in mind that mutation score is not independent from the implementation. Thus, if the objective is to give separate grades from tests and implementation, raw mutation scores are not the best option as they are not commensurable. We assume that it would be possible to set an exercise-specific threshold to identify certainly poor or suspicious work. However, this is where more research is needed.

Although many students submit their work just before the deadline, we assume mutation analysis to scale up and not to be computationally too expensive. For example, analysing a single submission in test set A took 12 seconds on average (see Section 4.1).

7. Future Research

In the future, we would like to see mutation analysis being used to provide formative feedback, i.e. feedback for learning. For example, if mutants are generated on source code level, programs which did not pass student's tests could be provided as feedback. However how to select which of the live mutants to show in an interesting research problem.

Testing can be made more effective by writing code that is easy to test. There are rules how to write testable code and metrics related to measuring the testability. One such metric is provided by a tool called TestabilityExplorer[5] [7]. In the future, we plan to take our data set and apply traditional code coverage, mutation score and TestabilityExplorer to understand how these three different metrics are related to each other. Follow up studies to see how students behave when the immediate feedback they get is based on mutation analysis and/or testability are needed.

References

[1] R. A. DeMillo, R. J. Lipton, and F. G. Sayward. Hints on test data selection: Help for the practicing programmer. *IEEE Computer*, 11:34–41, 1978.

[2] S. H. Edwards. Rethinking computer science education from a test-first perspective. In *Companion of the 18th annual ACM SIGPLAN conference on Object-oriented programming, systems, languages, and applications, Anaheim, California, USA, 26–30 October*, pages 148–155. ACM, New York, NY, USA, 2003. ISBN 1-58113-751-6.

[3] S. Elbaum, S. Person, J. Dokulil, and M. Jorde. Bug hunt: Making early software testing lessons engaging and affordable. In *ICSE '07: Proceedings of the 29th international conference on Software Engineering*, pages 688–697, Washington, DC, USA, 2007. IEEE Computer Society.

[4] M. H. Goldwasser. A gimmick to integrate software testing throughout the curriculum. *SIGCSE Bull.*, 34(1):271–275, 2002. ISSN 0097-8418.

[5] T. Greening. Emerging constructivist forces in computer science education: Shaping a new future. In T. Greening, editor, *Computer science education in the 21st century*, pages 47–80. Springer Verlag, 1999.

[6] M. Hauswirth, D. Zaparanuks, A. Malekpour, and M. Keikha. The javafest: a collaborative learning technique for java programming courses. In *PPPJ '08: Proceedings of the 6th international symposium on Principles and practice of programming in Java*, pages 3–12, New York, NY, USA, 2008. ACM. ISBN 978-1-60558-223-8.

[7] M. Hevery. Testability explorer: using byte-code analysis to engineer lasting social changes in an organization's software development process. In *OOPSLA Companion '08: Companion to the 23rd ACM SIGPLAN conference on Object-oriented programming systems languages and applications*, pages 747–748, New York, NY, USA, 2008. ACM.

[8] D. Jackson and M. Usher. Grading student programs using ASSYST. In *Proceedings of 28th ACM SIGCSE Symposium on Computer Science Education*, pages 335–339, 1997.

[9] Y.-S. Ma, J. Offutt, and Y. R. Kwon. Mujava: an automated class mutation system: Research articles. *Softw. Test. Verif. Reliab.*, 15(2):97–133, 2005. ISSN 0960-0833.

[10] B. Marick. How to misuse code coverage. In *Proceedings of the 16th International Conference on Testing Computer Software*, pages 16–18, 1999.

[11] W. Marrero and A. Settle. Testing first: emphasizing testing in early programming courses. In *ITiCSE '05: Proceedings of the 10th annual SIGCSE conference on Innovation and technology in computer science education*, pages 4–8, New York, NY, USA, 2005. ACM. ISBN 1-59593-024-8.

[12] D. Schuler and A. Zeller. Javalanche: efficient mutation testing for java. In *ESEC/FSE '09: Proceedings of the 7th joint meeting of the European software engineering conference and the ACM SIGSOFT symposium on The foundations of software engineering on European software engineering conference and foundations of software engineering symposium*, pages 297–298, New York, NY, USA, 2009. ACM. ISBN 978-1-60558-001-2.

[13] D. Schuler, V. Dallmeier, and A. Zeller. Efficient mutation testing by checking invariant violations. In *ISSTA '09: Proceedings of the eighteenth international symposium on Software testing and analysis*, pages 69–80, New York, NY, USA, 2009. ACM. ISBN 978-1-60558-338-9.

[14] J. Spacco and W. Pugh. Helping students appreciate test-driven development (tdd). In *OOPSLA '06: Companion to the 21st ACM SIGPLAN symposium on Object-oriented programming systems, languages, and applications*, pages 907–913, New York, NY, USA, 2006. ACM. ISBN 1-59593-491-X.

---

[5] http://code.google.com/p/testability-explorer/

Compiler Construction With A Dash of Concurrency and An Embedded Twist

Adam B. Mallen   Dennis Brylow

Department of Mathematics, Statistics, and Computer Science
Marquette University
Milwaukee, WI 53201-1881
{amallen,brylow}@mscs.mu.edu

Abstract

We describe the renovation of our compilers curriculum to meld together an established object-oriented textbook compiler with an inexpensive embedded target platform. The result is a modern compiler implementation course with aspects of concurrency and embedded systems, and a palpable increase in student enthusiasm. We discuss the trade-offs in retargeting our compiler, gauge the difficulty of supporting thread-level concurrency in our target language, and outline the resulting structure of the course and integration with the rest of our computer science curriculum.

Categories and Subject Descriptors   D.3.4 [*Programming Languages*]: Processors—Compilers

General Terms   Languages

1. Introduction

The study of programming language translation (compilers) remains a core component of the computer science curriculum [12]. At its best, a compiler course delves into the technology that not only has transformed the ways we build software in recent decades, but also drives much of our field's recent productivity gains.

This paper is about our efforts to reinvigorate our traditional compiler construction course by combining two proven instructional technologies: a well-established modern compilers textbook – Appel and Palsberg's "MiniJava" book [2] – and the wireless router hardware used by the Embedded Xinu educational operating system [3]. By selecting a target *platform* (a processor and operating system combination) rather than simply a target processor or simulator,

we are also able to extend the object-oriented MiniJava language to include support for basic thread concurrency and the Java `synchronized` construct.

Language-level concurrency support in a compilers course is difficult for several reasons. First, concurrent programming is inherently more complex than serial programming for students to reason about at any level. Second, despite the wide availability of thread-level concurrency support in modern languages like Java, popular compiler textbooks [1, 2, 11] do not cover the topic. (Aho et.al [1] cover instruction-level parallelism and concurrent garbage collection.) Finally, in a hands-on compilers course, the term project cannot reasonably explore concurrency without underlying runtime support for threading and synchronization; courses that target simulators or eschew a platform operating system are not generally able to provide this support.

In retargeting our instructional compiler project to a real embedded platform, we discovered that thread-level concurrency could be treated as a basic language feature, woven naturally throughout each stage of the term compiler construction project.

The contributions of this paper are threefold:

- A prototype that retargets a well-documented, object-oriented, instructional compiler to an embedded platform with a well-documented instructional operating system,

- An evaluation of our compilers course using the prototype as the model for the term-length student project, and

- An extension adding concurrent threading and synchronization appropriate for upper-division students.

The following sections of this paper present related work, followed by an explanation of the technical trade-offs explored while integrating two very different sets of educational software. Next, we outline the general structure of our course, with particular attention to the phases of the semester-length compiler project, and present an assessment of the results. Following that, we describe the concurrency features we have implemented to extend the compiler project in next year's course. Finally, we conclude.

Permission to make digital or hard copies of all or part of this work for personal or classroom use is granted without fee provided that copies are not made or distributed for profit or commercial advantage and that copies bear this notice and the full citation on the first page. To copy otherwise, to republish, to post on servers or to redistribute to lists, requires prior specific permission and/or a fee.
SPLASH'10,   October 17–21, 2010, Reno/Tahoe, Nevada, USA.
Copyright © 2010 ACM 978-1-4503-0240-1/10/10... $10.00

1.1 Prior and Related Work

Innovative compiler courses have been written about for decades, and cannot possibly be summarized here. Two recent projects with similarities to our own include the Bantam Java project, and the Chirp-Scribbler language.

Bantam Java [8] is a Java subset designed for education. It is a simpler design than the MiniJava compiler, and has a free manual intended to release instructors from a particular textbook choice. We chose MiniJava as our base for this proof-of-concept implementation, but we're currently working on duplicating our results with the Bantam Java system.

The Chirp-Scribbler language [15] was devised to teach programming language translation using the Scribbler robotics platform. This project has similar goals to our own, but the complexity of our source language and target platform are at a very different level from the Chirp-Scribbler project, which translates a stack-free, C-like imperative language into interpreted PBASIC.

On the opposite end of our project, Embedded Xinu is a reimplementation of the venerable Xinu operating system [7]. Xinu has been ported to more than half a dozen platforms, but Embedded Xinu is the first ANSI-standard C port for modern RISC hardware. Embedded Xinu is a core component of the Project Nexos curriculum [5], an NSF-sponsored development of inexpensive, portable curriculum materials for embedded systems education.

2. An Embedded Target Platform

The primary task in revamping the semester project in our compiler construction course was to target the educational compiler from a well-established textbook to a real embedded platform that could run the resulting executable. We chose Appel and Palsberg's popular *Modern Compiler Implementation in Java* text because, at its core, it is centered on a marvelous semester-length compiler project. For our embedded target platform, we chose the Embedded Xinu operating system [3, 4, 6], an inexpensive laboratory infrastructure in use at a growing number of universities for experimental systems courses.

In the next several subsections, we explain the modifications necessary to meld these two existing curriculum resources into a coherent whole.

2.1 Grammar Extensions

One of the inevitable tensions when designing a compilers course is to balance the simplicity and expressive power of the language. Syntax should be straightforward and familiar, yet powerful enough to build interesting testcases without unnecessary tedium. Like Java, *MiniJava* [2] suffers from a poverty of I/O primitives. MiniJava contains only the `System.out.println()` method for output; without overloading or variadic arguments, this stripped-down `println()` method can only print a single integer at a time.

As a result, MiniJava testcases consist of programs that take no input, and output only unornamented integer lists.

The desire for minimalism in Appel and Palsberg's text is understandable, but when teaching a compilers course with this book, the first embellishment an instructor is likely to make is to add more I/O – particularly to allow input, and to output non-integer data. The challenge is then to design I/O extensions that retain the most elegant property of MiniJava; MiniJava programs are a proper subset of Java, and thus can be compiled and run with the standard Java tools.

Working strictly within the constraints of the Java Standard Library then means that even the most rudimentary of input operations requires building support into the compiler for multiple special-purpose Java I/O classes, (`System.in`, `java.io.BufferedReader`, etc.) as well as additional grammar productions for `import` statements and some exception syntax. All of this must then be supported by the compiler's ultimate runtime as well.

One satisfactory solution to this problem of adapting the compiler language to a richer set of I/O functions is to create a special "helper class" with I/O methods. The helper class will contain method names reserved for the compiler to link up to underlying runtime I/O operations, but that can also be encoded as a companion `.java` source file for native Java testing. The I/O helper class concept has been used in several popular introductory Java texts, to ease students into the complex world of Java I/O libraries; here we reuse this idea to simplify construction of the compiler itself.

$$
\begin{array}{lll}
\textit{Statement} & \rightarrow & \ldots \\
& \rightarrow & \texttt{Xinu}.\textit{id} \, (\, \textit{ExpList}\,); \\
\textit{Exp} & \rightarrow & \ldots \\
& \rightarrow & \texttt{Xinu}.\textit{id} \, (\, \textit{ExpList}\,)
\end{array}
$$

Figure 1. External call productions added to MiniJava

Figure 1 gives the set of statement and expression productions we add to the MiniJava language so programs can access external runtime functions. This makes simple serial-based I/O possible for testcases run on our embedded target environment. Specifically, we add the ability to print strings with `Xinu.print(String s)`, the ability to print a new line with `Xinu.println()`, the ability to print an integer with `Xinu.printint(int x)`, and the ability to read in an integer input with `Xinu.readint()`. Though here we only add support for simple I/O operations, the external call mechanism makes it easier and more natural to extend the language with embellished I/O functions or additional operating system calls beyond I/O operations, as we shall see when we add thread operations in Section 5. Still, this minimal extension to the MiniJava language is sufficient to illustrate the changes required throughout the various phases of the compiler.

Figure 2 is the Java source code for the `Xinu` helper class. With this source, MiniJava test programs with Xinu

I/O extensions can be compiled and run with the standard Java tool set.

```java
import java.util.Scanner;
public class Xinu
{
    public static int readint()
    {
        Scanner s = new Scanner(System.in);
        return s.nextInt();
    }

    public static void printint(int x)
    {   System.out.println(x);    }

    public static void print(String s)
    {   System.out.print(s);    }

    public static void println()
    {   System.out.println();    }
}
```

Figure 2. Java Class for Xinu I/O Functions

2.2 Compiler Changes

The lexical analysis phase (scanner) of the compiler was extended to include `Xinu` as a basic token. The syntactic analysis phase (parser) of the compiler was extended with the grammar rules given in Figure 1 and produces abstract syntax tree (AST) nodes for the external call statement and external call expression productions which keep track of the name of the Xinu method being called.

Semantic analysis (type checking) requires an additional step for initializing the class and type environments. The class environment must be initialized with a type-descriptor containing each of the method types in class `Xinu`, and the type environment must be initialized with a binding of identifier `Xinu` to this class type.

The next major phase of compilation, translation, must map the AST representations of Xinu I/O functions to intermediate representation (IR) nodes that reference the corresponding underlying runtime functions. Care must be taken at this point to choose runtime function names that will not conflict with legitimate source language method names; we follow longstanding tradition and append an underscore to the runtime function names. The complete list of runtime support functions is given in Figure 3. The mapping of the I/O functions is self-explanatory, but also at this point we add in a dynamic memory allocation function to support the source language `new` operator for instantiating new objects and arrays. In addition, if the compiler is to support Java-like runtime checking for null pointers and array bounds, corresponding runtime error handlers must be mapped.

The instruction selection and register allocation phases of the compiler required no special modifications to target

Xinu function	Purpose
`syscall _readint(void)`	Parse in integer input.
`syscall _printint(int i)`	Print an integer.
`syscall _print(char *s)`	Print a string literal.
`syscall _println(void)`	Print a carriage return.
`int *new(int n, int f)`	Allocate object or array.
`void _BADPTR(void)`	Null pointer exception.
`void _BADSUB(void)`	Bounds exception.

Figure 3. MiniJava to Xinu Compatibility Layer

Embedded Xinu, and merely had to follow standard MIPS calling conventions.

The output of this MiniJava compiler is MIPS assembly language. The final steps are to assemble into machine language and link with the runtime system. Purists may insist on students also constructing their own assembler, but in the context of an undergraduate course where project time is always at a premium, this activity is really just more of the same after completing the earlier, more complex phases.

2.3 O/S Requirements

We use the Embedded Xinu *Mips Playground*, as first laid out in [4], to provide a lightweight bootstrapping environment for running MIPS code directly on the WRT54GL wireless router's embedded processor. The output of the compiler is linked directly into the kernel, which calls the MiniJava `main` program immediately after initialization, and the entire image is uploaded to the target device on demand.

The compatibility layer between MiniJava and Embedded Xinu consists primarily of short mappings between I/O function names. The two non-trivial cases are object/array allocation and integer input (Figure 4); the full C language Xinu code for integer input is given below.

```c
syscall _readint(void)
{
    int i = 0, c = 0;
    c = getchar();
    while (('\n'!=c) && ('\r'!=c) && (EOF!=c))
    {
        if (('0' <= c) && ('9' >= c))
        {   i = i * 10 + c - '0';    }
        c = getchar();
    }
    kprintf("\r\n");
    if (EOF == c) return c;
    return i;
}
```

Figure 4. Character-based Input From Xinu

3. Compiler Construction Course

Our compiler construction course is fifteen weeks, three credit hours, and is an upper-division elective taken primarily by computer science and engineering majors. Prerequisites include data structures, hardware systems (computer organization with assembly language), and a prior course on programming languages.

Our programming language and compilers sequence meets the "Programming Languages" requirements (PL1 through PL10) in the ACM/IEEE Model Curriculum [12]; COSC 170 combines aspects of model course $CS240_s$, *Programming Language Translation*, with model course CS340, *Compiler Construction*, from the Interim Revision [9].

Upon completion of the course, we expect that students will be able to: **Recognize** various classes of grammars, languages, and automata, and employ these to solve common software problems; **Explain** the major steps involved in compiling a high-level programming language down to a low-level target machine language; **Construct** and **use** the major components of a modern compiler; and **Work** together effectively in teams on a large project.

Project 1 is a simple Java-based interpreter, a gentle review of Java programming for students who have been away from the language for several terms, as well as a review of abstract syntax and recursive decent from the prerequisite course. The Project 2 scanner is constructed "by hand", a tokenizer built without the assistance of compiler automation tools. For Project 3, a full MiniJava scanner and parser is constructed using the JavaCC [13] parser/scanner generator tool. The instructor provides a complete grammar for the variant to be used in this term, but the grammar must be transformed into an unambiguous, right-recursive JavaCC specification with correct precedence and associativity.

The AST produced by the parser is then passed into the Project 4 type checker. From this stage on, each phase of the compiler uses a new JavaCC grammar (provided by the instructor) to parse in the input from the previous phase. This adds additional complexity over a monolithic compiler design, but has the advantage of enforcing clear interface boundaries between each phase. Also, by enforcing these boundaries, students can temporarily drop in the instructor's reference implementation for any phases of the compiler project that they cannot complete well enough to drive the next phase of the compiler. Project 5 translates the type-annotated AST into an IR tree format defined by the textbook. Project 6 tiles the IR tree with MIPS instructions, and outputs assembler with an infinite pool of temporaries.

For each project students are given skeleton code for the data structures and backbone of that phase of the compiler. The students are then expected to complete the visitor methods which define that pass of the compiler

In this version of the course, we generally do not have time for the students to construct a full RISC register allocator on their own. After two weeks of lectures on the topic, the

students instead complete a written homework assignment on register allocation by graph coloring with coalescing and spilling. The instructor provides a binary reference implementation of the full allocator that can produce MIPS code ready to be linked directly into the Embedded Xinu kernel. Final integration is posed as a "grand challenge", with the potential to replace the lowest project grade; two thirds of the students opted to attempt this, with good results.

The entire semester project sequence generally produces about 10-15K lines of code per team of two students – a substantial implementation effort, and often the largest system the students have worked on up to this point.

3.1 An Integrated Curriculum

Building a functional implementation of a MiniJava to Embedded Xinu compiler is a significant investment in both student and instructor time. For our department, this has been made significantly more attractive by integrating embedded aspects into courses throughout the undergraduate major.

Students use the Mips Playground on Embedded Xinu to learn assembly in sophomore year hardware systems [4]; they also learn activation record structure and standard calling conventions to build medium-sized assembler programs.

In the next semester, students build device drivers, concurrency, and interprocess communication systems as part of their own implementation of Embedded Xinu. [3].

Several students reach compilers having already taken an elective course in embedded networking [6].

While we are mindful to teach other architectures in computer organization, and to give them experience with other platforms in O/S, the end result of this curricular integration is that students arrive in compilers with a deep understanding of the system they are targeting with their term projects. In our case, this is made easy by leveraging our investment in a flexible experimental platform that serves many of our systems courses, but the advantages are generalizable well beyond specific lab choices. Our experiences and results support cross-cutting integration of instructional technologies across systems courses. Students arriving in a compilers course anywhere ought to have the opportunity to integrate prior learning experiences from computer organization, operating systems, programming languages, etc. This idea is not new, but we believe we are the first to demonstrate wide applicability with embedded hardware and an instructional operating system.

4. Assessment

The second author has taught compilers to hundreds of students at both a large, public university, and a mid-sized, private university. For our evaluation, we use 20 students at Marquette, broken into a control group (2007) and an experimental group (2009). Both courses have the same experienced instructor, same edition of the textbook, and the term-length compiler project detailed in the previous section.

They differ in the targeting of the compiler and the pacing of the middle projects: the 2007 group used a generic PowerPC platform; the 2009 group targeted the embedded MIPS wireless router running the Embedded Xinu system from a prior course, and had a shorter deadline for semantic analysis. The concurrency features we have now added to the compiler project will be evaluated in the next offering of the course this spring.

Qualitative evaluations showed a marked improvement in enthusiasm for the embedded compiler project in 2009. One student summed up general sentiments of the class in stating that he was "stoked" to get his compiler to produce code that would run directly on the embedded operating system he had worked on in previous terms.

Quantitative assessment (see Figure 5) showed improvements in minimum, maximum, and mean scores for P3 (the parser), and P5 (the translator). In the 2009 semester, all teams completed P6 (the instruction selector) and most went on to the "grand challenge" of getting all of their compiler phases to work together to produce code to run on the embedded target. In contrast, all but one of the teams in 2007 ran out of steam on P6, and completed neither their instruction selector nor the final integration. P2 in 2007 was not comparable with 2009, and is thus omitted from the table.

Measure	2007 Average	2009 Average
Project 1 - Warm up	88	83
Project 3 - Parser	72	74
Project 4 - Semantic	88	66
Project 5 - Translate	70	72
Project 6 - Select	25	96
Project 7 - Integration	0	66
Exam 1	64	78
Exam 2	66	71

Figure 5. Assessment Before and After

Results also showed drops in the overall scores for P1 (the unrelated warm-up interpreter,) and P4 (the type-checker). P1 is assigned on the first day of class, and is not impacted by the new embedded content. If anything, P1 data suggests that the 2009 cadre was initially no better prepared for the course material, and possibly at somewhat of a disadvantage.

The P4 deadline was shortened from four weeks to three in 2009 in order to allow more lecture and lab time for the final integration steps in P7. As expected, performance on this difficult phase dropped accordingly, but this was more than compensated for by improvements on P5, P6 and P7. As always, finite lecture time means reduced coverage in one area to improve or add coverage in another.

Exams scores for the two 2009 midterm exams were uniformly higher than in 2007.

In summary, targeting the embedded platform in 2009 seems to have qualitatively increased student interest, particularly in the back half of the compiler, and quantitatively improved performance both on practical programming projects and theoretical exams.

5. Concurrency

```
class Main {
    public static void main(String[] args) {
        TestThread myThr1 = new TestThread();
        TestThread myThr2 = new TestThread();
        Data dd = new Data();
        dd.y = 0;
        myThr1.d = dd;
        myThr2.d = dd;
        Xinu.threadCreate(myThr1);
        Xinu.threadCreate(myThr2);
    }
}
class TestThread extends Thread {
    Data d;
    int x;
    public void run() {
        x = d.foo();
        Xinu.printint(x);
    }
}
class Data {
    int y;
    public synchronized int foo() {
        int temp = y;
        temp = temp + 1;
        temp = this.write(temp);
        return y;
    }
    public synchronized int write(int z) {
        Xinu.yield();
        y = z;
        return y;
    }
}
```

Figure 6. Concurrent MiniJava Example Program

With the growing importance of parallel and concurrent programming, it is essential that students are exposed to the language-level concurrency support provided by many modern compilers. For this reason, we have extended our compiler project to include basic Java threads.

Our pedagogical model is clear: students will practice the use of thread creation and coordination in creating testcases with our Concurrent MiniJava language; using the Xinu.java helper class, they will learn how these testcases execute when compiled and run with real Java; finally, they will implement and test the compiler phases required to transform these testcases into concurrent threads running directly on the target machine.

In the spirit of MiniJava, our goal was to choose the minimum extension necessary to illustrate the concepts entailed in the compilation of these advanced concurrency features. In this way students can see the major issues involved without being bogged down by the details of a full implementation of Java's threads and synchronization.

Figure 6 shows a program written in Concurrent MiniJava that illustrates the need for synchronization primitives in a program with concurrent threads. The example spawns two threads with a reference to the same shared Data object. Each thread reads the value of the shared y variable from memory, changes it, writes the new value back to the shared variable, and prints.

If this program is correctly synchronized it should print 1 and then 2, with a final resulting value of 2 stored in y. However, because each thread yields between reading and writing the shared variable, this program could possibly result in an erroneous value of 1 stored in the shared variable if it is not properly coordinated with the synchronized keyword. This is a classic example of a race condition, and precisely the kind of common concurrent programming error that Java is designed to prevent.

The following subsections outline the changes necessary to support Concurrent MiniJava.

5.1 Threads

Concurrent MiniJava remains a proper subset of Java, so programmers declare threads by extending the built-in Thread class. One then override the run method inherited from the Thread class, adding the code to be executed when the thread of execution represented by this class runs.

Since the MiniJava compiler is not aware of built-in Java classes, the compiler must be informed implicitly that there is a Thread class. To avoid the complexity of making the compiler aware of the entire Java Thread class, the parser will generate an Abstract Syntax Tree (AST) node for a Thread class with an empty run method. Class declarations which extend Thread are thus a special case for the parser; Thread becomes a token for the scanner, and a class declaration which extends Thread is handled by the added *Thread-Decl* grammar production, as shown in Figure 7. This is necessary so that the parser can recognize if a Thread class is required and only add the AST node when needed.

As an alternative, we could require the programmer to declare a Thread class themselves, but when compiled with a regular Java compiler this declaration would override the built-in Thread class and result in a very different program.

Further changes must be made to account for declaration of the run() method since void return types are not allowed in MiniJava, except in the special case of the main method declaration. To handle this, we add a run() method declaration production to the grammar, as shown in Figure 7.

For students to create useful test cases and to see the effects of concurrency features on a compiler, we must support the creation and manipulation of multiple threads of execu-

Program	→	*MainClass (ClassDecl | ThreadDecl)*
ClassDecl	→	...
	→	class *id* extends *id* { *VarDecl** (*MethodDecl* | *RunDecl*)* }
ThreadDecl	→	class *id* extends Thread { *VarDecl** (*MethodDecl* | *RunDecl*)* }
RunDecl	→	public void run() { *VarDecl** Statement* }
MethodDecl	→	public (synchronized)? *Type id* (*FormalList*) { *VarDecl** Statement* return *Exp* ; }

Figure 7. Concurrent MiniJava Modifications

tion. We further extend Concurrent MiniJava with external call statements that spawn threads, yield control of the processor, and cause a thread to sleep for a given number of milliseconds. Figure 8 shows the required additions to the Xinu.java helper class. These new methods are also added to the initial class and type environments during the semantic analysis phase, as described previously in Section 2.2.

```
public class Xinu
{   ...
    public static void threadCreate(Thread t)
    {   t.start();   }
    public static void yield()
    {
        Thread t = Thread.currentThread();
        try
        { t.yield(); }
        catch(Exception e)
        { System.out.println(e); }
    }
    public static void sleep(int time)
    {
        Thread t = Thread.currentThread();
        try
        { t.sleep(time); }
        catch(Exception e)
        { System.out.println(e); }
    }
}
```

Figure 8. Xinu.java Thread Support

Likewise, each of these new functions is added to the Xinu compatibility layer (Section 2.3) and mapped to underlying runtime functions, as listed in Figure 9.

The Xinu.threadCreate method is mapped to the runtime _threadCreate which takes an object as a parameter and spawns a new thread that executes that object's run method. The default Thread class run method prevents the runtime error that would result from calling threadCreate on an object inheriting from Thread but not overriding run.

Xinu function	Purpose
`syscall _threadCreate(int* obj)`	Spawns a new thread.
`syscall _yield(void)`	Yields the processor.
`syscall _sleep(int time)`	Sleeps time milliseconds.

Figure 9. Compatibility Layer for Threads

5.2 Synchronization

The meat of language-level concurrency support is automatic synchronization to properly coordinate thread interactions with shared data. In Java, this is provided by the `synchronized` modifier. In the example code (Figure 6), this keyword invokes Java monitors that prevent interleaved execution of the threads from producing incorrect results. Java allows both `synchronized` blocks of statements and `synchronized` methods [10]; we add only the latter to Concurrent MiniJava under the continuing theme of simplicity.

Java's `synchronized` feature depends on the JVM monitor system [10], which has subtly different semantics from standard O/S semaphores. The following sections describe how Java-style synchronization is added to our MiniJava compiler, with matching monitors added to the Xinu kernel.

5.2.1 Monitors

Java monitors act as locks guarding fields and methods of an object [10]. Each Java object is associated with one monitor. The `synchronized` keyword requires a thread to acquire the monitor lock associated with a `synchronized` method's target object before executing the body. Two different `synchronized` methods belonging to the same object both depend on the same lock as the monitor is associated with the object, and not the methods.

A thread which has already acquired a lock does not wait when attempting to acquire that same lock – this is the primary difference between Java-style monitors and typical counting semaphores. Thus, in the example (Figure 6), `synchronized` method `foo` would wait indefinitely before calling `synchronized` method `write` using traditional semaphore semantics. As a corollary, any thread holding a lock must perform an *unlock* action once for each corresponding *lock* action before releasing the lock.

The monitors we add to Xinu contain an associated semaphore, a thread ownership ID, and a count tracking the number of `lock`s performed without corresponding `unlock`s. Thus, a monitor count begins at zero, every successful `lock` action increases the count by one, and every `unlock` action decreases the count by one. Figure 10 shows pseudocode for the `lock` and `unlock` functions we add to Xinu. Functions `wait` and `signal` are the traditional wait and signal semaphore operations. While not clear from the code, the `lock` and `unlock` functions are themselves "synchronized"

in the sense that they are not executed concurrently. While our example is for the Xinu O/S, equivalent support exists in many mainstream O/Ses.

```
syscall lock(monitor m)
{
    if (m->owner == NOOWNER) {
        m->owner = currentThread;
        (m->count)++;
        wait(m->semaphore);
    } else {
        if (m->owner == currentThread) {
            (m->count)++;
        } else {
            wait(m->semaphore);
            m->owner = currentThread;
            (m->count)++;
        }
    }
}

syscall unlock(monitor m)
{
    (m->count)--;
    if (m->count == 0) {
        m->owner = NOOWNER;
        signal(m->semaphore);
    }
}
```

Figure 10. Java-Style Monitors in Xinu

5.2.2 Compiling `synchronized`

Methods declared `synchronized` are tracked by the parser with an additional field in the *MethodDecl* AST node.

In the Xinu compatibility layer, the `new` function, which allocates memory for new object instances, must now also acquire a monitor from the operating system and associate it with the new object. The `_lock` and `_unlock` functions take an object as a parameter and call the lock and unlock functions described in Figure 10, passing the monitor associated with the given object as a parameter.

Figure 11 shows the extensions to the list of runtime support functions in the compatibility layer.

Xinu function	Purpose
`int *new(int n, int f)`	Allocate object or array and associated monitor.
`syscall _lock(int *obj)`	Lock the monitor associated with object.
`syscall _unlock(int *obj)`	Unlock the monitor associated with object.

Figure 11. Compatibility Layer for Monitors

During the translation phase the compiler wraps synchronized method bodies with *lock* and *unlock* actions, adding the compatibility layer calls at the beginning and end, respectively, of every synchronized method body. The compiler must ensure that the *lock* action precedes the evaluation of *any* part of the method body including the evaluation of the right hand side of local variable declarations. Similarly, *unlock* must come after *any* part of the method body including the evaluation of the return expression.

6. Conclusions

In summary, course assessment and anecdotal evidence demonstrate that adding an "embedded twist" to our traditional compilers course increased student interest and motivation for the semester. The course met its instructional goals with regards to student learning, and was scored exceptionally well in evaluations by students.

By leveraging our existing hands-on embedded system laboratory, we were also able to develop new material that will add thread-level concurrency support into our target language for each phase of the project in the next iteration of our compilers course. Our proposed Concurrent MiniJava language allows students to build testcases with multiple `Thread` objects that are a strict subset of Java, featuring both shared and local instance data, time-oriented primitives for sleeping and yielding, and Java-style monitor synchronization. This extension required only a handful of new grammar productions, type rules, and translation clauses – roughly on par with other common Java additions, like static methods or Strings. From the students' perspective, these concurrency features will add only a few more visitor pattern methods to each pass of the compiler, a net increase in student workload of about 500 lines of code per team (under 5%) over the semester.

Beyond the scope of this course, it is clear that weaving a coherent sequence of embedded projects throughout our department's core courses and electives has generated significant student enthusiasm, has sparked new avenues of undergraduate research, and has given our students a deeper understanding of computer systems at all levels.

The course technology developed in this effort is being posted on the Project Nexos Wiki [14], in hopes that it can be leveraged by others to bring about similar positive changes in their own departments.

6.1 Future Work

Plans are underway to extend our approach to the text-independent Bantam Java compiler, which is itself part of a larger collection of cross-curricular tools.

In the next iteration of our compilers course, we plan to assess the effectiveness of Concurrent MiniJava, not only for student learning outcomes in compilers, but also in deepening their understanding of concurrent programming issues.

As in original MiniJava, our current implementation does not deal with garbage collection; this is an advanced topic we would like to explore further.

Finally, the current implementation targets single core embedded devices. Genuine multi-core concurrency will be possible either with a multi-core version of Embedded Xinu, or retargeting to another suitable O/S with such support.

6.2 Acknowledgments

The authors are grateful to the students of our compiler construction courses for their fortitude, and to Tony Hosking for his model course syllabi and excellent register allocator.

References

[1] A. V. Aho, M. Lam, R. Sethi, and J. D. Ullman. *Compilers: Principles, Techniques and Tools.* Pearson, 2nd edition, 1985.

[2] A. W. Appel and J. Palsberg. *Modern Compiler Implementation in Java.* Cambridge, 2nd edition, 2002.

[3] D. Brylow. An experimental laboratory environment for teaching embedded operating systems. In *SIGCSE 2008*, volume 40, pages 192–196, 2008. ACM.

[4] D. Brylow. An experimental laboratory environment for teaching embedded hardware systems. In *WCAE 2007: Workshop on Computer Architecture Education*, pages 44–51. ACM Press, June 2007. ISBN: 978-1-59593-797-1.

[5] D. Brylow and B. Ramamurthy. Nexos: Next generation embedded operating system course and an innovative support environment. NSF CCLI Awards DUE-0737476 and DUE-0737243, 2008.

[6] D. Brylow and B. Ramamurthy. Nexos: A next generation embedded systems laboratory. *SIGBED Review*, 6(1), January 2009. ISSN 1551-3688.

[7] D. E. Comer. *Operating System Design: The XINU Approach.* Prentice Hall, 1984.

[8] M. L. Corliss and E. C. Lewis. Bantam: a customizable, Java-based, classroom compiler. In *SIGCSE '08*, pages 38–42, 2008. ACM. ISBN 978-1-59593-799-5.

[9] Joint ACM/AIS/IEEE-CS Task Force for Computing Curricula. Computer science curriculum 2008: An interim revision of CS 2001, December 2008.

[10] J. Gosling, B. Joy, G. Steele, and G. Bracha. *The Java Language Specification.* Addison Wesley, 3rd edition, 2005.

[11] S. Muchnick. *Advanced Compiler Design and Implementation.* Morgan Kaufmann, 1997.

[12] Joint IEEE Computer Society/ACM Task Force on the Model Curricula for Computing. Approved final draft of the computer science volume, Dec 2001.

[13] S. Viswanadha, S. Sankar, and S. Microsystems. Java compiler compiler, v5.0. Code available for download, 2009. URL https://javacc.dev.java.net/.

[14] Xinu Wiki. Project Nexos / Embedded Xinu Wiki, 2010. http://xinu.mscs.mu.edu/.

[15] L. Xu. Language engineering in the context of a popular, inexpensive robot platform. In *SIGCSE '08*, pages 43–47, 2008. ACM. ISBN 978-1-59593-799-5.

Understanding Abstraction:
A Means of Leveling the Playing Field in CS1?

Celina Gibbs

University of Victoria
Canada
celinag@cs.uvic.ca

Yvonne Coady

University of Victoria
Canada
ycoady@cs.uvic.ca

Abstract

Given the wide ranging treatment of IT in high schools, future generations of CS1 students are bound to arrive with dramatically different levels of exposure to programming constructs. Though exposure to language mechanisms is not the take-away point from CS1, this appears to create an uneven playing field in our introductory courses. The premise of our work is that by focusing on abstraction, students connect with opportunities to engage in creative and analytical processes, potentially achieving more intellectual satisfaction—even from simple formative exercises in a first assignment.

Our results show that of the 75 students in the study, on average 91% reported success with the implementation exercises in the *assignment*. However, when asked to reflect on their implementations at a higher level of abstraction, only 69% communicated solutions in ways that meaningfully generalized the specific task at hand. Further, success in abstracting their solution appeared to be less tightly linked with previous programming experience, and instead is most strongly related to the propensity to experiment with their own code.

Categories and Subject Descriptors K.3.2 [**Computers and Education**]: Computer and Information Science Education– computer science education, curriculum.

General Terms Algorithms, Design, Experimentation.

Keywords Computer Science education.

1. Introduction

First impressions are critical. Wide-eyed students arriving at university for the first time are ready to take on the task of unlocking the mysteries of the universe. How do the first impressions of a general CS1 fare in consideration of those needs? In particular, when an increasing number of our students are arriving with programming experience from high school already?

Given the myriad of factors involved in inferring first impressions from students, we start with the following

Permission to make digital or hard copies of all or part of this work for personal or classroom use is granted without fee provided that copies are not made or distributed for profit or commercial advantage and that copies bear this notice and the full citation on the first page. To copy otherwise, or republish, to post on servers or to redistribute to lists, requires prior specific permission and/or a fee.
SPLASH'10 October 17–21, 2010, Reno/Tahoe, Nevada, USA.
Copyright © 2010 ACM 978-1-4503-0240-1/10/10...$10.00.

assumptions about the ways in which students may perceive assigned homework in general:

1. Challenging, creative and analytical processes have the potential to be daunting but intellectually stimulating.
2. Drill like formative exercises to accomplish a one-time, relatively small task with seemingly no significant abstract component have the potential to be useful in the long run, but initially inane.

We further assume that writing code for a first assignment could fall into either category, most likely depending on the degree to which students can and do work to abstractly model their solutions. Given these assumptions, we then ask the question:

What do our students really take away from their initial impressions of CS1?

To explore this question we investigated the ability of students to reflect on their code and abstract their solutions. Based on their attempts to generalize their own code, our observations can be summarized by the following relationships:

1. Not all students who reported a successful implementation demonstrated the ability to articulate their solutions beyond the specific case.
2. Of the group that had difficulty abstracting, experience appeared to make a difference: those with previous experience tended to be too specific, while those without experience tended to be too vague.
3. Of the group of students who met with some success abstracting, experience did not appear to make a difference, however, initiative to experiment with their own implementation may have played a role.

Background and Related Work

Tension exists between taking on engaging tasks and needing to carefully foster first time programmers in CS1. Wing envisions an attitude where everyone is eager to learn [12], but Walker's observation that students often believe that CS is mindless button-pushing still holds [11]. Huang and Briggs demonstrated the importance of communicating to students early that CS is not just programming [7]. This can be exceedingly critical when, as Carter noted, the population in the typical classroom contains many students who are not CS Majors [5]. Though Dodds et al's findings show that many students who have taken CS in high school benefit from a challenging track for students who have experience [6], typical classes still mix experienced with non-experienced students.

Powers suggests engaging students early by revisiting topics at increasing intellectual levels over time [8]. Several researchers have shown that programming burdens can be supported for beginners though tools such as PlanAni [4] and Scratch [9, 15]. But by studying logs of results of compilers, Rodrigo found that at-risk students can be identified even before they have completed a programming assignment [10].

2. Experimental Setup

This study takes exercises from a successful first programming assignment appropriate for CS1 [14] and augments them with a prominent reflection component. This component supports the subsequent qualitative inquiry designed to identify first impressions.

Original Assignment

The original assignment introduces programming in an inviting context using the Scratch programming language [15]. This assignment leverages properties of geometry and graphics to introduce programming constructs such as conditionals and iteration through simple examples.

The first exercise provides a Scratch code segment, Figure 1(a), and asks the students to first predict what the code does and then suggests they test their prediction by running the program. In the next step students are asked to modify the program to produce a spiral shape comprised of six squares as shown in Figure 1(b). A written description of the solution suggests that the code to draw a square should be repeated six times with a slight turn after each drawing. Further, implementation specific information is provided by noting that the solution will *consist of adding a* ***repeat*** *loop which will enclose the existing* ***repeat*** *loop.*

The assignment then shows a subsequent pinwheel of an unspecified number of squares, explaining its implementation as a simple increase in the number of repetitions and a corresponding decrease in the rotation between squares and suggests a more generalized description of the solution:

> *The number of repetitions multiplied by the number of degrees the sprite turns before the next repetition should equal 360 in order to accomplish the overall circular shape.*

The next exercise asks the student to revert to the code that draws a single square and ask them to write the code to draw a row of six squares as shown in Figure 1(c). Students are asked to alter the code to draw a row of triangles and finally, a row of another polygon of their choosing.

Augmented Assignment

In the creation of the augmented assignment, modifications to the original were minimal in terms of the tasks students were asked to perform, but more substantial in terms of the required reflection on the tasks.

In order to place a larger focus on reflection, students were asked to hand in their solution in the form of a general algorithm, after they had time to play with their implementation and reflect on their code.

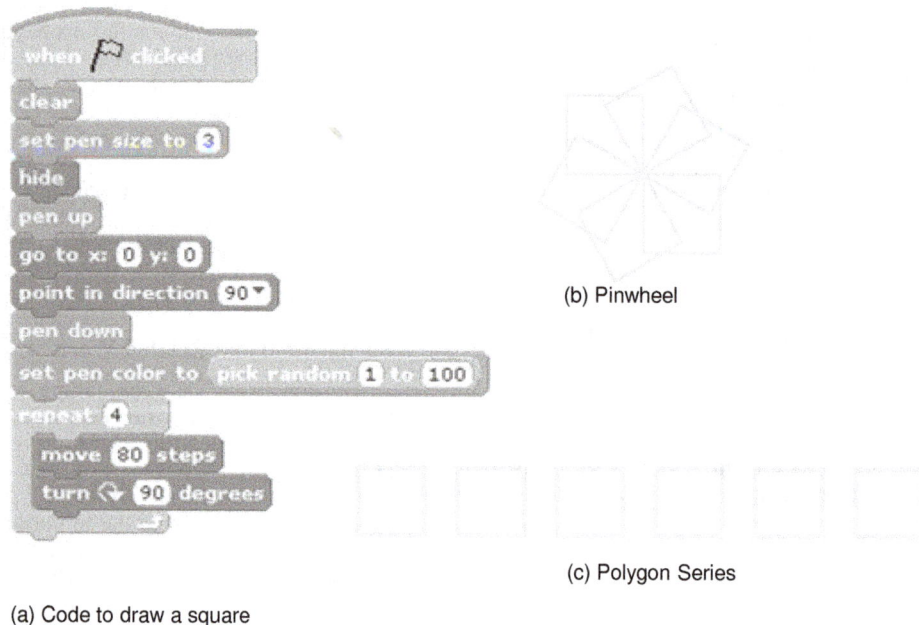

(b) Pinwheel

(c) Polygon Series

(a) Code to draw a square

Figure 1: Provided code (a), and associated exercises (b and c) from sample assignment [14].

Three exercises were given to students, two of which were taken directly from the original assignment, while the third was developed from a related exercise for comparison. For each exercise, students were asked to implement two or three instances of the problem with follow up questions for each in the form:

- *What is the general algorithm to solve the problem?*
- *Were each of your implementations successful?*
- *Did you experiment with other instances of the problem?*

In the pinwheel exercise (Figure 1(a)), students were asked to program a pinwheel with 6 and 36 squares. In the polygon sequence exercise (Figure 1(b)), students were asked to implement a row of squares, triangles and one other polygon.

In the third exercise students programmed a set of nested squares, such as the instance of six shown in Figure 2. In addition to the nesting, students were asked to maintain a constant factor of 2 in terms of the relationship between adjacent inner/outer squares.

Figure 2: Nested squares.

3. Raw Survey Results

A total of 75 students voluntarily participated in this study through an online survey format associated with their first CS1 assignment. Of the 75, 27 students self-identified as having some form of programming experience with the other 48 claiming no previous experience.

Table 1 provides a summary of the survey results showing that the majority of the students (average, 92%) experienced programming success in the Scratch environment and a large portion of students (average, 80%) experimented beyond the requirements of the assignment. It is interesting to note that these levels of success and experimentation decreased across the three exercises.

Table 1. Quantitative Results

exercise	success		experimented
pinwheel	n = 6	73	67
	n = 36	70	
polygon	n = 6, m = 4	70	56
	n = 6, m = 3	70	
nesting	nested	68	58
	scale	64	
Experienced Students: 27, Inexperienced Students: 48			

4. ANALYSIS

To assess impact of the reflective exercises in this assignment a systematic approach to evaluate solutions was developed in the form of a rubric shown in Table 2. This rubric consists of four categories of achievement, in which

each of the student's algorithms were assigned to one category.

Table 2 provides a description of this spectrum with a *0* for non-existent or straight code submission and a *3* for a generalized solution with clearly defined relationships in terms of variables and control flow. Categories *1* and *2* were reserved for submissions that fell between this range. A *1* was assigned to a solution that was too implementation specific, while a *2* was assigned to a generalized solution that was missing necessary detail or was not clear and concise.

Table 2. Rubric

Category	Evaluation Metric
0	incorrect, no submission, submitted implementation or description of implementation
1	solution too implementation/language specific, over complicated
2	solution too general, no clear definition of variable dependencies
3	generalized solution, clear steps and loops, variables and dependencies defined

Figure 3 shows a breakdown of the student population based on their programming experience. This large contingent of experienced students allows us to analyse the data from both perspectives.

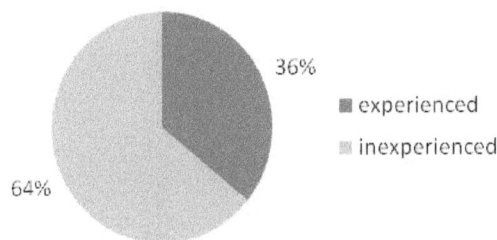

Figure 3. Student population by experience level.

Figure 4 (a, b, c) provides the results of the classification of the students' pinwheel, polygon and nesting algorithm submissions respectively.

Looking at just the submissions assigned a *3* on the rubric scale was, across the board, approximately 50% for the experienced population and 30% for the inexperienced. This percentage falls substantially below the 91% of the reported programming success from the students. The disparity in these results, demonstrates that implementation success is not a strong indicator of a student's ability to generalize and abstract.

Considering the submissions in the mid-points (*1, 2*) of the rubric spectrum, we see a possible trend across the students who did not achieve a suitable generalized solution (*3* on the rubric scale). Of these students, the experienced ones typically submitted solutions that were too detailed and implementation specific (*1* on the rubric scale) whereas the inexperienced students tended to be too general, or missing some important details (*2* on the rubric scale).

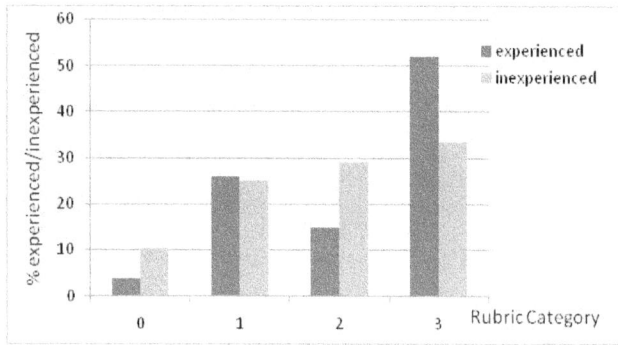

(a)

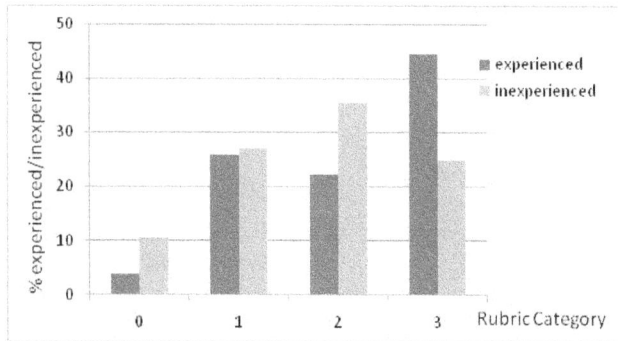

(b)

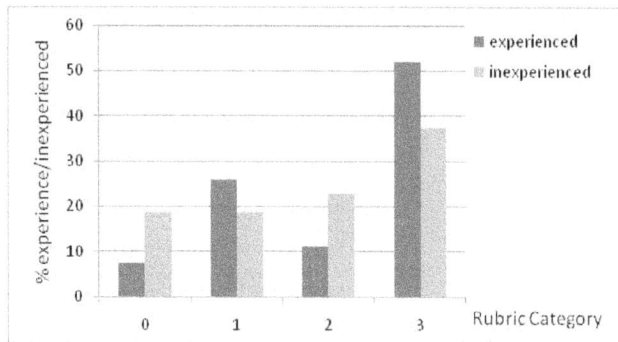

(c)

Figure 4. Pinwheel (a), Polygon (b) and Nested square (c) algorithms' rubric based evaluation.

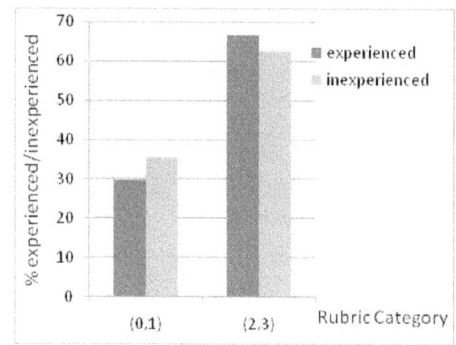

(a)

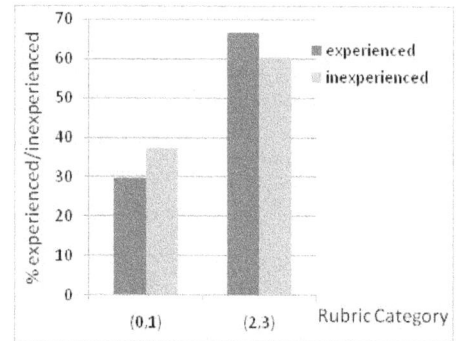

(b)

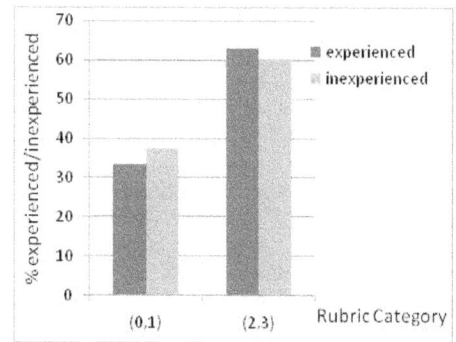

(c)

Figure 5. Coarse-grain evaluation of pinwheel (a), polygon (b) and nested square (c) algorithms.

This result leads us to consider a more coarse-grained representation of the rubric evaluation shown in Figure 5 (a, b, and c). This breakdown allows us to group students into two categories: those able to generalize (*2* and *3* on rubric scale) and those not able to (*1* and *2* on the rubric scale). From Figure 4 it was clear that the experienced students were more likely to come up with a suitable, generalized algorithm. Approximately a 20% difference is shown between the experienced students and the inexperienced students to achieve a *3* on the rubric scale. But this same data consoidated into the two categories in Figure 5 shows us that inexperience may not hinder ability to abstract.

Finally, Figure 6 (a, b, and c) decompose the data into the same categories as Figure 5, splitting the rubric into the upper and lower halves, but this time comparing the number of students who experimented with their implementation. This perspective allows us to consider the correlation between the ability of students to abstract a solution and their self-directed experimentation with their implementation.

From this breakdown, we see that a larger portion of the students who were able to generalize their solutions also experimented with their implementation.

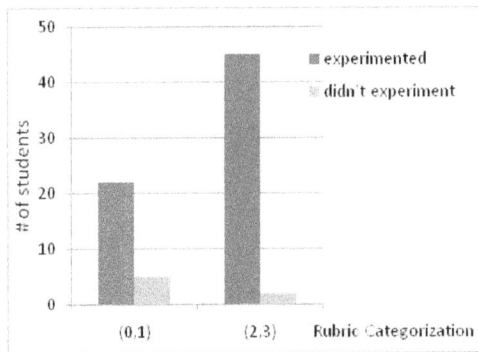

(a)

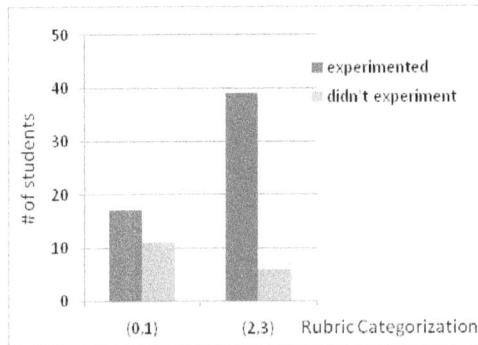

(b)

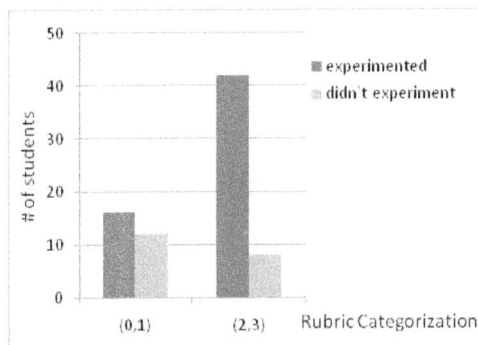

(c)

Figure 6. Correlation between experimentation and abstraction in the (a) pinwheel, (b) polygon and (c) nested square exercise.

5. DISCUSSION AND CONCLUSIONS

This case study begins with a set of assumptions and inquires into the meaning students may ascribe to their first assignment. Through this qualitative inquiry we believe we capture some information relevant to a first impression of CS1. Our results show that many of our students (31% of this study) are not able to abstract their solutions effectively. This may indicate that, though they were most likely successful with the given task, they did not connect with any deeper intellectual merit to the activity, and did not obtain an appreciation of the power of abstraction.

There are several risks to the validity of our inquiry. First, though Ahoniemi and Becker have shown the utility of rubrics in assessment [1, 3], our rubric was designed to unveil patterns or trends in responses, and contained overlap (for example, solutions that were both too specific in parts and too vague in others), which makes the categories less crisp.

Based on these results, we believe it is critical to include open-ended experimentation as a part of the process of understanding the intellectual intent of an assignment— even a first assignment in CS1. This experimentation is not just testing of the source, but testing of the extensibility of the model. As much as possible, we need to encourage students to take the extra steps to engage in exploration when building a model of their own solutions. Coupling assessment that involves this systematic inclusion of experimentation with Ala-Mutka's semi-automated assessment of source code [2], may actually allow this approach to scale in large CS1 classes.

References

[1] Ahoniemi, T., V. Karavirta, Analyzing the Use of a Rubric-Based Grading Tool, ITiCSE 2009.

[2] Ala-Mutka, K., and H.-M. Jarvinen. Assessment process for programming assignments. *Advanced Learning* Technologies, 2004. Proceedings. IEEE International *Conference on*, pages 181–185, 30 Aug.-1 Sept. 2004.

[3] Becker, K., Grading programming assignments using rubrics. In ITiCSE '03: *Proceedings of the 8th annual conference on Innovation and technology in computer science education*, pages 253–253. ACM, 2003.

[4] Byckling , P. and J. Sajaniemi, Roles of variables and programming skills improvement, In Proceedings of 37*th* SIGCSE *technical* symposium on computer science education 2006.

[5] Carter, L. Why Students with an Apparent Aptitude for Computer Science Don't Choose to Major in Computer Science. In *Proceedings of the 37th SIGCSE Technical Symposium on Computer Science Education*, pp. 27-31. March 2006.

[6] Dodds, Z., Alvarado, C., Kuenning, G., and Libeskind-Hadas, R. Breadth-First CS 1 for Scientists. In *Proceedings of the 12th Annual SIGCSE Conference on Innovation and Technology in Computer Science Education*, pp. 23-27. June 2007.

[7] Huang, T., and A. Briggs, A Unified Approach to Introductory Computer Science: Can One Size Fit All? In *Proceedings of the Annual SIGCSE Conference on Innovation and Technology in Computer Science Education* 2009.

[8] Powers, K. D. Breadth-Also: A Rationale and Implementation. In *Proceedings of the 34th SIGCSE Technical Symposium on Computer Science Education*, pp. 243-247. February 2003.

[9] Malan, D., AND Leitner, H. 2007. Scratch for Budding Computer Scientists. SIGCSE Bull. 39 (1), 223-227.

[10] Rodrigo, T., A. Amarra, S. Lim, R. Baker, T. Dy, S. Pascua, E. Tabanao, M. Jadud, M. Espejo-Lahoz, J. Sugay, Affective and Behavioral Predictors of Novice Programmer Achievement, ITiCSE 2009.

[11] Walker, H. M. What Image Do CS1/CS2 Present to our Students? In *ACM SIGCSE Bulletin*, vol. 39, no. 4. December 2007.

[12] Wing, J. M. Computational Thinking. In *Communications of the ACM*, vol. 49, no.3. 2006, pp. 33-35.

[13] Yorke, M., Formative assessment in higher education: moves towards theory and the enhancement of pedagogic practice. *Higher Education*, 45(4):477–501, 2003.

[14] Computer Science S-1, handout, http://isites.harvard.edu/fs/docs/icb.topic576139.files/n o3.cscis1.2009.pdf

[15] Scratch, www.scratch.mit.edu.

Teaching and Training
Developer-Testing Techniques and Tool Support

Tao Xie[1]   Jonathan de Halleux[2]   Nikolai Tillmann[2]   Wolfram Schulte[2]

[1]North Carolina State University, [2]Microsoft Research

[1]xie@csc.ncsu.edu, [2]{jhalleux,nikolait,schulte}@microsoft.com

Abstract

Developer testing is a type of testing where developers test their code as they write it, as opposed to testing done by a separate quality assurance organization. Developer testing has been widely recognized as an important and valuable means of improving software reliability, as it exposes faults early in the software development life cycle. Effectively conducting developer testing requires both effective tool support by tools and developer-testing skills by developers. In this paper, we describe our experiences and lessons learned in teaching and training developer-testing techniques and tool support in both university and industrial settings. We highlight differences in teaching and training in these two settings, and observations from interacting with practitioners in our process of teaching and training.

Categories and Subject Descriptors   D.2.5 [*Software Engineering*]: Testing and Debugging—Symbolic execution, Testing tools

General Terms   Reliability, Verification

Keywords   Testing, unit testing, parameterized unit testing, theories, symbolic execution, mock objects, Pex

1. Introduction

Developer testing, often in the form of unit testing, has been widely recognized as a valuable means of improving software reliability. In developer testing, developers test their code as they write it, as opposed to testing done by a separate quality assurance organization. The benefits of developer testing are two folds: (1) gain high confidence in the program unit under test (e.g., a class) while developers are writing it and (2) reduce fault-fixing cost by detecting faults early when they are freshly introduced in the program unit.

The popularity and benefits of developer testing have been well witnessed in the industry [24]; however, manual developer testing is known to be labor intensive. In addition, manual testing is often insufficient in comprehensively exercising behaviors of the program unit under test to expose its hidden faults. To address the issue, one of the common ways is to use testing tools to automate activities in developer testing. Developer-testing activities typically include generating test inputs, creating expected outputs, running test inputs, and verifying actual outputs. Developers can use existing testing frameworks such as NUnit [4] for .NET and JUnit [1] for Java to write unit-test inputs and their expected outputs. Then these frameworks can automate running test inputs and verifying actual outputs against the expected outputs.

To reduce the burden of manually creating test inputs, developers can use test-generation tools to generate test inputs automatically. Although great research advances have been made in automatic test generation, it is still a long way towards satisfactorily accomplishing effective test generation when testing common real-world code bases. Then when using test-generation tools, developers need to have the skills to understand the challenges that these tools face and provide guidance to the tools in attempting to address these challenges.

After test inputs are generated automatically, expected outputs for these test inputs are still missing. Developers could choose to write no explicit expected outputs but rely on uncaught exceptions or crashes to focus on robustness checking. To check functional correctness, developers need to write assertions within the test code or the code under test for asserting the expected program behaviors. Most modern (testing) frameworks provide some kind of `Debug.Assert(bool)` methods for developers to use. However, in practice, these assertions are usually written in an ad-hoc way, and less senior or experienced developers have no clear idea on where and for what purpose to write assertions.

To address the issue, two major approaches have been proposed. First, developers could write assertions to encode specifications such as design by contract [18] (a form of axiomatic specifications [13]) with tool support such as Code

Permission to make digital or hard copies of all or part of this work for personal or classroom use is granted without fee provided that copies are not made or distributed for profit or commercial advantage and that copies bear this notice and the full citation on the first page. To copy otherwise, to republish, to post on servers or to redistribute to lists, requires prior specific permission and/or a fee.

SPLASH'10,   October 17–21, 2010, Reno/Tahoe, Nevada, USA.

Copyright © 2010 ACM 978-1-4503-0240-1/10/10...$10.00

Contracts [2] for the code under test to check program behaviors. Second, developers write assertions in Parameterized Unit Tests (PUTs) [22], which are unit tests with parameters; these assertions often encode expected behaviors in the form of algebraic specifications [12]. In these two approaches of writing assertions, developers need to have good skills to write specifications to capture expected behaviors for the code under test.

As educators, we need to devise effective ways to teach students or practitioners to equip them with these preceding skills. In this paper, we describe our experiences in teaching and training developer-testing techniques and tool support in both university and industrial settings. We highlight differences in teaching and training in these two settings, and observations from interacting with practitioners in our process of teaching and training.

The rest of the paper is organized as follows. Section 2 presents the key developer-testing techniques and tool support covered in our teaching and training materials. Section 3 describes our teaching and training experiences in university settings. Section 3 describes our teaching and training experiences in industrial settings, including observations from interacting with practitioners in our process of teaching and training. Section 5 compares differences in the university and industrial settings for teaching and training. Section 6 discusses related issues. Section 7 concludes the paper.

2. Background

Parameterized unit testing [22] is a new methodology extending the current industry practice based on closed, traditional unit tests (i.e., test methods without input parameters). Test methods are generalized by allowing parameters to form Parameterized Unit Tests (PUTs). Below is an example PUT for testing one behavior of `List`'s `Add` method. In the PUT, the `Assume.IsTrue` method specifies an assumption: any test inputs violating the assumption are filtered out during test generation or execution; the `Assert.AreEqual` method specifies an assertion.

```
void TestAdd(List list, int item) {
  Assume.IsTrue(list != null);
  var count = list.Count;
  list.Add(item);
  Assert.AreEqual(count + 1, list.Count);
}
```

This generalization to form PUTs serves two main purposes. First, PUTs are specifications of the behaviors of the methods under test: they not only provide exemplary arguments to the methods under test, but ranges of such arguments. Second, PUTs describe a set of traditional unit tests that can be obtained by instantiating the parameterized test methods with given argument values. Instantiations via argument values should be chosen so that they exercise different code paths of the methods under test. Most unit testing framework have been extended to support parameterized

unit testing, provided that relevant argument values are specified by the user.

Dynamic Symbolic Execution (DSE) [11] (also called concolic testing [20]) is a recent technique to automatically supply such argument values. DSE combines static and dynamic analysis to automatically generate test inputs, e.g., argument values. Given a program that takes inputs, the goal of DSE is to generate test inputs that, upon execution of the program, will exercise as many reachable statements as possible. DSE is based on observing actual executions of the program under test. By leveraging observed concrete input/output values, DSE can simply concretize those operations that interact with the environment, or that are difficult to reason about (e.g., floating-point arithmetic), while previous approaches based on symbolic execution [15] would lose precision. Various implementations of DSE exist, ranging from academic open-source projects to industrial tools. Our teaching and training use the Pex tool [3, 21] from Microsoft Research, which tests .NET programs such as C# programs.

Environment isolation is conducted to test individual software components in isolation when they interact with environments. It makes testing more robust and scalable. Especially in the context of unit testing, where the intention is to test a single unit of functionality, all irrelevant environment dependencies should be mocked [17, 23], or simulated, so that the unit tests run quickly and give deterministic results. In contrast, the goal of integration testing is to test an integrated (sub)system, including all environment dependencies, at the same time.

Ideally, the code under unit testing should be written in a way that allows to substitute its constituent components at testing time, in order to isolate a feature under test. In other words, it should be possible to treat all components as test parameters, so that mocked implementations or simulations can be used to instantiate parameterized tests. One solution to the problem is to refactor the code [10], introducing explicit interface boundaries and allowing different interface implementations. When refactoring is not an option, e.g., when dealing with legacy code, other approaches can be used to detour environment-facing calls at testing time. Various tools exist to enable automatic code isolation, ranging from academic open-source projects to industrial tools. One such tool is Moles [8] from Microsoft Research.

3. Teaching and Training in University Settings

We next present an overview of our teaching and training experiences in university settings and then discuss our lessons learned from our experiences.

3.1 Overview

The teaching and training of developer-testing techniques and tool support were conducted by the first author in a graduate software testing course (CSC 712) at North Carolina State University for the 2008 Fall semester (20 students) and the 2009 Fall semester (18 students). The course schedule, homework and project assignments, lecture slides, and reading materials for these two semesters can be found here[1]. We next describe key teaching materials covered during the 2009 Fall semester (which are mostly similar to the ones covered during the 2008 Fall semester).

Lectures. There were two 75-minute lectures (Mondays and Wednesdays) each week for the 16-week semester. The lectures were given in a lab where every two students shared the same desktop with two monitors. We designed the lectures on Mondays to be mostly on testing foundations, particularly coverage criteria, based on selected materials and slides from the textbook "Introduction to Software Testing" by Ammann and Offutt [6]. We designed the lectures on Wednesdays to be mostly on testing techniques and tools including Pex for 10 weeks, Code Contracts [2] for 2 weeks, and (only briefly) NModel [14] (a model-based testing tool for C#) for 1 week. The instructor (the first author) gave both slide presentation (being more heavily used in Monday lectures) and live tool demonstration (being more heavily used in Wednesday lectures) during lecturing.

Quizzes and homework assignments. We designed four quizzes taken by students throughout the semester to assess students' mastery of lecture topics on testing foundations. To assess students' mastery of lecture topics on testing techniques and tools as well as testing foundations, we designed four homework assignments. Homework 1 included student surveys and their personal homepages. Homework 2 included exercises for familiarizing students with code development and testing in C#. Homework 3 included students' submission of candidate open source code to be tested in the term project. Homework 4 included exercises on applying the instructed test generalization techniques [16].

Term project. Based on the list of preferred teammate candidates that each student submitted together with their Homework 2, the teaching staff (i.e., the instructor and the teaching assistant) assigned students into teams, each of which included two students. As described earlier, in Homework 3, each formed team was asked to submit candidate open source code to be tested in the term project. In midsemester, each team was asked to submit a midterm project report describing the team's experience following the guidelines described in the sample paper skeleton[2] distributed to the students. Basically, each team was asked to write PUTs by performing test generalization on existing traditional unit tests for the chosen open source code under test and document their experiences. In the second half of the semester, each team was asked to write additional new PUTs to aug-

ment the PUTs written for the midterm report to achieve higher block coverage and possibly higher fault-detection capability, and document their additional experiences by expanding their midterm report to produce their final report.

3.2 Lessons Learned

We next describe some observations and lessons learned during our teaching and training in the university settings.

Integration of teaching testing foundations and testing techniques/tools was desirable for a testing course but could be challenging. In the design of our lecture topics, we arranged Mondays' lecture topics to be on coverage criteria and Wednesdays' lecture topics on testing techniques and tools. One potential risk of such design was that these two types of lecture topics might be difficult to be well integrated and students could have perception that the two types of lecture topics were too separated and isolated. We intended to alleviate the issue by demonstrating how achieving specific logic coverage criteria could be formulated as problems of achieving branch or path coverage with Pex [19]. However, such ways of using practical tools to demonstrate tool-assisted satisfaction of coverage criteria are limited to only logic coverage so far. More recently, we extended Pex to support mutant killing for mutation testing [26] and we plan to incorporate this new extension in our future offerings of the course to demonstrate tool-assisted satisfaction of mutation killing.

Another direction for the integration of teaching coverage criteria and practical tools could be to use and demonstrate coverage measurement tools when lecturing topics of coverage criteria. There exist a number of industrial-strength tools for measuring and reporting statement/block or branch coverage; however, they generally lack measurement tools for other more advanced types of coverage criteria such as dataflow coverage.

In addition, more thoughts and work would be needed to investigate how to weave in coverage criteria or more generally testing foundations when lecturing topics of testing techniques and tools. We already briefly introduced some basic background on constraint solving and theorem proving when lecturing the Pex tool and its techniques. Some technique and tool topics such as writing PUTs fed to Pex and writing code contracts fed to Pex and Code Contracts have strong formal foundations of algebraic specifications [12] and axiomatic specifications [13], respectively. The lecture topics of writing specifications were not explicitly listed in the testing textbook or its accompanying slides that we used [6] and thus not included in Mondays' lecture topics. However, we plan to collect teaching materials on writing algebraic specifications and axiomatic specifications, and include them in Mondays' lecture topics in our future offerings of the course.

A term project on testing realistic open source code could give students opportunities to gain testing experiences close to the real world but such a term project also had lim-

---

[1] http://research.csc.ncsu.edu/ase/courses/csc712/

[2] http://research.csc.ncsu.edu/ase/courses/csc712/
2009fall/wrap/project/generalization/testgeneralization.
pdf

itations on training *real* developer testing, where developers test their code as they write it. Open source code is abundant for students to choose and test. However, few open source projects are well documented or equipped with sufficient information for students to understand the full scale and details of expected behaviors of the code under test. Therefore, students could face significant challenges in writing down high-quality assertions for their newly written PUTs for the open source code under test. To alleviate the issue, we designed the term project to heavily focus on *test generalization* [16], where students tried to understand and recover the intended behaviors tested by traditional unit tests written by the open source code developers, and generalize these traditional unit tests to be PUTs. Such a procedure allowed students to gain not only program/test understanding skills but also generalization/abstraction skills. The last part of the term project was on writing new PUTs to achieve higher code coverage and likely higher fault-detection capability, requiring students to write new PUTs, without relying on or referring to existing traditional unit tests.

Our design of the term project allowed the students to heavily invest their course efforts on testing instead of writing production code (which they supposedly already learned from past programming and software engineering courses). The term project in fact simulated situations where third-party developers tested code not written by themselves, strictly speaking, not falling into the activities of developer testing. An alternative type of term projects could be to ask students to develop some new features of a software project while testing their newly implemented features (where students could possibly be requested to practice test driven development [7]). However, in this way, students would spend significant time on feature implementation (and thus less time on feature testing). In addition, it could be difficult to find an appropriate open source code base (e.g., not too complicated but realistic enough) to use in the term project.

We allowed students to search and choose open source code (to be tested in their term project) that satisfied the specified characteristics (e.g., equipped with traditional unit tests), rather than designating the same open source code across all the student teams in the class. Advantages of doing so included that different student teams could encounter different interesting observations and lessons learned by testing different open source code bases, and later sharing their different experiences with the whole class via final project presentations could be more beneficial for other students outside of their team. Disadvantages of doing so included that some student teams might choose open source code that might be inherently not amenable to applying Pex. For example, during the course offering of the 2008 Fall semester, a student team chose Math.NET[3], a mathematical library for symbolic algebraic and numerical/scientific computations, and in later phases of the term project, the team found out

that Pex could not be effectively applied on it because the library implementation involves intensive floating-point computation, which is currently not well supported by Pex's underlying constraint solver [9]. To alleviate the issue, we did request student teams to conduct an early try-out of Pex on part of the open source code under consideration to reduce the risk. In addition, we allowed a student team to change their open source code under test over the duration of the semester without imposing penalty grade points. Furthermore, the term project was designed to have multiple milestones and the submission of a later milestone was built upon the submissions from previous milestones so that students could incorporate feedback from the teaching staff on previous submissions to improve their later submissions.

Using industrial-strength tools and technologies not only reduced the "*debugging*" overhead imposed on both the students and teaching staff, but also gave students experiences that they could immediately benefit from when they took on their industrial jobs. In the homework and project assignments, we deliberately used industrial-strength tools, rather than academic research prototypes. Academic research prototypes often lack support for dealing with various types of code features frequently included in real-world code bases. Furthermore, these prototypes might often include faults and the prototype developers might be often too busy to provide timely technical support or fixing of reported faults. For our students asking questions via the Pex MSDN forums[4], the Pex developers (the second and third authors of this paper) provided timely technical support in using Pex, substantially reducing the support effort from the teaching staff.

Incorporating the training of research skills in the term project benefited students in their future research career as well as software development career. The major deliverables of the term project used for grading included the midterm project report and the final project report. To train students in technical writing, we gave a lecture on common technical writing issues[5]. To reduce barriers for students who were new to writing technical papers, we provided a detailed paper template, which describes the desired structure of the paper including what sections should be included and what contents should go to each section. In the second half of the 2008 Fall semester, we also distributed a sample midterm report that was the best among the student submissions and whose distribution permission was given by the authoring team. In the 2009 Fall semester, both a sample midterm report and final report were distributed to the class at the beginning of the semester. These mechanisms allowed students to learn from good example writing, reducing barriers for them to prepare their own reports. Such a term project including the research-oriented empirical study and its technical writ-

---

[3] http://www.mathdotnet.com/

[4] http://social.msdn.microsoft.com/Forums/en-US/pex/threads/

[5] http://people.engr.ncsu.edu/txie/advice/

178

ing also gave students first-hand experience on conducting empirical studies or empirical evaluations.

4. Teaching and Training in Industrial Settings

We next present an overview of our teaching and training experiences in industrial settings and then discuss our observations from interacting with practitioners and our lessons learned from the process of teaching and training.

4.1 Overview

The teaching and training of developer-testing techniques and tool support were conducted by the second and third authors in the form of one-day or half-day tutorials both within Microsoft (such as internal training of Microsoft developers) and outside Microsoft (such as invited tutorials at .NET user groups). The attendees of a tutorial could range approximately from 10 to 25 practitioners. For a tutorial outside Microsoft (normally with half-day duration), sometimes attendees might not have already installed Pex on their laptops while attending the tutorial, and therefore, the tutorial presentation was primarily the combination of slide presentation and live demonstration of Pex and Moles. However, for a tutorial within Microsoft (normally with full-day duration), the tutorial was given in a training lab at Microsoft, where each attendee was able to use a lab desktop computer installed with Pex and Moles. In this setting, the tutorial involved frequent hands-on exercises conducted by attendees, besides slide presentation and live demonstration of Pex and Moles. The tutorial slides on Pex and Moles can be found at the slide deck section of the Pex documentation web[6].

4.2 Observations

We next describe some observations while interacting with practitioners during our teaching and training, and other general occasions in promoting technology and tool adoption. These observations provide insights not only for teaching and training but also for design or improvement of testing techniques and tools. We illustrate our findings with conversations between developers and trainers; while these conversations are anecdotal in nature, they show quite typical developer mind sets that have been observed by the trainers frequently[7].

Assertion deficit syndrome conversations occurred between a developer and a trainer (i.e., one of the second and third authors) as below:

- Developer: "Your tool only finds null references."
- Trainer: "Do you have any assertions?"
- Developer: "Assertion???"

When a developer is equipped with a test-generation tool such as Pex, the developer is often attempted to click a button provided by the tool to run the tool to generate a large number of test inputs to test the code under test, and then wait for the testing results, which include the test failures reported by the tool. Without assertions written by the developer, either in the test code of PUTs or in the code under test as contracts, the test failures would be limited to uncaught exceptions or crashes. Developers need to be aware of what a test-generation tool could offer if no assertions are written to capture intended behaviors of the code under test. As a consequence, we suggest that training should emphasize the importance of assertions, including quizzes to study beneficial assertion patterns.

Hidden complexity of the code under test is often not realized by developers. Code similar to the following was actually brought to the attention of the trainers:

```
void Sum(int[] numbers) {
    string sum = "0";
    foreach(int number in numbers) {
      sum = (int.Parse(sum) + number).ToString()
    }
    if (sum == "123")
        throw new BugException();
}
```

The API method invocations of int.Parse and int.ToString could incur challenges for a test-generation tool that analyzes and explores code, since these API implementations could be very complicated, incurring hidden complexity for the tool. More and more convenient framework and library APIs (whose implementations hidden from API-client-code developers could be quite complicated though) are available and popularly used by developers. The hidden complexity of these invoked framework or library APIs causes a test-generation tool to take long to explore; even worse, when these framework or library API implementations are in native code (other than managed code in .NET or Java), a tool that analyzes and explores only managed code could not explore these API implementations. As a consequence, a portion of training should be devoted to the issue of hidden complexity, teaching how to interpret the tool feedback to identify such cases.

Unit testing utopia and **Test Driven Development (TDD) [7] dogma** was deeply established among some developers. A developer, being a unit testing enthusiast, stated that "I do not need test generation; I already practice unit testing (and/or TDD)". A developer, being a TDD convert, stated that "Test generation does not fit into the TDD process". It is not easy to change the philosophy of these developers. It should be emphasized during teaching and training that using a test-generation tool can complement manually writing traditional unit tests (without parameters) since manual generation of test inputs could be limited, missing important corner or extreme inputs, due to the inherent limitation

---

[6] http://research.microsoft.com/pex/documentation.aspx

[7] While there are a non-trivial number of practitioners in industry that would match the profiles described in this section, there are far more practitioners with great interest and passion in learning techniques that could improve the effectiveness and quality of their work.

of human-brain power. A longer-term ideal situation could be that developers write PUTs instead of traditional unit tests; if needed, developers could manually write test inputs to the written PUTs besides those automatically generated test inputs for the PUTs.

Writing PUTs and applying a test-generation tool could also be integrated into the TDD process. Developers could go through the iterations of (1) writing PUTs before writing the code implementation under test, (2) applying a test-generation tool to generate test inputs for the PUTs and inspecting the reported test failures, and (3) writing the code implementation under test to a just-enough extent to make the test failures disappear. One key difference between this new TDD process and the traditional TDD process is that, in contrast to written traditional unit tests, written PUTs of higher quality would often be much more difficult to "fool" with a naive code implementation under test. As a result, developers could spend more effort in writing code implementation under test and spend less effort in incrementally improving the quality of the test code. It remains an open question for future empirical studies whether such "bigger-jump" iterations of improving code implementation under test would compromise the originally acclaimed benefits of "more modularized, flexible, and extensible code" [7]. These benefits are supposedly provided through "taking small steps when required", but the new TDD process would incur larger steps than the traditional TDD process.

Interacting with generated tests triggered quite some questions from developers. First of all, a developer might not know what to do after tests are automatically generated. For example, a developer in front of 100 generated tests asked "What do we do with the generated tests?" It is important to teach developers on how to interact with the generated tests, e.g., inspecting the reported test failures, inspecting the coverage reports to understand the insufficiency of the generated test inputs (and/or PUTs if written), diagnosing causes for the insufficiency, and providing guidance to the tool to address the insufficiency.

Below are conversations between a developer and a trainer on desired naming of generated tests by a tool:

- Developer: "Your tool generated a test called Foo001. I don't like it."
- Trainer: "What did you expect?"
- Developer: "Foo_Should_Fail_When_The_Bar_Is_Negative."

When developers write traditional test methods manually, they use meaningful naming conventions to these test methods. It is natural for developers to expect to see meaningful naming for generated test methods. Note that if developers write PUTs, they have control on the naming of the PUTs and the developers would need to pay less attention to the naming of the generated traditional unit tests that invoke the PUTs. But if developers write no PUTs but rely on a tool to generate test inputs for robustness checking, e.g., throwing uncaught exceptions, the developers would pay attention to

the naming of the traditional unit tests generated by the tool. In such cases, tool builders could improve the naming of the generated traditional unit tests.

Below are conversations between a developer and a trainer on desired representative values for generated test inputs by a tool:

- Developer: "Your tool generated "\0""
- Trainer: "What did you expect?"
- Developer: "Marc."

It is important to explain to developers why and how "\0" is generated by a tool instead of a *normal* string like "Marc". Basically, a tool such as Pex relies on an underlying constraint solver such as the SMT solver Z3 [9] to solve the constraints of a path in the code under test. Constraint solvers are often designed to provide the simplest solution to satisfy the constraints. Developers could provide guidance to the tool by supplying some default values for the tool to use as starting points.

Isolate first development is crucial to make test generation work in real-world code bases in practice. In real-world code bases, a component under test (such as a method or a class) could have non-trivial dependencies on external environments such as file systems. The environment API implementations could be very complex or be written in native code rather than managed code being amenable to code exploration. Developers need to isolate the environment dependencies, e.g., with the assistance of a tool such as Moles [8]. Solving the dependency-isolation problem is orthogonal to and facilitates solving the test-generation problem: developers could use Moles without using Pex while manually writing test inputs, but could face challenges when using Pex without using Moles on environment-dependent code.

4.3 Lessons Learned

We next describe lessons learned while interacting with practitioners during our teaching and training in industrial settings.

Setting realistic expectations right away is very important. While it is important in an industrial setting to showcase the potential benefits of a new technology, automated tools will always have limitations, and these limitations must be clearly communicated. The developers have to be taught what the limitations are, how the developers can detect them when they hit such limitations, and how they can act on them. With regards to the fault-detection capabilities, it is important to emphasize the concept of assertions as specifications to specify the intended functionality of the code – in order to find violations of such specifications. With regards to the abilities of any code analysis tool, it is important to define the scope of their applicability. When they do not apply, the developers must be prepared to act on them, e.g., by manually writing traditional unit tests instead of PUTs, or by using code isolation frameworks in order to ensure that unit tests can run without environment dependencies. Training on these skills should be included in training sessions.

Trying to change deeply ingrained beliefs all at once is futile. Especially in an industrial setting, developers have usually become accustomed to particular development styles. Convincing them to change is difficult. It is important to highlight how a new advanced technology relates to earlier approaches, emphasizing on complementary aspects instead of differences or total replacement. For example, if a developer has adopted an approach of TDD, it should be emphasized how parameterized unit testing is a natural generalization of this approach, and not a radically new one or replacement.

5. Comparison of Teaching and Training at University and Industrial Settings

We observed three main differences on teaching and training developer-testing techniques and tool support at university and industrial settings.

First, students at university settings often do not have substantial experiences of industrial software development (especially C# software development given that Java has so far remained a popular teaching language at various universities), whereas practitioners at industrial settings often have substantial experiences (including C# software development). In our teaching and training, we used Pex for testing C# code. However, a non-trivial portion of the graduate students in our graduate course did not have C# programming experiences (with primarily Java programming experiences). To alleviate the issue, we designed a homework exercise in the beginning of the course on asking students to convert JUnit test code in Java to C# test code, getting them a quick start in getting familiar with C# coding.

Second, students at university settings have the incentives of studying well the teaching materials to earn good course grades besides learning various valuable skills, whereas practitioners at industrial settings often "come and watch", learning what is going on. At the university settings, adoption of tools or technologies being taught (after the course finishes) may not be heavily emphasized as a teaching objective; instead, emphasis is put on learning a wide range of skills ranging from abstract thinking, rigorous thinking, to understanding of testing techniques, writing of specifications in the form of PUTs, and effective usage of tools. At the industrial settings, adoption of tools or technologies being taught (after the tutorial finishes) could be an important training objective. Therefore, in training materials, it is desirable to incorporate more realistic and complex enough illustrative examples for applying the presented techniques and tool support in the industrial settings so that practitioners could be more easily convinced the utility of the techniques and tool support. On the other hand, in the university settings, illustrative examples used in the beginning of a course should have sufficiently low levels of complexity for students to understand and digest.

Third, teaching duration at university settings (being one semester long such as 16 weeks) is much longer than training duration at industrial settings (about half-day or full-day duration). At the university settings, substantial after-lecture exercises and projects as well as in-class discussion could be possible for students to digest and master the presented materials besides the slide presentation and live tool demonstration during lectures. In contrast, at the industrial settings, limited duration allowed presentation of only important knowledge points and brief summaries of important tool features.

6. Discussion

It is desirable that developers do not need to master sophisticated theories or technical details underlying tools when using the tools. For example, rather than demanding developers to write algebraic specifications [12] in a formal way, Pex allows developers to write intended behavior of the code under test in the form of PUTs (simply test methods with parameters), which in fact encode algebraic specifications. The internal details of dynamic symbolic execution as well as its underlying constraint solving and theorem proving of Z3 [9] exploited by the Pex tool are also not exposed via the tool interface to developers who are using Pex.

However, no state-of-the-art tool including Pex can deal with all complicated situations in real-world code bases automatically without human intervention or guidance. For example, sometimes a tool could fail to generate test inputs for covering a branch for one or more reasons. Understanding these reasons by the developers is required before the developers could provide guidance to the tool such as carrying out environment isolation, instrumenting some framework or library code that the code under test invokes, and writing factory methods that encode method sequences for generating desirable objects. While we are actively researching how to automatically provide better explanations when encountering problems [25], exposing some internal technical details of the tool to developers would be still needed (at least in the near future) to allow developers and a tool to cooperate for effectively carrying out testing tasks. Therefore, training developers with such skills remains important future work.

In our teaching at the university settings, coverage criteria were major lecture topics for testing foundations. It still remains an open question on how understanding these various coverage criteria could directly assist developers in carrying out developer testing, especially in the context of applying a powerful tool such as Pex. For example, given that a tool could be enhanced or pre-configured (by tool authors or vendors) to automatically achieve specific advanced coverage criteria [19], we hypothesize that the awareness and deep understanding of advanced coverage criteria could be less necessary in developer-testing practice. With the adoption of tools and methodologies such as Pex and PUTs, we hypothesize that much more emphasis should be placed on training developers on how to write high-quality specifications (e.g., in the form of PUTs) than manually understanding and applying various coverage criteria, which were originally the basis for test generation and selection (currently automated with a tool). However, there still remains an open question on how to effectively train such specification-writing skills.

7. Conclusion

Effectively conducting developer testing requires both effective tool support by tools and developer-testing skills by developers. As educators, we need to devise effective ways to teach students or practitioners to equip them with these skills. In this paper, we have described our experiences in teaching and training developer-testing techniques and tool support in both university and industrial settings. We highlight differences in teaching and training in these two settings, and observations from interacting with practitioners in our process of teaching and training.

In future work, we plan to conduct quantitative studies such as comparing measurable data before and after a course offering or training session. We plan to conduct comparison of teaching skills of developer testing with teaching skills of other testing types, or with teaching other software development skills. In addition, we plan to develop a set of educational tools for developers to learn developer testing. We have already released a website called "Pex for Fun" [5]. It currently provides different types of programming puzzles such as coding-duel puzzles. For a coding-duel puzzle, the user is requested to write and iteratively improve an implementation that matches a hidden implementation based on feedback provided by Pex in showing the behavioral differences (i.e., different program outputs) of the two implementations. Coding-duel puzzles can be used to train developers' programming skills and problem solving skills. We plan to extend "Pex for Fun" to include puzzles for training testing skills.

Acknowledgments. Tao Xie's work is supported in part by NSF grants CNS-0716579, CCF-0725190, CCF-0845272, CCF-0915400, and CNS-0958235, and Army Research Office grant W911NF-08-1-0443.

References

[1] JUnit. http://www.junit.org.

[2] Microsoft Research Code Contracts. http://research.microsoft.com/en-us/projects/contracts.

[3] Microsoft Research Pex. http://research.microsoft.com/Pex.

[4] NUnit. http://www.nunit.org/.

[5] Pex for fun. http://www.pexforfun.com/.

[6] P. Ammann and J. Offutt. *Introduction to Software Testing*. Cambridge University Press, 2008. http://www.introsoftwaretesting.com/.

[7] K. Beck. *Test Driven Development: By Example*. Addison-Wesley, 2003.

[8] J. de Halleux and N. Tillmann. Moles: tool-assisted environment isolation with closures. In *Proc. TOOLS*, pages 253–270, 2010.

[9] L. M. de Moura and N. Bjørner. Z3: An efficient SMT solver. In *Proc. TACAS*, pages 337–340, 2008.

[10] M. Fowler. *Refactoring: Improving the Design of Existing Code*. Addison Wesley, 1999.

[11] P. Godefroid, N. Klarlund, and K. Sen. DART: Directed automated random testing. In *Proc. PLDI*, pages 213–223, 2005.

[12] J. V. Guttag and J. J. Horning. The algebraic specification of abstract data types. *Acta Informatica*, 10:27–52, 1978.

[13] C. A. R. Hoare. An axiomatic basis for computer programming. *Commun. ACM*, 12(10):576–580, 1969.

[14] J. Jacky, M. Veanes, C. Campbell, and W. Schulte. *Model-based Software Testing and Analysis with C#*. Cambridge University Press, 2008.

[15] J. C. King. Symbolic execution and program testing. *Commun. ACM*, 19(7):385–394, 1976.

[16] M. R. Marri, S. Thummalapenta, T. Xie, N. Tillmann, and J. de Halleux. Retrofitting unit tests for parameterized unit testing. Technical Report TR-2010-9, North Carolina State University Department of Computer Science, Raleigh, NC, March 2010.

[17] M. R. Marri, T. Xie, N. Tillmann, J. de Halleux, and W. Schulte. An empirical study of testing file-system-dependent software with mock objects. In *Proc. AST, Business and Industry Case Studies*, pages 149–153, 2009.

[18] B. Meyer. *Object-Oriented Software Construction*. Prentice Hall, 1988.

[19] R. Pandita, T. Xie, N. Tillmann, and J. de Halleux. Guided test generation for coverage criteria. In *Proc. ICSM*, 2010.

[20] K. Sen, D. Marinov, and G. Agha. CUTE: A concolic unit testing engine for C. In *Proc. ESEC/FSE*, pages 263–272, 2005.

[21] N. Tillmann and J. de Halleux. Pex – white box test generation for .NET. In *Proc. TAP*, pages 134–153, 2008.

[22] N. Tillmann and W. Schulte. Parameterized unit tests. In *Proc. ESEC/FSE*, pages 253–262, 2005.

[23] N. Tillmann and W. Schulte. Mock-object generation with behavior. In *Proc. ASE*, pages 365–368, 2006.

[24] G. Venolia, R. DeLine, and T. LaToza. Software development at microsoft observed. Technical Report MSR-TR-2005-140, Microsoft Research, Redmond, WA, October 2005.

[25] X. Xiao, T. Xie, N. Tillmann, and J. de Halleux. Issue analysis for residual structural coverage in dynamic symbolic execution. Technical Report TR-2010-7, North Carolina State University Department of Computer Science, Raleigh, NC, March 2010.

[26] L. Zhang, T. Xie, L. Zhang, , N. Tillmann, J. de Halleux, and H. Mei. Test generation via dynamic symbolic execution for mutation testing. In *Proc. ICSM*, 2010.

Learning CUDA: Lab Exercises and Experiences

Nate Anderson, Jens Mache, William Watson

Lewis & Clark College
Portland, OR 97219, USA
{noa, jmache, wwatson}@lclark.edu

Abstract

Whereas the fastest supercomputer of 1998 could compute 1.34 trillion double precision floating point operations per second (TFLOPS) [7], today's consumer-level (sub-$500) graphics cards such as the NVidia GeForce GTX 480 can compute 1.35 TFLOPS (single precision) [8]. The rise of multi- and many-core processing has certainly introduced new urgency to teaching parallel programming. In this paper, we focus on lab exercises at the undergraduate level. Three undergraduate students and one faculty member spent several weeks on CUDA lab exercises, starting with the recent book by Kirk and Hwu [4]. We describe our experiences and lessons learned working with the book and its accompanying labs. We discuss extended labs including the game of life, curvature flow, and ray tracing, all of which may appeal to an even wider audience of today's learners.

Categories and Subject Descriptors D.1.3 [*Software*]: Programming Technique—Concurrent Programming; K.3.2 [*Computer and Information Science Education*]: Computer Science

General Terms Algorithms, Design, Human Factors, Languages, Measurement, Performance

Keywords parallel computing, GPGPU, CUDA, computer science education

1. Introduction

Since 2005/2006, processor manufacturers have shifted their method of scaling performance from increasing clock speeds to increasing the number of cores. Processors in the future are predicted to have hundreds of cores.

The rise of multi- and many-core processing has introduced new urgency to learning parallel programming. Whereas typical machines today have two cores, today's graphics cards can already run hundreds of threads in parallel. General-purpose computing on graphics processing units (GPGPU) broke into the mainstream with the introduction of NVIDIA's CUDA API in 2007.

In this paper, we focus on lab exercises at the undergraduate level. Three undergraduate students and one faculty member spent several weeks on CUDA lab exercises, starting with the book by Kirk and Hwu [4] which was published in February 2010. We describe our experiences and lessons learned working with the book and its accompanying labs in Section 3. After this, we share our experiences and suggestions in Section 4. We discuss possible extended labs in Section 5.

2. Background

The CUDA programming model is an extension of the C language. CUDA applications consist of two portions of code: functions to be executed on the CPU host, and functions to be executed on the GPU device. The entry functions of the device code are tagged with a *global* keyword, and are referred to as kernels. A kernel executes in parallel across a set of parallel threads in a Single Instruction Multiple Thread (SIMT) model [5]. Since the host and device codes execute in two different memory spaces, the host code must include special calls for host-to-device and device-to-host data transfers. Fig. 1 shows the sequence of steps involved in a typical CUDA kernel invocation.

When the device executes a kernel it runs within a grid with parameters defined in terms of number of blocks (up to two dimensions) and number of threads per block (up to three dimensions), but totalling no more than 512 threads per block. Streaming multiprocessors on the video card execute the thread blocks. The graphics card we used was the NVidia 9800GT, which has 14 streaming multiprocessors, each of which can execute 8 blocks or 768 threads at one time for a maximum of 10,762 concurrent threads.

3. Lab exercises

Working with the CUDA labs from the book by Kirk and Hwu [4], we changed the order to lab 1, lab 3, lab 4 and then lab 2, for the following reason: lab 2 mentions the topic

Permission to make digital or hard copies of all or part of this work for personal or classroom use is granted without fee provided that copies are not made or distributed for profit or commercial advantage and that copies bear this notice and the full citation on the first page. To copy otherwise, to republish, to post on servers or to redistribute to lists, requires prior specific permission and/or a fee.

SPLASH'10, October 17–21, 2010, Reno/Tahoe, Nevada, USA.
Copyright © 2010 ACM 978-1-4503-0240-1/10/10...$10.00

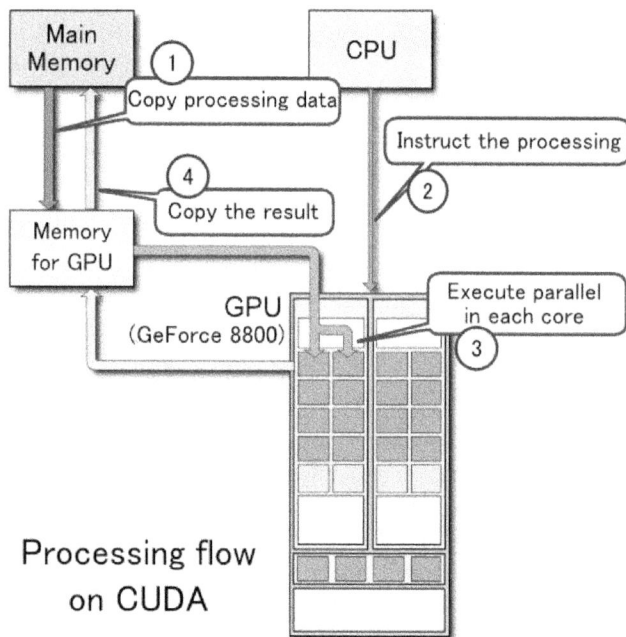

Figure 1. Steps in a typical CUDA kernel invocation [9]

```
void MM(const Matrix M, const Matrix N, Matrix P)
{
  Matrix Md = AllocateDeviceMatrix(M);
  Matrix Nd = AllocateDeviceMatrix(N);
  Matrix Pd = AllocateDeviceMatrix(P);
  CopyToDeviceMatrix(Md, M);
  CopyToDeviceMatrix(Nd, N);

  dim3 dimBlock(P.width, P.height);
  dim3 dimGrid(1, 1);
  MMKernel <<< dimGrid, dimBlock >>> (Md, Nd, Pd);

  CopyFromDeviceMatrix(P, Pd);
}

__global__ void MMKernel(Matrix M, Matrix N, Matrix P)
{
  ...
}
```

Figure 2. Code for the matrix multiplication lab1

of thread diversion which the book covers in Chapter 6. In contrast, lab 1 only depends on Chapter 3, and lab 3 and lab 4 both only depend on material up to Chapter 5 from the book.

3.1 A first lab (on matrix multiplication)

The programming staple "Hello, World!" has served as a basic introduction into sequential programming languages for years. The simple task of instructing a computer to print the two words represents a basic and welcoming introduction into giving the CPU and system instructions. Lab 1 from the book by Kirk and Hwu [4] seems to be a good GPU equivalent of the "Hello, World!" program. The properties of matrices are well suited to the CUDA architecture, and the problem of matrix multiplication serves as a simple introduction into giving instructions to the GPU and managing its interactions with the host CPU.

The purpose of lab 1 is to compute the multiplication of two matrices, the result of which will not contain a total number of elements greater than can be handled by a single block of threads. By default the lab manipulates 3 matrices of 16*16, resulting in the execution of 256 threads, which is within CUDA's maximum per-block thread count of 512.

Our experience with lab 1 was met with hesitation as although we were well aware of the process of multiplying matrix cells, the structure of CUDA devices and the extended language were still foreign. Lab 1 provided functions that handled the creation of matrices and host-to-device as well as device-to-host memory management. What it did not provide was the kernel execution code and the required statements of dim3 dimBlock and dimGrid structures that al-

lowed for proper execution, see Fig. 2 (lines 9 to 11). The dim3 structure is provided as a tool that helps define the structure of the kernel in terms of its components. dimBlock defines the number of threads per block, while dimGrid defines the number of blocks per grid. Completing the kernel code was a relatively easy process, given a proper understanding of the Matrix structure and how to access elements within the matrix in terms of a one-dimensional array.

The following testimonial is from one of the co-authors of this paper, an undergraduate computer science student with 2 years experience working in C and 2 years experience working with Java on topics including computer graphics, security, algorithms and software development. We refer to this student as Student 1.

> What I did not understand about the lesson structure of lab 1 was why the focus of editing the host code was the execution of the kernel, as only one block was used and no effort was made to address the properties of thread management. As the introductory exercise with CUDA, I feel that it may benefit some students more to familiarize themselves with the process of transferring memory and commands to and from the host and the device than the specifics of kernel execution. My perception that lab 1 is the "Hello, World!" of CUDA programming is hindered by the removal of the memory management and obstructed by the kernel execution section that can be more effectively learned from lab 3.
>
> This lab took approximately two hours of reading, half an hour to write the code and about two hours to debug the program in order to get it working.

3.2 A lab covering tiling and shared memory

Lab 3 from the book by Kirk and Hwu [4] is an extension of the principles of matrix multiplication with a focus on the proper deployment of the kernel execution and the management of tasks that require more than the maximum number of threads that can be handled by one streaming multiprocessor (SM) at a time. As each CUDA block can only handle up to 512 threads at a time, using only a single block fails for square matrices with dimensions over $22 * 22$ (as $22 * 22 = 484$ cells and $23 * 23 = 529$). We note that non-square matrices of $32 * 16$ would successfully execute, as this totals to 512 threads per block. For matrices over this limit, however, we are introduced to the concept of tiling. Tiling is the process by which larger problem sets are broken into smaller sections that can be managed within the constraints of the block and grid organization of CUDA. Rather than having threads identify themselves by calling only threadIdx (thread index), we determine a thread's position in a matrix by employing the block index as well (blockIdx). To determine the number of blocks needed by each axis we take the size of the matrix and divide it by the size of the block in threads and round up to include all cells. This method determines the properties of the two dim3 structures required to initiate a kernel, dimBlock and dimGrid, where dimGrid is the dimensions of the grid in number of blocks and dimBlock is the dimensions of each block in number of threads.

The following testimonial is also from Student 1.

I believe that lab 3 is a more effective learning tool for understanding the properties of kernel execution in CUDA. By forcing the student to manipulate the size of both the blocks and the grid the purpose of the dim3 structure becomes more clear. From this understanding calling the [Kernel] $<<< dimGrid, dimBlock >>>$ ([Arguments]); command [to execute the kernel on the device] becomes trivial.

While translating the lab 1 code to handle much larger matrices for lab 3 is relatively uncomplicated, the introduction of shared memory vs. global memory could benefit from some clarification. At the time of this writing, I have not yet successfully completed a shared memory implementation of the lab 3 tiled matrix multiplication. An example point of confusion is understanding what exactly happens when shared memory is defined within a thread, compared to how a given block manages shared memory. Breaking lab 3 into two distinct sub-problems (with and without the use of shared memory) may benefit students as the concepts of tiling and shared memory management can be taught independently.

This lab, having already completed lab 1, took significantly less time to complete [without shared memory], in terms of both coding and debugging. I spent approximately two hours reading and 45 minutes getting the code to execute correctly.

3.3 The convolution lab

The topic of lab 4 from the book by Kirk and Hwu [4] is matrix convolution. Convolution is important in image and signal processing applications. Because it requires the same action to be performed on every element in a given matrix, it works efficiently on the GPU. The largest hurdle that must be overcome when programming a convolution kernel is dealing with the edge cases. In our 5x5 convolution lab, each element uses the 24 elements around it, but if it is on or near an edge, it must substitute zeroes for the missing elements. The solution is to load the elements operated on by the block into shared memory but with a halo of required elements around it.

The following testimonial is from another co-author of this paper, an undergraduate computer science student with 3 years of C/C++ experience and 1 year of Java experience in areas including software development, algorithms, and computer graphics. We refer to this student as Student 2.

This lab was the most challenging for me both conceptually and in difficulty of programming. The solution code loaded one element of the shared memory per thread. With a 16 by 16 thread block, only the inner 12 by 12 threads would do any work after loading their elements. This makes the code simpler but less efficient. I attempted to load multiple elements per thread in order to use more of the threads on processing those elements later. For a 16 by 16 block, I created a 20 by 20 block of shared memory. This led to a much more complicated solution that took longer to debug than to program. Because I was more confident at writing code in CUDA after the previous labs, this difficulty was surprising. Debugging proved even more frustrating because the GPU running the program was also handling the graphics of the rest of the operating system, so some issues in the code caused visual artifacts or system crashes. The ideas behind convolution and haloing were new to me and I think I would have had an easier time with the lab if there had been a lecture beforehand.

This lab took me about an hour to code and 3 hours to debug, along with an hour of reading. The debugging time would have been cut down if I would have known how to use the debugger and had my errors not crashed the computer when the program ran.

3.4 The reduction lab

Lab 2 from the book by Kirk and Hwu [4] is the implementation of a parallel reduction algorithm. The kernel is given an array of 512 values and returns their sum. The concept introduced here is thread diversion. A naive implementation would cause threads in every warp to diverge, decreasing performance substantially. The following testimonial is also from Student 2.

I felt that it was easy to understand how divergent threads could be minimized and the lab itself was easy to code. Because it was limited to 512 elements, only one block was needed. The concepts behind the lab were easy to understand. I did this lab after Lab 4, so it might have been more challenging to someone with less CUDA experience.

I completed this lab in about one hour.

4. Experiences and suggestions

We believe that, due to their similar nature and their effectiveness as introductory examples into CUDA, lab 1 and lab 3 from the book by Kirk and Hwu [4] are best paired together. The continuity of moving between the two may help solidify the student's understanding of the basic operations of memory allocation and kernel execution. The matrix multiplication problem is the perfect framework in which these concepts can be communicated.

That being said, we believe that students may be more engaged with a more results-driven problem; the current reward for a successful complement of code is the command line stating "Test PASSED" rather than "Test FAILED". We believe that, while these labs are an effective tool for students to learn from, the benefit of CUDA and parallel processing is lost in the lack of feedback. One method we found interesting was the inclusion of timers to compare the CPU and GPU versions of the solution. As each lab includes a CPU version to compare the GPU version to, we wrapped a timer around each method call to measure the speedup. In lab 3, we manipulated the size of the matrix and calculated the results of two matrices that are 2048x2048 each. On an NVidia GeForce 9800 GT graphics card, our speedup was greater than 16 (compared to the CPU on a dual-core Intel Pentium G6950 PC) using global memory-only tiled matrix multiplication. (While the demonstrated run time was reduced from almost two and a half minutes to just eight seconds, we expect the speedup to increase when optimized with shared memory.) We believe that measuring the benefits of parallel processing is both an effective tool for motivating students and an opening for students to challenge themselves in the optimization of their code.

Visual feedback for correct solutions is another means to motivate students. Getting a "Test PASSED" message upon completion is not as satisfying as seeing something that the student creates. That is why we propose supplementing lab 4 (convolution) with a lab on the game of life (see [2]). Instead of looking at a 5 by 5 block of elements around the one being worked on, the game of life looks at a 3 by 3. It has similar challenges and would still need haloing to work efficiently, but provides visual feedback.

If labs 1 and 3 are paired together, we think that lab 2 could be more difficult. In the current order lab 2 is given before multiple blocks are used, and is quite limited as a result. If it is introduced after lab 3, students could be challenged with larger data sets or use more advanced techniques for improved performance [3].

5. Discussion

Due to the fact that CUDA kernels execute on a device that lacks the ability to make system calls (such as print statements), and that its debugger will not run on a GPU that is displaying graphics, CUDA represents a challenge when it comes to debugging. In our experience, we often ran into situations in which the computer would hang or a sloppy memory call would overwrite necessary system information and force us to restart the device and therefore the system. On top of this, the difficulty of accessing run time information on the device from the host running in graphical mode meant that kernel debugging could only be done by checking the results of the output from the device. This significantly slowed the pace of writing code, and we suggest that it be kept in mind when attempting to either learn or teach CUDA.

One additional idea for a lab could be the inclusion of a simple ray tracer for those students familiar with graphical concepts or those who are confident in their ability to translate code from C into CUDA-C. The nature of ray traced 3D graphics allows for pixels to be calculated independently of each other. We are currently working on a very simple ray tracer that we believe will address the viability and benefit of a CUDA based implementation. This project may make for a good final or semester lab as it provides more opportunities for parallel optimization as well as providing a graphical result as a reward for a successful implementation.

Another idea is curvature flow [6]. A theorem in differential geometry [1] that states that any simple closed curve moving under its curvature (each piece of the curve moves perpendicular to the curve with speed proportional to the curvature) collapses to a circle and then in on itself. Producing animations of the 3-dimensional version of this behavior is based on code similar to convolution, but can take hours on a CPU. Our future work includes translating this code to CUDA, and potentially turning it into an additional lab exercise which may appeal to an even wider audience of today's learners.

6. Conclusions

Whereas general-purpose parallel computing on graphics processing units (GPGPU) and the CUDA API have been around since 2007, is CUDA ready for the undergraduate classroom? After spending several weeks of independent study on CUDA lab exercises, our experiences are as follows:

- Parallel programming education on GPUs with CUDA looks very promising, even for the undergraduate classroom. CUDA labs are suitable for hands-on teaching of parallel programming to undergraduate students. (Ideally, students have seen C/C++, before. Debugging needs some getting used to.)

- The lab exercises from the recent book by Kirk and Hwu [4] are a very good resource. We discussed ideas for changing the overall order of the labs, the focus of lab1 and dividing lab3 into two parts.

- For motivation, we recommend to include timers and speed comparisons, early.

- For pedagogy, we recommend as much visual feedback as possible. Promising candidates for new labs are the Game of Life, ray tracing, and curvature flow.

Acknowledgments

This work is supported by an NSF REU and grant CNS-0720914. We would like to thank Ben Perkins for his participation in this study.

References

[1] K. Brakke. *The Motion of a Surface by its Mean Curvature.* Princeton University Press, 1978.

[2] M. Gardner. Mathematical games – the fantastic combinations of John Conway's new solitaire game "life". *Scientific American*, pages 120–123, October 1970.

[3] M. Harris. Optimizing parallel reduction in CUDA. URL http://developer.download.nvidia.com/compute/cuda/1_1/Website/projects/reduction/doc/reduction.pdf.

[4] D. Kirk and W.-M. Hwu. *Programming Massively Parallel Processors: A Hands-on Approach.* Morgan Kaufmann, 2010. URL http://www.elsevierdirect.com/morgan_kaufmann/kirk/.

[5] J. Nickolls, I. Buck, M. Garland, and K. Skadron. Scalable parallel programming with CUDA. *ACM Queue*, 6(2):40–53, 2008.

[6] J. Sethian. Curves moving under their curvature collapse. URL http://math.berkeley.edu/ sethian/2006/Applications/Geometry/curvecollapse.html.

[7] Top500. URL http://www.top500.org/sublist.

[8] S. Wasson. Nvidia's GeForce GTX 480 and 470 graphics processors, 2010. URL http://techreport.com/articles.x/18682/1.

[9] Wikipedia. URL http://en.wikipedia.org/wiki/File:CUDA_processing_flow_%28En%29.PNG.

Learning OOP With Weakly Typed Web Programming Languages Adding Concrete Strategies to a PHP Strategy Design Pattern

William B. Sanders, Ph.D.

University of Hartford
Multimedia Web Design & Development
Dana Hall 310
200 Bloomfield Avenue
West Hartford, CT 06117
wsanders@hartford.edu

Abstract

While strongly typed languages such as C++ and Java are taught using OOP principles and design patterns; weakly typed Web programming languages like PHP and JavaScript often are not because of weak typing. As the weakly typed languages themselves incorporate more OOP structures, such as type hinting in PHP 5.1, educators need to consider ways to include OOP practices in courses where weakly typed languages are taught. This paper suggests one way to introduce *OOP principles* is through design patterns. Using design patterns educators can introduce both design pattern structures and OOP principles while revealing the practicality of both.

Categories and Subject Descriptors I.7.1 [**WEB**]: Weakly typed Web Languages – design patterns, learning, applying OOP principles

General Terms Design.

Keywords PHP design patterns; learning experiment; lack of use by developers; weakly typed languages; demonstrating practicality; type hinting and programming to an interface.

1. Introduction

This paper uses the Strategy Design Pattern because the pattern lends itself to demonstrating the principles of 1) favoring composition over inheritance [2, 5] and 2) programming to the interface instead of the implementation [2, 5]. It also provides a simple and practical example of code change, re-use and extension. Likewise the implementation illustrates polymorphism,[1] single responsibility rule [4], and loose coupling [6]. The example project involves students building additional concrete strategies based on an initial example structure.

Most of the PHP texts concentrate on algorithms and processes for entering and retrieving data from MySQL databases. Included are many good practices for validating data, error checking, data security and other sound techniques for PHP programs. Some books do introduce OOP, but very few tackle the principles and instead focus

Permission to make digital or hard copies of all or part of this work for personal or classroom use is granted without fee provided that copies are not made or distributed for profit or commercial advantage and that copies bear this notice and the full citation on the first page. To copy otherwise, or republish, to post on servers or to redistribute to lists, requires prior specific permission and/or a fee.
SPLASH'10 October 17–21, 2010, Reno/Tahoe, Nevada, USA.
Copyright © 2010 ACM 978-1-4503-0240-1/10/10...$10.00.

on techniques for accomplishing practical tasks. Many of the more advanced practices, such as design patterns are either ignored or implemented incorrectly.

When students are introduced to design patterns in any programming language, they often find patterns to be overly difficult, and either set them aside, or they are frustrated. One technique for introducing design patterns is to provide a pattern stripped of ancillary practices such as error checking, validation and other housekeeping techniques required for good programming. The idea is to demonstrate the structure of the design pattern and then add the ancillary practices once the students understand the pattern.

The approach introduced here begins with a simple design pattern with no ancillary procedures but a single functional concrete implementation that does something. Students are invited to add a new class to the existing pattern. Once they have created and tested a new concrete strategy object, they can better see the principles behind OOP and design patterns. In this way, they can better see how it works and its practicality in that adding new functionality does not require the program to be re-written. It helps them see the principles they are required to understand as having been developed for practical goals in programming.

2. Beginning with a functional design pattern

For this paper, I use a simple Strategy Design Pattern as described by Gamma, Helm, Johnson and Vlissides (pp. 315-330) [2]. The Strategy pattern was selected because it is one of the main patterns that depend on delegation (p. 21) [2]. Gamma *et al*, point out that delegation "is a way of making composition as powerful for reuse as inheritance." *Favoring object composition over class inheritance* is one of the main principles in programming design patterns and an important one for students to understand.

All of the algorithms for accessing and using the database through SQL commands are very simple. By encapsulating each algorithm in a concrete strategy, two concepts can be better understood by students: (1) object composition, and (2) reuse/replacement. Instead of being a highly dependent set of classes sub-classed from the Context participant, each strategy implements the Strategy interface, opening the door for a far looser set of class relations suitable for reuse and change.

The purpose of the Strategy pattern is to allow algorithms to vary independently from the clients that use them. In this way the concrete strategies (algorithms) can be used independent of any single object. Further, with several different concrete strategies, the clients can select only those that they need and/or add more as required without disrupting the program. Figure 1 shows the class diagram for the Strategy pattern:

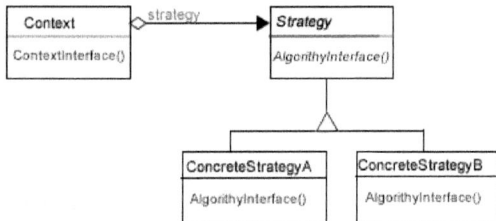

Figure 1: Strategy Design Pattern class diagram

The implementation of the Strategy pattern has only a single concrete strategy, but the students are shown the original class diagram to imply that they can add their own. Each of the class participants is explained and discussed, and then the students are shown the following implementation:

File name: Context.php

```php
<?php
class Context
{
    private $strategy;

    public                     function
__construct(IStrategy $strategy)
    {
        $this->strategy = $strategy;
    }

    public function algorithm(Array
$elements)
    {
        $this->strategy-
>algorithm($elements);
    }
}

?>
```

File name: IStrategy.php

```php
<?php

interface IStrategy
{
    public   function   algorithm(Array
$elements);
}

?>
```

File name: StratEnterData.php

```php
<?php
```

```php
ini_set("display_errors","2");
include_once('IStrategy.php');
ERROR_REPORTING(E_ALL);
/*Simulation of data entry using
print statements instead of SQL com-
mands */
class StratEnterData implements IS-
trategy
{
    public function algorithm(Array
$elements)
    {
        print              "<h3>Data
Entered:</h3>";
        print      "Name      entered:
$elements[0]<br/>";
        print  "Department  entered:
$elements[1]<br/>";
        print  "University  entered:
$elements[2]<br/>";
    }
}
?>
```

Implementation of this Strategy further requires both an input utility (an HTML5 application) and a Client class. To optimize the flexibility of the Client, instead calling it from the HTML page, it uses a PHP trigger file to call the Client with a specific request. As the students add their own concrete strategy classes, they can add requests to the Client and create their own trigger files to launch their own or others concrete implementations. To start they are provided with the following files.

File name: StrategyChoice.html

```html
<!DOCTYPE HTML>
<html>
<head>
<meta         http-equiv="Content-Type"
content="text/html; charset=UTF-8">
<style type="text/css">
h1 {
    color:#8C3123;
    font-family:"Arial Black";
    font-size:18px;
}
h2 {
    color:#B6D9C3;
    font-family:"Verdana";
    font-weight:bold;
    font-size:14px;
    background-color:#232B30;
}
body {
    color:#232B30;
    font-family:Verdana,        Arial,
Helvetica, sans-serif;
    font-size:11px;
    background-color:#C9C89F;
}
a, h3 {
    color:#BFA26B;
    font-family:"Verdana";
```

```
        font-weight:bold;
        font-size:12px;
        background-color:#232B30;
        text-decoration:none;
    }
    </style>
    </head>
    <body>
    <h2> Strategy          Design
Pattern</h2>
    <header>
      <h1>Enter   Name,  Department and
College:</h1>
    </header>
    <section>
      <form          action="Strat1.php"
method="post">
        Name:<br/>
        <input  type="text"  name="sname"
/>
        <br/>
        Department:<br/>
        <input   type="text"   name="dept"
/>
        <br/>
        College:<br/>
        <input              type="text"
name="college" />
        <input            type="submit"
value="Send" />
      </form>
    </section>
    <p/>
    <footer>
      <h3> PHP            Design
Patterns: <a
href="http://www.php5dp.com">http://ww
w.php5dp.com</a></h3>
    </footer>
    </body>
    </html>
```

File name: Client.php

```
<?php
ini_set("display_errors","2");
ERROR_REPORTING(E_ALL);
include_once('Context.php');
include_once('IStrategy.php');
include_once('StratEnterData.php');

class Client
{
//Encapsulate  variables  used  in
request
        private $snameNow;
        private $deptNow;
        private $collegeNow;

        private $context;
        private $collection;
/*Method  to read  entries  and place
into
  array to be sent to context */
```

```
      public function enterData()
      {
          $this-
>snameNow=$_POST['sname'];
          $this-
>deptNow=$_POST['dept'];
          $this-
>collegeNow=$_POST['college'];
          //Add to array
          $this->collection=
array($this->snameNow,  $this->deptNow,
$this->collegeNow);
          $this->context    =    new
Context(new StratEnterData());
          $this->context-
>algorithm($this->collection);
      }
    }
    ?>
```

File name (trigger file): Strat1.php

```
<?php
include_once('Client.php');
//Create new instance of Client
$strat1 = new Client();
//Send request to Context
$strat1->enterData();
?>
```

All of the students have the same set of files, and so no time is used initially with file creation.

3. *Making Additional Objects*

Instead, of going over the program and explaining all of the OOP concepts no concepts at all are introduced, but instead an *experiment* is suggested. *Would it be possible to add another concrete object as long as the same interface was used?* The students are shown the following concrete strategy class:

```
class  ConcreteStrategy    implements
IStrategy
    {
        public  function  algorithm(Array
$elements)
        {
            //operation
        }
    }
```

They are asked to make a successful concrete strategy class based on the generic class. They cannot change the Context class, the Strategy interface (IStrategy) nor the original concrete strategy class (StratEnterData), and the original concrete strategy still has to work correctly if called. They are required to change the following but no more:

- The name of the concrete strategy class (required)
- The nature and number of operations in the algorithm method (required)
- The number of elements in the array (required)

- Add a new form to the HTML program including a button to launch it (required)
- Add a method to the Client class to call their object (required)
- Add a new trigger file (required)

As students work on their project, the instructor helps by clarifying any points they misunderstand in general coding or the requirements of the task.

4. Explaining OOP and Design Pattern Principles after new Object has been created

Once all of the students have created a new object, they are shown how the functionality of their new object is an example of *composition being favored over inheritance*. Rather than creating a class and adding functionality by sub-classing, new functionality is created by implementing a new object using the same interface as the original. Explaining how the design pattern exemplifies *programming to the interface instead of the implementation* is a little trickier because the students assume that the interface being discussed is the IStrategy interface from which they implemented a new object. To some extent that is true, but a more subtle form of programming to the interface instead of the implementation occurs in the Client with the instantiation of the concrete strategy through the Context constructor. Using type-hinting in the Context constructor types any object as an IStrategy instead of a concrete strategy. (In some respects using an abstract class is more helpful because there is no interface construct to confuse the issue.) Ironically, while weakly typed languages are supposed to be easier to write because of weak typing, they can be much more difficult to explain because partial strong typing (type-hinting) is used.

Once the new object has been created and tested, students can see how loosely coupled their object (and everyone else's) is. As long as they implement the interface correctly, the algorithms they add will work. Adding, changing and even removing concrete strategies will not break the program. At the same time they can see how the **algorithm()** method can be implemented in many (poly) different forms (morphism) and *see* polymorphism at work.

The process also provides an opportunity to illustrate *unit testing* as the students develop objects that can be tested for proper functionality as they develop them. Likewise, the *single responsibility* principle can be discussed in that each concrete strategy can have a single reason to change. While this can be misleading if handled wrong (or a student manages to develop an example that

has more than a single reason to change), it provides an opportunity to focus on farming out responsibilities rather than crowding them all in a single inflexible class.

5. SPLASH Conference Interactive Component

For the SPLASH conference attending participants will be given the files through a URL where they can be downloaded. If they have PHP in their computers, they will be able to run and test the concrete implementation on their localhost. For those who do not have local accessibility to PHP 5.1+ on their computers, special guest accounts at the University of Hartford will be set up for them to use to test their concrete classes. The steps for creating the concrete strategy classes will be in a PowerPoint presentation. Once everyone has successfully created a concrete strategy, key principles to be discussed include:

- Programming to the interface instead of the implementation
- Favor composition over inheritance
- Unit testing
- Polymorphism
- Single responsibility principle

Most importantly, though, the opportunity will be used to discuss concepts session members believe to be important to explain to students and how this technique may or may not be helpful. Likewise, suggestions for improving the technique are invited as well.

References

1. Grady Booch, Robert A. Maksimchuk, Michael W. Engel, and Bobbi J. Young . *Object-Oriented Analysis and Design with Applications*. Addison-Wesley, Boston, MA, 2007. Third Edition

2. Erich Gamma, Richard Helm, Ralph Johnson, and John Vlissides. *Design Patterns: Elements of Reusable Object-Oriented Software*. Addison-Wesley, Boston, MA, 1995.

3. Paul Hamill. *Unit Test Frameworks*. O'Reilly, Sebastopol, CA, 2004

4. Robert C. Martin. *Agile Software Development, Principles, Patterns, and Practices*. Prentice Hall, Upper Saddle River, NJ, 2002.

5. William Sanders and Chandima Cumaranatunge. *ActionScript 3.0 Design Patterns*. O'Reilly, Sebastopol, CA, 2007

6. Karl Weick. The Management of Organizational Change among Loosely Coupled Elements. In Karl Weick, *Making Sense of the Organization* . Wiley-Blackwell, Indianapolis, IN, 2002.

Using a Web-Based Repository to Integrate Testing Tools into Programming Courses

Peter J. Clarke, Andrew A. Allen

School of Computing and Info. Sciences
Florida International University
Miami, FL 33199, USA
{clarkep, aalle004}@cis.fiu.edu

Tariq M. King

Dept. of Computer Science
North Dakota State University
Fargo, ND 58108, USA
tariq.king@ndsu.edu

Edward L. Jones

Dept. of Computer and Info. Sciences
Florida A&M University
Tallahassee, FL 32307, USA
ejones@cis.famu.edu

Prathiba Natesan

Department of Educational Psychology
University of North Texas
Denton, TX 76203, USA
prathiba.natesan@unt.edu

Abstract

Improving the quality of software developed in the 21st century is one of the major challenges in the software industry. Addressing this problem will require that academic institutions play a key role in training developers to produce high quality software. Unfortunately, students and instructors continue to be frustrated by the lack of support provided when selecting appropriate testing tools and program analyzers to verify programs under development.

In this paper we present an approach that integrates the use of software testing tools into programming and software engineering courses. The approach consists of three phases, developing an online repository with learning resources, training instructors in the area of testing techniques and tools, and integrating the use of testing tools into various programming courses. We also present the results of the first instructors' workshop and studies on integrating testing tools into two courses, CS2 and Software Engineering (SE).

Categories and Subject Descriptors   K.3.2 [*Computer and Information Science Education*]: Miscellaneous

General Terms   Experimentation

Keywords   Software Testing, Unit Testing, Programming Courses, Computer Science Education

Permission to make digital or hard copies of all or part of this work for personal or classroom use is granted without fee provided that copies are not made or distributed for profit or commercial advantage and that copies bear this notice and the full citation on the first page. To copy otherwise, to republish, to post on servers or to redistribute to lists, requires prior specific permission and/or a fee.

SPLASH'10,   October 17–21, 2010, Reno/Tahoe, Nevada, USA.
Copyright © 2010 ACM 978-1-4503-0240-1/10/10...$10.00

1. Introduction

The size and complexity of software systems continue to grow as software becomes more pervasive and ubiquitous. Ensuring the quality of these software systems in the 21st Century will require changes to the development strategies and improvement to the pedagogy used to teach these strategies in academia. Testing continues to be the primary technique used to ensure the development of high quality software, but recent studies [2, 30] indicate that major improvements in software testing are needed. Any comprehensive approach to improving the quality of software systems developed in the future requires that academic institutions play a vital role in training students how to test software, and making them aware of the tools available to support software testing. Unfortunately, students and instructors continue to be frustrated by the lack of support provided when selecting appropriate testing tools and program analyzers to verify programs under development.

Research data on the use of software testing tools by students and instructors to support pedagogy are scarce. During the last decade several researchers [14, 16, 19–21] have indicated that little or no coverage is given to software design and testing techniques in many academic CS programs. One of the first Computer Science (CS) and Information Technology (IT) courses that students encounter in many programs in the nation is "CS1 - Introduction to Programming". It is in CS1 that students should be exposed to the tools that have the potential to improve the quality of the code they write. Exposing students to testing techniques and tools during courses early in the CS/IT curricula would allow them to gain the necessary practice and experience required to produce high quality software. There are also reports that little attention is given to software testing even in software engineering (SE) courses. One aspect not fully addressed in the research papers on integrating testing into CS/IT courses is the preparation required to introduce programming course instructors to the area of software testing. To support the aforementioned claim, Lethbridge et al. [24] raise the broader question of how many instructors teaching core SE courses have a deep background in the field.

In this paper we present an approach that supports the integration of testing into programming courses supported by a web-based repository of testing tools. The approach consists of three phases: (1) developing an online portal of learning resources that supports pedagogy in the area of software testing; (2) holding a series of annual workshops for instructors to introduce them to software testing and the learning resources available through the online portal; and (3) integrating the use of testing tools into programming and SE courses. We report on the phases of the project mentioned above identifying the results obtained from the studies that have been conducted to date.

The remainder of the paper is organized as follows: in Section 2 we describe techniques in the literature that integrates testing into programming courses. Section 3 presents our approach and Section 4 describes the results of our first instructors' workshop and studies conducted in CS2 and SE courses. Section 5 describes the related work and we conclude in Section 6.

2. Testing in Programming Courses

Members of the academic community and software industry have expressed interest in integrating testing into the curricula of programming courses. The most recent approach being employed by instructors is Test Driven Learning (TDL), or teaching Test Driven Development (TDD). Such approaches involve using automated testing tools to motivate students to learn about software testing, while improving their testing skills and ability to develop quality software. In this section we describe some of the approaches being used by instructors to integrate testing into programming courses, and summarize the results of applying these approaches as reported in the literature.

2.1 Approaches

Goldwasser [16] proposed a technique that required minor modifications to the course structure to include the submission of test sets with the source code for assignments. The source code of each assignment is then executed on each test set submitted. This approach uses mainly black-box testing [27]. Goldwasser refers to this approach as a "little gimmick" and states that the approach can be applied to most programming courses at all level of the curriculum. A significant benefit for instructors cited in this approach is its amenability to existing programming assignments. This approach requires unambiguous specifications and automated

grading tools to support medium to large classes [16]. As such an instructor would need to learn how to create such assignments and use these tools.

Edwards [7, 8] observed that most beginner students use the trial-and-error approach to program correctness. However, even though natural and sufficient for simple programs, this approach does not lead to the development of higher order problem solving skills needed to develop more complex software. Students need practice applying the scientific method: observing the behavior of software, hypothesizing cause-effect relationships in the software, and experimenting to verify hypotheses. Software testing can play an important role in learning to develop software, but only when students are provided with a special environment that provides frequent feedback on their performance forming hypotheses and verifying them. Web-CAT, developed by Edwards, receives a student's program code and test set, and provides as feedback an overall score (grade) and three performance measures: (1) code correctness based on the number of student-supplied test cases that passed; (2) code test completeness based on code coverage; and (3) problem test completeness and validity based on a teacher-provided test set.

Janzen et al. [20] present test-driven learning (TDL) as a pedagogical tool and discuss the incorporation of TDL into multiple levels of the CS and SE curricula. They propose that TDL can be applied as early as the first day of the first programming course, but that it should not compete with other approaches in introductory courses. Instead, TDL should integrate well with other programming-first approaches such as imperative-first, objects-first, functional-first, event-driven, among others. An experiment was conducted in two CS1 sections, taught by the same instructor, to compare the scores between TDL students and non-TDL students.

Elbaum et al. [11] state that it continues to be difficult to integrate testing into early programming courses due to the lack of appropriate courseware materials that can be directly used by instructors. Therefore in an effort to promote early integration of software testing into early programming courses, the authors developed a hands-on web-based tutorial named *Bug Hunt*. The features of Bug Hunt provide both instructors and students with the ability to: (1) practice the fundamentals of testing while providing students with feedback; (2) review the material in the tutorial at their pace; (3) configure the tutorial to accommodate the instructor's requirements; and (4) automatically assess the students' performance by the instructor.

Schaub [31] describes an instructor's experience when introducing testing into a CS1 course that focuses on web application development. The author combines the use of a web API, an appropriate development environment, and a TDD methodology to emphasize design and testing. TDD was employed to get students to focus on the design of the core application API, while writing automated unit tests before implementing the application's functionality. For assignments, students were provided with a specification of the classes and methods to be developed, together with an initial unit test set that must pass for the solution to be considered acceptable. To reduce the effort needed for students to adopt unit testing techniques in CS1, the approach used by Schaub [31] did not require students to learn xUnit-style frameworks [33] in CS1 but instead write stand-alone unit tests as a console application.

The work by Desai et. al [5] demonstrate how TDD can be integrated into CS1/CS2 course curricula. The approach attempts to introduce testing without burdening the students by giving them full JUnit [15] test suites for projects and labs early. Initially, JUnit tests are supplied for a Java class similar to one the students would have to test, e.g., test cases were supplied for a *Triangle* class, and the students had to write the test cases for a *Rectangle* class. However, in subsequent projects students were expected to write all the tests themselves without the aid of test examples. Students were also taught the value of reusable automated unit tests as projects built upon previous ones. Therefore, some written tests did not have to change but just re-run to ensure that changes did not break any of the previously tested functionality. Two controlled experiments were conducted to evaluate the introduction of TDD into a CS1/CS2 course.

2.2 Summary of Results

Some observations from the aforementioned works on integrating testing into programming courses can be summarized as follows:

- Careful structuring of assignments is key in getting students to adopt the test-driven approach naturally.

- The use of adequate automatic grading tools is essential for: (1) reducing the instructor's course load, and (2) providing students with helpful feedback on the adequacy of the testing done in their assignments.

- Simply re-writing course materials to incorporate TDD, even though effective, is not ideal. Re-ordering and re-emphasis of topics is recommended.

- It can be difficult to determine what kind of curriculum changes are required, how drastically projects must change and what will be the effect on the students.

- Aside from the one-time setup cost, instructor effort is not necessarily increased with the introduction of TDL, and in some cases may even decrease thanks to the opportunity of automated grading.

3. Using WReSTT to Support Pedagogy

There have been several approaches used to integrate testing into programming courses as described in the previous section. Although these approaches expect instructors to participate in this process, there needs to be more work done to assist instructors in gaining the necessary knowledge on testing to support the integration. In addition to this knowledge transfer, it is important to complement this integration with appropriate tools, course materials and other resources. In this section we describe an approach consisting of three phases that integrates testing into programming courses.

3.1 Web-Based Repository

Phase one of our approach consists of developing an online portal of learning resources that supports pedagogy in the area of software testing. The main objective of the online portal is to increase the number of users at academic institutions that currently have access to vetted learning materials, including tutorials on software testing tools, that support the integration of testing into programming courses. We have created such a repository known as *Web-based Repository of Software Testing Tools (WReSTT)*[1] [35] that contains tutorials on software testing tools and links to other materials on software testing. WReSTT currently contains learning materials for the following tools:

- *Cobertura* - a free Java tool that calculates the percentage of code accessed by tests [3].

- *CppUnit* - a C++ unit testing framework [13].

- *EclEmma* - a free Java code coverage tool for Eclipse [17].

- *JDepend* - a tool that traverses Java class file directories and generates design quality metrics for each Java package [1].

- *JUnit* - a unit testing framework for the Java programming language [15].

- *SWAT* - the Simple Web Automation Toolkit (SWAT) is a library written in C# designed to provide an interface to interact with several different web browsers [32].

- *Rational Functional Tester* - an automated functional and regression testing tool [18].

Figure 1 shows the web page containing the learning materials for JUnit [15]. The top of the page contains links to the registration page, the forums, events related to the project, sponsors of the project, links to other learning materials, and the contact information for the page. The left side of the page is the sidebar that allows users to navigate around the portal and a list of participating institutions. The center page contains the content for JUnit, including a link to the official JUnit web site, and video tutorials on setting up JUnit in Eclipse and creating test cases for a simple example program. The right side of the page contains the links to other testing resources and recent events.

WReSTT was developed using Drupal [6], a content management system, and uses a four-tier architecture. WReSTT was designed to allow access to four types of users: develop-

---

[1] http://wrestt.cis.fiu.edu/

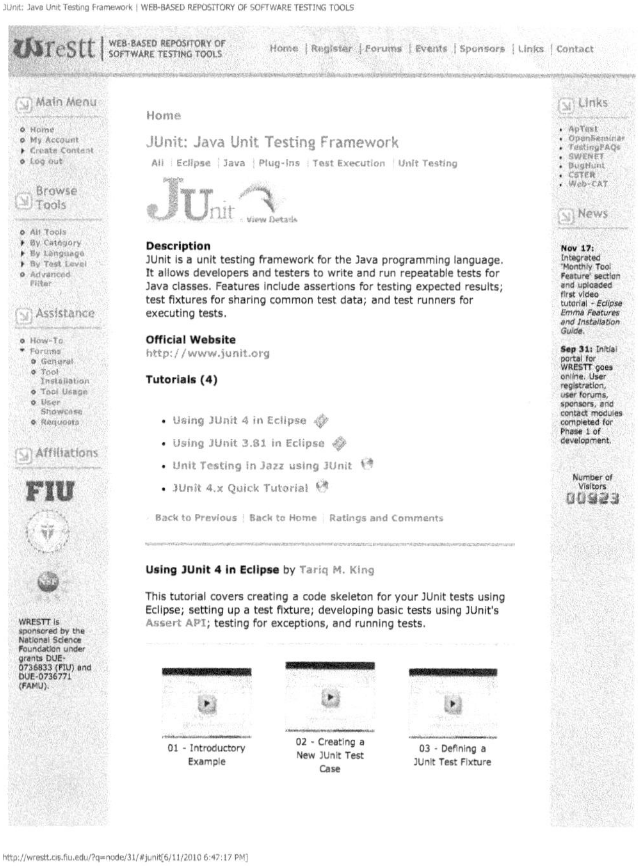

Figure 1. Web page in WReSTT showing the links and some of the tutorials for JUnit.

ers, moderators, instructors and students. Each type of user has access to a different set of facilities in WReSTT, e.g., instructors can monitor how frequently students in their classes access the tutorials for a specific tool. Data is maintained for each type of user thereby allowing the WReSTT team to monitor the use of the repository.

3.2 Instructors Workshop

Phase two of our approach consists of holding a series of annual workshops for instructors that introduce them to software testing and the learning resources available through WReSTT. The main objective of the instructor workshops is to provide a forum where CS/IT instructors can improve their knowledge of software testing and software testing tools to support pedagogy. The outcome for this objective is that instructors participating in a workshop will increase their knowledge of software testing and the use of software testing tools to support pedagogy. More specifically, it is expected that there be an improvement of at least 30% between the pretest and posttest scores of the workshop participants.

Our first workshop was conducted in the spring of 2009 and was attended by 17 instructors from various colleges and universities. The title of the workshop was "The First Workshop on Integrating Software Testing into Program-

ming Courses (CS1-CS3) (WISTPC 2009)". The workshop lasted for two days and during that time the instructors were exposed to the basic concepts of testing and the resources available on WReSTT. The resources on WReSTT presented during the workshop included: EclEmma [17], JUnit [15], SWAT [32], Rational Functional Tester [18] and Web-CAT [9]. Web-CAT is a plug-in-based web application that supports electronic submission and automated grading of programming assignments. The instructors attending the workshop were also introduced to features of WReSTT to support pedagogy including, registration, techniques to browse the tools, and posting to the forums. We present the results of the first workshop in Section 4.

3.3 Integrating Testing into Programming Courses

Phase three of our approach consists of two components. The first component is to perform experiments on integrating testing into programming courses at several academic institutions and making an evaluation of the integration process. The second component involves developing learning materials that can be used by other institutions, and embarking on a broad dissemination plan to get other institutions involved. All learning materials developed will be made available on WReSTT.

The main objectives of integrating testing into programming course are: (a) improve the students' conceptual understanding of the approaches used to test software; and (b) improve their practical software testing skills with respect to the testing tools in WReSTT. The expected outcomes of this objective are: (a) at least 80% of the students exposed to integrating testing into programming courses will be able to describe at least two approaches used to test programs using automated tools; and (b) at least 80% of the students will be able to demonstrate how to use at least two of the automated tools that support the testing techniques in (a).

The research team at Florida International University conducted studies on integrating testing into the CS2 and SE courses with the support of the resources in WReSTT. The general approach used in both courses was non-intrusive, that is, the courses were taught similar to previous classes, but the students in the treatment group were exposed to the learning material available in WReSTT.

In the CS2 course a teaching assistant (TA) was assigned to the course and the TA's responsibilities included: (1) teaching students how to develop unit test cases for their assignments; (2) teaching them how to use the results from code coverage to improve testing their programs; and (3) demonstrating how to use the learning materials for the testing tools on WReSTT. The TA was not available to help the students with understanding their assignments, since the students were expected to use the normal resources for the course, e.g., Professor and other course TAs. In the SE course WReSTT was introduced to the students prior to the topic of software testing being covered. The only requirement added to the course, to encourage students to use the

Question	Instructors' Workshop		Software Engineering Course	
	Pretest	*Posttest*	*Pretest*	*Posttest*
2. Have you ever used tools to support testing of programs?	N(7) Y(5)	N(1) Y(11)	N(15) Y(3)	N(6) Y(12)
3.b.i Unit Testing Tool Proficiency	Avg = 2.7 (6 responses)	Avg = 3.5 (8 responses)	Avg = 4 (1 response)	Avg = 1.7 (8 responses)
3.b.ii Web-based Testing Tool Proficiency	Avg = 3.5 (2 responses)	Avg = 2.6 (7 responses)	NA	NA
3.b.iii Functional Testing Tool Proficiency	Avg = 3.7 (3 responses)	Avg = 2.7 (6 responses)	NA	NA
3.b.iv Code Coverage Tool Proficiency	Avg = 3 (3 responses)	Avg = 3.3 (6 responses)	(0 responses)	Avg = 3 (4 responses)
4. Do you know of any online resources that provide information on software testing?	N(7) Y(5)	N(2) Y(10)	N(11) Y(7)	N(5) Y(13)
6. How beneficial do you think it is to use tools to support the testing of programs?	Avg = 3.9 (11 responses)	Avg = 4.6 (11 responses)	Avg = 4.3 (18 responses)	Avg = 4.6 (18 responses)
8. How well do you know any automated grading tools that encourage students in CS1- CS3 to test their programs before submission?	Avg = 2.2 (12 responses)	Avg = 2.8 (12 response)	NA	NA

Table 1. Results for the closed ended questions in the pretest/posttest instrument. N — No; Y — Yes; Avg — average of scores are out of 5; NA — Not Applicable in this study.

resources in WReSTT, was awarding bonus points to those student teams that used tools to automate the testing of the code for their projects. These tools needed to support unit testing and code coverage. We report on these studies in next section.

4. Case Study

In this section we describe the evaluation studies performed during WISTPC 2009[2], the Fall 2009 CS2 class and the Spring 2010 SE class. The evaluation for WISTPC 2009 focused on the effectiveness of improving the participants' knowledge of software testing and the use of software testing tools to support pedagogy. The studies in the CS2 and SE classes focused on improving the students' practical skills of testing programs by using automated testing tools. In the following sections we describe the instruments used to capture the data, present a summary of the results obtained, and discuss issues related to the evaluation for the studies.

4.1 Data Capture

Workshop: The data collected for the study reported in this paper is based on a pretest/posttest instrument that was administered to the participants of WISTPC 2009. The instrument consisted of nine questions that use both closed and open ended questions. There were four classes of questions: Q(1)-(3) focused on program testing and the use of testing tools, Q(4)-(5) on online resources available to support testing, Q(6)-(7) assessed the importance of tool support for software testing, and Q(8)-(9) knowledge of automated grading tools that encourages testing. The leftmost column of Table 1 shows the closed ended questions from

[2] http://wrestt.cis.fiu.edu/?q=node/27#wistpc09

the pretest/posttest instrument. The instrument was administered to the participants during the introduction session and closing session of the workshop. Seventeen instructors attended the workshop and they came from a cross-section of tertiary US educational institutions. Other evaluation instruments were administered during the workshop but we do not describe them in this paper since they focused on the logistics of the workshop and effectiveness of the presenters.

CS2 and SE Classes: The instruments used to collect data from the students in the CS2 and SE classes included pretest/posttest and for the SE class the grading rubric used during the demonstration of the class project. Thirty-one (31) students in the CS2 class volunteered for the study (treatment group). In the SE class eighteen (18) students participated in the study and were divided into eight (8) teams for the class project. There was no control group for the SE class. The pretest/posttest instrument consisted of seven questions, which were similar to the questions used in the instructors' workshop. The grading rubric contained criteria on the testing tool(s) used, and the type of tool(s) selected i.e., unit testing tool and/or code coverage tool. The testing tools were used mainly to support unit testing of classes during the implementation and testing phases of the project.

4.2 Results

Workshop: The effectiveness of the workshop was evaluated using a pretest/posttest instrument that included questions such as the participants' knowledge and proficiency of various tools and their perceptions of the usefulness of tools to support program testing. Table 1 shows the results for the closed ended questions used in the instrument. Columns 1 shows the question text, Columns 2 and 3 show the results for the pretest and posttest, respectively. Rows with ques-

Question	Instructors' Workshop			
	t	df	sig	Cohen's d
3.b.i Unit Testing Tool Proficiency	-2.449	4	0.070	-1.095
3.b.iii Functional Testing Tool Proficiency	0.200	1	0.874	0.141
3.b.iv Code Coverage Tool Proficiency	1.000	1	0.500	0.707
6. How beneficial do you think it is to use tools to support the testing of programs?	-3.730	10	0.004	-1.125
8. How well do you know any automated grading tools that encourage students in CS1-CS3 to test their programs before submission?	-2.390	10	0.038	-0.721

Table 2. Results after applying paired sample t-tests and Cohen's d effect size on the data collected.

tion numbers 2 and 4 show the number of responses with the value no (N) and yes (Y). The other rows in the table contain the average value (out of 5) for the responses given by the participants. For these questions the Likert scale of 1 to 5 was used, where 1 indicated barely competent, not at all beneficial, or no knowledge of the tool as the case may be, and 5 indicated extremely proficient, extremely beneficial, and very high knowledge about the tool.

At the end of the workshop, the percentage of participants who were exposed to tools that support testing of programs had increased from 58.33% to 91.67%. Similarly, the percentage of participants who were aware of online resources that provide information on software testing increased from 58.33% to 83.33%. Paired samples t-tests and Cohen's d effect size [4] were conducted and calculated respectively to test and measure the difference in the proficiency of using various tools, the perceptions of usefulness of the tools, and knowledge of automated grading tools. Owing to the small sample size and the use of several univariate statistical significance tests, the p-values of the tests were not used for inference [28]. Instead the p-values were simply used as indicators of a possible difference between the pretest and the posttest measurements and the Cohen's d values were used to quantify the magnitude of the difference.

As can be seen from the Table 2 Columns 2 through 5, the perceptions of participants about the usefulness of the tools to support program testing had the maximum effect size (1.12), indicating that there was a positive change of about 112% from before the workshop to after the workshop that the tools are indeed beneficial. Similarly, in their opinion, participants overall became more proficient in the use of unit testing tools (d=1.09) and gained more knowledge in automated grading tools that encourage their students to test their programs before submission (d=.72). However, participants felt that their proficiency level in using the functional testing tool and the code coverage tool worsened after attending the workshop. This is indeed an area of concern.

CS2 and SE Classes: Initially, 31 students volunteered for the study (treatment group) in the CS2 class. Of these, 10 students created user accounts on WReSTT, and the 10 accounts were accessed after registration. None of the students completed the study. It was apparent that students were not motivated to continue using the WReSTT testing resource in completing their assignments unless this was a course requirement and awarded credit for using the testing tools.

The results captured using the pretest and posttest for the SE class are shown in Table 1 Columns 4 and 5. The results show that after exposure to WReSTT there was a significant increase (400%) in the number of students that used tools to support the testing of programs. The contents of Table 1, row with question number 4, indicates that after the treatment more students (180% increase) were able to identify at least one online resource that provided information on software testing. The results for the SE course shown in the table were not statistically significant due either to the sample size or the effect of exposing students to the resources in WReSTT.

The data obtained from the grading rubric and observation of the project demonstrations indicated that five of the eight teams used testing tools during the validation of the team project. The five teams all used unit testing frameworks, these frameworks included JUnit [15], MbUnit [29], and Visual Studio Team System 2008 [26]. Two of the teams also used code coverage tools during testing, these tools included Cobertura [3] and the code coverage tool in Visual Studio Team System 2008 Test Edition [26]. The teams that used the unit testing tools did a better job at writing test cases and testing the overall system. In addition, these teams were more efficient when it came to demonstrating the execution of test cases i.e., they were able to execute the test drivers without any problems. The two teams that used the code coverage tools were able to explain the adequacy of the test cases with respect to the statement coverage achieved during testing. The students in these teams also stated that they were not able to get 100% code coverage due to the time constraints, that is, they did not have enough time to write the number of test cases required to get 100% code coverage.

4.3 Discussion

The expected outcome of the workshop was to improve the participants' knowledge of software testing and the use of software testing tools to support pedagogy by at least 30%. This outcome was achieved for the most part as stated in the previous subsection, specifically in the areas of (1) using tools to support program testing, and (2) being aware of online resources to support software testing. Although not shown in Tables 1 and 2 most participants were able to identify at least one tool to support unit testing, web-based testing, functional testing and code coverage upon completion of the workshop. In addition, most of the participants were also able to identify at least one online resource containing testing resources. A review of the answers to several of the questions on the pretest/posttest instrument revealed that some of the question may have been ambiguous. In the pretest, participants identified unit testing tools, e.g., JUnit [15], as automated grading tools that encourage students in programming courses to test their programs before submission. The results of the posttest revealed that the presentation at the workshop of coverage tools may have to be reviewed. The participants identified JUnit as a coverage tool when performing program testing. This may have been due to the fact that EclEmma [17] was introduced directly after the JUnit presentation and participants did not see the distinction. The presentation on the functional testing tool, Rational Functional Tester [18], appeared to have been overwhelming for the participants.

Introducing students in the SE class to software testing tools addresses the second objective and expected outcome described in Section 3.3. Recall the objective is to improve the students' practical software testing skills with respect to the testing tools in WReSTT. The expected outcome is at least 80% of the students will be able to demonstrate how to use at least two of the automated tools that support the testing techniques. The results obtained during the demonstration of the student projects showed that we have not yet accomplished this objective since only 63% of the student teams (50% of the students) were proficient in using a unit testing tool. These numbers were even lower for the code coverage tool. The reason for this poor result may be attributed to the fact that the course was taught by a PhD student who was teaching the course for the first time.

We plan to repeat the study in a future SE class with a more experienced instructor and continue to offer students incentives for using tools to support testing. We are also modifying the interface to the WReSTT web site to incorporate some of the social networking concepts such as allowing students to create a profile and a list of friends that may participate in testing tutorials. We plan to repeat CS2 class study in Fall 2010 and will integrate testing topics explicitly into the syllabus. Both the instructor and the teaching assistant for the course in the fall attended the recently held workshop for integrating testing in to programming courses (WISTPC 2010).

5. Related Work

Although instructors have been able to introduce testing into their programming courses with some success, there has been limited focus on providing instructors with the knowledge, tools, and guidelines necessary to make such a transition smooth and minimally intrusive. In Section 2 we reviewed several of the works related to integrating testing into programming courses and will not repeat them here. To the best of our knowledge, this is the first work that aims to provide both a central repository of software testing tools, and the training workshops necessary to help instructors successfully integrate these tools into their CS1-CS3 and SE courses. However, some researchers have proposed approaches similar to ours which we now describe as related work.

There have been several workshops and user group sessions on teaching software testing in the computer science course curricula [10, 22, 23]. The annual Workshop on Teaching Software Testing (WTST), Kaner et al. [22, 23], is concerned with teaching many of the practical aspects of university-caliber software testing to both academic and commercial students. Both academics who have experience teaching testing courses, and practitioners who teach professional testing seminars share their experiences and techniques with other instructors and graduate students. The Web-CAT User Group meetings, led by Edwards [10], allow users of an automated grading tool for programming and testing-related assignments to exchange their experiences using the tool, while attracting instructors that may be thinking of adopting the tool. Although not specifically geared towards introductory CS courses, such forums are similar to the WReSTT workshops as they also provide avenues for instructor education on effective software testing techniques and tools.

Lastly, many repositories and tutorials on software testing tools are accessible via the World-Wide Web [12, 25, 34]. These repositories contain a plethora of software testing tools and resources. However, the vast number of testing tools provided by these repositories make them inconvenient for use by instructors. WReSTT offers a practical solution by narrowing the scope of the tools and tutorials to those that both instructors and students have found useful in programming courses.

6. Concluding Remarks

In this paper we presented an approach to integrate testing tools into programming courses by providing a web-based repository of software testing tools, training instructors in the area of testing techniques and tools, and integrating the use of testing tools in various programming courses. The contents and structure of the web-based repository of software testing tools (WReSTT) was described in the paper. We have presented the results of the first instructors' workshop and the first study on integrating testing tools into CS2 and SE courses. We have recently held the second instructors' workshop and are currently performing additional studies in SE classes. Although the first set of results are promising, we are continuing to investigate innovative ways to integrate software testing into programming courses. We expected to redesign the WReSTT site to be more attractive to students and provide them with a features that support team-oriented learning.

Acknowledgments

This work was supported in part by the National Science Foundation under grants DUE-0736833 (FIU) and DUE-0736771 (FAMU). We would like to thank Yali Wu and

Barbara Espinoza and for their assistance in collecting the data, and the reviewers for their insightful comments on how to improve the paper.

References

[1] M. Clark. JDepend, May 2010. http://www.clarkware.com/software/JDepend.htm.

[2] "CNSS". Software 2015: A national software strategy to ensure u.s. security and competitiveness. Technical report, Center for National Software Studies, 2005.

[3] Cobertura Team. Cobertura, May 2010. http://cobertura.sourceforge.net/.

[4] J. Cohen. The earth is round (p < .05). *American Psychologist*, 49(12):997–1003, December 1994. http://web.math.umt.edu/wilson/Math444/Handouts/Cohen94_earth%20is%20round.pdf.

[5] C. Desai, D. S. Janzen, and J. Clements. Implications of integrating test-driven development into cs1/cs2 curricula. *SIGCSE Bull.*, 41(1):148–152, 2009. ISSN 0097-8418.

[6] Drupal Community. Drupal, 2008. http://drupal.org/.

[7] S. H. Edwards. Rethinking computer science education from a test-first perspective. In *Companion of the 18th Annual ACM SIGPLAN Conference on Object-Oriented Programming, Systems, Languages, and Applications (OOPSLA '03)*, pages 148–155, New York, USA, 2003. ACM Press.

[8] S. H. Edwards. Using software testing to move students from trial-and-error to reflection-in-action. In *Proceedings of the 35th SIGCSE Conference*, pages 26–30, New York, NY, USA, 2004. ACM. ISBN 1-58113-798-2.

[9] S. H. Edwards. Web-CAT: the Web-based Center for Automated Testing, 2009. http://web-cat.cs.vt.edu/.

[10] S. H. Edwards and M. A. Perez-Quinones. Web-cat user group, March 2008. BOF session at the 39th SIGCSE Technical Symposium on Computer Science Education.

[11] S. Elbaum, S. Person, J. Dokulil, and M. Jorde. Bug hunt: Making early software testing lessons engaging and affordable. In *ICSE '07: Proceedings of the 29th international conference on Software Engineering*, pages 688–697, Washington, DC, USA, 2007. IEEE Computer Society.

[12] D. Faught. TestingFAQs.org - an information resource for software testers, 2010. http://www.testingfaqs.org/.

[13] M. Feathers. CppUnit, May 2010. http://apps.sourceforge.net/mediawiki/cppunit/.

[14] S. Frezza. Integrating testing and design methods for undergraduates: teaching software testing in the context of software design. *Frontiers in Education, Annual*, 2:S1G1–4, 2002.

[15] E. Gamma and K. Beck. JUnit, 2008. http://www.junit.org/.

[16] M. H. Goldwasser. A gimmick to integrate software testing throughout the curriculum. In *Proceedings of the 33rd SIGCSE Conference*, pages 271–275. ACM, 2002.

[17] M. R. Hoffmann. EclEmma, 2008. http://www.eclemma.org/.

[18] IBM. Rational Functional Tester , 2008. http://www-01.ibm.com/software/awdtools/tester/functional/.

[19] U. Jackson, B. Z. Manaris, and R. A. McCauley. Strategies for effective integration of software engineering concepts and techniques into the undergraduate computer science curriculum. In *SIGCSE '97: Proceedings of the twenty-eighth SIGCSE technical symposium on Computer science education*, pages 360–364, New York, NY, USA, 1997. ACM.

[20] D. S. Janzen and H. Saiedian. Test-driven learning: intrinsic integration of testing into the CS/SE curriculum. *SIGCSE Bull.*, 38(1):254–258, 2006.

[21] E. L. Jones. Integrating testing into the curriculum — arsenic in small doses. *SIGCSE Bull.*, 33(1):337–341, 2001.

[22] C. Kaner, S. Barber, and R. Fiedler. Workshop on teaching software testing: Wtst 7, Jan. 2008. http://www.wtst.org/wtst7.html.

[23] C. Kaner, S. Barber, and R. Fiedler. Workshop on teaching software testing: Wtst 8, Jan. 2009. http://www.wtst.org/wtst8.html.

[24] T. C. Lethbridge, J. Diaz-Herrera, R. J. J. LeBlanc, and J. B. Thompson. Improving software practice through education: Challenges and future trends. In *FOSE '07: 2007 Future of Software Engineering*, pages 12–28, Washington, DC, USA, 2007. IEEE Computer Society.

[25] M. J. Lutz, W. M. McCracken, and S. Mengel. Swenet - network community for software engineering education, Sept 2009. http://www.swenet.org/.

[26] Microsoft Corporation. Visual Studio Team System 2008, May 2010. http://msdn.microsoft.com/en-us/library/ee338734(v=VS.90).aspx.

[27] G. J. Myers. *Art of Software Testing*. John Wiley & Sons, Inc., New York, NY, USA, second edition, 2004. ISBN 0471469122.

[28] P. Natesan and B. Thompson. Extending improvement-over-chance i-index effect size simulation studies to cover some small-sample cases. *Educational and Psychological Measurement*, 67(1):59–72, 2007.

[29] NUnit.org. MbUnit, May 2010. http://www.mbunit.com/.

[30] RTI. The economic impacts of inadequate infrastructure for software testing. Technical Report 7007.011, National Institute of Standards and Technology NIST, May 2002.

[31] S. Schaub. Teaching cs1 with web applications and test-driven development. *SIGCSE Bull.*, 41(2):113–117, 2009.

[32] Ultimate Software. SWAT, 2009. http://sourceforge.net/projects/ulti-swat/.

[33] Wikipedia. xUnit, 2009. http://en.wikipedia.org/wiki/XUnit.

[34] L. Williams and S. Heckman. OpenSeminar - software testing resources, 2010. http://openseminar.org/se/modules/7/index/screen.do.

[35] WReSTT Team. WReSTT: Web-based Repository for Software Testing Tools, 2009. http://wrestt.cis.fiu.edu/.

Panel

Designing the Next Educational Programming Language

Andrew Black

Portland State University

black@cs.pdx.edu

Kim. B. Bruce

Pomona College, CA

kim@cs.pomona.edu

James Noble

Victoria University of Wellington

kjx@ecs.vuw.ac.nz

Abstract

Object-oriented programming is widely taught in introductory computer science courses, however no existing object-oriented programming language is "the obvious choice" for a teaching language. This makes it harder to transfer skills, techniques, and teaching materials between courses and between institutions, and leaves employers uncertain what they should expect new graduates to know. We believe that the object-oriented programming languages community should take this opportunity to work together to select, shape, or design the next educational programming language, and propose a set of principles that the language should follow. The purpose of this panel is to start a dialog with the educational community to refine these principles and to consider next steps.

Categories and Subject Descriptors D.3.0 [*Programming Languages*]: General

General Terms Languages

Keywords object-oriented, introductory programming language, design, teaching

1. Introduction

In the 1980s, computer science and software engineering programs worldwide benefited from a surprising unanimity in their choice of programming language: Pascal. This unanimity benefited students and teachers, who were able to transfer their skills and techniques between institutions, and to use textbooks from a wide variety of sources. It was also of benefit to employers, who were able to rely on graduates having a shared basis in programming, and researchers, who had a *lingua franca* for presenting programs and their designs, analysis, and execution.

With the wide acceptance of object-orientation, the choice of introductory language became much less clear. Smalltalk, the obvious choice, was at first far too resource-intensive for an educational environment. Educators had to choose between "toy" languages (like Budd's *Little Smalltalk* [2]) and proprietary extensions like Object Pascal and Objective C. Just when Smalltalk became a feasible choice, Java and C++ appeared on the scene, further fragmenting the educational community. Java remains the most popular choice, but it is now a large and complex language with many features for supporting professional software engineering, and bearing the scars of 15 years' evolution. New languages such as C♯ and Scala have benefited from what we have learned from Java, but they too are large languages, also designed to support professional practice, and retain duplicative features for backwards compatibility with C++ or Java. Some institutions are adopting Python as a first language; however, others are wary of an introductory language that lacks declarations for data fields and a static type system. Scheme, Haskell, ML, GBeta, Smalltalk, and C++ — to name but a few — have been or are being used as introductory languages in particular contexts, but none has gained the widespread acceptance of Pascal or Java.

The programming languages community has successfully addressed this problem in the past. In the 1950s, there were a large number of attempts to produce an "algorithmic language": these attempts were unified and gave rise to ALGOL-60 [14, 15]. In the 1980s, functional programming languages were similarly diverse: these differences were resolved by designing Haskell [9]. In the 1990s there was at least one attempt to produce an object-oriented teaching language, Blue [11, 12], but it did not succeed, partly because many faculty wanted to use an "industrial-strength" language in their courses, and at that time Java seemed like a viable alternative. Given the last 20 years experience using C++, Java, and other "real" languages for teaching, perhaps it is time to reconsider and instead create a language designed for novices?

Permission to make digital or hard copies of all or part of this work for personal or classroom use is granted without fee provided that copies are not made or distributed for profit or commercial advantage and that copies bear this notice and the full citation on the first page. To copy otherwise, to republish, to post on servers or to redistribute to lists, requires prior specific permission and/or a fee.

SPLASH'10, October 17–21, 2010, Reno/Tahoe, Nevada, USA.
Copyright © 2010 ACM 978-1-4503-0240-1/10/10. . . $10.00

2. Principles

We have yet to begin sketching a language design. Instead we propose the following principles to guide the selection or design of the next educational programming language.

Paradigm The language should support object-oriented programming, because object-oriented languages are widely used in teaching, practice, and research. The language should use garbage collection, because machine-level issues such as storage management are a distraction for novices and should not intrude on teaching introductory programming [10, 12]. The language should have a purely functional subset, because the functional style is becoming increasingly important in teaching programming [6] and functions operating on immutable objects make it much simpler to support concurrency and distribution [5, 7].

Simplicity The language should be simple to learn and simple to use. The language should provide one "fairly clear way" to do most things. Like Modula-3, the language specification should follow C.A.R. Hoare's fifty-page rule [4]. The language should not build-in features that can be satisfactorily added through libraries [1].

Teaching Language The primary goal for the language is introductory teaching, covering at least the first year of study: program design, data structures, and algorithms. Ideally, the language should also be suitable for teaching intermediate topics also: software craft, personal development practices, and software design. If the language finds more advanced uses and employment outside the classroom, that will strengthen the argument to use it for teaching; however, advanced use is not a *primary* design goal.

Language Levels The language should support progressive teaching strategies, which use language subsets and extensions that can be matched to students' experience [6]. For example, one course could start with top-level functions, adding objects, types, mutable state, failure handling, and modules in separate language components. Teaching subsets can also allow error messages to be tailored to suit different levels of experience with the language.

Adaptable The language should support a range of curriculum approaches, including at least objects-first, imperative-first, functions-first, and breadth-first. Particularly because pointers are difficult to learn, the language must support a clear model of object references.

Best Practice The language should capture current best practice in programming and program design. Where possible, common bugs (i.e., those typically illustrated in introductory programming classes, or detected by findbugs) should be prevented by design.

Unsurprising The features of the language should be unsurprising. To quote C.A.R. Hoare again: *"the job of the language designer is consolidation"* [8]. As much as possible, programmers literate in two or more current industrial languages should be able to guess the meaning of code in the new language.

Evidence As far as possible, the design of the language should be based on evidence about features of existing languages — empirical results, formal studies, and teaching experience.

Ease of Implementation A graduate student should be able to construct a simple implementation of the language in six months. An experienced team should be able to construct an optimized, robust implementation in less than a year. Language implementations may be interpreted, compiled statically, or compiled dynamically.

Type System The language should be strongly typed: that is, there should be no unchecked run-time type errors. The language should support teaching with both static and dynamic type systems [3]. The execution of the language should not depend on a program's static types.

Formal Semantics The language should lend itself to reasoning about programs, and potentially to verification, especially as verification and checking technology makes its way into introductory IDEs. For these reasons, the language should have a well-defined formal semantics.

Portable The language and libraries should be independent of implementation technology and infrastructure. The next language should be able to be used on Unix/Linux, Windows, Mac OS X, and directly over the web. Most likely the language should run on top of common existing virtual machines (JVM, CLR, JavaScript).

Concurrency and Parallelism The language must support teaching concurrent and parallel programming, without mandating one particular approach. As a minimum, the language must support teaching message passing and shared memory concurrency, perhaps in different extensions.

Development Environment The language must be supported by novice-friendly development environments (such as BlueJ or Racket) and good debuggers.

Graphics and Multimedia The language should support programming with graphics and multimedia, and event-driven programming. Several teaching approaches rely on graphics and multimedia programming; they are also important application areas in their own right.

Software Engineering The language should support teaching good software engineering practices. This means that the language will need some support for software modularity, for handling failure, and for programming to interfaces. The language should provide explicit support for preconditions, postconditions, and invariants that would be automatically checked during (or before) program execution.

Performance Model The language should support a simple performance model for simple programs. The language must be able to support teaching students "how to predict, control, and/or explain the performance of their programs" [13].

Efficiency Efficiency is not a concern of this language design.

3. Call to Action

We call on the object-oriented programming language community to design a new language to meet this need.

We invite the community to bring together a relatively small group to investigate features to be included, and to solicit feedback on the language as the design progresses. We believe that, to promote and maintain a coherent vision, the core language design must remain vested in a small group. However, the language design process should be as open and transparent as possible, and the resulting language specification should be vested in the community.

4. Panel

Members of the panel will lay out the need for an educational programming language designed for teaching novices object-oriented programming, and trace the history of earlier attempts to design educational languages. The panel will focus on many of the principles that have been agreed to and why they are important for an educational language, as well as how the language design will proceed.

Supporters

In addition to the three authors of this document, the following people support this effort.

- Gilad Bracha, Ministry of Truth.
- John Boyland, University of Wisconsin-Milwaukee.
- Sophia Drossopoulou, Imperial College, London.
- Susan Eisenbach, Imperial College, London.
- Michael Kölling, The University of Kent.
- Doug Lea, SUNY Oswego.
- Jan Vitek, Purdue.

References

[1] A. P. Black, E. Jul, N. Hutchinson, and H. M. Levy. The development of the Emerald programming language. In *History of Programming Languages III*. ACM Press, 2007.

[2] T. Budd. *A Little Smalltalk*. Addison-Wesley, 1987.

[3] L. Cardelli. *Handbook of Computer Science and Engineering*, chapter Chapter 103: Type Systems. CRC Press, 1997.

[4] L. Cardelli, J. Donahue, L. Glassman, M. Jordan, B. Kalsow, and G. Nelson. Modula-3 reference manual. Technical Report Research Report 53, DEC Systems Research Center (SRC), 1995.

[5] J. Dean and S. Ghemawat. MapReduce: simplified data processing on large clusters. *Commun. ACM*, 51(1):107–113, 2008.

[6] M. Felleisen, R. B. Findler, M. Flatt, and S. Krishnamurthi. *How To Design Programs*. MIT Press, 2001.

[7] B. Goetz, T. Peierls, J. Block, J. Bowbeer, D. Holmes, and D. Lea. *Java Concurrency in Practice*. Addison Wesley Professional, 2006.

[8] C. Hoare. Hints on programming language design. Technical Report AIM-224, Stanford Artificial Intelligence Laboratory, 1973.

[9] P. Hudak, J. Hughes, S. P. Jones, and P. Wadler. A history of Haskell: being lazy with class. In *History of Programming Languages III*, pages 12–1–12–55. ACM Press, 2007.

[10] D. H. Ingalls. Design principles behind Smalltalk. *BYTE Magazine*, August 1981.

[11] M. Kölling and J. Rosenberg. Blue — a language for teaching object-oriented programming. In *ACM Conference on Computer Science Education (SIGCSE)*, 1996.

[12] M. Kölling, B. Koch, and J. Rosenberg. Requirements for a first year object-oriented teaching language. In *ACM Conference on Computer Science Education (SIGCSE)*, 1995.

[13] D. Lea, D. F. Bacon, and D. Grove. Languages and performance engineering: Method, instrumentation, and pedagogy. In *SIGPLAN Workshop on Programming Language Curriculum*, 2008.

[14] P. Naur. The European side of the development of ALGOL. In *History of Programming Languages I*, pages 92–139. ACM Press, 1981.

[15] A. J. Perlis. The American side of the development of ALGOL. In *History of Programming Languages I*, pages 75–91. ACM Press, 1981.

Posters & Student Research Chair's Welcome

SPLASH Posters provide an excellent forum for authors to present their work in an informal and interactive setting. Posters are ideal to showcase speculative, late-breaking results or to introduce interesting, innovative work. Posters sessions are highly interactive. They allow authors and interested participants to connect to each other and to engage in discussions about the work presented. Posters provide authors with a unique opportunity to draw attention to their work during the conference. Authors in other SPLASH technical tracks therefore are strongly encouraged to complement their submission with a poster about their work.

After its remarkable success in previous years, SPLASH is again hosting an ACM SIGPLAN Student Research Competition. The competition, sponsored by Microsoft Research, is an internationally recognized venue that enables undergraduate and graduate students to experience the research world, share their research results with other students and SPLASH attendees, and compete for prizes. The ACM SIGPLAN Student Research Competition shares the Poster session's goal to facilitate students' interaction with researchers and industry practitioners, providing both sides with the opportunity to learn of ongoing, current research. Additionally, the ACM SIGPLAN Student Research Competition affords students with experience in both formal presentations and evaluations.

On the following pages, you will find the SPLASH Poster and ACM SIGPLAN Student Research Competition abstracts, covering an interesting mix of topics from the domains of systems, applications, and programming languages. It is worth noting that students participating in the ACM SIGPLAN Student Research Competition submit their abstract as sole author. You can use the abstracts to receive a brief introduction to posters from both the SPLASH Posters and ACM SIGPLAN Student Research Competition on display during the poster session, or to find further information about the author and their work. The ACM SIGPLAN Student Research Competition abstracts can also be used to get a general overview of what the student will be presenting during their formal presentation the day after the poster session.

At this time, I would like to take the opportunity to thank everyone who has participated in making SPLASH Posters and the ACM SIGPLAN Student Research Competition a success. In particular, I would like to acknowledge the contributions of the SPLASH Poster and ACM SIGPLAN Student Research Competition members. The reviews helped considerably to select the best of the submissions, and give valuable feedback to the authors. I would also like to acknowledge Microsoft Research, once again, for their sponsorship of the ACM SIGPLAN Student Research Competition.

I look forward to seeing you in Reno/Tahoe, NV at SPLASH.

James H. Hill, M.S., Ph.D.
SPLASH 2010 Posters Chair
Dept. of Computer and Information Science
Indiana University-Purdue University Indianapolis
hillj@cs.iupui.edu

Designing Language-Oriented Programming Languages

Boaz Rosenan

Dept. of Mathematics and Computer Science
Open University of Israel
brosenan@cslab.openu.ac.il

Abstract

Today, language-oriented programming (LOP) is realized by using either language workbenches or internal DSLs, each with their own advantages and disadvantages. In this work, we design a host language for DSLs with language workbench features, thereby combining the two approaches and enjoying the best of both worlds.

Categories and Subject Descriptors D.3.2 [*Programming Languages*]: Language Classifications—Specialized application languages

General Terms Languages, Design

1. Introduction

Language-oriented programming (LOP) is a software development paradigm that places *domain-specific languages* (DSLs) at the center of the software development process [7, 1, 2]. With LOP, software is developed "from the middle out" [7], starting with a definition of a DSL, or several interoperable DSLs, going "up," implementing the software product using these DSLs, and going "down," implementing the DSLs themselves, and thus making the software executable.

DSLs play a key role in the realization of LOP, and consequently code developed using LOP is declarative, concise and close to the specification it is based on. DSLs are highly expressive, each DSL fitted to the problem domain it is designed to capture. DSLs increase reusability because the same DSL can be used to implement similar but different software products (e.g., different products in a software product line). Reusability is maximized when using several, interoperable DSLs. This increases granularity when sharing DSLs between software products, and thus improves reusability.

Fowler [2] makes a distinction between two kinds of DSLs: *external* and *internal*. *External DSLs* are DSLs that are implemented as compilers, translators or interpreters, and are thus *external* to the programming language in which they are implemented. *Internal DSLs* (also known as *embedded DSLs* [3]) are implemented using definitions in a pre-existing, usually general-purpose programming language, named the *host language*, and are thus internal to the host language.

These two kinds of DSLs have significant trade-offs. On the one hand, external DSLs provide their designers with full freedom in defining the desired syntax and semantics, while internal DSLs are bound to the syntax and semantics of the host language. On the other hand, internal DSLs reuse the compiler or interpreter of the host language, making their implementation much simpler in comparison with external DSLs. Internal DSLs are also better suited for DSL interoperability, since code in different DSLs written over the same host language is actually code in the host language.

Intuitively, external DSLs are better for going "up" in the LOP process, as they are potentially more expressive, while internal DSLs are better for going "down", as they are easier to implement. To make LOP an effective and practical paradigm, there is a need to balance the trade-offs between internal and external DSLs.

2. State of the Art

The limitations of both internal and external DSLs have biased the software industry in favor of conventional programming paradigms over LOP. Recent work attempts to remedy this by bridging the gap between internal and external DSLs through the use of language workbenches. *Language Workbenches* are Integrated Development Environments (IDEs) for defining, implementing and using external DSLs [2]. They address some of the limitations of external DSLs, allowing them to enjoy some of the features traditionally associated with internal DSLs. These include relieving the developer of the need to provide a parser for the DSL and supporting symbolic integration between DSLs [2]. They ease the definition and implementation of external DSLs by applying LOP to these tasks, i.e., by providing *meta-DSLs* for defining and implementing DSLs. A unique feature of language

Copyright is held by the author/owner(s).

SPLASH'10, October 17–21, 2010, Reno/Tahoe, Nevada, USA.
ACM 978-1-4503-0240-1/10/10.

workbenches is the fact they use projectional editing [2] as an alternative to parsing. With this, they edit the DSL abstract syntax tree (AST) directly by projection to a view, where the AST is considered a *model*. DSL interoperability is thus possible through interoperability between models. However, DSL implementation is still hard, and suffers from the limitations of code generation or those of interpretation (whichever is selected as the implementation method). The most notable language workbenches include MPS [1] and the Intentional Domain Workbench [6].

In contrast to language workbenches, our work takes the opposite direction, making internal DSLs enjoy features traditionally associated with external DSLs.

3. Approach

In this work we design a *host language* for *internal DSLs*, with properties currently associated mostly with language workbenches. These properties are: (1) the ability to define and use projectional editing, and (2) the ability to define and enforce *DSL schemas*, i.e., the set of rules defining valid DSL code. We call such a host language a *language-oriented programming language* (LOPL), as it is well suited to support LOP, just like object-oriented programming languages (OOPL) are suited to support OOP.

An LOPL can be based on the semantics of a non-LOP programming language, as long as that language meets certain criteria. First, it should be a good *host language* for internal DSLs. To allow projectional editing it needs to be able to reason about its own code, meaning that the language should to be *homoiconic* or *reflective*, at least to some extent. For projectional editing to be effective, the language should to be *minimalistic*, i.e., have a small number of node types in the AST representation of the code. This is important because projectional editing transforms this AST into visuals. Projection definitions can refer to a small number of node types, such as lists in Lisp, compound terms in Prolog or message-sends in Smalltalk. Projectional editing will be most effective if this small number of types comprises most of the AST. Since the code providing the projection definition needs to run at "design time," i.e., as the DSL code is being edited, *dynamic semantics* makes sense for LOPLs.

Static typing of the host language can help define and enforce DSL schemas. When used with projectional editing, static typing can make the editor "smarter," guiding the user to write valid DSL code to begin with. When using a dynamic host language, the type system can be implemented by using reflection.

4. Validation

To validate our approach, we developed *Cedalion* [4], an LOP language. Cedalion uses logic-programming as its core semantics, taking advantage of the homoiconic, minimalistic, and dynamic nature of Prolog. Another consideration for the selection of logic-programming is the ease of defining operational semantics for DSLs, in a clean and formal way.

Cedalion code is edited using a projectional editor, and the visualization of language constructs is customized by adding clauses to a predicate. Cedalion is statically typed, but its type system is implemented from within the language, as a set of predicates, rather then as part of the language. The predicates comprising the type system are activated from within the visualization mechanism, highlighting erroneous code and suggesting solutions.

LOP is realized in Cedalion by defining, implementing and using internal DSLs, using Cedalion as the host language. A DSL definition includes type signatures and projection definitions for all new constructs, while the implementation usually consists of deductions providing operational semantics for these constructs, as demonstrated by Menzies [5].

5. Conclusion

The main contribution of our work is in presenting a novel approach for bridging the gap between internal and external DSLs. Its uniqueness is in the direction we take: using internal DSLs, taking advantage of the ease of implementing them, while adding language-workbench features (namely projectional editing and enforcing a schema) to provide the freedom and safety in defining DSLs, qualities traditionally associated with external DSLs.

As a paradigm, LOP has a great potential in improving the way we write and maintain software. However, it is not widely adopted due to the limitations of DSLs, internal or external. LOP languages have the potential of changing that, with languages such as Cedalion paving the way.

References

[1] S. Dmitriev. Language oriented programming: The next programming paradigm. *JetBrains onBoard*, 1(2), 2004.

[2] M. Fowler. Language workbenches: The killer-app for domain specific languages. 2005. http://www.martinfowler.com/articles/languageWorkbench.html.

[3] P. Hudak. Building domain-specific embedded languages. *ACM Computing Surveys (CSUR)*, 28(4es), 1996.

[4] D. H. Lorenz and B. Rosenan. Cedalion: A language oriented programming language. In *IBM Programming Languages and Development Environments Seminar*, Haifa, Israel, Apr. 14 2010. IBM Research - Haifa.

[5] T. Menzies. DSLs: A logical approach, 2001. Lecture Notes, EECE 571F, http://courses.ece.ubc.ca/571f/lectures.html.

[6] C. Simonyi, M. Christerson, and S. Clifford. Intentional software. *ACM SIGPLAN Notices*, 41(10):451–464, 2006.

[7] M. P. Ward. Language-oriented programming. *Software-Concepts and Tools*, 15(4):147–161, 1994.

Metamodel Evolution through Metamodel Inference

Qichao Liu

Department of Computer and Information Sciences
University of Alabama at Birmingham
Birmingham, Alabama, USA

qichao@cis.uab.edu

Abstract

Serving as the schema of models, a metamodel defines the abstract syntax of models and the interrelationships between model elements. Model instances are often inaccessible due to metamodel evolution or the metamodel becoming lost. This poster describes our research recovering a metamodel from model instances to support metamodel driven evolution.

Categories and Subject Descriptors I.6.5 [**Simulation and modeling**]: Model Development

General Terms Algorithms, Design, Languages.

Keywords model-driven engineering; domain-specific modeling; grammar inference; metamodel

1. Background and Motivation

Model-driven engineering (MDE) is considered an alternative to traditional code-based software development due to its potential to increase software productivity and quality [1]. In MDE, a user defines a metamodel to represent a schema definition of the syntax and static semantics of a model. A programming language depends on a grammar similar to how a model depends on a metamodel. A metamodel serves as the grammar of a model and both grammars and metamodels represent a schema that defines the syntax of a language.

Under most conditions the schema needs to evolve to address new features resulting in previous instances being orphaned from the new definition. Lämmel and Verhoef [2] [3] addressed the schema evolution problem in the area of programming languages and their approach is to recover grammars from grammar-related artifacts and create a parser for language instances. In MDE, modeling language designers often need to modify metamodels even if they have created many instance models that depend on a previous metamodel. As a result, those former models that depend on the previous metamodel could not be interpreted and used by the modified metamodel which is a waste of model instances in most cases. The common approach toward addressing the metamodel evolution problem is to create model transformations that update existing model instances to be interpretable by the latest metamodel. This work requires that both the old and new metamodel are available for mapping and comparison. However, users usually make changes to a metamodel without restoring the old definition or more generally a metamodel may be lost due to the version change or hard disk crash. Without the old metamodel it is very hard to perform model transformation.

This research addresses the metamodel evolution problem in MDE through metamodel recovery from model instances so that users could perform model transformation with both the old and evolved metamodel and enable the latest metamodel to interpret existing model instances.

2. Limitations of Related Work

Sprinkle and Karsai proposed to update the domain models created by a domain-specific visual language (DSVL) using graph-rewriting (GR) techniques in [4]. Their approach could be considered as rewriting a domain model to another one as required by the new DSVL to make an old model evolve to conform to a new DSVL. However, the domain models created by a DSVL is represented using a graph structure and could not be applied to general domain-specific modeling environment.

There is a variety of work that has been done or is being conducted in the area of grammar inference. Traditionally, schema evolution has been related with the problem of database schema evolution to adapt to changes in the modeled reality. Grammar inference has been applied to DTD and XML Schema extraction from XML documents. For example XTRACT [5] can induce the DTD from a set of XML documents using its regular grammar induction engine. Our research is concentrated on recovering a metamodel from model instances contained in XML documents to address the metamodel schema evolution problem.

Favre [6] presented a generic metamodel-driven process, CacOphoNy that integrates software architecture and MDE. Although their work includes metamodel recovery, the approach requires manual intervention. Our research also incorporates MDE through the effort toward the metamodel recovery problem and our process is semi-automatic beyond the information from the model instances. Javed et al. [7] presented work on metamodel recovery using grammar inference which addressed the more general problem of metamodels lost due to disk crash. The work is greatly limited to a simple metamodel and is also platform dependent. Our research provides a general approach aiming at solving the problem of metamodel evolution.

3. Solution Approach: MRMI

The Metamodel Recovery from Model Instances (MRMI) research described in this poster is the first step toward addressing the metamodel evolution problem. The idea behind metamodel inference is to analyze the characteristics exhibited in the model

Copyright is held by the author/owner(s).
SPLASH'10 October 17-21, 2010, Reno/Tahoe, Nevada, USA.
ACM 978-1-4503-0240-1/10/10.

instances and infer a metamodel. As a result, we have implemented EMARS (Extended MetAmodel Recovery System) [8]. The modeling tool used in EMARS is GME [9] which could export a model instance into XML file and modeling concepts like "model" and "atom" are established as nodes in XML.

The metamodel inference begins with reading in a set of instance models in XML as input. An XSLT translator performs the XSL (Extensible Stylesheet) Transformation [10] on XML files. XSLT uses the XML Path Language (XPath) [11] to retrieve values of interest at specific nodes in an XML document. As the output of the XSLT translator, a domain-specific language (DSL) called model representation language (MRL) containing the essence of model instances is produced. MRL is composed of components of the model instance in a form that could be used by the metamodel inference process. The following is an example for 'model' definition in MRL. As such, a mapping is constructed from model instances in XML to MRL.

model folderX::X
{
* submodels Y, Y;*
* fields fieldX$_1$, fieldX$_2$;*
* connections;*
}

The MRL is then loaded into the LISA language development environment [12]. Our metamodel inference algorithm could infer the corresponding XML representation for MRL having an inferred metamodel as the output. This inferred metamodel could be loaded back into the modeling tool (e.g., GME) to view the previous model instances. Figure 1 illustrates the MRL example in GME.

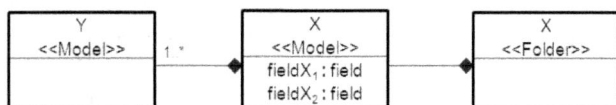

Figure 1. MRL example in GME

4. Results and Contribution

We have tested MRMI successfully on various simple domains with a small number of elements and our inference is almost exactly the same as the original metamodel. We have also tested the approach with some complex domains like ESML [13] with multiple viewpoints. Due to the large number of metamodeling elements used in ESML, the quality of our inference greatly relies on the quality of model instances used to do the inference. We applied MRMI on three instances created by the original ESML metamodel and over 90% of the metamodeling elements of the original are inferred accurately in our inference. Additionally, MRMI currently can infer accurate generalization of elements sharing common features and the cardinality is also inferred as being the same as the original. Detailed experimental results will be presented in the poster.

Our ultimate goal is to infer a metamodel exactly the same as the original which could be used to view model instances just like the original. However, the semantics contained in a metamodel could not be inferred from static model instances except the containment cardinality. Likewise, inference of OCL constraints is not possible with the proposed technique. OCL (Object Constraint Language) is used to describe domain semantics and can only be captured by dynamic class diagrams. Without OCL,

the inferred metamodel may reject model instances legally created by the original metamodel. The related work will be addressed in our future work.

The contribution of this paper is to present MRMI for metamodel recovery from model instances. A host of technologies such as XSLT, LISA and metamodel inference algorithm are utilized to solve the problem of inaccessible existing model instances due to metamodel evolution or the metamodel becoming lost. MRMI is the most succesful work in applying grammar inference in the field of MDE and also serves as our first step towards addressing the metamodel evolution problem.

Acknowledgments

This work is supported in part by NSF award CCF-0811630.

References

[1] Schmidt, D. C.: Guest Editor's Introduction - Model-Driven Engineering. IEEE Computer, vol. 39, no. 2, Feb. 2006, pp. 25-31.

[2] Lämmel, R., Verhoef, C.: Semi-automatic grammar recovery. Software-Practice & Experience, vol. 31, no. 15, Dec. 2001, pp.1395-1448.

[3] Lämmel, R., Verhoef, C.: Cracking the 500 language problem. IEEE Software, vol. 18, no. 6, Dec. 2001, pp.78-88.

[4] Sprinkle, J., Karsai, G.: A domain-specific visual language for domain model evolution. Journal of Visual Languages and Computing, vol. 15, no. 3-4, Aug. 2004, pp. 291-307.

[5] Garofalakis, M. N., Gionis, A., Rastogi, R., Seshadri, S., Shim, K.: XTRACT - A system for extracting document type descriptors from XML documents. In Proceedings of the ACM SIGMOD International Conference on Management of Data, ACM Press, Dallas Texas, USA, May. 2000, pp. 165-176.

[6] Favre, J-M.: CacOphoNy - Metamodel driven architecture reconstruction. In Proceedings of the 11th Working Conference on Reverse Engineering, Nov. 2004, pp. 204-213.

[7] Javed, F., Mernik, M., Gray, J., Bryant, B.: MARS - A metamodel recovery system using grammar inference. Information and Software Technology, vol. 50, no. 9-10, Aug. 2008, pp.948-968.

[8] Liu, Q., Bryant, B.R., Mernik, M.: Metamodel recovery from multi-tiered domains using extended MARS. In Proceedings of the 34th Annual International Computer Software and Applications Conference, Seoul, South Korea, Jul. 2010, pp. 279-288.

[9] The Generic Modeling Environment, http://www.isis.vanderbilt.edu.

[10] Clark, J.: XSL Transformations (XSLT) (Version 1). W3C Technical Report, Nov. 1999, http://www.w3.org/TR/1999/REC-xslt-19991116.

[11] Clark, J., DeRose, S.: XML path language (XPath) (Version 1.0). W3C Technical Report, Nov. 1999, http://www.w3.org/TR/1999/REC-xpath-19991116.

[12] Mernik, M., Lenič, M., Avdičaušević, E., Žumer V.: LISA - An interactive environment for programming language development. In Proceedings of the 11th International Conference on Compiler Construction, Apr. 2002, pp. 1-4.

[13] Karsai, G., Neema, S., Sharp, D.: Model-driven architecture for embedded software - A synopsis and an example. Science of Computer Programming, vol. 73, no. 1, Sep. 2008, pp.26-38.

Model Scalability
Using a Model Recording and Inference Engine

Yu Sun
Department of Computer and Information Sciences
University of Alabama at Birmingham
Birmingham, AL 35294

yusun@cis.uab.edu

Abstract
Model scalability is traditionally supported by manual editing or writing model transformation rules. However, this process presents challenges to those who are unfamiliar with a model transformation language or metamodel definitions. This poster describes an approach to scale models by recording and analyzing demonstrated operations by end-users.

Categories and Subject Descriptors D.2.2-2.6 [**Software Engineering**]: Design Tools and Techniques; Programming Environments; I.6.5 [**Simulation and Modeling**]: Model Development

General Terms Algorithms, Design, Languages.

Keywords Model scalability, demonstration, MT-Scribe.

1. Introduction
In software engineering, scalability is a significant property to reflect the ability of a system "to accommodate an increasing number of components, elements, and objects, to process a growing amount of work load in a graceful manner, and to handle enlargement readily" [1]. Enabling a reliable scale-up process is crucial for the long-term success of a system.

Recently, with the increasingly wider usage of models in software systems, model scalability has emerged as an important challenge. For instance, system design models (e.g., UML design models) often need to be scaled up to address large-scale system requirements and evaluate design decisions among a set of possible alternatives. In the context of Model-Driven Engineering, models can be used to describe and generate a software system (e.g., code generation from domain-specific models). Scaling these models often involves enlarging the actual system directly. Models can also play important roles in software maintenance (e.g., runtime models used to control and manage applications running in the cloud). Therefore, it is quite common to enlarge a model for the purpose of scaling application deployment and configuration.

While a number of modeling tools have already been developed to create and edit models for different purposes, a specific function to scale models has not been well-supported. In most situations, models are manually scaled by the basic operations provided by the editing environment. Manual scaling is often tedious and error-prone, especially when the model to be scaled is large and complex or the scaling process involves a tremendous amount of manual operations.

An alternative to efficiently scale models is to use model transformation languages [4], which are high-level domain-specific languages that can be used to specify model transformation tasks. The scaling process can be automated further, because scaling up a model from a base state to a complex state is in fact a model transformation process.

Although model transformation languages are very powerful and expressive to handle various kinds of model scalability tasks, scaling models using a transformation language is not always the perfect solution, due to the steep learning curve of the languages and the need to deeply understand the abstract syntax of the models (i.e., the metamodel definitions). Because many potential model users (e.g., requirements engineers, domain experts and cloud computing administrators) are not necessarily software engineers or programmers, learning transformation languages and understanding the formal metamodel definitions may be beyond their capability. Such challenges may prevent some of these model users from realizing model scalability tasks for which they have extensive domain experience.

The research described in this poster aims to simplify the implementation of model scaling, so that general end-users are enabled to realize model evolution tasks in an automated manner, without knowing any model transformation languages or metamodel definitions.

2. Related Work
The model scalability issue was first introduced in [2], where the authors used a model transformation framework to handle the model scaling task. As mentioned in the previous section, the major problems of this approach come from the inherent challenge of learning the transformation language, as well as understanding the metamodel definitions when specifying transformation rules.

Model Transformation By Example (MTBE) [5] is an innovative approach to address the challenges inherent from using model transformation languages. Instead of writing transformation rules manually, users are asked to build a prototypical set of interrelated mappings between the source and target model instances, and then the metamodel-level transformation rules are semi-automatically generated. This approach simplifies model transformation implementation to some extent, but is not appropriate for model scalability tasks, because: 1) it focuses on direct concept mapping between two different domains rather than scaling a model within the same domain; 2) they do not support attribute transformation, preventing the automatic setup of attributes needed in many scenarios. Another work has been described by Brosch et al. in [6], which uses an example-based approach to address model refactoring tasks. Because it supports model transformation within the same domain, it also has potential to be applied in model scalability scenarios. However, the user feedback step may not be at the proper level of abstraction in their approach, and complex attribute transformation is not provided.

Copyright is held by the author/owner(s).

SPLASH'10 October 17–21, 2010, Reno/Tahoe, Nevada, USA.
ACM 978-1-4503-0240-1/10/10.

3. Solution Approach: MTBD

Our solution to enable general users to implement model scalability tasks without learning a model transformation language or understanding metamodel definitions is to apply demonstration-based model transformation. Model Transformation By Demonstration (MTBD) [7] is a new model transformation approach that initially focused on model refactoring problems. Instead of manually using transformation languages to specify transformation rules, users are asked to demonstrate how the model transformation should be done by directly editing the source model to simulate the transformation process step-by-step. During the demonstration process, a recording and inference engine captures all the user operations and infers the user's intention in a model transformation task, generating a transformation pattern that summarizes the precondition of a transformation (i.e., *where* a transformation should be done) and the actions needed in a transformation (i.e., *how* a transformation should be done). This generated pattern can be executed by the engine in any model instance to carry out the same transformation process.

Considering model scalability tasks as model transformations, we have used MTBD to demonstrate how to scale a model and generate the pattern to automate the process. However, two major problems in the previous implementation of MTBD prevented it from being a practical approach to support model scalability. Firstly, the generated pattern is not generic. In other words, it works like a macro to exactly repeat the recorded operations. For instance, if we demonstrate how to scale up a model from 5 elements to 10 elements, the generated pattern will only be capable of processing another model with 5 elements and enlarging it to 10, but cannot work in any other cases. In addition, users are not enabled to provide more specific precondition to restrict which part of a model to scale up.

To solve these problems and make MTBD applicable to model scalability tasks, we extended the previous work in two ways. An additional step is performed after operation recording to enable users to identify generic (repeatable) operations in the demonstration. For example, increasing the elements from 5 to 10 requires a number of repeated operations to replicate the source model. Users can simply select these operations and the engine will automatically infer and recognize the smallest set of actions needed to replicate one extra element. Thus, the final generated transformation pattern is capable of increasing any number of new elements by repeating this set of operations. Furthermore, to specify a more restrictive precondition, users are asked to give additional feedback on the elements they just operated in the demonstration. To shield users from knowing metamodel definitions, they can simply select the specific element and define the desired condition for it.

4. Results and Contribution

The idea and extension of MTBD has been implemented as a plug-in called MT-Scribe for GEMS (Generic Eclipse Modeling System) [8], which is a modeling tool hosted within Eclipse. In our approach, users are only involved in editing a model instance to demonstrate the transformation process and give feedback after the demonstration. Although users now need to provide more information than the previous version, all of the other procedures (i.e., optimization, inference, generation, execution, and correctness checking) are automated without any manual refinement. No model transformation languages are used and the generated transformation patterns are invisible to users. Therefore, users are completely isolated from knowing a model transformation language and the metamodel definition. In addition, complex attribute operations can be inferred as well, making our approach more practical and transparent to end-users when compared to the related works.

We have applied our approach to successfully implement several practical model scalability tasks in different domains, without writing any transformation rules or code. To better evaluate the approach, we accomplished two examples using MTBD, which were already done by model transformation languages in [2] and [3]. It is found that the first example on Stochastic Reward Nets domain consumed 36 operations in the demonstration while over 170 lines of C-SAW code was used previously; 17 operations were demonstrated in another example in Event QoS Aspect domain, which was implemented by 32 lines of C-SAW code.

In the current implementation of MTBD, a tradeoff exists between simplicity and functionality, because a user's demonstration and feedback are not as expressive and accurate as the specific written transformation rules in a well-defined language. Adding additional feedback may undermine the simplicity of this approach. Therefore, finding a balance between the two to make MTBD as practical and powerful as possible is the main issue to be considered in future work.

5. Acknowledgement

This work is supported by an NSF CAREER award (CCF-0643725).

6. References

[1] Bondi, A.: Characteristics of scalability and their impact on performance. In Proceedings of the 2nd International Workshop on Software and Performance, Ottawa, Ontario, Canada, pp. 195-203, 2000.

[2] Gray, J., Lin, Y., Zhang, J., Nordstrom, S., Gokhale, A., Neema, S., Gokhale, S.: Replicators: Transformations to address model scalability. In Proceedings of the International Conference on Model-Driven Engineering Languages and Systems, Montego Bay, Jamaica, pp. 295-308, 2005.

[3] Lin, Y., Gray, J., Zhang, J., Nordstrom, S., Gokhale, A., Neema, S., Gokhale, S.: Model Replication: Transformations to Address Model Scalability. Software: Practice and Experience, vol. 38, no. 14, pp. 1475-1497, 2008.

[4] Sendall, S., Kozaczynski, W.: Model transformation - The heart and soul of model-driven software development. IEEE Software, Special Issue on Model Driven Software Development, vol. 20, no. 5, pp. 42-45, 2003.

[5] Balogh, Z., Varró, D.: Model transformation by example using inductive logic programming. Software and Systems Modeling, vol. 8, no. 3, pp. 347-364, 2009.

[6] Brosch, P., Langer, P., Seidl, M., Wieland, K., Wimmer, M., Kappel, G., Retschitzegger, W., Schwinger, W.: An Example is Worth a Thousand Words: Composite Operation Modeling By-Example. In Proceedings of International Conference on Model Driven Engineering Languages and Systems, Denver, CO, 2009.

[7] Sun, Y., White, J., Gray, J.: Model transformation by demonstration. In Proceedings of International Conference on Model Driven Engineering Languages and Systems, Denver, CO, pp. 712-726, 2009.

[8] Generic Eclipse Modeling System (GEMS). http://www.eclipse.org/gmt/gems/

Verifying Configuration Files

Ciera Jaspan

Carnegie Mellon University

ciera@cmu.edu

Abstract

Configuration files are commonly used to create applications by gluing together new or existing components. However, components may be missing, misconfigured, or connected improperly, resulting in exceptions and unusual runtime behavior. This research contributes a mechanism to statically verify configuration files alongside the component code.

Categories and Subject Descriptors   D.2.4 [*Software Engineering*]: Software/Program Verification

General Terms   Verification

Keywords   configuration files, relationships

1. Configuration Files

Configuration files are used by many software frameworks and platforms to describe how to connect components together in new ways to create an application. Apache Tomcat, Eclipse, Spring, and Ruby on Rails, all require developers on their platform to use configuration files to describe the component they are developing and how it connects with other components. While XML [3] is frequently used for these configuration files (and is by all the systems described above), systems may also define configuration files in a proprietary format.

When XML is used, the system will frequently provide a schema which describes the appropriate layout of the configuration file. However, these schemas can only be used to check the layout of the configuration file; they cannot check for more detailed semantic problems that might cause an exception or unexpected runtime behavior.

As an example, consider how a developer uses the Spring Web Application framework to create a simple web application [2]. In this framework, a developer must provide several components:

Listing 1. Definition of the Controller

```
1  package edu.cmu.cs.classquiz.web;
2  import org.springframework.web.servlet.mvc.*;
3
4  public class AddQuestionController
5    extends SimpleFormController {
6      protected ModelAndView onSubmit(Object command)
7        throws Exception {...}
8  }
```

Listing 2. Definition of the Validator

```
1  package edu.cmu.cs.classquiz.bus;
2  import org.springframework.validation.*;
3
4  public class QuestionValidator implements Validator {
5      public boolean supports(Class clazz) {
6        return clazz.equals(QuestionCommand.class);
7      }
8      public void validate(Object target, Errors errors) {...}
9  }
```

- A *controller* that handles submissions to a web form, as shown in Listing 1.

- A *command object* that represents the data being submitted to the web form.

- A *validator* that checks that the data submitted is valid, as shown in Listing 2.

These three components are connected through an XML file, such as the one shown in Listing 3.

While this configuration file appears simple, there are several constraints hidden within it:

- Since the class `AddQuestionController` derives from `SimpleFormController`, it must describe the properties shown in Listing 3.

- The type of the element referenced at line 6 in Listing 3 must be derived from `Validator`.

- The `Validator` must be able to validate the type defined at line 7, by way of returning true when its `supports` method is called.

Of course, all the classes described must exist, and there are more constraints about the other properties in lines 8-11. Unfortunately, the DTD schema declared in line 2 can only be used to check layout and not any interconnections between the XML elements or between XML elements and other code. Breaking any of the above constraints causes a

Copyright is held by the author/owner(s).

SPLASH'10,   October 17–21, 2010, Reno/Tahoe, Nevada, USA.

ACM 978-1-4503-0240-1/10/10.

Listing 3. Snippet of a Spring config file

```
1   <xml version="1.0" encoding="UTF-8"?>
2   <!DOCTYPE beans PUBLIC ''-//SPRING//DTD BEAN//EN'' ''http://www.springframework.org/dtd/spring-beans.dtd''>
3   <beans>
4     <bean id=''addQuestionValidator'' class=''edu.cmu.cs.classquiz.bus.QuestionValidator''/>
5     <bean id=''addQuestionForm'' class=''edu.cmu.cs.classquiz.web.AddQuestionController''>
6       <property name=validator><ref bean=''addQuestionValidator''/></property>
7       <property name=''commandClass''><value>edu.cmu.cs.classquiz.bus.QuestionCommand</value></property>
8       <property name=''commandName''><value>newQ</value></property>
9       <property name=''sessionForm''><value>true</value></property>
10      <property name=''formView''><value>add_question</value></property>
11      <property name=''successView''><value>view_questions.html</value></property>
12    </bean>
13  </beans>
```

runtime error either when the application is loaded, or worse, when the controller is invoked by a user submitting a form.

2. Collaboration Constraints and Relationships

The constraints described above are an example of a *collaboration constraint*, a state-based restriction on how multiple objects may interact. Prior work on collaboration constraints has used the FUSION tool to statically analyze code for violations of collaboration constraints [1]. In the FUSION system, framework developers specify collaboration constraints using *relationships*. A relationship is a user-defined predicate over objects that describes how they are related. For example, a relationship called Validator could connect together a `Validator` and a `SimpleFormController`. These relationships can then be used in logical predicates to describe pre- and post-conditions of operations.

This same specification system can be used to describe the collaboration constraints in configuration files. For example, there are three relationships between the validator, the controller, and the command: Validator(Validator, SimpleFormController), Validates(Validator, Class), and Submits(SimpleFormController, Class). Using these three relationships, the last constraint above can be specified as:

ctrlr instanceof SimpleFormController ⇒
   (Validator(valid, ctrlr) ∧ Validates(valid, cls) ∧
   Submits(ctrlr, cls))

That is, whenever, there is an object of type `SimpleFormController`, it must have a validator. Additionally, that validator must validate commands of the same type as the controller is submitting.

3. Querying Relationships

In [1], relationships are derived from the post-conditions of operations. For example, the Validates relationship would be derived as a post-condition of the `Validator.supports` method. However, the relationships Validator and Submits are *only* described in the configuration file.

To retrieve relationships from XML-based configuration files, the FUSION system allows framework developers to write XQuery that describes the relationships. Listing 4

shows sample XQuery code that retrieves the Validator relationship from any Spring configuration file. To verify this program, FUSION simply runs the XQuery to retrieve all the relationships from the configuration files and then runs the static analysis on the rest of the program as normal.

Listing 4. XQuery to retrieve the Validator relationship

```
1   let $beans := doc($doc)/beans/.
2   for $bean in $beans/bean*
3   let $validator in $bean/property[name="validator"]/ref
4   where isSubtype(type($bean),
5     "org.springframework.web.servlet.mvc.SimpleFormController")
6   return <Relationship name="Validator">
7         <Object name ="{name($validator)}"
8         type="{type($validator)}"/>
9         <Object name="{name($bean)}" type="{type($bean)}"/>
10     </Relationship>
```

4. Future Work

While this solution works, it is far from ideal. The XQuery in Listing 4 depends on several developer-defined functions, like type and name, in order to retrieve semantic information that is not built into XML. In particular, XML is missing concepts such as subtyping and object identity. As each framework may have its own XML semantics for these concepts, there is no general way to specify them in XML.

This is perhaps not a fault of the solution to use XQuery to retrieve relationships, or even of XML, but of using XML for configuration files. XML is a data format language, but configuration files do not describe a data format but a program. Therefore, configuration files should be written in a programming language, complete with a semantics that is interoperable with the semantics of the component programming language. Understanding the constraints and relationships in existing XML files is a first step towards the larger goal of creating a true configuration language.

References

[1] C. Jaspan and J. Aldrich. Checking framework interactions with relationships. In *ECOOP*, 2009.

[2] SpringSource. Spring Web Application Framework. http://www.springsource.org/.

[3] World Wide Web Consortium. Extensible Markup Language. http://www.w3.org/XML/.

OOGIE: Ownership Object Graph Interactive Editor

Talia Selitsky

Department of Computer Science,
Wayne State University
talias@wayne.edu

Abstract

We propose an interactive editor which allows developers to refine an initially extracted object graph into a hierarchical graph that matches their mental model of the runtime structure. The developer can expand or collapse selected hierarchies to control the level of visual detail. Such views of the runtime structure can be useful for code modification tasks.

Categories and Subject Descriptors D.2.3 [*Software Engineering*]: Coding Tools and Techniques—Object-oriented programming

General Terms Experimentation, Documentation

1. Problem and Motivation

Software architecture is important for developers to gain an understanding of the high-level structure of large code systems. This information is important for software evolution tasks such as fixing bugs, adding functionality, optimizing performance, and identifying security vulnerabilities. One type of software architecture view, or way of seeing the code, is the runtime view, which abstracts sets of objects into components and data structures. This is useful for tasks related to performance, reliability and security [1].

Recent work has demonstrated that the extraction of sound run-time architecture extraction from dynamic systems is possible [3]. Though the initial extraction does make a good estimate of the developer's mental model of the code [1], there are many possible decompositions. Tool support is needed to allow developers to refine the initial extraction into a decomposition that *better* fits their mental model.

2. Background

In hierarchical *ownership* object graphs, objects have nested domains, and objects representing sub-architecture. Rele-vant objects appear in the top-level domains. This type of graph has *ownership domains* which is an abstraction of the software code, that represents a conceptual group of objects. There are policies that govern how domains can reference other objects in other domains. Each object belongs to a single ownership domain that does not change at runtime. Each object can declare one or more public or private domains to hold internals objects. Object domains support hierarchy.

3. Related Work

We are developing our tool for the Scholia approach [3]. Scholia extracts an object graph that provides architectural abstraction by ownership hierarchy and by types.

A previous study was done to investigate whether diagrams depicting the runtime structure of objects in a system at compile time is useful. Abi-Antoun et al. found that developers do ask questions about object structure, such as containment, ownership, and aliasing. The study demonstrated that understanding runtime structure, e.g., object diagrams, is important in object-oriented code [2]. Since developers do ask questions that object graphs answer, improving object graph extraction would be helpful to developers since it could help them answer these questions.

Another study was done that revealed that developers do think in terms of objects and relations. The study also suggested that an extracted object diagram might not match a developers mental model of object structure exactly, and what kind of tool support could help the developer iteratively refine the initial object graph to better match their mental model of the runtime object-structure [1]. This study is what led us to the requirements for iterative refinement.

4. Uniqueness of the Approach

Our contribution is the creation of a tool that enables a developer to iteratively refine an object graph to better match their mental model. Developers impose a conceptual hierarchy on runtime objects. Hierarchy provides architectural abstraction, whereby architecturally significant objects appear near the top of the hierarchy and data structures are further down. Having obtained an hierarchical graph, a developer can control the level of visual detail by expanding and collapsing the sub-structures of selected objects.

Copyright is held by the author/owner(s).

SPLASH'10, October 17–21, 2010, Reno/Tahoe, Nevada, USA.
ACM 978-1-4503-0240-1/10/10.

To allow for iterative refinement, our tool supports the following features:

- Manipulate domains: The developer can divide the architecture into tiers of components. The developer can create new domains, and merge existing domains.
- Manipulate the object hierarchy: The developer can change the way that objects are grouped into components. She can move objects between domains, including domains from different tiers.
- Abstract objects by type: The initial extracted object graph creates a component for every type of object at every level in which it is created, which may be excessive. The tool supports operations that merge components into one and split a into several components, each of which includes different types of objects
- Summarize objects as connectors: Connectors are often treated as references between objects. But connectors that are higher level are in fact implemented by some objects in the program. For this reason, one of the requirements is an operation to treat one or more objects as a connector.

5. Results and Contributions

Tool implementation. We have developed a tool, OOGIE, that allows developers to refine an initial object graph into a hierarchical graph. Our tool consists of two parts. The left-hand side displays the objects and their domains in a hierarchical form. The right-hand side represents the software as a hierarchical object graph (see Fig. 1, where edges between objects are not shown). Our tool has the following features:

- Drag-and-drop objects: the developer can move objects between domains by dragging them from one domain in the tree to another. This change is reflected in the graph so that architects can better visualize the changes.
- Rename domains: object domain names are given through annotations. The name of the domain can be changed in order to better fit role of the domain.
- Collapse/expand sub-structures: The developer can choose to view an object's sub-structure, or hide it.

Example. We illustrate our approach on MicroDraw, which is representative of JHotDraw, an open source framework [5] which follows the Model-View-Controller architecture [4]. MODEL, VIEW, and CONTROLLER are the top-level tiers (Fig. 1).

An automated extraction algorithm extracts a mostly flat object graph, where all the objects are in one top-level tier. The automated extraction might determine however that some objects are strictly encapsulated within others. For example, it determines that the fSelectionListener object is owned by the drawingView object, and thus appears nested inside it. Then the developer decides to convey the Model-View-Controller design pattern. So she renames the top-level tier to MODEL and adds two other top-level domains, VIEW and CONTROLLER. She then drags some of the objects from the MODEL domain to either VIEW or CONTROLLER. Finally, the developer chooses to expose the sub-architecture

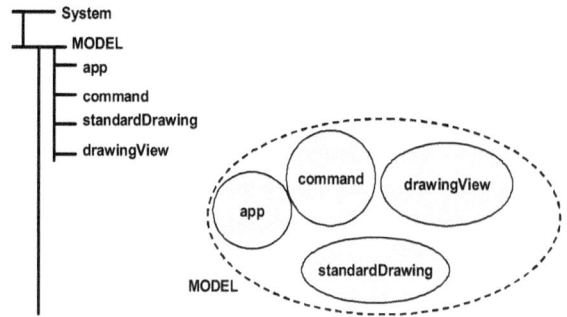

Figure 1. Initial extracted object graph of MicroDraw.

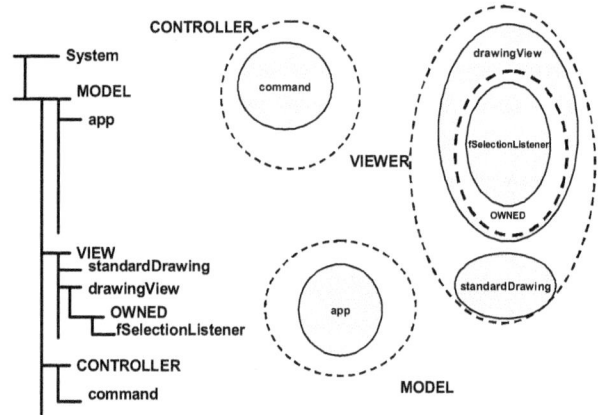

Figure 2. Object drawingView's sub-architecture.

of the drawingView object (Fig. 2), in order to highlight that the drawingView listens to notifications from other objects, such as command. This information would be valuable for another developer performing a code modification task.

Evaluation. We first did a cognitive dimensions analysis which exposed some weaknesses in the tool. We then conducted a pilot study with one subject who was already familiar with the testing code. From the pilot study, we found problems with the usability of the tool which we plan on addressing. In the future, we plan on conducting first a user study, and then a field study to test whether outside developers will be able to use our interactive editor to refine an extracted architecture to better fit their mental model.

References

[1] Abi-Antoun, M., Selitsky, T., and LaToza, T. Developer Refinement of Runtime Architectural Structure. In *SHARK*, 2010.

[2] Abi-Antoun, M., Ammar, N. and LaToza, T. Questions about Object Structure during Coding Activities. In *CHASE*, 2010.

[3] Abi-Antoun, M. and Aldrich, J. Static Extraction and Conformance Analysis of Hierarchical Runtime Architectural Structure using Annotations. In *OOPSLA*, 2009.

[4] Gamma, E., Helm, R., Johnson, R., and Vlissides, J. Design Patterns: Elements of Reusable Object-Oriented Software. Addison-Wesley, 1994.

[5] JHotDraw. www.jhotdraw.org, 1996. Version 5.3.

Extending Abstract GPU APIs to Shared Memory

Ferosh Jacob

University of Alabama, Department of Computer Science
Tuscaloosa, Alabama, USA
fjacob@ua.edu

Abstract

Parallel programming is used extensively for general-purpose computations. However, performance of parallel APIs varies for a given problem and a given architecture. This gives rise to the need for having an abstract way to express the parallel problems. This poster presents a new approach through which programmers can access these APIs without having to focus on the technical or platform-specific details. Our earlier approach of Abstract Application Programming Interface (API) targeted for Graphical Processing Unit (GPU) programming is extended to shared memory using OpenMP.

Categories and Subject Descriptors D.1.3 [*Concurrent Programming*]: Parallel programming

General Terms Algorithms, Design, Languages

1. Introduction

Parallel programming can be defined as the creation of code for computations that can be executed simultaneously. Currently, in order to write a program that will execute a block of code in parallel, a programmer must learn a parallel programming Application Programming Interface (API) that can be used to describe the computation. Even after the execution, the programmer must use other APIs or frameworks to evaluate the performance of their parallel program in other platforms.

Graphical Processing Units (GPUs) provide an excellent platform for executing parallel programs. In our earlier work [1], we introduced Abstract APIs for GPU programming. With Abstract APIs, GPU programs can be expressed in an abstract way ignorant of CUDA[1], or OpenCL[2] details.

[1] http://www.nvidia.com/object/CUDA_home_new.html

[2] http://www.khronos.org/OpenCL/

In this poster, we introduce a shared memory programming language to the Abstract APIs as a first-step toward enabling traditional C/Java programmers in writing parallel programs. With this new approach, a programmer can 1) select a block of code and specify the architecture on which it is to execute in order to understand the performance concerns, 2) set default values for the GPU configuration parameters in case of GPU execution, 3) generate CUDA, OpenCL, or OpenMP code. An analysis of CUDA and OpenCL was carried out and is explained in Section 2. The design details are explained in Section 3. This paper concludes by discussing some of the related works in Section 4.

2. Analysis of GPU and OpenMP programs

The analysis was done with the goal of verifying whether the CUDA and OpenCL programs could be represented by an Abstract API. In the CUDA analysis, priority was given to the data flow of a GPU program, while OpenCL was analyzed to identify the templates used in an OpenCL program.

Program analysis using CUDA and OpenCL: Data flow in the current context can be defined as the flow of data from GPU to CPU (or vice versa), the flow of data between multiple threads, and the flow of data within the GPU (e.g., shared to global or constant). As a general rule, for a GPU call from a CPU, the input variables should be copied from CPU to GPU before the GPU execution and output variables should be copied back to the CPU after execution. There can be exceptions as revealed by the analysis. For the analysis, 42 kernels were selected from 25 randomly selected programs that are provided as code samples from the installation package of NVIDIA CUDA (Detailed analysis of the programs can be found here[3]). OpenCL supports the execution of programs in heterogeneous platforms (e.g., both GPUs and CPUs). Every OpenCL program includes a considerable amount of code that is used to initialize a program. As with the data flow analysis, 15 programs were randomly selected from the code samples that are shipped with the NVIDIA OpenCL installation package. From the OpenCL examples, to make OpenCL programming easier and faster,

Copyright is held by the author/owner(s).

SPLASH'10, October 17–21, 2010, Reno/Tahoe, Nevada, USA.
ACM 978-1-4503-0240-1/10/10.

[3] http://cs.ua.edu/graduate/fjacob/software/analysis/

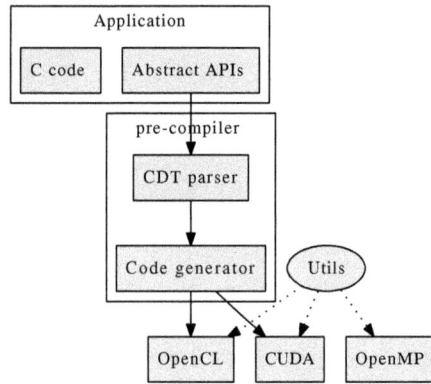

Figure 1. Design diagram for the Extended Abstract API

```
1  // Starting the parallel block  named block_1
2  parallelstart(transpose);
3
4  // Use of abstract API getLevel1
5  int xIndex = getLevel1();
6  // Use of abstract API getLevel2
7  int yIndex = getLevel2();
8
9  if (xIndex < width && yIndex < height){
10     int index_in  = xIndex + width * yIndex;
11     int index_out = yIndex + height * xIndex;
12     odata[index_out] = idata[index_in];
13 }
14 // Ending the parallel block
15 parallelend(transpose);
```

Figure 2. Abstract API representation of matrix transpose

the steps identified can be written as functions and included as libraries with the newly written code.

Supporting OpenMP: From the GPU examples, any GPU call can be considered as a three-step process: 1) copy or map the variables before the execution, 2) execute on the GPU, and 3) copy back or unmap the variables after the execution. An abstract representation of the three steps are 1) `copyin(vars1)` 2) `callkernel(vars2)`, and 3) `copyout(vars3)`. In the code, `vars1,vars2,vars3` refers to the list of variables that have to be copied to the GPU before execution, list of variables required for the call, and list of variables that have to be copied back to the CPU, respectively. In the case of OpenMP programs, the copy operations are not necessary as the execution is on the CPU itself and calling the kernel needs to be aware of the number of threads in which it has to be executed. The Abstract API to make a shared memory call is `callParallel(original_paramlist, num_threads)`. More details of the OpenMP transformation inside the method call are explained in Section 3.

3. Design of Abstract API supporting OpenMP

The overall design is shown as a block-diagram in Figure 1. Abstract APIs are function calls inside the program, hence as a pre-compiler step these function calls are expanded into the platform-specific details. Abstract API representation of the matrix transpose example is shown in Figure 2. The API `parallelstart` defines the start of a parallel block with a name, which would represent the name of the method call in case of OpenMP or kernel name in case of GPU programs. All the lines until the end of the parallel block defined by `parallelend` are replaced with the three steps (as defined in Section 2, in the case of GPU) or one step (in the case of shared memory). The input and output parameters can be calculated using static code analysis, similar to extract function refactoring. Corresponding code for the GPU and OpenMP are shown in the poster. As a design princi-

ple, the variables declared and used only inside the parallel blocks are defined private for the access of only one thread. If a variable is only read and never updated, it is defined READ_ONLY (in case of GPU).

4. Related Works and Conclusion

To the best of our knowledge, Abstract APIs [1] represents the first effort in providing an abstraction to both OpenCL and CUDA. However, there have been efforts in providing abstractions to CUDA [3, 4]. Another related work is [2], which converts OpenMP code to CUDA code. The work described in this poster enables the programmers to switch between CUDA, OpenCL and OpenMP code. A new domain-specific language (DSL) powerful enough to express programs independent of language details has been designed. As an initial stage, some of the OpenMP and CUDA features are not supported in the proposed design and is limited to the programming model differences in these architectures.

References

[1] F. Jacob, R. Arora, P. Bangalore, M. Mernik, and J. Gray, "Raising the level of abstraction of gpu-programming," in *Proceedings of the 16th International Conference on Parallel and Distributed Processing Techniques and Applications*, Las Vegas, Nevada, in press.

[2] S. Lee, S.-J. Min, and R. Eigenmann, "OpenMP to GPGPU: a compiler framework for automatic translation and optimization," in *Proceedings of the 14th ACM SIGPLAN symposium on Principles and practice of parallel programming*, New York, NY, USA, 2009, pp. 101–110.

[3] T. D. Han and T. S. Abdelrahman, "hiCUDA: A high-level directive-based language for GPU programming," in *Proceedings of 2nd Workshop on General Purpose Processing on Graphics Processing Units*, Washington, D.C., March 2009, pp. 52–61.

[4] S.-Z. Ueng, M. Lathara, S. S. Baghsorkhi, and W.-M. W. Hwu, "CUDA-lite: Reducing GPU programming complexity," in *Proceedings of the International Workshop on Languages and Compilers for Parallel Computing*, Edmonton, Canada, July 2008, pp. 1–15.

SPLASH Doctoral Symposium Chair's Welcome

On behalf of the SPLASH doctoral symposium committee, I hope you enjoy these papers from the proposers at the first SPLASH doctoral symposium, held in Reno/Sparks Nevada, October 18, 2010. We have received and selected papers from seven proposers, who received detailed feedback on their dissertation plans and ideas.

While this is the first SPLASH doctoral symposium, it continues the tradition of the OOPSLA doctoral symposia, dating back many years. As in previous years, doctoral students seeking feedback from our distinguished committee could submit as apprentices or as proposers. This year we had one student submit as an apprentice, and accepted her participation at the symposium. We had seven students submit as proposers, and accepted all seven as proposers. The proposers each have a two page paper, which appears later in this Companion. They also present their work to the committee during the symposium, and receive the committee's feedback.

Each paper submitted by a proposer was assigned to at least two committee members to review. Reviews are meant to provide constructive feedback and suggestions to the authors. In the end, we decided to accept all 7 submissions out of the 7 submitted.

My thanks, and the thanks of the students, I am sure, go to the distinguished committee who agreed to help the students in this year's doctoral symposium. They are (besides myself):

- Jonathan Aldrich, from Carnegie Mellon University,

- Kathryn McKinley, from the University of Texas at Austin, and

- Eli Tilevich, from Virginia Tech.

I thank all of them for their diligent work and careful thought and advice; I also appreciate their time and effort spent attending the doctoral symposium. It is our hope that the students we mentor through the doctoral symposium will mature and make great and long-lasting contributions to the SPLASH community.

Gary T. Leavens
SPLASH 2010 Doctoral Symposium Chair
University of Central Florida
leavens@eecs.ucf.edu

Encapsulation And Locality

A Foundation for Concurrency Support in Multi-Language Virtual Machines?

Stefan Marr[1]

Software Languages Lab
Vrije Universiteit Brussel, Belgium
stefan.marr@vub.ac.be

Abstract

We propose to search for common abstractions for different concurrency models to enable high-level language virtual machines (VMs) to support a wide range of different concurrency models. This would enable domain-specific solutions for the concurrency problem. Knowledge about concurrency in the VM will most likely lead to better implementation opportunities on top of the different upcoming many-core architectures. The idea is to investigate the concepts of encapsulation and locality to this end. Thus, we are going to experiment with different language abstractions for concurrency on top of a VM, which supports encapsulation and locality, to see how language designers could benefit, and how VMs could optimize programs using these concepts.

Categories and Subject Descriptors   D.3.4 [*Programming Languages*]: Processors;   D.1.3 [*Programming Techniques*]: Concurrent Programming

General Terms   Experimentation, Languages, Performance

Keywords   Multi-language virtual machines, concurrency, many-core, abstraction

1.   Problem Statement

High-level language virtual machines (VMs) use highly optimized just-in-time compilers and garbage collectors to provide performance characteristics comparable to classic low-level system programming languages. Recent improvements and additions to VMs like the Java Virtual Machine or Common Language Runtime enable efficient execution of a wide range of dynamic languages. These dynamic capabilities are used increasingly to build domain-specific languages (DSLs) on top of these VMs. In return, DSLs enable developers to tackle their problems at an even higher level of abstraction. However, VMs have not made the step into the many-core era by supporting language designers to utilize concurrency and parallelism.

The main question here is, are there common abstractions for the various concurrency models? To provide the necessary flexibility to language designers, a VM should support a wide range of different concurrency models. Shared memory with threads and locks is the standard, transactional memory promises to handle some of the software engineering challenges, actor-like message passing systems avoid typical low-level concurrency issues, and data-flow programming is a good fit for a number of computing problems. They all have application where they shine, and use-cases which are not supported that well. For a multi-language VM, choosing a single model does not seem to be appropriate.

Implementing an unsupported models on top of a VM comes usually with significant additional complexity as well as performance disadvantages. Examples are actor languages for the JVM, which need to compromise on the actor properties they provide[3]. Software transactional memory (STM) research suggests direct changes to the runtime systems to achieve the desired performance, too[1, 6].

To achieve real abstraction instead of merely adding one concurrency model after another, we are searching for fundamental commonalities. These commonalities should allow language developers to implement their ideas more easily, while giving the VM opportunities for optimizations.

By approaching the question of a common abstraction, the problem of integrating different concurrency models becomes most relevant, too. One fundamental questions is, how a module, that is written with shared-memory libraries, interacts with a module, which is based on the assumptions of non-shared memory and needs to enforce strong encapsulation. A typical scenario is legacy code written for shared-memory that needs to integrate seamlessly with new modules, which could utilizes an actor-based model that requires strict encapsulation.

Copyright is held by the author/owner(s).

SPLASH'10,   October 17–21, 2010, Reno/Tahoe, Nevada, USA.
ACM 978-1-4503-0240-1/10/10.

---

[1] Supported by a doctoral scholarship of the Institute for the Promotion of Innovation through Science and Technology in Flanders, Belgium.

2. Goal

The concepts we see as most relevant to provide such an abstraction are encapsulation and locality. Encapsulation refers to the guarantee given to an entity that its internal state is only accessible by itself. Locality refers to the notion of a spacial relation between entities. For instance, the objects encapsulated by an actor could be grouped together in memory. Our goal is to experiment with VM support for these concepts and evaluate their usefulness in a multi-language VM for many-core architectures.

To this end, concrete incarnations of the different concurrency models need to be analyzed to see how they could benefit from these two concepts. Furthermore, these abstractions have to be evaluated with respect to the different upcoming many-core architectures like Tilera's TILE architecture[5].

These experiments will either indicate the applicability of the chosen concepts to reach the desired goal, or will provide the necessary indications to choose more suitable ones. The results will allow us to design concrete low-level constructs, which need to be supported by multi-language VMs to allow an implementation of a wide range of different concurrency models on top of them. Furthermore, these results should provide us with the understanding to propose concrete optimization strategies for the VM implementations on the different many-core architectures.

To facilitate interoperability between different concurrency models a framework needs to be provided, which either predefines certain rules, or gives language designers the means to specify how other modules, libraries, or languages are supposed to interact with their language. Currently, the literature discusses a number of pair-wise combinations of different concurrency models to propose possible semantics for their interaction. However, for the proposed abstraction such a semantics has to be more general.

3. Research Approach

As a foundation for this research, we started with an literature survey including the implementation strategies for *partitioned global address space* (PGAS) languages. They use the notion of locality to divide a global address space based on physical computational nodes. Furthermore, their implementations typically combine shared memory concurrency with a message-passing infrastructure, and thus, utilize different concurrency models to implement a language on top. The candidates for non-shared-memory, actor-like languages are E and AmbientTalk[4]. They represent a very compelling approach for object-oriented languages. For functional languages, Erlang is know for its concurrent nature. Based on this literature study we will choose a number of language concepts to experiment with.

Our goal is to implement the chosen language abstractions prototypically on top of an existing virtual machine. The next step is to incorporate support for encapsulation and locality at the VM level. Thus, we will design a VM model, with an extended instruction set and presumably a sketch for a memory model semantics. Based on these facilities, we want to rebuild the same language abstractions. This will enable us to assess the different engineering efforts to build domain-specific language abstractions on top. Furthermore, we also expect to get an initial intuition about the performance related aspects on a Tilera 64-core processor.

With respect to the interoperability between different concurrency models, we plan to investigate how VM support could be designed to provide enough flexibility to language designers but also provide the necessary guarantees to the different concurrency models. Furthermore, we will investigate how the notion of locality can facilitate VM implementations on many-core architectures. Here a relevant question is how can the concept of locality be represented flexibly in the VM with respect to its granularity.

To investigate the generality of our approach, the experiments need to be extended to at least one other model. STM seems to be a relevant candidate. While researchers struggles to reduce the overhead to an acceptable level, hardware vendors start to provide the foundations for hardware-assisted TM. Thus, they provide mechanisms which are itself limited, but improve the performance of STM systems on top[2]. Based on their proposals, we see a strong correlation of STM to the notion of locality. Similar mechanisms could be provided based the VM support for locality and encapsulation. This would allow to implement sophisticated STM systems on top of that. Even such the restricted VM support would directly facilitate the implementation of concurrent data structures.

References

[1] A.-R. Adl-Tabatabai, B. T. Lewis, V. Menon, B. R. Murphy, B. Saha, and T. Shpeisman. Compiler and runtime support for efficient software transactional memory. In *Proc. of PLDI'06*, pages 26–37. ACM, 2006.

[2] D. Dice, Y. Lev, M. Moir, and D. Nussbaum. Early experience with a commercial hardware transactional memory implementation. In *Proc. of ASPLOS'09*, pages 157–168. ACM, 2009.

[3] R. K. Karmani, A. Shali, and G. Agha. Actor frameworks for the jvm platform: A comparative analysis. In *Proc. of PPPJ'09*. ACM, 2009.

[4] T. Van Cutsem, S. Mostinckx, E. G. Boix, J. Dedecker, and W. De Meuter. Ambienttalk: Object-oriented event-driven programming in mobile ad hoc networks. *Proc. of SCCC'07*, 2007.

[5] D. Wentzlaff, P. Griffin, H. Hoffmann, L. Bao, B. Edwards, C. Ramey, M. Mattina, C.-C. Miao, J. F. Brown III, and A. Agarwal. On-chip interconnection architecture of the tile processor. *IEEE Micro*, 27(5):15–31, 2007.

[6] P. Wu, M. M. Michael, C. von Praun, T. Nakaike, R. Bordawekar, H. W. Cain, C. Cascaval, S. Chatterjee, S. Chiras, R. Hou, M. Mergen, X. Shen, M. F. Spear, H. Y. Wang, and K. Wang. Compiler and runtime techniques for software transactional memory optimization. *Concurrency and Computation: Practice & Experience*, 21(1), 2008.

Unsticking the Web

Joshua Sunshine

Carnegie Mellon University

sunshine@cs.cmu.edu

Abstract

A single web page in a complex web application has many possible runtime states. Functions, like JavaScript event handlers, that operate on such pages are therefore difficult to write correctly. I propose DynXML, a new language for the web which safely and naturally mutates XML trees. Any dynamic web application written in DynXML is statically guaranteed to be free of structural defects – code that transforms the page in a way that is unexpected by other code or relies on an element of the page that is of the wrong type or does not exist. I specified DynXML formally and proved it sound. I intend to show its expressiveness by implementing several web application design patterns and a subsection of a popular JavaScript framework. I will analyze web application defects to validate the importance of structural defects.

Categories and Subject Descriptors F.3.1 [*LOGICS AND MEANINGS OF PROGRAMS*]: Mechanical Verification

General Terms Languages, Verification

1. Introduction

The web today relies heavily on client-side code whose primary purpose is to modify a web page represented as an XML document. The major examples of this paradigm are JavaScript changing HTML pages and ActionScript mutating MXML-based Flash interfaces. These client side programming languages and the tools built on top of them do not provide guarantees about the state of the pages they modify. The consequences of this phenomenon are varied — browser crashes, unresponsive applications, and lost data.

Consider a user composing an email in a webmail client. He composes the message and clicks send, which triggers a JavaScript event handler. This event handler expects the page to contain a certain element, which is missing because of the particular path, chosen possibly from thousands, he

used to travel to the page state. The email isn't sent and the browser may even crash causing him to lose his data. One can see evidence of this problem by observing the hundreds of errors logged in the browser's error console after a long browsing session.

DynXML employs a type-based approach, which could provide basic safety guarantees to the programmer, while retaining the automatability of type systems. In order to do so, DynXML builds on the regular expression types of Hosoya and Pierce [3]. However, this and other prior XML-related language research [1, 2] focused on purely functional query and transformation. While this paradigm is natural in many XML processing applications, in the setting of dynamic web applications, a functional approach would introduce copying inefficiencies and require a drastically different programming style. This work, therefore, focuses on reasoning about the imperative modification of XML trees.

Imperative update underlies the central challenge of this work: that the structure of an XML tree can change as it is modified. Therefore, the type system must track the state of an XML tree flow-sensitively, reason about the side effects of functions on trees, and control aliasing to ensure that elements of the page are not unexpectedly changed. Furthermore, dynamic web pages contain embedded event handlers that are invoked in response to end-user actions; we must ensure that when these handlers are invoked, the web page is in the expected state, and that the handlers leave the web page in a potentially changed but still well-formed state.

2. Language

I use the simple bookstore shown in Figure 1 to illustrate the features of DynXML. The top section contains the book title, description and price. The bottom section has two alternate states: 1) the purchasing state, which contains a textbox allowing the user to enter the quantity of books to buy and a button to process the purchase; and 2) the rating state, which allows a user who has already purchased the book to select a rating from a dropdown list and to push a button to submit.

The type of a page can be represented as a type such as a DTD or XML Schema. DynXML's syntax borrows from the regular expression types of Hosoya and Pierce. The type constructor n[...] classifies XML nodes with the label n (i.e. <n>...</n>). Types can also include regular expression

Copyright is held by the author/owner(s).

SPLASH'10, October 17–21, 2010, Reno/Tahoe, Nevada, USA.
ACM 978-1-4503-0240-1/10/10.

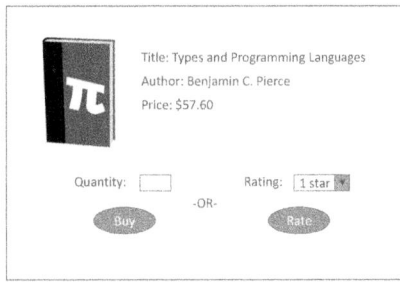

Figure 1. Schematic of book store page.

```
1  type quantity = textbox[], //quantity textbox
2    button[(quantity page)→(rating page)]];
3  type rating = dropdown[option[int]*, //rating
4    button[(rating page)→(thanks page)]];
```

Listing 1. Code describing type of book store item page.

operators like * (repetition); ? (option); , (sequence); and | (union). The type table[(tr[td[($int|str$)]])*] is the type of all one column tables whose cells each include an integer or a string. The types of the bottom section of the book store item page in DynXML are in Listing 1. The type quantity and rating are the types for the last element of the page when it is in the purchasing state and the rating state.

The arrow types embedded in the buttons in Listing 1 illustrate one of DynXML's most interesting features. They are manifestations of the event handlers introduced in Section 1. I treat event handlers as functions which are passed the page as an argument and return it as the result. The right and left halves of the arrow type are not fixed types, but instead flow-sensitive *permissions*. I use permissions to track the precise type of XML trees as they are modified. This precise type is the system's best estimate of the most specific current type for the expression referenced by the permission, and is expressed using the regular expression types introduced earlier in this section.

Permissions are linear resources that cannot be duplicated, so they can be used to ensure that an XML tree is not modified through aliased pointers. If a permission to a tree is not passed to a function, then it is certain that the function will not modify that tree. Permissions, like types in most programming languages, are stated in code only at function boundaries. Within a function the system maintains a list of permissions in the *permission context*, each of which is automatically updated as changes are made to the XML documents referred to by the permissions. Therefore, the system is modular— an implementation of DynXML should be able to check each method independently.

3. Validation

This work makes three primary claims that DynXML is sound, expressive, and solves a significant problem. Each claim is presented in detail and the validation that will support it follows immediately.

Sound: I can develop and formalize a programming language for building web applications, DynXML, in which web applications written are guarantee web applications do not contain structural defects and prove that the system will not produce false negatives.

Validation: In preliminary work I've developed and formalized a type system for DynXML that statically prevents structural defects and proved it sound [4].

Important Problem: Structural defects are common and result in severe failure. Validation: I will study the errors that exist in released web applications, and the severity of the failures that result from those errors. The study will employ a Firefox plugin to log the JavaScript error console, user events, and document object model (DOM) changes of internet users as they browse in their everyday lives. I identify failure in this study through JavaScript exceptions, which are symptomatic of failure and are logged in the browsers error console. I examine the JavaScript source to identify the error that results in the exception and, where possible, the fault that causes the error. The biggest challenge in this study is to determine the severity of failures. I do so by inferring the page changes the user expects from the user events that precede the exception and checking the DOM changes around the exception for correspondence to that expectation. DynXML prevents structural defects and I hope to show that structural defects are common and the resulting failures can be severe.

Expressive: DynXML can express the most important web application programming idioms, behaviors and techniques.

Validation: I will evaluate DynXML's expressiveness in a series of case studies. First I will implement some of the buggy code found in the bug study to ensure that DynXML properly statically determines the error. Second, I will implement the most widely used web application design patterns which serve as the primary building blocks for most web applications. Finally, I will implement a few of the most popular interaction techniques from JQuery and script.aculo.us to ensure that DynXML can support the richest techniques.

References

[1] G. Bierman, E. Meijer, and W. Schulte. The essence of data access in CΩ. In *Proc. European Conference on Object-Oriented Programming*, pages 287–311, 2005.

[2] J. Cheney. FLUX: functional updates for XML. In *Proc. Intl. Conference on Functional Programming*, pages 3–14, 2008.

[3] H. Hosoya, J. Vouillon, and B. C. Pierce. Regular expression types for XML. *ACM Trans. Program. Lang. Syst.*, 27(1):46–90, 2005.

[4] J. Sunshine and J. Aldrich. Dynxml: Safely programming the dynamic web. In *Proc. Workshop on Analysis and Programming Languages for Web Applications and Cloud Applications*, 2010.

Towards Feature Modularization

Márcio Ribeiro   Paulo Borba

Informatics Center, Federal University of Pernambuco, 50740-540, Recife – PE – Brazil

{mmr3, phmb}@cin.ufpe.br

Abstract

Virtual Separation of Concerns was introduced as a way to reduce drawbacks of implementing product line variability with preprocessors. Developers can focus on certain features and hide others of no interest. However, features eventually share elements, which might break feature modularity, since modifications in a feature result in problems for another. In this thesis we propose the concept of emergent feature modularization. The idea consists of establishing contracts among features to prevent the developer from breaking other features when performing a maintenance task.

Categories and Subject Descriptors D.2.3 [*Software Engineering*]: Coding Tools and Techniques

General Terms Design

Keywords Product Lines, Modularity, Preprocessors

1. Introduction

In a Software Product Line (SPL), features are often implemented using mechanisms like preprocessors [2], so that directives such as #ifdef and #endif encompass code associated with features. Despite their widespread use, several drawbacks are known, including no support for separation of concerns. Virtual Separation of Concerns (VSoC) [2] allows developers to hide feature code not relevant to the current task, being important to reduce some of the preprocessors drawbacks. The idea is to provide developers a way to focus on a feature without being distracted by other ones.

Although VSoC is helpful to visualize a feature individually, it does not modularize features to the extent of supporting independent feature maintenance and development [3], since developers know nothing about what is hidden. In fact, when maintaining a feature, a developer might introduce errors into the hidden features, since these features eventually share elements (variables and methods) with the feature being maintained. For instance, the new value of a variable might be correct to the maintained feature, but incorrect to another that uses this variable. Thus, we have a problem due to the lack of feature modularization: the modification of a feature leads to errors in another. And this problem is worse since this error would only be noticed when running the product built with the problematic feature.

This thesis proposes the concept of *Emergent Feature Modularization* [4], which consists of establishing contracts among feature implementations. We call our approach emergent because the components and interfaces here are neither predefined nor have a rigid structure. Instead, they emerge on demand to give support for specific feature development or maintenance tasks. Notice that we also achieve the hiding benefits towards feature comprehensibility. However, while still hiding completely the feature code, our emergent interfaces abstract its details. At the same time, they provide valuable information to maintain a feature and keep other features and their possible combinations safe. Our intent is to provide enough information to prevent developers of breaking other features, even when they are working on parallel.

Our hypothesis is that, by using the emergent interfaces, developers achieve modularity and, consequently, make fewer mistakes during SPL maintenance, improving their productivity. In particular, our research questions are the following. **Q1**: Do emergent interfaces provide better support during feature maintenance?; **Q2**: Do emergent interfaces allow developers to analyze less code?

2. Emergent Feature Modularization

The top of Figure 1 shows two features of Mobile Media[1]: Music and the Copy optional feature (implemented with preprocessors). We do not provide the Copy feature code on purpose to simulate VSoC, so that the developer is not concerned about other features like, for this example, Copy. To some extent, hiding features is worthwhile to the feature comprehensibility benefit, since it may help developers to comprehend a feature individually. Despite this advantage, VSoC does not provide enough support for feature modularization, which also means modifying features separately [3].

Copyright is held by the author/owner(s).

SPLASH'10,   October 17–21, 2010, Reno/Tahoe, Nevada, USA.
ACM 978-1-4503-0240-1/10/10.

[1] http://mobilemedia.cvs.sourceforge.net/

Because there is no information about the hidden code, when maintaining the `Music` feature, problems may occur in `Copy`. So, the independent *changeability* benefit is not achieved. For example, since the `screen` variable is used only at the `MMController` constructor, a developer may decide to change `MMController(screen)` to `MMController(new MMScreen(..))` and delete the `screen` declaration. Since the `Copy` feature uses `screen`, an error will occur when a developer eventually compiles the product with the problematic feature combination (with `Copy`).

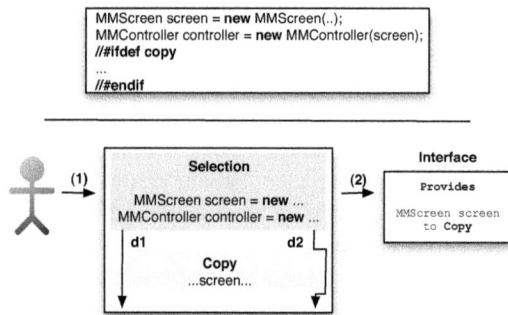

Figure 1. Copy feature hidden / Emergent Interface.

In this context, sharing information about two or more features may be a confusing point for two developers, so that achieving the *parallel development* is difficult. This happens because there is no "*mutual agreement between the creator and accessor*" [5]. Since this contract does not exist, developers of a feature might actually break another one.

To solve these problems, we propose the concept of emergent feature modularization, which consists of establishing, according to a given development task, interfaces among features. This is based on an uncommon way to think about components and interfaces: they are not predefined, nor have a rigid structure, but are computed on demand, to give support for feature development. For example, in a maintenance, the feature code to be changed is a component, named *Selection*. The backward/forward paths of the code surrounding it are components too. Paths consider the different feature combinations by the feature model. They are named *dataflows*, since data is exchanged among features. Interfaces capture data dependencies between these components, and give support to maintaining *Selection* without having to understand the details of code associated to the *dataflows*.

Thus, before changing the `Music` feature, developers select the code to be maintained. In this case, since `Copy` is optional, two *dataflows* are considered according to the feature model: **d1:** Music $\wedge$ Copy and **d2:** Music $\wedge$ ($\neg$ Copy). They are illustrated through arrows on the bottom of Figure 1. After the selection, interfaces emerge to basically show data dependencies between components. The *dataflows* are used to catch dependencies between the selection and code of other features. Figure 1 shows an emergent interface, stating that the *Selection* component provides `screen` to the Copy fea-

ture. This interface allows us to change *Selection* abstracting details of surrounding features (which are still hidden). At the same time, they provide information to the *Selection* developer, so that he might avoid implementations that cause problems to other features. Now, when looking at the interface, he would think twice before continuing the refactoring. Now we present the ongoing work and some results.

More evidences to our problem. We are trying to collect semantic errors caused by the lack of feature modularization. Also, the problem addressed here gets worse depending on the number of features within methods. For this reason, we are computing for some C and Java product lines metrics like the number of `#ifdefs` per method; and the number of variables declared in a feature and used in another one.

Tool. We are building a tool (which is based on *Colored IDE* [2]) to compute emergent interfaces.

Evaluation. For **Q1**, we should collect real scenarios of SPL maintenance, like adding, removing, and changing features. By using these scenarios, we intend to conduct an experiment with students to evaluate if our proposal allows developers to commit fewer mistakes. For **Q2**, since our approach provides information about what is hidden, we count the lines of code of the hidden feature and of our interfaces. Our interfaces should be smaller. Otherwise, it seems to be easier for the developer to analyze the hidden code directly.

How do we go beyond? We still have the VSoC benefits since hidden feature details are abstracted. At the same time we provide summarized information to maintain a feature and keep the hidden ones safe. Therefore, emergent interfaces help developers to change a feature without breaking others. Thus, we may achieve not only the comprehensibility benefit, but also the independent changeability. Some works check for type errors of all SPL variants [1]. Our intent is to make developers aware about other features before initiating the maintenance, avoiding errors that would be only caught afterwards by these checking-based works. Finally, we are also concerned with system behavior, rather than only with static type information. For example, interfaces may state that a feature needs a particular value for a variable.

References

[1] C. Kästner and S. Apel. Type-checking software product lines - a formal approach. In *Proceedings of the 23rd ASE'08*, pages 258–267. IEEE Computer Society, September 2008.

[2] C. Kästner, S. Apel, and M. Kuhlemann. Granularity in Software Product Lines. In *Proceedings of the 30th ICSE'08*, pages 311–320, New York, NY, USA, 2008. ACM.

[3] D. L. Parnas. On the criteria to be used in decomposing systems into modules. *CACM*, 15(12):1053–1058, 1972.

[4] M. Ribeiro, H. Pacheco, L. Teixeira, and P. Borba. Emergent Feature Modularization. In *Proceedings of the Onward! 2010*, New York, NY, USA, 2010. ACM. To appear.

[5] W. Wulf and M. Shaw. Global variable considered harmful. *SIGPLAN Notices*, 8(2):28–34, 1973. ISSN 0362-1340.

Enabling Expressive Aspect Oriented
Modular Reasoning by Translucid Contracts

Mehdi Bagherzadeh

Iowa State University, Ames, IA, USA
mbagherz@iastate.edu

Abstract

Making assertions about the program's control flow is important for reasoning purposes, e.g. ensuring that an advice proceeds to the original join point. Obliviousness of the base modules to the aspects in aspect oriented languages, like AspectJ, makes it difficult to make such assertions in a modular manner. Base-aspect interfaces like crosscutting interfaces (XPIs), augmented with blackbox behavioral contracts save modularity of the reasoning process to some extent, but are not expressive enough to specify base-aspect control interactions in their full generality. Translucid contracts are proposed to specify and enforce typical control flow properties.

Categories and Subject Descriptors D.2.4 [*Software/Program Verification*]: Programming by contract, Assertion checkers; F.3.1 [*Specifying and Verifying and Reasoning about Programs*]: Assertions, Invariants, Pre and postconditions, Specification techniques

General Terms Design, Languages, Verification

Keywords Modular Reasoning, Translucid Contracts

1. Introduction

Aspect oriented (AO) languages modularize crosscutting concerns by localizing them into aspects. Aspects are woven into the base modules, making them capable of modifying the behavior of the base, obliviously. Base-aspect obliviousness troubles modular reasoning [1] by requiring whole program analysis whereas in the modular reasoning, to reason about a module, only its implementation and at most the interface of the referred modules are needed.

Problems and Existing Work:. Explicit base-aspect interfaces (AO interfaces) [1, 5–8] like crosscutting interfaces (XPI) [7], combined with the behavioral contracts, par-

tially save modularity of the reasoning process. Reliance of the existing work on *blackbox* behavioral contracts is their Achilles' heel (detailed discussion of related work could be found in [3]). Blackbox contracts only specify the input-output relation of aspects' advice and are not capable of exposing internal states [4], necessary for specific classes of control flow assertions, e.g. Rinard's direct interference patterns [10]. To illustrate consider the canonical figure editor example in Figure 1, implemented in AspectJ. The requirement is to update the display after `Point` is changed by `setX`. The example uses XPI `Changed` (lines 7–12) augmented with the blackbox contract (lines 10–11) to specify the behavior of the base-aspect interaction.

First Problem:. Suppose the call to **proceed** in `Update` on line 16 is inadvertently forgotten. Without proceed, the body of `setX` will never be executed. Note the incapability of the blackbox behavioral contract of alerting such a problem. Behavioral contracts in AO interfaces are not expressive enough to specify the control interactions which are concerned about the internal states of the aspects.

Second Problem:. Suppose there is another concern `Logging` which logs changes to the `Point` caused by `setX`. A missing **proceed** in `Update`, has two different outcomes here, dependent on the order of the composition of the aspects. In one composition where `Update` runs first, `Logging` would be skipped whereas in the reverse composition it would not. Behavioral contracts are not able to convey information about the composition of the aspects.

2. Solution

Translucid contracts [2] solve the two afore-mentioned problems. Greybox based [4] translucid contracts are abstract algorithms, abstract enough to hide the details as much as the blackbox specification does while revealing the internal states as much as the whitebox (source code) does.

To illustrate consider the same figure editor example in Figure 2, written in Ptolemy [9] with a translucid contract on lines 11–16. Ptolemy introduces quantified typed events as the explicit AO interface. Events can be defined (**event** declaration, lines 9–17), announced with arbitrary event body (**announce**, lines 5–6) along with contextual infor-

Copyright is held by the author/owner(s).

SPLASH'10, October 17–21, 2010, Reno/Tahoe, Nevada, USA.
ACM 978-1-4503-0240-1/10/10.

```
1  class Fig { }                  7  aspect Changed{                    13  aspect Update{
2  class Point extends Fig {      8    pointcut jp(Fig fe):              14    void around (Fig fe):
3    int x; int y;                9      call(void Fig+.set*(..))&& target(fe);  15      Changed.jp(fe){
4    void setX(int x){           10    requires fe != null               16        proceed(fe);
5      this.x = x;}              11    ensures  fe != null               17        Display.update(fe);}
6  }                             12  }                                  18  }
```

Figure 1. A behavioral contract for AO interfaces using XPI [7]

```
1  class Fig { }                  9   Fig event Changed {              18  class Update {
2  class Point extends Fig {     10    Fig fe;                          19    Update(){ register(this) }
3    int x; int y;               11    requires fe != null              20    Fig update(thunk Fig rest,
4    Fig setX(int x){            12    assumes {                        21                   Fig fe){
5      announce Changed(this){   13      invoke(next);                  22      invoke(rest);
6        this.x = x; this}       14      establishes fe == old(fe)      23      refining establishes fe == old(fe){
7    }                           15    }                                24        Display.update(fe); fe}
8  }                             16    ensures  fe != null              25    }
                                 17  }                                  26    when Changed do update;}
```

Figure 2. A translucid contract for AO interfaces in Ptolemy [9]

mation (**this**, line 5) and handled (lines 20–25) using registration (**register**, line 19) and quantification mechanisms (**when** − **do**, line 26). **refining** expression (line 23–24) refines its blackbox specification on line 23. In Ptolemy aspects are called *handlers* and **invoke** expression is the AspectJ's equivalent of **proceed** which calls the next handler.

The **assumes** part in Figure 2 on lines 12–15 reveals the internal states of the handlers. For example revealed call to **invoke** on line 13 requires refining handlers to evaluate the only allowed call to **invoke** in their implementation as the very first expression. Translucid contracts combine blackbox (line 14) and whitebox specifications (line 13).

Translucid Contracts Obligations:. Two obligations must be met by translucid contracts: (i) they are required to reveal all the calls to **invoke** and (ii) all registered handlers for a an event type must refine the contract of the event type.

Specification of Control Effects:. Whitebox parts make translucid contracts flexible enough to reveal internal implementation details of the refining handlers. In Figure 2, revealing the call to **invoke** on line 13 assures base developer that the call to **invoke** will not be missed in the refining handlers, avoiding the first problem, in Section 1.

Reasoning about Composition of Handlers:. Assertions can be made about composition of the handlers regardless of their number and order, e.g., considering obligation (i) it is assured that all the handler will run, avoiding the second problem in Section 1. Obligation (ii) gives us an upper bound on the compositional behavior of the refining handlers [3].

Verification Technique:. Refinement technique is an adapted version of the structural refinement [11]. Briefly for any blackbox part in the translucid contract there must be a refining part in the implementation. For a whitebox part, there must be a textually matching part in the implementation. Handler update in Figure 2 refines the contract on lines 11–16 as line 22 matches the whitebox on line 13 and refining statement on lines 23–24 claims to refine the black-

box part on line 14. Pre- and postconditions of update are the same as pre- and postconditions on lines 12 and 17. Run time probes take care of the refinement requirements [3].

Future Work:. The hope is to increase expressiveness of the translucid contracts to enable specification of more complex control flow properties in large scale applications. Translucid contracts can also be used to enable expressive data flow reasoning about AO programs.

References

[1] J. Aldrich. Open modules: Modular reasoning about advice. In *ECOOP '05*.

[2] M. Bagherzadeh, H. Rajan, and G. T. Leavens. Translucid contracts for aspect-oriented interfaces. In *FOAL '10*.

[3] M. Bagherzadeh, H. Rajan, G. T. Leavens, and S. Mooney. Translucid contracts for aspect-oriented interfaces. Technical Report 10-02, Iowa State U., Dept. of Computer Sc., 2009.

[4] M. Büchi and W. Weck. The greybox approach: When blackbox specifications hide too much. Technical Report 297, Turku Center for Computer Science, 1999.

[5] S. Gudmundson and G. Kiczales. Addressing practical software development issues in AspectJ with a pointcut interface. In *In Advanced Separation of Concerns*, 2001.

[6] K. J. Hoffman and P. Eugster. Bridging Java and AspectJ through explicit join points. In *PPPJ '07*.

[7] K. J. Sullivan *et al.* Modular aspect-oriented design with XPIs. *TOSEM '09*, 20(2).

[8] G. Kiczales and M. Mezini. Aspect-oriented programming and modular reasoning. In *ICSE '05*, pages 49–58.

[9] H. Rajan and G. T. Leavens. Ptolemy: A language with quantified, typed events. In *ECOOP '08*.

[10] M. Rinard, A. Salcianu, and S. Bugrara. A classification system and analysis for aspect-oriented programs. In *FSE'04*.

[11] S. M. Shaner, G. T. Leavens, and D. A. Naumann. Modular verification of higher-order methods with mandatory calls specified by model programs. In *OOPSLA*, 2007.

Metamodel-Driven Evolution

Qichao Liu

Department of Computer and Information Sciences
University of Alabama at Birmingham
Birmingham, Alabama, USA

qichao@cis.uab.edu

Abstract

With the rapid development of model-driven engineering (MDE), domain-specific modeling is becoming a popular software development technique. In MDE, a metamodel represents a schema definition of the syntax and static semantics in a similar manner to how a grammar defines a programming language. In most cases, users need to modify a metamodel to incorporate new concerns resulting in failure of applying existing instances. The research described in this paper makes a contribution toward metamodel driven evolution.

Categories and Subject Descriptors I.6.5 [**Simulation and modeling**]: Model Development

General Terms Algorithms, Design, Languages.

Keywords model-driven engineering; domain-specific modeling; grammar inference; metamodel; model-transformation

1. Background and Motivation

In software engineering, new techniques and methodologies are often developed with the aim of improving productivity. Model-driven engineering (MDE) is a software development methodology that is focused on creating abstractions that represent an alternative to the classical code-based development.

In MDE, models are created according to the schema defined by a metamodel. Similar to how a programming language is dependent on a grammar, a model is defined by a metamodel. Under most cases, users need to modify the metamodel once they are not satisfied with using existing model instances. As a result, the metamodel evolves and all the model instances need to be redesigned. In industry, a model instance could be very complex and the number of instances could scale greatly. To adapt existing models to a new metamodel schema can be a very error-prone and tedious task.

The research described in this abstract makes a contribution in the area of metamodel-driven evolution. A specific focus is on techniques to enable an evolved metamodel to interpret previous model instances and to convert them to the new definition. Our research is based on three core areas: 1) metamodel recovery; 2) metamodel comparison and mapping; 3) model transformation.

2. Related Work

Much existing work is described in the literature on the topic of grammar evolution. Lämmel and Verhoef [1] addressed the schema evolution problem in the area of programming languages and their approach is to recover grammars from grammar-related artifacts and create a parser for language instances. Our research is focused on recovering a metamodel from model instances to address the schema evolution problem.

Model mapping and comparison is widely explored with a rich amount of model comparison work. However, the majority of model differentiation focuses on UML diagrams [2] instead of domain-specific models. Our research deals with metamodel mapping and comparison in the domain-specific modeling environment, which could not only evaluate the metamodel recovery work but also be used in model transformation.

In the direction of addressing the schema evolution problem through model transformation, Sprinkle and Karsai [3] proposed to use graph-rewriting (GR) techniques to update the domain models created by a domain-specific visual language (DSVL). However, the domain models created by a DSVL are represented using a graph structure and the approach works only when the intermediate transformation steps exist. Our research focuses on more general domain-specific modeling environments and we use metamodel based model transformation. Javed et al. [4] presented work on metamodel recovery using grammar inference to address the more general problem of metamodels lost. However the work is just an initial effort related to the metamodel evolution problem which is platform dependent and limited to small domains. Our research will provide a more general and detailed approach solving the problem of metamodel evolution.

3. Goals and Objectives

This research aims to make a contribution to the metamodel-driven evolution problem. More specifically, the research will enable users to adapt model instances without concern for the different metamodel versions. As our first step, the Metamodel Recovery from Model Instances (MRMI) research described in this paper is to infer a metamodel using a set of model instances. The metamodel inference will be a semi-automatic method applicable to multiple modeling environments. The objective for the second step is to explore an efficient algorithm of Metamodel Comparison and Mapping (MCM). MCM will assist in evaluating metamodel recovery in the first step and explore differences and mappings between the old and new metamodel that could be used in our model transformations. The objective for the last step which is also our ultimate goal is to apply Metamodel Based Model Transformation (MBMT) to transform exiting models to evolved ones that could be reused by the latest metamodel.

Copyright is held by the author/owner(s).
SPLASH'10 October 17-21, 2010, Reno/Tahoe, Nevada, USA.
ACM 978-1-4503-0240-1/10/10.

4. Proposed Methodology

Figure 1 illustrates an overview of our proposed methodology. This research contributes to the problem of metamodel-driven evolution specifically in three steps: 1) Applying MRMI to solve the general problem of metamodel recovery where existing metamodels are changed or might be even missing; 2) Applying MCM to evaluate the inferred metamodel and guide model transformation; 3) Applying MBMT to transform existing model instances to those which could be used by the latest metamodel.

For MRMI, we created MARS (MetAmodel Recovery System) [5] to read in a set of model instances defined by the old metamodel, analyze the characteristics exhibited in the model instances and recover the old schema. The metamodel inference engine takes a set of instance models in XML file as input and has an inferred metamodel in XML file as the output after applying our metamodel inference algorithm. This inferred metamodel could be loaded back into the modeling tool (e.g., GME [6]) to view the previous model instances.

As an automated differentiation algorithm MCM addresses the challenges of a manual approach of metamodel comparison that is infeasible in the presence of a large metamodel containing a great number of elements. Because we use GME as our modeling tool, metamodels can be treated as labeled graphs, such that we need MCM to compare two graphs (i.e., a 'Diff' for graphs). Our metamodel comparison algorithm will be efficient, simple and suited for metamodels rather than general graphs.

Described as "The Heart and Soul of Model-Driven Software Development" in [7], model transformation is the last step. A variety of model transformation approaches and examples have been presented in the community. In our research, the transformation from previous models to new models that conform to the evolved metamodel could be treated as metamodel-based transformation and the transformation description will be expressed with the existence of both the inferred and evolved metamodels. Instead of asking users to manually write the transformation rules to adapt the old models, the rules could be automatically inferred and generated based on the metamodel comparison results obtained in the second step.

5. Experimental Evaluation

MRMI will be evaluated by MCM that provides an automatic evaluation report of the inference. The report could present detailed comparison between the original and the inferred metamodel, for instance recall and precision. The evaluation of MBMT will be based on the completeness and correctness of model transformation: we need to guarantee that the set of models MBMT transformed are the same as the source models used in MRMI at steps 1 and 2 in Figure 2; the number of input and output models of MBMT remains the same; the transformed models could be interpreted by the latest metamodel; the model transformation rules are automatically generated in MBMT.

6. Current Results

The current focus of the work is the implementation of MRMI. An extended MARS [8] with a new metamodel inference algorithm has been designed to make the metamodel recovery more general and more accurate. Current evaluation of MRMI is based on a manual comparison between the inferred and the original metamodels. Our work is implemented in the modeling tool GME

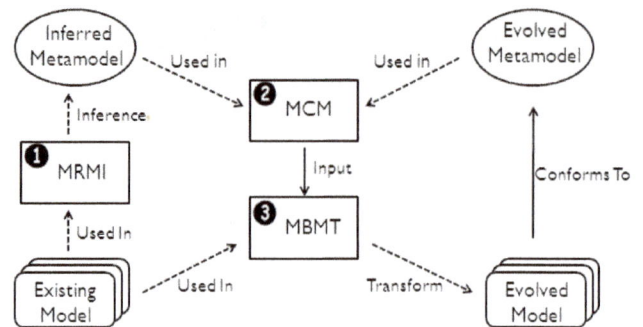

Figure 1. Overview of Proposed Methodology

and we have applied our approach successfully to several GME domains. For simple domains like Finite State Machine, our inference is almost exactly the same as the original metamodel. When it comes to complex domains with a large number of metamodeling elements, the quality of MRMI greatly relies on the model instances we applied. According to a manually operated statistical report about the performance of metamodel inference, the inferred metamodel has a similarity of over 90% with the original if the model instances used are of high quality exhibiting most features in the original metamodel. The current MRMI could also infer good generalization of elements sharing common features. However, the semantics contained in a metamodel could not be inferred except the containment cardinality and inference of OCL constraints is not possible with the proposed technique.

Acknowledgments

This work is supported in part by NSF award CCF-0811630.

References

[1] Lämmel, R., Verhoef, C.: Semi-automatic grammar recovery. Software-Practice & Experience, vol. 31, no. 15, Dec. 2001, pp.1395-1448.

[2] Girschick, M.: Difference detection and visualization in UML class diagrams. Technical report, TU Darmstadt, 2006.

[3] Sprinkle, J., Karsai, G.: A domain-specific visual language for domain model evolution. Journal of Visual Languages and Computing, vol. 15, no. 3-4, Aug. 2004, pp. 291-307.

[4] Javed, F., Mernik, M., Gray, J., Bryant, B.: MARS - A metamodel recovery system using grammar inference. Information and Software Technology, vol. 50, no. 9-10, Aug. 2008, pp.948-968.

[5] Liu, Q., Javed, F., Mernik, M., Bryant, B. R., Gray, J., Sprague, A., Hrnčič, D.: MARS - Metamodel recovery from multi-tiered models using grammar inference. Third IEEE Int'l. Symp, Theoretical Aspects of Software Engineering, 2009, pp. 325-326.

[6] The Generic Modeling Environment, http://www.isis.vanderbilt.edu.

[7] Sendall, S., Kozaczynski, W.: Model transformation - The heart and soul of model-driven software development. IEEE Software, Special Issue on Model Driven Software Development, vol. 20, no. 5, Sep./Oct. 2003, pp. 42-45.

[8] Liu, Q., Bryant, B.R., Mernik, M.: Metamodel recovery from multi-tiered domains using extended MARS. In Proceedings of the 34th Annual International Computer Software and Applications Conference, Seoul, South Korea, Jul. 2010.

Supporting the Evolution of Software Knowledge with Adaptive Software Artifacts

Filipe Figueiredo Correia

Faculdade de Engenharia
Universidade do Porto
filipe.correia@fe.up.pt

Abstract

The knowledge of software developers materializes itself as software artifacts, that may be seen at two different levels (information and structure), which are difficult to change independently from each other. This work explores how the expression of software knowledge using adaptive software techniques, may support the creation of adaptive software artifacts, to improve the effectiveness of capturing knowledge under constant evolution.

Some work already exists in the context of the Weaki Wiki, which will be extended into a full environment supporting the creation and evolution of software artifacts beyond their initial form. We intend to validate this work experimentally.

Categories and Subject Descriptors D.2.6 [*Programming Environments*]: Integrated environments; D.2.7 [*Distribution, Maintenance, and Enhancement*]: Documentation

General Terms Design, Documentation, Experimentation

Keywords knowledge capture, software artifacts, adaptive software, development tools, software forges

1. Introduction

Software artifacts are commonly captured as standalone files, sometimes managed by advanced integrated development environments, but web-based systems, such as wikis and software forges, have been increasing their use in recent years due to their collaborative nature and ease of use.

Regardless of the medium, artifacts are a form of captured (i.e., recorded) knowledge, but while software knowledge evolves freely in the minds of the project's team members, artifacts are not always as easy to adapt. Consider a development team, that starts by recording software requirements as documents. Although initially informal, this information will need to end up distilled into a concrete software system. With this goal in mind, developers choose to create additional artifacts — such as user-stories, models and design documentation — giving information a more concrete and unambiguous form. When creating a domain model of the system, developers resource to the descriptive documents that already capture the knowledge they need, even if in an unstructured way. They create these new models completely from scratch rather than reusing or adapting the actual documents. This implies that the concepts and entities that they describe aren't causally connected to the elements of the newly created models, which may stem concerns like consistency and traceability.

The goal of this work is to give new capabilities to artifacts supported by Web-based environments. In concrete, we will leverage existing techniques for adaptive software to allow developers to evolve existing artifacts, and to capture new artifacts by reusing and molding the information of existing ones, so that the causal-connections between them are maintained.

2. Evolving Software Knowledge and Artifacts

Developers are *knowledge-workers*, as their activity revolves around acquiring, processing and capturing knowledge, with the ultimate goal of obtaining instructions to be executed by a computer [7].

Two levels may be considered within software artifacts: the *information* and the *meta-information*, also referred to as *structure*. While the former refers to the particular subject that the artifact intends to represent, the later describes the information itself, contextualizing it, and conferring it additional semantics. While some structure is not changeable, artifacts frequently allow the creation of additional structural elements, that are open to being authored. The process of capturing such structures is one of carefully organizing and classifying knowledge.

The allowed expressiveness is an important factor when choosing which type of artifact to use. Document artifacts, for example, allow one to capture virtually any topic, as their structure is domain-agnostic, enforcing only a layout form. For this reason, richer artifacts are usually included in documentation, for a better balance, between flexibility and expressiveness [1].

Moreover, software systems can hardly be seen as immutable entities. The difficulty in identifying all the requirements right from the start is well known in industrial environments. Although this is sometimes blamed upon the lack of the stakeholders' knowledge [6], it's inevitable that the knowledge of stakeholders and developers will change throughout the project, which implies that artifacts usually need to be adapted to new understandings. Our key concern is that, although knowledge may evolve, software artifacts are usually more difficult to adapt accordingly, especially when structural changes are needed.

3. Techniques for Adaptive Software

Adaptable systems are those that can be efficiently molded according to changed circumstances. One way of creating an adaptive system is through a meta-architecture: one in which the program manipulates itself as if it were data. Meta-architectures usually describe the system's domain, or part of it, by establishing different levels of (meta-)data, that comply to each other.

Several approaches to the creation of adaptable systems exist. Dynamic approaches, like those using the Adaptive Object-Model (AOM) pattern [8], allow systems to be adapted at runtime. The system interprets a high-level description of its domain, and adapts its behavior to any changes introduced to that description.

Copyright is held by the author/owner(s).
SPLASH'10, October 17–21, 2010, Reno/Tahoe, Nevada, USA.
ACM 978-1-4503-0240-1/10/10.

An alternative to dynamic approaches is Generative Programming: the high-level description of a system is used to automatically create executable code, or a code skeleton that will be further completed by the developers. Adaptability is thus introduced at compile-time, requiring a full generation/compilation cycle.

4. Research Problem and Goals

Software development tools support the evolution of artifacts to some extent, but they normally assume that artifacts have a fixed format. Artifacts that could be easily evolved throughout the project's lifetime, in what concerns both their contents and structure would bring benefits to knowledge capture activities. Information usually first appears as informal, and only gradually becomes more structured, and captured into richer artifacts. A classic example is how requirements are often first captured as descriptive documents, and only afterwards materialize as models, issue-tracking tickets, and source-code, among others.

The existing techniques for adaptive software allow developers to build software systems supporting domain adaptability. The same techniques may help us build development tools supporting software artifacts that are more adaptable.

We believe that supporting the expression of software knowledge through adaptive software artifacts will improve the effectiveness of capturing knowledge under evolution.

Our objective is to find an approach, to be supported by software development tools, that allows software artifacts to be easily changed, in what concerns both their contents and their structure. With this purpose in mind, we will:

- Identify the difficulties in the creation and evolution of software artifacts from a knowledge capture standpoint;
- Build a theory on how these needs may be fulfilled;
- Create new tools, or extend existing ones, that better support the capture and evolution of captured software knowledge.

5. Research Approach

Research in software engineering needs to go beyond concrete implementations and tools and consider the human side of software development, and all of the context that underlies it. Given the amount of possibilities that this entails, research strategies usually encompass different methods, which are combined to improve the knowledge on the subject.

In the course of this work we will conduct quasi-experiments on an academic environment, and case-studies on an industrial environment. In the first phase, both will be done with an exploratory aim, to collect new insights on the problems underlying the creation and evolution of software artifacts. Later, the research will take a confirmatory goal: industrial case-studies will provide feedback and drive the development of tools; and together with the academic quasi-experiments they will be used to assess our claims.

To explore the phenomenas that artifacts go through during software development, we will try to answer the following questions:

- Which difficulties are found by developers during the capture and evolution of contents?
- What are the effects of such difficulties?
- How hindered is expressiveness when artifacts need to evolve?

To answer these questions, and again later to assess the results, a set of metrics will be used:

- How much *technical debt* and *software aging* exist?
- How *long* do capture activities take?
- How *expressive* can developers be?

6. Current Work

Wikis are nowadays very popular in software development. They are an effective approach to collaborative knowledge capture, and used extensively to support software documentation artifacts.

Weaki is a wiki engine developed in the context of this doctoral work, which supports the incremental capture and evolution of structured document artifacts [2]. For now, its development has focused on dealing with evolving document structures, and increasing awareness by the users towards the structure of contents. Although it possesses no specific features for software development at this time, our goal is to apply it to this domain, allowing the integration of some of the most common types of software artifacts, and supporting evolution beyond their original form.

We plan to support its development using an AOM design. A framework for the development of AOM-based systems has been under development, and will be used for this purpose [5].

Patterns have also been mined from existing literature and tools, and will also be used during development [3, 4].

7. Research Plan

The remaining of this research work will encompass these phases:

- **Identify further needs of knowledge capture and evolution in the context of software projects.** The recognition of these needs will be made through literature review, case-studies and quasi-experiments. The approaches currently used to handle them will be documented as patterns;

- **Create a prototype environment.** Taking the development of Weaki further, an environment will be created for managing software artifacts, that will allow their expression, and their evolution beyond an initial structure;

- **Validate the approach.** Quasi-experiments and case-studies will be used to validate the use of adaptive software artifacts and their benefits in a context of evolving software knowledge;

- **Document and consolidate the obtained results.** The results previously obtained will be analyzed and documented.

References

[1] A. Aguiar and G. David. WikiWiki weaving heterogeneous software artifacts. In *Proceedings of the 2005 international symposium on Wikis*, pages 67–74, San Diego, California, 2005. ACM.

[2] F. F. Correia, H. S. Ferreira, N. Flores, and A. Aguiar. Incremental knowledge acquisition in software development using a Weakly-Typed wiki. In *Proceedings of the 5th International Symposium on Wikis and Open Collaboration*, Orlando, Florida, USA, Oct. 2009. ACM.

[3] F. F. Correia, H. S. Ferreira, N. Flores, and A. Aguiar. Patterns for consistent software documentation. In *Proceedings of the Pattern Languages of Programs*, Chicago, Illinois, USA, Aug. 2009.

[4] H. S. Ferreira, F. F. Correia, and L. Welicki. Patterns for data and metadata evolution in adaptive Object-Models. In *Proceedings of the Pattern Languages of Programs*, Nashville, Tennessee, USA, Oct. 2008. ACM.

[5] H. S. Ferreira, F. F. Correia, and A. Aguiar. Design for an adaptive Object-Model framework: An overview. In *4th Workshop on Models@run.time at MODELS 09*, pages 71–80, Oct. 2009. URL http://ceur-ws.org/Vol-509/MRT09_proceedings.pdf.

[6] R. Garud, S. Jain, and P. Tuertscher. Incomplete by design and designing for incompleteness. In *Design Requirements Engineering: A Ten-Year Perspective*, pages 137–156. Springer, 2009.

[7] P. N. Robillard. The role of knowledge in software development. *Communications of the ACM*, 42(1):87–92, 1999.

[8] J. W. Yoder, F. Balaguer, and R. Johnson. Architecture and design of adaptive object-models. *ACM SIG-PLAN Notices*, 36(12):50–60, Dec. 2001.

Dynamic Tainting for Deployed Java Programs

Du Li

Deptartment of Computer Science and Engineering
University of Nebraska-Lincoln
Lincoln, NE 68588-0115
dli@cse.unl.edu

Abstract

Dynamic tainting is a powerful technique that has been used to detect computer attacks, generate test cases, analyze data scopes, and protect memory. However, existing tainting techniques suffer from excessive runtime overheads that can be as high as 30 to 50 times, making them unsuitable for applications in deployed systems. The goal of our work is to provide an efficient and low-overhead tainting framework that can be used in deployed environments.

To accomplish this goal, we propose to implement a framework that supports dynamic tainting as a feature of a Java Virtual Machine (JVM). In this approach, the tainting code can be injected by the JVM without needing to instrument the source code. It can also support customizable and configurable tainting. The overhead of tainting can be controlled by sampling and different tainting granularity. For example, the framework can taint all the data as needed when the workload is low. It can also taint only a subset of interesting data to reduce the overhead. Ultimately, we envision that our proposed framework will be instrumental in various dynamic monitoring methodologies including runtime verification.

Categories and Subject Descriptors D.2.5 [*Software Engineering*]: Testing and Debugging—Debugging aids, Testing tools; D.3.4 [*Programming Languages*]: Processors—Debuggers, Runtime environments

General Terms Language, Performance, Experimentation

Keywords Tainting, Java Virtual Machine

1. Introduction

Dynamic tainting has been used in various testing and debugging techniques to trace an execution of a program to determine which parts of computation are affected by predefined tainting sources. Currently most existing tainting tools such as *Dytan* [5], which is based on *PIN* [6] and *Taintcheck*, which is based on *Valgrind* [9] can incur 20 to 50 times overhead because they are built on third-party infrastructures. Furthermore, these infrastructures must be set up to replicate the real operating environments before these tainting tools can be used, requiring potential users to expend additional efforts to properly set up these tools. These factors make these tools only useful for testing and debugging purposes; they cannot feasibly be used with deployed software.

In mission critical systems, the ability to detect faults at runtime plays a critical role in enabling system adaptability and self-healing, runtime verification, and fault tolerance. Dynamic tainting during deployment can allow runtime detection of software components that have been affected by a failed component. This information can then be used to bypass some of these affected modules or replace them with "safer" modules, designed to operate the system in safe-mode [8] as part of system recovery. Clause *et al.* [4] and Chang *et al.* [3] have shown tainting tools that incur small runtime overhead can be quite useful in deployed systems.

2. Our Approach

Our goal is to implement an efficient tainting analysis framework for Java that can be used in deployed systems. To achieve this goal, the framework must meet the following requirements. First, our framework must be able to run in deployed environments without needing additional infrastructure components. To meet this requirement, we will implement our framework as part of a high-performance JVM. Users can utilize our framework by simply setting a configuration flag. Second, its overhead must be low enough to be used in deployed systems without significantly degrading their performances. We plan to meet this requirement by leveraging existing runtime components that are regularly used as part of normal VM operations. As such, the overhead of our framework should be small. Last, the framework must be configurable and adaptive to meet the runtime and user's performance requirements. We plan to meet this requirement by: (i) allowing users to specify particular data sources that

Copyright is held by the author/owner(s).
SPLASH'10, October 17–21, 2010, Reno/Tahoe, Nevada, USA.
ACM 978-1-4503-0240-1/10/10.

must be tainted; (ii) allowing users to specify predicates to initiate tainting; and (iii) providing user-configurable sampling interfaces.

2.1 Implementation Plan

We plan to leverage existing JVM's runtime systems to accomplish our goal. The first major component that we will investigate is the dynamic compiler. The tainting related code can be injected and optimized by the Just-In-Time (JIT) compiler. According to our preliminary investigation, optimized codes run 5 to 10 times faster than unoptimized codes. So we can expect the performance of tainting process to be significantly improved with optimization of the JIT compiler. We will also investigate recent work on high performance program analysis [2].

We will investigate the use of read/write barrier mechanism used to support data tracking. Our previous work has shown that the overhead to perform read/write barriers on primitive and reference data is less than 30% in large programs. We expect that barriers will dominate the overhead.

We will also investigate the use of garbage collector to process the tainting information. This may require additional steps in the garbage collection process. Furthermore, we may need to abandon the incremental approach in favor of full-heap collectors [1]. This aspect of our implementation will be heavily investigated.

In addition to these existing features, the proposed framework exploits information maintained by the JVM to guide tainting process, making our taint analysis more accurate and efficient. For example, if we need to taint data in a specific service request in a large application server, we simply turn on the tainting feature when the request begins. When the service is completed or rolled back, we can turn off the tainting feature to reduce the overhead. We also plan to support predicate-based approach to trigger tainting when certain events occur. The knowledge about application comes from two sources: code emitted by the JIT compiler and information obtained through static program analysis. The analysis results are then used to guide the tainting process to make it smarter and faster.

Our approach also considers trade-offs between performance and accuracy. As we previously discussed, the runtime overhead is a major performance penalty for our tainting analysis framework. Most of the existing tainting tools use best-effort strategy. So in some scenario, when the amount of data to be tainted is enormous, the overhead is inevitably high. We plan to use adaptive policy instead of best-effort policy allowing users to identify interesting data to taint; making a trade-off between completeness and performance. We also monitor the system's load and the tainting overhead. When the system is heavily loaded and the tainting overhead is high, for example, our technique can dynamically adjust the sampling granularity to ensure the system overall performance is not lower than a specified threshold.

3. Conclusion

In this paper, we outline our plan to create a tainting analysis framework that is applicable to deployed systems. Our approach can reduce the overhead and improve the flexibility of tainting analysis. Our framework will be implemented in a high performance JVM. We will leverage its existing runtime systems to ease the development and reduce the overhead. We anticipate that our tainting framework will be efficient, accurate, and configurable, which are important factors for its applicability in deployed systems.

Acknowledgments

This work is supported in part by the National Science Foundation through award CNS-0411043 and CNS-0720757. I would like to thank my advisor, Dr. Witawas Srisa-an for his guidance and support of this research. I would also like to thank the reviewers for their valuable comments.

References

[1] Aftandilian, Edward E. and Guyer, Samuel Z. 2009. GC Assertions: Using the Garbage Collector to Check Heap Properties. In Proceedings of the ACM Conference on Programming Language Design and Implementation. 235-244.

[2] Bond, M. D., Baker, G. Z., and Guyer, S. Z. 2010. Breadcrumbs: Efficient Context Sensitivity for Dynamic Bug Detection Analyses. In Proceedings of the ACM Conference on Programming Language Design and Implementation. 13-24.

[3] Chang, W., Streiff, B., and Lin, C. 2008. Efficient and Extensible Security Enforcement Using Dynamic Data Flow Analysis. In Proceedings of the ACM Conference on Computer and Communications Security. 39-50.

[4] Clause, J., Doudalis, I., Orso, A., and Prvulovic, M. 2007. Effective Memory Protection Using Dynamic Tainting. In Proceedings of IEEE/ACM International Conference on Automated Software Engineering. 284-292.

[5] Clause, J., Li, W., and Orso, A. 2007. Dytan: A Generic Dynamic Taint Analysis Framework. In Proceedings of the ACM International Symposium on Software Testing and Analysis. 196-206.

[6] Luk, C., Cohn, R., Muth, R., Patil, H., Klauser, A., Lowney, G., Wallace, S., Reddi, V. J., and Hazelwood, K. 2005. Pin: Building Customized Program Analysis Tools with Dynamic Instrumentation. In Proceedings of the ACM Conference on Programming Language Design and Implementation. 190-200.

[7] Nethercote, N. and Seward, J. 2007. Valgrind: A Framework for Heavyweight Dynamic Binary Instrumentation. In Proceedings of the ACM Conference on Programming Language Design and Implementation. 89-100.

[8] Rathinam, S., Sengupta, R. 2004. A Safe Flight Algorithm for Unmanned Aerial Vehicles. In Proceedings of the IEEE Aerospace Conference.

[9] Seward, J. and Nethercote, N. 2005. Using Valgrind to Detect Undefined Value Errors with Bit-precision. In Proceedings of the Annual Conference on USENIX Annual Technical Conference. 17-30.

Typelets

Duraisamy S. Pradeep Kumar

College of Engineering, Guindy
Anna University
Chennai, India.
ds.pradeepkumar@yahoo.com

Abstract

Numbers play an important role in every-day life. In a very large-scale program, type system helps to detect the programming errors at compile time. However, the existing type system lack in defining type properties based on numeric values. Typelets ensures types based on numbers rather than predefined assumptions.

Categories and Subject Descriptors   D.3.3 [**Programming Languages**]: Language Constructs

General Terms   Languages, Verification.

Keywords   typelets; dependent types

1.   Introduction

Numbers play an important role in every-day life. In a very large-scale program, types help to organize the program and make changes to it reliably. The existing type system fixes the reasoning of objects based on fixed typing assumptions thereby they lack in defining type properties based on numeric values. For instance, number of aliases or socket connections etc., permitted per-object or group-of objects cannot be defined by the type system of existing programming language because it does not distinguish   between number of current aliases/connections and permitted alias/connections count.

Typelets: The typelets are small type based on numbers used to express constraints on objects.

Typelet is an extension to the Alias Count [3]. For example, in this paper, the typelets is classified under ourteen categories, which at present can be possible by either designing a type-checker to detect and prevent errors in a language independent manner or else designing certain programming patterns/methodologies/type annotations.

The fourteen categories are as follows:

1. number of aliases permitted per-object or group-of objects

2. number of concurrent threads permitted
3. number of locks a thread can acquire at particular time
4. number of references permitted from outside to inside and inside to outside the owners' boundary
5. number of objects permitted for a class
6. number of role-binding permitted for an object
7. number of subclasses permitted for a class
8. number of objects within a container
9. number of socket connections permitted per object
10. number of SQL connections permitted per object
11. number of reads/writes to a shared state
12. time constraint – amount of time a resource can be handled by a thread before releasing or how long certain information can be retained within the application
13. number of copies of an object must exist in the world at particular period of time in a distributed environment
14. number of times an object canbe copied/cloned

Typelets shall help us to create a good design environment. More importantly, designing a flexible mechanism based on typelets will help us to answer an important question like, how many times? The main advantage of typelets is that:

1. Typelets helps to design flexible and easy understood architectural specification [1] design method and easy implementation of the system.

2. Typelets shall enforce the static security check at compilation phase itself and thus it can reduce the runtime risk.

3. Typelets provides a simple method to add dependent type [4] kind of functionality to Java.

2.   Typelet as Annotations

Annotations provide additional semantics about a program that is not part of the program itself. They help the developers to understand the intent behind the implementation detail. Typelet specifications are added to

Copyright is held by the author/owner(s).
SPLASH'10 October 17–21, 2010, Reno/Tahoe, Nevada, USA.
ACM 978-1-4503-0240-1/10/10.

Java code in the form of annotations in comments, similar to JML [2].

Typelets are specified within comments. Typelets begin with an @ sign followed by typelet name followed by "equalto" (=) sign specifying the numbers.

E.g.
```
//@ <Typelet_Name> = <Number_Values>      (Or)
   /*@ <Typelet_Name> = <Number_Values>*/
```

Sample Program (Singleton Pattern):

```
/* @objectCount= 1 */
class B
{      static variable = 14;            }
main()
{
   B obj1 = new B();     //OK Permitted
   B obj2 = new B();     //Error – class B cannot have
                         //two objects
}
```

The above program shows the singleton pattern [5], here creation of more than one object is not allowed since the typelet *'objectCount'* gives the permission to create only one object for the class B.

Sample Program (Alias – Circular Linked List):

```
//@aliasCount = 2
class LinkedList
{      …;
       *forward;
}
main()
{
LinkedList head = new LinkedList();
LinkedList /* aliasCount =1*/ node1 = new LinkedList();
LinkedList /* aliasCount =1*/ node2 = new LinkedList();

   Iterator iterator = head.Iterator();        //reference 1
   head.forward = node1;
   node1.forward = node2;
   node2.forward = head;             //reference 2
LinkedList unknownAlias = new LinkedList();
(*)   unknownAlias.forward = head;
                        //reference 3  (ERROR)
}
```

The above program shows the class LinkedList, where at any point of time a node can have only 2 or less alias references as given by *'aliasCount'*. The aliasCount can also be specified at the time of object creation. The * line shows the error, where the reference from *unknownAlias.forward*

pointing to head will add third   reference to the head node, which is not permitted.

Typelets is a generic solution to most of the problem based on number system. Typelets are inheritable, where the subclass typelet value must be lessthan or equalto the super-class typelet value.
   i.e.

```
/* @objectCount= 3 */
class SuperClass
{      …;   }

/* @objectCount = n */
class SubClass extends SuperClass
{      …;   }
```

Where value of *n* must be less than or equalto 3 (n<=3), where 3 is the typelet value of the superclass.

Thus typelet design shall help developers to specify software architectural details that can also be extended safely to the subclass by at compile time itself.

3.   Conclusion and Future Work

In this paper the typelets are specified using numbers, which helps in designing more flexible and secure environment which has compile time analysis mechanisms. The future plan is to extend the work to study many other possibilities that can be provided at compile time for program analysis. The possibility of adding modal logics to typelets is also to be explored

Acknowledgments

I am grateful to Dr. Gary T. Leavens, for his motivation in developing typelets. I also thank my Parents, my brothers and sisters and my friends for their continuous support.

References

[1]   J. Aldrich. Using Types to Enforce Architectural Structure. PhD thesis, University of Washington, August 2003.

[2]   Gary T. Leavens, Albert L. Baker, and Clyde Ruby. Preliminary design of JML: A behavioural interface specification language for Java. ACM SIGSOFT Software Engineering Notes, 31(3), March 2006.

[3]   D S Pradeep Kumar. Alias Count Facilitate Ownership Transfer. In Poster Session, OOPSLA'08

[4]   H. Xi and F. Pfenning. Dependent types in practical   programming. In Twenty-Sixth ACM Symposium on   Principles of Programming Languages, pages 214{227, San Antonio, Texas, Jan. 1999.

[5]   Gamma, E., Helm, R., Johnson, R. and Vlissides, J. Design Patterns: elements of reusable object-oriented software,   Addison-Wesley, Reading, MA, 1995.

The Spoofax Language Workbench

Lennart C. L. Kats

Delft University of Technology

l.c.l.kats@tudelft.nl

Eelco Visser

Delft University of Technology

visser@acm.org

Abstract

Spoofax is a language workbench for efficient, agile development of textual domain-specific languages with state-of-the-art IDE support. It provides a comprehensive environment that integrates syntax definition, program transformation, code generation, and declarative specification of IDE components.

Categories and Subject Descriptors D.2.3 [*Software Engineering*]: Coding Tools and Techniques; D.2.6 [*Software Engineering*]: Programming Environments

General Terms Languages

1. Introduction

Domain-specific languages (DSLs) provide high expressive power focused on a particular problem domain. They provide linguistic abstractions and specialized syntax specifically designed for a domain, allowing developers to avoid boilerplate code and low-level implementation details.

The development of new DSLs comprises many tasks, ranging from syntax definition to code generation to the construction of an integrated development environment (IDE). Language engineering tools are essential for productivity in each of these tasks.

The Spoofax language workbench [2] is a platform for the development of textual domain-specific languages with state-of-the-art IDE support. Spoofax provides a comprehensive environment that integrates syntax definition, program transformation, code generation, and declarative specification of IDE components. The environment supports agile development of languages by allowing incremental, iterative development of languages and showing editors for the language under development alongside its definition (Figure 1). These editors can be used to view the abstract syntax of a program or to directly apply transformations on a selection of text.

Spoofax is based on Eclipse, an extensible programming environment that offers many language-generic development facilities such as plugins for version control, build management, and issue tracking. Spoofax language definitions take the form of Eclipse plugin projects, and can be distributed to "end developers" using the Eclipse update site mechanism.

2. Syntax Definition

The grammar forms the heart of the definition of any textual language. It specifies the concrete syntax (keywords etc.) and the abstract syntax (data structure for analysis and transformations) of a language. In Spoofax, the syntax is also used to derive customizable editor services, such as a default syntax highlighting service and an outline view service.

We use the modular syntax definition formalism SDF2 [3] for the specification of grammars. SDF grammars are highly modular, combine lexical and context-free syntax into one formalism, and can define concrete and abstract syntax together in production rules. Grammar productions in SDF take the form $p_1 \ldots p_n$ -> s and specify that a sequence of strings matching symbols p_1 to p_n matches the symbol s. Productions can be annotated with a constructor name n to uniquely identify them in the abstract syntax using the `{cons(n)}` annotation. Other annotations include `{left}` and `{right}` to specify the associativity of operators, and `{deprecated}` to indicate deprecated syntax.

Figure 1 (left) shows the SDF syntax for a datamodeling language (Figure 1, upper right). The first production rule defines `Start`, the start symbol of the grammar. It matches the `module` keyword, followed by an identifier, and a list of `Definitions`. Each `Definition` is a database entity with an identifier name and a list of `Property` symbols.

3. Editor Services

Modern IDEs increase developer productivity by incorporating many different kinds of *editor services* specific to the syntax and semantics of a language. They assist developers in understanding and navigating through the code, they direct developers to inconsistent or incomplete areas of code, and they even help with editing code by providing automatic indentation, bracket insertion, and content completion. As a consequence, developers that have grown accustomed to these services are growing less accepting of languages that do not have solid IDE support.

Editor services have a prominent role in Spoofax and can be specified using declarative editor descriptor languages. Spoofax generates default, customizable editor service descriptors based on the syntax of the language. Figure 2 illustrates an editor descriptor for the syntax highlighting of the entity language. It consists of two modules: `EntityLang-Colorer`, which specifies a custom color for types, and `EntityLang-Colorer.generated`, which contains generated default colors. Other editor services follow the same pattern, combining custom specifications with generated specifications that are based on static defaults and heuristic rules, each specified in its own file.

4. Code Generation

We use the Stratego program transformation language [1] to describe the semantics of a language. Stratego is based on rewrite rules for first-order terms, and strategies that control the application of these rules. Basic rewrite rules take the form

r : t_1 -> t_2 `where` s

with r the name of the rule, t_1 and t_2 first-order terms, and s an optional *strategy expression*. A rule applies to a term when its left-

Copyright is held by the author/owner(s).

SPLASH'10, October 17–21, 2010, Reno/Tahoe, Nevada, USA.

ACM 978-1-4503-0240-1/10/10.

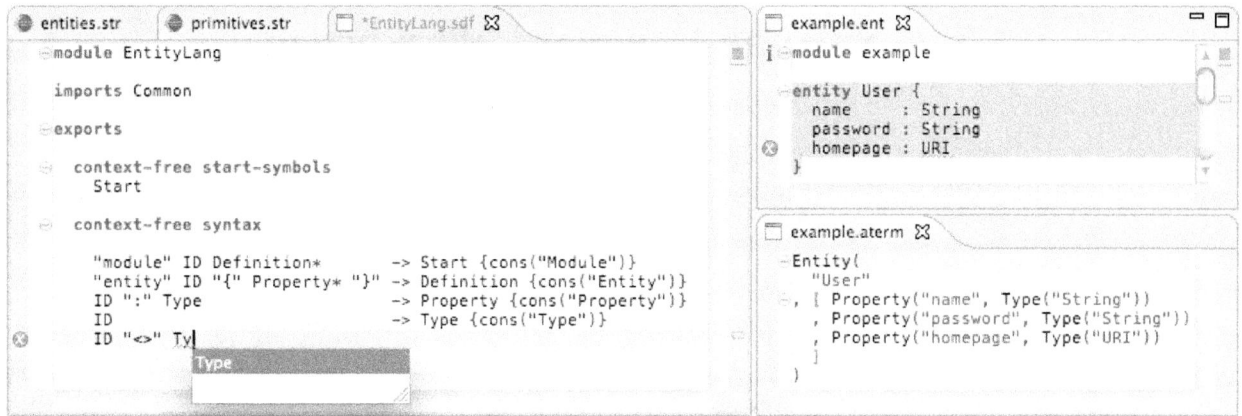

Figure 1. Multiple editors, side by side, in the same Eclipse IDE instance: the definition of an entity language (left), an editor for the entity language itself (upper right), and the abstract syntax of the selected entity (lower right).

hand side t_1 matches the term, and the condition s succeeds, resulting in the instantiation of the right-hand side pattern t_2. During development, the abstract syntax view can be used as a reference for the first-order term representation of a language's abstract syntax (lower-right of Figure 1).

Figure 3 shows rewrite rules that generate Java code for the entity language. These rules match against the abstract syntax of the language and generate string expressions for matching elements using the $[...] string interpolation syntax. String interpolation expressions construct a string of all literal characters between the quotes, except for escapes between [...]. Other transformation rules, not shown here, may rewrite to abstract syntax or may use syntax-checked concrete syntax expressions [4].

Code generation rules can be used to transform the DSL to a compilable form. They can be applied automatically as files are saved, or manually when triggered by the user. They can also be used to create *views* of the language, similar to the abstract syntax view of Figure 1. By default, views are automatically kept up-to-date and regenerated in the background as the source is changed.

5. Analysis and Transformation

Stratego rewrite rules are also used to specify semantic editor services, such as error markers, reference resolving, and content completion. Figure 4 shows two rules that check for semantic errors in the entity language. These rules use one or more conditions in their `where` clause to match elements of a program that contain errors.[1] At the right-hand side they include a tuple of the offending term – where the error marker would be placed in the editor – and the error message. As an example, the upper right editor of Figure 1 contains an error marker for the `"URI"` term in the User entity.

6. Conclusion

The Spoofax language workbench supports agile development of new programming languages by allowing selective, incremental development of editor services that can be dynamically loaded, evaluated, and tuned in the same environment. Using high-level languages to specify the syntax and semantics of a language, it provides a language development solution that greatly increases productivity of language engineers compared to using handwritten components or separate language engineering tools.

---

[1] For reasons of space, we do not include a full description and definition of these conditions here, but rather refer the reader to [2] for a comprehensive description of analyses and check rules.

```
module EntityLang-Colorer
imports EntityLang-Colorer.generated
colorer
  Type : blue

module EntityLang-Colorer.generated
colorer
  keyword    : magenta bold
  identifier : default
  string     : blue
  ...
```

Figure 2. Syntax highlighting rules for the entity language.

```
to-java:
  Entity(x, p*) ->
  $[ class [x] {
        [p2*]
     }
  ]
  where p2* := <to-java> p*

to-java:
  Property(x, Type(t)) -> $[
     private [t] [x];
     public [t] get_[x] { return [x]; }
     public void set_[x] ([t] [x]) { this.[x] = [x]; }
  ]
```

Figure 3. Code generation rules.

```
constraint-error:
  Property(x, Type(t)) -> (t, $[Unknown type [t]])
  where
     not(!t => "String");
     not(!t => "Int");
     not(<GetEntity> t)

constraint-warning:
  Entity(x, _) -> (x, $[Must start with a capital])
  where
     not(<string-starts-with-capital> x)
```

Figure 4. Semantic check rules for the entity language.

References

[1] M. Bravenboer, K. T. Kalleberg, R. Vermaas, and E. Visser. Stratego/XT 0.17. A language and toolset for program transformation. *Sci. of Comp. Programming*, 72(1-2):52–70, June 2008.

[2] L. C. L. Kats and E. Visser. The Spoofax language workbench. Rules for declarative specification of languages and IDEs. In M. Rinard, editor, *OOPSLA 2010*. ACM, 2010.

[3] E. Visser. A family of syntax definition formalisms. Technical Report P9706, Progr. Research Group, University of Amsterdam, July 1997.

[4] E. Visser. Meta-programming with concrete object syntax. In *GPCE 2002*, volume 2487 of *LNCS*, pages 299–315. Springer-Verlag, 2002.

Many-Core Virtual Machines

Decoupling Abstract from Concrete Concurrency

Stefan Marr[1]   Theo D'Hondt

Software Languages Lab
Vrije Universiteit Brussel, Belgium
stefan.marr@vub.ac.be

Abstract

We propose to search for common abstractions for concurrency models to enable multi-language virtual machines to support a wide range of them. This would enable domain-specific solutions for concurrency problems. Furthermore, such an abstraction could improve portability of virtual machines to the vastly different upcoming many-core architectures.

Categories and Subject Descriptors   D.3.4 [*Programming Languages*]: Processors;   D.1.3 [*Programming Techniques*]: Concurrent Programming

General Terms   Design, Languages, Performance

Keywords   Multi-language virtual machines, concurrency, many-core, abstraction, machine model, parallel programming models

1.   Problem Statement

Since the processor manufacturers reached the boundaries of what is feasible to achieve computational speedups in terms of increased clock rates, they changed their scaling dimension from *clock rate* to *core count*, i. e., the number of computing units on a single chip. With this change, they are still able to deliver more computing power with every new processor generation by shifting the burden of realizing speedups to the software developers[9]. However, for the development of end-user applications, today's systems still lack comprehensive support to make concurrency accessible and its complexity manageable.

The most widely used programming model for concurrency is shared memory with threads and locks. Unfortunately, this model has very narrow limits. Even though fine-grained locks have proven to allow high-performance concurrency, programming complexity increases fast with a rising number of threads and shared resources. Therefore, this model does not scale up to the degree of concurrency in many-core system. The use of disciplined concurrency models avoiding shared state, is almost the only choice to cope with the inherent complexity. With the actor model and software transactional memory, there are promising candidates available. However, the general forms of these models also have their problems, thus, we expect domain-specific solutions for the different application domains to become an important approach to handle concurrency.

Another aspect of the changing processor designs is an increase in the diversity of processor architectures. Processor designers experiment with various different approaches to arrange cores on the chip and to connect them to the memory system, using various different caching strategies, and possibly explicit inter-core communication. For instance, the Cell B.E., Intel's Larrabee[6], and Tilera's TILE architecture[11] are fundamentally different especially with respect to their memory architecture.

High-level language virtual machines (VMs) like the *Java Virtual Machine* (JVM) and *Microsoft's Common Language Runtime* (CLR) have become the major means to tackle these kind of problems and are used as multi-language runtime environments. Ongoing efforts like the introduction of the `invokedynamic` bytecode extend the capabilities of this platform to handle a large number of different programming paradigms[5].

However, concurrency is a concept for which VMs do not provide sufficient abstraction. The JVM and CLR have rudimentary support for threads and locks in their instruction set architectures, and Erlang as notable exception provides explicit support for the actor model in its BEAM opcodes set[3]. But there is no VM which exposes more than one concurrency model to the programmer or provides means to abstract from the different concrete concurrency models provided by the hardware. We expect that VMs have to

Copyright is held by the author/owner(s).
SPLASH'10,   October 17–21, 2010, Reno/Tahoe, Nevada, USA.
ACM 978-1-4503-0240-1/10/10.

[1] Supported by a doctoral scholarship of the Institute for the Promotion of Innovation through Science and Technology in Flanders, Belgium.

handle both aspects to be able to provide software developers with the necessary, possibly domain-specific tools to cope with concurrency.

2. Research Goal

Our main goal is to identify common abstractions of different abstract concurrency models which are also appropriate to be mapped efficiently onto the various upcoming many-core architectures[4]. Thus, the concurrency models on the different levels of implementation are to be decoupled. For this, we will experiment with an VM with explicit support for some form of disciplined concurrency. The VM has to provide appropriate abstractions to generalize the broad range of abstract concurrency models to be usable as a foundation for new language designs.

The analysis and design is approached iteratively to find an appropriate compromise between the different instances of the currently most important concurrency models as well as between these models itself. Currently, actors[1, 8], software transactional memory[7], and shared-memory models are most important. The analysis and design process will iterate over the different concurrency models and chose a suitable compromise for the different instances of the current model under investigation. The compromise will be guided from the viewpoint of the language designer as well as from the viewpoint of the VM implementer.

Important is also the mapping on a concrete concurrency model provided by a specific hardware architecture. The simplest, but still important one is an intra-core communication. This is the standard case for single-core processors, possible with multiple hardware threads. The next step is a uniform memory access model like it is used for current multi-core systems and could be used for subsets of cores on many-core systems as well. For real many-core systems only a non-uniform memory access model is feasible. At least this three concrete models have to be considered in the iterations to be able to provide a suitable mapping from the VM to different hardware architectures. Distributed systems, i. e., systems based on a number of physical nodes connected by a network are not regarded by this project. Instead, the main focus of this research are on the challenges with respect to processor internal communication and the influence of the different many-core architectures.

The results of this research should enable us to decouple abstract and concrete concurrency models by using an VM with inherent concurrency support. New abstract concurrency models can be implemented on top of the VM and a new concrete concurrency model or a new many-core architecture can be supported by the generalization the VM provides.

3. Current State and Future Work

Currently, we completed the initial phase of literature studies and prototyping of ideas. Thus, we investigated the state of the art in concurrency support for virtual machines[3] and experimented with support for threads and locks, as well as actor abstractions on the instruction set level[4]. Our experiments included also an analysis of high-level concurrency constructs with a focus on barrier synchronization. However, they turned out to be to divers and their high-level character did not match the requirements for a concept that needs to be directly supported by virtual machines.

Our future work will be based on the work of Ungar and Adams[10]. With this multi- and many-core virtual machine, we have a foundation for experimenting on the TILE architecture as well as commodity multi-core systems.

Furthermore, we will investigate the notions of locality and encapsulation as fundamental concepts to concurrency. Encapsulation refers to the guarantee given to an entity, for instance an object or an actor, that its internal state is only accessible by itself. Locality refers to the notion of a spacial relation between entities. For instance, the objects grouped together in an partitioned global address space model. We aim to evaluate their capabilities to facilitate virtual machine support for different concurrency models[2].

References

[1] G. Agha. *ACTORS: A Model of Concurrent Computation in Distributed Systems*. MIT Press, 1986.

[2] S. Marr. Encapsulation and locality: A foundation for concurrency support in multi-language virtual machines? In *Proc. of SPLASH 2010 - Doctoral Symposium*, 2010. (to appear).

[3] S. Marr, M. Haupt, and T. D'Hondt. Intermediate language design of high-level language virtual machines: Towards comprehensive concurrency support. In *Proc. of VMIL'09*, pages 3:1–3:2. ACM, October 2009. (extended abstract).

[4] S. Marr, M. Haupt, S. Timbermont, B. Adams, T. D'Hondt, P. Costanza, and W. D. Meuter. Virtual machine support for many-core architectures: Decoupling abstract from concrete concurrency models. In *Prof. of PLACES'09*, 2010.

[5] J. R. Rose. Bytecodes meet combinators: Invokedynamic on the jvm. In *Proc. of VMIL'09*, pages 1–11. ACM, 2009.

[6] L. Seiler, D. Carmean, E. Sprangle, T. Forsyth, M. Abrash, P. Dubey, S. Junkins, A. Lake, J. Sugerman, R. Cavin, R. Espasa, E. Grochowski, T. Juan, and P. Hanrahan. Larrabee: A many-core x86 architecture for visual computing. *ACM Trans. Graph.*, 27(3):1–15, 2008.

[7] N. Shavit and D. Touitou. Software transactional memory. In *Proc. of PODC'95*, pages 204–213. ACM, 1995.

[8] S. Srinivasan and A. Mycroft. Kilim: Isolation-typed actors for java. In *Proc. of ECOOP'08*, pages 104–128, 2008.

[9] H. Sutter. The free lunch is over: A fundamental turn toward concurrency in software. *Dr. Dobbs Journal*, 30(3), 2005.

[10] D. Ungar and S. S. Adams. Hosting an object heap on many-core hardware: An exploration. In *Proc. of DLS'09*, 2009.

[11] D. Wentzlaff, P. Griffin, H. Hoffmann, L. Bao, B. Edwards, C. Ramey, M. Mattina, C.-C. Miao, J. F. B. III, and A. Agarwal. On-chip interconnection architecture of the tile processor. *IEEE Micro*, 27(5):15–31, 2007.

Guiding Modelers through Conflict Resolution: A Recommender for Model Versioning *

Petra Brosch   Martina Seidl   Konrad Wieland

Business Informatics Group
Vienna University of Technology, Austria
{lastname}@big.tuwien.ac.at

Abstract

Like traditional code, software models are usually developed in teams requiring collaboration support in terms of version control systems (VCS). One use case of such a system is integrating concurrently evolved versions of one model into one consistent version. When the modifications are contradicting, then the VCS reports the conflict, but the cumbersome resolution process is left to the user. We present a recommender system which suggests automatically executable conflict resolution patterns.

Categories and Subject Descriptors   D.2.9 [*Software Engineering*]: Management—Programming teams

General Terms   Design, Languages

1. Introduction

When multiple developers concurrently work on the same artifact, conflicting modifications are very likely to be performed. Merging the different versions poses a very time-intensive, repetitive challenge in order to obtain a consistent artifact which integrates the work of all involved developers. To support the merging process, version control systems provide conflict detection components which highlight potential conflicts. The following task of conflict resolution is then manually carried out by one developer, preventing him/her from doing productive work. In order to unburden and support developers, if the artifact under consider-

* This work has been partly funded by the Austrian Federal Ministry of Transport, Innovation, and Technology and the Austrian Research Promotion Agency under grant FIT-IT-819584 and by the fFORTE WIT Program of the Vienna University of Technology and the Austrian Federal Ministry of Science and Research.

Copyright is held by the author/owner(s).
SPLASH'10,   October 17–21, 2010, Reno/Tahoe, Nevada, USA.
ACM 978-1-4503-0240-1/10/10.

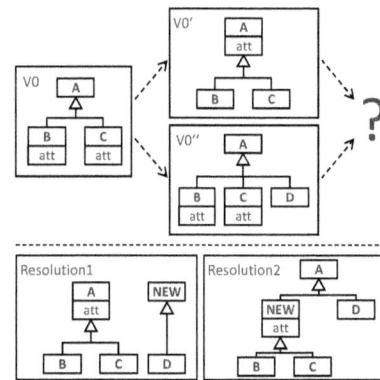

Figure 1. Motivating Example

ation is a software model, we present a recommender system which suggests automatically executable conflict resolution patterns applicable to the given scenario. The recommender system is integrated into the adaptable model versioning system AMOR [1] which offers an enhanced conflict detection component. This component reports not only conflicts where atomic changes like add, update, and delete are involved, but also composite operations like refactorings which imply a multitude of possible resolution approaches.

2. Conflicts in Model Versioning

In the context of optimistic model versioning, where multiple modelers are allowed to modify the same artifact at the same time, *conflicts due to overlapping changes* occur whenever two or more modelers modify an artifact in a contradicting manner, i.e., if the involved operations are sequentially applied, the result is dependent on the order of the operations. Another kind of conflicts are *violations* occurring in the model, which integrates the valid versions of different modelers. For a detailed discussion on the notion of conflicts in model versioning, we kindly refer to [2].

An example scenario is shown in Fig. 1. The base version V0 contains a UML Class Diagram consisting of the classes B and C which both contain an attribute att and which are both subclasses of the class A. Then one modeler performs

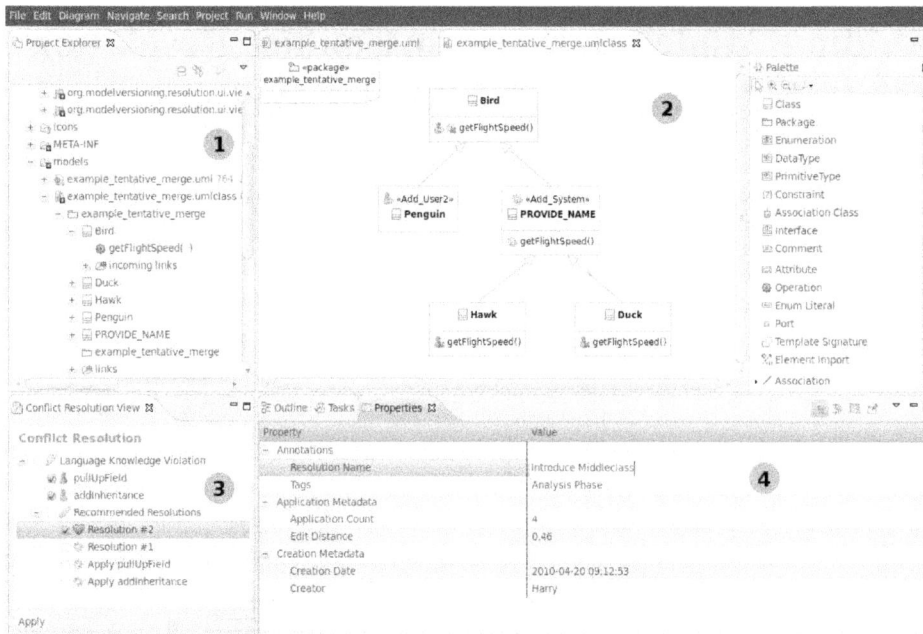

Figure 2. AMOR Conflict Resolver

a refactoring pullUpField and shifts the common attribute to the superclass. At the same time, another modeler introduces the new class D which is also a subclass of A. A naive merge incorporating all changes would result in a model, where D inherits the attribute att. The conflict detection component of AMOR is able to report such a conflict due to the violation of one precondition of the refactoring, i.e., all subclasses must have an attribute with the given name. Then multiple resolution strategies are possible, including the trivial solutions like abandoning the modifications of one modeler or including all modifications. More sophisticated resolution strategies are shown in the lower half of Fig. 1.

In order to support the modeler in charge of conflict resolution we propose a recommender system offering resolution patterns. The recommendations should facilitate the resolution process since they are automatically executable, but also offer guidance by showing different strategies to eliminate a conflict.

3. Realization

The proposed recommender system is based on the Eclipse Modeling Framework and Eclipse Team Support. It extends the manual conflict resolution facilities of AMOR as shown in Fig. 2 which implements the basic interplay with the versioning server (cf. (1) in Fig. 2) and offers the possibility to remodel artifacts to resolve conflicts (2). The actual recommender system (3) supports the conflict resolution by providing a list of automatically applicable resolutions patterns for each conflict looked up from a repository of conflicts. The resolution patterns in this repository are either defined manually or are automatically mined as described in [1]. The

proposed resolution patterns may be previewed, rolled back, and manually refined. For easier identification of conflicting operations in the preview mode, the conflicting operations are marked with the dedicated user symbol combined with annotations indicating the application of *add*, *delete*, and *update* on the respective model elements. Recommended resolution strategies are marked accordingly with a system symbol (the cog). Previewing many operations at once may on the one hand overflow the model, but on the other hand may be necessary to understand changes. Therefore, the user may decide which operation should be displayed.

The recommended resolutions are ranked by their relevance. The relevance is calculated by a combination of the edit distance between the current conflict situation and the stored one, the number of applications so far, and the impact of the user who created the conflict resolution, by aggregating the application count of all resolutions created by this user. Resolution specific information is displayed in a dedicated property view (4). The property view contains metadata about the resolution's origin, application and edit distance. Furthermore, since automatically derived resolutions do not have a name, users may enhance the resolution pattern by providing a meaningful name and tags.

References

[1] P. Brosch, G. Kappel, P. Langer, M. Seidl, K. Wieland, M. Wimmer, and H. Kargl. Adaptable Model Versioning in Action. In *Modellierung*, LNI. GI, 2010.

[2] P. Brosch, P. Langer, M. Seidl, K. Wieland, and M. Wimmer. Colex: A Web-based Collaborative Conflict Lexicon. In *Int. Workshop on Model Comparison in Practice*. ACM, 2010.

Reconciling Concurrency and Modularity with Pāṇini's Asynchronous Typed Events

Yuheng Long   Hridesh Rajan   Sean L. Mooney

Dept. of Computer Science, Iowa State University

{csgzlong,hridesh,smooney@iastate.edu}

Abstract

This poster presents our language design called Pāṇini. It focuses on Pāṇini's asynchronous, typed event which reconciles the modularity goal promoted by the implicit invocation design style with the scalability goal of exposing concurrency between the execution of subjects and observers.

Categories and Subject Descriptors   D.3.2 [*Language Classifications*]: Concurrent, distributed, and parallel languages; D.3.3 [*Language Constructs and Features*]: Concurrent programming structures, Patterns

General Terms   Languages, Design, Performance

Keywords   Safe Implicit Concurrency, Modularity

1. Introduction

We present our implicitly concurrent language Pāṇini [3]. The overall goal of its design is to discourage the use of explicitly concurrent features such as threads and locks. Using explicitly concurrent features can complicate program design, development, verification, and maintenance. Instead Pāṇini's design encourages programmers to construct their system to improve modularity in its design. If programmers use Pāṇini's features to improve modularity, they automatically receive concurrency.

This poster will demonstrate Pāṇini's asynchronous, typed events [3]. This language feature aims to achieve a synergy between modularity in program design and concurrency for implicit-invocation design style. In this design style components are decoupled using the event abstraction. Some components, called *Subjects*, announce events. Other components, called *Observers*, express interest to receive event notifications. So subjects are able to invoke observers without becoming name-dependent on them.

Copyright is held by the author/owner(s).
SPLASH'10,   October 17–21, 2010, Reno/Tahoe, Nevada, USA.
ACM 978-1-4503-0240-1/10/10.

The event abstraction has been proposed before as a mean for introducing distributed concurrency, e.g. by Schmidt's reactor pattern [7], Actor-based model as in Erlang [1]. These ideas work well with a distributed memory model, where concurrent tasks are isolated. However, languages with shared memory models introduce its own challenges to concurrent execution of subjects and observers.

The novelty of Pāṇini's language design, its semantics and implementation is that it addresses the challenges due to shared memory models. The resulting design thus allows programmers to modularize their programs using the implicit-invocation style and in doing so exposes safe, predictable concurrency between subjects and observers.

2. Pāṇini's Language Design

Pāṇini is designed as an extension of Java. Main new abstraction in Pāṇini is an event type (**event**). For subjects, it is an abstraction of all observers and vice-versa for subjects. Thus, unlike object-oriented observer pattern [2], in Pāṇini, we have a two-way decoupling of components. An example event type is shown below.

```
1 event Available {
2   Request r;
3 }
```

For a hypothetical chain-of-responsibility like scenario, this declaration gives a type to events named `Available`. This event type has a context variable of type `Request`. Context variables are reflective information about events. Just like observer design pattern, in Pāṇini, components may also announce events using the **announce** expressions.

```
4 class Client {
5   void makeRequest (...) { ....
6     Request req = ...
7     announce Available(req);
8   }
9 }
```

Two advantages are noteworthy here. First, unlike typical usage of observer design pattern, where programmers often have to put together boiler-plate infrastructure for events, in Pāṇini, event announcements are declarative. Second, Pāṇini's compiler would check for correctness of event announcements and is often able to optimize announcements behind the scene to produce faster code.

Unlike observer pattern: observers must explicitly register with each subject (and thus are coupled with them), in Pāṇini, registration is declarative. Following illustrates.

```
10 class Handler1 {
11   ...
12   when Available do handle;
13   void handle(Request r) {
14   if(canHandle(r)) doHandle(r);
15 }}
```

In this listing on line 12 is an example of *binding* declaration in Pāṇini. This declarations says to run the method `handle` when events of type `Available` are announced.

Let us now assume a variation of chain-of-responsibility pattern where there are several handlers (`Handler1 ... HandlerN`) capable of handling request. This chain could be an implicit source of concurrency in this application, however, exploiting this concurrency in a safe manner would require analyzing these N handlers and determining if their concurrent execution can create data-races. Furthermore, to be able to understand this system's operation it would be nice to determine a sequential order of execution of these handlers and reason about the system execution that follows this order. This would avoid complications that normally arise due to interleaving between concurrent tasks.

Pāṇini relieves programmers of these tasks. During compilation, Pāṇini's compiler creates a summary of the effects of observers. This summary is computed by analyzing the control-flow graph to determine reads, writes, event announcements and registrations. When an observer registers at runtime, Pāṇini's runtime system uses this summary to compare whether concurrent execution of this observer with other already registered observers for the same event is likely to create a data-race. This is done by comparing the effect summaries of observers. Based on this comparison a safe order of execution of observers is automatically created that maximizes available implicit concurrency in the program. Pāṇini does this book-keeping during registration because registration is infrequent compared to announcement.

When an event is signalled as in the listing above, all of its observers are run in the order determined at registration. This introduces safe implicit concurrency.

2.1 Benefits of Pāṇini's Design

Main benefit of Pāṇini's design is that it allows developers to introduce implicit concurrency in their program (and thus achieve scalability in their applications) while producing modular software designs. Pāṇini does not have locks so it is deadlock free. It uses automatic conflict detection that ensures race freedom and guarantees sequential semantics. Another key benefit is that all of the concurrency-related logic is encapsulated behind the language features. This avoids any threat of incorrect or non-deterministic concurrency, thus allowing programmers to concentrate on creating a good, maintainable modular design. Additional concurrency between modules is automatically exposed.

2.2 Advantages of Pāṇini's Design over Related Ideas

Pāṇini is similar to our previous work on Ptolemy [5], but Pāṇini provides concurrency advantages. It is also similar to the ideas promoted for distributed concurrency [1, 7], however, Pāṇini's design also accounts for conflicting effects between observers in a typical shared memory model. Compared to Jade [6] that allows implicit concurrency for explicit calls, Pāṇini allows implicit concurrency for implicit invocation. Unlike message-passing languages such as Erlang [1], the communication between implicitly concurrent handlers is not limited to value types or record of value types.

3. Conclusion

In the design of Pāṇini, we have developed the notion of asynchronous, typed events that are especially helpful for programs where modules are decoupled using implicit-invocation design style [4]. Event announcements provide implicit concurrency in program designs when events are signaled and consumed. We have tried out several examples, where Pāṇini improves both program design and potential available concurrency. Furthermore, performance of Pāṇini programs is comparable to hand-tuned explicitly concurrent programs. Thus, an important property of Pāṇini's design is that, for systems utilizing implicit-invocation design style, it makes scalability a by-product of modularity.

Pāṇini is available from `http://paninij.org`.

Acknowledgments. This work was supported in part by the US NSF under grant CCF-08-46059.

References

[1] J. Armstrong, R. Williams, M. Virding, and C. Wikstroem. *Concurrent Programming in ERLANG*. Prentice-Hal, 1996.

[2] E. Gamma, R. Helm, R. Johnson, and J. Vlissides. *Design Patterns: Elements of Reusable Object-Oriented Software*. Addison-Wesley Longman Publishing Co., Inc., 1995.

[3] Y. Long, S. L. Mooney, T. Sondag, and H. Rajan. Implicit invocation meets safe, implicit concurrency. In *GPCE '10: Ninth International Conference on Generative Programming and Component Engineering*, October 2010.

[4] D. Notkin, D. Garlan, W. G. Griswold, and K. J. Sullivan. Adding Implicit Invocation to Languages: Three Approaches. In *JSSST International Symposium on Object Technologies for Advanced Software*, pages 489–510, 1993.

[5] H. Rajan and G. T. Leavens. Ptolemy: A language with quantified, typed events. In *ECOOP*, pages 155–179, 2008.

[6] M. C. Rinard and M. S. Lam. The design, implementation, and evaluation of Jade. *ACM Trans. Program. Lang. Syst.*, 20(3):483–545, 1998.

[7] D. C. Schmidt. Reactor: an object behavioral pattern for concurrent event demultiplexing and event handler dispatching. *Pattern languages of program design*, pages 529–545, 1995.

Translucid Contracts for Modular Reasoning about Aspect-oriented Programs

Mehdi Bagherzadeh[β], Hridesh Rajan[β], Gary T. Leavens[θ] and Sean Mooney[β]

[β]Iowa State University, Ames, IA, USA   [θ]University of Central Florida, Orlando, FL, USA
{mbagherz, hridesh, smooney}@iastate.edu   leavens@eecs.ucf.edu

Abstract

Several proposals have advocated notion of aspect-oriented (AO) interfaces to solve modular reasoning problems, but have not shown how to specify these interfaces to facilitate modular reasoning. Our work on translucid contracts shows how to specify AO interfaces which allow modular understanding and enforcement of control flow interactions.

Categories and Subject Descriptors D.2.4 [*Software/Program Verification*]: Programming by contract

General Terms Design, Languages, Verification

Keywords Modular Reasoning, Translucid Contracts

1. Introduction

In aspect-oriented (AO) languages like AspectJ, an aspect can affect the control flow of the base modules and consequently complicate modular reasoning. Several notions of explicit AO interfaces have been proposed to improve modular reasoning about AO programs [1, 3–6]. The research question behind this work is whether marrying such interfaces with a design by contract methodology can be effective for improving reasoning about AO programs.

Related Work and Problems. Design by contract (DBC) for AO languages has been explored before [4, 7], however, existing work relies on behavioral contracts (explained in more detail in [2]). Such behavioral contracts specify, for each of the aspect's advice methods, the relationship between its inputs and outputs, and treat the implementation of the aspect as a black box, hiding all the aspect's internal states from base modules and from other aspects. To illustrate, consider the code in Figure 1 from the canonical drawing editor example with functionality to draw points and a display updating functionality.

Figure 1 uses crosscutting interface (XPI) `Changed` as the AO interface [4]. The key idea behind XPI is to establish a design rule interface that serves to decouple the base design and the aspect design and governs exposure of execution phenomena as join points, how they are exposed through the join point model of the given language, and constraints on behavior across join points. For example, XPI `Changed` specifies the pointcut `jp`, on lines 8–9, which is exposed by class `Point` and advised by aspect `Update` (line 14).

A significant advantage of AO interfaces like XPIs is that they provide a syntactic location to specify contracts between the aspect and the base code [4], independent of both. Following previous work [4, 7], we added an example black-box behavioral contract to the `Changed` interface (lines 10–11). The behavioral contract is written in terms of precondition (*requires* clause) and postcondition (*ensures* clause). The contract states that any aspect, e.g. `Update` on lines 13–18, advising the base at the pointcut `jp` (lines 8-9) must ensure that object `fe` is non-null before advice is applied and stays non-null after advice is finished.

First Problem. The first problem with specifying aspect interfaces using behavioral contracts is that they are insufficient to specify the control effects of the advice in full generality [2]. For example if **proceed** on line 15 is inadvertently missed the contract in Figure 1 for AO interface `Changed` doesn't alert us. missing proceed would skip the evaluation of the expression **this**.x = x in setX.

Second Problem. The second problem with such behavioral contracts is that they don't help us in effectively reasoning about the effects of aspects on each other. Consider another example concern, say `Logging` aspect which logs changes of `Point` caused by setX. For this concern, different orders of composition with the `Update` concern, when **proceed** is missing on line 15, could lead to different results. In one composition where `Update` runs first followed by `Logging`, the evaluation of `Logging` will be skipped, whereas `Logging` would work in the reverse order of composition. An aspect developer can not, by just looking at the behavioral contract of the AO interface, reason about the composition of such aspects. Rather the developer must be aware of the effects of all aspects that apply to the AO

Copyright is held by the author/owner(s).

SPLASH'10, October 17–21, 2010, Reno/Tahoe, Nevada, USA.
ACM 978-1-4503-0240-1/10/10.

```
1  class Fig { }                          7  aspect Changed{                          13 aspect Update{
2  class Point extends Fig {              8   pointcut jp(Fig fe):                    14  void around (Fig fe): Changed.jp(fe){
3   int x; int y;                         9    call(void Fig+.set*(..)) && target(fe);  15   proceed(fe);
4   void setX(int x){                     10  requires fe != null                     16   Display.update(fe);
5    this.x = x;}                         11  ensures  fe != null                     17  }
6  }                                      12 }                                        18 }
```

Figure 1. A behavioral contract for aspect interfaces using XPI [4]

```
1  class Fig { }                  10 Fig event Changed {            19 class Update {
2  class Point extends Fig {      11  Fig fe;                       20  Update(){ register(this) }
3   int x; int y;                 12  requires fe != null           21  Fig update(thunk Fig rest,
4   Fig setX(int x){              13  assumes {                     22                Fig fe){
5    announce Changed(this){      14   invoke(next);                23   invoke(rest);
6     this.x = x; this            15   establishes fe == old(fe)    24   refining establishes fe == old(fe){
7    }                            16  }                             25    Display.update(fe); fe}
8   }                             17  ensures  fe != null           26  }
9  }                              18 }                              27  when Changed do update;}
```

Figure 2. A translucid contract for aspect interfaces in Ptolemy [6]

interface [1, 3]. Furthermore, if any of these aspect modules changes one must reason about every other aspect that applies to the same AO interface.

2. Translucid Contracts

To solve these problems, we are developing the notion of *translucid contracts* [2]. A translucid contract for an AO interface can be thought of as an abstract algorithm describing the behavior of aspects that apply to that AO interface. The algorithm is abstract in the sense that it may suppress many actual implementation details, only specifying their effects using specification expressions. This allows the specifier to decide to hide some details, while revealing others. We use a restricted form of refinement that requires structural similarity, to allow specification of control effects.

To illustrate, consider the translucid contract shown in Figure 2 on lines 12–17. Examples in Figure 1 and Figure 2 are the same except that the former uses behavioral contracts and is implemented in AspectJ whereas the latter is implemented in Ptolemy and uses translucid contracts. Ptolemy introduces quantified typed events [6] which share similarities with AO interfaces like XPIs. In Ptolemy events are defined using **event** type declaration (lines 10–18). Context variables are part of event declaration (line 11). Events are announced using **announce** (line 5) expression which also specifies event body (line 6). Observers explicitly register themselves using **register** (line 20) and use binding declarations (line 27) to specify the method to be run upon the announcement of a specific event. Expression **invoke** (line 23) is Ptolemy's equivalent for AspectJ's **proceed**. A **refining** expression supposedly refines its specification. Unlike AO languages, Ptolemy decouples subject and observer. Subject and observer are coupled to the event types.

Contrary to the behavioral contract, internal states of the handler methods that run when the event Changed is announced are exposed in the translucid contract. In particular, any occurrence of **invoke** expression in the handler *must*

be made explicit in the contract. The contract must be refined by each conforming handler method which handles the event type. This in turn allows the developer of the class Point announcing Changed, to understand the control effects of the handler methods by just inspecting the specification of Changed. For example, from lines 14 in Figure 2 one may conclude that, irrespective of the concrete handler methods, the body for the method setX will always be run.

Making the **invoke** expression explicit also benefits other handlers that may run when the event is announced. Consider the logging concern discussed earlier. Since the contract of Changed describes the control flow effects of the handlers, reasoning about the composition of the handler for logging and other handler methods becomes possible without knowing about all explicit handlers as the contract forces all refining handlers to evaluate **invoke** (line 14) [2].

Our analysis shows that translucid contracts are expressive enough to represent all of the Rinard *et al.*'s categories of control flow interactions. We also show how to apply our ideas to other notions of aspect-oriented interfaces [2].

References

[1] J. Aldrich. Open modules: Modular reasoning about advice. In *ECOOP '05*.

[2] M. Bagherzadeh, H. Rajan, and G. T. Leavens. Translucid contracts for aspect-oriented interfaces. In *FOAL '10*.

[3] C. Clifton and G. T. Leavens. MiniMAO$_1$: Investigating the semantics of proceed. *SCP '06*, 63(3).

[4] K. J. Sullivan *et al.* Modular aspect-oriented design with XPIs. *TOSEM '09*, 20(2).

[5] G. Kiczales and M. Mezini. Aspect-oriented programming and modular reasoning. In *ICSE '05*, pages 49–58.

[6] H. Rajan and G. T. Leavens. Ptolemy: A language with quantified, typed events. In *ECOOP '08*.

[7] J. Zhao and M. Rinard. Pipa: A behavioral interface specification language for AspectJ. In *FASE '03*.

Towards a Tool-based Development Methodology for Sense/Compute/Control Applications

Damien Cassou   Julien Bruneau   Julien Mercadal   Quentin Enard   Emilie Balland
Nicolas Loriant   Charles Consel
University of Bordeaux / INRIA / LaBRI, France
first-name.last-name@inria.fr

Abstract

This poster presents a design language and a tool suite covering the development life-cycle of a *Sense/Compute/Control (SCC) application*. This language makes it possible to define the architecture of an application, following an architectural pattern commonly used in SCC applications. Our underlying methodology assigns roles to the stakeholders, providing separation of concerns. Our tool suite includes a compiler that takes design artifacts written in our language as input. The compiler generates customized support for subsequent development stages, namely implementation and test. In doing so, it ensures the conformance between the architecture and the code. Our tool suite also includes a simulator for testing SCC applications, without requiring code modification. Our methodology has been applied to a wide spectrum of areas, such as building automation, advanced telecommunications, and health-care.

Categories and Subject Descriptors D.2.11 [*Software Engineering*]: Software Architectures—Domain-specific architectures; D.3.4 [*Software Engineering*]: Processors—Code generation

General Terms Design, Languages

Keywords Domain-Specific Languages, Architecture Description Languages, Generative Programming, Methodology

1. Introduction

Sense/Compute/Control (SCC) applications are applications that interact with a physical or computing environment. SCC applications are being deployed in a growing number of areas, including building automation, assisted living, robotics, ubiquitous computing, and autonomic computing. These systems involve a wide range of devices and software components, communicate using a variety of protocols, and rely on intricate distributed systems technologies. Besides requiring expertise on underlying technologies, developing an SCC application also involves domain-specific architectural knowledge to collect information relevant for the application, process it and perform actions. To improve the development of SCC applications, we propose a tool-based methodology that relies on the architectural description for guiding each development phase.

2. DiaSuite methodology

Figure 1 illustrates the different stages of our development methodology and its associated tools.[1]

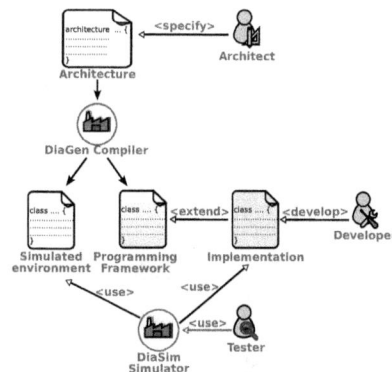

Figure 1. Development support provided by DiaSuite.

2.1 Specifying the architecture

To specify the architecture of an SCC application, we propose DiaSpec, a domain-specific Architecture Description Language (ADL). This domain-specific ADL is associated with an architectural pattern illustrated in Figure 2 that consists of three types of components: *entities* send information sensed from the environment to the context layer through data sources; *contexts* refine (aggregate and filter) the sensed

Copyright is held by the author/owner(s).
SPLASH'10, October 17–21, 2010, Reno/Tahoe, Nevada, USA.
ACM 978-1-4503-0240-1/10/10.

---

[1] http://diasuite.inria.fr

information provided by the entities; *controllers* interpret the information provided by the contexts to issue orders to the entities; finally, entities trigger actions on the environment. Our domain-specific ADL also includes declarations dedicated to error handling. These architecture-level declarations provide a separation between functional and error-handling concerns [6].

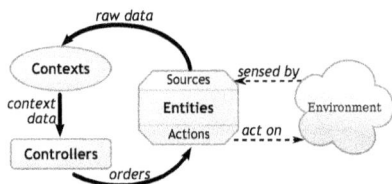

Figure 2. SCC Architectural pattern used in DiaSuite.

2.2 Implementation

We leverage the architecture description to provide dedicated support to the developers. This support takes the form of a Java programming framework, generated by the DiaGen compiler [3]. This framework guides the developer by providing high-level abstractions of low-level details (*e.g.,* the distributed systems technology) and ensures the conformance of the resulting implementation with the architectural specification. The generated programming framework also contains support for signaling, propagating and treating errors, which makes the programming of error handling more rigorous and systematic [6].

2.3 Testing

DiaGen generates a simulation support to test SCC applications before their actual deployment. An application is simulated with DiaSim [2], without requiring any code modification. DiaSim provides a graphical editor to define simulation scenarios and a 2D-renderer to monitor simulated applications. Furthermore, simulated and real entities can be mixed. This hybrid simulation enables an application to migrate incrementally to an actual environment.

3. Ongoing and future work

We have successfully applied our methodology to a variety of SCC applications in areas including advanced telecommunications [1], home/building automation [4], and healthcare [5]. Presently, this work is being expanded in various directions.

Enhancing the design phase. One direction consists of widening the scope of the DiaSpec language by introducing non-functional concerns (*e.g.,* fault-tolerance, safety and security) at the architectural level. For example, we are exploring how to enrich the error-handling mechanism with fault tolerance strategies.

Enhancing the testing phase. An ongoing work aims to simplify the testing phase by automatically generating a ded-

icated unit-testing framework. In accordance with the architect, a tester could then describe the desired behavior of each component separately, even before the implementation has started. Another direction concerns the simulation tool. Simulating natural phenomena like heat propagation can be quite complex as they involve mathematical equations. We are actively working on easing simulation of these phenomena by leveraging Acumen [7], a DSL for describing differential equations.

Enhancing the evolution phase. Our approach permits late changes to the architecture; a change in the architecture triggers a compile-time error in the developer's code. We believe the architect could be provided with refactoring tools that would ease changes in the developers' code.

References

[1] B. Bertran, C. Consel, W. Jouve, H. Guan, and P. Kadionik. SIP as a universal communication bus: A methodology and an experimental study. In *ICC'10: Proceedings of the 9th International Conference on Communications*, Cape Town, South Africa, 2010.

[2] J. Bruneau, W. Jouve, and C. Consel. DiaSim: A parameterized simulator for pervasive computing applications. In *Mobiquitous'09: Proceedings of the 6th International Conference on Mobile and Ubiquitous Systems: Computing, Networking and Services*, pages 1–10, Toronto Canada, 2009. IEEE Computer Society.

[3] D. Cassou, B. Bertran, N. Loriant, and C. Consel. A generative programming approach to developing pervasive computing systems. In *GPCE'09: Proceedings of the 8th International Conference on Generative Programming and Component Engineering*, pages 137–146, Denver, CO, USA, 2009. ACM.

[4] D. Cassou, J. Bruneau, and C. Consel. A tool suite to prototype pervasive computing applications (demo). In *PERCOM'10: Proceedings of the 8th International Conference on Pervasive Computing and Communications*, pages 1–3. IEEE Computer Society, 2010.

[5] Z. Drey, J. Mercadal, and C. Consel. A taxonomy-driven approach to visually prototyping pervasive computing applications. In *DSL WC'09: Proceedings of the 1st Working Conference on Domain-Specific Languages*, volume 5658, pages 78–99, 2009.

[6] J. Mercadal, Q. Enard, C. Consel, and N. Loriant. A domain-specific approach to architecturing error handling in pervasive computing. In *OOPSLA'10: Proceedings of the 25th International Conference on Object Oriented Programming Systems Languages and Applications (To appear)*, Reno, NV, USA, 2010.

[7] A. Y. Zhu, J. Inoue, M. L. Peralta, W. Taha, M. K. O'Malley, and D. Powell. Implementing haptic feedback environments from high-level descriptions. In *ICESS'09: Proceedings of the 6th International Conference on Embedded Software and Systems*, pages 482–489, Washington, DC, USA, 2009. IEEE Computer Society.

Almost Free Concurrency! (Using GOF Patterns)

Sean L. Mooney   Hridesh Rajan   Steven M. Kautz   Wayne Rowcliffe

Dept. of Computer Science, Iowa State University

[smooney, hridesh, smkautz, wrowclif]@iastate.edu

Abstract

We present a framework that provides concurrency-enhanced versions of the GOF object-oriented design patterns. The main benefit of our work is that if programmers improve program modularity by applying standard GOF design patterns while using the reusable pattern implementations from our framework, they receive implicit concurrency for free.

Categories and Subject Descriptors D.2.2 [*Design Tools and Techniques*]: Object-oriented design methods

General Terms Design, Human Factors, Languages

Keywords Modularity, concurrency, design patterns

1. Introduction

Although much library support exists for exploiting concurrency in embarrassingly parallel applications, finding opportunities for concurrency in a general purpose program and then implementing the concurrent design correctly and efficiently remains a challenge [5]. Potential concurrency isn't generally as obvious in general purpose programs as it is in scientific applications.

Our goal is to help programmers take advantage of implicit concurrency in their programs by providing a library of concurrency-enhanced implementations of standard Gang-of-Four (GOF) object-oriented design patterns [1]. GOF patterns are design structures that are commonly used to improve the modularity of object-oriented software. These patterns describe strategies to decouple components (participants) and specify how these participants should interact.

Our main insight is that the interactions between participants dictated by these patterns can be exploited to *automatically and safely* expose implicit concurrency between the participants. For example, the decorator pattern organizes components in a chain in which each component adds behavior to the previous component in the chain. If the added be-

havior of components in this chain is independent or can be split into dependent and independent parts, processing of independent added behaviors can be performed concurrently. Similarly, the builder pattern decouples the creation logic of complex products from their usage. If object creation is expensive, e.g. creating an object based on the contents of a file on disk, this pattern can allow object creation to interleave with other computation in the program.

Our main result is that for 18 out of 23 GOF patterns the decoupling of components specified by the pattern can be effectively used to expose implicit potential concurrency. The implication of our results is that applying these 18 patterns concomitantly improves the design and potentially available concurrency. As a result, when programmers practice good software design they receive implicit concurrency for free.

2. Related Ideas

Most related to this work is Mattson *et al.*'s work on parallel patterns [4] and Schmidt *et al.*'s work on the ACE framework [6]. Mattson *et al.* provide guidelines on how to structure a concurrent application, but require programmers to explicitly create threads and manage locks. Similarly, Lea [3] used a pattern-oriented approach to develop a set of concurrency utilities for the Java language that were subsequently incorporated into the standard libraries. These utilities provide a substantial improvement over the primitive features originally included with the Java platform, but the programmer must still identify potential concurrency and choose how to create and manage tasks and their synchronization mechanisms.

Schmidt *et al.*'s work on the ACE framework [6] also provides guidelines on structuring distributed, and thus potentially concurrent, applications. Their work also provides a reusable library for distributed concurrency, but leaves the synchronization tasks to the programmers. ACE is also targeted towards typically isolated tasks.

The basic difference between our work and prior work on parallel patterns is that we are proposing to exploit existing well-known design idioms to expose potential concurrency, whereas previous efforts propose new idioms that are particularly suited for explicit concurrency. Thus, we believe that the training efforts to use our framework will be minimal because OO programmers are typically already familiar with

Copyright is held by the author/owner(s).

SPLASH'10, October 17–21, 2010, Reno/Tahoe, Nevada. USA.
ACM 978-1-4503-0240-1/10/10.

GOF patterns. Our work is also related to the Galois system by Kulkarni *et al.* [2] where it is argued that exposing optimistic concurrency requires better abstraction. Their work is geared towards the iterator pattern, whereas we handle many more cases.

3. Illustration

We have briefly discussed the case for the decorator and builder patterns. Here we illustrate the design and usage of our framework via the composite pattern [1, p. 163].

The composite pattern is used to represent hierarchical structures in such a way that individual elements (leaves) of the structure and compositions of elements can be treated uniformly. Both individual and composite elements implement a common interface representing one or more operations on the structure. A client can invoke one of the operations without knowledge of whether an object is a leaf or composite element.

Operations on composites typically involve tree traversal to gather information about the structure. The value at a node often depends on the values computed from child nodes, but generally not on the values of sibling nodes. This fact suggests an opportunity for concurrency.

A simple and familiar composite structure is a file system, where directories are composites and files are leaves. An example of such a structure is shown in Figure 1.

```
1  interface FileSystemComponent{ //Common Interface
2    int sizeOperation();   // An operation on the structure
3  } //Other methods: add, remove, getChild, count elided.
4  class Directory implements FileSystemComponent{ //Composite
5    protected List<FileSystemComponent> children = ...
6    public int sizeOperation() { return 0; }
7  } // Other methods elided.
8  class File implements FileSystemComponent { // Leaf
9    protected int size;
10   public int sizeOperation() { return size; }
11 } // Other methods elided.
```

Figure 1. Composite Elements and Individual Elements.

Performing an operation on the structure involves a recursive traversal as shown in Figure 2.

```
1  int getTotalSize(FileSystemComponent c){
2    int size = c.sizeOperation();
3    for (int i = 0; i < c.getChildCount(); i++)
4      size += getTotalSize(c.getChild(i));
5    return size;
6  }
```

Figure 2. Recursive Traversal of Composite Structure.

To adapt the file hierarchy structure for concurrent operations we require node types to extend the generic class ConcurrentComponent from our framework. It provides methods for managing children along with the method operation(), shown in Figure 3, where Result and Arg are generic type parameters representing the result type and argument type for the operation. The operation() method initiates the concurrent traversal by creating the initial task and submitting it to the thread pool used to execute the tasks.

Application-specific behavior is added by implementing the abstract methods shown in Figure 3. In particular, the

method sequentialOperation() represents the operation to be performed on leaf nodes, and the combine() method determines how the children's results are assembled into a result for the parent node.

```
1  public abstract class ConcurrentComponent <Arg,Result>{
2    private static ForkJoinPool pool = new ForkJoinPool();
3    // Performs operation on a leaf
4    protected abstract Result sequentialOperation(Arg args);
5    // Distributes args value for child nodes
6    protected abstract Arg[] split(Arg args);
7    // Assembles the results from child nodes for parent
8    protected abstract Result combine(List<Result> results);

10   public Result operation(Arg args){
11     ConcurrentComponentTask<Arg,Result> task =
12       new ConcurrentComponentTask<Arg,Result>(this, args);
13     return pool.invoke(t);
14   }
15 } // other details elided
```

Figure 3. Library Class ConcurrentComponent.

The ConcurrentComponentTask class is a subtype of RecursiveTask from the fork-join framework. The key method is compute(), which is executed in the fork-join thread pool and returns a result via the join() method. For leaves, compute() delegates to sequentialOperation(). For composites, a new ConcurrentComponentTask is created for each child, and the results are assembled using the combine() method when they become available.

4. Conclusion

We have introduced a concurrent design pattern framework that provides concurrency-enhanced versions of 18 out of 23 GOF design patterns. Our motivation for the design and implementation of this framework was to exploit well-defined protocols of design patterns to automatically expose implicit concurrency in object-oriented software. For the 18 patterns that we have adapted, concurrency concerns are completely encapsulated inside our framework.

Acknowledgments This work was supported in part by the US National Science Foundation under grant 08-46059.

References

[1] E. Gamma, R. Helm, R. Johnson, and J. Vlissides. *Design Patterns: Elements of Reusable Object-Oriented Software.* Addison-Wesley Longman Publishing Co., Inc., 1995.

[2] M. Kulkarni, K. Pingali, B. Walter, G. Ramanarayanan, K. Bala, and L. P. Chew. Optimistic parallelism requires abstractions. In *PLDI*, pages 211–222, 2007.

[3] D. Lea. *Concurrent Programming in Java. Second Edition: Design Principles and Patterns.* Addison-Wesley Longman Publishing Co., Inc., Boston, MA, USA, 1999.

[4] T. G. Mattson, B. A. Sanders, and B. L. Massingill. *A Pattern Language for Parallel Programming.* Addison Wesley Software Patterns Series, 2004.

[5] J. Ousterhout. Why threads are a bad idea (for most purposes). In *ATEC*, January 1996.

[6] D. C. Schmidt, H. Rohnert, M. Stal, and D. Schultz. *Pattern-Oriented Software Architecture: Patterns for Concurrent and Networked Objects.* John Wiley & Sons, Inc., 2000.

Hamster - Making Grid Middleware Fault-Tolerant

Rafael Farias

University of Pernambuco
Rua Benfica 455, Recife/PE, Brazil
rafael.lucas@gmail.com

Francisco Soares-Neto

University of Pernambuco
Rua Benfica 455, Recife/PE, Brazil
xfrancisco.soares@gmail.com

Fernando Castor

Federal University of Pernambuco
Av. Prof. L. Freire s/n, Recife/PE, Brazil
castor@cin.ufpe.br

Abstract

Organizations which use grid computing have to deal with events such as a machine turned off or a failed component. Some of these events can completely break a grid. We propose a mechanism to maximize resource usage by monitoring grid middleware components and making them capable of recovering from failures.

Categories and Subject Descriptors Software [*Operating Systems*]: Reliability: Fault-tolerance

General Terms Reliability

1. Introduction

In developing countries, such as Brazil, universities and companies often do not have financial resources to acquire super computers or powerful servers to meet their computing needs. Notwithstanding, these organizations usually have a great amount of average workstations that sit idle for large periods of time. By leveraging grid computing, these organizations can solve tasks that would require a large amount of processing at a low cost. Unfortunately, computational grids are prone to faults.

Existing proposals[1][2] to decrease the impact of faults in grid computing environments focus on the nodes that run the grid applications. In general, they use some kind of checkpointing mechanism that saves and recovers the state of each node as required. They are not, however, capable of handling failures of the nodes responsible for the grid middleware, the nodes that maintain the grid infrastructure. Faults of these nodes might require a full restart of the grid. This might be a very expensive operation, potentially spanning hundreds of nodes deployed across different domains.

This paper presents Hamster, a monitoring and recovery mechanism for grid middleware. Its main goal is to maximize the use of available resources, recovering faulty middleware components and avoiding resource idleness or, worse, a complete grid stop. Hamster comprises a number of services that complement existing application-level checkpointing mechanisms. It has been integrated into the OurGrid middleware platform.

2. Requirements

The development of a mechanism such as Hamster poses a number of challenges to developers. First, Hamster must make the grid highly available. It might make some compromises, as long as it avoids wasting resources while maintaining scalability and performance. It must be light, not requiring too much memory, CPU power, or network bandwidth. Moreover, it has to respond quickly to failures because if it takes too long, resources might be wasted. It should be capable of dealing with very large grids, comprising potentially thousands of nodes running in parallel. Hamster should also present high availability even when multiple grid components fail. Also, it has to monitor itself and be capable of recovering its own components when they fail.

Another important requirement is that it should be easy to configure, execute, and integrate with existing grid middleware platforms. This requirement is difficult to meet but is crucial for the reliability of the service. Hamster has to be compatible with different architectures for grid computing middleware with minimum changes. It should also be adaptable enough to consider differences in the recovery procedures required by different grid platforms.

3. Reliable Grid Computing with Hamster

Hamster is a grid middleware monitoring and recovery mechanism that aims to avoid resource idleness that stems from failures of grid middleware components. Since the failure of such components can stop the whole grid, this event should be avoided at all costs. Hamster attempts to achieve this by monitoring grid components and, when they fail, recovering from the failure in the way that is less damaging to the grid as a whole. The monitoring that Hamster performs focuses on the components that manage the computational grid. When such a component fails, Hamster acts by first trying to micro-reboot the component and, if this is not possible, restarting it while trying to recover the component's state just before the failure. When recovery is not possible in the former environment of the failed component, it is necessary to transfer the faulty component to another machine where it can run without errors. When this component migration is necessary, Hamster automatically reconfigures the grid so that other grid components that need to know about this change maintain consistent information.

Although different grid middleware platforms have different kinds of components, some of them are common to most or all of these platforms. Job schedulers, application brokers, resource providers, and communication substrates can be considered basic grid components. Each of these components has different requirements, in terms of failure recovery. Hamster considers that some mechanism is already in place to handle resource provider's failures, since most previous work on fault tolerance for grids has focused on these components. In addition, scheduler recovery is not a difficult task unless the later is actually part of a component with additional responsibilities.

To handle failures of application brokers, Hamster intercepts all the jobs submitted by users and saves them in stable storage, together with all the data and programs required to execute these

Copyright is held by the author/owner(s).

SPLASH'10 October 17–21, 2010, Reno/Tahoe, Nevada, USA.
ACM 978-1-4503-0240-1/10/10.

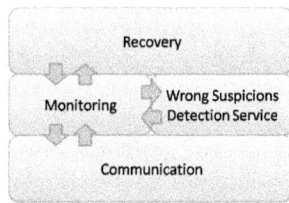

Figure 1. Hamster mechanism modules

jobs. The resulting job list is periodically partitioned and distributed across the Hamster components. The amount of redundancy of this distribution is set by Hamster users. When the broker fails, as soon as it starts running again, Hamster attempts to retrieve the parts of the list of jobs and, as they are obtained, submits the jobs for execution. The recovered parts of the job list are organized so that the jobs are executed as much as possible in the order in which they were originally submitted. It is important to stress, though, that Hamster does not guarantee that the jobs will be executed in this order.

When either the communication substrate component or the application broker fail and later recover, the remaining grid nodes will need to know whether they have been migrated by Hamster. If so, information about their new addresses is propagated to all grid components to guarantee a consistent view. If for some reason this information cannot be updated (e.g., due to inconsistent TCP connections) or grid components must be started in a certain order, Hamster initiates an automated grid restart, initiating each grid component in the expected order.

As mentioned on Section 2, faults can happen not only to the grid infrastructure, but also to Hamster itself. Faults of Hamster components are detected by other Hamster components (monitors) and by the grid middleware components monitored by the faulty Hamster component. In the first case, other monitors consider the machine where the faulty Hamster component was running as suspicious, and try, periodically, to send a reconnection request. If the faulty machine does not reply to the request, it is considered faulty and Hamster will try to transfer the grid components from the faulty node to another machines. In the second case, the grid components monitored by the faulty monitor become independent of Hamster's monitoring network, not influencing the grid operation.

3.1 Architecture

Figure 1 presents the main sub-components of the Hamster architecture. The Hamster components that are part of the Hamster monitoring network exchange heartbeat messages among themselves and with their monitored grid components through the Communication sub-component. This way, it is possible to detect if the machine where a grid component is being executed has failed or if a grid component by itself has failed. This processing is done by the Monitoring sub-component. In case of a failure detection, the Recovery sub-component is triggered. Hamster uses a Wrong suspicion detection service sub-component to stop false positives in failure detection from damaging the consistency of the grid and avoid unnecessary recovery actions, such as requesting the recovery of a correct grid component. To the best of our knowledge, this is the first work to propose wrong suspicion handling as a service in fault-tolerant distributed systems.

The Hamster components are identified by the IP address of the machine where they are executed. Moreover, each Hamster component monitor is part of a user-defined group. Groups comprise identifiers of machines located within the same physical location. This information is used to decide about the machine to which a recovered component should be transferred. That is meant to avoid

the recovery of a faulty component on a machine that is inaccessible to the original user of the component. For example, an application broker recovered in a different lab, to which its original user has no access, would impede this user from getting the results he needed.

4. Hamster for OurGrid

OurGrid[4] is a well-known grid computing middleware platform. It comprises four components: the PEER component manages the global grid resources, distributing work among those who offer resources; the BROKER component is responsible for submitting user jobs and displaying their results back to the users who requested them; the WORKER component is responsible for executing the user application that was submitted by a BROKER and directed by a PEER, i.e, each resource provider executes a WORKER component; and the OPENFIRE component is the responsible for grid user management and communication. Each grid node might run up to one instance of each component.

Fault injection tests in OurGrid have shown us the need for a service such as the one provided by Hamster. Both failures of some grid components and wrong suspicions in failure detection resulted in failures of OurGrid-based grids. We have incorporated Hamster into OurGrid by extending some of its modules to interact with the other parts of Hamster. It was made by adapting Ourgrid's code by adding a module which would be responsible for communicating with our mechanism. The added module is a generic interface with Hamster. The resulting middleware exhibited a sensible increase in reliability.

5. Conclusion and Future Works

This paper presented Hamster, a mechanism to make grid middleware fault-tolerant. We hope, with this mechanism, to improve the reliability of grid computing systems and maximize their resource usage. Any application that can benefit from grid computing, such as weather forecast, financial market prediction, and DNA analysis, can leverage Hamster. Hamster is under development and the current prototype is available at http://code.google.com/p/gridmonitor/. Our next step is to make an evaluation of Hamster to assess its influence on factors such as memory consumption, network usage, overhead on the grid middleware's latency and throughput.

Acknowledgments

We would like to thank the anonymous referees for the insightful comments. We'd also like to thank the OurGrid team for answering our many questions. Francisco is supported by CNPq/Brazil. Rafael is supported by CAPES/Brazil. Fernando is partially supported by CNPq, grant 308383/2008-7. This work is partially supported by INES, funded by CNPq and FACEPE, grants 573964/2008-4 and APQ-1037-1.03/08.

References

[1] R. Y. de Camargo, F. Kon, R. Cerqueira: Strategies for Checkpoint Storage on Opportunistic Grids. IEEE Distributed Systems Online 7(9): (2006)

[2] D. Diaz, X. C. Pardo, M. J. Martin, P. Gonzalez: Application-Level Fault-Tolerance Solutions for Grid Computing. CCGRID 2008: 554-559.(2008)

[3] A. Goldchleger, F. Kon, A. Goldman, M. Finger, G. C. Bezerra: InteGrade: object-oriented Grid middleware leveraging the idle computing power of desktop machines. Concurrency - Practice and Experience 16(5): 449-459 (2004)

[4] W. Cirne, F. V. Brasileiro, N. Andrade, L. Costa, A. Andrade, R. Novaes, M. Mowbray: Labs of the World, Unite!!! J. Grid Comput. 4(3): 225-246 (2006)

Onward! Panel Welcome

Welcome to Onward! 2010. This year, we are delighted to bring you another environmentally focused Panel called "Software for a Sustainable World." Last year at Onward we heard a panel discuss "Why is Software not yet Green?" This year, the Onward Green Panel will focus on Software Systems that support sustainability – e.g. Systems that helps us reduce energy consumption, or manages energy output, or gives us better data on consumption. We will explore how Smart Grids can impact us, how we can make saving energy easier and less intrusive, and other tools for large enterprise business or the home consumer. Perhaps, "software is not yet green", but we can create software to produce a more sustainable future. We look forward to seeing you at the Panel for this very important and timely discussion.

Aki Namioka
Onward! 2010 Panel Chair

Steven Fraser
Cisco Research Center

Ruth Lennon
Letterkenny Institute of Technology

Dave Thomas
Bedarra Research Labs

Collaboration

Steven Fraser
Director
Cisco Research Center
Cisco Systems
San Jose, CA

Hannah Faye Chua
Research Assistant Professor
School of Public Health
University of Michigan
Ann Arbor, MI

Gail Harris
Principal Consultant
Instantiated Software Inc.
Toronto, ON

Orit Hazzan
Associate Professor
Technion, Israel
Institute of Technology
Haifa, Israel

Jean Tabaka
Agile Coach
Rally Software Development
Boulder, CO

Rob Tucker
Principal, Leadership
Research Institute
Rancho Santa Fe, CA

Dave West
Professor,
School of Business
Highlands University of NM
Las Vegas, NM

Abstract

Collaboration, the art of working together, is an essential part of system development, often learned on the job rather than by academic training. Aspects of collaboration include: tangible and intangible "results" – the fruits of collaboration; community governance – the norms of ownership and usage; and modes of production – the processes for incubating and developing "results". This panel will bring together a diverse set of experts from industry and academia to share their opinions and strategies for collaboration.

Categories & Subject Descriptors:
K.0 Computing Milieux
K.4.3 Organizational Impacts

General Terms: Design

Keywords: Collaboration, partnerships, tools, technologies

1. Steven Fraser *(panel impresario)*, *sdfraser@acm.org*

STEVEN FRASER is the Director of the Cisco Research Center in San Jose California (www.cisco.com/research) with responsibilities for developing university research collaborations and facilitating technology transfer between researchers and Cisco Business Units. Previously, Steven was a member of Qualcomm's Learning Center in San Diego, California enabling technical learning and development in software engineering best practices. Steven held a variety of technology roles at Bell-Northern Research and Nortel including Process Architect, Senior Manager (Global External Research), and Design Process Advisor. In 1994, he was a Visiting Scientist at the Software Engineering Institute (SEI) at Carnegie Mellon University (CMU) collaborating on the development of team-based domain analysis (software reuse) techniques. Fraser was the XP2006 General Chair, the Corporate Support Chair for OOPSLA'07

and OOPSLA'08, Tutorial Chair for both XP2008 and ICSE 2009 and co-Publicity Chair for XP2010. Steven is a frequent impresario of conference panels and special events. With a doctorate in Electrical Engineering from McGill University in Montréal, he is a member of the ACM and a senior member of the IEEE.

Aspects of collaboration in the context of software engineering have been described as topics of interest for almost forty years – beginning with the "The Psychology of Computer Programming" by Gerald Weinberg (1971), and "The Mythical Man-Month" by Fred Brooks (1975); – continuing through the 1980s with Tom DeMarco and Tim Lister's "Peopleware" (1987); into the 1990's with Larry Constantine's "Work Organization: Paradigms for Project Management and Organization" (1993); Eric S. Raymond's "The Cathedral and the Bazaar" (1999); and more recently with Kent Beck's "Extreme Programming Explained" (2000), Steven Weber's "The Success of Open Source" (2004), and Jean Tabaka's "Collaboration Explained" (2006).

Within the past ten years we have seen an increasing emergence of self-organizing collaborative teams from groups originally driven by "command and control" centric decision-making. We continue to learn how issues of scale and scope can be best addressed – in part by considering issues of governance which may place constraints on future usage and ownership of the fruits of collaboration (e.g., proprietary ownership or GNU General Public Licensing).

Collaboration depends on *inter* and *intra* team communications, and a shared context determined by a common set of norms, beliefs, vocabulary, and goals. Trust and reputation are factors that build on a shared context.

While tools exist to foster a shared context for geographically distributed teams (e.g., tele-presence and web conferencing), it is still hard to match the fidelity of face-to-face interaction. However, even face-to-face teams can require

Copyright is held by the author/owner(s).
SPLASH'10, October 17–21, 2010, Reno, NV, USA.
978-1-4503-0240-1/10/10...$10

catalysts such as "facilitation" to overcome challenges such as sustaining trust, avoiding groupthink (including false consensus), and a lack of requisite variety (diversity of opinion and composition).

Tweets, blogs, social websites (e.g. Facebook), ultra portable networked digital cameras (both still and video), shared calendaring, location based services, and other emergent devices and services continue to combine in new ways to change the way we learn, communicate, play, work – and collaborate!

2. Hannah Faye Chua, *hfc.work@gmail.com*

HANNAH FAYE CHUA is a Research Assistant Professor at the University of Michigan's School of Public Health. She is also a Faculty Associate at the Research Center for Group Dynamics at the University's Institute for Social Research and an Adjunct Assistant Professor in Psychology. She completed her PhD in Psychology at the University of Michigan. Her research interests include understanding the mechanisms involved in persuasion (effective tailored communications), social cognition (how people think about social events), emotions and decision making, and cultural differences in thinking and behavior, using behavioral, eye tracking and neuroimaging methods.

Collaboration involves people or groups with different expertise from either the same team or different teams to work on a project and achieve goals together. Each person has a unique role or contribution to the 'new team'. Communication is especially important when people are using different vocabulary or when people have different expectations about processes. Communication could be greatly enhanced with satisfactory use of technology.

3. Gail Harris, *Gail.Harris@instantiated.ca*

GAIL HARRIS is a Principal of Instantiated Software, a small company whose primary business is applying agile methodologies and open- source technologies to deliver custom-developed applications to start-up companies. Between development projects, Gail does project of complex enterprise systems for large organizations, as well requirements engineering and business analysis. Before joining Instantiated Gail was a consultant with various firms, large and small, providing software development expertise to government and industry. Gail has been a contributor to OOPSLA since 1997, served in various capacities on many OOPSLA committees since 2002, and was conference chair in 2008. She is also marketing a squash club management system that includes a sophisticated player rating system.

Can you remember the last time you worked alone, really alone – maybe at school? My collaborations have taken different forms such as team member, technical lead, project manager, or oversight of a third party doing development. Although the end result may have been an implemented system in most or all of these endeavors, the day to day experiences along the way have included both successes and failures. That is, one day I may have had a harmonious, productive meeting while the next day may have included a stressful fiasco needing management intervention to resolve the conflict. The most spectacular failures usually were caused either by following a tactic of controlling all the details or of insisting on my solution. I hadn't set out to be closed minded or a micro-manager, and yet upon reflection, my behaviors exemplified these methods.

Some of the successful tactics I have used include showing respect for my colleagues and of sharing responsibility. Showing respect started with a particular frame of mind, one where I accepted that others are knowledgeable, that they may have a different perspective borne from different experiences and their knowledge is worthy of my attention. By listening to my colleagues ideas and concerns, addressing those points where I disagreed, and generally working to communicate, I showed respect. Sharing responsibility started with discussing how tasks will be shared, sometimes using the "responsibility ladder" from Roger Martin, to decide things like if I will get or give specific help at certain points, or present options, or make a recommendation, or make a decision and inform stakeholders afterward. Sharing responsibility means showing trust in others abilities to do the work. These tactics have led to conflict-free, productive collaborations.

I'm still looking for that "perfect" experience. The rewards and personal satisfaction at the end of the project come from the efforts made each day to respect others and share responsibility.

4. Orit Hazzan, *oritha@techunix.technion.ac.il*

ORIT HAZZAN is an Associate Professor in the Department of Education in Technology and Science at Technion - the Israel Institute of Technology. In May 2004 her book *Human Aspects of Software Engineering* was published, co-authored with the late Jim Tomayko. Orit's second book *Agile Software Engineering,* co-authored with Yael Dubinsky, was published by Springer in 2008. In parallel to her research work, Orit is a consultant for several software projects in the Israeli software industry. She presents her research at conferences on software engineering in general (ICSE, SPLASH, and Agile) and computer science and software engineering education in particular (SIGCSE).

Based on my coaching experience of software teams, my perspective on collaboration in software development environments is inspired by the importance attributed to the human aspects of software engineering and highlights connections to transparency and to reward allocation.

With respect to *transparency*, it seems that transparency increases team members' collaboration and lack of collaboration can be explained by showing that that the project environment is not transparent. This mutual relationship between collaboration and transparency is embedded within the context of Game Theory in general and the Prisoner Dilemma framework in particular, as is explained in what follows: Many software development environments require team collaboration. However, due to software intangibility, team members are often unable to ensure that their cooperation will be reciprocated. In accordance with the Prisoner's Dilemma, even if there is a desire to collaborate, each team member may prefer not to collaborate. Alternatively, a transparent development process fosters collaboration.

With respect to *reward allocation*, as it turns out, if a given financial bonus is to be distributed among team members, different team members and teams would prefer different forms of reward allocation (for example, based on individual contributions or shared equally among team members). The different forms, however, are largely determined by the intensity of team members' conflicts between their desire to excel on the individual level and their need to collaborate.

As can be seen, collaboration in software teams is a sensitive issue and should not be neglected when team members are asked to collaborate.

5. Jean Tabaka, *jtabaka@rallydev.com*

JEAN TABAKA is an Agile Fellow with Rally Software and is continuing on her 30 year path of learning about software development principles, processes, and practices for people. She seeks a humane approach to bringing high value to our communities of creators and consumers. This has led her to move into Kanban and Lean approaches that reach beyond traditional Agile frameworks. Jean holds a Masters in Computer Science from Johns Hopkins University. She is the author of "Collaboration Explained" and a variety of articles on Agile, organizational change, team dynamics, systems thinking, Lean thinking, and other associated topics. Jean blogs at www.rallydev.com/agileblog and can be followed on twitter as @jeantabaka. When home in Boulder, CO, she'd invite you over for some wine and some music while gazing across her backyard over a Flat Iron Mountains sunset. Meanwhile, you can find her at jean.tabaka@rallydev.com.

My work in collaboration began at a team level for Agile teams. In the past 5 years, my perspective and practices have expanded in principles, in models, and in reach. This has led me to work more at the Agile Organization level. I have been working to apply collaborative vision and decision models such as A3s, value stream maps, PDCA and ORID sessions. I've also helped bring personal visioning aligned with corporate visioning as a powerful means to create common ground. All of this has affirmed my belief in the power of great facilitation and a conviction in the power of collaborative work and participatory decision-making up and down organizations as well across them.

6. Rob Tucker, *rob.tucker@lri.com*

ROB TUCKER is a Principal at Leadership Research Institute. He works as an executive coach and facilitator for organizations focused on science, technology and engineering. In the past ten years, Rob's work has taken him all over the world with more than eighty client organizations. Prior to joining LRI, Rob's background was in research, earning a Ph.D. in technical communication from the Annenberg School at the University of Southern California. His doctoral work examined best practices in "science translation," – the communication of highly technical material to non-scientific audiences. In his ten years with LRI, Rob has focused his work in two primary commercial sectors – Finance and Technology. His work with financial organizations included coaching and facilitation for a number of global investment banks, holding banks, and other financial entities. His work in the technology field includes coaching, content development, and facilitation for large-scale engineering and technical clients, including global hardware and software development organizations. He has worked extensively in Asia, Europe and the emerging geographies (with coaching and facilitation in India, Brazil and Argentina). Rob is an avid technology fan, the proud parent of two sons, and a passionate reader in the fields of neuroscience, history, and macroeconomics.

LEADERSHIP, COLLABORATION AND ORGANIZATIONAL STRUCTURE: Using examples from his client work in R&D and large (>500) software development organizations, Rob will share key lessons learned for effective - discussing: What's the right balance between centralized and decentralized decision-making? ... At what phases or stages of project development are different leadership styles conducive or hostile to effective collaboration?

7. Dave West, *dmwest@nmhu.edu*

DAVID WEST is a Professor in the School of Business at New Mexico Highlands University, where he developed an agile-based curriculum in software, business, and information system design. He created the object curriculum and founded and served as the Director of the Object Lab, a co-operative effort with local corporations dedicated to researching and promoting object technology, at the University of St. Thomas. In addition to academia, Dave works as a consultant, agile coach and systems designer and has more than thirty years experience as a software development professional.

Unlike the professional world; in academia "collaboration" is spelled c-h-e-a-t-i-n-g. Our new BS and MS programs reject the academic view and stress both collaboration and the knowledge, skills, and experience necessary to become a solid collaborator. We work in an open studio (a one-room classroom) with first year and fifth year students working in the same room and on the same teams. All work – development work for outside (paying) companies and educational learning is done in teams and pairs. Outcomes are public, in the same sense that an agile team can see – based on progress charts and other information radiators – what the team is doing and which individuals are contributing.

Our real goal is to create a community, not just graduates. To this end we bring in working professionals to pair with students; we require students to present papers at refereed professional conferences; and all required student papers go through a writer's workshop process until such time as they are deemed 'finished.' We also teach listening and observations skills – including the kind of participant observation used by cultural anthropologists. All students also experience and come to understand the value that customers, managers, coaches, and team members bring to a project via their ability to collaborate.

This program reflects the importance we place on collaboration skills, the educational foundation for those skills, and the experience that add the tacit knowledge required. It also is grounded in the ideas of Peter Naur, that software development is Theory Building – i.e. whole team consensus on the nature of an "affair in the world" and how a bit of software can "handle or support it." Theory is totally dependent on collaborative thinking and collaborative action.

SPLASH Panels Welcome

Welcome to SPLASH 2010! This year we expect the Panels to be just as informative, entertaining, and controversial as ever. OOPSLA Panels are known for their highly participatory nature, and lively discussion between Panelists and audience is expected.

We will start Tuesday evening, with a revival of TOOTS (The Object-Oriented Trivia Show). It was so popular in 2009, that we had to bring it back. On Wednesday, Steve Fraser will lead us in a discussion about Collaboration – a timeless and important topic. And on Thursday afternoon, Dave Thomas will participate in the increasingly important subject of OO and Multi-Core. This is an exciting line-up and we hope you can come and join the discussions.

Aki Namioka
Onward'10 Panel Chair

Ruth Lennon
Letterkenny Institute of Technology

Steven Fraser
Cisco Research Center

Dave Thomas
Bedarra Reserach Labs

The Object-Oriented Trivia Show (TOOTS)

Jeff Gray
University of Alabama
Department of Computer Science
Tuscaloosa, AL USA

gray@cs.ua.edu

Jules White
Virginia Tech
Dept. of Electrical and Computer Engineering
Blacksburg, VA USA

julesw@vt.edu

ABSTRACT

OOPSLA has a longstanding tradition of being a forum for discussing the cutting edge of technology in a fun and participatory environment. The type of events sponsored by OOPSLA sometimes border on the unconventional. This event represents an atypical panel that conforms to the concept of a game show that is focused on questions and answers related to SPLASH, OOPSLA, and Onward! themes. The goal of the panel is to provide an educational opportunity for attendees to learn about a broad range of topics in a style that encourages audience participation.

Categories and Subject Descriptors D.1.5 [**Programming Techniques**]: Object-oriented Programming; D.2.2 [**Software Engineering**]: Design Tools and Techniques; D.2.3 [**Software Engineering**]: Coding Tools and Techniques

General Terms Design, Languages.

Keywords Objects, Game Show.

1. Overview of the OOPSLA Trivia Show

OOPSLA (and now SPLASH) has one of the most diverse collections of attendees among all computer science conferences. At SPLASH, academic researchers working on theoretical areas of language design may share a conversation with a developer from industry who is working with the latest agile development tools. Moreover, a SPLASH first-timer will have the opportunity at a workshop or social event to converse with a veteran researcher, such as Turing Award Winner Barbara Liskov (at OOPSLA 2009). This game show panel continues this tradition by encouraging students, faculty, and industry researchers to collaborate, compete, and share their knowledge related to the SPLASH research themes and history. The objective of this panel is to educate the audience on diverse topics important to the SPLASH/OOPSLA/Onward! communities, foster new relationships between participants competing as teams, and provide technology takeaways in a style that is entertaining. To meet this objective, the panel will conform

Copyright is held by the author/owner(s).
SPLASH'10 October 17–21, 2010, Reno/Tahoe, Nevada, USA.
ACM 978-1-4503-0240-1/10/10.

to the concept of a game show that is focused on topics related to research and history related to the conference.

The results of current and past TOOTS panels is archived at: *http://www.cs.ua.edu/~gray/external/toots*

2. TOOTS Rules

The panel will follow the general rules of the Jeopardy game show, with a few variations. The list below summarizes some of the particular rules that will be observed in the panel:

- All responses must be given in the form of a question. Each team gets one warning when this rule is violated. Subsequent violations will be counted as an incorrect response, even if the content of the response is correct.

- There will be three teams, each with three players. The teams will represent attendees from industry, academia, and students.

- When a team answers a question incorrectly, one of the team members must leave the game (typically, the member that suggested the incorrect response). A member of the audience from the same group may join the team to keep each team size at three. Thus, the concept of panel member replacement, as typical in a Fish Bowl arrangement, is adopted to improve audience participation.

- Each audience member will be given a number when entering the room. Numbers will be drawn at random to select new participants.

- Once eliminated, a participant cannot come back into the game.

- The teams have 30 seconds to provide an answer. Any question that is unanswered will be asked to the audience at large. Thus, a fourth team is represented by the general audience, who also have the opportunity to respond and have their cumulative score recorded.

- There will be three rounds of play with each round having five categories and each category having five questions of increasing difficulty and value. The initial two rounds will be similar, but the final third round represents a single question.

- In the final round, a single category will be revealed and the participants must wage a portion of their current score. The answer is then revealed to the contestants and they must provide the correct question within one minute. The score of each team is updated based on the correctness of their answer and the value that they waged.

- After the final round, the team with the highest score is declared the winner.

- All decisions relating to the correctness of a team response will be determined by the Judge.

- At the end of the contest, all participants will be asked to join their team on stage for photos that will be used to archive the event. All members of the winning team will receive a token prize.

3. Sample Question Areas

Because SPLASH has attendees from diverse backgrounds and experience levels, the questions will be defined broadly to cover many topics of interest at different levels of difficulty. The questions will be designed in a manner to educate a general audience in an engaging way. When possible, questions involving multimedia will be offered, such as short video clips, images, and sounds.

A total of two full rounds (25 questions per round) and a final round will provide 51 questions for consideration in the contest. The following represent a sample of the categories that will be covered:

- OOPSLA History: Trivia from past OOPSLAs

- SPLASH 2010 Research Trivia: Questions based on the papers published in the proceedings of OOPSLA and Onward! 2010

- Popular Topics from SPLASH: Design Patterns, Enterprise Middleware, OO Language Design

- Crash: Factoids about various failed software projects

- Rosetta Stone: Challenges to interpret legacy, obfuscated, and strange code

4. Key Participants

The participants of the panel come from three separate groups: the question curators (who design the game show content), the contestants, and the organizers (who moderate and coordinate the production of the game show).

Question Curators

The committee of "Question Curators" assists in defining questions for each category and ensuring the correctness of each answer. This committee will be comprised of members who are well-known in the SPLASH community from both industry and academia.

Contestants

The three contestant teams will represent the categories of the primary constituents at OOPSLA: industry, academia, and students. Contestants representing the teams from industry and academia are leaders in the OOPSLA community and those who had a prominent role in previous OOPSLAs. The student team will be seeded with participants who are SPLASH student volunteers, or student authors of OOPSLA 2010 papers. Due to the "Fish Bowl" format, when questions are answered incorrectly the contestants will also be dynamically replaced by members of the general audience. As noted in Section 2, there is a fourth team that is composed of the entire general audience (i.e., the general audience has the opportunity to provide a response to each question that goes unanswered).

Organizers

Jeff Gray is an Associate Professor in the Department of Computer Science at the University of Alabama where he co-directs the research in the Software Composition and Modeling (SoftCom) laboratory. His research interests are in aspect-oriented software development, model-driven engineering, domain-specific languages, and generative programming. He is an NSF CAREER award winner and the 2008 Carnegie Foundation Professor of the Year (Alabama). Jeff was the 2009 Program co-Chair of the conference on Software Language Engineering (SLE), the 2009 Organizing Chair of the conference on Aspect-Oriented Software Development (AOSD), and serves as the 2010 SPLASH workshops chair. Jeff has attended every OOPSLA since 1995. Over the past 9 years, he has co-organized the popular OOPSLA workshop on Domain-Specific Modeling (DSM), as well as organizing an OOPSLA 2008 panel on Domain-Specific Languages and the OOPSLA 2009 TOOTS panel.

Dr. Jules White is an Assistant Professor of Electrical and Computer Engineering at Virginia Tech. Dr. White's research focuses on using a combination of modeling and constraint/heuristic/metaheuristic optimization techniques to automate the generation, deployment, and configuration of software. His research on automating the diagnosis of software product-line configuration errors won the "best paper" award at the 2008 International Conference on Software Product-lines, sponsored by the Carnegie Mellon Software Engineering Institute. He is the project leader of the Eclipse Foundation's Generic Eclipse Modeling System.

As formal participants, Jeff will serve as the moderator and Jules will play the role of judge, score keeper, and award presenter.

SPLASH and Onward! Workshop Chairs' Welcome

SPLASH and Onward! workshops are a great way to grow your knowledge and expand your professional network. They are highly interactive events that provide a creative and collaborative environment where attendees meet to discuss and solve challenging problems related to a variety of new emerging technologies and research areas.

Over the past two decades, the OOPSLA workshops provided an incubator for exploring many of the ideas that went on to shape general software practice (e.g., design patterns, UML, aspect-oriented software development, and agile methods). That tradition continues this year within the new charter for SPLASH, and incorporates the visionary focus of Onward!

This year, SPLASH and Onward! offer 15 workshops that represent a diverse set of technology and research topics. Some workshops are in their first offering, and others have been around for over a decade (e.g., the Domain-Specific Modeling workshop is celebrating its 10th year). Example areas covered by the workshops include cloud computing, model-driven engineering and domain-specific modeling, virtual machines, pedagogical concerns, parallel and high performance computing, software product lines, ontologies, foundations of OO, and agile methods. PLATEAU returns to Onward! this year, continuing to bridge the fields of programming languages and human-computer interaction. In addition to the 15 workshops, the popular CloudCamp event is also offered again at the conference. The following summaries included in this companion provide an introduction to the goals and objectives of each workshop.

We welcome you to these workshops with the hope that the discussions are productive and fruitful, and assist in fostering new collaborations that extend beyond the borders of the conference!

Each workshop proposal received three reviews from the SPLASH Workshop Selection Committee. We would like to thank the following members of this committee:

- Alessandro Garcia (PUC-Rio, Brazil)
- Aniruddha Gokhale (Vanderbilt University, USA)
- Christa Schwanninger (Siemens, Germany)
- Elisa Baniassad (The Australian National University, Australia)
- Ruzanna Chitchyan (Lancaster University, UK)
- Sergiu Dascalu (University of Nevada, USA)
- Steve Marney (HP Enterprise Services, USA)

In addition, Bruce Horn (Powerset, USA) served on the Onward! workshop committee.

SPLASH Workshop Chair:
Jeff Gray
University of Alabama
Department of Computer Science
Tuscaloosa, AL USA
gray@cs.ua.edu

Onward! Workshop Chair:
Jonathan Edwards
MIT, Computer Science
and Artificial Intelligence Lab
Cambridge, MA USA
edwards@csail.mit.edu

Evaluation and Usability of Programming Languages and Tools (PLATEAU)

Emerson Murphy-Hill

North Carolina State University
emerson@csc.ncsu.edu

Shane Markstrum

Bucknell University
shane.markstrum@bucknell.edu

Craig Anslow

Victoria University of Wellington
craig@ecs.vuw.ac.nz

Abstract

Programming languages exist to enable programmers to develop software effectively. But how *efficiently* programmers can write software depends on the usability of the languages and tools that they develop with. The aim of this workshop is to discuss methods, metrics and techniques for evaluating the usability of languages and language tools. The supposed benefits of such languages and tools cover a large space, including making programs easier to read, write, and maintain; allowing programmers to write more flexible and powerful programs; and restricting programs to make them more safe and secure. We plan to gather the intersection of researchers in the programming language, programming tool, and human-computer interaction communities to share their research and discuss the future of evaluation and usability of programming languages and tools. We are also interested in the input of other members of the programming research community working on related areas, such as refactoring, design patterns, program analysis, program comprehension, software visualization, end-user programming, and other programming language paradigms.

Categories and Subject Descriptors   D.3.0 [*Programming Languages*]: Standards
; H.1.2 [*User/Machine Systems*]: Human Factors

General Terms   Human Factors, Languages

Keywords   Evaluation, Programming Languages, Tools, Usability

1. Main Themes and Goals

At the Programming Languages Grand Challenges panel at POPL 2009, Greg Morrisett claimed that one of the great neglected areas in programming languages research is the bridge between programming languages and human-computer interaction: the evaluation of the usability of programming languages and tools. This is evident by the recent research programs of major languages conferences such as POPL, PLDI, OOPSLA, and ECOOP. The object-oriented conferences tend to have at least one or two papers in the areas of corpus analysis or evaluation methodologies, but the authors of the papers seem to avoid using the results of their studies to make conclusions about the languages or tools themselves. Software engineering and human-computer interaction conferences tend to have

better support of language usability analysis (CHI 2009 had three tracks that showcase research in this direction), but have limited visibility to the programming languages community.

Following on to our previous workshop of the same name at OOPSLA 2009, this workshop aims to begin filling that void by developing and stimulating discussion of usability and evaluation of programming languages and tools with respect to language design and related areas. We will consider: empirical studies of programming languages; methodologies and philosophies behind language and tool evaluation; software design metrics and their relations to the underlying language; user studies of language features and software engineering tools; visual techniques for understanding programming languages; critical comparisons of programming paradigms, such as object-oriented vs. functional; and tools to support evaluating programming languages. We have two goals:

1. Develop a research community that shares ideas and collaborates on research related to the evaluation and usability of languages and tools.

2. Encourage the languages and tools communities to think more critically about how usability affects the design and adoption of languages and tools.

2. Organizers

The logistical organisation of this workshop will be done by the following organizers.

- **Emerson Murphy-Hill** is an Assistant Professor in the Computer Science department at North Carolina State University, researching how software developers find and adopt software tools. He recieved is Ph.D. from Portland State University in 2009. His research interests include human-computer interaction and software tools.

- **Shane Markstrum** is an Assistant Professor in the Computer Science department at Bucknell University. He received his Ph.D. from the University of California, Los Angeles in 2009. His research interests include domain-specific languages and tools for extensible type systems; and building tool support for non-traditional language constructs.

- **Craig Anslow** is a PhD student in the School of Engineering and Computer Science, Victoria University of Wellington, New Zealand. His PhD topic is *Multi-touch Table User Interfaces for Collaborative Visual Software Analytics* and is supervised by James Noble and Stuart Marshall. Craig has experience in building applications to support the evaluation of programming languages using information visualization and multi-touch techniques.

Copyright is held by the author/owner(s).
SPLASH'10   October 17–21, 2010, Reno/Tahoe, Nevada, USA.
ACM 978-1-4503-0240-1/10/10.

3. Program Committee

Along with the organizers, the following people will form the Program Committee (PC) for the workshop and will help promote the workshop in the programming languages and human-computer interaction communities.

- **Andrew P. Black** is a Professor of Computer Science, Portland State University, USA. His research interests are in the area of programming languages, operating systems, object-oriented systems and distributed computing, and more specifically in the region where they overlap (such as language design for distributed object-oriented computing). Andrew has been on the PC of OOPSLA ('08, '05) and Chair of ECOOP ('05) and PC member ('07, '06, '05, '03).

- **Rob DeLine** is a member of the Human Interactions in Programming group at Microsoft Research in Seattle, WA. His recent research has included recommender systems for team newcomers, the use of spatial memory to navigate large code bases, and knowledge retainment in long-lived projects. He is the co-creator, along with Randy Pausch, of the Alice rapid prototyping system. Prior to joining Microsoft Research, he received a Ph.D. in Computer Science from Carnegie Mellon University and an M.S. in Computer Science from the University of Virginia.

- **Christine A. Halverson** is a Research Staff Member in Social Computing at IBM's T. J. Watson Research Center. She is generally interested in understanding collaborative work, with and without technology support. Currently she is working on the PERCS project to understand the world of high performance computing - programmers, users and support staff. Christine holds a Ph.D. in Cognitive Science from the University of California, San Diego for work done in Distributed Cognition.

- **Donna Malayeri** is a postdoctoral researcher in the Scala group at Ecole Polytechnique Federale de Lausanne (EPFL), Switzerland. She received her Ph.D. in 2009 from Carnegie Mellon University in Pittsburgh, PA. Her thesis explored the role of type systems in developing extensible software. She served on the program committee for PLATEAU 2009 and has been an external reviewer for a number of international top-tier conferences and journals.

- **Rob Miller** is an Associate Professor in the MIT EECS department and a member of the Computer Science and Artificial Intelligence Laboratory. His current research concerns usable programming systems and usable security.

- **James Noble** is a Professor of Computer Science and Software Engineering within the School of Engineering and Computer Science, Victoria University of Wellington, New Zealand. His research areas include Software Design, Programming Languages, Design Patterns; Human-Computer Interaction; Software Visualisation and Visual Languages; and the philosophy of Computer Science and Software Engineering.

- **Vibha Sazawal** is Clare Boothe Luce Assistant Professor in the Department of Computer Science at the University of Maryland, College Park. Her research areas include Human-Computer Interaction and Software Design.

- **Christopher Scaffidi** is an Assistant Professor in the Computer Science department at Oregon State University. His research interests have led him to study platform-independent abstractions called "topes" which he believes will ultimately serve as a "lingua franca" for exchanging data between scripts, spreadsheets and other kinds of code.

- **Jeffrey Stylos** is a User Experience Researcher at Microsoft. His research interests include Human-Computer Interaction and Software Engineering.

- **Ewan Tempero** is an Associate Professor in the Department of Computer Science, University of Auckland, New Zealand. His main area of research is measuring software design quality. To support this kind of research he manages the Qualitas Corpus, a standard corpus of open-source Java software for use in empirical studies of software. The underlying goal of this research is to make programmers more productive, that is, help the people who actually produce code to do so faster, with less effort, fewer errors, and with more enjoyment than currently.

- **Christoph Treude** is a PhD student in Computer Science at the University of Victoria in Canada, working with Dr. Margaret-Anne (Peggy) Storey and Dr. Jens Weber. He received his undergraduate degree at the University of Siegen in Germany and spent one year as an exchange student at the University of British Columbia, Canada.

- **Ben Wiedermann** researches program analysis and programming language design. His recent work has contributed new ways for programmers to write modular, efficient, distributed programs. He currently is investigating program analysis and language design for security and for multi-lingual programs. He obtained his PhD from The University of Texas (UT) at Austin in December 2009 and is continuing at UT as a postdoctoral fellow.

4. Participant Preparation

Workshop participants should submit a short position paper. Position papers will be made available through the workshop website and participants are encouraged to have read the position papers before attending the workshop. Participants are also asked to prepare a presentation to support their position paper. We will accept papers (from 4 to 6 pages) that describe work-in-progress or recently completed work based on the themes and goals of the workshop or related topics, report on experiences gained, question accepted wisdom, raise challenging open problems, or propose speculative new approaches. People who do not submit papers will be allowed to attend as well.

5. Activities and Format

This workshop will be run as a full-day workshop at Onward! 2010. We will have an introduction and keynote session in the morning followed by the presentation of workshop papers. The last session of the day will include some workshop papers followed by a specialevent. If we have time we will prepare a poster for the SPLASH/Onward! Welcome Reception.

6. Post-workshop Activities

We will publish our participant's papers as a technical report. We aim to continue hosting this workshop in future years.

9th Workshop on Parallel/High-performance Object-oriented Scientific Computing

Kei Davis

Los Alamos National Laboratory
kei@lanl.gov

Joerg Striegnitz

University Of Applied Sciences Regensburg
joerg.striegnitz@informatik.fh-Regensburg.de

Abstract

Categories and Subject Descriptors   I [*I.0*]

General Terms   Languages, Performance

Keywords   object oriented, parallel computing, scientific computing

1.   Main Theme and Goals

While object-oriented programming has been embraced in industry, particularly in the form of C++, Java, and Python, its acceptance by the parallel scientific programming community has been relatively slow. Nonetheless, various factors practically dictate the use of language features that provide higher level abstractions than do C or older FORTRAN standards. These include increasingly complex physics models, numerical algorithms, and hardware, e.g. deep memory hierarchies, ever-increasing numbers of processors, the advent of multi-core processors; more recently the use of heterogeneous architectures using the IBM Cell/BE or GP-GPUs, and soon the experimentation with many-core processors.

Challenges in scientific computing include scalability, performance, domain decomposition, scheduling, memory management, coupling large codes, load balancing, exploiting computational accelerators, and others that can benefit from OO abstraction.

Our goal is to bring researchers 'out of the woodwork' to present their latest and greatest innovations and developments in exploiting object-oriented abstraction in parallel high-performance scientific computing to a like-minded, inquisitive audience of peers. The emphasis is on how object-oriented programming can benefit scientific computing specifically: new or novel frameworks, approaches, techniques, or idioms that use object orientation. Multi-paradigmatic approaches are also of definite interest. Presentations of work in progress are welcome. In previous POOSC workshops have had participants whose primary purpose was to get feedback on their nascent research ideas; we regard this as an ideal use of the workshop format.

Specific areas of interest include, but are not limited to,

- alternatives or extensions, including multi-paradigmatic approaches, to mainstream object-oriented languages (e.g. C++, Java, Python);

- performance issues and their realized or proposed resolution;

- issues specific to handling or abstracting parallelism, including the handling or abstraction of heterogeneous, multicore, or accelerated microarchitectures;

- higher level languages (e.g. domain specific languages) or their embedding into OO languages to support parallelism or specific tasks in scientific computing;

- frameworks and tools for object-oriented scientific computing;

- proposed or realized solutions to problems hindering acceptance of object-oriented scientific computing;

- position papers and grand visions (of relevance).

The workshop will consist of a sequences of presentations each followed by a discussion session. The workshop will conclude with an overall discussion. We expect the majority of the participants to give presentations.

Full papers are not required for acceptance/presentation, but they are strongly encouraged.

For authors of accepted presentations who require justification for travel the organizers can provide official letters of invitation.

Copyright is held by the author/owner(s).

SPLASH'10,   October 17–21, 2010, Reno/Tahoe, Nevada, USA.
ACM 978-1-4503-0240-1/10/10.

The 10th Workshop on Domain-Specific Modeling

Juha-Pekka Tolvanen

MetaCase
Ylistonmaentie 31
FI-40500 Jyvaskyla, Finland

jpt@metacase.com

Jonathan Sprinkle

University of Arizona
ECE Department
1230 E. Speedway Blvd.
Tucson, AZ, USA

sprinkle@ECE.Arizona.Edu

Matti Rossi

Aalto University School of
Economics
Runeberginkatu 22-24
FI-00100 Helsinki, Finland

Matti.Rossi@aalto.fi

Steven Kelly

MetaCase
Ylistonmaentie 31
FI-40500 Jyvaskyla, Finland

stevek@metacase.com

Abstract

Domain-Specific Modeling raises the level of abstraction beyond programming by specifying the solution directly using visual models to express domain concepts. In many cases, final products can be generated automatically from these high-level specifications. This automation is possible because both the language and generators fit the requirements of only one domain. This paper introduces Domain-Specific Modeling and describes the related 2-day workshop (17th and 18th October 2010).

Categories and Subject Descriptors D 3.2 [**Languages**]: Specialized application languages, very high-level languages;
D 2.2 [**Design Tools and Techniques**]: *Computer-aided software engineering* (CASE)

General Term Design, Languages

Keywords Modeling Languages; Metamodeling; Domain-Specific Languages; Code Generation

1. Introduction

The primary drawback of most software and system modeling tools is that they are constrained to work with a fixed notation. That is, the tool vendor has defined a notation and environment that must be used in a prescribed way, regardless of the unique requirements of the user. Such inflexibility forces the user to adopt a language that may not be suitable in all cases for their distinct needs. Examples of such modeling tools include early flowchart tools, or more recent environments supporting object-oriented modeling. What is desired by most users is a customized modeling environment that has been tailored to contain the concepts needed in the user's problem domain.

Raising the level of abstraction may often lead to a corresponding increase in productivity. In the past this has occurred when programming languages evolved towards a higher level of abstraction. Today, Domain-Specific Modeling (DSM) languages provide a viable solution for continuing to raise the level of abstraction beyond coding, making development faster and easier.

Industrial experiences of DSM consistently show it to be several times faster than current practices, including current UML-based implementations of MDA. As Booch et al. [1] state, "the full value of MDA is only achieved when the modeling concepts map directly to domain concepts rather than computer technology concepts." Accordingly, in DSM the models are constructed using

Copyright is held by the author/owner(s).
SPLASH'10 October 17–21, 2010, Reno/Tahoe, Nevada, USA.
ACM 978-1-4503-0240-1/10/10.

concepts that represent things in the problem domain, not concepts of a given programming language [8]. The modeling language follows the domain abstractions and semantics, allowing developers to perceive themselves as working directly with domain concepts. The models represent simultaneously the design, implementation and documentation of the system, and the final products may be generated from the high-level models with domain-specific code generators. This automation is possible because of domain-specificity: both the modeling language and code generators correspond to the requirements of a narrow domain, often in a single company.

This paper introduces DSM by describing a general framework for defining domain-specific modeling languages and code generators for a specific purpose. This is followed by describing the focus and topics of the 10th workshop on Domain-Specific Modeling [12].

2. Defining and using domain-specific languages

Three things are necessary to achieve full automatic code generation from domain modeling: firstly, a modeling tool supporting a domain-specific modeling language; secondly, a code generator; and lastly, a domain-specific framework. Figure 1 shows these three elements at two levels: the definition level and the use level.

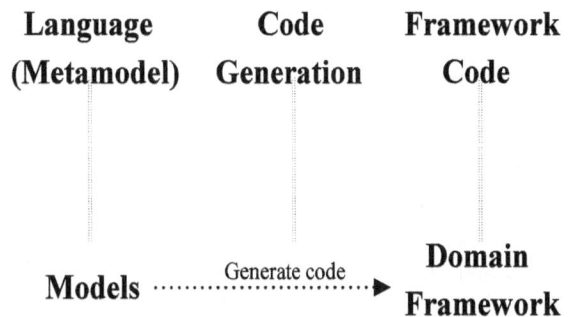

Figure 1. Framework for domain-specific modeling

The top-level (representing the definition) is made once by the organization for a given domain. This forms the start-up cost of the DSM approach [9]. Normally, one or two experts will define the modeling language (i.e., a metamodel) and related code generation, normally with a metamodeling tool [3, 6]. The metamodel is the implementation of the domain-specific modeling language, and includes the concepts and rules directly from the domain. The framework code will often be reused from earlier projects in the domain, with some added or modified code specifically for the DSM creation project.

The bottom-level process represents the use of a domain-specific modeling language and code generator.

This level is performed many times, once for each product, by normal developers. Development time can often be further reduced by reusing parts of the DSM model that are common to several products. The code generation and use of a domain framework or platform services require no effort by the developer. Together, these savings form the primary payback of the DSM approach. This is unlike many visual modeling languages that are fixed to a specific notation that maps to semantically well-defined concepts of programming languages (e.g., UML). In these languages, developers must leap straight from requirements into implementation concepts, and map back and forth between domain concepts, UML concepts, and code: this requires significant resources, and potentially introduces errors.

In DSM, the specification models are built from instances of the domain concepts specified in accordance with the rules in the language metamodel. The code generator walks through the model and transforms the concept structures into code. In some cases the code will be fully self-contained; more often, significant parts of the code will be calls to reusable components and the domain framework. Because the code is generated, syntax and logic errors do not normally occur, and the resultant improvement in quality forms a significant secondary payback of the DSM approach [2].

3. Workshop focus and topics

DSM has been successfully applied in many different domains [9], including automotive manufacturing [7], digital signal processing [10], mobile devices [2], telecommunication [4, 11], finance [4], and electrical utilities [4]. More investigation is still needed in order to advance the acceptance and viability of DSM.

There are general characteristics about these domains that suggest scenarios when DSM would be useful. Each of these examples represents a type of configuration problem with numerous choices (e.g., multiple "knobs" are available for tuning a system). Furthermore, each of these examples is based upon an underlying execution platform that may often change. The accidental complexities associated with evolving source code in the presence of platform adaptation are very hard to accomplish using ad hoc techniques based on low-level manual coding. This makes a system brittle because of the tight coupling to the execution platform. Moreover, these systems are constantly evolving by virtue of changes in the hardware and software platform, and due to changes in requirements. Therefore, there is a need to incorporate several degrees of concern separation through higher levels of system representation.

The goals of the workshop are to collect and exchange experiences related to building and using DSMs; continue building and extending the DSM community; and address in focus groups the issues raised in the presented papers and at previous workshops. The workshop examines DSM in different ways, including:

- Full papers describing ideas at either a practical or theoretical level
- Experience reports on applying DSM.
- Position papers describing work in progress or an author's position regarding current DSM practice
- DSM demonstrations describing a particular language, generator or tool for a particular domain

The presentations of papers and demonstrations form the basis for discussion in the group work sessions, and results of the group work sessions, along with presentation slides, will be available on the workshop website [12] together with the papers. Topics addressed in the workshop include:

- Industry/academic experience reports describing success/failure in implementing and using DSM languages/tools
- Approaches to identify constructs for DSM languages
- Novel features in language workbenches / tools to support DSM
- Approaches to implement metamodel-based modeling languages
- Metamodeling frameworks and languages
- Modularization technologies for DSM
- Novel approaches for DSM code generation
- Issues of support/maintenance for DSM-built systems
- Evolution of languages along with their domain
- Organizational/process issues in DSM adoption and use
- Demonstrations of working DSM solutions (languages, generators, frameworks, tools)
- Identification of domains where DSM can be most productive in the future (e.g. embedded systems, product families, multi-platform systems)

References

[1] Booch, G., Brown, A., Iyengar, S., Rumbaugh, J., and Selic, B., *MDA Journal*, May 2004.

[2] Gray, J., Tolvanen, J.-P., Kelly, S. Gokhale, A., Neema, S., and Sprinkle, J,, "Domain-Specific Modeling," *CRC Handbook on Dynamic System Modeling*, (Paul Fishwick, ed.), CRC Press, 2007.

[3] Kelly, S., Rossi, M., and Tolvanen, J.-P., What is Needed in a MetaCASE Environment?, *Journal of Enterprise Modelling and Information Systems Architectures*, Vol 1., 1, 2005

[4] Kelly, S., and Tolvanen, J-P, *Domain-Specific Modeling*, Wiley, 2008.

[5] Kieburtz, R., McKinney, L., Bell, J., Hook, J., Kotov, A., Lewis, J., Oliva, D., Sheard, T., Smith, I., and Walton, L., A Software Engineering Experiment in Software Component Generation, *Proceedings of 18th International Conference on Software Engineering*, Berlin, IEEE Computer Society Press, March, 1996.

[6] Lédeczi, A., Bakay, A., Maroti, M., Völgyesi, P., Nordstrom, G., Sprinkle, J., and Karsai, G., Composing Domain-Specific Design Environments, *IEEE Computer*, November 2001.

[7] Long, E., Misra, A., and Sztipanovits, J., Increasing Productivity at Saturn, *IEEE Computer*, August 1998, pp. 35-43.

[8] Pohjonen, R., and Kelly, S., Domain-Specific Modeling, *Dr. Dobbs Journal*, August 2002.

[9] Sprinkle, J., Mernik, M., Tolvanen, J-P., and Spinellis, D., What Kinds of Nails Need a Domain-Specific Hammer?, *IEEE Software*, July/Aug, 2009, pp. 15-18.

[10] Sztipanovits, J., Karsai, G., and Bapty, T., Self-Adaptive Software for Signal Processing, *Communications of the ACM*, May 1998, pp. 66-73.

[11] Weiss, D., and Lai, C. T. R., *Software Product-line Engineering*, Addison Wesley Longman, 1999.

[12] Workshop on Domain-Specific Modeling (DSM'10), http://www.dsmforum.org/events/DSM10

The 2nd Workshop on
Human Aspects of Software Engineering (HAoSE2010)

Orit Hazzan

Department of Education in Technology and Science
Technion – Israel Institute of Technology
oritha@techunix.technion.ac.il

Yael Dubinsky

IBM Research - Haifa Lab

dubinsky@il.ibm.com

Abstract

Continuing the OOPSLA 2009 workshop's success, we aim at strengthening the community's interest in and fostering the research on human aspects of software engineering – the focus of this workshop. The importance of this topic stems from the recognition that the more the software world is developed, the more it is accepted by the software engineering community that the *people* involved in software development processes deserve more attention. In this spirit, this workshop highlights the world of software engineering from the perspective of the main actors involved in software development processes: individuals, teams, customers, organizations, and other stake holders. Needless to say, the code and technology are main actors in this process as well; indeed, they are addressed and analyzed from the human perspective. Since the SPLASH community deals with software engineering processes, it should not neglect their human aspects. The workshop offers one venue in which the topic can be discussed.

Categories and Subject Descriptors D.2.9 [Software Engineering]: Management – Programming teams

General Terms Management, Measurement, Performance, Design, Economics, Human Factors, Legal Aspects.

Keywords human aspects of software engineering, teamwork, cognitive aspects, social aspects, managerial aspects.

1. Motivation

It is widely accepted today that software engineering should not address only technological aspects, but rather, it should refer also to the work environment and to the professional framework. Accordingly, we suggest examining the field of software engineering through the following three perspectives that create what we named The *HOT Framework for Software Engineering*:

- The **H**uman perspective, which includes cognitive and social aspects, and refers to learning and interpersonal (teammates, customers, management) processes;

- The **O**rganizational perspective, which includes managerial and cultural aspects, and refers to the workspace and issues that extend beyond the team;

- The **T**echnological perspective, which includes practical and technical aspects, and refers to how-to and code-related issues.

Figure 1 presents a schematic view of the HOT framework.

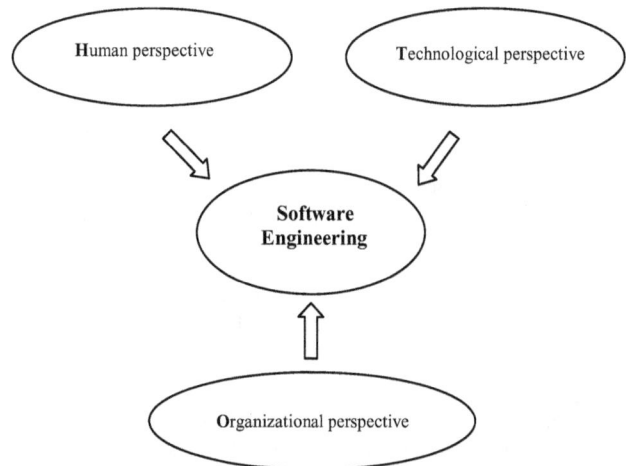

Figure 1. The HOT Framework for Software Engineering

The workshop focuses on the human perspective and the organizational perspective. It continues the interest expressed in the First Workshop on Human Aspects of Software Engineering (HAoSE2009) facilitated in OOPSLA 2009

2. Workshop goals

- The participants share their research work on human aspects of software engineering;

- The participants maintain and extend the community that explores human aspects of software engineering;

- The participants investigate research methods that fit for the exploration of human aspects of software engineering;

- The participants explore cognitive, social and organizational aspects of software engineering;

- The participants deepen their understanding of how human aspects of software engineering influence software development processes.

Copyright is held by the author/owner(s).
SPLASH'10 October 17–21, 2010, Reno/Tahoe, Nevada, USA.
ACM 978-1-4503-0240-1/10/10.

3. The workshop website

http://edu.technion.ac.il/Faculty/OritH/HomePage/HAOSE_OOP SLA_Workshop/index.htm

The workshop website will be updated right after the workshop with the workshop outcomes: topics of discussion, teamwork products, decisions regarding future activities, new ideas emerged in the workshop, and any other interested idea that will come up in the workshop.

4. Organizers

DR. ORIT HAZZAN (primary organizer a contact person) is an associate professor at the Department of Education in Technology and Science of the Technion – Israel Institute of Technology. In May 2004 she published her book *Human Aspects of Software Engineering*, co-authored with the late Jim Tomayko. Her second book – *Agile Software Engineering* – co-authored with Yael Dubinsky, was published by Springer in 2008. In parallel to her research work, she is a consultant for several software projects in the Israeli software industry. She presents her research at computer science and software engineering education conferences (e.g., SIGCSE), as well as at conferences on software engineering in general (such as, ICSE) and the Agile Conference).

DR. YAEL DUBINSKY is affiliated with the Software and Services group in IBM Haifa Research Lab (HRL). For more than ten years she is also the instructor of project-based courses in the Department of Computer Science at Technion IIT. She has published her work at conferences and journals related to software engineering and information systems, and has experience in organizing workshops and tutorials in leading conferences. Yael has a significant experience with guiding agile implementation processes in the industry and academia. Her book on Agile Software Engineering, which she co-author with Orit Hazzan, was published by Springer at 2008.

The organizers' work about the workshop theme can be found at the Agile Software Development Methods at the Technion website:

http://edu.technion.ac.il/Courses/cs_methods/eXtremeProgrammi ng/XP_Technion.htm

5. Activities and Format

A full day workshop.

The workshop consists of theory- and practice-based presentations, group work and discussions. Workshop activities include:

experience sharing with respect to case studies in which human aspects play a central role, examination of different software engineering topics from the human perspective, exploration of how the awareness to human aspects of SE may foster organizational processes, and teaching human aspects of SE in software organizations and in the academia.

Timetable

Hour	Topic
9:00-9:20	Introduction
9:20-10:30	Part A [The session theme will be determined according to the accepted papers] - paper presentation(s) - collaborative activity
10:30-11:00	Coffee Break
11:00-12:30	Part B [The session theme will be determined according to the accepted papers] - paper presentation(s) - group work
12:30-14:00	Lunch
14:00-15:30	Part C [The session theme will be determined according to the accepted papers] - paper presentation(s) - collaborative activity
15:30-16:00	Coffee Break
16:00-17:30	Part D Discussion: Future activities and follow up the workshop

6. Additional Information

Hazzan, O. and Dubinsky, Y. (2008). *Agile Software Engineering*, Undergraduate Topics in Computer Science' (UTiCS) Series, Springer.

Tomayko, J. and Hazzan, O. (2004). *Human Aspects of Software Engineering*, Charles River Media.

VMIL 2010

4th Workshop on Virtual Machines and Intermediate Languages

Hridesh Rajan[λ], Michael Haupt[φ], Christoph Bockisch[β], Robert Dyer[λ]

[λ]Iowa State University, [φ]Hasso Plattner Institute, University of Potsdam, and [β]Universiteit Twente

[λ]{hridesh,rdyer}@iastate.edu, [φ]michael.haupt@hpi.uni-potsdam.de, and [β]c.m.bockisch@cs.utwente.nl

Abstract

The VMIL workshop is a forum for research in virtual machines (VMs) and intermediate languages. It is dedicated to identifying programming mechanisms and constructs that are currently realized as code transformations or implemented in libraries but should rather be supported at VM level. Candidates include modularity mechanisms (aspects, context-dependent layers), concurrency (threads and locking, actors, software transactional memory), transactions, etc. Topics of interest include the investigation of which such mechanisms are worthwhile candidates for integration with the run-time environment, how said mechanisms can be elegantly (and reusably) expressed at the intermediate language level (e.g., in bytecode), how their implementations can be optimized, and how VM architectures might be shaped to facilitate such implementation efforts.

Categories and Subject Descriptors D.3.4 [*Programming Languages*]: Processors—run-time environments

General Terms Design, Languages, Performance

Keywords Virtual machine, intermediate language

1. Motivations and Themes

An increasing number of high-level programming language implementations is realized using standard virtual machines (VMs). Recent examples of this trend include the Clojure (Lisp) and Potato (Squeak Smalltalk) projects, which are implemented on top of the Java Virtual Machine (JVM); and also F# (ML) and IronPython, which target the .NET CLR. Making diverse languages–possibly even adopting different paradigms–available on a robust and efficient common platform leverages language interoperability.

Copyright is held by the author/owner(s).
SPLASH'10, October 17–21, 2010, Reno/Tahoe, Nevada, USA.
ACM 978-1-4503-0240-1/10/10.

Standard VM vendors have started to adopt extensions supporting this trend. For instance, the Oracle standard JVM will include the *INVOKEDYNAMIC* instruction, which will facilitate a simpler implementation of dynamic programming languages on the JVM.

The observation that many language constructs are supported in library code, or through code transformations leading to over-generalized results, has led to efforts to make the core mechanisms of certain programming paradigms available at the level of the VM implementation. Dedicated support for language constructs enables sophisticated optimization by direct access to the running system. This approach has been adopted by several projects aiming at providing support for aspect-oriented programming or dynamic dispatch in general-purpose VMs (Steamloom, Nu, ALIA4J).

The main themes of this workshop are to investigate which programming language mechanisms are worthwhile candidates for integration with the run-time environment, how said mechanisms can be declaratively (and re-usably) expressed at the intermediate language level (e.g., in bytecode), how their implementations can be optimized, and how VM architectures might be shaped to facilitate such implementation efforts. Possible candidates for investigation include modularity mechanisms (aspects, context-dependent layers), concurrency (threads and locking, actors, software transactional memory), transactions, paradigm-specific abstractions, and combinations of paradigms.

The areas of interest include, but are not limited to, compilation-based and interpreter-based VMs as well as intermediate-language designs with better support for investigated language mechanisms, compilation techniques from high-level languages to enhanced intermediate languages as well as native machine code, optimization strategies for reduction of run-time overhead due to either compilation or interpretation, advanced caching and memory management schemes in support of the mechanisms, and additional VM components required to manage them.

2. Goals and Expected Results

We intend to solicit both technical and position papers. Our expectation is to receive contributions that, on the one hand, point out mechanisms and concepts worth to be supported at the level of the execution environment; and, on the other, provide more detailed descriptions of implementation approaches for such mechanisms and concepts. These papers should motivate new researchers to include the workshop topics into their research. To accomplish this, we will make all papers available on the workshop web page; and we intend to publish the workshop proceedings—consisting of selected high-quality papers and extended abstracts of the remaining accepted papers—in the ACM digital library. The proceedings of the first three VMIL workshops have already been published in the ACM digital library. We also intend to open the workshop to researchers without accepted papers.

It is our intention to receive submissions from researchers new to the field as well as experienced researchers and practitioners. For the former, we want to offer a platform for discussing their ideas and receiving feedback on them. This will be supported by question and answer sessions as well as by a session of group discussions.

3. Organizers and Program Committee

Hridesh Rajan   is an Assistant Professor of Computer Science at the Iowa State University. He received his Ph.D. from the University of Virginia in 2005. He is the recipient of a 2009 US National Science Foundation CAREER award and a 2010 Early Achievement in Research Award from Iowa State University. He has published in several conferences such as ECOOP, ESOP, ICSE, ESEC/FSE, ASE, AOSD, and IEEE Software. He has served on the program committees of Onward, AOSD, OOPSLA, NWeSP, ACP4IS, FOAL, and as a referee for top journals in his area such as IEEE Transactions on Software Engineering, ACM Transactions on Software Engineering and Methodology, and IEEE Software. He has also served as an external referee for several international conferences namely IEEE Infocom, ESEC/FSE, ICSE, OOPSLA, Formal Methods (FM), COMPSAC, etc. and program committee of the FOAL, VMIL, and ACP4IS workshops. He was also co-organizer and co-chair of the 2007-09 editions of this workshop. He is a member of IEEE, IEEE Computer Society, ACM, SIGSOFT, and SIGPLAN.

Michael Haupt   is a post-doctoral researcher in the Software Architecture Group at Hasso-Plattner-Institut in Potsdam. His research interests are in improving the modularity of systems software architectures as well as in implementing programming languages, in which latter area his main focus is on faithfully regarding programming paradigms' core mechanisms as primary subjects of language implementation effort. Michael holds a doctoral degree from Technische Universit"at Darmstadt, where he has worked on the Steamloom VM to provide run-time support for AOP languages. He has published papers on this and other AOSD-related subjects in the L'Objet and IEEE Software journals as well as in the AOSD, VEE, OOPSLA, and ECOOP conference series. Michael has served as PC member for ECOOP

2008 and 2010, as reviewer for TAOSD, and has been supporting reviewer for the AOSD, ECOOP, ICSE, FSE, MODELS, and VEE conference series. He has co-organized the Dynamic Aspects Workshop series in conjunction with the AOSD conferences, and the previous two editions of the VMIL. Michael is a member of the ACM.

Christoph Bockisch   is an assistant professor on Software Composition with a research focus on the design and implementation of programming languages with advanced dispatch mechanisms. He received his doctoral degree from the Technische Universität Darmstadt in 2008. Christoph is one of two project supervisors and lead programmers of the ALIA4J project, which comprises the STEAMLOOM^{ALIA} VM, the successor of Steamloom. He authored and co-authored several papers about compilation techniques and VM support for aspect-oriented programming languages, published amongst others by the OOPSLA, AOSD, and VEE conferences. To provide VM support, Christoph researches extensions to high-performing Java VMs based on just-in time compilation. He furthermore researches meta-models for the definition of arbitrary dispatch mechanisms to act as a first-class representation. Christoph was co-organizer and co-chair of all prior editions of the VMIL workshop and he was program co-chair of the AOSD-Europe Summer School 2009. He was reviewer for the TAOSD and TSE journal, member of the program committee of the ODAL workshop 2006, and supporting reviewer for the conferences Compiler Construction, AOSD, and ECOOP and for the TOSEM journal. Christoph was and continues to be involved in teaching courses to graduate students about aspect-oriented software development, concepts of programming languages and VM.

Robert Dyer   is a fourth year Ph. D. student with a research focus on the design of intermediate language models and VM support for advanced modularization techniques. He is currently the lead developer on the Nu project, which includes an intermediate language model and VM support for aspect-oriented programming languages. He has authored and co-authored papers about advanced intermediate languages and dedicated VM caching mechanisms in the ACM TOSEM journal and AOSD conference. He was co-organizer of the previous two editions of the VMIL workshop. Robert served as a supporting reviewer for the OOPSLA and AOSD conferences and FOAL workshop. He is a student member of ACM, SIGSOFT, and SIGPLAN.

Program Committee
Walter Binder (University of Lugano, Switzerland)
Steve Blackburn (Australian National University, Australia)
Erik Ernst (University of Aarhus, Denmark)
Naveen Kumar (Intel Corporation, USA)
Doug Simon (Oracle, Switzerland)
Roel Wuyts (IMEC, Belgium)

KOPLE— Knowledge-Oriented Product Line Engineering

Haitham S. Hamza

Software Eng. Competence Center
Cairo University
Giza 12613, Egypt
hshamza@acm.org

Jabier Martínez

European Software Institute
Zamudio E-48170, Spain
Jabier.Martinez@esi.es

Joseba Laka Mugartza

European Software Institute
Zamudio E-48170, Spain
joseba.laka@esi.es

Abstract

The maturity of Knowledge Engineering (KE) theory and practice presents a real opportunity for advancing the state-of-the-art and state-of-the-practice in software Product-line Engineering (PLE). Several challenges that face the adoption and implementation of PLE in practice can be addressed by exploiting advanced techniques from KE. This paper introduces the concept of KOPLE and describes the related one-day workshop that will be held in conjunction with SPLASH 2010.

Categories and Subject Descriptors D.2.13 [*Software Engineering*]: Reusable Software, Domain Engineering

General Terms Design

Keywords Assets Mining; Domain Modeling; Knowledge Engineering; Product-Line Engineering

1. The Concept of Knowledge-Oriented PLE

Software Product Line Engineering (PLE) has emerged as an effective and practical technology to exploit systematic reuse in developing software applications. PLE exploits systematic reuse by identifying and methodically reusing software artifacts to develop different but related software systems. A software product-line can be defined as *"a set of software-intensive systems sharing a common, managed set of features that satisfy the specific needs of a particular market segment or mission and that are developed from a common set of core assets in a particular way"* [1].

To reap the real benefits of PLEs, organizations must adopt methods and techniques to identify reusable artifacts and reuse them in an orderly and systematic fashion. Methods and techniques that can be used to identify common features of different products in a domain and craft their commonalties into reusable assets are known as Domain Engineering and analysis [3] [4].

Developing product lines requires analysis skills to identify, model, and encode domain and product knowledge into artifacts that can be systematically reused across the development life-cycle. Practical implementations of PLE show that the intensive activities for PLE can be very beneficial for understanding the business domain. Indeed, analysis and modeling activities during the engineering of a product line serve as a base to distill and codify the *tacit business and technical knowledge* within the organization and the domain. As such, knowledge plays a fundamental role in the development of PLEs. Unfortunately, this role is not explicitly addressed in the PLE community.

The PLE community has been focusing mostly on the technical issues related to the modeling, analysis, and development of product-lines. However, less attention has been devoted to explore the knowledge aspects of PLE. Several practical challenges and problems that hinder the adoption of PLE in practice can be effectively addressed if viewed from knowledge perspective. Examples of challenges that can be addressed from a knowledge perspective include: domain knowledge identification and structuring, and product features modeling and analysis.

The above *knowledge-oriented* perspective of PLEs calls for new techniques to deal effectively and efficiently with the knowledge in the context of PLEs. Accordingly, we introduce the concept of *Knowledge-Oriented Product Line Engineering* (KOPLE) that refers to *research activities that extends and/or exploits knowledge engineering theories, techniques, and methods to address key challenges related to the development and implementation of PLEs.*

As a first step towards the assembly of a KOPLE research community and to bring the attention of the PLE community to this overlooked issue, we organize the first KOPLE workshop that will be held in conjunction with SPLASH 2010. The KOPLE workshop aims at exploring the interplay between KE and PLE. The workshop investigates how knowledge engineering can improve the theory and practice of PLE and vice versa.

Copyright is held by the author/owner(s).

SPLASH'10, October 17–21, 2010, Reno/Tahoe, Nevada, USA.
ACM 978-1-4503-0240-1/10/10.

2. Overview of KOPLE Related Research

Over the last decade, there have been an increasing research efforts in exploiting the potential of various knowledge engineering techniques in PLE and visa versa (see for example: [2], [5] – [12]).In [2], a lightweight product line engineering method is used along with agile techniques to develop tool that supports the visual composition of web services. In [5], the asset mining for product lines is described with focus on architecture reconstruction which can be used, in return, to support product line evolution.

In [8], an ontology-based approach is proposed for analyzing commonality and variability of features in PLE. Also, in [10], ontologies are used to enhance the reuse of domain and enterprise engineering assets. Source code mining is proposed in [12] in order to enhance the maintainability of product lines. In [9], a semantic modeling approach for PLE is proposed and demonstrated. Other studies also focused on feature asset mining and service identification in product lines using various techniques such as formal concept analysis and concept lattice.

These research efforts; however, are scattered, and thus they have a limited impact on advancing both the PLE and the KE research community. Workshops and other research forums are needed in order to jointly identify key challenges and problems in both communities, and explore how each community can benefit from the other. This workshop presents one of the early starts in this direction.

3. Workshop Objectives and Scope

The goals of this workshop are to identify and exchange research and industrial experiences related to the use of knowledge engineering in various aspects of PLE and visa versa; jump start a research community that focus on KOPLE; form focus groups to investigate key challenges identified and raised in the presented papers; and initiate a *Working Group* that focuses on knowledge issues related to PLE to further develop this area and its practice.

The workshop examines various issues and challenges related to KOPLE via the following venues: (1) Full papers describing theoretical and practical ideas and concepts, (2) Experience reports from industry that implement KOPLE or address its challenges in practical settings, (3) Position papers presenting work in progress or novel ideas at high level, and (4) Demonstration of practical implementation, tool support, etc. The results of the work groups, along with presentation slides will be made available on the workshop website [14].

The workshop focuses on various topics related to both PLE and KE communities such as:

- Mining knowledge from existing assets
- Use of ontology in developing PLE
- Use of PLE concepts for semantic web and web services

- KE techniques for PLE scoping and testing
- Knowledge-based commonality and variability modeling languages and techniques
- Industry case studies and experience reports in developing knowledge-oriented PLE
- Tool support for knowledge-oriented PLE
- Economical aspects of adopting knowledge-oriented PLE

References

[1] P. Clements and L. Northrop. Software Product Lines: Practice and Patterns. Addison-Wesley, 2007.

[2] M. Karam, S. Dascalu, H. Safa, R. Santina, and Z. Koteich, "A Product-line Architecture for Web Service-based Visual Composition of Web Applications," *J. of Systems and Software*, vol. 81, no. 6, pp. 855-867, 2008.

[3] H. Mili, et.al., Reuse-based software engineering, John Wiley & Sons, Inc. 2002.

[4] J. Neighbors, "Software Construction using components," PhD Thesis, Dept. of Info. and Computer Sc., U. of California, Irvine, 19981.

[5] L. OBrien, F. Hansen, R. Seacord, D. Smith, D., "Mining and Managing Software Assets," *Proc. of the 10th Int. Workshop on Software Tech. and Eng. Practice (STEP 2002)*, Washington, DC, 2002.

[6] T. Eisenbarth, R. Koschke, and D. Simon,"Feature-Driven Program Understanding Using Concept Analysis of Execution Traces," *Proc. of the Int. Workshop on Program Comprehension*, pp. 300-309, Toronto, Canada, May 2001.

[7] T. Eisenbarth and D. Simon, "Guiding Feature Asset Mining for Software Product Line Development,"*In Proc. of 1st Int. Workshop on Product Line Eng.: The Early Steps: Planning, Modeling, and Managing*, pp. 1-4, Erfurt, Germany, September 2001.

[8] S.-B. Lee, J.-W. Kim, C.-Y. Song, and D.-K. Baik, "An Approach to Analyzing Commonality and Variability of Features using Ontology in a Software Product Line Eng.," *Proc. of 5th ACIS Int. Conf. on Software Eng. Research, Management & Applications (SERA 2007)*, pp.727-734, 2007.

[9] M. Roshchin, P. Graubmann, and V. Kamaev, "Semantic Modeling for Product Line Engineering," *Int. J. of Information Theories and Applications*, vol. 15, pp. 387 – 390, 2008.

[10] A. Caplinskas and A. Lupeikiene, "The Role of Ontologies in Reusing Domain and Enterprise Engineering Assets," *Informatica vol. 14, no. 4/2003*, pp. 455-470, 2005.

[11] D.-S. Kang, C.-Y. Song, D.-K. Baik, "A Method of Service Identification for Product Line," *Proc. of Third Int. Conf. on Convergence and Hybrid Information Technology (ICCIT '08)*, pp. 1040 - 1045, 2008.

[12] M. Jiang, J. Zhang , H. Zhao, and Y. Zhou, "Enhancing Software Product Line Maintenance with Source Code Mining," Lecture Notes in Computer Science, Springer Berlin, pp. 538-547, 2008.

[14] Workshop on Konwledge-Oriented Product-Line Engineering: http://www.esi.es/workshop/KOPLE2010

Concurrency for the Application Programmer

Vijay Saraswat

IBM TJ Watson Research Center

vijay@saraswat.org

Doug Lea

SUNY, Oswego

dl@cs.oswego.edu

Abstract

Forced by architectural and commercial considerations, programmers now have to confront multi-core systems, heterogeneity, clusters, clouds.

What does this revolution mean for the application programmer, typically removed from the hardware through many layers of middle-ware (often on top of managed run-time environments)? How should the capabilities of heterogeneous processors (including GPUs, FPGAs, streaming processors) and heterogeneous memory (including non-coherent memory) be made available to the application programmer? Should abstractions for the application programmer focus primarily on application-level concurrency rather than implementation-level concurrency? Should application-level concurrency abstractions be fundamentally determinate? Fundamentally declarative? Resilient in the face of node- and network- failure? How can high-performance concurrent programs be written in garbage-collected languages? How can they *not* be written in garbage-collected languages?

This workshop aims to bring together practitioners and thinkers to address all topics around concurrency for the application programmer.

Categories and Subject Descriptors K.3 Computers and Education [*K.3.2 Computer and Information Science Education*]: Curriculum

General Terms Algorithms, Design, Experimentation, Measurement, Performance, Theory

Keywords Concurrency, Parallelism, Curricula, Multicore, Applications

1. Introduction

The concurrency revolution is upon us. Forced by architectural and commercial considerations, programmers now have to confront multi-core systems, heterogeneity, clusters, clouds. Programmers must address the challenge of productively and reliably implementing computational systems that deal internally with a large number of threads and massive amounts of data. Fundamental notions (what does it mean to read and write a shared memory location?) must be addressed. Long-standing data-access models (e.g. ACID transactions, relational querying) must be revisited (e.g. to take advantage of mostly read-only data, streaming).

What does this revolution mean for the application programmer? Typically such a programmer is removed from the hardware through many layers of middle-ware (often on top of managed run-time environments), and works with high levels of abstraction (e.g. in high-level or custom, domain-specific languages or frameworks such as J2EE).

Nevertheless the need to get performance and scale and exploit heterogenous and non-uniform architectures are as vital for such programmers as for the systems programmer. Application programmers face the additional challenge that they have to contend for the same computational resources with layers of the system on top of which they are built. This can cause significant problem with performance transparency and performance portability. (For instance it is well known that some kinds of Single-program/Multiple data programs are very susceptible to jitter that might be introduced by unpredictably scheduled computations on the same system, such as network interrupts, garbage collections etc.)

On the other hand, application programmers can often take advantage of regularities in their domains to simplify the computational task. For instance Hadoop is a concurrent application framework that permits its users to specify sequential pieces of code that are scaled out to run in parallel across multiple nodes of a cluster (data-parallelism). Typically the Map/Reduce computations realized in Hadoop are determinate. It is much easier to build tooling for determinate systems (as opposed to general concurrent, reactive concurrent systems).

This workshop aims to bring together practitioners and thinkers to address the topic of concurrency for the application programmer. Speficially the following questions are targeted:

> How should the capabilities of heterogeneous processors (including GPUs, FPGAs, streaming processors) and heterogeneous memory (including non-coherent memory) be made available to the application programmer? Should abstractions for the application programmer focus primarily on application-level concurrency rather than implementation-level concurrency? Should application-level concurrency abstractions be fundamentally determinate? Fundamentally declarative? Resilient in the face of node- and network- failure? How can high-performance concurrent programs be written in garbage-collected languages? How can they *not* be written in garbage-collected languages?

The workshop will be organized around the presentation of position papers selected by the PC, and a panel discussion. The results of the workshop will be made available online.

The Program Committee for this workshop consists of Bob Blainey (IBM), Joshua Bloch (Google), Ras Bodik (UC Berkeley), Amol Ghoting (IBM), Kevlin Henney (Curbralan Ltd), David Holmes (Oracle), Jim Larus (Microsoft), Doug Lea (SUNY Oswego – co-chair), Martin Odersky (EPFL), Bill Pugh (U Maryland), Vijay Saraswat (IBM – co-chair), Adam Welc (Intel).

Copyright is held by the author/owner(s).

SPLASH'10, October 17–21, 2010, Reno/Tahoe, Nevada, USA.
ACM 978-1-4503-0240-1/10/10.

Ontology-Driven Software Engineering 2010

Sergio de Cesare

Brunel University
United Kingdom

Frederik Gailly

Ghent University
Belgium

Grant Holland

Grant Holland and
Associates
U.S.A.

Mark Lycett

Brunel University
United Kingdom

Chris Partridge

BORO Program
United Kingdom

sergio.decesare@brunel.ac.uk frederik.gailly@ugent.be grant.holland@gmail.com mark.lycett@brunel.ac.uk partridgec@borogroup.co.uk

Abstract

Ontologies (i.e. formalized models of real world domains and systems) are becoming mainstream in the representation and management of data, information and knowledge. In software engineering, however, the adoption of ontology-driven methods and techniques is still at an initial stage of definition and gestation. A series of initiatives by both academic and industrial groups have highlighted the potential benefits that would derive from software development driven by ontologies. These benefits include improved model/code traceability, artifact reusability and increased levels of system interoperability and integration. In general ODiSE here refers to the different ways in which ontologies can contribute to improving Software Engineering – its processes and its artifacts. The broad themes of the workshop include: (1) Ontology as a means to inform all phases of the development lifecycle; (2) Ontology as means to increase software traceability; and (3) Methods, techniques and tools for ODiSE. The workshop aims to bring together researchers and practitioners with diverse cultural and professional backgrounds in order to discuss and analyze the different perspectives, issues and challenges of Ontology-Driven Software Engineering.

Categories and Subject Descriptors D.2.13 [**Software Engineering**]: Reusable Software – domain engineering, reusable libraries, reuse models.

General Terms: Algorithms, Management, Measurement, Documentation, Design, Languages, Theory.

Keywords: Ontology; software engineering; semantics; model development and transformation.

1. Theme and Goals

Ontologies (i.e. formalized models of real world domains and systems) are becoming mainstream in the representation and management of data, information and knowledge.

Copyright is held by the author/owner(s).
SPLASH'10   October 17–21, 2010, Reno/Tahoe, Nevada, USA.
ACM 978-1-4503-0240-1/10/10.

In software engineering, however, the adoption of ontology-driven methods and techniques is still at an initial stage of definition and gestation. A series of initiatives by both academic and industrial groups have highlighted the potential benefits that would derive from software development driven by ontologies. These benefits include:

- Improved understanding of the relation between (system) concepts and the domain.
- Improved ability to automatically reason over aspects of requirements, design and implementation.
- Potential to better cater for differences in requirements/use and/or adapt to context.
- Enhanced communication, trust and consistency.
- Improved interoperability and reusability.

The main theme of this workshop is Ontology-Driven Software Engineering (ODiSE: pronounced odyssey). ODiSE here refers to the different ways in which ontologies (i.e., formalized conceptual models of real world domains) can contribute to improving Software Engineering – its processes and its artifacts. This use of the term encompasses different and interrelated aspects of Software Engineering as a discipline. For example: (1) ontological principles can be used as the basis of improved development languages; (2) ontologies can help improve the way in which software development projects are organized; and (3) ontological domain models can drive or refine typical development phases, such as requirements, design and implementation.

The motivation for organizing a workshop on ODiSE derives from the increased interest that ontologies have generated in recent years within the software community. The relevance of ontologies in Software Engineering is exemplified, for instance, by the successful OOPSLA 2007 workshop on 'Semantic-Based Systems Development', various OMG and W3C initiatives, and commercial products based on 'semantic technologies'. However, regardless of such developments, these efforts still represent pioneering initiatives in the field of Software Engineering. As the state-of-the-art stands, ODiSE is still in its infancy. The adoption of theory and technologies developed by the Semantic Web community to enhance Software Engineering appears promising, with many areas that are worth investigating and exploring.

This workshop is the 7th in a series of OOPSLA/SPLASH workshops on the general theme of ontologies in systems development, evolution and integration. More specifically this is the second event titled Ontology-Driven Software Engineering. After a successful first edition, ODiSE 2010 will focus on the specific themes that emerged in 2009. The general areas that the workshop will address are:

- Ontology as a means to inform the process of gathering requirements.

- Ontology as a means to inform architecture development directly from requirements specifications.

- Ontology as a means to inform the software design directly from the architecture specification.

- Ontology as a means to model the software development process and the software product itself.

- Ontologies as run-time artifacts or to inform the design of run-time artifacts.

- The role of ontology reasoning in the software engineering process.
- The role of ontologies in model-driven development.
- Comparison of different ODiSE mechanisms (e.g. domain-specific modeling, profiling, etc.).
- Comparison of the role of core ontologies vs. domain ontologies in ODiSE.
- Ontology driven development of service software.
- Methodological issues for ODiSE.
- Problems of semantic mismatch between traditional software modeling paradigms, approaches, techniques, etc. and ontological modeling.

ODiSE 2010 aims to bring together researchers and practitioners with diverse cultural and professional backgrounds in order to discuss and analyze the different perspectives, issues and challenges of Ontology-Driven Software Engineering.

Curricula in Concurrency and Parallelism

Vijay Saraswat

IBM TJ Watson Research Center

vijay@saraswat.org

Kim Bruce

Pomona College

kim@cs.pomona.edu

Abstract

The concurrency era has exploded on us. Multicore systems are now everywhere – in our laptops, desktops, graphic cards, video game consoles. Symmetric multi-processors and clusters dominate the server and high performance computing market and are the foundation for cloud computing.

There is an urgent need to ensure that newly trained Computer Science graduates are well versed in the principles and practice of concurrent and parallel programming. Hence there is a growing groundswell of interest in revisiting undergraduate and graduate curricular design issues around concurrency.

This workshop aims to bring together practitioners and thinkers to address this topic. This is the second edition of the workshop first run at OOPSLA 09. Like the previous workshop, it will be organized around the presentation of position papers selected by the PC, and a panel discussion. The results of the workshop will be made available online.

Categories and Subject Descriptors   K.3 Computers and Education [*K.3.2 Computer and Information Science Education*]: Curriculum

General Terms   Algorithms, Design, Experimentation, Measurement, Performance, Theory

Keywords   Concurrency, Parallelism, Curricula, Multicore

1. Introduction

The goal of this workshop is to bring together practitioners and thinkers to address the issue of redesigning undergraduate and graduate **curricula for concurrency**.

Given the current state of the art in computer design, and expected industry trends, it is critical that Computer Science professionals be trained in the fundamental skills of concurrent programming. For instance, the practicing programmer must have realistic performance models for multicores, symmetric multiprocessors and clusters. S/he must understand fundamental issues around concurrency, atomicity, synchronization, ordering and affinity. S/he must understand fundamental abstractions (e.g. data parallelism, dependency graphs) and design principles (e.g. recursive parallel decomposition) and their domains of applicability. S/he must understand how to choose the right architecture to fit the concurrent processing problem at hand (e.g. fat-cores for branching code;

GPGPUs for data-parallel, non-branching, regular access codes, clusters for scale-out).

Abstractions and performance models that were considered well-understood in the sequential world must be revisited in the light of changes wrought by concurrency. For instance, How does concurrent garbage collection interact with atomic operations? How can programmers be trained to discipline their use of the beguiling expressiveness of arbitrary graphs of mutable objects (popularized by modern OO languages) to ensure their parallel code is determinate and deadlock-free? In some cases basic and long-held beliefs about what hardware does for you need to be revisited (e.g. the hardware may speculate, run scout threads to identify critical loads, track dependent reads and writes to support atomic operations, etc.)

These new demands impose a significant challenge to current pedagogical frameworks. The 2008 ACM Curriculum Guideline Revision acknowledges the "growing relevance of concurrency." However a large number of questions remain to be adequately addressed.

- What are the "fundamental ideas" of concurrency and parallelism that every Computer Science graduate should know? That every college graduate should know?

- Should concurrency and parallelism be taught "top-down" (via high-level abstractions such as operations on collections) or bottom up (with low-level tools such as threads and locks)?

- Should sequential programming be taught as a "special case" of concurrent and parallel programming?

- Should concurrency and parallelism issues be addressed in introductory computer science courses?

- Should concurrency and parallelism topics be "sprinkled" in existing courses (e.g. in architecture, systems, programming languages, algorithms) – if so which topics in those courses should be taken out to make room? Should these topics be taught in their own separate stream?

This workshop aims to bring together practitioners and thinkers to address this topic. It will be organized around the presentation of position papers selected by the PC, and a panel discussion. The results of the workshop will be made available online at

Practical answers to these questions must take into account the realities of educational institutions. For instance, the student populations and practices at a primarily teaching-oriented four-year college are quite different from those at a top-ten research university. Concurrency ideas are new to many senior faculty and hence there is a significant need for re-training.

The workshop seeks to provide a forum for practitioners and thinkers to discuss these issues. As in the first workshop, the central goal is to establish those areas in which a rough consensus exists, and identify those in which further thought and debate is warranted. The first workshop was successful in fostering a dialog between

Copyright is held by the author/owner(s).

SPLASH'10,   October 17–21, 2010, Reno/Tahoe, Nevada, USA.
ACM 978-1-4503-0240-1/10/10.

computer scientists and educators from a variety of teaching colleges. It led to a BOF at SIGCSE last month.

The website for this meeting is

```
http://www.cs.pomona.edu/~kim/CCP2010.html
```

The Program Committee for this workshop consists of Guy Blelloch, Kim Bruce, Dan Ernst, Shriram Krishnamurthi, Tim Mattson, Vijay Saraswat, Michael Scott, and Guy L. Steele, Jr.

SPLASH 2010 Workshop on Flexible Modeling Tools

Doug Kimelman

IBM T.J. Watson Research Center
PO Box 704
Yorktown Heights, NY, 10598
dnk@us.ibm.com

André van der Hoek

University of California, Irvine
5029 Donald Bren Hall
Irvine, CA 92697, USA
andre@ics.uci.edu

Harold Ossher

IBM T.J. Watson Research Center
PO Box 704
Yorktown Heights, NY, 10598
ossher@us.ibm.com

Margaret-Anne Storey

University of Victoria
PO Box 3055, STN CSC
Victoria, B.C. Canada V8W 3P6
mstorey@uvic.ca

Abstract

"*Flexible modeling tools*" hold the promise of bridging the gap between formal modeling and free-form authoring. This workshop will bring together researchers and practitioners to explore ideas and showcase early results in this emerging field.

Both formal modeling and free-form authoring offer important benefits for software architects and designers, as well as others. Unfortunately, contemporary tools often force users to choose one style of work over the other. During the exploratory phases of design, it is more common to use white boards than modeling tools. During the early stages of architectural analysis, it is more common to use office tools like PowerPoint and Excel. These tools offer ease of use, freedom from strict representation rules, and the ability to readily prepare attractive presentations for a variety of stakeholders. However, users miss out on the clarity, consistency, and completeness that can accrue from using modeling tools, as well as the powerful visualization, navigation, manipulation, and guidance that semantics-driven tools can provide.

At this workshop, people who build tools and people who use tools for software development will discuss the reasons for the current state of the practice, and will focus on tool users' needs and tool capabilities to address those needs. Papers and live demonstrations will present work on free-form authoring tools, formal modeling tools, and hybrid tools that aim to achieve the benefits of both.

Categories and Subject Descriptors D.2.2 [**Software Engineering**]: Design Tools and Techniques – computer-aided software engineering.

General Terms Design, Human Factors.

Keywords modeling tools; authoring tools; sketching; flexible modeling

1. Introduction

Most activities during the software lifecycle involve producing and manipulating representations of information. These range from domain analysis (such as business analysis) during the early stages of requirements engineering, through architectural and lower-level design, to coding, testing, deployment and beyond. Many of these activities, and the tools that support them, have long been of interest to the SPLASH community. The information representations are models, and hence these are modeling activities, though not typically called that in all cases. Many modeling tools exist to support modeling activities. They have a variety of advantages, such as syntax and static semantics checking, providing multiple views of models for visualization and convenience of manipulation, providing domain-specific assistance (e.g., "content assist") based on model structure, providing documentation of the modeling decisions, ensuring consistency of the models, and facilitating integration with other formal tools and processes, such as model-driven engineering (MDE) and model checking.

Despite these advantages, however, formal modeling tools are often not used for many of these activities. During the exploratory phases of design, it is more common to use white boards, pen and paper or other informal mechanisms. Free-form diagrams serve as the centerpiece of discussion and can easily evolve as discussion proceeds. During the

Copyright is held by the author/owner(s).
SPLASH'10 October 17–21, 2010, Reno/Tahoe, Nevada, USA.
ACM 978-1-4503-0240-1/10/10.

early stages of requirements engineering, when stakeholders are being interviewed and domain understanding is being built, it is also more common to use office tools (word processors, spreadsheets and drawing/presentation tools). Free-form textual documents, tables and diagrams serve as working documents and can easily be fashioned into presentations to stakeholders that are such an important part of this activity. The documents and presentations are easy to share with stakeholders. Users are also not forced to commit too early to specific choices, and thus have freedom during highly iterative, exploratory activities.

Formal modeling tools and more informal but flexible, free-form approaches thus have complementary strengths and weaknesses. Practitioners throughout the software lifecycle must currently choose between them for each specific task. Whichever they choose, they lose the advantages of the other, with attendant frustration, loss of productivity, traceability, or even quality.

What can be done about this unfortunate dichotomy? Tools that blend the advantages of modeling tools and the more free-form approaches offer the prospect of allowing users to make trade-offs between flexibility and precision/formality and to move smoothly between them. We refer to these as *flexible modeling tools*. They might be modeling tools with added flexibility, or office tools with added modeling support, or tools of a new kind. Some work has already been done in this area, much of it quite recently, for example: software design sketching tools, modeling tools that allow free-form annotation and tagging, and tools that support progression from unstructured text or diagrams to more formal representations. Successful workshops at CASCON 2009 and ICSE 2010 showed that there is considerable and diverse interest in this area. These workshops in particular began to lay the groundwork for understanding the problem, and provided some hints at possible solutions (position papers from these workshops are downloadable from the workshop web sites). But many more discussions are needed to understand how to design flexible modeling tools.

This workshop will bring together researchers from the SPLASH community who understand tool users' needs, usability, user interface design and tool infrastructure to explore these questions. The concrete goals of this workshop are to explore in depth the current dichotomy and its implications for users, leading to a list of key issues, and to discuss obstacles to flexible modeling and means to overcome them, leading to a new research agenda in flexible modeling tools.

2. Presentation Topics

Position papers on topics relevant to the dichotomy between modeling tools and more free-form tools will be presented. Topics could include: analysis of specific problems with existing tools, detailed requirements for flexible modeling tools, analysis of usability tradeoffs involved in flexible modeling, descriptions of approaches for architecting and building flexible modeling tools, and descriptions of actual examples of such tools.

As well, there will be live demonstrations of working prototypes of flexible modeling tools, focusing on essential capabilities of the tools.

3. Workshop Format

The workshop will consist of a few brief presentations from a subset of the accepted position papers and demonstrations. Each presentation will be accompanied by considerable discussion. To fuel this discussion, all participants will be asked to prepare:

a) Two problems they have experienced with existing modeling tools, or two tasks or situations for which modeling tools would be helpful but are not used typically used; and

b) Two features/differences in behavior or ideas for radical new tools they would like to see.

In addition, there will be an area where all accepted papers and demonstrations can be displayed as posters, to be viewed by all participants throughout the day.

Finally, all participants are encouraged to bring working prototypes of tools along with them. If there is sufficient interest, a SPLASH BOF will be organized to provide an opportunity to discuss and showcase tools and some of the workshop results in greater depth.

4. Further Information

For further information, please see the workshop website at http://www.ics.uci.edu/~nlopezgi/flexitools.

5. Organizers

Doug Kimelman, IBM T.J. Watson Research Center, USA
Harold Ossher, IBM T.J. Watson Research Center, USA
André van der Hoek, University of California, Irvine, USA
Margaret-Anne Storey, University of Victoria, Canada

6. Program Committee

Elisa Baniassad, The Australian National University
Krzysztof Czarnecki, University of Waterloo, Canada
Rob DeLine, Microsoft Research, USA
Michael Desmond, IBM Research, USA
Miryung Kim, University of Texas at Austin, USA
Andrew Ko, University of Washington, USA
Michele Lanza, University of Lugano, Switzerland
Crista Lopes, University of California, Irvine, USA
Marian Petre, Open University, UK
Dave Thomas, Bedarra Research Labs, Canada

2010 International Workshop on Foundations of Object-Oriented Languages (FOOL'10)

SPLASH/OOPSLA'10 Workshop Summary

Jonathan Aldrich

Carnegie Mellon University

jonathan.aldrich@cs.cmu.edu

Jeremy Siek

University of Colorado at Boulder

jeremy.siek@colorado.edu

Abstract

The search for sound principles for object-oriented languages has given rise to considerable research during the last few decades, leading to a better understanding of the key concepts of object-oriented languages and to important developments in type theory, semantics, program verification, and program development. The purpose of this workshop is to provide a forum for discussing new ideas in the foundations of object-oriented languages and provide feedback to authors. Submissions to this workshop were invited in the general area of foundations of object-oriented languages, including but not limited to language semantics, type systems, program analysis and verification, programming calculi, concurrent and distributed languages, database languages, and language-based security.

Categories and Subject Descriptors D.3.1 [*Programming Languages*]: Formal Definitions and Theory

General Terms Languages, Security, Theory, Verification

Keywords foundations, object-orientation, programming languages, type theory, semantics, analysis, verification, concurrency, distributed systems, databases, security

1. Main Theme and Goals

The theme of the workshop is the general area of foundations of object-oriented languages; topics of interest include language semantics, type systems, program analysis and verification, programming calculi, concurrent and distributed languages, database languages, and language-based security. Papers are welcome to include formal descriptions and proofs, but these are not required; the key consideration is that papers should present novel and valuable ideas relating to foundations for object-oriented languages. The main focus in selecting workshop contributions will be the intrinsic interest and timeliness of the work, so authors are encouraged to submit polished descriptions of work in progress as well as papers describing completed projects. In addition to the sharing of research ideas, another goal of the workshop is to provide feedback to the authors, helping them prepare their papers for submission to top-tier conferences.

2. Papers and Activities

FOOL is a 1-day workshop that includes presentations of accepted papers as well as invited speakers and other technical sessions.

FOOL does not have formal proceedings, to enable authors to present preliminary work that they wish to later publish formally in a conference venue. Papers are peer-reviewed by the program committee above, however, and are posted online at the FOOL workshop site as an informal record of the workshop. Many past FOOL papers have had significant influence on object-oriented programming language research and revised versions appear in prominent conferences and journals. The home page of FOOL is at

    http://www.cs.cmu.edu/~aldrich/FOOL/,

and the web page for FOOL'10 is at

    http://ecee.colorado.edu/~siek/FOOL2010/

3. Location at SPLASH/OOPSLA

While FOOL has traditionally been held in conjunction with POPL, the steering committee felt that the the object-oriented research community that is centered on OOPSLA and SPLASH would also provide a strong positive research community. Furthermore, FOOL fills a need for a foundational language workshop at SPLASH. We look forward to synergizes between these communities as SPLASH and OOPSLA host FOOL this year.

Copyright is held by the author/owner(s).

SPLASH'10,   October 17–21, 2010, Reno/Tahoe, Nevada, USA.
ACM 978-1-4503-0240-1/10/10.

4. Organization

FOOL is guided by a steering committee as follows:

- Jonathan Aldrich (Chair, Carnegie Mellon University)
- Viviana Bono (Universitá di Torino)
- Kathleen Fisher (AT&T Labs)
- Atsushi Igarashi (Kyoto University)
- Benjamin Pierce (University of Pennsylvania)
- John Reppy (University of Chicago)
- Christopher Stone (Harvey Mudd College)
- Philip Wadler (University of Edinburgh)

The program committee this year is as follows:

- Jeremy Siek (Chair, University of Colorado at Boulder)
- Davide Ancona (Universitá di Genova, Italy)
- Juan Chen (Microsoft Research, USA)
- Derek Dreyer (MPI-SWS, Germany)
- Atsushi Igarashi (Kyoto University, Japan)
- Donna Malayeri (EPFL, Switzerland)
- Nate Nystrom (University of Texas Arlington, USA)
- Frank Piessens (Katholieke Universiteit Leuven, Belgium)
- Chieri Saito (Kyoto University, Japan)
- Sam Tobin-Hochstadt (Northeastern, USA)
- Elena Zucca (Universitá di Genova, Italy)

Building the Right Cloud Solutions

Lars Arne Skår
Miles Consulting
Norway
lars@miles.no

Ruth Lennon
Letterkenny Institute
of Technology, Ireland
ruth.lennon@lyit.ie

E. Michael Maximilien
Almaden Services Research,
IBM Almaden Research Center, San Jose,
CA 95120, USA
maxim@us.ibm.com

Arne Jørgen Berre
Sintef
Norway
arne.j.berre@sintef.no

Abstract

Given that cloud computing is still one of, if not *the* most hyped buzzword in technology these days, we think it is important to bring the community of developers together to discuss and share the initial experiences in building the cloud solutions that makes the most sense in todays reality. According to NIST[2], the four deployment models of cloud computing are community clouds, private clouds, public clouds and hybrid clouds. The workshop aims to discuss and share experiences and state of the practice in deploying these cloud models.

Categories and Subject Descriptors D.2. [**Software engineering**]: General – *standards*, Coding tools and techniques, Testing and debugging, Programming environments, Management, Interoperability, Reusable software
General Terms Management, Performance, Design, Economics, Reliability, Security, Human Factors, Standardization, Legal Aspects.
Keywords Cloud, SOA, Web Services, Service Orientation, SaaS, Communities.

1. Main theme and goals

Cloud computing is one of these topics that everybody is talking about, but very few actually use yet. Our impression is that the early adopters are startup companies that are attracted to the economics and scalability capabilities, and innovators who use this for personal use or simply play with it due to their interest in modern technology.

The importance of Cloud Technologies have been promoted by Obama[1] and others. NIST[2] describes four deployment models for the cloud: Private Cloud, Community Cloud, Public Cloud and Hybrid Cloud. We could easily classify the submitted articles and presentations from last years workshop on cloud computing at OOPSLA09 into these deployment models.

Of these – the idea of a community cloud shows the most promising, yet challenging area. NIST[2] defines Community Clouds as a 'cloud infrastructure shared by several organizations and supports a specific community that has a shared concern'. Private clouds are likely to be the most common approach by businesses today due to still unresolved issues around data ownership and security. Private clouds are defined as a data center that has capabilities similar to a public cloud but is operated and owned by a business entity. Hybrid clouds is defined as using a public cloud in combination with a private data center. A use case for hybrid clouds could be offloading

Copyright is held by the author/owner(s).
SPLASH'10 October 17–21, 2010, Reno/Tahoe, Nevada, USA.
ACM 978-1-4503-0240-1/10/10.

work to a cloud-based solutions. Public clouds, like EC2 and S3 offered from Amazon can be considered fairly established, although the availability and variation in the market is increasing rapidly. So is the confidence among early adopters.

Many of the providers of cloud technologies and many hosts for cloud reside in the US. While this ensures conformity to American regulations such as HIPAA it does cause challenges within the European and wider community. Which laws apply to the storage of data by a European company in an American host providers cloud centre for instance. Governance and provenance are key issues that may be resolved through community based cloud development.

One example of this is the GS1 Product Recall[3]. GS1 is a global not for profit organisation aimed at improving supply chain efficiencies. This cloud based recall system will be extended to Canada running on the HP Cloud Computing Platform. Some of the most important advantages of this expansion are non-functional. The mitigation of consumer safety concerns has taken priority in this case. EMC[4] hold approx 31% of Thailands total external midrange storage market and have a strong policy for the future development of community clouds through their 'ready-to-go/ready-to-grow' packages. Interoperability solutions such as this will appear more prevalent in the future.

Clearly the move to community clouds requires investigation to tease out such issues as security, reliability, etc. However the ability to quickly transform data to the appropriate formats for each regulatory body of any given country could vastly increase the ability of companies to import and export services from a wider market area.

Modern thinking would also require investigation into the carbon impact of such technologies. The advantage of cloud technologies lies in the distribution of computing resources on a pay as you go basis. Thus an organization is not always aware of the location of hosting nor the impact on their carbon footprint. Given the extensibility of web services to include non-functional requirements it would become easy to place a regional requirement into the contract thus reducing the possible carbon footprint.

In this context, the proposed workshop aims to tackle the research problems (as well as practical experiences) around methods, techniques, concepts, models, languages, tools and technology that enable cloud computing. Of particular interest are the architectural, technical, and developmental models for the cloud showing how they combine synergistically to enable distributed computing on the scale required by today's cloud-hosted enterprise systems. The workshop aims to bring together researchers and industry practitioners (e.g. leading modelers, architects, system vendors, open-source projects, developers, and end-users) exploring Design Principles and Practices when applying services in conjunction with Cloud computing technologies, and promote and foster a greater understanding of how the service cloud can assist business to business and enterprise application integration, thus helping people develop and manage business processes more efficiently and effectively.

We particularly welcome practitioners in ongoing projects to establish one of the mentioned cloud types. Also vendors who are willing to engage in the workshop and share their visions as well as experiences in developing their cloud offerings – as long as it is free from marketing or sales pitches.

2. Organizers

Lars Arne Skår - CTO of Miles - a consulting company based in Norway. Lars is a system architect with about 20 years experience with a strong focus on system integration, quality and effective processes in system development. He's been co-organizing the SOA best practices workshop at OOPSLA since 2006. Co-organized this at OOPSLA09.

Ruth Lennon – lecturer in Letterkenny Institute of Technology. She has lectured for over 10 years and has provided consultancy on a number of commercial and EU funded projects. She has been on the organizing committee of the SOA best practices workshop at OOPSLA for the past two years. Ruth will focus on the advantages of services and Cloud to SMEs in the workshops. Co-organized this cloud workshop at OOPSLA09.

E. Michael Maximilien – Research staff member of Almaden Services Research at IBM Almaden Research Center, San Jose, USA. Doing research in cloud computing, Web APIs compositions mashups, Web services, social software, and agile software development.

Arne Berre – chief scientist at SINTEF, Norway. He has a PhD in Computer Science from NTNU, Norway. Working on model-based and object-oriented programming at SINTEF since 1985, he is now active in the standardization of UML and MDA within OMG. Currently he is heading the Norwegian computing society's group on application integration, methodologies and architecture. Co-organized this cloud workshop at OOPSLA09.

3. Results from previous workshops

At OOPSLA09 we ran a series of 2 full day workshops on cloud computing; one with an emphasis on design aspects, the other on implementation and operation aspects. About 40 participants attended these workshops – 2 posters were created based on intense discussions in groups.

Findings include:

- Still a lack of knowledge and experience in using cloud computing technologies
- Understanding where and when to abstract is important (cloud implicate a certain way of abstracting)
- You need to design differently for the cloud

- Legacy problems still exists
- SLAs are important in the cloud (and the cloud vendors tend to have a less committing view on SLAs today)
- Management – monitoring is challenging
- Virtual clouds may lower barriers within specific domains
- On-demand and flexible cost structures are key for cloud

4. Topics for discussions

We will start off with the following list of potential topics to discuss during the workshop:

1. SAAS, IAAS & PAAS for the Business Community
2. Gated Community Clouds
3. Ecosystem among Cloud computing providers
4. Domain Driven Quality of services (QoS) and services level agreements (SLAs)
5. Analysis and modelling of security, privacy, and trust in the Community Cloud, hybrid cloud and public cloud
6. Policy-based service-oriented systems in the service cloud
7. Service lifecycle management and infrastructure lifecycle managing for the different cloud deployment models
8. Models for governance in the Cloud
9. Service discovery, composition, execution, monitoring, and mediation in cloud environments

These topics indicate the general focus of the workshop, however, related contributions are also welcome.

5. Results from the workshop

A poster will be produced from the workshop to be presented at the SPLASH poster session. The purpose of the poster is to enable conference attendees that could not attend the workshop session to review the output of the workshop. The intent is also to promote discussion on the web site; www.soacloudbestpratices.com/CloudWorkshops.html, which will continue to be hosted after the workshop has finished. The discussions and results of the workshop will be made available via podcast on the workshop web site. A questionnaire will be carried out to assess the value of the workshop and evaluate the future direction of the workshop.

References

[1] Daniel Terdiman, "White House Unveils Cloud Computing Initiative", Geek Gestalt, CNET, 15 Sept. 2009, http://news.cnet.com/8301-13772_3-10353479-52.html.

[2] Peter Mell and Tim Grance "The NIST Definition of Cloud Computing", National Institute of Standards and Technology, Information Technology Laboratory, (2009), http://csrc.nist.gov/groups/SNS/cloud-computing/cloud-def-v15.doc.

[3] Anon, "HP Develops Cloud Service with GS1 Canada to Enhance Product Recall Process", 24 Aug. 2009, http://www.hp.com/hpinfo/newsroom/press/2009/090824xb.html.

[4] Suchit Leesa-nguansuk, "EMC Eases Path to Corporate Clouds", Bangkok Post, Tech News, 10 Mar. 2010, http://www.bangkokpost.com/tech/technews/34206/emc-eases-path-to-corporate-clouds.

Workshop: Architecture in an Agile World

Dennis Mancl

Alcatel-Lucent
Murray Hill, NJ, USA
dennis.mancl@alcatel-lucent.com

Steven D. Fraser

Cisco Systems
San Jose, CA, USA
sdfraser@acm.org

Bill Opdyke

JP Morgan Chase
Chicago, IL, USA
opdyke@acm.org

Abstract

Agility is important in the business world – but in many problem domains, *architecture* is valuable too. The combination of agile and architecture-driven approaches is often essential to success – it creates some opportunities for discovering potential problems early in the development cycle.

Categories and Subject Descriptors: D.2.9 Management – programming teams; K.4.3 Organizational Impacts – computer-supported collaborative work; K.6.3 Software Management – software process

General Terms: Management

Keywords: agile; architecture

1. Agility and Architecture

Agility is important in the business world – but in many problem domains, *architecture* is valuable too. The combination of agile and architecture-driven approaches is often essential to success – it creates some opportunities for discovering potential problems early in the development cycle.

For example, Agile development techniques are best for highlighting issues that are linked to the "uncertainties in customer requirements." Architecture practices can also help surface some of the key "technical unknowns" in a complex product development effort.

The Architecture in an Agile World workshop is exploring the issues and obstacles in doing agile development – with an eye on building and maintaining a sound architecture. The discussion in this workshop attacks the following subjects:

- Understanding some of the risks and opportunities of blending agile and architecture-driven software development practices.

- Determining how architects establish credibility with software development teams.
- Definitions of some key characteristics of good architects and good agilists.
- Discussion of why agile groups have problems with architecture-driven processes and why architects have problems with agile project organizations.
- How both agile and architecture-driven practices are used in cloud computing and software as a service.
- Exploration of some of the "good practices" that should be part of the toolkit of agilists and architects – "how to get just the right amount of architecture."

2. Why Agility and Architecture?

The world is moving faster than ever, and our software development techniques are struggling to keep up. We feel we need to have an agile feature set, but without a well-defined and understandable architecture, we feel like everything is in chaos. How do we manage the balance between architecture and agility?

This workshop explores the clash between agile and architecture-centric philosophies, and some practical ideas for combining the two approaches. This workshop continues a discussion started in an OOPSLA 2009 workshop and panel session.

The report of the OOPSLA 2009 workshop can be found at http://mysite.verizon.net/dennis.mancl/oopsla09/index.html.

3. What do we know about Agility and Architecture?

The obvious conclusion in the OOPSLA 2009 workshop was that "pure agile" and "pure architecture-driven" approaches are not the way to go.

- In a "pure agile" approach, the system would have an "emergent architecture" – because the most extreme agilists would consider any serious up-front architecture planning and modeling as unnecessary big design up front.
- In a "pure architecture-driven" approach, all architecture choices should be made using a top-down devel-

Copyright is held by the author/owner(s).
SPLASH'10 October 17–21, 2010, Reno/Tahoe, Nevada, USA.
ACM 978-1-4503-0240-1/10/10.

opment approach instead of using code-level experimentation and refactoring.

Some early attention to architecture planning will contribute to better communication within a development team. Even in a one-person project, architecture planning helps – it gives the developer an opportunity to think through important development issues, instead of merely implementing his or her first idea.

4.   The architect's role in an Agile world

In an agile world, an architect (or any development team member who is involved with software architecture or high-level design) has to be connected with development teams.

An architect needs to overcome the perception of being an "outsider" to the development work. One agile approach to reduce the distance between architects and developers is to include architects as members of a development team, with specific development and testing tasks assigned to them in each development iteration. There is at least one big benefit of this model: it makes the architects into users of their own documents and models, so they aren't just off in an "ivory tower." Also, as a member of an agile team, they will have frequent discussions with other development team members, which should improve communication about the architecture.

On the other hand, the idea of "making an architect a member of a development team" is not perfect. Some architects have poor development skills. The distractions of the development process may limit the amount of time they can spend on architecture planning. In some large systems, it is necessary for architects to spend time thinking about larger issues – not just the development tasks of a single development team.

5.   Building bridges between architects and agilists

Agile development teams have many complaints about architects. The top two problems:

- Agilists feel that architects are "always trying to push everyone around."
- In addition, agilists feel that architects often "overdesign."

These are valid complaints. Architects really do try to control things too much – and an agile viewpoint could really help architects do their job better.

Architects often complain about agile teams – some issues related to lack of forward vision and feedback:

- Most agile teams have trouble answering the question: "How much road do you have to pave ahead of you?" If the design vision only extends to the end of the next iteration, it might be easy for the design to fall off a cliff.
- Sometimes agile teams fail to get adequate feedback from stakeholders and customers. It isn't always the agile team's fault – but teams should always try to do better.

6.   Which issues are we going to discuss?

The SPLASH 2010 workshop will have a similar discussion agenda, but it will inevitably find some different issues and new conclusions – which will be reported in the workshop poster and final report. Please check the workshop website after the conference for the results:

http://mysite.verizon.net/dennis.mancl/splash10/index.html

Workshop on Experimental Evaluation of Software and Systems in Computer Science (Evaluate 2010)

Steven M. Blackburn

School of Computer Science
Australian National University
Acton, ACT, Australia
steve.blackburn@anu.edu.au

Amer Diwan

Department of Computer Science
University of Colorado at Boulder
Boulder, CO, USA
amer.diwan@colorado.edu

Matthias Hauswirth

Faculty of Informatics
University of Lugano
Lugano, TI, Switzerland
matthias.hauswirth@usi.ch

Atif M. Memon

Department of Computer Science
University of Maryland
College Park, MD, USA
atif@cs.umd.edu

Peter F. Sweeney

Thomas J. Watson Research Center
IBM
Hawthorne, NY, USA
pfs@us.ibm.com

Abstract

We call ourselves 'computer scientists', but are we scientists? If we are scientists, then we must practice the scientific method. This includes a solid experimental evaluation. In our experience, our experimental methodology is ad hoc at best, and nonexistent at worst.

This workshop brings together experts from different areas of computer science to discuss, explore, and attempt to identify the principles of sound experimental evaluation.

Categories and Subject Descriptors C.4 [*Performance of Systems*]; D.2.0 [*Software Engineering*]: General; D.3.4 [*Programming Languages*]: Processors; D.4.8 [*Operating Systems*]: Performance

General Terms Experimentation, Measurement

Keywords Evaluation Methodology

1. Motivation

In the last few years, researchers have identified some disturbing flaws in the way that experiments are performed in computer science.

An OOSPLA 2006 paper [1] pointed out that the complex interaction between Java applications and the architecture, compiler, virtual machine, and memory management required more extensive evaluation than C, C++, and Fortan applications. The authors took steps towards improving methodologies for choosing and evaluating benchmarks.

An OOPSLA 2007 paper [2] pointed out that the current state-of-the-art approach to evaluating Java applications was flawed. The authors went on to propose a more rigorous methodology based on confidence intervals from statistics and then used this methodology to demonstrate the previous reported evaluations were erroneous.

An ASPLOS 2009 paper [3] pointed out that there are common artifacts in one's experimental setup, such as the environment size and link order of binary files, that are typically ignored, but can significantly impact the outcome of one's experiment for C applications.

A PLDI 2010 paper [4] demonstrated that the current state-of-the-art Java profilers, which everyone is using to understand the performance of Java applications, are fundamentally broken. Specifically, the profilers often disagree on the identity of hot methods. If two profilers disagree, at least one, if not both of them, must be incorrect.

All four of these papers are pointing out that the experimental methodologies, which we as a computer science community are using, are seriously flawed. If the field of computer science is going to be a 'science', we must have proper evaluation methodologies that allow us to experimentally understand a system's behavior and performance.

2. Format

This workshop brings together experts from different areas of computer science to discuss, explore, and attempt to identify the principles of sound experimental evaluation.

Copyright is held by the author/owner(s).
SPLASH'10, October 17–21, 2010, Reno/Tahoe, Nevada, USA.
ACM 978-1-4503-0240-1/10/10.

The workshop will consist of discussion sessions, which focus on themes such as data collection, data analysis, and reproducibility, with the goal to answer the following questions:

- What are the issues that are preventing proper experimental evaluation?

- How can we resolve these issues?

- We need more research in evaluation methodology. What should that research be?

- We need better tools to do sound experimental evaluation. How do we encourage investment in such tools?

- What are the principles and best practices that people are using in the different areas of computer science?

- How does the computer science curriculum need to be changed to prepare the next generation of computer scientists?

This workshop will not be a mini-conference, and it will not have any proceedings. We are asking each participant to submit a short position statement, no more than 1000 words, on the state of experimental evaluation in computer science. We will distribute those position statements among the participants before the workshop.

The workshop will start out with a keynote by Cliff Click of Azul Systems. He will provide an industry perspective on experimental evaluation. Moreover, we plan to host a video panel discussion on experimental evaluation in different areas of computer science. The panel will consist of leaders in evaluation methodologies in their respective fields: Chris Drummond (machine learning), Ioana Manolescu (databases), and Ellen Voorhees (information retrieval).

3. Organizers

- Steven M. Blackburn, Australian National University

- Amer Diwan, University of Colorado / Google

- Matthias Hauswirth, University of Lugano

- Atif M. Memon, University of Maryland

- Peter F. Sweeney, IBM Research

4. Workshop Home Page

http://evaluate2010.inf.usi.ch/

5. Post-Workshop Activities

We will establish a collaborative resource, probably in the form of a web site, which will disseminate the findings of the workshop, and which will serve as an ongoing community platform. This resource will be reachable from the workshop home page.

References

[1] Stephen M. Blackburn, Robin Garner, Chris Hoffmann, Asjad M. Khang, Kathryn S. McKinley, Rotem Bentzur, Amer Diwan, Daniel Feinberg, Daniel Frampton, Samuel Z. Guyer, Martin Hirzel, Antony Hosking, Maria Jump, Han Lee, J. Eliot B. Moss, B. Moss, Aashish Phansalkar, Darko Stefanović, Thomas VanDrunen, Daniel von Dincklage, and Ben Wiedermann. The dacapo benchmarks: java benchmarking development and analysis. In *OOPSLA '06: Proceedings of the 21st annual ACM SIGPLAN conference on Object-oriented programming systems, languages, and applications*, pages 169–190, New York, NY, USA, 2006. ACM.

[2] Andy Georges, Dries Buytaert, and Lieven Eeckhout. Statistically rigorous java performance evaluation. In *OOPSLA '07: Proceedings of the 22nd annual ACM SIGPLAN conference on Object-oriented programming systems and applications*, pages 57–76, New York, NY, USA, 2007. ACM.

[3] Todd Mytkowicz, Amer Diwan, Matthias Hauswirth, and Peter F. Sweeney. Producing wrong data without doing anything obviously wrong! In *ASPLOS '09: Proceeding of the 14th international conference on Architectural support for programming languages and operating systems*, pages 265–276, New York, NY, USA, 2009. ACM.

[4] Todd Mytkowicz, Amer Diwan, Matthias Hauswirth, and Peter F. Sweeney. Evaluating the accuracy of Java profilers. In *PLDI '10: Proceedings of the 2010 ACM SIGPLAN conference on Programming language design and implementation*, pages 187–197, New York, NY, USA, 2010. ACM.

Programming Support Innovations for Emerging Distributed Applications (PSI EtA—$\psi\eta$)

A SPLASH 2010 workshop summary

Eli Tilevich

Virginia Tech

tilevich@cs.vt.edu

Patrick Eugster

Purdue University

peugster@cs.purdue.edu

Abstract

Distribution has become a necessity for the majority of computing domains, but developing distributed applications remains a highly delicate and complex task. Several emerging distributed computing and application domains, including cloud computing, service-oriented computing, stream processing, sensor networks, and context-aware computing, pose unprecedented challenges to the programmer. Applications in these domains can deliver tangible benefits to the user once they enter the mainstream of industrial software development. What is hindering the wide adoption and use of these applications is the prevalence of ad-hoc programming practices in their software development process. The goal of this workshop is to explore programming support innovations that can address the incongruence between the advanced programming requirements of emerging distributed applications and the current state of the art of their programming support. To that end, the workshop will provide a venue for free and open discussions among academic researchers and industry practitioners of distributed applications.

Categories and Subject Descriptors D.1.3 [*Programming Techniques*]: Concurrent Programming—distributed programming; D.2.11 [*Software Engineering*]: Software Architecture—domain-specific architectures; languages; D.2.13 [*Software Engineering*]: Reusable Software—domain engineering; D.3.2 [*Programming Languages*]: Language Classifications—concurrent, distributed, and parallel languages; extensible language usages; D.3.3 [*Programming Languages*]: Language Construct and Features—modules, packages; D.3.4 [*Programming Languages*]: Processors—code generation; D.4.7 [*Operating Systems*]: Organization and Design—distributed system; C.2.1 [*Computer-Communication Networks*]: Network Architecture and Design—distributed networks; C.2.4 [*Computer-Communication Networks*]: Distributed Systems—client/server; distributed applications

General Terms Design, Experimentation, Languages

Keywords programming support, distributed computing, service-oriented computing, cloud computing, stream processing, sensor networks, context-aware computing, cyber-physical systems, geo-spatial systems, data-intensive computing, programming frameworks, domain specific languages, code generators, middleware systems, program transformation systems, extensible languages, component technologies, product-line architectures, advanced separation of concerns

1. Main Theme and Goals

This workshop will provide an avenue for researchers and practitioners to explore and address some of the most salient challenges of developing emerging distributed applications.

1.1 Emerging Distributed Applications

Distribution has namely become required for the majority of application domains, and several emerging domains pose unprecedented challenges to the programmer. Examples include: service-oriented computing, cloud computing, stream processing, sensor networks, context-aware computing, cyber-physical systems, geo-spatial systems, data-intensive computing.

Addressing challenges that arise in the development of applications for such emerging distributed settings requires innovation with respect to programming support, including abstractions, techniques, and tools. This workshop aims at filling this gap.

Copyright is held by the author/owner(s).

SPLASH'10, October 17–21, 2010, Reno/Tahoe, Nevada, USA.
ACM 978-1-4503-0240-1/10/10.

1.2 Contributions Sought

Possible topics for contributions include, but are not limited to: programming frameworks, domain specific languages, code generators, middleware systems, program transformation systems, extensible languages, component technologies, product-line architectures, advanced separation of concerns.

Distributed applications present some of the most salient challenges for researchers and practitioners alike. A large number of top quality recent research publications are concerned with this subject directly or indirectly (e.g., at software engineering conferences ICSE, FSE, at programming languages conferences PLDI, POPL, ECOOP, OOPSLA, and at systems conferences EuroSys, SOSP, NSDI, SIG-COMM). The software industry has introduced numerous commercial applications addressing various challenges of distributed application development, including programing languages, libraries, frameworks, and middleware support. This recent surge of interest in programming support of the emerging distributed applications in these separate communities brings about two insights. Firstly, the challenges of providing adequate programming support are widespread and cut through a wide spectrum of computing technologies. Secondly, truly synergistic approaches may be necessary to address these challenges.

We are convinced that the time is ripe for a cross-domain effort to address the outstanding challenges and to improve the state of the art in programming support for emerging distributed applications. Of particular interest are fundamental approaches which can benefit *several* different distributed application domains, as different settings have common characteristics in addition to diverging ones. The history of programming abstractions has shown that often solutions developed for one domain can be successfully applied to conquer programming challenges of another domain. Therefore, there is great potential benefit in considering a wide array of different distributed application domains during a single workshop. We expect that considering a diverse set of domains from both the practitioner and researcher perspectives will engender unprecedented opportunities for cross-pollination across different fields and communities.

As a specific example, consider sensor networks and context-aware computing. Both research areas may be viewed as two sides of the same coin — one an infrastructure providing contextual information, while the other applications exploiting that information — and may thus have to deal with similar problems and thus share support. Yet, neither implies the other, and it is important to understand the specific characteristics of each. This workshop aims at promoting the collaboration among different communities by providing a forum for exchanging ideas and for presenting cross-domain research. Applying existing approaches and techniques in one domain to another requires that their assumptions, benefits, and fundamental trade-offs be thoroughly understood.

2. Organizers

PSI-EtA is organized by two program committee chairs:

- Eli Tilevich (Virginia Tech)
- Patrick Eugster (Purdue University)

Eli Tilevich is an assistant professor in the Department of Computer Science at Virginia Tech, where he leads the Software Innovations Lab. Its mission is to tame the complexity of developing and maintaining emerging complex computer systems through novel software technologies. Eli's research interests lie on the intersection of systems and software engineering, with a particular emphasis on distributed systems. Some of his recent publications appeared in ECOOP'09, ICDCS'09, OOPSLA'09, Middleware'09, and AOSD'10. In 2010, he is serving as a PC member of ICDCS, ICSM, SPLASH, and the SPLASH Doctoral Symposium. In 2009, he chaired the Second ACM Workshop on Hot Topics in Software Upgrades (HotSWUp'09), which was organized at OOPSLA 2009. Eli is the primary organizer of the workshop and point of contact.

Patrick Eugster is an assistant professor in the Department of Computer Science at Purdue University, and head of the Distributed Programming Group. Patrick's area of expertise lies in the intersection of programming languages and distributed systems. Some of his recent publications in the former area appeared in ESOP'09, PLDI'09, ECOOP'09, or COORDINATION'10, and in the latter area in DSN'09, SRDS'10, Sensys'10, or Middleware'10. Patrick is a recipient of the NSF CAREER award. He served as workshop chair for ECOOP 2008, a conference series with a strong tradition of workshops. He also served on its PC, first in 2006 and last in 2011, as well as on several other conference PCs.

Technical Program Committee

- Gustavo Alonso, *ETH Zürich*
- Godmar Back, *Virginia Tech*
- Shigeru Chiba, *Tokyo Institute of Technology*
- Charles Consel, *INRIA / University of Bordeaux*
- John Field, *IBM Research*
- Buğra Gedik, *IBM Research*
- Jon Howell, *Microsoft Research*
- Hans-Arno Jacobsen, *University of Toronto*
- Christine Julien, *UT Austin*
- Valérie Issarny, *INRIA Paris - Rocquencourt*
- Chandra Krintz, *UCSB*
- Erik Meijer, *Microsoft Research*
- Richard Schantz, *BBN Technologies*
- Liuba Shrira, *Brandeis University*
- Mario Südholt, *Ecole des Mines de Nantes*

Stop the Software Architecture Erosion:

Tutorial SplashCon 2010

Bernhard Merkle

SICK AG
Research & Development
Software Engineering
Erwin-Sick-Str.1
79183 Waldkirch, Germany
bernhard.merkle@gmail.com

Abstract

During the evolution of a software system, it becomes more and more difficult to understand the originally planned software architecture. Often an architectural degeneration happens because of various reasons during the development phases.

In this tutorial we will be looking how to avoid such architectural decay and degeneration and how continuous monitoring can improve the situation and avoid architectural violations. In addition we will look at "refactoring in the large" and how refactoring can be simulated. We will also look at some popular open source projects like ant, findbugs and eclipse (CDT/JDT) and see if and how far architectural erosions happens/ed there.

The participants will analyze a system and search with tool support for erosion areas and subsequently simulate virtual refactoring for improving the software. At the end participants will improve the system and have a good feeling how far an automated and tool supported approach can lead to better results.

Categories and Subject Descriptors D.2.11 [**Software Architecture**]:

General Terms Architecture, Design, Refactoring.

Keywords *software, architecture, design, erosion, refactoring, simulation, refactoring, static code analysis*

Permission to make digital or hard copies of all or part of this work for personal or classroom use is granted without fee provided that copies are not made or distributed for profit or commercial advantage and that copies bear this notice and the full citation on the first page. To copy otherwise, or republish, to post on servers or to redistribute to lists, requires prior specific permission and/or a fee.
SPLASH'10 October 17–21, 2010, Reno/Tahoe, Nevada, USA.
Copyright © 2010 ACM 978-1-4503-0240-1/10/10…$10.00.

1. Architecture Analysis

The main and most important use case is "deviation analysis". Architects are interested where the "is"-architecture (current code base) deviates from the "should"-architecture (current code base). We need several ingredients as shown in Figure [1]:

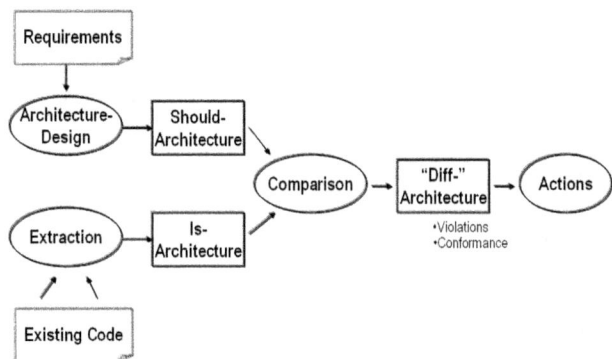

For the "is"-architecture we need to extract the information mostly from the source code in an efficient way. This information is aggregated and stored for later evaluation.

Figure 1. Reflexion model: is- and should-architecture

For the "should"-architecture we need a valid architecture model. Concepts like interface, public/private parts, components, subsystems and layers can be described with an Architecture Description Languages (ADL) additionally with the allowed dependencies. Subsequently both data sets are compared by a tool and we get a report of violations or conformance versus the architecture.

The reflexion model distinguishes between:

- "Convergences": Dependencies which should be present and are present in the is-architecture
- "Divergences": Dependencies which should **not** be present but are present in the is-architecture
- "Absence": Dependencies which should be present and are **not** present in the is-architecture.

Depending on the information you can then take actions and plan refactorings. Note that it is important to visualize the results in a condensed way. We do not want to see e.g. all violations between all classes. First it is important to aggregate them on the right level (e.g. inter component dependencies) and then drill down to lower levels. The amount of violations gives a first rough indication for the developer if it will be easy or difficult to cut a certain dependency. Also the numbers indicate how much the software depends on a certain framework. Additional Filter and navigation facilities are necessary in practice to manage large amounts of packages / classes.

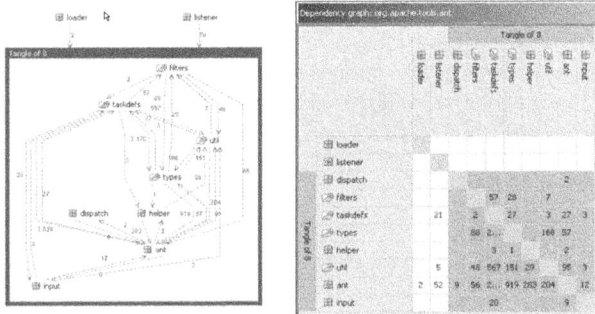

Figure 2. Graphical and numerical dependency visualizations

How to visualize the results (graphically/numerically) depends on the situation. Sometimes a graphical view is beneficial and sometimes a table with numbers is more appropriate. Figure [2] shows both alternative visualization methods: the graphical view uses the number of dependency as physical strength between to nodes. This spring-embedder algorithm can be used to visualize tight coupled packages in a very good way.

2. Architecture Analysis Tools

2.1.1 SotoArc / hello2morrow

SotoArc is a product from hello2morrow. Various languages like C/C++, C#, Java are supported. A parser ex-

tracts source code information and stores it in a mysql database for later analysis. Figure [3] show a screenshot of SotoArc with a possible should-architecture of findbugs. Dependencies between various layers and subsystems are represented as colored arrows counterclockwise, where green means a valid and red an invalid dependency. On the left side the creation of the should-architecture is shown. Most modeling operation are pattern based (e.g. following a java package style structure) and done via menus or wizard. SotoArc has algorithms to offer breaking of cycles; also the most important metrics are displayed. In SotoArc "virtual refactorings" are possible. Restructurings can be

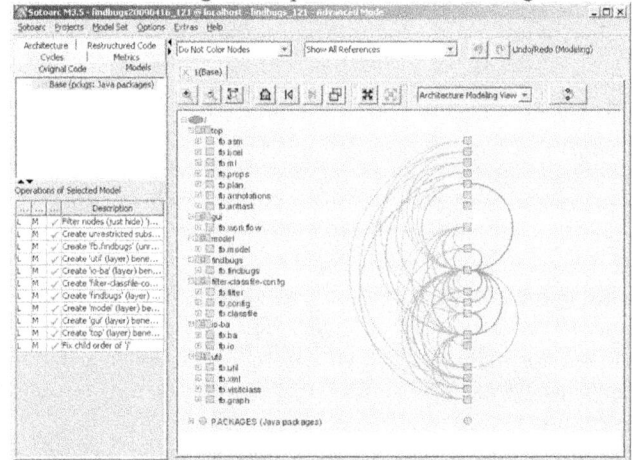

simulated before actually performed on the code base which is a major advantage. For trend analysis, extensive metrics and arbitrary model query support there is a more powerful Sotograph which uses the same mysql database information.

Figure 3. SotoArc ./ hello2morrow

2.1.2 Bauhaus / Axivion

Another interesting tool is Bauhaus from Axivion. It supports the "usual" languages like C/C++, Java but also COBOL, VB and various others. Bauhaus stores its information about the system in iml files (intermediate language) and rfg (resource flow graph). Based in this information various analysis can be performed. Figure [4] shows a deviation analysis with the should-architecture on the left side and the is-architecture on the right side. Modeling the should-architecture is done via the GUI or python scripts. Metrics, trend analysis and user defined queries are also possible. Also you can write your own coding guidelines as the full information

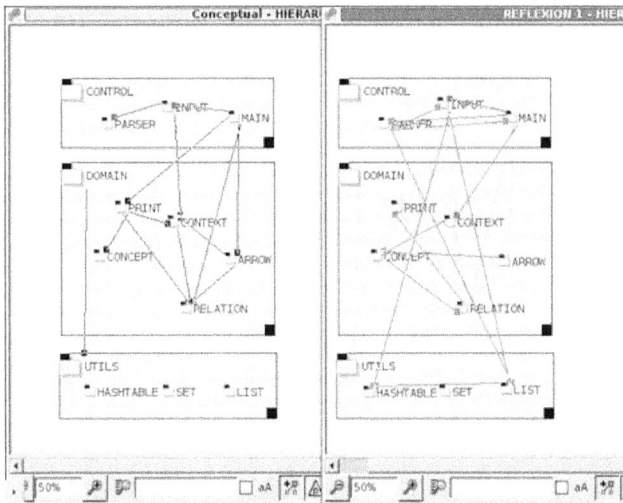

Figure 4. Bauhaus / Axivion

about the AST is still available. The MISRA-C guidelines e.g. have been implemented and are available as additional plug-in. The author expects that more and more tools will integrate the three levels of static analysis into one environment over time. Another interesting facility in Bauhaus is support for code clone detection, even modified code clones can be detected to a certain degree (e.g. renamed comments, renamed variables etc). Code duplication and clones often cause problems and new bugs during the maintenance phase of a product.

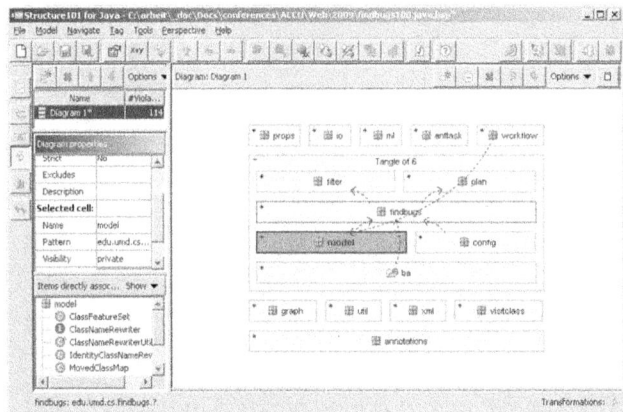

Figure 5. Structure101 / headway

2.1.3 Structure101 / Headway

Structure101 is a product from Headway software and supports multiple languages (C/C++, Java, .NET). There is also a "generic" support module which allows integrating any programming language, for up to date information check their website. Figure [5] again shows the architecture of findbugs, modeled in Structure101. Upward arrows are

architecture violations; the tool allows drilling down to the class where the violation happens. The should-architecture is defined within the architecture perspective. Beside the graphical view there is also support for DSM (dependency structure matrix). Refactorings can be simulated via transformation rules. A trend analysis tracks changes over time and the complexity view lists the most important metrics. To integrate the architecture analysis within your IDE there is also an eclipse and IntelliJ IDEA plug-in.

3. Summary

There is definitely a need for software architecture analysis. Every project suffers an architectural erosion or decay at some point and also open source projects are no exception as we saw. Compared with code- and design-level lint tools, the amount of messages can be better managed on the architecture level. Good tool support is necessary to be able to find violations efficiently and to simulate refactorings. We expect that over the next years, tools will start to combine the different level of static analysis and also integrate much more directly into the IDE.

References

[1] Martin, R. 2006 *Agile Software Development, Patterns and Principles.* Addison-Wesley Professional.

[2] Brown, J. 1998 *AntiPatterns: Refactoring Software, Architectures, and Projects in Crisis.* Wiley.

[3] http://standards.ieee.org/reading/ieee/std_public/description/se/1471-2000_desc.html

[4] Kruchten, P. 2003 *The Rational Unified Process: An Introduction, 3 edition.* Addison-Wesley Professional.

[5] Medvidovic, J. 2000: A Classification and Comparison Framework for Software Architecture Description Languages: IEEE Transactions on Software Engineering Volume 26 , Issue 1 (January 2000)

[6] http://www.eclipse.org/MoDisco/

[7] http://www.hello2morrow.com/products/sotoarc

[8] http://www.axivion.com/

[9] http://www.headwaysoftware.com/products/structure101

[10] Sangal, N., Jordan, E., Sinha, V., and Jackson, D. 2005. Using dependency models to manage complex software architecture. In *Proceedings of the 20th Annual ACM SIGPLAN Conference on Object-Oriented Programming, Systems, Languages, and Applications* (San Diego, CA, USA, October 16 - 20, 2005). OOPSLA '05. ACM, New York

XUnit Test Patterns and Smells

Improving the ROI of Test Code

Gerard Meszaros

Solution Frameworks

Splash2010@xunitpatterns.com

Abstract

High quality automated unit tests are one of the key development practices that enable incremental development and delivery of software by reducing the number of bugs introduced into code as it is evolved. But writing lots of tests is not enough as the tests need to be maintained over the life of the software. This maintenance cost can quickly outweigh the benefits provided by the tests.

XUnit is the generic name for the family of unit test frameworks that are now available in almost every programming language. JUnit, NUnit, MsTest and CppUnit are some of the better known members of the xUnit family. This tutorial provides the participants with a vocabulary of smells and patterns with which to reason about the quality of their xUnit test code and a set of reusable test code design patterns that can be used to eliminate the smells. Participants will be able to write tests that are easier to understand and maintain.

Categories and Subject Descriptors

D.2.2 [**Software Engineering**]:Design Tools and Techniques - Patterns

D.2.5 [**Software Engineering**]: Testing and Debugging - Debugging aids

General Terms Verification.

Keywords   code smells, unit testing, test patterns, test smells

1. Tutorial Attributes

1.1 Level:

Intermediate.

1.2 Attendee Background:

While some exposure and prior usage of one of the members of the XUnit family of test automation frameworks (e.g. JUnit, VbUnit, RUnit, CppUnit, etc.) is beneficial, even people new to automated testing using XUnit will get benefits.

1.3 Target audience:

XUnit Test Patterns and Smells will be of most interest to developers, development leads, coaches and architects working in a Test-First or Test-Driven Development environment. It is not, however, an introduction to the use of XUnit in general or any one member of the family in particular.

1.4 Tutorial objective:

1.4.1 Participants will learn:

- The difference between well-written automated unit tests and poorly written ones

- To recognize common code smells that make test code hard to understand and maintain.

- To recognize common behavior smells that increase the cost of running tests and interpreting the test results

- Test design patterns to avoid the behavior smells and which lead to highly repeatable and robust tests.

- Test coding idioms that make tests easier to understand and less fragile.

1.5 Presentation format:

The tutorial is presentation based frequently punctuated with short (5 minute) hands-on exercises that help the participants "experience" the smells and patterns. The material is presented as a sequence of mini case studies. Each case study starts with a sample of test code or test results and we discuss the "test smells" present in the tests and their impact on achieving our goal of repeatable, robust, fully-automated tests. Then we dig into the root causes of the smell(s) and present a set of alternative patterns that can be used to address them.

Exercises will be done in small groups. Ideally, participants will be able to form into groups of 3-4 to discuss the smells, causes and patterns in each exercise. The exercises are paper-based so laptop computers are not mandatory.

2. Tutorial Outline

- Motivation
  - Goals of Automated Unit Testing
  - Economics of Test Maintenance
  - What Does it Take to be Successful?
- Introduction to Concepts
  - Patterns
  - Smells
  - Debt

Copyright is held by the author/owner(s).

SPLASH'10   October 17–21, 2010, Ren Tahoe, Nevada, USA.

ACM 978-1-4503-0240-1/10/10.

- Code Smells & Remedies
  - o Case Study
  - o Obscure Test
    - Expected Object
    - Custom Assertion
    - Guard Assertion
    - Implicit Teardown
    - Automated Teardown
    - Transaction Rollback Teardown
    - Generated Value
    - Creation Method
  - o Rapid Test Writing using DSLs
- Behavior Smells
  - o Slow Tests
    - Lazy Setup
    - SuiteFixture Setup
    - Setup Decoriatio
  - o Erratic Test
    - Test Stubs and Mock Objects
  - o Fragile Test
    - Interface Sensitivity
    - Behavior Sensitivity
    - Data Sensitivity
    - Context Sensitivity
    - o Frequent Debugging
    - o Manual Intervention
- Project Smells
  - o Developers Not Writing Tests
  - o Bugs in Product(ion)
  - o Buggy Tests
  - o High Test Maintenance Cost
- Wrap-up
  - o How to use these Patterns

3. About the Presenter

Gerard Meszaros is an independent consultant specializing is agile development processes. Gerard wrote his first programs on punch cards in the late 1970's and joined Nortel's R&D subsidiary in 1981 as a software developer and later development manager, project manager and software architect. More recently, he built his first unit testing framework in 1996 and has been doing automated unit testing ever since. Along the way, he has become an expert in test automation patterns, refactoring of software and tests, and design for testability. Gerard has applied automated unit and acceptance testing on projects ranging from full-on eXtreme Programming to traditional waterfall development. His book [1] was published by Addison Wesley in May 2007 as part of the Martin Fowler Signature series and won a Jolt Productivity Award in the Best Technical Book category in 2008.

References

[2] Meszaros, Gerard, *xUnit Test Patterns – Refactoring Test Code* Reading Mass. Addison-Wesley Professional 2007

Language Extension and Composition
with Language Workbenches

Markus Völter

Independent/Itemis, Germany
http://www.voelter.de
voelter@acm.org

Eelco Visser

Delft University of Technology, The Netherlands
http://eelcovisser.org
visser@acm.org

Abstract

Domain-specific languages (DSLs) provide high expressive power focused on a particular problem domain. They provide linguistic abstractions and specialized syntax specifically designed for a domain, allowing developers to avoid boilerplate code and low-level implementation details.

Language workbenches are tools that integrate all aspects of the definition of domain-specific or general-purpose software languages and the creation of a programming environment from such a definition. To count as a language workbench, a tool needs to satisfy basic requirements for the integrated definition of syntax, semantics, and editor services, and preferably also support language extension and composition. Within these requirements there is ample room for variation in the design of a language workbench.

In this tutorial, we give an introduction to the state of the art in textual DSLs and language workbenches. We discuss the main requirements and variation points in the design of language workbenches, and describe two points in the design space using two state-of-the-art language workbenches. Spoofax is an example of a parser-based language workbench, while MPS represents language workbenches based on projectional editors.

Categories and Subject Descriptors D.2.3 [*Software Engineering*]: Coding Tools and Techniques; D.2.6 [*Software Engineering*]: Programming Environments; D.3.4 [*Programming Languages*]: Processors

General Terms Languages

Keywords Language Workbench, Domain-Specific Language, Meta-tooling, IDE, Projectional Editing, Parsing, Textual Language, Eclipse, Stratego, SDF, Spoofax, SGLR, MPS,

Copyright is held by the author/owner(s).

SPLASH'10, October 17–21, 2010, Reno/Tahoe, Nevada, USA.
ACM 978-1-4503-0240-1/10/10.

1. Domain Specific Languages

Domain-specific languages (DSLs) provide high expressive power focused on a particular problem domain. They provide linguistic abstractions and specialized syntax specifically designed for a domain, allowing developers to avoid boilerplate code and low-level implementation details. The syntax can be graphical, textual, or even a mixture of the two. DSL code (often called a "model") is typically executed by an interpreter, or transformed into programming language code for subsequent execution. In addition to aligning notations closely with the domain, DSLs allow error messages using domain terminology and optimizations based on domain knowledge.

Since DSLs typically focus on a single aspect of software implementation, models in multiple DSLs or combinations of models and regular programs are needed to cover all aspects of a complete software system. Thus, DSL models need to interact with models expressed with other DSLs and with programs in general purpose programming languages. This requires the extension of domain-specific checking and optimization to combinations of languages.

To enhance acceptance of DSLs with their prospective users (programmers or domain experts), the languages must come with good IDE support, as we know it from tools like Eclipse, Visual Studio or IntelliJ. Modern IDEs increase developer productivity by incorporating many different kinds of editor services specific to the syntax and semantics of a language. They assist developers in understanding and navigating through the code, they direct developers to inconsistent or incomplete areas of code, and they even help with editing code by providing automatic indentation, bracket insertion, and content completion.

The development of new DSLs comprises many tasks, ranging from syntax definition to code generation to the construction of an integrated development environment (IDE). Language engineering tools are essential for productivity in each of these tasks. Specifically for project-specific DSLs, which are by their nature limited in scope, development must be efficient, so DSLs can be developed as part of real-world development projects.

2. Language Workbenches

Language workbenches [3] are tools that integrate all aspects of the definition of domain-specific or general-purpose software languages and the creation of a programming environment from such a definition. To count as a language workbench, a tool needs to satisfy the following basic requirements and preferably also support language extension and composition. Within these requirements there is ample room for variation in the design of a language workbench.

2.1 Basic Requirements

A language workbench should at least support the definition of individual languages. A language definition consists of the definition of the syntax and semantics of the language, as well as the editor services that form the IDE.

Syntax definition: defines the concrete notation used for models and their underlying structure, which is the basis for analysis and transformation.

Semantics definition: defines the analyses and transformations applied to the structures defined by the syntax definition, including error checking, transformations such as refactorings, and code generation to translate a model to an implementation in a target language.

Editor services definition: defines the editor services that bind the language to an integrated development environment (IDE), including syntax highlighting, outline view, bracket matching, automatic indentation, reference resolving, content completion, error marking, and refactoring. Editor services often depend on syntactic or semantic analyses of the structure of edited models.

Language workbenches typically provide high-level, declarative DSLs to make language definition efficient.

2.2 Extension and Composition

The next step beyond support for the basic language definition requirements is support for language extension and composition to cater for language evolution and software projects consisting of models in multiple languages.

Language extension: existing languages can be extended with new concepts, adapting them to more specific contexts.

Language composition: languages for different domains can composed, either by symbolic integration such that language concepts in one language can reference concepts defined in other languages, or by embedding, such that concepts from one language can be embedded in another one.

2.3 Variation Points

There are many decisions that must be made in the design of a language workbenches. The following is a list of variation points in the design space:

Concrete syntax: The main dividing line is between graphical and textual notations. While in the long run we want to be able to mix the two, currently most tools are either focused on one, or at least have a strong bias. In this tutorial, we focus on textual notations.

Parser-based vs. projectional: Textual notations can either be implemented based on parsers or based on a projectional editor.

Derivation of editor services: Some editor services can be automatically derived from the language specification (e.g. code completion), others may have to be customized by the developer (outline view icons, or custom syntax highlighting).

Storage: Storage can either be file-based, using existing version control tools for team collaboration, or repository-based, often supporting real-time collaboration by various users. Furthermore, storage can be based on the abstract or the concrete syntax.

Inconsistent definitions: The model editor may or may not allow models to be in an inconsistent or erroneous state. Supporting (temporary) inconsistencies improves agility of software development, not requiring the developer to tend to each detail immediately.

In the tutorial we discuss two state-of-the-art language workbenches. Spoofax is an example of a parser-based language workbench, while MPS represents language workbenches based on projectional editors.

3. Spoofax

The Spoofax language workbench [1, 6] is a platform for the development of textual (parser-based) domain-specific languages with state-of-the-art IDE support. Spoofax provides a comprehensive environment that integrates syntax definition, program transformation, code generation, and declarative specification of IDE components. The environment supports agile development of languages by allowing incremental, iterative development of languages and showing editors for the language under development alongside its definition. These editors can be used to view the abstract syntax of a program or to directly apply transformations on a selection of text. Spoofax is based on Eclipse, an extensible programming environment that offers many language-generic development facilities such as plugins for version control, build management, and issue tracking. Spoofax language definitions take the form of Eclipse plugin projects, and can be distributed to "end developers" using the Eclipse update site mechanism.

3.1 Syntax Definition

The grammar forms the heart of the definition of any textual language. It specifies the concrete syntax (keywords etc.) and the abstract syntax (data structure for analysis and transformations) of a language. In Spoofax, the syntax is also used to derive customizable editor services, such as a default syntax highlighting service and an outline view service. Spoofax uses the modular syntax definition formalism SDF2 [4, 8] for the specification of grammars. SDF grammars are highly modular, combine lexical and context-free syntax into one formalism, and can define concrete and abstract syntax together in production rules.

3.2 Semantics Definition

Spoofax uses the Stratego program transformation language [2] to describe the semantics of a language. Stratego is based on rewrite rules for first-order terms, and strategies that control the application of these rules. During development, the abstract syntax view can be used as a reference for the first-order term representation of a language's abstract syntax. Rewrite rules may use string interpolation to conveniently generate text from textual templates. Alternatively, rules may rewrite to abstract syntax or may use syntax-checked concrete syntax expressions [9]. Code generation rules can be used to transform the DSL to a compilable form. They can be applied automatically as files are saved, or manually when triggered by the user. They can also be used to create views of the language. By default, views are automatically kept up-to-date and regenerated in the background as the source is changed. Stratego rewrite rules are also used to specify semantic editor services, such as error checking, reference resolving, and content completion.

3.3 Editor Services

Spoofax provides declarative editor descriptor languages for the definition of editor services. For many editor services, Spoofax generates default editor service descriptors from the syntax of the language, which can be combined with custom user-defined specifications in such a way that default descriptors can be re-generated when the syntax definition changes. Semantic editor services such as code generators and refactorings are declared by binding a user interface action to a semantics definition in Stratego.

3.4 Language Extension and Composition

Spoofax supports extension and composition of languages through the modularity of its underlying SDF and Stratego languages.

The syntax definition formalism SDF supports the full class of context-free grammars, which is the only class of grammars that is closed under composition. The definition of lexical syntax is integrated with the definition of context-free grammars, instead of using a separate language based on regular grammars for the definition of tokens. As a result, also lexical syntax definitions of SDF are closed under composition.

The semantics definitions in Stratego are also modular. The definitions of rules and strategies can be modularly extended to support new language constructs. More precise extensions can be achieved by extending hook definitions or instantiating parameters of transformation strategies. However, such extensions requires anticipation of extensibility in the design of the base language by including proper extension points.

Composition of languages is typically handled by means of a normalizing ('desugaring') transformation, which translates statements in an embedded language to an implementation in a common core language.

4. JetBrains MPS

JetBrains' Meta Programming System is a projectional language workbench [5] that has been developed over the last couple of years by JetBrains and is now available open source under Apache 2.0. MPS comes with an integration into popular version control systems. While the code is represented as XML files, the tool provides diff and merge facilities on the level of the concrete, projected syntax. Starting with version 1.5, MPS also comes with a facility to define debuggers for DSLs. The tool has been used extensively within JetBrains and is slowly getting traction outside of the company [7, 11]. An extensive, detailed tutorial for MPS can be found here [10]. An illustration of the capabilities of the tool is provided by the screencasts and papers listed on the mbeddr.com website [11].

4.1 Syntax Definition

MPS is a projectional editor. Consequently, language definition does not involve a grammar. Instead, language definition starts by defining the structure of the language through concepts. Secondly, projection rules, also known as editors, define the textual, tabular or graphical rendering of concepts.

The projectional approach has a couple of nice characteristics, in addition to fulfilling the requirements for language workbenches described above:

- Notations are more flexible than ASCII/ANSI/Unicode. Graphical, semi-graphical and textual notations can be mixed and combined. For example, a graphical tool for editing state machines can embed a textual expression language for editing the guard conditions on transitions.

- Since the model is stored independently from its concrete notation, it is possible to represent the same model in different ways simply by providing several projections. Different viewpoints of the overall program can be stored in one model, but editing can still be viewpoint specific. It is also possible to store out-of-band data, i.e. annotations on the core model/program, such as documentation, pointers to requirements (traceability), or feature dependencies in the context of product lines.

4.2 Semantics Definition

In MPS, the structure of a program can be restricted using various kinds of constraints: scopes, determine the set of possible targets for references, type system rules calculate types based on typing rules and an inference engine, and constraints check domain-specific properties of programs.

Transformations can be defined between arbitrary languages. Transformations are mappings from one language structure onto another one, i.e. transforming the underlying graph structure of a model. However, the concrete syntax of the target language can be used in transformations, making them look more like code generators.

Transformations can be cascaded and the MPS transformation engine incrementally reduces code until it cannot be reduced any further, at which point a text file is generated for subsequent compilation.

4.3 Editor Services

In parser-based environments where users basically enter text into a buffer, sophisticated editor services are optional — one can, in principle, use a simple text editor for editing. In a projectional environment this is different because editing requires the projection engine. Consequently, language definition requires the definition of IDE services. MPS does not even attempt to draw a line between the two: the definition of a language and it's editors automatically entails the creation of services for code completion, syntax highlighting, error markers, go-to-definition, and find references. While all of these can be customized, editor services can not be removed, since it would make editing models impossible.

4.4 Language Extension and Composition

In MPS, language definition is similar to object oriented programming in the sense that language concepts correspond to classes and models to objects. Thus, the principles for extension and composition from OO programming can be applied to languages. A language can inherit from another language, making the concepts from the base language available in the sub-language. The sub-language can then add new concepts, making the sub-language an extended version of the base language. Concepts in the sub-language can also extend concepts in the base language. This is the primary means of language extension: a base language might define a Procedure concept that contains a list of Statements. By defining sub-concepts of Statement, a sub-language can essentially plug into the base language, providing other kinds of statements usable in procedures.

The equivalent of delegation can be used to embed languages. A language can use another language and then define concepts that contain (as children) concepts from the used language. No special steps have to be taken to be able to integrate the languages syntactically, because no grammar and no parser is used.

There is another way of extending languages that closely resembles aspect oriented programming. A language can "contribute" additional properties to concepts defined in other languages, without invasively modifying this other language. This is very useful for all kinds of annotations such as documentation or traces to requirements.

Finally, the upcoming MPS 2.0 will allow sub-languages to define new notations for concepts inherited from a base language.

More details on language composition and extension with MPS can be found here [12].

References

[1] The Spoofax project. http://www.spoofax.org/.

[2] M. Bravenboer, K. T. Kalleberg, R. Vermaas, and E. Visser. Stratego/XT 0.17. A language and toolset for program transformation. *Sci. of Comp. Programming*, 72(1-2):52–70, June 2008.

[3] M. Fowler. Language workbenches: The killer-app for domain specific languages? http://martinfowler.com/articles/languageWorkbench.html, 2005.

[4] J. Heering, P. R. H. Hendriks, P. Klint, and J. Rekers. The syntax definition formalism SDF: Reference manual. *SIGPLAN Not.*, 24(11):43–75, 1989.

[5] JetBrains. Meta Programming System. http://www.jetbrains.com/mps/.

[6] L. C. L. Kats and E. Visser. The Spoofax language workbench. Rules for declarative specification of languages and IDEs. In M. Rinard, editor, *Proceedings of the 25th Annual ACM SIGPLAN Conference on Object-Oriented Programming, Systems, Languages, and Applications, OOPSLA 2010, October 17-21, 2010, Reno, NV, USA*, 2010.

[7] Realaxy LTD. Realaxy action script editor. http://www.realaxy.com/.

[8] E. Visser. A family of syntax definition formalisms. In M. G. J. van den Brand et al., editors, *ASF+SDF 1995. A Workshop on Generating Tools from Algebraic Specifications*, pages 89–126. Technical Report P9504, Programming Research Group, University of Amsterdam, May 1995.

[9] E. Visser. Meta-programming with concrete object syntax. In D. Batory, C. Consel, and W. Taha, editors, *Generative Programming and Component Engineering (GPCE 2002)*, volume 2487 of *LNCS*, pages 299–315. Springer-Verlag, October 2002.

[10] M. Völter. LWC 11 MPS Submission. http://code.google.com/p/mps-lwc11/wiki/GettingStarted.

[11] M. Völter and B. Merkle. mbeddr.com. http://mbeddr.com.

[12] M. Völter and K. Solomatov. Language composition with projectional language workbenches illustrated with mps. http://www.voelter.de/data/pub/VoelterSolomatov_SLE2010_Language%20ModularizationAndCompositionLWBs.pdf.

Better Planning via Tasking as a Team

Christopher P. O'Connor

University of Michigan
Institute for Social Research
Ann Arbor, MI 48109
cpoconno@umich.edu

Abstract

Do you find your story estimation sessions taking too much time away from development? Do you have stories that go over their estimates by a significant amount or turn into multiple stories? Then this session is for you. In this session we will look at various methods to improve tasking by better leveraging the team as a whole to strive toward more clearly defined and more granular stories. We will address common pitfalls such as stories that are really epics, overly vague stories as well as how to identify good stories and improve the definition of done for your stories.

Categories and Subject Descriptors   D.2.9 [*Management*]: life cycle, cost estimation, time estimation, programming teams, productivity, software quality assurance (SQA)

General Terms   Management

Keywords   Agile development, agile teams, scrum, XP

1. Summary

This tutorial will be a journey through different ways to approach working with stories to achieve better planning sessions and end up with a better plan. All of the teams I have worked with overs the years have struggled with various aspects of stories, from writing stories to breaking down stories. We will look at how and when dividing your team into different size groups affects story breakdown sessions. We will also discuss common problems teams run into during planning and story development.

Here are some examples of questions we will explore: Should you gather the entire team or break into groups? Who needs to be involved? How detailed do your stories need to be? Is there value in driving down to the implementation level? We will explore answers by actually running story development sessions and applying different techniques. While much of this tutorial will resonate most with developers, all roles can benefit from understanding and participating.

Stories are core to an agile team. When a team can generate a good set of stories to work from, they are well on their way to being a productive and cohesive agile team. Story development is a key activity to achieving this. Unfortunately the larger the team the more challenging it is to have a productive story development session. How do we balance this with current agile mantra which encourages us to involve as much of the team as possible? The answer depends on not only on size but also where your team is at from an agile maturity stand point. Traditionally agile gives us estimation and planning game to achieve a working plan for our iteration. This leaves the production of the stories up to the team. Business Analysts, Solution Architects, and Product Owners are usually the first up when it comes to story development. Stories at this level usually fall into what is referred to in agile as the theme or epic level. More often than not these stories are not executable by the developers without further breakdown and development.

A good development session actually show us signs of trouble in the proceeding step. Are your stories consistently vague? Too large? Does the team have trouble estimating stories? Do sessions often break down into technical discussions? Each of these symptoms points to different issues surrounding story development. Involving not only the story originators mentioned above but also team roles responsible for quality assurance and deployment is essential to successful story development. If you are missing or unable to involve the different team roles and members you are making it harder for the team. Stories developed in isolation are more likely to produce the aforementioned symptoms. This goes back to an old agile tenant: A story is just a place holder for a conversation. This conversation requires the entire spectrum of agile team roles working in conjunction. In the end a good measure of the session is the plan it produces.

Achieving a valuable plan requires solid, well-defined stories. Creating and refining those stories takes time and resources. Many teams attempt to save on both by reducing

Permission to make digital or hard copies of all or part of this work for personal or classroom use is granted without fee provided that copies are not made or distributed for profit or commercial advantage and that copies bear this notice and the full citation on the first page. To copy otherwise, to republish, to post on servers or to redistribute to lists, requires prior specific permission and/or a fee.
SPLASH'10,   October 17–21, 2010, Reno/Tahoe, Nevada, USA.
Copyright © 2010 ACM 978-1-4503-0240-1/10/10... $10.00

the number of people involved. This is a trap many inexperienced agile teams fall into, especially when there are examples of teams that manage to get away with this. So how do we avoid having everyone at every meeting while not falling into this trap?

Traditionally the team leaves the final breakdown of the story into tasks in the hands of the pair of developers who end up working on the card. While this approach works fine in many cases it is not the only or the best method in all situations. Consider breaking down work in small, cross functional, groups. Be sure to invite - leaning towards insisting on - representatives from roles other than developers such as quality assurance, business analyst roles, and people involved with deployment. This avoids bringing the session to a halt due to having too many people while avoiding being blocked. With larger teams you have to figure out what a small group means for your team. This takes practice - dont be discouraged by sessions which go over time or dont make it through enough stories at first. Worry if the trend continues.

During this style of story development session, each group works through the stories planned for the iteration and ac-

tually talks through at a high level the development tasks involved in implementing a given story. This gives the QA role better insight into how and what to test. The BA role is available for questions that come up and can help keep the team focused on achieving the business goal. The team members now all have at least some idea how this section of code will work. Compare this to the standard method - QA reviews the finished product which is a black box to them. The BA has to depend on correct interpretation of the story.

Another approach is to break into pairs and have each pair come up with a set of tasks to achieve a given card. Set a timer or assign a facilitator to make sure any one card doesnt take a disproportionate amount of time. Five minutes is usually plenty. Afterward bring the team back together and have each pair walk through their plan. This approach helps ensure one voice does not rule the design and helps avoid long technical discussions.

After running through sessions using the techniques in this session, I hope that you will not only have a better understanding of when, how, and why to apply them to your teams, but that you will also find it positively influences your team and the plan you produce as a result.

Xtext - Implement your Language Faster than the Quick and Dirty way

Tutorial Summary

Moritz Eysholdt

itemis AG

moritz.eysholdt@itemis.de

Heiko Behrens

itemis AG

heiko.behrens@itemis.de

Abstract

Whether there is an (emerging or legacy) Domain-Specific Language to increase the expressiveness of your coworkers or whether you are about to invent a new General Purpose Prgramming Language: Tool support that goes beyond a parser/compiler is essential to make other people adopt your language and to be more productive. Xtext is an award-winning[1] framework to build such tooling.

In this tutorial we explain how to define a language and a statically typed, EMF-based Abstract Syntax Tree using only a grammar. We then generate a parser, a serializer and a smart editor from it. The editor provides many features out-of-the-box, such as syntax highlighting, content-assist, folding, jump-to-declaration and reverse-reference lookup across multiple files. Then, it is shown how literally every aspects of the language and its complementary tool support can be customized using Dependency Injection, especially how this can be done for linking, formatting and validation. As an outlook, we will demonstrate how to integrate a custom language with Java, how Xtext maintains a workspace-wide index of named elements and how to implement incremental code generation or attach an interpreter.

Categories and Subject Descriptors D.2.6 [*Software Engineering*]: Programming Environments—Eclipse, Xtext

General Terms Design, Languages

Keywords Modeling, MDSD, DSL, Xtext, Eclipse, EMF

---

[1] Eclipse Community Award 2010 for the most innovative Eclipse project

Permission to make digital or hard copies of all or part of this work for personal or classroom use is granted without fee provided that copies are not made or distributed for profit or commercial advantage and that copies bear this notice and the full citation on the first page. To copy otherwise, to republish, to post on servers or to redistribute to lists, requires prior specific permission and/or a fee.

SPLASH'10, October 17–21, 2010, Reno/Tahoe, Nevada, USA.

Copyright © 2010 ACM 978-1-4503-0240-1/10/10...$10.00

1. Introduction

Xtext[1] is a framework which allows you to quickly develop tooling for a textual language. The kind of language can range from small Domain-Specific Languages (DSL [3]) to full-blown General Purpose Languages (GPL). This also includes textual configurations files or human-readable requirement documents. The motivation for having good tooling is to increase the readability, writability and understandability of documents written in those languages. Starting with a grammar definition, Xtext generates a parser, serializer and a smart editor for the language. All these generated artifacts can be configured or customized via dependency injection.

2. Motivation

This section explains why quality and of languages is important as well as how Xtext can help.

2.1 Why Languages Matter

Formal languages are a direct way of communication between human beings and computer systems. As with all languages, a clearly defined set of vocabulary is needed to avoid misunderstandings. An appropriate slang or dialect can be helpful to increase the efficiency of the conversation. Xtext focuses on scenarios where a human being uses a formal language to instruct a computer system. For those scenarios, there are the following requirements for a good language:

- Developers spent a large amount of their time writing code in that language. Hence, they should be efficient in doing so.

- Developers need to understand the concepts of the language to be able to express their intend in it. This implies that the language must be compatible with the developer's mind- and skill-set.

- Developers need to understand the code that other developers have written. This is because their own code has to interact with the code of other developers. A lack of understanding will lead to faulty code.

- The requirement to understand code can be refined as the need to read, browse, navigate, search and compare code.

- Code often is in production for a long time. If developers build up a large code-base over time, this is a large investment persisted in written code. To ensure the value of this investment doesn't decrease over time, the code-base should sustain a maximum of flexibility:

  - Fixes need to be applied and enhancements need to be made.

  - It should be possible to migrate the code. This can be an automatic transformation to a new version of the language or to a different notation.

  - Dependencies to runtime technology should be kept to a minimum to ensure exchangeability of runtime components.

In summary, it is important to care which language or which languages are used to write code. Especially when a lot of code has to be written.

These requirements have, for example, led to various flavors of languages: There are General Purpose Languages (GPL), Domain-Specific Languages (DSL), and also the notation of a configuration file can be perceived as a custom language.

However, the requirement for a language to be machine-processable without circumstances has often drawn away the language designer's attention from the actual users of the language. XML-based languages are a popular tradeoff since they are easily processable using generic libraries while their notation is to some degree human-readable at the same time. However, a BNF-based syntax for such a language can improve readability a lot.

2.2 Why Tooling Matters

First, there is tooling to execute code written in a certain language or to transform it to a different notation which is executable. This part is often built on top of a parser and a compiler or generator.

Second, there is tooling to assist the developer in working with code written in this language. This tooling should make it as easy as possible for the developer to read, write, browse, navigate, search, edit and compare code.

A direct result of these complementary needs is the emergence of modern Integrated Development Environments (IDEs). They integrate booth sets of tools in a convenient manner while emphasizing the editing support with features such as:

Syntax Highlighting: It allows faster reading of the code by emphasizing its structure.

Content Assist: At every possible curser position within a document the editor should provide a menu with suggestions what the user could type next. The suggestions must take into account the notation's syntax. The menu should, for example, suggest keywords and names of elements which can be referenced. This should avoid the user's need to open up other files to look up element names she wants to refer to. Furthermore, this provides a convenient way for the user to familiarize herself with the notation's syntax.

Instant validation: The user should get feedback as she types into the editor. Erroneous elements should be highlighted and an error annotation should display a message about the error's cause. This speeds up the work of a developer noticeable since it allows to detect errors early and avoids unnecessary build and test cycles that would otherwise reveal these errors. Three kinds of errors can be distinguished:

Syntax Errors: They occur if the document cannot be parsed correctly.

Linker Errors: They occur if a cross reference cannot be resolved. I.e., if an element is referenced which does not exist or is not accessible in a given scope.

Domain-Specific Errors: Any kind of error that is specific to the language's semantic. For example, if the language makes use of a concept such as inheritance, cycles are most-likely illegal.

Automatic Fixes for Errors: For some errors, automatic fixes can be provided. Example: For a broken cross-reference a new element declaration can be created or a typo can be fixed.

File-Local "Semantic" Search: There should be a search mechanism to search within a file based on the elements names. The search should only consider the element's names since it is intended for quick navigation within the file. For example, when the user wants to navigate to an element which is named "Alarm" and uses a text-based search, the user will also find all occurrences of "Alarm" in comments, references to "Alarm" etc. This search mechanism, however, will directly lead to the declaration of the element.

Cross-File "Semantic" Search: There should be a search mechanism to search among the names of all elements from any file within the workspace. If the user selects an element from the search results, an editor should open up and show the file in which the element is declared. The element should be selected in the editor.

Navigation "Open Declaration": If an element is referenced within the code, the user should be able to navigate from this particular mention directly to the element's declaration.

Search "Find References": For every element declaration, this search should list all references to this element. If the user wants to modify existing code, this search helps to understand the impact and possible side-effects before applying the modification.

Automatic Formatting: This mechanism should automatically arrange whitespace, line-breaks and indentation in a document to have it formatted nicely and consistently.

Template Proposals: The user should be able to define custom templates of (small) code snippets that can quickly be invoked while typing.

All features listed above should be usable with keyboard-shortcuts, i.e. without the mouse.

2.3 What Xtext can do

Xtext is a framework that dramatically reduces the effort of building good tooling for a language. From a grammar, Xtext can generate a parser, a serializer and a smart editor. All concerns of Xtext itself and of the code generated by Xtext can be customized via dependency injection. For the most concerns, Xtext's default behavior usually is just fine. For concerns that need customization (validation, linking/scoping, etc.), Xtext provides and easy-to-use API.

Xtext heavily utilizes the Eclipse Modeling Framework (EMF [5]). In fact, the Abstract Syntax Tree created by Xtext's parser is an EMF model. The corresponding Ecore model can automatically be derived from the grammar or be specified explicitly. Thereby, Xtext allows easy integration with tools from the Eclipse Modeling ecosystem, such as Model-to-Model or Model-to-Text transformation languages. Another example is to integrate Xtext with graphical tools such as GMF [2].

3. About

The Xtext tutorial is conducted by Moritz Eysholdt and Heiko Behrens.

3.1 Moritz Eysholdt

Moritz Eysholdt is a developer and software architect at *itemis AG* in northern Germany where he develops tools and frameworks related to model-driven software development. Current fields of activity are textual DSLs, patching models and co-adapting models to their evolving meta models. Moritz gives talks on these topics at software conferences and is a committer for the Eclipse projects TMF Xtext, M2T Xpand, EMF Compare and openArchitectureWare.

3.2 Heiko Behrens

Heiko Behrens works as a software architect and consultant for *itemis AG* in Kiel (Germany). His current focus is on domain-specific languages where he is involved with the design and implementation of Xtext. He is a committer for the Eclipse Modeling Project and openArchitectureWare.

3.3 About itemis AG

Employing 140 people, *itemis AG* has its headquarters in Lünen (close to Dortmund), Germany and branches in Canada, Switzerland and France. As a Strategic Member of the Eclipse Foundation *itemis AG* employs several Eclipse committers of which four are working full time on the Xtext project.

Model-Driven Software Development [4] and domain-specific languages [3] are the main focus of *itemis*. This knowledge is mainly applied in the fields of enterprise applications, embedded systems and mobile devices (e.g. based on the iPhone and Android platform).

4. Attendee Background

To attend this tutorial, knowledge about grammars (e.g. BNF), Java, Eclipse and the Eclipse Modeling Framework (EMF) is helpful.

5. Tutorial Contents

During this tutorial, the attendees learn:

- How to define a grammar and a statically typed AST for a simple language. The Ecore model for AST is derived from the grammar. The details of Xtext's grammar syntax are explained. There is an exercise to gather hands-on experience.

- How to run a workflow that generates parser, serializer and a smart editor from the grammar. The workflow, which configures code generation, is explained. It is shown how to launch the newly built Eclipse editor.

- How to customize generated code via dependency injection, which is based on Google Guice. Covered by an exercise, we will customize the scoping for a language that affects content assist and linking.

- How to implement a custom validation rule for a language. For this, Xtext's Java-based abstraction for EValidators is used. There is an exercise for this.

- How to integrate an Xtext language with the Java language to refer to Java classes, fields and methods. We will also show how to implement an incremental code generator and how to attach an interpreter to a custom language.

References

[1] Xtext framework, `http://eclipse.org/Xtext`

[2] M. Eysholdt and J. Rupprecht. Migrating a Large Modeling Environment from XML/UML to Xtext/GMF. *Proceedings of SPLASH'10*, 2010.

[3] M. Fowler. Domain Specific Languages. *Addison-Wesley Professional*, 2010.

[4] T. Stahl and M. Völter. *Model-Driven Software Development*. Wiley, 2006.

[5] D. Steinberg, F. Budinsky, M. Paternostro, and E. Merks. *EMF: Eclipse Modeling Framework 2.0*. Addison-Wesley Professional, 2009.

Bridging Software Languages and Ontology Technologies

Tutorial Summary

Fernando Silva Parreiras
Tobias Walter

Institute for Web Science and
Technologies, University of
Koblenz-Landau
D-56070 Koblenz, Germany
{parreiras,walter}@uni-koblenz.de

Christian Wende

Institute for Software- and
Multimedia-Technology, Dresden
University of Technology
D-01062 Dresden, Germany
c.wende@tu-dresden.de

Edward Thomas

Department of Computing Science,
The University of Aberdeen
Aberdeen AB24 3UE
e.thomas@abdn.ac.uk

Abstract

Current model-driven development approaches allow for a more productive way of developing software systems. However, building tools and languages for software development still suffer a neglect of semantics in modeling and metamodeling.

An interest to strengthen semantics in modeling and metamodeling that gained scientific and commercial attention is the integration of ontology technology and software development. Ontology formalisms for consistency validation and dynamic classification as well as semantic web technologies for enabling shared terminologies and automated reasoning provide means for leveraging metamodeling and language engineering.

This tutorial summary (1) enlightens the potential of ontology and semantic web technology for modeling and metamodeling in software development, positioning it among modeling standards like UML, and MOF; and (2) illustrates ontology-enabled software development with real application scenarios in areas like software design patterns, domain-specific languages and variability management.

Categories and Subject Descriptors D.2.2 [*Software Engineering*]: Design Tools and Techniques—Computer-aided software engineering (CASE)

General Terms Design, Languages

Keywords Semantic Web, Ontology Technology, Software Languages, UML, DSL, Model-Driven Development

Permission to make digital or hard copies of all or part of this work for personal or classroom use is granted without fee provided that copies are not made or distributed for profit or commercial advantage and that copies bear this notice and the full citation on the first page. To copy otherwise, to republish, to post on servers or to redistribute to lists, requires prior specific permission and/or a fee.
SPLASH'10, October 17–21, 2010, Reno/Tahoe, Nevada, USA.
Copyright © 2010 ACM 978-1-4503-0240-1/10/10. . . $10.00

1. Introduction

Semantic web technologies comprises a stack of standard and tools using metadata, logic and ontology languages, i.e., languages to describe formally a domain of discourse. Among ontology languages, the Web Ontology Language (OWL) [17] is the most prominent for Semantic Web applications, providing a class definition language for ontologies.

Indeed, OWL provides important features complementary to class-based model design that improve software languages: it allows different ways of describing classes; it handles these descriptions as first-class entities; it provides additional constructs like transitive closure for properties; and it enables dynamic classification of objects based upon class descriptions.

OWL has been applied into software engineering for many years in the form of Description Logic languages to achieve improvements on the maintainability and extensibility [9]. For example, the knowledge encoded in OWL evolves independently of the execution logic, i.e., developers maintain class descriptions in the ontology and not in the software. Moreover, developers may use class descriptions to semantically query the domain. Semantic query plays an important role where shared terminologies, interoperability and consistency detection are required.

This tutorial summary addresses the following question: What are the features and services provided by ontology technologies that can be used to improve software languages? What are the applications of these features and services in software language engineering?

We organize this tutorial summary as follows: Section 2 enlightens the potential of ontology and semantic web technology for modeling and metamodeling of software languages, positioning it among modeling standards like UML, and MOF. Section 2 illustrates ontology-enabled software languages with real application scenarios in areas like software design patterns, domain-specific languages, business process modeling and variability management.

2. Ontologies in Software Languages

Class-based modeling languages (e.g. UML class diagrams or MOF) and OWL comprise some constituents that are similar in many respects like classes, associations, properties, packages, generalization and instances [11].

Nevertheless, OWL offers a more expressive and extensible manner of modeling data and provides flexible ways to describe classes and, based on such descriptions, it enables type inference. Indeed, OWL provides various means for describing classes, which may also be nested into each other such that explicit typing is not compulsory. One may denote a class by a class identifier, an exhaustive enumeration of individuals, property restrictions, an intersection of class descriptions, a union of class descriptions, or the complement of a class description.

For example, software developers can use reasoning services (Sect. 2.2) to *dynamically classify* objects based on conditions specified in class descriptions (Sect. 3.1). Language users can count on *explanation services* (Sect. 2.2) for debugging and learning domain concepts (Sect. 3.2). Lastly, software developers might want to use class descriptions to integrate software languages and use *query answering* for retrieving information of multiple languages (Sect. 3.6).

Non-class-based modeling languages requires ad-hoc transformations into OWL for taking advantage of reasoning services. For example, while OWL contains elements like classes, properties and individuals, a business process modeling language contains elements like process, task, gateways, activities, states, etc.

Applications of OWL ontologies in those cases usually relies on *satisfiability checking* reasoning service to verify whether the integrity of model elements is fulfilled in all possible states. For example, software product line developers can carry out *satisfiability checking* to verify whether every feature of the feature model is instantiable (Sect. 3.4). Process modelers can verify whether a specific process model refining an abstract one is valid, i.e., they can verify whether the execution set of the abstract process model holds for every execution set of the refined process model (Sect. 3.3).

2.1 Demystifying OWL

In this section, we compare how the Semantic Web and Software Engineering worlds differ in terms of their world assumption (respectively, open world versus closed world). We show how an ontology can, either in whole (as locally closed world) or in part (locally closed domain) be made to behave under the closed world assumption. We also look at negation as failure in the context of ontologies.

The Semantic Web adopts an open world assumption, this extends to the ontology language OWL, and to the reasoners and tools which work with it. In simple terms, this means that any fact that cannot be proven to be true by the known data, cannot be assumed to be false unless it is directly contradicted by other data in the ontology. For example,

given an OWL axiom which states that all cows eat only plants, and that sheep are animals (in DL syntax: $Cows \sqsubseteq \forall eats.Plant$ and $Sheep \sqsubseteq Animals$), asserting that some cow eats some sheep does not cause a contradiction, since it has not been stated anywhere that animals cannot also be plants ($Animals \sqsubseteq /Plants$). In fact, a reasoner will infer exactly this fact from the given knowledge.

It is possible in OWL to close the domain of a particular class, by asserting that that class is equivalent to exactly the set of all its members. This prevents the reasoner from inferring that any other individual (either a named individual, or an inferred individual) is a member of this class. A reasoner can be used to close the domain of a class or a property, affecting the outcome of various reasoning tasks on the ontology [16].

By closing the domain of an entire ontology, we can simulate a closed world assumption. This involves closing the domain of every class and property in an ontology. This compares to the closed world assumption in Software Engineering, but it has performance implications when closing the domain of a complex ontology.

An alternative to closed world assumption is to use negation as failure (NAF) in the Semantic Web context. The results from using NAF can differ from using a true (locally) closed world (or domain) approach, and a closed domain and NAF can be combined in ontology reasoning to allow default behaviour and other techniques to be performed (See [16]).

OWL2 comprises a family of description logic languages, called profiles, which offer different levels of expressiveness and tractability. By using different language profiles where different levels of performance and expressivity are required, and by exploiting quality-guaranteed transformations between these languages, hybrid reasoners such as TrOWL [16] can reduce the complexity of a given domain model, increasing performance.

1. *OWL2-QL* The primary application for *OWL2-QL* are for ontologies with large abox datasets. It supports storing and querying this data using an SQL database, using query expansion to perform complete query answering with respect to the semantics of OWL and the tbox of the ontology.

2. *OWL2-EL* OWL2-EL is a profile of OWL2 specifically designed for high performance TBox reasoning. It supports consistency, classification, class expression subsumption and instance checking in polynomial time (cf. 2NexpTime for OWL2-DL).

3. *OWL2-RL* OWL2-RL is the subset of OWL2 which amenable to expression as a set of rules. These rules are run over a set of ground facts (the concrete axioms given in the ontology file) to infer every axiom which can be derived from those facts under OWL2 RDF semantics.

4. *OWL2-DL* OWL2-DL can be regarded as the full expressivity of OWL2 available under OWL2 direct semantics.

It is the most expressive profile in OWL2 and it corresponds to the description logic $\mathcal{SROIQ}$.

OWL presents complementary constructs to UML and OCL, allowing, for example, property transitivity, which is very useful for querying large and complex models.

By targeting different profiles of OWL2 to different aspects of a reasoning problem, improved performance can be achieved. For example, taking a very large ontology, classifying it, and performing query answering in OWL2-DL may be too costly in time and memory. By transforming that ontology into an OWL2-EL and OWL2-QL representations, these tasks become much more tractable (PTIME-complete and NLogSpace-complete, instead of 2NEXPTIME-complete).

2.2 Reasoning Services for Model Design

OWL ontologies can be operated on by reasoners providing services like consistency checking, concept satisfiability, instance classification and concept classification.

Reasoners provide the following standard reasoning services:

Consistency Checking The reasoning service consistency checking checks if a given model is consistent with regard to their language metamodel.

Satisfiability Checking The satisfiability checking service finds all unsatisfiable concepts in a given language metamodel. A concept metamodel is unsatisfiable if it represents an empty set of instances.

Classification The classification service returns for a given instance a set of metamodel concepts which contain/describe the instance. The instance conforms to all concepts in the result of the classification service. The classification service is used to dynamically classify elements in models to find its most specific type.

Subsumption The subsumption checking service checks whether a concept is superconcept or subconcept of another given (anonymous) concept.

In addition, some reasoners provide a set of non-standard reasoning services:

Query Answering SPARQL [14] is a prominent query language for querying OWL ontologies. SPARQL queries are able to operate on both, the schema level (metamodel layer) and on the instance level (model layer).

Explanation Services The generation of explanations for inferences computed by a reasoner is now recognized as highly desirable functionality. If the inference leads to some inconsistency or unsatisfiable classes, the explanation service results some debugging relevant facts and the information how to repair the model.

3. Applications of Ontology Technologies in Software Languages

3.1 Improving General Purpose Software Design Patterns

In general, the Software Design Pattern deal with variation and delegation of concepts in software models. However, as already documented by [5], the Strategy Pattern has a drawback. The clients must be aware of variations and of the criteria to select between them at runtime. Hence, the question arises of how the selection of specific classes could be determined using only their descriptions rather than by weaving the descriptions into client classes.

In [15], we present an approach to decouple class selection from the definition of client classes by exploiting OWL-DL modeling and reasoning. It enables the identification of patterns integrating UML class diagrams with software design patterns and OWL like, for example, the Selector Pattern.

The application of the Selector Pattern presents the following consequences: (1) reuse – The knowledge represented in OWL-DL can be reused independently of platform or programming language; (2) flexibility – The knowledge encoded in OWL-DL can be modeled and evolved independently of the execution logic; and (3) testability – The OWL-DL part of the model can be automatically tested by logical unit tests, independently of the UML development.

The application of our approach can be extended to other design patterns concerning variant management and control of execution and method selection. Design patterns that factor out commonality of related objects, like Prototype, Factory Method and Template Method, are good candidates.

3.2 Ontology-Based Domain-Specific Languages

Domain-specific languages (DSL) are used to model and develop systems of different application domains. However, there is an agreement about the challenges faced by current DSL approaches: (1) tooling (debuggers, testing engines), (2) interoperability, (3) semantics, (4) learning curve and (5) domain analysis. Improving tooling enhances user experience while formal semantics is the basis for interoperability and formal domain analysis.

In [18, 19], we propose an Ontology Based DSL Framework that allows for defining DSLs enriched by formal class descriptions. It allows DSL designers to check consistency of the model and helps DSL users to verify and debug DSL programs by using reasoning explanation. Moreover, novice DSL users may rely on reasoning services to suggest domain concepts according to the language definition.

The integrated metamodel MOF+OWL allows for a formal and logical representation of the solution domain. Thus, DSL designers count on an expressive language that allows for modeling logical constraints over DSL metamodels. Consistency of metamodels and constraints can be checked by reasoners and inferences are clarified by explanation services. The nature of the logical restrictions allowed by OWL enables progressive evaluation of DSL program consistency.

Moreover, the integration MOF+SPARQL enables DSL users to define SPARQL-like queries with the DSL metamodel to query objects in DSL programs. These queries are the interface between DSL user and reasoning services. For example, a DSL user may use a query defined in the DSL metamodel to query all classes that describe an object in the DSL program.

3.3 Ontology-Based Analysis in Variability Modelling

In software product lines [13], *feature models* are used to capture common and variable features in a family of related software products. Feature modeling originates from the FODA study [8]. In addition to simple relationships in hierarchical feature models as *mandatory*, *optional*, *alternative* or *exclusive-alternative* features several extensions were proposed. Most notably are propositional cross-tree relations (*requires*, *conflicts*) [1], cardinality-based features and groups [4], and feature attributes [3]. Using these constructs, feature models impose several constraints and relationships among features and, thus, specify all valid variants of the product line. During variant configuration *variant models* select a subset of the features in a product line's feature model to specify a concrete product.

Analysis in variability modelling checks the consistency of feature models, propositional feature terms and variant models w.r.t. the constraints and relationships specified for a concrete product-line and is an important area of research. For a recent, extensive overview of existing approaches on feature model analysis we refer to [2].

In this use case we discuss the application of ontology technology to validate feature and variant models and provide guidance in variant configurations. Based on existing approaches for the description logic based representation and analysis of feature models [20] we cover the following topics:

- Automated translation of hierarchical feature models with propositional cross-tree relations to OWL ontologies that represent their structural and semantics constraints,

- Automated translation of propositional feature terms and variant models to OWL ontologies,

- Application of OWL reasoning services to validate feature models, propositional feature terms, or variant models and to provide guidance in variant configuration,

- Integration of ontology-based analysis in variability modelling with the model-driven technology using the tool FeatureMapper [7],

- Exemplary applications of ontology-based variability modelling in SPLE, and

- Open challenges and issues in analysis of variability modelling.

3.4 Modeling and Querying Process Models with OWL

Process models capture the dynamic behavior of an application or system. In software modeling they are represented by graphical models like BPMN Diagrams or UML Activity Diagrams. The corresponding metamodels prove flexible means to describe process models for various applications. However, process models are often ambiguous with inappropriate modeling constraints and even missing semantics.

The process model in OWL gives an explicit description of the execution order dependencies of activities [6]. Hence, this information is used for process retrieval. A query describes the relevant ordering conditions like which activity has to follow (directly or indirectly) another activity. For instance a process that executes the activity $FillOrder$ before $MakePayment$ with an arbitrary number of activities between them, is given by the query process description $\exists TOT.(FillOrder \sqcap \exists TOT.MakePayment)$. The transitive object property TOT is used to indicate the indirect connection of the activities. The result are all processes that are subsumed by this general process description.

Besides ordering constraints, this semantic query processing allows the retrieval of processes that contain specialized or refined activities. For instance the result of the demonstrated query also contains all processes with subactivities of $FillOrder$ and $MakePayment$. The corresponding class expressions in the OWL model are specializations of the class expression given by the query expression. Finally, the usage of in the queries allows handling of modality for activity occurrences in a process, like a query that expresses that the activity $ShipOrder$ has to occur or might occur.

3.5 Metamodeling

The UML allows for capturing information about multiple views of systems like static structure and dynamic behavior. Since it is hard to capture all aspects of software into only one model, UML includes numerous types of diagrams to be used according to the software development task.

Since the semantics of UML constructs is textually described in the UML specification, it is hard to guarantee the same behavior across multiple implementers. Moreover, since UML enables multiple views of systems, it is important to have a consistent view over all UML diagrams. We have used the integration MOF+OWL [12] to model OWL descriptions at the metamodeling level. Metamodeling with OWL helps to disambiguate UML constructs and allow to specify logical constraints only textually described yet.

We have analyzed the different types of relationships in the UML2 Specification [10] and identified constraints that could benefit from our approach. For example, where property transitivity is required, e.g., in specifying constructs like Activity, State, StateMachine and Transition, our approach allows for defining additional operations that are not easily expressible in OCL.

3.6 Enabling Linked Data Capabilities to Software Languages

In the software development process, there are standards for general-purpose modeling languages and domain-specific languages, capable of capturing information about different views of systems like static structure and dynamic behavior. In a networked and federated development environment, modeling artifacts need to be linked, adapted and analyzed to meet the information requirements of multiple stakeholders.

We propose an approach for linking, transforming and querying models expressed in MOF compliant languages, including OMG standards and domain-specific languages. We define structural mappings between MOF and OWL and propose the usage of semantic web technologies for linking and querying software models.

We show that the usage of OWL for specifying metamodels is a viable solution to achieve interoperability and shared conceptualizations. The role of OWL is not to replace MOF or the Object Constraint Language because OWL addresses distinct requirements, specially concerning networked environments. OWL should compose the spectrum of software modeling languages in a unified architecture.

4. Conclusion

In tutorial summary paper we present an overview of the main features of ontology technologies for software languages and exemplify this features and services with case studies being developed under EU STReP MOST that use ontology technologies.

References

[1] D. S. Batory. Feature models, grammars, and propositional formulas. In J. H. Obbink and K. Pohl, editors, *SPLC*, volume 3714 of *LNCS*, pages 7–20. Springer, 2005.

[2] D. Benavides, S. Segura, and A. Ruiz-Cortés. Automated analysis of feature models 20 years later: A literature review. *Inf. Syst.*, 35(6):615–636, 2010.

[3] K. Czarnecki and C. Kim. Cardinality-based Feature Modeling and Constraints: A Progress Report. In *OOPSLA05 Workshop on Software Factories, October 17, 2005, San Diego, California, USA.*, 2005.

[4] K. Czarnecki, S. Helsen, and U. Eisenecker. Formalizing Cardinality-based Feature Models and their Specialization. *Software Process: Improvement and Practice*, 10(1):7–29, 2005.

[5] E. Gamma, R. Helm, R. Johnson, and J. Vlissides. *Design patterns: elements of reusable object-oriented software.* Addison-Wesley, Boston, MA, USA, 1995.

[6] G. Gröner and S. Staab. Modeling and Query Patterns for Process Retrieval in OWL. In A. Bernstein, D. R. Karger, T. Heath, L. Feigenbaum, D. Maynard, E. Motta, and K. Thirunarayan, editors, *International Semantic Web Conference*, volume 5823 of *LNCS*, pages 243–259. Springer, 2009.

[7] F. Heidenreich, J. Kopcsek, and C. Wende. Featuremapper: mapping features to models. In *ICSE Companion '08: Companion of the 30th international conference on Software engineering*, pages 943–944, New York, NY, USA, 2008. ACM.

[8] K. C. Kang, S. G. Cohen, J. A. Hess, W. E. Novak, and A. S. Peterson. Feature-Oriented Domain Analysis (FODA) Feasibility Study. Technical report, Carnegie-Mellon University Software Engineering Institute, November 1990.

[9] D. L. McGuinness. Configuration. In F. Baader, D. Calvanese, D. L. McGuinness, D. Nardi, and P. F. Patel-Schneider, editors, *The Description Logic Handbook*, chapter 12, pages 397–414. Cambridge University Press, 2003.

[10] OMG. *Unified Modeling Language: Superstructure, version 2.1.2.* Object Modeling Group, November 2007.

[11] OMG. *Ontology Definition Metamodel (ODM) Version 1.0.* Object Modeling Group, May 2009.

[12] F. S. Parreiras and S. Staab. Using ontologies with UML class-based modeling: The Twouse approach. *Data & Knowledge Engineering*, In Press, Accepted Manuscript, 2010.

[13] K. Pohl, G. Böckle, and F. Van Der Linden. *Software Product Line Engineering: Foundations, Principles, and Techniques.* Springer-Verlag, 2005.

[14] E. Prud'hommeaux and A. Seaborne. SPARQL Query Language for RDF. Technical report, W3C, 2008.

[15] F. Silva Parreiras, S. Staab, and A. Winter. Improving design patterns by description logics: A use case with abstract factory and strategy. In *Modellierung 2008*, volume P-127 of *LNI*, pages 89–104. GI, 2008.

[16] E. Thomas, J. Z. Pan, and Y. Ren. Trowl: Tractable owl 2 reasoning infrastructure. In L. Aroyo, G. Antoniou, E. Hyvönen, A. ten Teije, H. Stuckenschmidt, L. Cabral, and T. Tudorache, editors, *The Semantic Web: Research and Applications, 7th Extended Semantic Web Conference, ESWC 2010, Heraklion, Crete, Greece, May 30 - June 3, 2010, Proceedings, Part II*, volume 6089 of *LNCS*, pages 431–435. Springer, 2010.

[17] W3C OWL Working Group. OWL 2 Web Ontology Language Document Overview. W3C Recommendation 27 October 2009, 2009.

[18] T. Walter, F. Silva Parreiras, and S. Staab. OntoDSL: An Ontology-Based Framework for Domain-Specific Languages. In *Model Driven Engineering Languages and Systems, 12th International Conference, MODELS 2009*, volume 5795, pages 408–422. Springer, 2009.

[19] T. Walter, F. Silva Parreiras, J. Ebert, and S. Staab. Joint Language and Domain Engineering. In *Proc. of 6th European Conference on Modelling Foundations and Applications, ECMFA 2010, Paris, France, June 15-18, 2010*, LCNS. Springer, 2010.

[20] H. H. Wang, Y. F. Li, J. Sun, H. Zhang, and J. Pan. Verifying feature models using OWL. *Web Semant.*, 5(2):117–129, 2007.

An Architecturally-Evident Coding Style:
Making Your Design Visible in Your Code

George H. Fairbanks

Rhino Research
george.fairbanks@rhinoresearch.com

Abstract

Because of Eric Evans' Domain Driven Design, software developers are already familiar with embedding their domain models in their code. But the architecture and design is usually hard to see from the code. How can you improve that? This tutorial describes an architecturally-evident coding style that lets you drop hints to code readers so that they can correctly infer the design. You will learn why some design intent (the intensional part) is always lost between your design/architecture and your code. It builds upon ideas like Kent Beck's Intention Revealing Method Name pattern and provides a set of lightweight coding patterns and idioms that let you express your design intent in the code.

Categories and Subject Descriptors   D.2.11 [*Software Engineering*]: Software Architectures

General Terms   Design, Documentation

Keywords   software architecture, software design, design intent, coding style, pattern

1. Presenter Bio

George Fairbanks is the president of Rhino Research, a software architecture training and consulting company. He holds a Ph.D. in Software Engineering from Carnegie Mellon University, where he was advised by David Garlan and Bill Scherlis. His dissertation introduced design fragments, a new way to specify and assure the correct use of frameworks through static analysis. He has publications on frameworks and software architecture in selective academic conferences, including OOPSLA and ICSE. He has written production code for telephone switches, plugins for the Eclipse IDE, Android phone applications, and everything for his own web dot-com startup. He maintains a network of Linux servers in his spare time. This tutorial is based on a chapter from his book *Just Enough Software Architecture: A Risk-Driven Approach* [4].

2. Target Audience

This is an intermediate-level tutorial aimed at software developers and architects. Ideal participants are active software developers who are fluent with software architecture concepts. However,

Copyright is held by the author/owner(s).
SPLASH'10   October 17–21, 2010, Ren   Tahoe, Nevada, USA.
ACM 978-1-4503-0240-1/10/10.

background ideas (e.g., essentials of software architecture) will be covered sufficiently so that any software developer can participate. This tutorial is primarily slide-based lecture and some code examples will be shown.

3. Tutorial Objectives

Participants will learn some of the basics of software architecture just in case they do not already know them, things like the standard set of abstractions (modules, components, connectors, ports, styles/patterns) and relationships (designation, refinement, dependencies, partitions).

They will then learn what parts of the design or architecture can be straightforwardly translated into code and what parts cannot — the extensional parts (enumerated) go easily but the intensional parts (universally quantified) do not. So general rules such as "Never do validation in the UI" cannot easily be expressed in Java.

Given that, they learn the specific kinds of design intent that are valuable to express in the code and corresponding hard and soft mechanisms to make it visible.

Finally, participants learn about software frameworks as one particular difficulty, because frameworks usually impose their own idea of architecture on the code.

4. Summary of Contents

Kent Beck [1]and Eric Evans [3] have written about how you can express your design in the code. This session is based on a chapter from my book (which is going to the publisher in a few weeks). If others have written about expressing architecture in code then please let me know so I can add those references to the book.

A few years ago, Amnon Eden and Rick Kazman published a paper that prescribed a distinction between architecture and design [2]. They said that architecture included the intensional elements, the ones that were universally quantified (like "no client can circumvent the cache"), and that these cannot be expressed in mainstream programming languages. The code can respect intensional constraints but you cannot, for example, write that constraint as a Java expression (though you could in a rules-based language like Prolog). This is one large category of design intent that the developer knows when writing the code but that cannot be expressed in the programming language directly, so that design intent is lost.

The inspiration for this material comes from David Garlan who commented to me that source code differs in its ability to convey its architecture to readers. I have subsequently elaborated on his insight to develop a set of patterns that make the architecture more visible.

4.1 Inventory of hard and soft mechanisms to convey intent.

Hard mechanisms are machine checkable (e.g., the type system) while soft mechanisms rely on humans (e.g., method naming patterns).

4.2 Architectural design intent from the module viewtype

Source code is itself in the module viewtype so code expresses most elements from the module viewtype rather well. Most languages, however, lack a full-featured module system. Some express modules only via the directory structure where source files are saved, assuming that one directory means one module. They cannot express the dependencies between modules that are important parts of the architecture model. Programming languages commonly have relatively simple module visibility restrictions that can force you to break encapsulation.

Programming languages let you declare data structures and classes but not the larger architectural elements like component, connector, and port types. It is difficult to see what set of classes makes up a component or connector type. Classes and interfaces can express what services are provided, but not what services are required. While you can talk about the dependencies code has, it is usually awkward or impossible to express those dependencies in the code itself.

Protocols for interaction are an obvious concern and visible in architecture models but have no first-class representation in source code, though code comments often discuss legal calling sequences. Protocols can be expressed using annotations, which are increasingly common in object-oriented languages. Annotations are also being used to express other architectural properties.

4.3 Architectural design intent from the runtime viewtype

The entire runtime viewtype is hard to envision from looking at source code because you must read through the code and mentally animate the runtime instances. This mental animation is made harder with branching, looping, and input parameters. When relevant code is not co-located it is easy to overlook places where new components are instantiated or where connections are made.

A runtime view of the system can look like a sea of objects. Boundaries between components are hard to discern because the code does not let you declare anything larger than a class. Connectors are hard to see too because identical communication mechanisms, such as method calls or the observer pattern, are used both within and between components. Connectors may have no runtime representation at all. Communication between components does not happen just at ports, but often from any number of objects inside the components.

Runtime constraints and styles are exceptionally difficult to see from the source code. Constraints and styles usually refer to components and connectors rather than objects, so inferring them is doubly hard. First, components and connectors must be identified from the sea of objects and second the rules governing their runtime arrangement must be inferred.

4.4 Architectural design intent from the allocation viewtype

The runtime viewtype is merely difficult to infer from source code, but it is usually impossible to infer the allocation viewtype. Natural language is used to describe how code should be deployed, if it is written down at all. Most code is deployed in one large chunk on a single machine, but not always. The kind of machine and the network properties will impact the system's performance, and in cases it may be possible to express these properties in the code.

4.5 Patterns for expressing this design intent

Not everything can be expressed but we can express quite a bit. Method names can embed architectural intent, such as properties of connectors (compare "read()" with "readAsynchronous()"). The "reification" pattern is heavily used to make explicit what was implicit: The class hierarchy (or "tag" interfaces) can express component and connector types so that they stand out from other classes. Classes can also represent ports and can check protocol state and compliance.

5. Structure of Contents

The example that runs throughout is for a natural-language email processing system. Processing proceeds using a pipe and filter network of linguistic classifiers. Each filter in the network shares a common superclass and there is just one pipe class. Because all components are subclasses of the Component class, you can easily find them all by using your IDE's "browse hierarchy" view. Creation of these filters is localized in one method, as is the creation of the network, so you can envision the runtime structure from looking at the code.

Section 1: What is software architecture? This section provides background information on software architecture, including basic concepts (quality attributes, architecture drivers, architecture as a skeleton) and a conceptual model (views and viewtypes, domain-design-code).

Section 2: Design intent and how it is lost. It shows how design and implementations are the same and how they differ. Specifically, it describes how intensional [2] design elements (such as "No update may circumvent the cache") are hard to convey in the code, while extensional elements can be expressed.

Section 3: Techniques for expressing architecture in code. It teaches the Model-In-Code Principle: Expressing a model in the system's code helps comprehension and evolution. This principle applies equally to the domain (well-accepted in OO/agile circles) as well as to the design / architecture (accepted in architecture circles). However, design concepts like Layers and Components are not automatically visible, but you can follow a set of intention revealing patterns and idioms to do so. This tutorial describes patterns for package organization, subclassing, naming (classes, variables), first-class connectors, and initialization.

Section 4: Architecture and frameworks. More often than not, developers build code within an application framework (like Spring, Eclipse, OSGi, or Enterprise Java Beans). In some ways this helps express architecture, and in other ways it obfuscates it.

References

[1] K. Beck. *Smalltalk Best Practice Patterns*. Prentice Hall PTR, 1996.

[2] A. H. Eden and R. Kazman. Architecture, design, implementation. *International Conference on Software Engineering (ICSE)*, pages 149–159, 2003.

[3] E. Evans. *Domain-Driven Design: Tackling Complexity in the Heart of Software*. Addison-Wesley Professional, 2003.

[4] G. Fairbanks. *Just Enough Software Architecture: A Risk-Driven Approach*. Marshall & Brainerd, 2010.

Rulemakers and Toolmakers:
Adaptive Object-Models as an Agile Division of Labor

Ultimate Agility: Let your Users Do Your Work!

Joseph Yoder

The Refactory, Inc
joe@refactory.com

Rebecca Wirfs-Brock

Wirfs-Brock Associates
rebecca@wirfs-brock.com

Abstract

Agile practices liberate us from the straightjackets of top-down design. But, the ease with which requirements can change encourages users to overwhelm us with requests for features. The result: featuritis, which promotes hasty construction of poorly designed software to support those features. The design of an expressive domain model might get lost in the rush to write working code. Adaptive Object-Models support changeable domain modules by casting business rules as interpreted data and representing objects, properties and relationships in external declarations. Now users can change the system domain models themselves as their business dictates without having to deal with programmers at all. It's the ultimate in agility!

Categories and Subject Descriptors D.3.3 [**Programming Languages**]: Language Constructs and Features – abstract data types, frameworks, polymorphism, patterns, control structures; D.1.5 [**Programming Techniques**]: Object-oriented Programming; D.2.2 [**Design Tools and Techniques**]: Object-oriented design methods, User Interfaces; D.2.11 [**Software Architectures**]: Domain-Specific Architectures, Patterns.

General Terms Design, Human Factors, Language.

Keywords *Agile, Design, Architecture, Domain Specific Languages, Patterns, Adapting, Adaptive Object-Models.*

1. Introduction

An Adaptive Object-Model is an instance-based software system that represents domain-specific classes, attributes, relationships, and behavior as metadata [1,7,8]. The system is a model represented by instances rather than classes. AOM domain objects are constructed from externally stored definitions (metadata) that are interpreted at run time. Users change the metadata (object model) to reflect changes in the domain.

Typically in an Adaptive Object-Model, metadata describing this object model is stored in a database and interpreted at runtime. Consequently, the object model is adaptable; when the descriptive information is modified, the system immediately reflects those changes similar to a UML Virtual Machine described by [4].

Copyright is held by the author/owner(s).
SPLASH'10 October 17–21, 2010, Reno/Tahoe, Nevada, USA.
ACM 978-1-4503-0240-1/10/10.

When a change in requirements causes the model to be redefined, metadata descriptions are modified. They can be reflected in a running system without any programmatic changes. Often, tools are provided with AOM systems to allow end users or domain experts to edit and change these Adaptive Object-Model metadata descriptions. This is similar to Domain Specific Languages (DSLs).

Agile processes are very useful for creating and evolving AOMs. Specifically, since AOMs are similar to frameworks which should be used before they are embellished, it is prudent to only evolve the AOM architecture as the specific business needs evolve. Getting concrete user scenarios and creating tests is an important way to insure that the needed domain flexibility is added and validated properly. Ultimately, as the AOM evolves and as a DSL grows, the system is such that it can adapt to changing requirements by changing some of the core Entities, Properties, Relationships and Rules.

2. Architectural Style of Adaptive Object-Models

The design of Adaptive Object-Models differs from most object-oriented designs. Normally, object-oriented design would have classes for describing the different types of business entities and associates attributes and methods with them. The classes model the business, so a change in the business causes a change to the code, which leads to a new version of the application. An Adaptive Object-Model does not model these business entities as classes. Rather, they are modeled by descriptions (metadata) that are interpreted at run-time. Thus, whenever a business change is needed, these descriptions are changed which are then immediately reflected in the running application.

Adaptive Object-Model architectures are usually made up of several smaller patterns. TYPE OBJECT [3] provides a way to dynamically define new business entities for the system. TYPE OBJECT is used to separate an Entity from an EntityType. Entities have Attributes, which are implemented with the PROPERTY pattern [1]. The TYPE OBJECT pattern is applied a second time in order to define the legal types of Attributes, called AttributeTypes. As is common in Entity-Relationship modeling, an Adaptive Object-Model usually separates attributes from relationships.

The STRATEGY pattern [2] is used to define the behavior of EntityTypes. These strategies can evolve into RuleObjects or a rule-based language that gets interpreted at runtime. Finally, there is usually support for non-programmers to define the new types of objects, attributes and behaviors needed for the specified domain.

Adaptive Object-Models are usually built from applying one or more of the above patterns in conjunction with other design patterns such as COMPOSITE, INTERPRETER, and BUILDER [2]. COMPOSITE is used for building dynamic tree structure types or rules. For example, if the entities need to be composed in a dynamic tree-like structure, the COMPOSITE pattern is applied. BUILDERS and INTERPRETERS are commonly used for constructing domain objects from the meta-model or interpreting results.

Currently many writings on and experiences about AOMs can be found at www.adaptiveobjectmodel.com.

3. Tutorial Outline

Agile practitioners value incremental delivery of working software. This typically means that there is not a long, involved design phase that precedes implementation. Design simplicity is also important. At first glance, Adaptive Object-Model based systems seem to fly in the face of these values. Yet we have found that under the right conditions, choosing to implement an Adaptive Object-Model architecture has made our users happier and have given them back the control they need to confidently revise, extend and grow their software on their own.

The centerpiece of this tutorial will be a presentation of the highlights of several real-world systems the authors have worked on. Our examination of each will showcase ways in which the incorporation of an Adaptive Object-Model Architecture made the systems more adaptable and our users more agile, thereby justifying the additional effort and complexity of this approach. The Adaptive Object-Model Architecture will be presented as a system that represents classes, attributes, relationships, and behavior as metadata. Additionally, a review of a process for developing AOMs will be examined.

4. Tutorial Objectives

The following are expected learning outcomes:
- See how to let users build and modify complex structures like business rules themselves, so that you, the programmer don't have to anymore.
- Learn when and when not to use this architecture.
- Obtain a core understanding of AOM Architecture.
- See how to make new types of objects with attributes, relationships, and behavior through using the TypeObject, Properties, EntitiyRelationship, and RuleObject patterns.
- Understand when to consider AOM architectures for building end-user adaptable software.
- Understand the basics of using metadata to represent objects, properties and relationships.
- Be able to identify the risks of exposing programming and model extension facilities to users, and how to mitigate these risks.
- Learn how a system that is a model based on instances rather than classes allows users to more quickly change the system by simply changing the metadata (object model) to reflect changes in the domain.
- Review the process for developing highly adaptive systems and how important an agile process is for these architectures.

5. Attendee Background

Attendees are required to have a core understanding of Object Principles. Pattern experience is helpful. Agile is a plus along with an understanding of principle of Doman Specific Languages (DSLs). Primary focus will deal with teams developing DSLs.

6. Presenters Biography

Joseph Yoder currently resides in Urbana, Illinois. He teaches Agile Methods such as XP, Design Patterns, Object Design, Refactoring, and Testing in industrial settings and mentors developers on these concepts. Joseph currently oversees a team of developers who have constructed an order fulfillment system based on enterprise architecture using the .NET environment. His other recent work includes working in both the Java and .NET environments, and deploying Domain-Specific Languages for clients. Joe thinks software is still too hard to change. He wants to do something about this and believes that putting the ability to change software in the hands of the people with the knowledge to change it seems to be on promising avenue to solve this problem.

Rebecca Wirfs-Brock, president of Wirfs-Brock Associates and past IEEE Software Design Columnist, is an internationally known and respected object practitioner. She is a past board member of the Agile Alliance, co-founder of the Agile Open Northwest Conference, and president of the Agile Open Northwest non-profit board. Rebecca worked on an AOM system for a telecommunications company and was involved in the meta-side of Smalltalk while an engineer at Tektronix. She invented the way of thinking about objects known as Responsibility-Driven Design and is the lead author of *Object Design: Roles, Responsibilities[and Collaborations*[5], and the classic *Designing Object-Oriented Software*[6]. Through her writing, teaching, consulting, and speaking she popularizes the use of informal techniques and thinking tools for architects, designers, and analysts.

References

[1] Foote B, J. Yoder. *Metadata and Active Object-Models*. Proceedings of Plop98. Technical Report #wucs-98-25, Dept. of Computer Science, Washington University Department of Computer Science, October 1998.

[2] Gamma, E.; R. Helm, R. Johnson, J. Vlissides. *Design Patterns: Elements of Reusable Object Oriented Software*. Addison-Wesley. 1995.

[3] Johnson, R., R. Wolf. *Type Object*. Pattern Languages of Program Design 3. Addison-Wesley, 1998.

[4] Riehle, D., Fraleigh S., Bucka-Lassen D., Omorogbe N. The Architecture of a UML Virtual Machine. Proceedings of the 2001 Conference on Object-Oriented Program Systems, Languages and Applications (OOPSLA '01), October 2001.

[5] Wirfs-Brock, R.; McKean, A. *Object Design: Roles, Responsibilities and Collaborations*. Addison-Wesley, 2003

[6] Wirfs-Brock, R.; Wilkerson, B.; Wiener, L. *Designing Object-Oriented Software*. Prentice Hall, 1990.

[7] Yoder, J.; F. Balaguer; R. Johnson. *Architecture and Design of Adaptive Object-Models*. Proceedings of the ACM SIGPLAN Conference on Object Oriented Programming, Systems, Languages and Applications (OOPSLA 2001), Tampa, Florida, USA, 2001.

[8] Yoder, J.; R. Johnson. *The Adaptive Object-Model Architectural Style*. IFIP 17th World Computer Congress - TC2 Stream / 3rd IEEE/IFIP Conference on Software Architecture: System Design, Development and Maintenance (WICSA 2002), Montréal, Québec, Canada, 2002

iPhone Application Development

Javier Gonzalez-Sanchez

Arizona State University
University Drive and Mill Avenue
Tempe, AZ. 85281
javiergs@asu.edu

Maria Elena Chavez-Echeagaray

Arizona State Univesity
University Drive and Mill Avenue
Tempe, AZ. 85281
helenchavez@asu.edu

Abstract

iPhone is a pretty new device. In 2008 Apple sold 13.7 millions of devices. In the same year the software development kit for iPhone was downloaded about 800,000 times (according with Apple records) and right now there are 50,000 iPhone Developers subscribed to the Official iPhone Developer Program. That is why iPhone is a new and widely extended platform to develop object-oriented applications.

iPhone platform involve several and amazing technologies that make programming a cool activity for both experts and novices.

Using XCode under Mac OS X as our IDE, and Objective-C and iPhone API as our programming tools we will create iPhone applications (from basic to medium level), which finally can be loaded into an iPhone. We'll start with the classical "Hello World" and continue to develop applications using graphical user interfaces, handling multi-touch and motion detection, communication interfaces, and different media.

Categories and Subject Descriptors D.3.2 [**Programming Languages**]: Language classifications --- Object-oriented languages, Specialized applications languages, D.1.5 [**Programming Techniques**]: Object-oriented programming.

General Terms Design,, Standardization, Languages, Theory.

Keywords iPhone; iPhone SDK; iPhone API; XCode; Objective-C; Applications development; Apple technology.

1. Introduction

iPhone is a fairly new device that incorporates several technologies (phone, video, audio, images, and web among others). It was awarded the best device in 2007 according to Times Magazine, and was the big winner in the 2008 British Technology Awards. iPhone also claimed the award for Gadget of the Year, won the Best Mobile Technology, Most Stylish Technology, and Technological Innovation of the Year awards.

iPhone has captive the interest of different types of users and created a new emerging market in various environments. Today, thousands of programmers want to provide applications on the iPhone, which take advantages of the amazing features of the device: multi-touch interface, sensors and a camera.

2. Tutorial Presentation History

This tutorial has been presented at the last two OOPSLA (2008 and 2009) beside that, this material has been presented in others forums mainly at Mexico and locally in Arizona. This has helped to improve the content, activities and time management. Last year we worked with iPhone SDK 3.0, now we are working with SDK 3.1.3.

3. Tutorial Objectives

Through this tutorial, the attendee will:

- Learn about iPhone software architecture.
- Learn about iPhone Development tools and Objective-C programming language.
- iPhone Application Framework.
- Graphics and Media Overview.
- User Interface Design and key practices for iPhone Applications.
- Location, Acceleration, Orientation and System Information.
- Fundamentals of iPhone for Web Developers.

4. Development tools

Now that we have everything ready, we can start working with the development tools. As we mentioned before, in order to develop an iPhone application, we will need to use the following development tools:

1. One of the most important elements on the SDK is XCode - Apple's Integrated Development Environment (IDE). XCode includes tools to create and debug, compile and performance tune.
2. Interface Builder provides you with an environment to facilitate the development of your GUI's and to give functionality to GUI's components.
3. Another element is the simulator that allows you to run your iPhone programs on your Mac.

NOTE: the free SDK does not allow you to upload your applications to your iPhone (or iPod Touch) or distribute your software in Apples' iPhone App Store. In order to do this, you have to get the Standard ($99) or the Enterprise ($299) version of the SDK

Copyright is held by the author/owner(s).
SPLASH'10   October 17–21, 2010, Ren Tahoe, Nevada, USA.
ACM 978-1-4503-0240-1/10/10.

4.1 XCode

The focus of your development experience is the XCode application. XCode is an integrated development environment (IDE) that provides all of the tools you need to create and manage your iPhone projects and source files, build your code into an executable, and run and debug your code either in iPhone simulator or on a device.

To create a new iPhone application, you start by creating a new project in XCode. A project manages all of the information associated with your application, including the source files, build settings, and rules needed to put all of the pieces together. The heart of every XCode project is the project window.

XCode comes with an advanced text editor, which supports features such as code completion, syntax coloring, code folding (to hide code blocks temporarily), and inline annotations for errors, warnings, and notes.

The build system in XCode provides both appropriate default settings and the ability to customize the environment. And if you need documentation, the Research Assistant provides context-sensitive documentation while the XCode documentation window lets you browse and search for information.

When you build your application in XCode, you have a choice of building it for iPhone simulator or for a device. The simulator provides a local environment for testing your applications to make sure they behave essentially the way you want. After you are satisfied with your application's basic behavior, you can tell XCode to build it and run it on an iPhone or iPod touch connected to your computer. Running on a device provides the ultimate test environment, and XCode lets you attach the built-in debugger to the code running on the device.

4.2 Interface Builder

Interface Builder is the tool you use to assemble your application's user interface visually.

Using Interface Builder, you assemble your application's window by dragging and dropping pre-configured components onto it. The components include standard system controls such as switches, text fields, and buttons, and also custom views to represent the views your application provides. After you have placed the components on the window's surface, you can position them by dragging them around, configure their attributes using the inspector, and establish the relationships between those objects and your code. When your interface looks the way you want it, you save the contents to a nib file, which is a custom resource file format.

The nib files you create in Interface Builder contain all the information that the UI Kit needs to recreate the same objects in your application at running time. Loading a nib file creates run time versions of all the objects stored in the file, configuring them exactly as they were in Interface Builder. It also uses the connection information you specified to establish connections between the newly created objects and any existing objects in your application. These connections provide your code with pointers to the nib file objects and also provide the information that the objects themselves need to communicate user's actions to your code.

5. Objective-C Language

The Objective-C language is a simple computer language designed to enable sophisticated object-oriented programming. Objective-C extends the standard ANSI C language by providing syntax for defining classes, methods, and properties, as well as other constructs that promote dynamic extension of classes. The class syntax and design are based mostly on Smalltalk, one of the first object-oriented programming languages.

If you have programmed with object-oriented languages before, the following information should help you learn the basic syntax of Objective-C. Many of the traditional object-oriented concepts, such as encapsulation, inheritance, and polymorphism, are all present in Objective-C.

If you have never programmed using an object-oriented language before, you need to have at least a basic understanding of the associated concepts before proceeding. The use of objects and object-oriented constructs is fundamental to the design of iPhone applications, and understanding how they interact is critical to creating your applications.

References

The iPhone Dev Center provides access to technical resources and information to assist you in developing with the latest technologies in iPhone OS.

http://developer.apple.com/iphone.

Skills for the Agile Designer:

Seeing, Shaping, and Discussing Design Ideas

Rebeca Wirfs-Brock

Wirfs-Brock Associates
rebecca@wirfs-brock.com

Abstract

Agile teams incrementally develop solutions. So the pace of design work can be more intense and episodic. Agile designers need to be able to quickly see the essence of a problem and shape reasonable solutions. And when ideas don't pan out or requirements shift, they must be comfortable revising their designs. This SPLASH tutorial introduces several techniques and some vocabulary for sharing design ideas, characterizing (and then designing to accommodate) variability, responding to design advice, and tracking design work and technical debt.

Categories and Subject Descriptors D.2.2 [Design Tools and Techniques]: Modules and interfaces

General Terms Design, Experimentation.

Keywords Agile software design, commonality-variability analysis, control styles, design categories, design thinking, design vocabulary, designers' stories, hot spot cards, role stereotypes, trust regions.

1. Introduction

Good software designers share many habits and traits whether they work on agile teams or not. Although agile techniques and practices vary, successful agile designers are passionate about incrementally producing high-quality design solutions [5]. They aim to design and implement solutions for the current problems at hand simply and efficiently, connecting their design work to real, not presumed, needs. They view development as a team sport. They aren't just heads-down coders. They know to give and ask for constructive design advice. Seasoned agile designers try to strike a balance. They know the difference between core and revealing design tasks and work accordingly. When unanticipated problems crop up, they adapt their work rhythms.

Permission to make digital or hard copies of all or part of this work for personal or classroom use is granted without fee provided that copies are not made or distributed for profit or commercial advantage and that copies bear this notice and the full citation on the first page. To copy otherwise, or republish, to post on servers or to redistribute to lists, requires prior specific permission and/or a fee.
SPLASH'10 October 17–21, 2010, Reno/Tahoe, Nevada, USA.
Copyright © 2010 ACM 978-1-4503-0240-1/10/10...$5.00.

2. Agile Design

So what is different about agile design? Agile teams typically incrementally develop solutions. So the pace of design work can be more intense and episodic. Agile designers need to be able to quickly see the essence of a problem and shape reasonable solutions. And when ideas don't pan out or requirements shift, they must be comfortable revising their designs. Agile designers figure out just enough design at the most responsible moments. Coding and designing go hand-in-hand. Excessive design speculation or goldplating is rare. Design tasks aren't typically long solo excursions culminating in complex solutions only understood by the designer and implemented by others. Designs ideas are shared and improved on during a project. Collective code ownership and design collaboration is common.

While agile design does not require drastically different design or technical skills, it benefits greatly from teamwork, cooperation, openness, and honesty.

3. Agile Design Techniques

This SPLASH tutorial introduces several techniques for sharing design ideas, having design discussions, characterizing (and then designing to accommodate) problem variability, responding to design advice, and tracking design work and technical debt. Three of these techniques are designers' stories, commonality-variability analysis, and categorizing design tasks.

3.1 Designers' stories

A designer's story allows individuals to put their spin on the nature of the system to be designed and built [6]. At the start of a new project or a major release cycle is a good time to write designers' stories.

In pre-agile days, I often would write privately to collect my thoughts. I'd look back into my project journal and remark how naïve I was. But in hindsight, it wasn't realistic to expect great design insights early in a project. Instead a more achievable outcome was to recognize and make sense of the design concerns that were swirling around in my head. The very act of writing sets in motion active thinking about the discoveries and investigations that might be needed, what I suspected to be true, and relevant past experiences. Story writing helped me own and engage in the design problem.

Now, on agile projects, I encourage developers to write and share designers' stories. The technique is simple. Even those who only like writing code can write a designer story if it is short, sweet, to the point, and only takes 15 minutes. I ask people to write their stories on paper. This makes them look rough, less polished, and more approachable A designer's story is short—two paragraphs or less is ideal and discusses what you the designer think are your system's essential characteristics, challenges, and pressing concerns. In it you might touch on these questions:

- What is your software supposed to do, really? Is it similar to anything you have done before? Are there insights or cautionary tales from past experiences that you are thinking about?
- What will make your design a success?
- What are the challenging parts? Is anything easy?
- Are there things you want to investigate?

After people have written their stories, we read them out loud. Each person on the team gets to voice their ideas before thought leaders, loud mouths, and dominant personalities jump in to shape the group's design beliefs and concerns.

3.2 Commonality-Variability Analysis

At the Agile 2007 conference, Steve Freeman and Mike Hill presented a tutorial [2] on how developers could untangle complex written requirements and write better automated tests. The tangled acceptance tests they presented are realistic distillations of what designers encounter and inspired me expose agile designers to commonality-variability analysis.

Commonality-variability analysis isn't design. It is what is done in preparation for thinking about an appropriate design [1]. Most of the time on agile projects, designers don't work through complex examples prior to coding. But commonality-variability analysis is especially appropriate when many special cases and variations need to be supported. It isn't done in isolation. It requires domain expertise and insights from both designers and other project stakeholders.

Commonality-variability analysis helps you sort through the significance of complex requirements before investing in complex design solutions. Using overly complex acceptance tests alone to drive your design can lead to ill-formed solutions. The goal of performing commonality-variability analysis is to understand inherent complexity and find meaningful, stable domain concepts.

James Coplien and Gertrud Bjørnvig note, "The structuring tasks in design build on the deepest building blocks of human cognition: being able to distinguish what is common from what changes." Designers often spot commonalities that business people do not. Rather than considering them equally significant, we should discern whether they are meaningful in the problem domain or just byproducts of our pattern-making and abstraction skills? Either way, we must deal with them in our designs. But if they represent important domain abstractions, we should engage domain experts in commonality-variability analysis discussions.

A useful technique, invented by Wolfgang Pree [3], is to record and summarize variations on "hot spot" cards. Cards are divided into three sections as shown in figure 1:

Rental Rate Calculation

The cost of a car rental is based on fees assessed based on type of car, mileage, and customer membership status.

Standard member = 3 days * daily rate + 6 hrs * hourly rate + (cost per mile * miles).

Low member = 56 * hourly rate + (cost per mile * miles)

Figure 1. A hot spot card is divided into three parts.
- The top section names the hot spot.
- The middle section summarizes the functionality that varies.
- The bottom section is used to show at least two examples of the variation (there may be more).

Most find it easier to understand the dimensions of a common abstraction after seeing several concrete examples. The value of "hot spot" cards is that like CRC cards, they only have room for capturing the essence. If more detail is needed, it can be written elsewhere. But forming concepts and abstractions requires elaboration followed by distillation.

3.3 Categorizing Design Work

You can be prepared with a toolkit full of agile techniques and practices, but design is never predictable. There are always surprises, additional complexity, and new twists. To keep on track, it can be help to categorize iteration tasks according to design effort and significance and treat them accordingly [6]. Tasks can contribute to solving:

1. Core design problems—the core is the core because without it there is no reason to build the rest. Your software won't meet its users' needs without a well-designed core. Core design problems absolutely, positively must be dealt with.
2. Revealing design problems—when pursued, these problems lead to a deep understanding about your software. Just because some part of a design is tricky or difficult, however, doesn't make it revealing.
3. The rest. Although not trivial (well, not all the time), the rest requires far less creativity or inspiration.

Each category warrants a different approach and has a different rhythm to its solution. Core problems must be solved. You've got to give them proper attention. Revealing problems are squishy and hard to characterize or even know when they are solved. Each time you look into a revealing problem it teaches you something. Revealing problems can't be solved in tidy ways—they must be tamed (and consequently are difficult to estimate). But the rest can't be ignored either. The rest is always present and pressing. If you don't budget your time, it can soak up all spare cycles.

At the start of each iteration or sprint, teams can sort their tasks into "core" and "the rest". If there are working on revealing tasks, they probably should be identified as being part of a design spike. If they are serious excursions that require innovation and experimentation, they probably are better managed separately from the more routine work found in the backlog. Depending on your design, you might nominate as core:

- Important system functionality
- Key algorithms
- Mechanisms that increase reliability such as exception handling and recovery, synchronization and connection with other systems, performance tuning, caching…

To decide whether something is core ask what are the consequences of "fudging" on that part? Would the project fail or other parts of your design be severely compromised? Then it's core.

When a team disagrees about whether certain tasks are core or not, it is good to dig deeper. It may be that someone isn't getting listened to (so in order to be heard they want to elevate the importance of particular tasks that they find comfortable or familiar). Or, it may be that they know something you don't.

Whether you classify something as "core" or "the rest", you still have to deal with it—it's just a matter of emphasis. In any iteration give design tasks the attention they deserve and be clear on the team's priorities and general approach to tackling core design issues.

At the end of an iteration, reflect on which tasks are soaking up time (but they aren't core design tasks), which things are not getting the attention they deserve, and what should be done about them. You also may choose to assign core design tasks as "paired tasks" (e.g. requiring that two heads look at core problems), but allow any of the "rest" to be done solo.

4. Shared Vocabulary

Agile designers benefit from using a common vocabulary to describe their design choices. Designers who work together need common ways to describe what they are thinking about and characterize their designs. Control styles, role stereotypes, and trust boundaries are three ways of "seeing" and describing complex software.

4.1 Control Styles

Deciding on and developing a consistent control style is one of the most important decisions designers make. A control center is a place where design elements charged with controlling and coordinating reside [6]. Developing a control style involves decisions about:

- How to control and coordinate software tasks;
- Where to place responsibilities for making domain-specific decisions, and
- How to manage unusual expected conditions (the design of exception detection and recovery).

While many frameworks make some of these decisions for you, there is much room for judgment (and lots of options to explore). It isn't just a matter of style. Control design affects complexity and ease or difficulty of your design to change. Your goal should be to develop a dominant, simple enough pattern for distributing the flow of control and sequencing of actions among collaborating objects.

A control style can be centralized, delegated, or dispersed. But there is a continuum of solutions. One design can be said to be more centralized or delegated than another.

If you adopt a centralized control style you place major decision-making responsibilities in only a few objects—those stereotyped as controllers. The decisions these controllers make can be simple or complex, but with more cen-

tralized control schemes, most objects that are used by controllers tended to be devoid of any significant decision-making capabilities. They do their job (or hold onto their information), but generally they are told by the controller how to do so.

If you choose a delegated control style, you make a concerted effort to delegate decisions to other objects. Decisions made by controlling objects will be limited to deciding what should be done (and handling exceptions). Following this style, objects with control responsibilities tend to be coordinators rather than control every action.

Choosing a dispersed control style means distributing decision-making across many design elements involved in a task. You could consider a pipes-and-filters architecture or chain-of-responsibilities patterns to be a dispersed control style.

Nothing is inherently good about any particular style. They all have plusses, minuses, and things to watch out for.

4.2 Role Stereotypes

Agile designers need to see and describe their ideas to others. If you share the same way of talking about your design inventions and objects, then you'll improve how you communicate. Role stereotypes, from Responsibility-Driven Design are a fundamental way of seeing objects' behaviors [6,7]. A stereotype is a "purposeful oversimplification" that you can use to identify the gist of a new class or component's behavior. Later on you can use stereotypes to characterize your implementation or somebody else's design.

Here is a synopsis of six stereotypes:

Information holder—knows and provides information.

Structurer—maintains relationships between objects and information about those relationships.

Service provider—performs work and in general offers services.

Controller—makes decisions and closely directs others' actions.

Coordinator—still makes decisions, but primarily delegates tasks to others and keeps out of the way (there's a spectrum of behaviors from overly-dominating controller to laissez-fair coordinator).

Interfacer—transforms information and requests between distinct parts of a system. There are user interfacer objects, for example, and external interfacers that may wrap other systems and objectify their services. But interfacers can be go-betweens from layers or subsystems, too.

4.3 Trust regions

A trust region is an area where trusted collaborations occur between design elements [6]. A trust boundary isolates a trust region from non-trusted collaborators and clients.

During a sequence of communications between collaborators within a trust region there is no need to re-check information once it has been validated. Requests can be assumed to be at the right time and contain the right information (whether or not they satisfy constraints is another question). This leads to simpler designs.

If you carve your software into trust regions you can design accordingly. Determining trust regions for an enterprise application is pretty straightforward. Any request from an external source or a user is assumed to be untrusted. Usually, objects in the same layer are within the same trust region. There is an obvious trust boundary between an HTTP request and any servlet.

Another trust boundary to not forget is between the domain layer and the database or any external service or gateway. There's no guarantee that a domain repository can create a well-formed domain object from the data it retrieves from the database if other applications have corrupted that data. Data might be available, but it could violate integrity constraints.

An interesting design consideration is whether components should be trusted or not. If a collaborator can't be trusted, it doesn't mean that it is inherently unreliable. But a more defensive collaboration style may be warranted.

Generally, objects or components located with the same trust region communicate collegially, although they still encounter exceptions and errors as they do their work. Within a system there are several cases to consider:

- Collaborations among objects or components that interface to the user and the rest of the system (unless information it is verified before it is sent to the rest of the system, it shouldn't be trusted to be valid);
- Collaborations with external systems;
- Collaborations among different layers or subsystems; and
- Collaboration among elements you design and those designed by someone else.

References

[1] Coplien,J; Bjørnvig, G. *Lean Architecture for Agile Software Development.* Wiley, 2010.

[2] Freeman, S; Hill, M. Style and Taste in Writing Fit Documents presentation at Agile 2008, http://www.exdriven.co.uk/fitstyleandtaste/Style%20and%20Taste.pdf

[3] Pree, W. "Hot-Spot-Driven Framework Development", Proceedings of the Summer School on Reusable Architectures in Object-Oriented software Development, 1995.

[4] Wirfs-Brock, R.; Wilkerson, B.; Wiener, L. *Designing Object-Oriented Software.* Prentice Hall, 1990.

[5] Wirfs-Brock, R. "Designing with an Agile Attitude", IEEE Software, March/April 2009, Volume 25, Number 2.

[6] Wirfs-Brock, R.; McKean, A. *Object Design: Roles, Responsibilities and Collaborations.* Addison-Wesley, 2003

[7] Wirfs-Brock, R. "The Responsible Designer", *IEEE Software*, November/December 2009, Volume 26, Number 6.

Author Index

www.ingramcontent.com/pod-product-compliance
Lightning Source LLC
Chambersburg PA
CBHW080912220326

41598CB00034B/5550